THE GREAT PYRAMID

PLATE I.

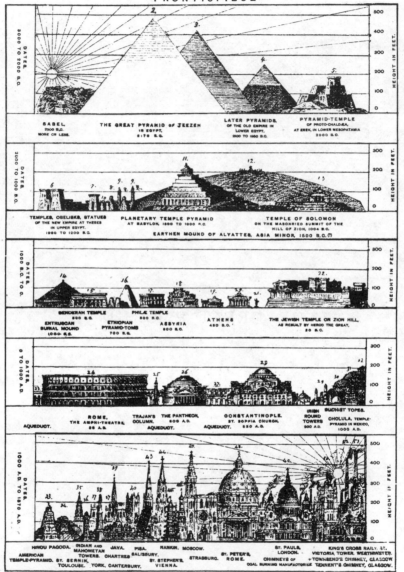

THE STONE ARCHITECTURE OF ALL AGES, IN TIME, AND IN HEIGHT.

PIAZZI SMYTH, DEL.

THE GREAT PYRAMID

ITS SECRETS AND MYSTERIES REVEALED

FOURTH AND MUCH ENLARGED EDITION

With Twenty-five Explanatory Plates

GIVING MAPS, PLANS, ELEVATIONS, AND SECTIONS

OF ALL THE MORE DIFFICULT AND CRUCIAL

PARTS OF THE STRUCTURE

BY

PIAZZI SMYTH, F.R.S.E., F.R.A.S.

ASTRONOMER-ROYAL FOR SCOTLAND

WITH A NEW FOREWORD BY FATMA TURKKAN

BELL PUBLISHING COMPANY
NEW YORK

Originally published in 1880 as *Our Inheritance in the Great Pyramid*.
Special material Copyright © MCMLXXVIII by Crown Publishers, Inc.
All rights reserved.
This edition is published by Bell Publishing Company
a division of Crown Publishers, Inc.
BELL 1978 PRINTING
a b c d e f g h

Smyth, Charles Piazzi, 1819-1900.
  The great pyramid.
  Reprint of the 1880 ed. published by W. Isbister, London under
title: Our inheritance in the great pyramid.
  1. Giza. Great Pyramid of Cheops—Miscellanea.
I. Title.
DT63.5.S725 1977   932   78-13686
ISBN 0-517-26403-X

FOREWORD.

On the rocky plateau of Giza, fifteen miles from Cairo, rise the three great pyramids of the Fourth Dynasty (2615–2500 B.C.). Each was built during the lifetime of a pharaoh. The Great Pyramid, that of Cheops, consists of well over two million limestone blocks, some weighing over fifteen tons. The 203 rows of stones rise 755 feet, fitted together with simple wooden joints. Serene they stand, against the Egyptian sky as a bold defiance against time, an affirmation of man's longing for immortality, and a challenge to future generations.

In 1864, in the wake of the scientific interest engendered by Napoleon's 1798 expedition to Egypt, a Scottish astronomer minutely explored these tombs. Through an elaborate system of mathematical calculations based on the dimensions, capacities, and proportions of its outer and inner structure, he unravelled what he called a divinely inspired Christian chronicle of man's history—past and future.

Piazzi Smyth, Astronomer-Royal of Scotland, was not the first traveler to puzzle over the origin and purpose of these desert tombs. Julius Honorius, a Roman historian of the fifth century A.D., believed that these artificial mountains were ancient granaries, and later, Arab writers of the Middle Ages associated the pyramids with the Biblical narrative of the Flood. They believed the Egyptians had constructed them as repositories for their scientific knowledge and wisdom in anticipation of the disaster.

FOREWORD.

Centuries later, in the 1850s, a London bookseller, John Taylor, introduced a similar theory which viewed the pyramid as a divine storehouse designed prophetically in anticipation of the Great Flood. His erudite references, elaborate mathematical calculations, and highly technical diagrams were brought to the forefront of intellectual controversy in the following decade by that eminent academician and member of the Royal Society of Edinburgh—Piazzi Smyth.

Convinced of the sacred origin of the pyramids, Smyth and his wife traveled to Egypt in 1864 to verify the crucial measurements of the aging structures. A vivid, enthusiastic description and summation of his theories was later set down in *Our Inheritance in The Great Pyramid*. Within its pages he carefully analyzed the "three keys" for grasping the mystery of the pyramids—pure mathematics, applied mathematics, and various revelations from the Bible. It is this ground-breaking and historic work that is here being reissued as *The Great Pyramid: Its Secrets and Mysteries Revealed*.

Starting with the basic exterior measurements of base, height, and width and those of the interior chambers which included the angle of the Descending Passage to the King's sarcophagus, Smyth established twenty-two mathematical and astronomical relationships for the Great Pyramid. The most important revealed the use (ages before its so-called discovery by the Greeks) of pi (π), the crucial concept of the ratio of the circumference of a circle to its diameter, in the buildings proportions. In addition, he recognized the extraordinary fact that the pyramid was, in many respects, a structural duplication of the solar system. Smyth's more controversial discovery was of a unique unit of measurement which he called the "pyramid inch." He believed this was first used by the builders of the Great Pyramid and was equal to 1.001 of a British inch.

A modern reading of Smyth's pyramid theories reveals a fervent Scottish puritanism. They display an obsession with sin and purity which can be understood best in the context of

FOREWORD.

his era—uneasy, pre-Darwin, Victorian England. The discovery of the usage of such complex architectural mathematics by the human species prior to recorded Christian history, was difficult for the Church to reconcile snugly with its dogma.

But the Victorian era was not the first to seek a spiritual place for these silent white monuments in the sand. The early Egyptians considered the pyramidal shape as a grand representation of the Primeval Mound of their Creation myth. In the later Pyramid Texts, scrolls of blessings entombed with the dead king, there are direct references to the ascension of the Pharaoh to the Heavens by steps (the Step Pyramid being a predecessor of the Giza Pyramids).

The mortuary complex thus played the double function of tomb and spiritual vessel. Smyth and many later pyramid theorists followed in their footsteps and imputed a cyclical death-and-rebirth philosophy to the origin of the pyramids. But their overly literal interpretation of the Pharaonic monument as a Christian calendar, was carried to extremes.

In later years, Smyth's many accomplishments would be viewed in varying ways by successive waves of scientists and scholars, first applauded, then reviled, then reaffirmed. Actually, his work at Giza marked the first systematic analysis of these ancient structures with modern scientific equipment—specialized measuring rods, clinometers, and the use of the newly invented technique of magnesium-light photography. Moreover, he was the first to unearth the rocky outcrop upon which the pyramid rested to obtain more accurate measurements of its perimeter. Controversial, and neglected, and praised by turns, *The Great Pyramid* is not only an important document in the history of Egyptian studies as it developed in the nineteenth century, but also an example of scientific thought in the Victorian era, and a fascinating account of man's continued pursuit of the mysteries of the past.

FATMA TURKKAN
New York City, June, 1978

TO THE MEMORY OF THE LATE

JOHN TAYLOR,

GOWER STREET, LONDON

(DEPARTED JULY, 1864, AGED 83 YEARS),

AUTHOR OF

'THE GREAT PYRAMID: WHY WAS IT BUILT? AND WHO BUILT IT?"

THE NOW *FOURTH* EDITION OF

THIS FURTHER ATTEMPT TO APPLY ACTUAL

SCIENTIFIC EXAMINATION

TO TEST HIS

EXCEEDINGLY MOMENTOUS THEORY

AND MOST PRECIOUS DISCOVERY OF THE AGE FOR ALL MANKIND,

IF TRUE,—

IS DEDICATED BY

THE FRIEND OF HIS FEW LAST DAYS,

BUT ADMIRER OF ALL HIS LONG AND EARNEST CHRISTIAN LIFE,

PIAZZI SMYTH.

EDINBURGH, 1880.

PREFACE.

WHEN the late worthy John Taylor (publisher to the London University) produced, in 1859, his larger work entitled *The Great Pyramid: why was it built, and who built it?* and afterwards, in January, 1864, his smaller pamphlet, *The Battle of the Standards (of Linear Measure): the ancient of four thousand years against the modern of the last fifty years—the less perfect of the two,*—he opened up for archæology a purer, nobler, more intellectual pathway to light than that study had ever enjoyed before.

But academic archæology would not accept it; indeed the whole reading world stood askance; and I can hardly now explain how it came about that something induced me, in February, 1864, to commence an independent examination of Mr. Taylor's theory; and my publication in September of that year (*i.e.* the first edition of the present book) contained the findings so arrived at. Findings, in many points confirmatory of the principal thread of Mr. Taylor's chief and most startling discovery; but exhibiting in the general literature of the subject, and on which, unfortunately, he had been obliged to depend too much, a lamentable deficiency in the accurateness of almost all the numerical data required; and which necessary exactitude, nothing but practical examination and instrumental measure *at the place* could hope properly to supply.

Meanwhile John Taylor died, and with almost his last breath emphatically confided this, the most important labour of his long life-toil, to my most unworthy hands; and yet hands not altogether unused to *some* of the operations *next* required. How, then, with little help from any one, save a single subscription volunteered by a kind friend* in Edinburgh, my Wife and self did, on very scanty private means, sail for Egypt in November, 1864; and did, through a four months' residence on the Great Pyramid hill in 1865, employ a variety of surveying and astronomical instruments, in obtaining many measures of the mighty monument; some of them to far more exactness than had ever been attempted before, and others descending to numerous details unnoticed by former observers, though still leaving other large parts to the future efforts of the nation—all this was described by me, first in abstract to the Royal Society, Edinburgh, in April, 1866; and afterwards, at much greater length to the world in my three-volumed book, " Life and Work at the Great Pyramid " in 1867.†

That last publication, even from the very oppositions it called up, helped to spread a knowledge both of the importance of the question at issue, and the only means for solving it; especially as against the modern hieroglyphic scholars, the so-called Egyptologists; who, though exceedingly learned in *their* lettered way touch-

---

* Andrew Coventry, Esq., died, much regretted, August 11, 1877.

† Pages 1,653. Plates 36. Published by Edmonston and Douglas, now " Douglas and Foulis," Edinburgh.

ing Egyptian remains of more recent times, have never much troubled themselves to examine the far more ancient, as well as purer, Great Pyramid in the mechanical and scientific manner now required.

Indeed, the literary Egyptologists seem, by their criticisms, rather angered than otherwise, to hear that such precise and strictly provable data, in merely modern instrumental measure, when at last collected by others than themselves, are most successful in showing a radical difference throughout between the Great, and every other, Pyramid in Egyptian land. In fact these measures tend to establish that the Great Pyramid, though *in* Egypt, is not, and never was, *of* Egypt— that is, of, belonging to, or instructing about Pharaonic, idolatrous, and chiefly Theban, Egypt. Also, that though built in the earliest ages, far before written history, the Great Pyramid was yet prophetically in tended—by inspiration afforded to the architect from the one and only living God, who rules in heaven, and announced vengeance against the sculptured idols of Egypt (Ezekiel xxx. 13)—to remain quiescent during those earlier ages ; and only, in a manner, to come forth at this time to subserve a high purpose for these latter days. That it, the Great Pyramid, was never even remotely understood, either by the Egyptian, or any other branch of the Cainite and anti-Israelite family of nations. But that it is able nevertheless to explain its grand, even Messianic, mission, most unmistakably. Not, indeed, in the usual manner of less ancient monuments, by the use of any written language, whether hieroglyphic or vulgar, but by aid of the mathematical and physical science of modern times applied to show the significance residing in the exact amount of its *ancient* length, breadth and angles; a means most efficacious both for preventing the parable being read too soon in the history of an, at first, unlearned world; but for insuring its being correctly read, and by all nations, when the fulness of prophetic time, in a science age, has at last arrived.

This confirmation of the main view arrived at by John Taylor, *viz.* that in the Great Pyramid the world now possesses a *Monument* of Inspiration, as it has long possessed a *Book* of Inspiration, one dating altogether, and the other partly, from primeval times—brought by degrees many able intellectualists of the mathematical and Christian, rather than the Egyptological and rationalistic, order into the field. And some of them have succeeded, or are succeeding, in demonstrating the purpose and meaning of so many successive parts of the structure, according to the measures taken in 1865, —that if a second and amended edition of my original work was called for in 1874, and a third in 1877, much more is a fourth required now, when there are so many additional discoveries by other workers to be cited; and when the whole is gaining shape, acquiring purpose and now almost day by day illustrating our modern history, our Israelitic brotherhood with America, the future of Egypt, Syria, and the way of the Kings of the East, in these eventful times so truly foreseen, and absolutely monumentalized of old, by supernaturally inspired men, by prophets of the living God.

CONTENTS.

PART I.

GEOGRAPHY AND THE EXTERIOR OF THE GREAT PYRAMID.

PART II.

HISTORY AND THE INTERIOR OF THE GREAT PYRAMID.

PART III.

NATIONAL WEIGHTS AND MEASURES, AND ALSO THOSE OF THE GREAT PYRAMID.

CONTENTS.

PART IV.

MORE THAN SCIENCE AT THE GREAT PYRAMID.

PART V.

THE PERSONAL AND THE FUTURE AT THE GREAT PYRAMID.

APPENDICES.

GREAT PYRAMID GRAPHICAL ILLUSTRATIONS.

(ENGRAVED BY ALEX. RITCHIE, EDINBURGH.)
(TO BE FOUND FOLLOWING PAGE 224)

SUPPLEMENTARY
ILLUSTRATIONS

THE THREE KEYS

REQUIRED FOR THE OPENING OF THE GREAT PYRAMID.

————————

KEY THE FIRST.

THE key of *pure mathematics*, as supplied chiefly in mediæval and modern times, and mostly by the labours of private philosophers in their own studies, sometimes to absolute truth, sometimes to such close approaches thereto, as to be certain up to the last figure of any fraction yet arrived at; as, for one example much used and illustrated in the Great Pyramid,— ϖ, or the value of the circumference of a circle in terms of its diameter, =

3·14159	26535	89793	23846	26433
03279	50288	41971	69399	37510
58209	74944	59230	78164	06286

+ &c., &c., &c.

KEY THE SECOND.

The key of *applied mathematics*, or of astronomical and physical science, as furnished by the latest and best approximations of all the first-class nations of the world; who have been working publicly for centuries and at a cost of millions of money, and have attained, or are on the point of attaining, an accuracy, sometimes only in the second figure, sometimes in the third, fourth, fifth, or even lower figures, according to the greater, or less, difficulty in nature of the question concerned. As thus:—

Polar diameter of the earth = between 500,378,000 and 500,560,000 British inches.

Mean equatorial diameter of the earth between 502,080,000 and 502,230,000 British inches.

Mean density of the earth between 5·3 and 6·5; the two latest determinations by powerful government institutions.

Mean distance of the earth from the sun between 91 and 93 millions of miles, British.

Obliquity of the ecliptic in 1877 A.D. = 23° 27′ 17″·9 to 23° 27′ 19″·0.

Length of the solar tropical year in mean solar days = 365·24222 to 365·24224.

Precession of the equinoxes in years, = 25,816 to 25,870.

KEY THE THIRD.

The key of positive human history—past, present, and future—as supplied in some of its leading points and chief religious connections by Divine Revelation to certain chosen and inspired men of the Hebrew race, through ancient and mediæval times; but now to be found, by all the world, collected in

THE OLD AND NEW TESTAMENTS.

There is no twisting, no forcing needed in using any of these Keys; and least of all, is any *alteration* of them required for this particular purpose.

Wherefore no man who either vainly maintains a sensibly different value of π, or demands in these latter days new principles of Astronomy, or insists on having private interpretations of the open and published word of Scripture, need hope to arrive at the true explanation of

THE GREAT PYRAMID.

PART I.
THE GEOGRAPHY, AND THE EXTERIOR, OF THE GREAT PYRAMID.

"THE GREAT, THE MIGHTY GOD, THE LORD OF HOSTS, IS HIS NAME, GREAT IN COUNSEL, AND MIGHTY IN WORK: . . . WHICH HAS SET SIGNS AND WONDERS IN THE LAND OF EGYPT, EVEN UNTO THIS DAY."

JEREMIAH XXXII. 18—20.

"O LORD GOD OF HOSTS . . . THE HEAVENS ARE THINE, THE EARTH ALSO IS THINE; AS FOR THE WORLD, AND THE FULLNESS THEREOF, THOU HAST FOUNDED THEM."

PSALM LXXXIX. 8, 11.

"BECAUSE THAT WHICH MAY BE KNOWN OF GOD IS MANIFEST IN THEM; FOR GOD HATH SHOWED IT UNTO THEM. FOR THE INVISIBLE THINGS OF HIM FROM THE CREATION OF THE WORLD ARE CLEARLY SEEN, BEING UNDERSTOOD BY THE THINGS THAT ARE MADE."

ROMANS I. 19, 20.

"DAVID, IN A CHOICE OF EVILS SIMILAR TO THESE, SAID, 'LET ME FALL INTO THE HANDS OF THE LORD, FOR VERY GREAT ARE HIS MERCIES; BUT LET ME NOT FALL INTO THE HAND OF MAN' (I CHRON. XXI. 13). THE PEOPLE OF ENGLAND KNOW WHAT IT IS TO EXPERIENCE SOMEWHAT OF THE LATTER CALAMITY; AND THOUGH THEY ARE BOUND TO ACKNOWLEDGE THAT THEIR LONG-PROTRACTED GRIEFS ARE TO BE PREFERRED TO THE SHORT BUT SEVERE SUFFERINGS WHICH THE NATIONS OF THE CONTINENT HAD TO ENDURE, THEY MUST FEEL, AFTER ALL, THAT IT IS A DEEP AFFLICTION WHICH MANY HAVE HAD TO BEAR. BUT LET THEM WITH FAITH AND PATIENCE ENDURE THEIR TROUBLES A LITTLE LONGER. THEIR REDEMPTION DRAWETH NIGH."

JOHN TAYLOR'S WEALTH THE NAME AND NUMBER OF THE BEAST, P. 149.

THE EASTERN FACE OF THE GREAT PYRAMID SEEN RISING ABOVE THE
LUSH NILE VALLEY, 1975.
Photo By Mariette Pathy Allen.

THE EXCAVATED CEMETERY WEST OF CHEOPS' PYRAMID AT GIZA.
Photo courtesy of Museum of Fine Arts, Boston.

INTREPID TOURISTS SCALING THE EASTERN FACE OF THE GREAT
PYRAMID, 1975.
Photo by Mariette Pathy Allen.

A PORTION OF THE VAST EXCAVATIONS BEING DONE IN THE
SOUTHERN SECTOR OF THE GIZA COMPLEX, 1975.
Photo by Mariette Pathy Allen.

THE TWO ENTRANCES TO THE GREAT PYRAMID. THE ORIGINAL (UPPER
LEFT) WAS NOT REDISCOVERED UNTIL AFTER THE FORCED ENTRANCE
(LOWER RIGHT) LED INTRUDERS TO INTERIOR PASSAGEWAYS. PHOTO
TAKEN IN 1975.
Photo by Mariette Pathy Allen.

THE SPHINX WITH GREAT PYRAMID IN THE BACKGROUND, 1975.
Photo by Mariette Pathy Allen.

CHAPTER I.

Of the General Question of the Great Pyramid.

THE ancient pyramids of Egypt form somewhat of a long clustering group of gigantic monuments, extending chiefly over about a degree of latitude. They begin in the north, at the apex, or southern head of the triangular - shaped " Delta " land of " Lower Egypt," and stretch thence further southward along almost seventy miles of the western side of the Nile.

Within that nearly meridian distance, one traveller claims to have noted thirty-five, another rashly says sixty-seven; and another still, but in his case going beyond what is strictly Egypt, and ascending its colossal river as far as Meroe, Noori, and Barkal in Ethiopia, mentions one hundred and thirty as existing there. But they are mediæval rather than ancient, small instead of large, and with very little about them either in form or material to remind of the more typical early examples entirely in stone; or those really mathematically shaped *old pyramids*, which, though few in number, are what have made the world-wide fame of their land's architecture from before the beginning of history.

Now it is precisely with those grander specimens only, or the oldest examples of the country (not more, even including some that are positively ruinous, than thirty-eight in number), that we have to do in this book; and selecting even further amongst them, we find, that of all the more important instances that have yet attracted the attention of mankind as being really typical, there are none to equal the combined fame and antiquity, the purity of shape and excellence of both preservation and construction, of the several stone pyramids near Jeezeh; * a hill in view of the ancient Memphis, and not far, though separated by the river, from the present city of Cairo.

The Jeezeh pyramidal group is situated, like all the others, on the western, or more thoroughly African, lone, and desert, side of the river; but close to the southern apex, and as it were the very point of origin of the sector-shaped plain of Lower Egypt. The group, in its strangely massive, yet crystalline shaped, architecture, is conspicuously planted there on the utmost north-eastern edge of an elevated rocky steppe; so that while it overlooks on one side the sand-strewn wastes extending back to the great Sahara, it beholds on the other the green and fertile plains of Nile, about 130 feet in level below. But amongst these Jeezeh Pyramids, again, there is one that transcends in intellectual value all the rest; one that has been involuntarily by all the world named for ages past the "Great Pyramid"; and which stands out, the more it is examined into, distinct and distinguished from all its fellows by its not only giant, but particular, size, its wondrous internal structure, its superior age, more frequent historical notice by men of various nations,

---

* The following varieties of orthography, by different authors, may lead to the correct pronunciation, viz.: Gyzeh, Ghizeh, Gizeh, Jeezeh, Gheezeh, Jizeh, Djiza, Dsjise, Dschiseh, Geezeh, El-Geezeh, Dzireth, &c., &c.

"Jeezeh, or Geezeh, is the proper way of spelling this word in English," writes Dr. J. A. S. Grant, from his Sanatorium, Palais Matatia, in Cairo, in March, 1877.

and yet, the hitherto inscrutable destiny of its purpose ; the greatest of the seven old wonders of the world in the days of the Greeks, and the only one of them all, which is still in existence on the surface of the earth.

With many of the smaller and later pyramids there is little doubt about their objects ; for, built by the Egyptians as sepulchres for the great Egyptian dead, such dead, both Pharaohs and their relatives, were buried in them, and with all the written particulars, pictorial accompaniments, and idolatrous adornments of that too graphic religion, which the fictile nation on the Nile ever delighted in. But as we approach, ascending the stream of ancient time, in any careful chronological survey of pyramidal structures, to the " Great Pyramid," Egyptian emblems are gradually left behind ; and in, and throughout, that mighty builded mass, which all history and all tradition, both ancient and modern, agree in representing as the first in point of date of the whole Jeezeh, and even the whole Egyptian,* group, the earliest stone building also positively known to have been erected in any country, —we find in all its *finished* parts not a vestige of heathenism, nor the smallest indulgence in anything approaching to idolatry ; no Egyptology of the kind denounced by Moses and the prophets of Israel ; nor even the most distant allusion to Sabaism, and its elemental worship of sun, or moon, or any of the starry host of heaven.

* There are some disputations still touching the possibly greater antiquity of another pyramid, viz., the so-called (but not really) Great Pyramid, or " pyramid of degrees," at Sakkara (see Plate V.) ; but though it is, without any doubt, most rudely and clumsily built, those qualities do not by any means invariably and necessarily imply greater age, in Egypt ; and the building has no other point wherein it can presume to compare with *the* Great Pyramid of Jeezeh, through all of *its* features of positive and exact mensuration ; while these are the chief, and almost only, tests which are to be employed as we proceed in this book ; though at first starting, we are compelled to lay down a few statements in simple words only.

I have specified "finished parts," because in certain unfinished, internal portions of the constructive masonry of the Great Pyramid broken into by Colonel Howard-Vyse in 1837, there are some rude Egyptian markings, in a few daubs of red paint only, and for a mere temporary mechanical purpose to be presently explained ; and I also except, as a matter of course, any inscriptions inflicted on the same pyramid by modern travellers, even though they have attempted, like the Prussian *savants* of 1843 A.D., to cut their names in their own happily shallow ideas of the ancient hieroglyphics of the old, thorough-paced, Egyptian idolaters elsewhere. But with these simple exceptions we can most positively say, that both exterior and interior are absolutely free from all engraved or sculptured work, as well as from everything relating to any known form of idolatry or erring man's theotechnic devices. From all those hieratic emblems, therefore, which from first to last have utterly overlaid every Egyptian temple proper, as well as all Egypt's obelisks, sphinxes, statues, tombs, and whatever other monuments they, the Egyptians, did build up at any certain historical and Pharaonic epoch in connection with their peculiar, and, alas ! degrading religion.

Was the Great Pyramid, then, erected before the invention of hieroglyphics, and previous to the birth of the false Egyptian religion ?

No ! for there, both history, tradition, and recent exploratory discoveries elsewhere, testified to by many travellers and antiquaries, are perfectly in accord ; and assure us that the Egyptian nation was established, was powerful, and its spiritually vile hieratic system largely developed, though not arrived at its full proportions, at the time of the erection of the Great Pyramid ; that that structure was even raised by the labour of the Egyptian population ruled over at the time by an

Egyptian king ;* but under some remarkable compulsion and constraint which positively forbade them from putting their unmistakable decorations and elsewhere accustomed inscriptions on the finished building; more especially too from identifying it in any manner, direct or indirect, with their impure and even bestial form of worship.

* This very important conclusion results from the " quarry marks " of the workmen (see Colonel Howard-Vyse's volumes, " Pyramids of Gizeh," London, 1840), being found in red paint on concealed parts of the stones, and in interior places of the structural mass of masonry never intended to be seen.   The marks are superficial and rude in the extreme, but are evidently in the Egyptian language or manner freely handled ; and in so far prove that they were put in by Egyptians, and of the age or under the reign of that Egyptian king variously called Shofo, Khufu and Cheops. They are excessively rough, no doubt, but quite sufficient for their alleged purpose, viz. checks for workmen, whereby to recognize a stone duly prepared according to orders at the quarry, miles away, and to see it properly placed in its intended position in the building.

Still further that these marks were not meant as ornaments in the structure, or put on after the stones were built into it, is abundantly evidenced by some of them being upside down, and some having been partly pared away in adjusting the block into its position (see Colonel Howard-Vyse's plates of them) ; and, finally, by the learned Dr. Birch's interpretation of a number of the marks, which seem from thence to be mostly short dates, and directions to the workmen as to which stones were for the south, and which for the north, wall.

These markings, moreover, have only been discovered in those dark holes or hollows, the so-called " chambers," but much rather " hollows of construction," broken into by Colonel Howard-Vyse above the " King's Chamber " of the Great Pyramid.   There, also, you see other traces of the steps of mere practcial work, such as the "bat-holes" in the stones, by which the heavy blocks were doubtless lifted to their places, and everything is left perfectly rough.   Nor was there the least occasion for finishing it up, rubbing out the marks, or polishing off the holes, for these void spaces were sealed up, or had been built up outside in solid masonry (excepting only the lowest one, known for a century as "Davison's Chamber," and having its own small passage of approach from the south-east corner of the Grand Gallery), and were never intended to be used as chambers for human visitation or living purposes.   In all the other chambers and passages, on the contrary, intended to be visited, and approached by admirably constructed white-stone passages, the masonry was finished off with the skill and polish almost of a jeweller ; and in them neither quarry marks nor "bat holes," nor painted marks, nor hieroglyphics of any sort or kind, are to be seen : excepting always those modern hieroglyphics which Dr. Lepsius put up over the entrance into the Great Pyramid, " on a space five feet in breadth by four feet in height," in praise of the then sovereign of Prussia ; and which have recently misled a learned Chinese envoy, by name Pin-ch'-un, into most absurdly claiming a connection between the Great Pyramid and the early monuments of his own country.   (See *Athenæum*, May 21, 1870 p. 677.)

According to Herodotus, Manetho, and other ancient authorities, the Egyptians hated, and yet implicitly obeyed, the mysterious, and coercive though non-military, power that made them work on the Great Pyramid ; and when that power was again relaxed or removed, though they still hated its name to such a degree as to forbear from even mentioning it except by a peculiar circumlocution,—yet with involuntary bending to the sway of a really superior intelligence once amongst them, they took to imitating in other buildings, as well as they could, though without understanding, a few of the more ordinary mechanical features of that great work on which they had been so long employed ; and they even rejoiced for a time to adapt them, so far as they could be adapted, to their own more favourite ends, egotistic glorifications, and other such congenial ideas.

Hence the numerous *quasi*-copies, for *sepulchral* purposes, of the Great Pyramid, which are now, in the shape of other pyramids, to be observed further south, along that western side of Egypt; always betraying, though, on close examination, the most profound ignorance of their noble model's chiefest internal features, as well as of all its niceties of angle and cosmic harmonies of linear measurement.   And such mere failures, as those later *tombic* pyramids, are never found, even then, at any very great number of miles away from the site, nor any great number of years behind the date, of the colossal parent work on the Jeezeh hill.

The ostensible architectural idea, indeed, of that one grand primeval monument, though expensively copied during a few centuries, yet never wholly or permanently took the fancy of the ancient Egyptians.   It had, or rather simulated before them to have, some one or two suitabilities to their favourite employment of lasting sepulture, and its accompanying rites ; so they tried

what they knew of it, for such purpose.   But they soon
found that it did not admit of their troops of priests,
nor the easy introduction of their unwieldy " sacred "
animals.   Nor bulls, nor crocodiles, nor the requisite
multitudes of abject worshippers, could enter a pyramid
with the facility of their own temples ; and so, on the
whole, mature Egypt preferred *them*.   Those accordingly more open and columned, as well as symbolically
sculptured and multitudinously inscribed structures, of
their own entire elaboration, are the only ones which
we now find to have held, from their first invention, an
uninterrupted reign through all the course of ancient
and mediæval Egyptian history, or that period when
Egypt was most rich, most powerful, most wicked ;
and to reflect themselves continuously in the placid,
natural Nile, from   one   end   of   the   long-drawn
Hamitic land to the other.   They, therefore, those
Karnac   and   Philœ temples, with   all   their   sins   of
idolatry on their heads, are, architecturally, Egypt.
Thebes, too, with its hundred adorned Pylon temple-
gates, and statues, and basso-relievos, and incised outlines of false gods, must be confessed to be intensely
Egypt.   But the Great Pyramid is, in its origin and
nature, something pure and perfectly different.

Under   whose   direction,   then,   and   for   what   purpose, was the Great Pyramid built; whence did so
foreign, and really untasteful, an idea to Egypt
come ; who was the mysterious carrier of it to that
land ; and under what sort of special compulsion was
it that, in his day, to his command though he was not
their king, the Egyptians, King and people all alike,
laboured for years in a cause which they appreciated
not ; and gave, in that primeval age of generally
sparse, and pastoral, population only, their unrivalled
mechanical skill and compacted numerical strength
for an end which they did not at the time understand ; and which they never even came to under-

stand, much less to like, in all their subsequent national ages?

This has been indeed a mystery of mysteries, but may yet prove fruitful in the present advancing age of knowledge of all kinds to inquire into further : for though theories without number have been tried and failed in, by ancient Greeks and mediæval Arabians, by French, English, Germans, and Americans, their failures partly pave, and render so much the safer, for us the road by which we must set out. Pave it poorly, perhaps, or not very far ; for their whole result has, up to the present time, been little more than this, that the authors of those attempts are either found to be repeating idle tales, told them by those who knew no more about the subject than themselves ; or skipping all the really crucial points of application for their theories which they should have attended to ; or, finally, like some of the best and ablest men who have given themselves to the question, fairly admitting that they were entirely beaten.

Hence the *exclusive* notion of temples to the sun and moon, or for sacred fire, or holy water, or burial-places, and nothing but burial-places, of kings, or granaries for Joseph, or astronomical observatories, or defences to Egypt against being invaded by the sands of the African desert, or places of resort for mankind in a second deluge, or of safety when the heavens should fall, have been for a long time past proved untenable ; and the Great Pyramid stands out now, far more clearly than it did in the time of Herodotus (no less than 2,400 years ago), as both a prehistoric monument, and yet rivalling some of the best things of modern times, not only in practical execution and workmanship, but in its eminently grand design and pure conception ; or in forming a testimony which, though in Egypt, is yet not at all of, or according to, historical Egypt, and whose true and full explanation must be still to come.

Under these circumstances it is, that a new idea, based not on ancient hieroglyphics, profane learning, old Egyptian sculpture, or modern Egyptology springing therefrom, but on new scientific measures of the still remaining actual facts of ancient masonic construction in number, weight, and measure, was recently given to the world by the late Mr. John Taylor, of London, in a book published in 1859.* He had not visited the Pyramid himself, but had been for thirty years previously collecting and comparing all the published accounts, and specially all the better-certified mensurations (for some were certainly poor indeed) of those who had been there; and while so engaged, gradually and quite spontaneously (as he described to me by letter), the new theory opened out before him.

Though mainly a rigid induction from tangible facts of scientific bearing and character, Mr. Taylor's result was undoubtedly assisted by means of the mental and spiritual point of view from whence he commenced his researches, and which is, in the main, simply this :—

That whereas other writers have generally esteemed that the unknown existency who directed the building of the Great Pyramid (and to whom the Egyptians, in their traditions and for ages afterwards, gave an immoral and even abominable character) must, therefore, have been very bad indeed,—so that the world at large, from that time to this, has ever been fond of standing on, kicking, and insulting that dead lion whom they really knew nothing of,—he, Mr. John Taylor, seeing how religiously *bad* the idol-serving Egyptians themselves were, was led to conclude that he, whom *they* hated (and could never sufficiently abuse) might perhaps have been pre-eminently good; or was, at all events, of a *different and very much purer religious faith*

* The Great Pyramid : why was it built? and who built it? " (Longmans and Co.)

from that of the land of Ham. Then, remembering, with *mutatis mutandis*, what Christ himself says respecting the suspicion to be attached when all the *world* speaks *well* of any one, Mr. Taylor followed up this idea by what the Old Testament does record touching the most vital and distinguishing part of the Israelitish religion; and which is therein described, some centuries after the building of the Great Pyramid, as notoriously an "abomination *to the Egyptians*": and combining this with certain unmistakable and undisputed by any one, historical facts, he successfully deduced sound and Christian reasons for believing that the directors of the building, or rather the author of its design and those who under his more immediate guidance controlled the actual builders of the Great Pyramid, were by no means Egyptians, but of the *chosen race*, descendants of Shem, and in the line of, though preceding, Abraham; so early indeed as to be closer to Noah than to Abraham. Men, at all events, who had been enabled by Divine favour to appreciate the appointed idea, as to the absolute necessity of a sacrifice and atonement for the sins of man by the blood and the act of a Divine Mediator, as in the most modern and Evangelical form of Christianity. This very crucial idea was nevertheless of an antiquity coeval with the contest between Abel and Cain, and had descended through the Flood to certain predestined families of mankind; but yet was an idea or principle in religion which no one of Egyptian born would ever contemplate with a moment's patience. For every ancient Egyptian, from first to last, and every Pharaoh of them more especially, just as with the Ninevites and Babylonians generally, was an unmitigated Cainite in thought, act, and feeling to the very backbone; confident of and professing nothing so much, or so constantly, as his own perfect righteousness, and absolute freedom by his own innate purity, and by his own invariable, complete, and unswerving rectitude throughout his whole life, from every kind of sin, large or small, against God or man.

On this ground it was that Mr. Taylor took his stand; and, after disobeying the world's long-formed public opinion of too passively obedient accord with profane Egyptian tradition, and after thereby also setting at nought some of the most time-honoured prejudices of modern Egyptological scholars, so far as to give a full, fair, and impartial examination to the whole case from the beginning, announced that he had discovered in some of the arrangements and measures of the Great Pyramid—when corrected for injuries of intervening time—certain scientific results, which speak of neither Egyptian nor Babylonian, nor Roman nor Greek, but of something much more than, as well as quite different from, any ordinary human ways. For, besides coming forth *suddenly* in the primeval history of its own times without any preliminary period of childhood, or known ages of evolution and preparation, the actual facts at the Great Pyramid, in the shape of builded proofs of an exact numerical knowledge of the grander cosmical phenomena of both earth and heavens, not only rise above, and far above, the extremely limited and almost infantine knowledge of science humanly attained to by any of the Gentile nations of 4,000, 3,000, 2,000, nay, 1,000 years ago; but they are also, in whatever of the physical secrets of Nature they chiefly apply to, essentially above the best knowledge of man in our own time as well.

This is indeed a startling assertion, if true; but, from its subject, admits of the completest and most positive refutation, if untrue. For the exact science of the present day, compared with that of only a few hundred years ago, is a marvel of development; and is capable of giving out no uncertain sound, both in asserting itself, and stating not only the fact, but the order and time of, the invention of all the practical means humanly necessary, to the minutest steps of all separate discoveries yet made. Much more then can this modern science of the mathematical kind speak with positiveness, when comparing its own presently extended knowledge against the little that was known to man, by his own efforts and by his then school methods, in those early epochs before accurate and numerical physical science had begun, or could have begun, to be seriously cultivated at all; that is, in the truly primeval day when men were few on the earth, and the Great Pyramid was built, finished, sealed up, and left as we see it now, dilapidations only excepted, awaiting its intended purpose, whatever that was to be, in a long subsequent day.

Let us proceed then to exactly such a scientific examination of all known Pyramid facts. Rather a dull proceeding perhaps at the beginning, to some, but necessary to all who would understand ; and not too difficult for any, if taken step by step, and in order, more or less as follows.

CHAPTER II.

GEOMETRICAL PROPORTIONS

Of the outer surfaces of the Great Pyramid.

John Taylor's First Discovery.

MR. TAYLOR'S first-discovered theorem with regard to the Great Pyramid's *shape*, as derived from modern measures and calculations of it, is, that the Pyramid's height, in the *original condition of the monument*, when each one of its four sloping triangular sides was made into a perfect plane by means of the polished outer, sloping, surface of the bevelled casing stones (see Plates VIII. and XX.), and when those sides, being continued up to their mutual intersections, terminated at, and formed the summit in, a point,— that its central, vertical height then was, to twice the breadth of its square base, as nearly as can be expressed by good monumental work, *as the diameter to the circumference of a circle.*

Or, that the vertical height of that Pyramid was to the length of one side of its base, when multiplied by 2, as the diameter to the circumference of a circle; *i.e.* as 1 : 3·14159 + &c.; this last number being no other than our " Key the first " of page xv.

Or, again, as shown more recently by Mr. St. John Day, the area of the Great Pyramid's right section (*i.e.* a vertical, central section parallel to one of the sides of the horizontal base) is to the area of the base, as 1 to the same 3·14159, &c.

Or, as the same fact admits again of being differently expressed, the vertical height of the Great Pyramid is the radius of a theoretical circle, the length of whose curved circumference is equal to the sum of the lengths of the four straight sides of the actual and practical square base of the building.

Now this is neither more nor less than that celebrated practical problem of the mediæval and modern ages of Europe, " the squaring of the circle "; and the thing was thus practically done, truly and properly at the Great Pyramid, thousands of years before those mediæval days of our forefathers. For it was so accomplished by the architect who designed that pyramid, when,—over and above deciding that the building was to be a square-based pyramid,—with, of course, all the necessary mathematical innate relations which every square-based pyramid *must* have,—he also ordained that its height, which otherwise might have been anything, was to bear such a particular proportion to its breadth of base, as should bring out the nearest possible value of π as above mentioned; and which proportion not one out of any number of square-based pyramids would be otherwise necessarily endued with; and not one out of all the thirty-seven other measured pyramids in Egypt has been proved to be endowed with even approximately.

If, therefore, the quantity is really found built into the Great Pyramid with exactness, as well as magnitude, characterizing and utilizing the *whole* of that vast mass, it not only discriminates that building at once from all the other pyramids of Egypt, but proves that such a distinguishing feature must have been the result either of some most marvellous accident, or of some deep wisdom and settled, determined purpose; in this case, too, not less than 3,000 years in advance of the learned world in the building's own time. And that wisdom of the Great Pyramid's founder was apparently working in a peculiar confidence of scientific knowledge and historical trust, not for its contemporaries, to whom it explained nothing and showed very little, but for a most distant posterity; knowing well that a fundamental mathematical truth like π, would infallibly come to be understood both in and by itself alone, and be appreciated in the fact without any written inscription, in that then distant day when mathematics should at last be extensively and successfully cultivated amongst mankind, even as they are now.

A most just conclusion too; for experience has shown that neither mathematics nor mechanics can progress in any country in modern times without knowing well the numerical value and calculational quantity of π. In testimony whereof I may mention that in Dr. Olinthus Gregory's "Mathematics for Practical Men," third edition thereof by H. Law, C.E., at page 64 of Appendix, there is a Table 5, of "useful factors in calculation" (the calculations, be it remembered, of the hard-headed, strong-handed, exemplary working-men who construct our steam-engines, iron ships, railways, docks, and all other modern engineering), and consisting in each case of the few first figures, of that invaluable, but theoretically interminable, number or proportion π, or $3\cdot14159$, &c., in no less than fifty-four different mathematical forms.

Inquiry into the Data.

Now of this scientific value of π there is, and can be, in the present day, no doubt in any good school or university all the world over; neither of the Great Pyramid's chronological priority over all the existing architectural monuments raised, and much more over all known books ever written, anywhere by any of the sons of men ; nor again that the numbers which Mr. Taylor gives for the vertical height and double breadth of base of the Great Pyramid do realise the π proportion very closely.   But, as we are to take nothing for granted that we can inquire into ourselves in this book, it becomes our duty to ask what foundation John Taylor may have had, for the numbers which he has employed being really those which the Great Pyramid was anciently constructed to represent, or does contain within itself, when duly measured and corrected for modern dilapidations.

In this research I soon found it necessary to read rather extensively in a particular branch of literature, where the respective authors are not only numerous, but their accounts of mensurations, as a rule, most strangely contradictory.   Colonel Howard-Vyse, in the second volume of his important work,* published in 1840, gives either extracts from, or abstracts made with admirable fairness of, no less than seventy-one European and thirty-two Asiatic authors.   Many more are now to be added to the list, and it is extremely instructive to read and compare them all.   Unless, indeed, a very great number be read, no sufficient idea can be formed as to how little faith is often to be placed in the narratives even of highly, though too exclusively mentally, educated men of modern university, and competitive examination, times, on a very simple practical matter.

Thus it would be easy to string together a series of so-called measures, made by successive travellers (each of whom has published a book), on the same parts of the Great Pyramid, which should show its blocks of solid stone expanding and contracting between different visits to it, like elastic india-rubber air-bags.   But it will suffice for the present to indicate the necessity of

* " The Pyramids of Gizeh."   (Frazer, Regent Street, London.)

weighing the evidence in every case most scrupulously; to have a large quantity of evidence, a great variety of observers, and to place in the first rank of authors to be studied in the original, closely in every word they have written, but not necessarily to be always followed therein :

Professor John Greaves, the Oxford astronomer in 1638.

The magnificent French, or Napoleon Bonaparte, Expedition in 1799.

The princely Colonel Howard-Vyse in 1837 ; and

The learned, experienced, and amiable Sir Gardner Wilkinson from 1840 to 1858.

At present the Great Pyramid is, externally to the sight, a rough, huge mass ; a gigantic cairn, as it were ; but of a strikingly crystalline figure on the whole ; and, on closer examination, regularly and masterly, built of worked and cemented limestone blocks, in extensive and admirably horizontal sheets, or courses of masonry; * their outer, and now broken-off edges necessarily form- ing in these days a sort of rectangular steps up the sloping sides ; and, with a platform of sensible area on the top, forming at a distance an abnormally blunted summit. But this spurious or adventitious flattened top, as well as the spurious and adventitious steps on the sides, have all of them merely resulted from the mediæval dilapidations and forcible removal of the Pyramid's once polished white-stone casing (with its outer surface bevelled smoothly to the general slope, see Plate VIII.), which had stood for more than 3,000 years, and had in its day given to the structure

---

* To what extent these sheets of masonry are absolutely continuous throughout the mass can never be known until the whole structure is taken to pieces ; nor, happily, is it necessary to be known, so long as we see each stratum recording itself similarly on each of the four sides, ex- cepting only the small interruption of a portion of rock at the north-east corner, and also a hole filled with rubble work which is now reported by Dr. Grant, about a third of the way up one of the sides.

almost mathematical truth and perfection. This state of things was that described by Greek, Roman, and early Arabian writers; and it existed until the Caliphs of Egypt, about the year 1,000 A.D., profiting by the effects of a severe, and for Egypt very unusual, earthquake, recorded to have happened in 908 A.D., began methodically to strip off the polished and bevelled casing-stone blocks ; built two bridges to convey them more easily to the river, after chipping off the prismoidal angles and edges ; and then employed them in building mosques and palaces ; for the lining of the great " Joseph " well, and for other public structures which still adorn their favourite city El Kahireh, or the victorious—the Cairo of vulgar English.*

It is evidently then the original, not the present, size and shape which we require, and must have, for testing Mr. Taylor's proposition ; and for approximating, by whatever degree of exactitude may be reached, to whether it was accident or intention which decided the shape of the building ; and he has well pointed out that no one had any pretence to have obtained the old base-side length until the French Academicians, in 1799, cleared away the hills of sand and débris at the north-east and north-west corners, and reached beneath them the levelled surface of the living rock itself on which the Pyramid was originally founded. There, discovering two rectangular hollows carefully and truly cut into the rock, as if for " sockets " for the basal corner-stones, the said Academicians measured the dis-

* Very recently my friends Mr. Waynman Dixon and Dr. Grant have visited the celebrated Mosque of Sooltan Hassan, in Cairo, to see if any of the component blocks forming its walls could be identified as having belonged to the Great Pyramid. They found them to be undoubtedly of the same Mokattam stone, but too well squared to retain any of the outside bevelled, and, perhaps, inscribed, surface. The inquiry was, however, put a rude stop to by the Mohammedan janitors, before it had reached some of the more likely places near the top of the Mosque, wherein to meet with an accidentally or carelessly left oblique surface of the other far older building.

tance between those sockets with much geodesic refinement, and found it to be equal to 763·62 English feet.
The same distance being measured thirty-seven years
afterwards by Colonel Howard-Vyse, guided by another
equally sure direction of the original building, as 764·0
English feet,—we may take for the *present* solution of
our problem, where a proportion is all that is now
required, the mean, or 763·81 feet, as close enough *for
a first approximation only* to the ancient base-breadth.

But the ancient height of the Great Pyramid, which
we also need to have for instituting the calculation, is
not at all easy to measure directly with any sufficient
approach to exactness; chiefly because so very much
of the original top has actually been knocked away in
mediæval times as to leave a platform described by the
Arabs as "large enough for eleven camels to lie down;"
far therefore beneath the precise aerial place and height
where once the four triangular sloping sides, or external
flanks, of the building were continued up to, and terminated in, a sharp point.   In fact, the key-stone of the
whole theory of the Great Pyramid would have been entirely wanting to poor John Taylor's first efforts, but for
Colonel Howard-Vyse's most providential finding of
two of the ancient "casing-stones" *in situ,* with their
sloping faces, at the foot of the Pyramid (see Plate VIII.);
for they enable the problem to be attacked in a different
manner, and without any dependence on the missing
portion at the top ; or by angular, as contrasted to, but
afterwards made to furnish an idea of, linear, measure.
For such angle can give forth by *computation* a *complete*
vertical height, to be used with the already obtained,
by *measure*, complete base-breadth.

Beginnings of Objections by certain captious Individuals to the earliest Data on which the Modern Scientific Theory of the Great Pyramid rests.

After reading my first paper on this casing-stone part of the problem to the Royal Society, Edinburgh, before going to Egypt, I was seriously warned that two very shrewd and experienced members there had utterly condemned it. One of them, an engineer, saying "that he had twice passed through Egypt, been to the Pyramids, saw no symptoms of casing-stones, and therefore would not believe in anything about them." The other, an Indian naval officer, had also been to the Pyramids on a visit, and " found such heaps of rubbish about the great one, that he could not see how any man *could* measure even its base side length with any degree of correctness, much less the angles of casing-stones which he also could not see."

The First Objector.

Both these speeches are only too faithful examples of the small extent of information on which many persons, of commanding social rank, will even yet persist in speaking most authoritatively on both the present, and the long past, state of the Great Pyramid. Yet the first doubter about the casing-stones should at least have read the accounts of Herodotus, Strabo, Pliny, and many of the early Arabian authors too, who described what they saw before their eyes when the casing was still complete, eminently smooth, and by all men called beautiful. Next the doubter should have taken up Colonel Howard-Vyse's own book, descriptive, in details vocal with simple, naïve truth, both of how he succeeded, after immense labour with hundreds of workmen, in digging down to, finding, and measuring

probably the last two of the northern side's bevelled
blocks ; (still were they *in situ*, and adhering closely by
their original cement to the pavement base of the building ;) and then how he failed, though he covered them
up again with a mound of rubbish, pending an application to our Government to remove them to the British
Museum,—how he failed to save them from the hammers of Mohammedan prowlers by night ; deadly jealous
as they were of Christians obtaining anything really
valuable from the country *they* rule over.

Besides which, the large amount of casing-stones,
bevelled externally to the slope, still existing upon other
pyramids, as on the two large ones of Dashoor (see
Plate V.) ; the well-preserved ones of the second Jeezeh
Pyramid, conspicuous near its summit, and on a bright
day "shining resplendently afar," as says M. Jomard
(see Plates VIII. and IV.) ; and the granite ones of the
third pyramid, so excessively hard that modern workmen have not cared to have much to do with them   all
this, which has long been known, and more particulars
which I have presently to relate, should effect much in
convincing unwilling minds as to what was the *original*
state of the outside of the Great Pyramid.   While a
similar case of spoliation to what that building experienced in A.D. 840, was perpetrated only a few years
ago, on the south stone pyramid of Dashoor by Defter-
dar Mohammed Bey, in order to procure blocks of ready-
cut stones of extra whiteness wherewith to build himself
a palace near Cairo.*   All these well-known social and

---

* There is even a large consumption of ancient building-stones in the
accidents of modern Egyptian life, let alone the oft burning of lime-stone
blocks into lime, for mortar and plaster-work.   Thus I was astonished
in 1864 at the massive outside stair to his house which one of the Sheikhs
of the nearest Pyramid village had made, evidently with stone blocks
from the tombs of the Great Pyramid Hill, and certainly never cut out
in any natural quarry by modern Arab hand.   But in 1873 I am informed
by Mr. Waynman Dixon that that village has been in the interval
entirely washed away by a high Nile inundation, and that its inhabitants

historic recorded facts should have qualified the opposition of Objector No. One, even in the year 1864.

The Second Objector.

Then the doubter about the possibility of other men
succeeding in measuring what would have puzzled him
as he looked on idly, and never had held a measuring
rod of any kind in his hand, should have read the whole
account of the active and hard-working French Academicians in Egypt; of which the following extract, from p. 63
of "Antiquités, Description," vol. ii.,* is worthy of being
more generally known than it seems to be: viz. that after
digging down through the rubbish heaped up about the
lower part of the building, " They recognised perfectly
the esplanade upon which the Great Pyramid had been
originally established; and discovered happily, at the
north-east angle, a large hollow socket (*encastrement*)
worked in the rock, cut rectangularly and uninjured,
where the corner-stone (of that one basal angle) had
been placed; it is an irregular square, which is 118
British inches broad in one direction, 137·8 British
inches in another, and 7·9 of the same inches deep" all
over its floor (measures since then tested by myself, but
only after several days spent in digging and clearing the
locality over again by a civil engineer with a party of
Arabs). The French *savants* "made the same research
at the north-west angle, and there also discovered a

have since then built themselves a new village much closer to the Great
Pyramid Hill, and in so far nearer to their hitherto inexhaustible supply
of grand stones, cut and squared to their hand.

  * " Ils reconnurent parfaitement l'esplanade sur laquelle a été établie
la pyramide, et découvrirent heureusement à l'angle nord-est un large
encastrement, creusé dans le roc, rectangulairement dressé et intact, où
avait posé la pierre angulaire; c'est un carré irrégulier qui a 3 mètres;
dans un sens, 3·52 mètres dans l'autre, et de profondeur 0·207 mètres; ils
firent les mêmes recherches à l'angle nord-ouest, et ils y retrouvèrent
aussi un encastrement semblable au premier; tous·deux étaient bien de
niveau. C'est entre les deux points les plus extérieurs de ces enforce-
ments et avec beaucoup de soins et de précautions qu'ils mesurèrent la
base. Ils la trouvèrent de 233·747 mètres."

hollow socket (*encastrement*) similar to the former : the two were on the same level. It was between the two exterior points of these hollows, and with much care and precaution, that they measured the base-side length. They found it 763·62 British feet."

The "encastrement," so brought to light in the basal rock at the north-east angle, is duly figured in plan amongst the large French plates ; and, as I have since verified at the place, has the inner corner curiously pared away (see Plate VII.), evidently indicating the well-shaped rectangular *outer* corner to be the true starting-point for measure ; and because, also, it was originally the terminal point of the Pyramid's substance at that lower angle or foot. From the outer corner of the north-east to the outer corner of the north-west "encastrements" of their happy discovery it therefore was, that the skilful French surveyors extended their measuring bars, and with the result given above.

They also triangulated the ground round about, and from thence measured the altitude of the *present* depressed and flat-topped summit of the Great Pyramid with an accuracy which would have been quite enough for any ordinary remnant of archæological structure. But the Great Pyramid has to undergo severer tests ; and as there was no *ancient* fiducial mark up there to enable the *savants* to supply the exact quantity of the now missing portion of the original summit, we have, after all, for restoring that, to return to the angular inclined plane of the two original casing-stones below, so happily uncovered by Colonel Howard-Vyse in 1837, and proved by him to have been the very beginning of the northern upward-sloping side of the building.

Howard-Vyse's Casing-stones.

The extreme value residing in these angular relics was not only because they were of the number of the

original casing-stones, and actually *in situ* and undisturbed, and therefore showing what was once the
veritable outside of the Great Pyramid, viz. smooth,
polished, dense white lime-stone, almost like marble,
in a sloping plane; but because they exhibited such
matchless workmanship : as correct and true almost as
modern work by optical instrument-makers, but performed in this instance on blocks of a height of nearly
5 feet, a breadth of 8 feet, and a length, perhaps, of 12
feet; with the finest of joints, said to be no thicker,
even including a film of white cement, than " silver
paper." The angle of the inclined or bevelled outer
surface, measured very carefully by Mr. Brettell, civil
engineer, for the Colonel, came out 51° 50'; and being
computed from linear measures of the sides, made for
him by another engineer, came out 51° 52' 15.5".*
Results not indeed identical, and which might have
been made better, with more care at the time ; but yet,
extremely accordant with one another, as compared
with the French angular determination (before there
was anything on which to determine accurately, other
than the present ruined and dilapidated sides of the
edifice) of 51° 19' 4"; or of previous modern observers,
who are actually and incomprehensibly found anywhere, and most variously, between 40° and 60°.

John Taylor's Proposition supported by Howard-Vyse's Casing-stone Angle.

On the whole, then, taking everything into fair consideration, the ancient angle of the Great Pyramid's
slope may be considered to be certainly somewhere
between the two measured quantities of 51° 50' and
51° 52' 15.5", while there are many other reasons for
believing that it *must* have been 51° 51' and some
seconds. How many mere seconds, the modern

* Sir John Herschel, *Athenæum*, April 23, 1860.

observations are not competent altogether to decide; and a second of space is an exceedingly small quantity even in the most refined astronomical observations. But if we assume for the time 14·3″, and employ the whole angle, viz. 51° 51′ 14·3″, with the base-side as already given from linear measure = 763·81 British feet, to compute the *original* height-quantity which we have been struggling after so long, we have for that element 486·2567 of the same linear units. And from these values for the ancient height and base-breadth, computing the proportion of diameter to circumference, there appears 486·2567 : 763·81 × 2 : : 1 : 3·14159, &c.* And this result in so far shows that the Great Pyramid does represent, as closely as the very best modern measures can be trusted, the true value of π; a quantity which men in general, and all human science too, did not begin to trouble themselves about until long, long ages, languages, and nations had passed away after the building of the Great Pyramid; and after the sealing up, too, of that grand primeval and prehistoric monument, of an age, which was the *Patriarchal* age of the earth according to Scripture.

Subsequent Confirmations of the above grand Datum.

Hence the first stage of our trial terminates itself with as eminent a confirmation as the case can possibly admit of, touching the truth of John Taylor's theory, proposition, or statement; and now begins the second stage, wherein I can add the absolute weight of direct personal examination, as well as of practical researches

---

* John Taylor's numbers for the vertical height and the base-breadth of the Great Pyramid were 486 and 764 feet; evidently the nearest possible approximation by whole feet. Further, we should mention that the height of the Great Pyramid, trigonometrically measured by the French *savants*, is perfectly agreeable to the above computed result; for when it is increased by something more than 30 feet, to allow for the evidently missing portion at the summit, it amounts to the same thing.

carried on at the place by myself for a longer time and
with better measuring instruments than any of my
predecessors had at their command. I was not indeed
so fortunate as Colonel Howard-Vyse in finding anything like such large, entire, unmoved, and well-
preserved casing-stones as he did; but was enabled to
prove, that the enormous rubbish mounds now formed
on each of the four base sides of the Pyramid consist
mainly of innumerable fragments of the old casing-
stones, distinguishable both by the superior quality of
their component stone and their prepared angle of slope
always conformable, within very narrow limits, to
Colonel Howard-Vyse's determination. And a number
of these almost " vocal " fragments were deposited by
me, on my return, in the museum of the Royal Society,
Edinburgh.

Also, by careful measures of the angle of the *whole*
Pyramid along all four of its corner or " arris " lines
from top to bottom, observed with a powerful astronomical circle and telescope, as more particularly
described in my larger book, " Life and Work at the
Great Pyramid," in 1865, the same result came out.
For that *corner* angle so measured (see Plate XX.) was
found to be 41° 59′ 45″ nearly : and that gives by computation (according to the necessary innate relations of
the parts of a square-based pyramid), for the *side* slope
of this " Great " one, 51° 51′ and some seconds ; or
without any doubt the representative of the angle
Colonel Howard-Vyse did observe on the *side* directly ;
and the one which, if it is there, necessarily makes the
Great Pyramid, in and by its *whole* figure, express the
value of that most scientific desideratum π.

Nor has the proving of the matter stopped with me.
For other explorers have now been induced to search
the rubbish mounds about the Pyramid, and have
seldom left without carrying off some fragment, wherein

two evidently anciently worked sides met, not at a right
angle, but at the angle of either 51° 51′ or 128° 9′,
nearly : one being the angle at the foot, the other at
the head, of every casing-stone of a π pyramid, if built,
as the Great Pyramid is, but some other Pyramids are
not, in accurately horizontal courses of masonry.

I learn, too, from a recent American book of travel,
that my former Arab assistant in measuring the Great
Pyramid, Alee Dobree by name, and who was very
quick in seizing the idea of angle expressed in numerical
amount when I first explained it to him in 1865,—that
he is now driving quite a trade, and most unexceptionably, with the travellers who visit the Monument, by
selling them " casing-stone fragments with the angle;"
which fragments he is able, by the gift of a sharp and
appreciating eye, to pick out of the very same hills of
rubbish they walk carelessly over.

Yet even all his feats in that way have been far tran-
scended by my friend, Mr. Waynman Dixon, C.E.,
who, taking advantage of an extensive cutting into the
Great Pyramid rubbish mounds by the Egyptian
Government merely for material wherewith to make
the road by which the Empress of France visited the
Monument in 1869, discovered almost a whole casing-
stone. Not a very large one, indeed, and a loose block
only, but with portions more or less of all its six,
original, worked sides ; or a completer example than is
known at the present moment to exist anywhere else all
the world over.

This most unique specimen Mr. Waynman Dixon
graciously sent from Egypt as a present to me, and I
have deposited it under a glass case in the official
residence of the Astronomer-Royal for Scotland, where
it has been closely measured, and its ascending angle
found to be certainly between 51° 53′ 15″ and 51° 49′ 55″;
or as close as could be expected, from the block's

size and fractured condition, to that typical 51° 51' 14"
about which all the fragments of the Great Pyramid
are found to collect.

But none of the fragments of the other pyramids of
Egypt do so. Their casing-stones were sometimes
worked with equal hand-skill, so as to preserve one
particular angle very closely over the whole surface of
a large building, but it is always a wrong angle. The
ability of head was wanting there, and meaningless
angles of 43°, 50°, 57°, 63°, and even 73° occupied, and
wasted the time of their workmen, if a mathematical
demonstration, and not a mere architectural adornment, was really their object.

Closer up in the very neighbourhood of the Great
Pyramid, as on the hill of Jeezeh itself, some of the
subsequent smaller imitation pyramids could hardly
fail to be nearer their original, and were in fact within
half, or three-quarters, of a degree of its particular
angle. But they are constant all over their surfaces,
and on every side, at that deviation; and that so very
large a one, as to throw *their* numerical value of π into
utter error; and leave the Great Pyramid the sole
example throughout all Egypt of any building whatever, giving, by its whole proportions, or entire
geometry, and within the closest limits of the best
modern measures of it, the one, and only true practical
expression for π which modern science admits.

CHAPTER III.

STANDARD OF LENGTH,

Employed in laying out the Great Pyramid.

A Foot Standard unsuitable for π on the Great Pyramid's Scale of particular Size.

IN the process of recomputing Mr. Taylor's circumferential analogy of the Great Pyramid on p. 27, after his own manner, by linear vertical height and linear horizontal base-breadth, the quantities which we worked upon, were expressed in English feet; * but it is not therefore intended to imply that they, or indeed any foot-measures, were employed by the ancient builders.

Certainly the length, want of meaning, and inconvenience of the fractions obliged to be introduced in order to represent the true, or π, proportion of the one pyramid element to the other, in these particular, absolute, linear terms, tend to forbid the idea. No doubt that a foot is something of a natural and very common measure,† and *may* have been (I do not say that it was) extensively used in the patriarchal world for many agricultural and other operations, which, if lowly, "are innocent and hurt not"; but still there is good reason

---

* Viz. vertical height = 486·2567 feet, and length of one side of base = 763·81 feet.

† The natural or naked foot of man is shorter, say about 10·5 in place of 12 inches; but the practical foot of civilised man, sandalled, shoed, or booted, is often more than 12 inches long.

for disputing whether a "foot" was ever lifted up against that grandest building of all antiquity, the Great Pyramid, by any of the constructors, or applied to it by the authors, thereof.

If then a foot measure was not likely, and the profane Egyptian cubit (whose length was close to 20·7 British inches) gave similarly inconvenient fractions, what sort of standard of linear measure *was* likely to have been employed at the building, or rather by the very builder and architect of the whole design of the Great Pyramid?

What Standard would *suit* π *on the Scale of the Great Pyramid?*

As a first step in such an inquiry, let us see whether an equally exact proportion between linear height and twice base-breadth, to what our long fractions of feet gave, cannot be obtained from some simpler numbers. Take, for instance, 116·5 : 366·0. These do not give the value of π exactly, as no simple numbers can, when the proportion itself belongs really to the incommensurables; but it is an astonishingly close approach, and an admirable clearing away of fractional troubles in all approximate work, for such plain and small numbers to make; and the exceedingly trifling fraction * by which the one should be increased, or the other decreased, does not, in the existing state of our pyramidal knowledge thus far, make much practical difference upon most of the questions which we shall have presently to take up.

Are there, however, any other reasons than such of mere arithmetical convenience, why we should attach much significance, in the design of the Great Pyramid, to these particular numbers?

---

* Either 116·5014 : 366·0000, or
116·5000 : 365·9956, would be closer,
but not so convenient in multiplication and division.

There are some reasons of really grand suggestions.

In the *first* place, 366, which represents here (for our arbitrary diameter of a circle 116·5) the π circumferential analogy of that circle, is also the nearest *even* number of days in a year ; or more precisely, of mean solar days in a mean tropical solar year (of the earth) ; or, again, of day-steps in the circle of the earth's year, which year is the most important of all circles to the physical life of man.

We now know, by modern science, that the exact number of these day-steps in such terrestrial year is, at this present time in the history of man upon earth, 365·2422 + an almost endless fraction of unascertained length. So that the proportion of the day to the year is in a manner another incommensurable ; in practice, though not in theory, as interminable as π itself; and yet for the ordinary purposes of life, all civilized nations now use 365 even; except in leap-year, when they do, evenly also, make their year to consist of 366 days.

In the *second* place, it may be stated, that that portion of the Pyramid employed as the chief datum of linear measure in the problem under discussion, viz. the length of each side of its square base as determined by the "socket" measurements, both of the French *savants* and Colonel Howard-Vyse, when it comes to be divided into 366 parts, seems to give each of them a length approaching to one round and even ten-millionth of the earth's semi-axis of rotation, or nearly 25 British inches. Equivalent, therefore, *if further and independent confirmation shall be obtained*, to the architect having laid out the size of the Great Pyramid's base with a measuring-rod 25 inches long, symbolical in modern science of the earth's diurnal rotation on its axis, in his hand, —and in his head, the number of days and parts of a day so produced in a year of the earth's revolution round the sun; coupled with the intellectual and in-

structive intention to represent that number of days, in
terms of that rod, on each base-side of the building.

A Day and Year Standard indicated, with remarkable, and harmonious, Earth Commensurability.

Now this is a feature, in all sober truth, if that
quantity of length was really used intentionally as a
standard of measure, of the most extraordinary importance ; for it is only since Newton's time that men knew
anything exact about, or have attributed anything
peculiar in its size to, the earth's axis of rotation as
different from any other diameter thereof.   It is, therefore, to man, evidently a result of modern, very modern,
science alone; and every modern civilised nation has,
during the present century, been obliged to perform
gigantic trigonometrical operations and "degree measurings," in order to arrive at any approach to accurate
knowledge of the true length of that Polar earth-line, or
rotation axis of the earth ; and they are still pursuing
the inquiry with most extensive establishments of
well-trained surveyors and scientific calculators.

Their best results hitherto oscillate generally about
500,500,000 English inches within very narrow limits,
though some of the results, from unavoidable errors of
even the most advanced modern scientific mensurations,
are as great as 500,560,000, and others as small as
500,378,000.

Such, then, is the range of uncertainty in which
England, France, Germany, America, and Russia are
placed at this moment with regard to the size of the
world they live on.   And yet they are immensely closer
in accord, and nearer to the truth, than they were only
fifty years ago ; while 1,000, 2,000, or 3,000 years since,
even the most scientific of men knew nothing but what
was childish about the size of that earth-ball on which

it had pleased God to place His last and most wondrous act of creation—man—to dwell, and play his part, for, who knows, how short a season.

Is it possible, then, that at a much earlier date still than 3,000 years ago, or on the primeval occasion of the founding of the Great Pyramid in 2170 B.C., the author of the design of that building could have known both the size, shape and motions of the earth exactly, and have intentionally chosen the unique diameter of its axis of rotation as a physically significant reference for the standard of measure to be employed in that building?

Humanly, or by human science finding it out then, and in that age, of course was utterly impossible. But if the thing was inserted there in grandly monumental fact—too grand, too often repeated, and too methodic to be owing to accident,—there was something of the supernatural in its origination. And if traces of the supernatural in goodness and truth are attributable only to God and to His Divine inspiration, then this most ancient, yet still existing monumentalization of super-human *contemporary* cosmical knowledge *of that time*, must be one of the most remarkable facts that occurred at the beginning of the post-diluvial career of man, out-side of Scripture history; and stands next in importance to Scripture itself for all intellectual and religious man-kind to inquire into, as to how, and for what end, it was allowed or aided by the Almighty both to take place, and in a manner which has enabled it to last down to these days.

More rigid Inquiry into the Absolute Length of a Base-side of the Great Pyramid.

The first thing, therefore, for us to do now, is to ascertain if the alleged fact *is* there ; or rather, to what

degree of accuracy it is there ; for in all practical work
of physical science and nicety of measurement, good
scientific men know that nothing whatever can be ascertained absolutely, but only within certain limits of error ;
those limits becoming smaller as observation improves,
but never entirely vanishing.

Is, then, the ten-millionth part of the earth's semi-
axis of rotation, or 25·025 British inches (according to
the best modern estimate of that axis, which in a manner,
and with the shining of the sun to help, *makes* the days,
of the earth, being 500,500,000 British inches long),*
multiplied by 365·2422 (the now known number of solar
days in a year), the true length of a side of the square
base of the ancient Great Pyramid ; and if it is not, by
how much does it differ ?

The foregoing theoretically proposed quantity, or
inches 25·025 × 365·2422, evidently amounts to 9140·
British inches, nearly.   And at the time of the first
edition of this book being published, the only admis-
sible, because the only *socket-founded*, determinations of
the base-side lengths that I was acquainted with were,
1st, the French one (see p. 25) = 763·62 English feet
= 9163·44 British inches ; and, 2nd, Colonel Howard-
Vyse's, of 764 English feet = 9,168 British inches ; and
both of them are far too large.

This error did not affect our determination in the last
chapter for the π *shape* of the Great Pyramid; because
we computed the height, in terms of this same base-
breadth, by reference to an *angle* observed quite independently of any linear measure.   But now we require to

* If, instead of that mean and best number, we take either of the
extreme measures of the Earth's Polar axis already indicated, the ten-
millionth length will be either 25·028 or 25·019 British inches ; trifling
variations only from 25·025 ; while the ten-millionth of the *Equatorial*
diameter of the earth, and which would have no meaning as touching
the succession of days and nights, would amount to 25·113 British inches
at least, a very sensibly different quantity even to practical working-men.

know more positively whether the numerical length then used was real, or figurative only; and when I was actually at the Great Pyramid in 1865, Messrs. Aiton and Inglis, engineers, succeeded in uncovering all four of the Great Pyramid's corner sockets (as duly detailed in my book, "Life and Work"), and then proceeded to measure from socket to socket every one of the four sides of the base : and with what result? They made them all shorter, far shorter; to me it was at first incredibly shorter, than both the French and Howard-Vyse determinations; for it was equal only to 9,110 British inches on the mean of the four sides.

Either their measures then must have been very bad and too short; or those of the French and Colonel Howard-Vyse were also bad, but too long. And why was there so much badness amongst them? Mainly because the ground to be measured over is covered, and heaped, and thrown into horrible confusion of ups and downs by those hills of rubbish, formed by the fragments of casing-stones, of which we had so much to say in the last chapter. Very useful were they then, for the angular fragments they yielded, on being dug into and turned inside out; but dreadfully obstructive are they now, when an accurate linear measure over a long distance is wanted; and when, like all distance-measuring in surveying work, it must be in a straight and level line only, for ultimate use or reference. Each measurer hoped that he had cleverly corrected his really up-and-down measures over the hills and down into the hollows of rubbish, to what they would have been if the ground had been level—but when their severally independent results are brought together, behold how they differ! And this, remember, is modern science, so critical of the antique ages of the world.

After much consideration I was inclined to divide the errors very nearly evenly between the several parties, in

my book "Life and Work," published in 1867 : adopting, therefore, neither the 9,168 or 9,163 on one side,
nor the 9,110 on the other, but 9,142. And in 1869,
when the Royal Engineer surveyors, returning from the
Sinai survey, went (according to orders) to the Great
Pyramid, and announced, through their colonel at
home, that the mean length of a side of its square base,
from socket to socket, was 9,130 British inches, they
were nearer to the *theoretical* 9,140 than to any of the
other *measured* results.*

But as there are internal features of evidence showing
that none of the measures, not even the last, were
accurate enough to be depended on to the third place
of figures (whether measured upon only one side, or all
four sides, of the base considered *square* by everybody),
all men are at this very moment left by the last
Pyramid base-side measurers of modern times in this
predicament—viz. the theoretical length of 9,140
inches, which would imply such almost unutterable
wisdom, or such inconceivably happy accident, for that
primeval time, on the part of the designer of the Great
Pyramid, is really found *amongst*, or as though it were
the thing really and centrally certified to, by the best
conclusions of modern measure. It is, indeed, notably

---

* The Great Pyramid's base-side length, " by the Ordnance Surveyors," was recently quoted from Sir H. James by the Warden of the
Standards in *Nature* as 9,120 Br. inches. But this was an error; for on
page 7, line 4 *ab imo*, Sir H. James (then Colonel, afterwards General),
R.E., states distinctly, in his " Notes on the Great Pyramid," that the
" mean length of the sides obtained by the Ordnance Surveyors was
9,130 inches; " and it is only when he goes on, at home and in the
closet, to take the mean of his men's 9,130, with Aiton and Inglis's
9,110,—wholly excluding the French surveyors and Colonel Howard-
Vyse,—that he announces that " 9,120 inches was therefore the true
length of the side of the Great Pyramid when it stood perfect." The
reason of this dishonourable shelving of the most honourable older
observers, with their larger, and almost historic, results, is shown in the
next line, where the Colonel develops his strangely mistaken theory of
the much later Greek cubit having decided the length of the early Great
Pyramid base-side, and *requiring* such a length as 9,120 inches; of which
more anon.

confirmed by them; or may be asserted upon and by means of them, within such limits as *they* can confirm anything; and if those limits are coarse, that coarseness is entirely the fault of the modern measurers, not of the ancient building; which, founded on a rock (and an admirably firm and nearly unfissured hill of dense rock of nummulitic limestone, in nearly horizontal strata), could not possibly have expanded and contracted between the successive modern dates of 1799, 1837, 1865, and 1869, A.D., as the recent measures seem at first, most absurdly, to imply. The variations, therefore, first from 9,163 to 9,168, then to 9,110, and then to 9,130, must be merely the *plus* and *minus* errors of the modern measurers: or of men intending honestly to do well if they could, but erring involuntarily, sometimes to one side and sometimes to the other of absolute exactitude.

The Earth-Axis, and Year-commensurable, Result further indicated.

Of course better measures than all that have been yet taken, might be made in the present age of science, and should be instituted forthwith, to clear up so notable a point in the primeval history of man; but the expense to be incurred in the preliminary clearing of the ground from those obstructing rubbish-heaps of broken stones, to allow of accurate measuring apparatus being brought to bear effectually, is beyond the means of any private and poor scientific man; and the Great Pyramid is not a favourite subject either with rich men or the powerful governments of wealthy nations: while the invaluable corner sockets, never properly covered up since 1865, are daily being trodden and cruelly broken down at their edges out of shape and out of size; so that we are not likely to see speedily, if ever, any better measures of the Great Pyramid's base-side length than those already obtained.*

But as *they*, when considered by any experienced computer fully, honestly, and fairly, do *include* the theoretical 9,140 British inches, we are already justified so far (and we shall have in a future chapter signal confirmation from the interior of the Pyramid), in upholding the high degree of probability that the reason why the Great Pyramid (made already of a particular *shape* to enunciate the value of the mathematical term π) had also been made of a particular *size*, was,—in part, to set forth the essence of all true chronology for man in recording the order of his works, and in understanding the chief physical basis on which alone he is ordained to prosecute them, upon this earth. For evidently this *was* accomplished there, by showing that the number of times that the Pyramid's standard of linear measure would go into the length of a side of its square base, was equal to the number of days and parts of a day, in the course of a year. That standard of linear measure, being, moreover, with a marvellously complete appropriateness of symbology, the ten-millionth (or, in mathematical expression, the 10th part) of the length of the earth's semi-axis of rotation : or of half of that axis, by the earth's rotating upon which before the sun, that particular number of days for work and nights for rest is constantly being produced for all humanity in the course of the earth's annual revolution around the sun.

* In December, 1874, on returning from his grand expedition to Mauritius for observing the transit of the planet Venus across the disc of the sun, Lord Lindsay caused his then assistant, Mr. David Gill, now H.M. Astronomer at the Cape of Good Hope, to execute a most elaborate triangulation and survey around the Great Pyramid's base, so as to determine the length of each side, to an accuracy perfectly astonishing. But year after year has passed away without any result being published, and time has meanwhile marched on to October, 1879, thus far unimproved.

Hence there is here wheel within wheel of appropriate and wise meaning, far above all the then contemporary knowledge of man, and indicating far more than any mere single case of simple coincidence of numbers. A grouping, indeed it is, of some of the earth and heaven relations established by the Creator for the accompaniments of Adamic human life, implying something vastly beyond mechanical accident on the part of the unknown ancient architect; though modern Egypt-ologists and the ancient Egyptians, and all the rest of the pagan world too, both see, and saw, nothing in it. The affair was, moreover, perfectly open, because it was on the surface, during all antiquity ; and especially open during the days of the Greek philosophers in Alexandria, when the Great Pyramid was still complete in size and finish, with its bevelled casing-stones forming the then outside finished surface of the whole ; and the ground round about so eminently free from both the present obstructions, and all others too accompanying ordinary masons' work, that Strabo declared the building looked as if it had descended upon its site ready formed from Heaven, and had not been erected by man's laborious toil at all.*

* The question which chiefly troubled poor Strabo was—" What *have* the builders done with their *chips?*   Here is the most enormous building in the world, constructed almost entirely of stones squared by man's hand, so that the involuntary production of chips must have been immense; but none of them are to be seen ; all round the Great Pyramid is a level area swept as clean as if no stones at all had ever been chipped or squared upon it."   Yet what *he* could not discover, time and the weather of 1,800 years since his day have abundantly revealed; for the said primeval chippings by the original masons (a totally different affair from, and on an enormously larger scale than the hills of rubbish of the casing-stone fragments of Mohammedan time now to be seen about the building), were all thrown over the northern edge of the Pyramid hill, or firmly banked up against the natural cliff on that side, and levelled on the top so as to extend the esplanade on the northern front of the monument.   And there, a good photograph from the north-east sand-plain shows them still to be; discriminating admirably between the natural hill, and this adventitious addition to it. (See Plate VI)

Any of those learned Alexandrians, therefore, Greek mythologists and idolaters though they were, by merely dividing the Pyramid's base-side length by the number of days in a year, might have acquired to themselves, with both ease and accuracy, the most valuable scientific standard of length contained in the whole physical earth; but none of them did so; or rather was *allowed* so to do; and Christians have now no need to bow to anything Grecian, for learning either the laws of the Heavens or the facts of the Great Pyramid.

Beginning of Reference to the Great Pyramid's Numbers.

And the affair grows in wonder the further we inquire into it.   For Mr. Taylor, led by the numbers of British inches which measure the earth's polar-axis length— and other men, also led by the dominance of fives in the Pyramid's construction (as that it has five angles and five sides, including the lower plane of the base mathematically as one)—ventured the suggestion, that the author of the Great Pyramid's design both employed decimal and quinary arithmetic; and had, and used, as his smaller unit of measure, one fifth of a fifth part of his particular cubit, forming thereby, let us say in English, an *inch*.   An inch, larger indeed than a British inch, but only by a thousandth part, *i.e.* about half a hair's breadth; an apparently unimportant quantity, and yet it is that which enables the round, and at the same time grand, *Pyramid* number of *five* hundred millions of them, viz. Pyramid, not British, inches, even, to measure the length of the earth's polar diameter with exactitude.

With these truly earth-commensurable inches, the *day standard* of linear measure for the side of the base of the Great Pyramid is 5 × 5, or just 25 of them; and that length, while it will be shown presently to be fully deserving of the appellation, amongst all Christians, of

" Sacred Cubit," we shall in the meanwhile only call
the cubit of the Great Pyramid's scientific design.   But
in *its own inches*, the side of the Great Pyramid's base,
we must remember, will no longer now measure 9,140,
but 9,131·05. Next, as there are four sides to the
Pyramid's base, the united length of all of them evidently equals 36,524·2 of the same Pyramid inches; or,
at the rate of a round hundred of *those* inches to a day,
the whole perimeter of the building (already shown to
represent the theoretical π circle) is here found to
symbolize once again, in day lengths, 365·242, or the
practical day and night circle of the year, so essential
to the life and labours of man, and ordained to him
by the grace of an omniscient God.

Now, is it not most strange,—or rather, is it not
ominously significant, that the ancient profane cubit of
idolatrous and Pharaonic Egypt, 20·7 British inches
long nearly, if applied either to the Great Pyramid's
base-side, or base diagonals, or vertical height, or aiiis-
lines, or any other known radical length of the building,
brings out no notable physical fact, no mathematical
truth? While the other length of 25·025 British inches
(which the profane Egyptians, and the Jupiter, Juno,
and Venus worshipping Greeks and Romans, when in
Egypt, knew nothing of) brings out in this and other
cases so many of the most important coincidences
with the laws of Heaven and the ordinances of this
earth we inhabit, as make the ancient monument, at
once, speak both intelligibly, most intellectually and
religiously as well, to the scientific understanding of all
Christian men of the *present* day; but preferentially to
the men of Great Britain, than to any other European
nationality.

Why, it seems almost to imply—so far as the closeness of a 25 British inch length, to being a true key for
opening this part of the design of the Great Pyramid,

is concerned—that there was more of intercommunica-
tion in idea and knowledge between the architect of the
Great Pyramid, and the *origines* of the Anglo-Saxon
race, whoever they were and wherever they met, than
between the said architect or designer of the one Great
Pyramid in Egypt, and all the native Egyptian people
of all the ancient ages, with their invariable 20·7 inch
cubit, and their false gods of their own invention. A
standard of measure, that profane Egyptian cubit, which
has had no doubt a strangely long existence in the world,
or more than 4,000 years, but which explains nothing
for or about the Great Pyramid; nor for the Egyptians,
except their early connection with Babel; and they, the
Hamitic holders of that linear standard, idolaters worse
than Babylonian, and, if possible, more intensely Cainite
in religion.

Neither can any other pyramid in Egypt presume
for a moment to compete with the Great Pyramid in
this all-important earth-axial 25-inch standard, and
365·242 day, matter. That is none of their base-side
lengths, when divided by the number of days in a year,
are able to show that crucial 10th of the earth's axis
quantity, or anything near it, or anything else of cosmical
importance. The general instinct, therefore, of the whole
human race through all ages, in so readily and universally allowing, as it did, to the first Pyramid the surname of "Great," has been gloriously borne out, beyond
all that had been expected, by the application of modern
measure and scientific research. That method has,
indeed, and as we have just seen, its uncertainties, but
within comparatively narrow, and strictly assignable,
limits; so that while the ancient base-side length of the
Great Monument *has* been quoted so low as 9,110, it *has*
also been quoted so high as 9,168 British-inches, and in
a manner to lead to the inference that 9,140 of those
inches must be very nearly indeed the true quantity.

But what are the measures of the base-side lengths of the greatest of the other Pyramids of Egypt, taken in the same terms?

When measured by Colonel Howard-Vyse and his assistant, Mr. Perring (the authors of the 9,168 measure for the Great Pyramid, and therefore rather liable to err in excess than defect)—they, that is the respective *ancient* base-side lengths of those other pyramids, are reported thus:—

Second Pyramid of Jeezeh (see Plate IV.)   .. = 8,493 British inches.
North Stone Pyramid of Dashoor (see Plate V.) = 8,633   ,,
South Stone Pyramid of Dashoor ..   .. = 7,400   ,,
The chief, or " Great," Pyramid of Saccara .. = 4,727   ,,
Third Pyramid of Jeezeh ..   .. = 4,254   ,,
The chief Pyramid of Abooseir ..   ..   .. = 4,317   ,,
Northern Brick Pyramid of Dashoor ..   .. = 4,200   ,,
Southern Brick Pyramid of Dashoor ..   .. = 4,110   ,,
Pyramid-base of Mustabat el Pharaoon ..   .. = 3,708   ,,
Foundation for a Pyramid at Aboo-Roash .. = 3,840   ,,

And so we might go on through all the thirty-seven, continually diminishing, until the last of them, one of the Pyramids of Abooseir, has a base-side length of only 905 British inches.

The Great Pyramid's Linear Standard contrasted with the French Mètre.

We have thus arrived by a comparatively short and easy path, and dealing only as yet with the externals of the monument, at the same chief result touching the Great Pyramid's standards and units of linear measure, and a probability of whence the British inch was derived in primeval days of purity, restricted numbers of mankind, and blameless patriarchal worship before idolatry began,—which Mr. Taylor equally obtained, but by a more circuitous process; and what a result it is, in whatever point of view we look upon it, or by whatever fair road we have attained to it!

The nations of the world three thousand years ago, of their own selves and by their own knowledge, cared little about their national measures beyond their daily, social use as such ; and knew nothing but what was childish with regard to the size of the earth ; so that all our present exact acquaintance with it, as a reference for standards of length, is confined within the history of the last hundred years. The great attempt of the French people, in their first Revolution, to abolish alike the Christian religion, and the hereditary weights and measures of all nations, and to replace the former by a worship of philosophy, and the latter by their " mètre," " French mètre," scheme depending in a most unfortunate and ill-advised manner of their own Academicians upon the exterior of the earth, as well as to substitute for the Biblical week of seven days an artificial period of ten days,—is only eighty years old. And how did they, the French philosophers, endeavour to carry out the metrological part of their scheme ? By assuming as their unit and standard of length, the 1-10,000,000th part of a " quadrant of the earth's *curved surface*," mere outside rind ! Well may we ask with surprise if that was all that science, trusting in itself, was able to do for them. For the grasp and understanding of the subject, that took a curved, a crooked, line drawn on the earth's exterior in place of the straight, internal axis of rotation, was, truly inferior in the extreme. Sir John Herschel has well said, but *after* John Taylor's statement about the Great Pyramid had lighted up his mind with the exquisite thought, of how near after all the British hereditary inch is to an integral earth-measure, and the best earth-measure that he had ever heard of,—Sir John Herschel, we repeat, has said, " So long as the human mind continues to be human, and retains a power of geometry, so long will the diameter be thought of more primary importance

than the circumference of a circle"; and when we come
to a spheroid, and in motion, the central axis of all
its dynamical labour should hold a vastly superior importance still. Wherefore the Parisian superficial, and
curved, mètre idea, continues the great British scientist
yet more emphatically, "was not a blunder only : it was
a *sin* against geometrical simplicity."

Again, those French philosophers of eighty years
ago, in fixing on the Meridional quadrant of *surface* for
their mètre's derivation, had no idea that within the
last fifteen years the progress of geodesy would have
shown that the earth's equator was not a circle,
but a rather irregular curvilinear figure,* perhaps
ellipsoidal on the whole, so that it has many different
lengths of equatorial diameters, and therefore also
different lengths of quadrants of the Meridian in
different longitudes. *They*, the *savants* of Paris, could
not indeed foresee these things of the present day, or
a state of geodesic science beyond them ; and yet these
things were all taken into account, or provided for, or
certainly not sinned against, by the grand, and as yet
mysterious, mind that directed the building of the Great
Pyramid 4,040 years ago ; and the reference for the
ruling standard, the 10th, or ten-millionth, part of the
earth's polar semi-axis, then adopted, is now shown, by
the general progress of all learning, to be the only sound
and truly scientific reference which the earth itself
possesses.

Through those long mediæval periods, too, of darkness, confusion, and war, when our nation thought of
no such things as mathematics, geodesy, and linear
standards, another, if not the same, master-mind, very
much like Providence, prevented our *hereditary* and
quasi-Pyramid, *smaller unit of measure*, the inch, from

---

* See M. de Schubert in *Transactions of Imp. Acad. of St. Petersburg ;*
and Sir G. B. Airy, Astro.-R., in *Monthly Notices of Royal Astron. Soc.*

losing more than the thousandth part of itself. For this is the result, if it turns out as John Taylor believed—and as he was the first of men in these latter days both to believe and to publish his belief—that the Great Pyramid is the one necessarily material and memorial centre from which those practical things, weights and measures, in a primeval age, somewhere between the time of Noah and Abraham, take whatever chronology you will, were *Divinely* distributed. To whom?   Perhaps to the *origines* of all peoples; though in that case certainly refused by some.   Yet when accepted by others, such standards were carried by them in peculiar faith and with utmost regard from land to land of their early wanderings; they thereby acting under Providential control, for some special purposes perhaps of a grand future testimony, of a kind totally above their, as well as our, imagining, and which is yet to make its appearance on the stage of this world's history.

CHAPTER IV.

THE EARTH-SIZE AND SUN-DISTANCE,

Monumentalized in the Great Pyramid.

HAVING established thus much, though to a certain degree of approximation only as yet, touching the angular shape, size, and linear standard of the Great Pyramid, it may be worth our while to bestow some special attention on another analogy between that building and the astronomical earth, published by John Taylor; and which, on being examined soon afterwards by Sir John Herschel,* was honourably declared by him to be, so far as he then knew, an apparently direct relation, in even and harmonious numbers, between the size of the earth-globe and the size of the Great Pyramid. Of a rather striking kind too, as regarded the cosmical claims of the hypothesis; though at the same time he expressed his belief that it was only approximate.

A most useful caution; and keeping it fully in view, let us test the supposition over again and in terms of those very pyramidal units and standards which we ourselves have now obtained; for inasmuch as they allow us to speak of the Great Pyramid in the actual primal measures apparently employed by its architect in planning the design, we may thereby be enabled to put his work to a stricter test and more immediate proof.

The analogy is, when put into the form subsequently

---

* *Athenæum*, April, 1860; and Mr. Taylor's "Battle of the Standards," 1864. See the Appendix to the Second Edition of his "Great Pyramid." Longmans & Co.

chosen by Sir John Herschel, "a band encircling the
earth, of the breadth of the base of the Great Pyramid,
contains one hundred thousand million square feet."
The built size, in fact, of the Great Pyramid is here
stated to bear such a remarkably round and even number, as its proportion to the created size of the natural
earth, at and for the epoch of its known and civilized
human habitation (for that is a very necessary limitation
both of time and circumstance to keep in view, in these
days of both geologists and natural philosophers undertaking to discuss periods of many hundreds of millions
of years, both past and to come), that an argument for
intention rather than accident may spring therefrom, if
it hold closely in fact and in sequence to other coincidences independently ascertained.

The feet to be used on such an occasion can hardly
be any other than Pyramid feet, or 12 Pyramid inches
set in a line; and the part of the earth for the colossal
band to encircle, what should that be?

Though it is allowable enough, and very useful too in
approximate work, to speak of the earth as a sphere,
whose every great circle, or section through its centre,
will have the same length of circumference,—we cannot
so do, or content ourselves therewith, either in accurate
modern science on one side, or in any advanced stage of
Pyramid investigation on the other. Especially when
some of our earliest discoveries there, indicated that
its design successfully discriminated between the axis of
rotation diameter, and any and every other possible
diameter through the really spheroidal, or ellipsoidal,
or chiefly flattened-at-the-poles figure, of the great mass
of the earth.

Let us come to some very clear conclusion then on
the size and shape of our planet, the earth, in Pyramid
units of measure too, before we attempt the solution of
any further problem supposed to connect the two.

Of the Length of the Earth's Polar Axis.

Expressed in Pyramid inches (each of them 0·001 of an inch longer than the national British inch), the polar diameter, or axis of rotation of the earth, has been stated by different observers of the best modern schools of the present time to be either 499,878,000 or 500,060,000 Pyramid inches in length, or any and almost every quantity between those limits. The matter, cannot, in fact, be determined much closer by the best measures of the best men in the present day; and although one nation publishes its own results to an arithmetical refinement of nine places of figures, that is not physical exactness; and it cannot convince any other nation of its correctness beyond the first three places of figures. Some of them may agree to four places, few or none of them to five or six or more places. Therefore, in this case and all other similar ones throughout this book, I shall try to simplify all numerical statements of measures by only entering the significant numbers as far as they can be certainly depended upon. Hence the 000 with which the above statements terminate are merely to give the proper value to the preceding figures, and not to indicate that any one man's measures of the earth gave forth an even number of inches in units, tens, hundreds, or thousands.

" But why do they not ascertain what the length of the earth's axis is, and state it exactly?" may ask many a reader, not directly experienced in practical scientific measurement. Well, by all means let any and every such reader ask, and ask again, that question in the proper quarter. Let him ask, for instance, at the Ordnance Survey Office in Southampton, and from the Trigonometrical Survey of India, where generations after generations of Engineer officers have been taken away from their proper military duties, and kept at nothing but observations and calculations to get at the size and shape of the earth all their lives long. They have lived and died at that employment alone, and are still succeeded at the task by others, and yet it is not completed. In fact, the expense of the methods and the men employed, is increasing every day. And not in our country alone, but in every state on the Continent, is similar work going on, and with less chance than ever of one exact, absolute, and universally admitted conclusion being ever arrived at.

Neither is this any fault of those individuals; it is the nature of human science, because it is human and not Divine. Human practical science can only go on by approximations, though it work at one and the same simple subject for ages. And though the subject itself in nature and to the eye of its Creator is absolutely simple, human science makes it so complicated and difficult as it advances with its successive inductive approximations and application of more difficult mathematics, that the matter is crushed in the end by its own weight ; and at last falls out of the range of all ordinary men to deal with, or even to be interested in.

Not only, too, do the experts of two different countries produce different *measured* results for the size of one and the same earth's axis of rotation, but they produce different results in *computing* the *same* observations; until even one and the same computer will produce varying quantities out of the same data by different methods of computation and analytical treatment; the absolute correctness of any of which methods he does not pretend to guarantee, though he can say a great deal for them all, in the present advanced state of the science.

Latest Determination of the Earth's Polar Axis.

A good example of this condition of our best knowledge of the earth's size was given by a volume published by the Ordnance Survey in 1866. It contained some splendid computations by Colonel Clarke, R.E., the chief mathematician of the establishment, and gave perhaps the most highly advanced results of all earth surveys then made by any, and every, nation. Yet he presents his final results in two different shapes, and by one of them makes the polar axis of the earth (reduced here from British into Pyramid inches) to measure by one mode of computation 499,982,000, and by another 500,022,000; leaving the reader to choose which he likes, or any mean between the two.

That publication was, in its day, a most creditable advance upon everything before it; but now, in place of being contented with either one or other or both of those results, all European countries are engaged on further more numerous, more extensive, more tedious, and more costly measurements of the earth; which measurements, after the consumption of more millions of money, may enable the successors of the parties concerned, in the course of the next century or two, to amend the above numbers by some very small fractional part; but whether it will be practically sensible, there is no saying.

In a work entitled " The Metric System," by President Barnard, of Columbia College, New York, 1872, that able analytical mathematician and forcible writer, at pages 94 to 105, sets forth admirably, and in good plain words, the inconceivable practical difficulties which small irregularities in the earth's figure throw in the way of modern science, ever really determining the size and shape of the whole earth, to any much further degree of plain certainty than it has already arrived at. And, wonderfully extensive, dreadfully expensive too, as have been already the geodesic operations of all nations, taken together, during the last hundred years,—he considers that all their resulting data, expressed by him shortly as "40 latitudes," must eventually be increased to not less than 4,000 such, before the observed materials for computing the earth's size will be worthily ready for the then mathematicians to begin their unwieldy, unenviable, and humanly almost impossible, discussions of high, future-day science upon; supposing always that the governments of the several countries, and the people of the same, will still be found agreeable to pay for it all.

Equatorial, and other, Diameters of the Earth.

Meanwhile we have already assumed as the polar-axis length for computation in the Pyramid comparisons, 500,000,000 Pyramid inches; and that being a quantity which this recent Ordnance publication may, and to a certain extent does, and must, largely confirm, but cannot overthrow, let us hasten on to an equally close knowledge of what the other diameters of the earth may measure.

These lengths depend partly on what amount of elliptical compression the computers assume, as either $\frac{1}{290}$, $\frac{1}{300}$, or $\frac{1}{310}$, from special measures of it; and partly what shape they assign to the section of the earth at the equator, where a species of transverse elliptical compression is supposed to exist (not absolutely, but only with a certain slightly different degree of probability that it is *so*, rather than not) by the Ordnance book; but to an extent that may make one of the equatorial diameters 150,000 Pyramid inches longer than another.

Without then attempting to decide any one's correctness, I have represented these extremes in the accompanying table, and placed between them the very set of earth-measures which I had computed as *probably* nearest the truth in the first edition of " Our Inheritance in the Great Pyramid."

Table of the Earth's Several Diameters, in Pyramid Inches.

Parts of the Earth referred to.	Result with Clarke's smallest equatorial diam. 1866.	Result adopted in " Our Inherit- ance." First edition, 1864.	Result with Clarke's largest equatorial diam. 1866.
Polar Diameter ..	500,000,000	500,000,000	500,000,000
Diameter in Lat. 60 ..	500,396,000	500,420,000	500,435,000
,, ,, 45 ..	500,792,000	500,840,000	500,869,000
,, ,, 30 ..	501,186,000	501,257,000	501,301,000
,, at Equator	501,577,000	501,672,000	501,730,000

John Taylor's Analogy tested.

With these data at our command, let us return to the Taylor-Herschel Pyramid analogy, which asserts that " a band of the width of the Great Pyramid's base-breadth encircling the earth, contains 100,000,000,000 square feet."

An equatorial band is the only one which could en circle the earth in a great circle, and at the same time in one and the same parallel of latitude. We proceed, therefore, thus : from the equatorial *diameters* given above, we compute the equatorial *circumferences* by multiplying them by that almost magic number to work calculations with, the π of the Great Pyramid and modern mathematics, or 3·14159, &c. Reduce them to Pyramid feet by dividing by 12, and next multiply by the already determined Pyramid base-breadth in Pyramid feet, viz. $\frac{9131·05}{12}$ = 760·921 ; the following results then come out, viz. :—

They all give smaller figures than the required 100,000,000,000; for the smaller equatorial diameter gives 99,919,000,000, and the largest equatorial diameter gives 99,949,000,000.

Not absolutely true, therefore, with any allowable equatorial diameter, further than the first three places.

An interesting approximation,* therefore, but by its very want of being closer, indicating that there may be something still grander than the size of the earth alone, to be typified by the completer measures of the Great Pyramid, and by viewing them in a different set of relations ; just as, when the point of suspension of a steel-yard is changed, and all its indications are immediately multiplied in value.

Grander Pyramid, and Solar, Analogy.

Something then further than earth-size reference had been deemed possible in the Great Pyramid, but was only at last obtained when Mr. William Petrie, C.E., after studying the mensurations detailed in "Life and Work," in October, 1867, deduced the mean distance of the earth from the sun, or the sun from the earth ; in fact " the Sun-distance," to be the quantity hitherto vaguely expected only.   An enormous length of line, even in the heavens, is this sun-distance ; and before which the mere size of the earth vanishes into almost nothingness ; yet is it a distance from the great centre of light, of heat, and support of all physical, terrestrial life, on which man's existence eminently depends, on which all his science is intimately based,

* Even one very close approximation by mere accident is not, however, so frequently met with as some persons imagine.   For whereas in 1869 one of the Ordnance officers attempted to turn the Pyramid cubit into ridicule as an earth-measure,—" Because," said he, " the British foot is as closely commensurable a measure of an equatorial degree of longitude, in terms of the year and its days too, as the Pyramid cubit of the earth's polar semi-axis (i.e. five places of numbers); and we know that that relation of the modern foot must be purely accidental,"—yet when I came to test the assertion by calculating the matter out, I found that the officer had taken Colonel Clarke's maximum equatorial radius on the ellipsoidal theory, had used it as though it had been the mean radius, and did not get the full number he required for his assertions even then.   So that his number, instead of coming out to 365,242·, only reached 365,234·, but had no right to be quoted higher than 365,183· ; and there all the scoffer's reasoning and analogy ended, while the Pyramid's continued to go forward to greater things.

and concerning which it behoves him to know fully as much as it may have pleased the Creator to permit him to learn. The merciful Creator who has further written for our benefit by the Word of Inspiration that "the Lord God is a Sun and Shield" (Psalm lxxxiv. 11); if not also that "The Highest hath placed His Tabernacle in the Sun." *

Mr. Petrie had remarked, and naturally enough, that the circle typified by the base of the Great Pyramid has already been proved to symbolize a year, or the earth's annual revolution around the sun; and the radius of that typical circle had also been shown to be the ancient vertical height of the Great Pyramid, the most important and unique line which can be drawn within the whole edifice.

Then that line, said he further, must represent also the radius of the earth's mean orbit round the sun, however far away that may be; and in the proportion of 10^9, or 1 to 1,000,000,000; because, amongst other reasons, 10 : 9 is practically, in one mode of viewing it, the shape of the Great Pyramid. For this building, nothwithstanding, or rather by virtue of, its π angle at the *sides*, has practically and necessarily, and closer than any of the modern scientific measures have come to each other, just such another angle at the *corners* (see Figs. 1 and 2, in Plate XX.), that for every *ten* units which its structure advances inward on the diagonal of the base to central, nocturnal darkness, it practically rises upwards, or points to sunshine, daylight and sky, by *nine*. Nine, too, out of the ten characteristic parts (viz. five angles and five sides), being the number of those ten parts which the sun

* In our authorised version, Psalm xix. 4, the rendering is,—" In them hath He set a tabernacle for the Sun, . . . and there is nothing hid from the heat thereof." But the Vulgate, as quoted by Padre Secchi at p. xvi. of his grand work " Le Soleil," sets forth " In Sole posuit tabernaculum suum Altissimus."

shines on in such a shaped Pyramid, and in such a latitude, at noon, through the greater part of the year; when the sun "sits on the Pyramid with all its rays," and the building is then said, as it throws no shadow at all, "to devour it." *

The Pyramid Sun-distance.

To computation Mr. Petrie instantly proceeded, reducing the 5,813 Pyramid inches of the Great Pyramid's height to British inches, multiplying them by 10^9, and reducing those inches to British miles,—when he worked out the quantity 91,840,000 (nearly) of those miles. Alas! sighed he, the analogy does not hold even in the second place of figures, for the real sun-distance by modern astronomy has been held during the last half-century to be 95,233,055 miles.†

So he threw his papers on one side, thinking he had erred altogether in the very conception, and then attended to other matters; until one fine morning he (a professional man then almost wholly and intensely occupied with chemical engineering, besides his own

---

* This 10 : 9 shape of the Great Pyramid was independently discovered soon afterwards by Sir Henry James and Mr. O'Farrell, of the Ordnance Survey Office; and it is interesting to notice that the side angle computed from it amounts to 51° 50′ 39″·1 ; the π angle being 51° 51′ 14″.3 ; and the angle from Mr. Taylor's interpretation of Herodotus, or to the effect of the Great Pyramid having been built to represent an area on the side, equal to the height squared, 51° 49′ 25″. The vertical heights in Pyramid inches are at the same time, using the same base-side length for them all—by the 10 : 9 hypothesis, 5,811 ; by the π hypothesis, 5,813 ; and by the Herodotus-Taylor hypothesis = 5,807.

† Mr. Petrie may have used, and indeed did use, and I believe still upholds (though on what I am compelled to consider an unfortunately mistaken and unfounded idea) a rather greater measure, viz. 5,826 Pyramid inches, for the Great Pyramid's vertical height; in which case his sun-distance comes out also greater than our 91,840,000 British miles. But so slightly greater, in comparison, that the general nature of his grand result, together with its confuting testimony against the 95,233,055 miles sun-distance of modern science and all high-class European astronomy up to within fifteen years ago, remains sensibly just the same.

serious and exalted religious avocations) chanced to
hear, that although the above number, ninety-five millions odd, had been held to for so long by all the modern
world,—mainly because it had been produced by the
calculations of the then last Venus-transit across the
sun's disc, by a late first-rate German astronomer (calculations so vast, so difficult, and with such a prestige
of accuracy and power about them, that no living man
cared to dispute their results),—yet the astronomical
world had been forced to awaken during the last twelve
years to a new responsibility, and not only admit that
the number might possibly be erroneous, even very
erroneous (or actually in the second place of figures),
but to institute many series of difficult observations on
either side of the world at the same time, for endeavouring to determine what the correction should be.

Some of such observations, too, actually had just
then been collected from either hemisphere, and the
daily press was full of their new-computed results.
And what were they?

Why, one group of astronomers of several nations
declared the true mean sun-distance to be about ninety-
one to ninety-one and a half millions of miles ; and another group of the same and other nations declared it
to be from ninety-two and a half to ninety-three millions of miles.   And while they were fighting together
as to whose results were the better (an actual duel with
swords was expected at one time between M. Le Verrier
and the late lamented M. De Launay), Mr. Petrie steps
in and shows that the Great Pyramid result, which he
had formerly allowed to drop from his hands, out of his
exceeding respect to all modern science from the beginning of learning up to the year 1855 A.D., is *between*
these two latest, and supposed best, of all the conclusions or so-called determinations ; indeed, it is almost
exactly the mean between the contending parties, and

forms therefore in itself, and in all its grand simplicity
and antiquity, a single representation of the whole of
the numerous, laborious, and most costly sun-distance
results of all humankind even up to the present age.*

Granting then that modern science is now, *i.e.* not in
that past day of 1855 or 1860 A.D., but in 1874, 1877,
and 1879 A.D., so far advanced that it may talk, at
least on a *mean* of its *best* results, with some degree
of confidence at last of what may not improbably be
very near to the true, real, celestial sun-distance,—the
practically correct figures for it were given, and built
up monumentally, by the Great Pyramid's design,
4,040 years ago; or before any nations of mankind had
begun to run their independent, self-willed, theotechnic,
and idolatrous courses. And if we desired any additional proof, to the records of the history of science in
general, and of the sun-distance problem in particular,†

* A word of advice may be looked for here; seeing that, in spite of
our steel-yard comparison and allusion to the principle of limits on
page 56, some critics have remarked,—" You claimed in Chapter II. that
the size of the Great Pyramid was regulated by the number of days in
the year and the length of the ten-seventh part of the Earth's semi-axis
of rotation; and now you want to say that it was regulated by the
height of the ten-ninth part of the Sun's mean distance from the Earth.
Do you then give up the former?" By no means; there are good
symbologies pointing distinctly to both in the building; and there are,
here and there, in the solar system, man knows not how, some remarkable *harmonies* of measure and proportion; and these two are apparently
of them. Not to absolute exactitude very probably, but to within a
smaller fractional quantity than the science of modern times has yet
measured to. Such harmonies too are not lasting, if we look either to
eternity, or to merely the millions of millions of years which the new
mathematical physicists claim to be able to calculate for; but they, the
said harmonies, do sensibly hold through all the *human* historical period of
the earth, and for fully as long as the Scriptures indicate that the human
period of rule may have still to run on. See " The Approaching End of
the Age," by the Rev. J. Grattan Guiness, 1878. See also another line
of the argument in the author's review of Mr. Proctor's late Pyramid
criticisms, in " Life from the Dead " for June, 1877; published by
W. H. Guest, Warwick Lane, Paternoster Row, London.

† In the age of the Greeks, the distance attributed to the sun from the
earth began with the infantine quantity of about ten miles; it increased
slowly to 10,000; still more slowly to 2,500,000; then, after a long delay,
increased to 36,000,000, under German Kepler; to 78,000,000 in the days
of Louis XIV., through means of the South-African, or trans-equatorial

that such knowledge could not have been obtained in that early day, when men were few and weak upon the earth, and confined to inhabit an extremely small portion only of its surface,—except their knowledge came from Divine inspiration,—the modern astronomers are now splendidly, though involuntarily, affording it. Giving, indeed, proof heaped on proof, in the enormous, multitudinous, almost ruinously costly preparations which they are making, at the expense of their respective nations, to observe the transit of the planet Venus over the sun's disc: this being merely the most favourable known step for them in their endeavours towards getting the sun-distance number of modern science, a trifle better, perhaps, in the end of 1874.

Modern Astronomers are involuntarily proving that Man, unaided by supernatural Divine Power, could not possibly have measured the Sun-distance accurately in the Age of the Great Pyramid; and yet it is recorded there with exceeding accuracy!

These preparations for observing the next Venus-sun transit by modern astronomers have already (1873) been going on for several years, and nothing of their kind so costly, so scientific, so extensive, was ever seen on the face of the earth before. From Europe to America, and from the most northern nation's old Hyperborean strongholds to the most distant and the newest colonies in the Southern Hemisphere, the busy hum resounds. Steam navigation, iron ships, electric telegraphs, exquisite telescopes, both reflecting and refracting, photographic machines of enormous power, chemicals of wondrous nicety as well as deadly subtlety,

observations of the Abbé La Caille; and only at length reached the full quantity, and then clumsily overpassed it, at the beginning of the present century, under the leadership of German mathematical astronomy.

refined "regulator" clocks, and still more refined chronographs, transit instruments, equatorials, spectroscopes, polariscopes, altitude-azimuth circles, all these modern inventions and many others, with all the learning of the universities, and numerous officers and men both of the army and navy, are pressed into the cause ; preparatory computations, too, with much printing, engraving and publication, have been going on for years : and all will be carried out almost regardless of expense, of time, of danger, of obstacles, to the most distant parts of the earth ; and where necessary, to parts, some of them in the tropics, and some in frozen oceans ; which neither Greeks nor Romans in all their days, nor even our own fathers only seventy years ago, knew anything of.

But all this accumulated destination of power, of wealth, of numbers, of risk, co-operated in too by every civilized nation, is stated to be absolutely necessary; nothing of it can be spared, nothing omitted, if we are to enrich ourselves, in the present age, with a better result for the sun-distance than mankind was ever informed, much less possessed, of before; excepting always that one grand monumentalization of it laid up in the primeval Great Pyramid; but concerning which no official man seems to be allowed to breathe a word at this time in London society and all the circle of its scientific associations; associations so aristocratic or rather autocratic and even tyrannous in their bearing to the Witness which dates from before history, and yet themselves scarcely more than a century old. So the expeditions will set forth gloriously next year, the favourites of Government and representatives of this boasted nineteenth century. Home astronomical observatories, attending to many other phenomena of the sky, may meanwhile languish and decay, left with only worn-out instruments and superannuated staff to carry

on their now underrated duties. Nay, indeed, looking
to the tax-gathering-from-the-people origination of
the funds for all this Venus-transit display, there are
financial reformers in the country, only too ready to
remark, that while the said expeditions are spending
the national wealth upon distant coasts, at home large
populations may be starving, public interests be neglected, or delayed indefinitely; and the crimes, as well
as calamities, arising out of ignorance uneducated,
crowding in squalid residences, cities unsanitary, and
the innate wickedness of human nature when left to its
own devices uncorrected, will go on wholesale, making
our morning papers hideous. But for all that, the
happy, chosen parties will sail with their magnificent
treasuries of newest instrumental detail; and, if the
usual consequences of grand scientific researches, of
the more difficult order, follow, the science of the
modern world will have occasion to boast, after the affair
is over, of having improved its number for expressing
the sun-distance—a little; and its acquaintance with
certain disturbing phenomena increasing the transcendent difficulty of the observations, and throwing new
doubts over the final result—a great deal.

The Great Pyramid before Science.

What a solemn witness to all these unequal efforts of
mankind is not the Great Pyramid, which has seen all
human actions from the beginning; from the time when
men broke away in opposition to both the Divine rule
and inspired teachings of patriarchal life, and wilfully
went after their own inventions!

Placed in the midst among all men, and especially
those of the earliest inhabited regions of the post-
diluvial earth, thus has been standing the Great Pyramid from Dispersion times; and they, the men so

honoured, never knowing anything of its knowledge
capacity, or suspecting its profound meaning. Yet
these things, or the types and measures of many of
them, so far as we have seen them here, were on its
surface all the time. Any one, therefore, through all
history, who should have known, if he could have
known indeed, the true sun-distance, had only to compare the Great Pyramid's height therewith, reasoning
at the same time on its shape, in order to be enabled
to perceive that the measure of that all-important physical, astronomical, metrological, and anthropological
quantity was nailed up there from ancient days; and
in figures more exact than any that modern observations have done more than merely approximate to
as yet.

In this grand earth and sun symbology, too, the Great
Pyramid is not only more favourably circumstanced than
all the other Pyramids of Egypt,—but none of *them* can
pretend to have any place in the question. To be privileged even to enter the lists, *two* data of monumental
possession are necessary. One, is the π shape, to give
both the 10^9 proportion and the radius to circumference
of circle relation. The other, an absolute amount of
vertical height, which, in the case of the Great Pyramid, is by no one now assumed as less than 5,808, or
more than 5,832, and believed to be most close to 5,819,
British inches.

Now, as to the π shape, it has already been shown,
in Chapter II., that not only none of the other Pyramids
of all Egypt have that, but they persist in keeping to
other shapes.

While as to their vertical heights, these are all far too
small; the highest amongst them (as determined by
Colonel Howard-Vyse and Mr. Perring) having measured
in their complete *ancient* condition, as follows and no
more :—

Second Pyramid of Jeezeh, Vertical Height = 5,451 British inches.
North Stone Pyramid of Dashoor   ..   .. = 4,111   ,,
South Stone Pyramid of Dashoor   ..   .. = 4,029   ,,
South Brick Pyramid of Dashoor   ..   .. = 3,208   ,,
Chief Pyramid of Abooseir   ..   ..   .. = 2,734   ,,
Third Pyramid of Jeezeh   ..   ..   .. = 2,616   ,,
North Brick Pyramid of Dashoor   ..   .. = 2,586   ,,
Chief Pyramid of Saccara   ..   ..   .. = 2,405   ,,
Middle Pyramid of Abooseir ..   ..   .. = 2,056   ,,
and at last, as see Plates IV. and V.,
Pyramid-base of Mustabat el Pharaoon   .. =   720   ,,
and Small Pyramid of Abooseir   ..   .. =   564   ,,

Nor has any stone building whatever been erected in any age, even up to this present hour, high enough to compete with the Great Pyramid's glory in this one particular. (See Plate I., the Frontispiece, representing all the buildings of the world, in time and in height.)

But again we shall have to tell, and from facts ascertained and ascertainable in just as eminently practical a manner, that all that wonderful scientific information (more than wonderful for the age and circumstances under which it was placed there) was not introduced into the Great Pyramid for strengthening men in science; much less was it to promote the worldly fame of the introducer.

Science is there, but almost solely, as it would now seem, to prove to these latter scientific days of the earth, that the building so designed in the beginning of the Noachian world, when human science was not, has now a right, a title, an authority, to speak to men of these times, and even to the most scientific of them, on another and far higher subject; or of things unseen, yet quick and powerful, piercing even to the dividing asunder of the soul and spirit, and discerning the thoughts and intents of the heart.

Postscript in 1877 A.D.

So far was written in 1873. The Venus-Transit therein alluded to, came off most successfully as to innumerable observations and multitudes of photographs of it being taken in December, 1874; and what is the result now, in February, 1877, on the world's present knowledge, by modern science, of the sun's true distance from the earth?

Nothing! Yes, indeed, with one solitary exception, presently to be alluded to, nothing! And yet rooms full of computers have been working away ever since at the necessary computations; but the further they go, the more unexpected difficulties they find. The optical phenomena connected with the physical nature of the sun's disc, and the disc of the planet, offer a host of difficulties. Photography, too, it was expected was going to be of so much facile, and even hasty, assistance, and yet the *British Journal of Photography*, of February 9, 1877, contains the following :—

"It is stated on good authority that the measurements of the photographs of the Venus-transit—those for instance taken by the French parties—are not progressing favourably. More than 1,000 plates are to be investigated microscopically, and at the present moment only forty-seven have been disposed of. Unforeseen difficulties are said to have arisen."

Some of these may be guessed at, from the notices at page 182 of the Royal Astronomical Society's Anniversary Report of February, 1877, wherein it is mentioned that in the special calculations to get the means for correcting the *distortion* of the photographs at certain of the stations, no less than 2,800 pages of ordinary foolscap size have been closely covered with figures. One skilful measurer of the distorted photographs, kept at his task for seven months, made no less than 38,000 microscopic measures, and then his eyesight failed. Three hundred other British pictures have still to be measured in this distressing manner, and the corrections for distortion at five of their stations have still to be investigated.

Then the Tables of the Moon, after 200 years of observations of that luminary at the Royal Observatory, Greenwich,—are not yet accurate enough for the Longitudes of the Venus-Transit Stations; and finally, the earth itself is accused of no longer rotating with the full amount of equability expected by theory.

In short, those who hold the observational documents, and the powers of place, will not at present give out anything in the way of the new sun-distance number; nor say when their results *will* be ready, nor what they will cost the nation by the time they *are* published.

Under these circumstances it is almost needless to refer to the little, though honourable, exception mentioned above; and to relate how a notable member of the French Academy of Sciences has by his own means alone, computed some of the observations of *two* of the French Venus-Transit Stations, viz. Pekin, and the Island of St. Paul in the Indian Ocean; and having from them deduced a sun-distance number, this has been declared by Monsieur l'Abbé and Chanoine Moigno, in his scientific journal *Les Mondes*, to be almost identical with the ancient sun-distance of the Great Pyramid.

It is useless to make anything of this just now; because the holders-back of the store-houses full of observations from *all* the stations, are ready at any moment to overwhelm *M. Puiseux*, and declare that his one result is not to be taken as *the* result of the whole world of science at the Venus-Transit of December, 1874. They, the holders-back of what is wanted to be known, are the only authoritative sources of information to be looked to; and they are, in some instances at least, more occupied " in giving honour one to another," than in working disinterestedly and unselfishly at the required computations: for this is what we read at page 344 of the journal *Nature*, February 15, 1877 :—

"A medal to commemorate the part taken by the Institute of France in the observation of the transit of Venus has been struck at the National Mint. It bears the representation (rather too commemorative also of the profane and indecent classic idolatries) of a female (in the utmost state of nudity) passing close before the car of Apollo (who appears much surprised, and not particularly pleased, thereat), with the motto in Latin, *Quo distant spatio, sidera juncta docent.* Each member of the Institute has received a silver medal, as well as the heads of the mission; the assistants received a bronze one. A medal has been cast in gold and presented to M. Dumas, the president of the Transit Commission. The expenses were defrayed by subscriptions among the members of the Institute."

The position therefore, for sun-distance information, is rather this. The Venus-Transit alluded to *has* taken place. More money has been spent upon it than was spent on all the previous sun-distance measurings from the foundation of the world, put together; and still, more than two years afterwards, the world's knowledge of the sun-distance is defective in the *second* place of figures. How many more millions of money and thousands of years will it therefore take for modern science and all its votaries to reach an accuracy in the items of, say, five or six, places of figures?

And yet far more than that will be required, if the collective science of mankind is ever to answer, with regard to the sun-distance, that other and further question put so pointedly by the Almighty himself to Job (xxxviii. 18), touching merely the Earth-size,—

"Hast thou perceived the breadth of the Earth? Declare if thou knowest it *all.*"

Further Postscript in 1879 A.D.

"Oh! as for that," says modern science, "give my adepts time and money enough, and they'll not only do all that, but much more too. Education, continued uninterruptedly, can raise man up to any efficiency whatever."

But are you sure that the prescribed time for man and his independent trial on earth has not now almost run out? See what a downward turn, at least all these special Venus-Transit affairs, that were to have eclipsed the Great Pyramid sun-distance entirely, have been taking, even since our last report, as thus :—

1st. The Astronomer-Royal (at Greenwich) was called on by the Admiralty, impatient of further years of delay, to report, for the information of Parliament, what he and all his splendidly appointed Venus-Transit parties of three years previous, made their new sun-distance? He reported accordingly, but on their optical measures only, and said the distance was 93 millions and some hundreds of thousands of miles.

2nd. On these papers reaching the Cape of Good Hope, they were overhauled by the Astronomer there, declared to have been erroneously computed on some points, and the true result stated to be 91 millions and some hundreds of thousands of miles.

3rd. On that criticism returning to Greenwich, the Cape Astronomer was vehemently accused. But, on going over their own work again, the home parties found it expedient to alter their previously reported result, and in the same direction, though not to the full quantity, indicated to them from South Africa.

4th. In the spring of 1877 the Astronomer-Royal announced that a better plan for modern science to determine the sun-distance by, than any Venus-Transit, was an opposition of the Planet Mars, if observed that year, and in a particular manner at a station near the Equator. An expedition was accordingly sent out; no less than 14 fixed observatories in Europe, America and Australia were engaged to co-operate with it ; the de-sired observations were made, but the result, though indicated, is neither yet finally declared, nor apparently much cared, or waited for now, by anyone.

5th. In June, 1878, the *photographic* results of the Venus-Transit at the British stations in 1874, were reported to the Royal Astronomical Society, London ; but found to be so bad, some of them inferring the solar-distance to be even greater than infinity, that they were almost hooted at by everyone.

6th. Meanwhile the greater part of the French, and all the German, Italian, American and Russian obser-vations of 1874, are still hanging fire as to what their respective values of the sun-distance are to be. Indeed, the parties there concerned are beginning to say, that they do not intend to give out anything, until they shall also have observed and computed the next Venus-Transit which is to occur in 1882. And,

Finally, so far as the British work is concerned, by a Report of the Astronomer-Royal in February, 1879,* it appears that H.M. Government, pressed on all sides by the bad commercial times, extensive strikes of workmen all over the country, desertions of soldiers, bursting of naval guns, colonial disasters, wars and threatenings of wars in three parts of the globe at once, have stopped any further supplies to Venus-Transit work. Wherefore the said Astronomer-Royal is left, with only one captain out of all his late naval and military expeditional staff, to finish off those once o'er-vaulting, now unfortunate calculations, and get them printed where or how he can.

Still, therefore, the Great Pyramid stands, very much as it did before the late Venus-Transit expeditions, in

* See p. 262 of the *Monthly Notices of the Royal Astronomical Society*, London ; Vol. xxxix., No. 4.

all the strength of the human power of the nineteenth century, arose,—with its own primeval sun-distance undisturbed ; a silent, but solemn, witness among men of something more than mere natural history development having occurred at the building operations on the Jeezeh hill, in the early ages of mankind.

CHAPTER V.

GEOGRAPHICAL INDICATIONS;

From the position of Great Pyramid.

AFTER our last chapter, it may not improbably be demanded by some of my readers, to be shown a few easier and shorter proofs, if they exist, of some practical science of much more ordinary kind, having been *intended* by the primeval designer of the Great Pyramid,—before they can freely, and of their own understanding, admit the probably non-accidental character of such abstruse numerical coincidences as have hitherto been chiefly dealt with.

The request is most reasonable, and the accomplished facts of the Pyramid itself enable me to furnish more than one answer immediately, in both Chorography and Geography, as well as Astronomy.

Orientation of the Sides of the Great Pyramid.

To begin, the reader may be reminded, that the square base of the Great Pyramid is very truly oriented, or placed with its sides facing astronomically due north, south, east, and west; and this fact at once abolishes certain theories to the effect that all the phenomena of that Pyramid have to do with pure geometry alone; for to pure geometry, as well as to algebra and arithmetic, all azimuths or orientations are alike; whereas one most particular astronomical azimuth or direction was picked out for the sides of the base of the Great Pyramid.

In the early ages of the world the very correct orientation of a large pile must have been not a little difficult to the rude astronomy of the period. Yet with such precision had the operations been primevally performed on the Great Pyramid, that the French Academicians in A.D. 1799 were not a little astonished at the closeness. Their Citizen Nouet, " in the month Nivose of their Republican year 7," made refined astronomical observations to test the error, and found it to be only 19′ 58″; but with the qualification added by M. Jomard, that as M. Nouet had only the ruined exterior of the Pyramid before him to test, the real error of the original surface might have been less. In this conclusion M. Jomard was doubtless correct; for in the similar sort of measure of the angle of the slope of the side, with the base, of the Pyramid, it was proved afterwards (and as we have already shown in Chapter II.), on the discovery of the casing-stones, that his compatriot, spite of all his modern science, had erred to a very much larger extent than the original builders.

As it was, however, then, in this particular question of astronomical orientation, all the Academician authors of the great Napoleonic compilation expressed themselves delighted with the physical and historical proof which the ancient Pyramid seemed to give them, when compared with their own modern French observations of the Polar star, " That the azimuthal direction of the earth's axis of rotation had not *sensibly* altered, relatively to the sides of the great Pyramid's base, during probably 4,000 years."

Possibility of Azimuthal Change in the Crust of the Earth.

Now some alteration of that kind, one way or the other, has long been a mooted question among astronomers, though chiefly for its bearing on geography, general physics, and geology. In its surface character and linear nature, therefore, it must be kept entirely distinct from the more perfectly astronomical phenomenon, and which few but astronomers attend very closely to—viz. the *angular* direction of the earth's axis *in space,* carrying with it the whole substance of the earth at the same time, and without disturbing the relative position of any of its parts.   It is in this latter angular phenomenon, that the mysterious effect of *the precession of the equinoxes* comes prominently into view, with its slow but accumulating chronological changes from age to age in the apparent times and places of the risings and settings of the stars.   But in the former rather geographical, telluric, and more especially surface-differential, light in which the problem was discussed by the French *savants* of the Revolution, it had also been clearly seen long before, and held to be a worthy cynosure of historical study, by the penetrating genius of the English Dr. Hooke.

For it was this early and ill-paid, but invaluable Secretary of the Royal Society of London, who in his discourse on earthquakes, about the year 1677 A.D., remarks, "Whether the axis of the earth's rotation hath and doth continually, by a slow progression, vary its position with respect to the parts of the earth ; and if so, how much and which way, which must vary both the meridian lines of places, and also their particular latitudes ? that it had been very desirable, if from some monuments or records in antiquity, somewhat could have been discovered of certainty and exactness ; that by comparing that or them with accurate observations now made, or to be made, somewhat of certainty of information could have been procured." And he proceeds thus : " But I fear we shall find them all insufficient in accurateness to be any ways relied upon. However, if there can be found anything certain and accurately done, either as to the fixing of a meridian line on some stone building or structure now in being, or to the positive or certain latitude of any known place, though possibly these observations or

constructions were made without any regard or notion
of such an hypothesis; yet some of them, compared
with the present state of things, might give much
light to this inquiry. Upon this account I perused Mr.
Greaves' description of the Great Pyramid in Egypt,
that being fabled to have been built for an astronomical
observatory, as Mr. Greaves also takes notice. I
perused his book, I say, hoping I should have found,
among many other curious observations he there gives
us concerning them, some observations perfectly made,
to find whether it stands east, west, north, and south,
or whether it varies from that respect of its sides to any
other part or quarter of the world; as likewise how much,
and which way they now stand. But to my wonder, he
being an astronomical professor, I do not find that he
had any regard at all to the same, but seems to be
wholly taken up with one inquiry, which was about the
measure or bigness of the whole and its parts; and the
other matters mentioned are only by-the-bye and accidental, which shows how useful theories may be for the
future to such as shall make observations; nay, though
they should not be true, for that it will hint many
inquiries to be taken notice of, which would otherwise not be thought of at all, or at least but little regarded, and but superficially and negligently taken
notice of. I find indeed that he mentions the south
and north sides thereof, but not as if he had taken any
notice whether they were exactly facing the south or
north, which he might easily have done. Nor do I find
that he had taken the exact latitude of them; which
methinks had been very proper to have been retained
upon record with their other description."

Dr. Hooke, however—in mitigation of whose acer-
bity there is much to be said in excuse, for nature
made him, so his biographer asserts, " short of stature,
thin, and crooked "—this real phenomenon, Dr. Hooke,
" who seldom retired to bed till two or three o'clock in

the morning, and frequently pursued his studies during the whole night," would not have been so hard upon his predecessor in difficult times if he had known, and as we may be able by-and-by, to set forth, what extraordinarily useful work it was that Professor Greaves zealously engaged in when at the Great Pyramid. The Doctor's diatribes should rather have been at Greaves's successors to-be, those who were to visit the Great Pyramid in easy, intellectual, scientific times, and then and there do nothing, or mere mischief worse than nothing. Hence it seems to have remained to myself, in 1865, to attempt, at least, to determine with something like modern accuracy the astronomical azimuth of the Great Pyramid; and not only upon its fiducial socket-marks, as defining the ends and directions of the sides of the base, but, still more importantly, on its *internal passages.*

These passages, long, white-stoned, straight, and of exquisite workmanship, evidently received much of the care of the ancient architect; and though for some deep reasons, enquired into further on,* they were not established by him in the central vertical, and right, plane of the whole Great Pyramid, were yet placed parallel thereto; or, *for infinite distance,* in the selfsame natural orientation, with astonishing precision.

Popular Ideas of Astronomical Orientation.

In page 26 of George R. Gliddon's "Otia Ægyptiaca," that generally acute author does indeed fight against the idea of any astronomical skill in the ancient architect, by suggesting mystically that all this exactness of orientation indicates, amongst the builders of the "pre-antiquity" day of the Great Pyramid, "an acquaintance with the laws of the magnet." Yet had that been all the founders were possessed of to guide them, the orientation of their great and lasting work might have been in

* See Part IV., Ch. XIX.

error by ten, or twenty, or thirty degrees or more, in place of only twenty minutes, and, perhaps, far less.

Quite recently too, or within the last six months, on the occasion of a public lecture being given on the Great Pyramid at Ramsgate, an attempt was made by a gentleman-proprietor of the neighbourhood to invalidate the whole of the Great Pyramid subject, because forsooth the lecturer had said nothing about "the Variation of the Compass"; and without that being known, he sententiously informed the Mayor, that " all the rest of the measures were without any value."

I fear that gentleman must have been misled, like a very worthy friend of mine, a judge too of a great city, and in his day a brilliant classical and philosophical university student,—by having purchased, as a superior means of obtaining true *time* accurately, a miniature sun-dial mounted on a magnetic needle.

"What can be more perfect ?" said he. "Wherever you are, if only the sun shines, the gnomon of the dial is placed due north and south for you by the magic power of the needle, and you have only to read off the time on the hour circle."

So then I had to explain, what I thought every child of the present scientific age knew long ago; viz. that the end of the magnetic needle marked by the maker NORTH, only points to the real NORTH direction of the earth and the heavens *feebly*, *erroneously*, and *varyingly*.

So feebly, that the smallest imperfection of the central pivot may vitiate the direction of an ordinary waistcoat-pocket compass by several degrees.

So erroneously, either from the magnetic axis of the needle, not coinciding with the shape of the needle, or from the observer having a key or a knife, or a bit of iron or magnetic and attractive rock in his pocket or the neighbourhood, that the needle may be again deflected from its proper position by whole degrees.

And so varyingly, because there are daily, monthly, yearly, and century changes going on in the magnetic elements themselves : wherefore not only are they different in one part of the country from another, but in the same part they differ from age to age ; and in the lifetime of the Great Pyramid, the variation of the compass there may have oscillated from west to east of true north 40°, 50°, 60°, and several times over.

The more an *astronomer* looks into the pointings of a magnetic needle, the more full of serious uncertainties and vagaries he finds it.   But the more he examines by mechanical instruments and astronomical observations into the north and south of the axis of the world or the polar point of the heavens, the more admirably certain does he find *it* and its laws, even to any amount of microscopic refinement.

No astronomer, therefore, in a fixed observatory ever thinks of referring to a magnetic needle for the direction of the north.   The very idea, by whomsoever brought up, is simply an absurdity.   And of course, in my own observations at the Great Pyramid in 1865, I had nothing to do with occult magnetism and its rude, uncertain pointings, but employed exclusively, for the polar direction, an astronomical alt-azimuth instrument of very solid construction, and reading to seconds.   In that way comparing the socket-defined sides of the base, and also the signal-defined axis of the entrance passage, with the azimuth of *Alpha Ursæ Minoris*, the Pole-star, at the time of its greatest elongation west ; and afterwards reducing that observed place, by the proper methods of calculation, to the vertical of the pole itself, the cynosure was reached.

And with what result ? Though a tender-hearted antiquary has asked, " Was it not cruel to test any primeval work of 4,000 years ago, by such exalted scientific instruments, and abstruse books of logarithms, as those of the Victorian age in which we live ? "

Well, it might be attended with undesired results, if some of the most be-praised works of the present day should ever come to be examined by the advanced instruments of precision of 4,000 years *hence ;* but the only effect which the trial of my Playfair astronomical instrument from the Royal Observatory, Edinburgh, had at the Great Pyramid, was to reduce the alleged error of its ancient orientation from 19′ 58″ to 4′ 30″.*

Further Test by Latitude.

In so far, then, this last and latest result of direct observation declares with high probability,—that any relative azimuthal change between the northern direction of the earth's rotation axis, and a line drawn by man upon its crust 4,000 years ago, such as Dr. Hooke and the French Academicians so greatly desiderated, must, if anything of such change exist at all, be confined within very narrow limits indeed.

This conclusion has its assigned reason here and thus far, solely from observations of angular *direction* on the horizontal plane of the earth's surface at the place; and without any very distinct proof being arrived at yet, touching—that though we find the Great Pyramid's sides at present nearly accordant in angle with the cardinal points of astronomy, they were *intended* to be so placed by the primeval builder *for his own day*.

But indication will be afforded presently respecting another test of nearly the same thing, not by angle, but by distance on the surface; and further, that the architect did propose to place the Great Pyramid in the astronomical latitude of 30° north, whether that exact quantity was to be practical or theoretical; while my own astronomical observations in 1865 have proved, from the results of several nights' work, that it stands so *near* to 30°, as to be in the latitude parallel 29° 58′ 51″.

* The particulars of both observations and computations may be seen in vol. ii. of my " Life and Work at the Great Pyramid, 1867."

A sensible defalcation this, from 30°, it is true, but not all of it necessarily error; for if the original designer had wished that men should see with their bodily, rather than their mental eyes, the pole of the sky, from the foot of the Great Pyramid, at an altitude before them of 30°, he would have had to take account of the refraction of the atmosphere; and that would have necessitated the building standing not in 30°, but in 29° 58′ 22″. Whence we are entitled to say, that the latitude of the Great Pyramid is actually by observation *between* the two very limits assignable, but not to be discriminated, by theory as it is at present.

The precise middle point, however, between the two theoretical latitudes being 29° 59′ 11″, and the observed place being 29° 58′ 51″, there is a difference of twenty seconds which may have to be accounted for. Though Dr. Hooke's question upon it would pretty certainly have been, can the earth's axis have shifted so *little* in 4,000 years with regard to its crust, that the latitudes of places have altered no more in that length of time than a miserable 20″ of space.

Unfortunately none of the Greek, Roman, Indian, Alexandrian, or any of the older observatories of the world, had their latitudes determined in their day closely enough to furnish additional illustrations for this purpose. Even in Professor Greaves's time, two hundred and forty years ago, a whole minute of altitude was thought to be an almost superhuman refinement of measure; so that he mentions somewhat fearfully and with bated breath, how a celebrated Italian astronomer, Gaspar Bertius, had credibly informed him when in Rome, "that by repeated observations with a large instrument of Clavius' he had ascertained that the altitude of the pole there, was 41° and 46′." And yet if the spot where Bertius observed, were anywhere near either St. Peter's, or the Collegio Romano, whose latitudes have been well measured in modern times, his result must have been no less than 7′ in error.

At Greenwich, the oldest and best supported of modern European observatories, there has been a continued decrease in its observed latitude with the increase of the time. So that taking up at random the large volumes of its published observations now before me, I find the latitude successively stated as—

$$\text{In } 1776 = 51° \ 28' \ 40·0''$$
$$\text{In } 1834 = 51° \ 28' \ 39·0''$$
$$\text{In } 1856 = 51° \ 28' \ 38·2''$$

This change of 1·8″ in eighty years, implies a quicker rate of decrease than the 20″ at the Great Pyramid in 4,000 years,—if the observations were perfect; but they are not; and it is said, I believe, that small errors in both the instruments and the tables of refraction employed, *may* be found eventually to explain away the apparent Latitude change.*

Hence all the known practical astronomy of the modern world cannot help us in this matter; and if we apply to physical astronomy, some of its great mathematicians of the day who are supposed to be able to compute anything, and have announced long since how many millions of millions of millions of years the solar system is going to last, these great computers also announced a few years ago that they had found the interior of the earth to be solid, and as stiff as hammered steel; so that *no* change of latitude *could* take place. But within the last year, they have concluded again that the interior of the earth is fluid, and steadied only by vortex motion of that fluid; also that in the earlier

---

* In the Royal Astronomical Society's Report for 1878, it is mentioned that the new value for the latitude of the Royal Observatory, Greenwich, has been found, in 1877, from the mean of nearly 9,000 observations, to be 51° 28′ 38·60″. But again in the Annual Report for 1879, the issue of a new star-catalogue is stated to be delayed, by the recent discovery that the last change made in the Greenwich refraction tables, was wrong, and that all the declinations of the stars in the catalogue, as well as probably the latitude of the Observatory, will have to be altered.

geological ages, long before man appeared on the scene, great changes of latitude did take place in those almost infinitely long periods; and that, therefore, some *small* change of the same sort may have been experienced within human history; but it can only be a *very* small change, even as the Great Pyramid has already indicated.

Testimony, from the Great Pyramid's Geographical Position, against some recent Earth Theorizers.

In angular distance, then, from the equator, as well as in orientation of aspect, the land of Egypt, by the witness of the Great Pyramid, even if it has changed its latitude a very little, has certainly not changed sensibly for all ordinary, practical men at their usual avocations, in respect to the axis of the earth, during the last 4,000 years.

What therefore can mean some of our observers at home, observers too of the present day, who stand up for having, themselves during their own lifetimes, witnessed the sun at solstice rise and set in an *exceedingly* different direction by the naked eye from what it does now? I have looked over the papers of two such enthusiasts recently (one in England and the other in Scotland), but without being able to convince them of their involuntary self-deception.*

Again, in the Rev. Bourchier Wrey Savile's work, "The Truth of the Bible," published in 1871, that usually very learned and painstaking author (and much to be commended in some subjects) implies, on page 76, that the direction of the sun at the summer solstice is now, at Stonehenge, no less than *twelve degrees* different from what it was at the time of the erection of that monument, which is probably

---

* I am happy to say, in 1879, that the Scottish case has come all right; or the ultra-honest old gentleman recently assured me that six more years' experience had shown him how to guard against his earlier error in making the observation on the sloping side of a hill, and he is convinced now that there is nothing wrong about the Sun.

not more than a third as old as the Great Pyramid.
And he quotes freely from, as well as on his own part
confirms, a person now dead, one Mr. Evan Hopkins (not
the Cambridge mathematician and geologist Hopkins,
but a Civil Engineer long in Australia), in asserting
"that the superficial film of our globe is moving from
south to north in a spiral path, at the rate of seven
furlongs in longitude west, and three furlongs in latitude north, every year; whence, he says, the presently
southern part of England must have been under a
tropical climate only 5,500 years ago."

This astounding assertion is further supposed, by
those parties, to be supported by a quotation from one
of the Greenwich Observatory Reports in 1861, wherein
Sir George B. Airy remarks that "the transit circle and
collimators still present those appearances of agreement
between themselves, and of change with respect to the
stars, which seem explicable only on one of two sup-
positions—that the ground itself shifts with respect to
the general earth, or that the axis of rotation changes
its position." But I can venture to be professionally
confident that Sir G. B. Airy did not mean to support
any such assertion as Mr. Evan Hopkins's and Mr.
W. B. Savile's, by that mere curiosity of transcendental
refinement in *one year's* instrumental observation, which
he was alluding to in one number of a serial document;
a something of possible change, too, which is so excessively small (an angle subtending perhaps the apparent
thickness of a spider's line at the distance of fifty feet),
that no one can be perfectly certain that it ever exists;
a something which small heat expansions of the instrument may easily produce; and which, if found at any
given epoch, does not go on accumulating continually
in one direction with the progress of time, as it would
do if dependent on a grand cosmical cause.

To confirm, too, this much more sober view of the

nearly solid earth we live upon, the Great Pyramid adds all its own elder and most weighty testimony to that both of Greenwich and every public observatory with good astronomical instruments throughout Europe, by declaring the world's surface to be remarkably constant to the cardinal directions, *for as long as it has been accurately observed.* And thus it may come to pass at last, that there will yet be monumentally proved, from the earliest human times to the present, to be more of " the truth of the Bible " bound up with both the scientific definition, and exactly observed constancy through long ages, of astronomical orientations, as well as geographical directions and positions,—than has yet entered into many persons' modern philosophies.

True Primeval Astronomical Orientation, as in the Great Pyramid, opposed, but in vain, by all early idolatrous Structures elsewhere.

The Great Pyramid, then, as we have already shown (besides proving it a non-idolatrous, as well as primeval, monument), did set a clear and recognizable scientific rule in building, by so successfully *orienting* its sides to the cardinal directions of high astronomy. This plan was followed also wherever that Pyramid's example, by overshadowing grandeur, was felt to be compulsory; as it evidently was by all sorts of buildings on the hill of Jeezeh, and in the adjacent parts of Lower Egypt,— but, nowhere else.

At Thebes, for instance, the glory, as well as shame, of Upper Egypt, and far more characteristic of the Pharaonic, mediæval, and most wickedly powerful period of the nation, also in Nubia further away and later still, the temples and tombs are put down or founded at every possible azimuth, towards almost every quarter of the sky; and those temples and tombs are all of them undoubtedly idolatrous, Egyptologic, and speak lamentably to human theotechnic inventions.

In Mesopotamia, again, and the spiritually rebellious region of Babel, the Chaldean Temples, dedicated glaringly both to false gods, and all the Sabæan hosts of heaven, are not laid out at random ; or in general contempt of, or indifference to, all astronomical orientation, like the Theban temples of Egypt, but in another and an opposition sort of astronomical orientation to the Great Pyramid example. For while the bases of these Euphratian structures, though rectangular, are not square, they are set forth with their sides as far as possible *from* any and every cardinal point, *i.e.* at an angle of 45° therefrom; and steadily as well as persistently kept thereat from one end of the Inter-amnian country to the other.

The Rev. Canon Rawlinson of Oxford has, indeed, endeavoured to maintain that it was a matter of indifference for the astronomical observations of those Chaldean buildings, whether they were oriented upon, or at 45° away from, the cardinal points,—but in that case the astronomical observations made there must have been of as totally different a character from those of the Great Pyramid, as from those of any of our modern meridian observatories, where the exceedingly true meridian direction in which they observe, is everything. And when we study the Great Pyramid itself still further, important results follow to its prestige and geographical power upon earth, from new and most remarkable developments arising precisely out of its true and very north and south, with east and west, bearings, as well as from its regular figure.

Geographical Aptitudes of the Great Pyramid.

With the general's glance of a Napoleon Bonaparte himself, his Academician *savants* in Egypt, in 1799,

perceived how grand, truthful, and effective a trigonometrical surveying signal the pointed shape of the Great
Pyramid gratuitously presented them with ; and they
not only used it for that purpose, as it loomed far and
wide over the country, but employed it as a grander
order of signal also, to mark the *zero meridian* of *longitude* for all Egypt.

In coming to this conclusion, they could hardly but
have perceived something of the peculiar position of the
Great Pyramid at the southern apex of the Delta-land
of Egypt ; and recognized that the vertical plane of the
Pyramid's passages produced northward, passed through
the northernmost point of Egypt's Mediterranean coast ;
besides forming the country's central and most commanding meridian line. While the N.E. and N.W.
diagonals of the building similarly produced, enclosed
the fertile Delta's either side in a symmetrical and well-
balanced manner. (See Plate II.)   But the first very
particular publication on this branch of the subject was
by Mr. Henry Mitchell, Chief Hydrographer to the
United States Coast Survey.

That gentleman having been sent, in 1868, to report
on the progress of the Suez Canal, was much struck
with the regularity of a certain general convex curvature along the whole of Egypt's, "Lower Egypt's,"
northern coast.   To his mind, and by the light of his
science, it was a splendid example, on that very account,
of a growing and advancing coast-line, developing in
successive curves all struck one after and beyond the
other from a certain central point of physical origination in the interior.

And whereabouts there, was that physical centre of
natural origin and formation ?

With the curvature of the northern coast, really the
Delta-land of the Nile, on a good map before him (see,
in a very small way, our Fig. 1, Plate II.), Mr. Mitchell

sought, with variations of direction and radius carried southward, until he had got all the prominent coast-points to be evenly swept by his arc; and then looking to see where his southern centre was, found it upon the Great Pyramid : immediately deciding in his mind, "that that monument stands in a more important physical situation than any other building yet erected by man."

On coming to refinements, Mr. Mitchell did indeed allow that his radii were not able to distinguish between the Great Pyramid and any of its near companions on the same hill-top. But the Great Pyramid had already settled that differential matter for itself; for while it is absolutely the northernmost of *all* the Pyramids (in spite of one apparent, but false, exception to be explained further on), it is the only one which comes at all close—and it comes *very* close—to the northern cliff of the Jeezeh hill. Almost overhangs it, and the Delta too; so that the Great Pyramid thence looks out with most commanding gaze over the open-fan-shaped, fertile, and human-food producing land of Lower Egypt; looking over it, too, from the sectorial land's very " centre of physical origin"; or as from over the handle of the fan, outward to the far-off curved sea-coast. All the other Pyramids are away back on the table-land, so far to the south of the Great one that they lose that grand view from the front or northern edge of the hill. They even appear, one might almost say, in a mere menial, inferior position, away there behind, as being in a manner the suite and following train only, of the Great building; that mysterious Great one who is the unquestioned owner there, and seems to have thoughts, beyond their thoughts, as he gazes, Napoleon-wise, over that primevally fertile, historic, triangular plain right away before and immediately below him.

So very close was the Great Pyramid placed to the

northern brink of its hill, that the edges of the cliff
might have broken off, under the terrible pressure, had
not the builders banked up there most firmly the immense mounds of rubbish which came from their work;
and which Strabo looked so particularly for, 1,850 years
ago, but could not find.*   Here they were, however,
and still are, utilised in enabling the Great Pyramid to
stand on the very utmost verge of its commanding hill,
within the limits of the *two* required latitudes, 30° and
29° 58′ 23″, as well as over the centre of the land's
physical and radial formation; and at the same time
on the sure and proverbially wise foundation of rock.†

Now Lower Egypt being, as already described, of a
sector shape, the building which stands at, or just
raised above, its sectorial centre must be, as Mr. Henry
Mitchell has acutely remarked, at one and the same time
both at the border thereof, and in its *quasi* middle; or,
just as was to be that prophetic monument, pure and
undefiled in its religion though in an idolatrous land,
alluded to by Isaiah (ch. xix.), the monument which
was fore-ordained as both "an altar to the Lord in the
midst of the land of Egypt, and a pillar at the border
thereof"; destined moreover to become a most special
witness in the latter days, before the consummation of
all things, to the same Lord, and to what He hath
purposed upon mankind.

Whether the Great Pyramid will eventually succeed
in proving itself to be really the one and only monument alluded to under those glorious terms or not, it

---

* See Note to p. 41, Ch. III.

† " Certainly the rubbish *has* been thrown over the cliff, but not, in *my*
opinion, with any idea of banking up the cliff to support the Great
Pyramid."—*Dr. J. A. S. Grant*, Cairo, 1877.   Yet the late excellent
man, Alan Stevenson, C.E., builder of the Skerryvore Lighthouse, wrote
me a voluntary and even emphatic testimony, that that, to his professional judgment, *intentional* banking up of the Northern cliff, was with
him the final argument to convince him of the sacred and scientific,
rather than the tombic and Egyptologic, theory of the Great Pyramid.

has thus far undoubtedly most unique claims for representing much that is in them, both as to its circumstances of mechanical fact and surrounding chorography;
while its general characteristics of situation, not unworthy of the one and only known, existing monument
of Inspiration, by no means end there. For proceeding
along the globe due north and due south of the Great
Pyramid, it has been found by a good physical geo-
grapher as well as engineer, Mr. William Petrie, that
there is more earth and less sea in that meridian than
in any other meridian all the equator round. Hence,
therefore, the Great Pyramid's meridian is caused to be
as essentially marked by nature, in a general manner,
across the world from Pole to Pole, or rather from the
North Cape of Norway to the diamond fields and Zulu-
land of South Africa, as a prime meridian for all
nations measuring their longitude from, or for that
modern cynosure " the unification of longitude,"—as it
is more minutely marked by art and defined by human
work within the limits of the Lower Egyptian plain,
by the pointed building itself alone.

Again, taking the distribution of land and sea in
parallels of *latitude*, there is more land-surface in the
Great Pyramid's general parallel of 30°, than in any
other degree; so that the two grand, solid, man-inhabited
earth-lines, the one, of most land in any Meridian, and
the other of most land in any Latitude, cross on the
Great Pyramid. And finally, on carefully summing up
the areas of all the dry land habitable by man all the
wide world over, the centre of the whole falls within
the Great Pyramid's special territory of Lower Egypt.*

But, as Commodore Whiting, U.S. Navy, writes to
me recently from America, the Great Pyramid's further,
and even chief claim in his eyes to attention as a Zero

* See my "Equal Surface Projection," published in 1870 by Edmonston and Douglas, Edinburgh. See also Fig. 2 of Plate II., in this book.

of all nations' Longitude, is not merely that it is so eminently set in the midst, among all the busier haunts of men, on its own side of the earth ; but that its *Nether*-Meridian, or the continuation of its Egyptian Meridian round the *opposite* side of the world, forms the most suitable possible line of locality for circumnavigators of the globe to change their day of reckoning, as they pass it, accordingly as they are proceeding from East to West, or from West to East ; because, that *Nether*-Meridian of the Great Pyramid ranges its whole length from South to North Pole, excepting only near Behring's frozen Straits, through foaming, tossing, sea : realizing therefore almost exactly the precise *Nether*-Meridian long desired by the late most eminent Captain Maury, in his grand, and world-wide facilitations of the Navigation of all Nations.

Of the Mental Accompaniments of these several Facts.

It is useless for the Egyptological objectors to these growing ideas about the Great Pyramid's scientific commemorabilities, to go on railing at me and denouncing them, and declaring that the ancient Egyptians, the mere slaves of Pharaoh, did not know anything about the general arrangement of earth and sea surface over the globe ; and were certainly ignorant of the existence of America, Australia, New Zealand, or Japan ; while they figured the earth in their hieroglyphics as a *flat* cake of bread, and therefore could not have made the above calculation rightly,—for I have never accused, and do not propose to tax, those profane Egyptians with having had anything to do with the *design* of the Great Pyramid ; and I have no intention of limiting my accounts of what mathematical science may find in the measured facts of that most unique building of all the world and all time, merely to what

modern Egyptologists, from their most questionable
studies, may choose to tell us that the vile animal-
worshippers of old Egypt either did, or much rather
did not, know; for, generally speaking, ancient Egyptian
knowledge of science, or indeed noble intellectualism
of any kind (see the late Sir George Cornewall Lewis
for that) has been rated by the world vastly too high.

The actual, central geographical fact, as we have
stated it, is there in the Great Pyramid, and also in
the world, for every one who likes to test on absolute
grounds; to try its truth and application for our own
times first, and then to reduce it to the days of the
Pyramid, if there have been sensible changes in the
distribution of sea and land on the whole, going on
within the interval.

But, whatever amount of such changes may have
taken place in the millions of years of the geological periods of the earth before the advent of man,
there would seem to have been none of general geographical importance since then; and, indeed, for
the special period of the more certified human, or
division into nation, time of the world (*i.e.* since both
the Deluge and the Dispersion), there is every reason
to believe that the dry land surface spot which was
central 4,000 years ago is central still, and will continue to be so until the end of man's trial on earth,
according to all the scriptural indications thereof. And
if we be further enabled before long to illustrate that
the directors of the building of the Great Pyramid were
not natives of Egypt, nor worshippers with them, but
came into Egypt out of a country having a different
latitude and longitude, and went back again to that
country of theirs immediately after they had built the
Great Pyramid in all its surpassing purity and perfection; and that there, in their own country, though no
mean architects, yet they built no second Pyramid,—

will not that go far to indicate that, assisted by a higher power, they had been taught, and well knew of early time, that there was only one proper and fully appropriate spot all the wide, and *round*, world over, whereon to found that most deeply significant structure they had received orders to erect on a certain plan, and not for their own, neither for any Egyptian, purposes, viz. the Great Pyramid?

But if the *exterior* of that earth-central building, though in these last days in which we live, almost ruinous under the successive attacks of twenty nations, leads so abundantly, when carefully studied and scientifically measured, even in spite of all those dilapidations, to ennobling views (the like of which too were never made out in all past time for any other building of the whole world, not even for a single one of the other Pyramids of Egypt, which, all of them, err utterly in angle, size, and position), what may we not expect from the Great Pyramid's better-preserved *interior?*

We will first, however, conclude this earliest *Part* or Division of our book with a handy table of some of the principal measures touching the " Geography and Exterior " of the Great Pyramid.

Compendium of the Principal and Leading Measures connected with the Geography and Exterior of the GREAT PYRAMID, *as collected in* 1877 A.D.

POSITION.

Latitude = 29° 58' 51".
Longitude = 0° 0' 0" Pyr.
Elevation of pavement base :—   Pyr. inches.
    Above the neighbouring alluvial plain as now covered
      by sand ..   .. =   1,500
    Above the average water-level ..   .. =   1,750
    Above the Mediterranean Sea level   ..   ..   .. =   2,580
Elevation of the lowest subterranean construction, or subterranean excavated chamber above the average water-level of the country ..   .. =   250

HEIGHT-SIZE.

	Pyr. Inches.
Present dilapidated height, vertical, about .. .. .. =	5,450
Ancient vertical height of apex completed, above pavement =	5,813·01
Ancient inclined height at middle of sides, from pavement to completed apex .. .. =	7,391·55
Ancient inclined height at the corners, pavement to apex =	8,687·87
Ancient vertical height of apex above the lowest subterranean chamber.. .. .. =	7,015

BREADTH-SIZE.

Present dilapidated base-side length, about	8,950
Ancient and present base-side *socket*-length	9,131·05
Ancient and present base-*diagonal* socket-length	12,913·26
Sum of the two base-diagonals to the nearest inch	25,827
Present platform on top of Great Pyramid, in length of side, roughly	400

(It is flat, except in so far as it has four or five large stones upon it, the remains of a once higher course of masonry.)

Ancient length of side of Great Pyramid, with casing-stone thickness complete, at the level of the present truncated summit platform, roughly	580
Pavement in front, and round the base of Great Pyramid, formed of stones 21 inches thick, breadth at centre of North front	402
A chasm or crack in both pavement and rock beneath, near that North front, extends to a depth of, more or less ..	570

SHAPE AND MATERIAL.

	°	′	″
Ancient angle of rise of the casing-stones, and the whole Great Pyramid, when measured at the side =	51	51	14·3
Ancient angle of rise of the whole Great Pyramid, when measured at the corners or arris lines .. .. =	41	59	18·7
Ancient angle of Great Pyramid at the summit, *sideways* .. .. =	76	17	31·4
Ancient angle of Great Pyramid at the summit, *diagonally* or corner-ways .. .. =	96	1	22·6

Casing-stone materials—compact white lime-stone from the Mokattam Mountain quarries on the east side of the Nile, with a density = 0·367 (earth's mean density = 1).

General structural material of all the ruder part of the masonry—nummulitic lime-stone of the Pyramid's own hill, with a density = 0·412.

Number of sides of the whole building, including the square base as one—4 triangular and 1 square .. .. =	5
Number of corners of the whole building—4 on the ground and 1 anciently aloft .. .. =	5

THE GREAT PYRAMID.

MASONRY COURSES.

These courses of squared and cemented blocks of stone in horizontal sheets, one above the other, form the mass of the building of the Great Pyramid. They vary much in height one from the other, as thus:—

Number of Course in Ascending.	Height of each Course, in Inches, roughly.	Whole Height from Pavement. Inches.	Number of Course in Ascending.	Height of each Course, in Inches, roughly.	Whole Height from Pavement. Inches.	Number of Course in Ascending.	Height of each Course, in Inches, roughly.	Whole Height from Pavement. Inches.
Pavement	0	0	35	24	1152	70	31	2236
1			36	50	1202	71	28	2264
2	79	79	37	41	1243	72	28	2292
3	56	135	38	39	1282	73	27	2319
4	48	183	39	38	1320	74	26	2345
5	40	223	40	34	1354	75	31	2376
6	40	263	41	32	1386	76	28	2404
7	38	301	42	32	1418	77	26	2430
8	39	340	43	28	1446	78	24	2454
9	38	378	44	32	1478	79	24	2478
10	36	414	45	42	1520	80	24	2502
11	34	448	46	37	1557	81	22	2524
12	33	481	47	28	1585	82	24	2548
13	30	511	48	35	1620	83	24	2572
14	30	541	49	36	1656	84	26	2598
15	28	569	50	30	1686	85	26	2624
16	30	599	51	28	1714	86	25	2649
17	28	627	52	30	1744	87	25	2674
18	26	653	53	26	1770	88	24	2698
19	32	685	54	27	1797	89	24	2722
20	38	723	55	24	1821	90	25	2747
21	24	747	56	26	1847	91	36	2783
22	23	770	57	22	1869	92	33	2816
23	35	805	58	26	1895	93	31	2847
24	33	838	59	27	1922	94	28	2875
25	31	869	60	30	1952	95	26	2901
26	38	907	61	28	1980	96	25	2926
27	26	933	62	26	2006	97	24	2950
28	28	961	63	26	2032	98	24	2974
29	31	992	64	26	2058	99	41	3015
30	30	1022	65	28	2086	100	37	3052
31	26	1048	66	26	2112	101	34	3086
32	28	1076	67	26	2138	102	32	3118
33	28	1104	68	34	2172	103	30	3148
34	24	1128	69	33	2205	104	28	3176

Number of Course in Ascending.	Height of each Course in Inches, roughly.	Whole height from Pavement. Inches.	Number of Course in Ascending.	Height of each Course in Inches, roughly.	Whole Height from Pavement. Inches.	Number of Course in Ascending.	Height of each Course in Inches, roughly.	Whole height from Pavement. Inches.
105	27	3203	140	25	4078	175	20	4859
106	27	3230	141	22	4100	176	21	4880
107	26	3256	142	22	4122	177	20	4900
108	25	3281	143	22	4144	178	20	4920
109	29	3310	144	22	4166	179	21	4941
110	25	3335	145	28	4194	180	20	4961
111	24	3359	146	27	4221	181	26	4987
112	24	3383	147	24	4245	182	25	5012
113	24	3407	148	22	4267	183	23	5035
114	23	3430	149	22	4289	184	24	5059
115	23	3453	150	21	4310	185	22	5081
116	23	3476	151	26	4336	186	21	5102
117	25	3501	152	26	4362	187	21	5123
118	23	3524	153	25	4387	188	20	5143
119	35	3559	154	22	4409	189	21	5164
120	31	3590	155	21	4430	190	21	5185
121	29	3619	156	21	4451	191	21	5206
122	28	3647	157	21	4472	192	21	5227
123	26	3673	158	21	4493	193	21	5248
124	26	3699	159	21	4514	194	20	5268
125	24	3723	160	22	4536	195	21	5289
126	24	3747	161	21	4557	196	22	5311
127	23	3770	162	21	4578	197	24	5335
128	23	3793	163	24	4602	198	22	5357
129	23	3816	164	23	4625	199	22	5379
130	23	3839	165	25	4650	200	22	5401
131	27	3866	166	22	4672	201	22	5423
132	25	3891	167	22	4694	202	22	5445
133	23	3914	168	21	4715	203	21	fragment.
134	22	3936	169	21	4736	204	19	fragment.
135	22	3958	170	20	4756	205		wanting.
136	22	3980	171	21	4777	206		—
137	25	4005	172	20	4797	207		—
138	23	4028	173	21	4818	208		—
139	25	4053	174	21	4839	209		—

Supposed complete number of courses, including the original topmost corner-stone = 211; with whole height = 5813 Pyramid inches.

AREA, WEIGHT, &c.

	Pyr. Acres.
Ancient area of square base of Great Pyramid .. .. =	13·340

Ancient area of the square Pavement, on which the Great
    Pyramid is supposed to stand, but which has only been
    tested as yet on the Northern side, concluded probably =   16·00

The whole building from very base to apex is not solid masonry; but as clearly shown by the N. East basal corner, and indicated more or less at a point or two in the wall, and the descending entrance passage, includes some portions of the live-rock of the hill. Such portion having been, however, trimmed rectangularly, and made to conform in height and level with the nearest true masonry course.

Solid cubits of masonry contained in Great Pyramid's
    whole   ..   .. =   10,340,000

Tons (Pyramid) of squared, cemented building material =   5,274,000

UNITS OF MEASURE REFERRED TO.

1 Pyramid inch   =   1·001 British inch.

1 Pyramid cubit   = $\begin{cases} 25\text{·}025 \text{ British inches.} \\ 25\text{·}000 \text{ Pyramid inches.} \end{cases}$

1 Pyramid acre   =   0·9992 British acre.

1 Pyramid ton   =   1·1499 British avoirdupois ton.

See further, Plates III. to VIII., and XX. to XXII. inclusive.

PART II.

OF THE HISTORY, AND THE INTERIOR, OF THE GREAT PYRAMID.

"WHO HATH MEASURED THE WATERS IN THE HOLLOW OF HIS HAND, AND METED OUT HEAVEN WITH THE SPAN, AND COMPREHENDED THE DUST OF THE EARTH IN A MEASURE, AND WEIGHED THE MOUNTAINS IN SCALES, AND THE HILLS IN A BALANCE?

"WHO HATH DIRECTED THE SPIRIT OF THE LORD, OR BEING HIS COUNSELLOR HATH TAUGHT HIM?"—ISAIAH XL. 12, 13.

IVORY FIGURINE OF KING CHEOPS.
Courtesy of Cairo Museum.

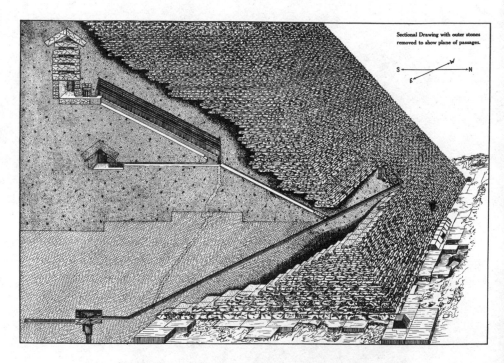

Sectional Drawing with outer stones
removed to show plane of passages.

SECTIONAL DRAWING OF THE INTERIOR OF THE GREAT PYRAMID.
Courtesy of Howard B. Rand, author of *THE CHALLENGE OF THE GREAT
PYRAMID*, published by Destiny Publishers, Merrimac, Mass. 01880.

MAIN PASSAGE OF THE GREAT PYRAMID, 1908.
Courtesy of New York Public Library Picture Collection.

LIMESTONE RELIEF, PROBABLY FROM THE TEMPLE OF GREAT PYRAMID AT
GIZA, FOURTH DYNASTY.
Courtesy of Museum of Fine Arts, Boston.

THE QUEEN'S CHAMBER OF THE GREAT PYRAMID.
Courtesy of André Pochan Collection.

THE GRANITE SARCOPHAGUS IN THE KING'S CHAMBER.
Courtesy of André Pochan Collection.

CHAPTER VI.

AN ENTRY MADE ;

First partially in Classic, then in Saracen, times.

THERE is little enough of hollow interior to enter into, in any of the Egyptian Pyramids, as they are generally all but solid masses of masonry. And yet what very little there is, will be found quite characteristic enough to raise up a most radical distinction of kind, as well as degree, between the Great Pyramid and every other monument, large or small, Pyramidal or otherwise, in all the continent of Africa, and Asia as well.

What the earlier of the Ancients knew about the Interior of the Great Pyramid.

The progress of profane historical knowledge of outside men, with regard to what constituted the hollow interior of the Great Pyramid, from the earliest times after the very building operation itself had ceased (say 2,150 years B.C.), down to later Greek and Roman eras,—was both slow and peculiar. Had we now before us, in one meridianal section of the monument, all that such very ancient knowledge had arrived at, the tale would amount to little more than this—that when the Great Pyramid stood on the Jeezeh hill in the primeval age of the world in white masonry, unassailed; a simple, apparently solid, crystalline shape, with the secret of its inner nature untouched; clothed too, complete on

every side, with its bevelled sheet of polished casing-
stones, the whole structure rising from a duly levelled
area of also white rock-surface in four grand triangular
flanks up to a single pointed summit,—that then it contained within, or beneath its foot (trending down from
the north, and entering at a point about 49 feet above
the ground, near the middle of that northern side)
merely an inclined descending passage of very small
bore, leading to a sort of subterranean, excavated
chamber in the rock, about 100 feet vertically under
the centre of the base of the whole built monument.

This one subterranean chamber did really exist, in
so far as it had been *begun* to be carved out, deep in the
heart of the rock, with admirable skill.   For the workmen, having cut their sloping way down to the necessary
depth by the passage, commenced with the chamber's
ceiling, making *it* exquisitely smooth, and on so large
a scale as 46 feet long by 28 broad.   Then sinking down
the walls from its edges in vertical planes, there was
every promise of their having presently, at that notable
100-foot depth inside, or rather underneath the surface
of the otherwise solid limestone mountain, a rectangular hollow space, or chamber, whose walls, ceiling, *and*
floor should all be perfect, pattern planes.   But when
the said men, the original workers it must be presumed,
had cut downwards from the ceiling to a depth of about
4 feet at the west end, and 13 feet at the east end, they
stopped in the very midst of their occupation.   A small,
very small, bored passage was pushed on into the rock
merely a few feet further towards the south, and then
that was also left unfinished ; a similar abortive attempt
was likewise made downwards, but with the only result,
that the whole floor, from one end of the chamber to
the other, was left a lamentable scene of holes, rocks,
and up-and-down, fragmentary confusion.   Verily (seeing
that the whole light of day was reduced down there to

a mere star-like point at the upper end of the long
entrance-passage, nearly 340 feet long), verily, it was
an answering locality for "the stones of darkness and
the shadow of death." (See Plate VI. and Plate IX.)

This one item, moreover, of a subterranean, unfinished chamber, with a sloping passage of approach,
there is good reason for believing, was *all* that the native
and profane Pharaonic Egyptians themselves knew of,
from within a generation after the Great Pyramid had
been built, to the latest times of their nation; excepting
only certain comparatively modern men of a fanatic invading army, who broke into the building, probably near
the epoch of Judah's Babylonian captivity, so late as
600 B.C.; and for them, see further on to our Part IV.

That the ancient, idolatrous, Egyptians themselves,
as a people (probably from 2100 B.C., down to their
most theotechnic Theban kingdom about 1700 B.C.;
thence to their conquest while still worshipping bulls,
goats, cats, and crocodiles by Persian Cambyses in
525 B.C.; then conquered again, when worshipping
onions, dogs and wolves as well, by Grecian Alexander
in 338 B.C.; and then by Julius Cæsar, when no better,
in 48 B.C.), that they all knew thus much, we may
readily allow, because they could hardly have known
less of the interior than their latest conquerors, the
Romans; and there is, or was recently, credible proof,
in the shape of good uncial letters marked in carbon,
and recorded to have been seen by Signor Caviglia
when he first recovered in modern times the re-entry to
that lower part of the Pyramid, that *they*, the Imperial
Romans, were once inside the subterranean chamber,
and did so mark its smooth ceiling, standing and scram-
bling amongst the stones of its unfinished floor.

There appears also, as it is asserted by a few modern
Egyptologists of rather a sanguine turn of mind, no
small probability that some kinds of Pyramids with this

single characteristic—viz. a descending entrance-passage
and subterranean, or, if you will, call it positively, as
they are so fond of doing, a tombic or sepulchral, chamber—were indigenous in Egypt *before* the erection of the
Great Pyramid.   In such case, therefore, that building
may have been begun so far, in seeming deference to
some contemporary, and by no means secret, native
ideas about burial; though as will be seen now, the
Great Monument did not care to complete *them;* nor to
carry out the either intended, or pretended, sepulchral
chamber to such a condition of floor state, that any
funeral sarcophagus could have been decently, and in
order, established there: while no remains of any kind
of coffin *have* ever been reported to have been found
either in that chamber or the passage leading to it.

In the undoubtedly subsequent second and third
Jeezeh Pyramids, on the contrary, their subterranean
rooms *were* finished, floors and all; and sarcophagi
were introduced.   *Their* architects, moreover, attempted
to make those chambers, the only interiors those pyramids possessed, notably object-worthy.   But it was
only with useless, confusing complication, without any
very sensible purpose; unless when it was to allow
a second king to make himself a burial-chamber
in the Pyramid cellar already occupied by a predecessor; and then it was bad.   Gradually, therefore,
as the researches of Colonel Howard-Vyse have shown,
on the fourth, fifth, sixth, seventh, eighth, and ninth
Jeezeh Pyramids (all these being, moreover, very
small ones: see Plate IV.), the native Egyptians
dropped nearly everything else that they had been
exercised on, or had been allowed to learn, at the building of the Great Monument, except the one single,
descending and generally sloping passage, with an unfinished subterranean chamber at its farther end.   Such
a passage and chamber, but well-finished chamber, and

therefore more probably copied from old native custom, they always made under their own little Pyramids; used them distinctly for burial purposes; and that use of them and nothing but it, they kept to, so long as they practised their petty pyramid-building at all (down to, perhaps, 1800 B.C.).   (See Plate V.)

Lepsius's Law of early Egyptian Pyramid Building.

Still further, that the making of such descending passages with subterranean chambers, and using them for sepulture, is precisely what the profane Egyptians usually did when they were their own masters and the directors of their own works ; and that they did little else even in subsequent times of increased national numbers and wealth, except it was to decorate them with images of false gods, boasting inscriptions in hieroglyphic writing, and portraits of themselves, is also testified to from quite another quarter.   For all the Egyptologists of our age, French, English, German, and American, have hailed the advent, on their stage of time, of the so-called " Lepsius's Law of the Egyptian Pyramid Building " ; they universally declaring that it satisfies absolutely all the observed or known phenomena.   And it may do so for every known case of every Pyramid throughout the land of Egypt, *except* the Great Pyramid ; and there it is antagonized at every point.

Taking, however, the cases which the law does apply to, viz. all the smaller, profane Egyptian examples, this alleged " law " of Lepsius pronounces, that the sole object of any of *its* Pyramids was, to form a royal tomb—subterranean as a matter of course—and that operations began, by making an inclined descending passage leading down into the subjacent rock, and there, at the end of it (many feet under the surface),

cutting out an underground chamber. The scheme for
the interior thus begun below, went on also *growing*
above ground for exterior purposes every year of the
King's reign, by the placing there of a new or additional
layer of building-stones, and piling them layer above
layer over, and around, a central, square-based nucleus
upon the levelled ground, vertically above the one, commencing, subterranean apartment. And this succeeding superincumbent mass of masonry was finally finished
off, on that king's death, by his successor ; who then
deposited his predecessor's body, embalmed and in a
grand sarcophagus, in the underground chamber ; next
stopped up the passage leading thereto, cased in the
rude converging exterior sides of the whole building
with bevelled casing-stones so as to give it a smooth,
as well as pyramidal, form, and left it in fact a
finished, Lepsian, profane-Egyptian, and Pharaonic,
or Royal tombic Pyramid to all posterity.* No mean

---

* In Dr. Lepsius's Letter 7, March, 1843, that eminent Egyptologist
says distinctly enough, with regard to the above theory,—" I discovered
the riddle of pyramidal construction on which I had long been employed " ; but in the letterpress attached to Frith's large photographs of
Egypt (1860 ?), by Mrs. Poole and R. S. Poole, the discovery is given
categorically to another person. As the passage is accompanied with a
very clear description of the theory, there may be advantage in giving it
entire from this opposite side ; as then proving beyond all doubt *how
much* of the whole internal arrangement of the Great Pyramid, as *now*
known and presently to be described, this approved pyramidal theory of
the most learned modern Egyptologists really accounts for :—

" The principle of their (the ancient Egyptians) pyramid construction
was discovered by Mr. James Wild, the architect who accompanied the
Prussian expedition. A rocky site was first chosen, and a space made
smooth, except a slight eminence in the centre, to form a peg upon which
the structure should be fixed. Within the rock, and usually below the
level of the future base, a sepulchral chamber was excavated, with a passage, inclining downwards, leading to it from the north. Upon the rock
was first raised a moderate mass of masonry, of nearly a cubic form, but
having its four sides inclined inwards ; upon this a similar mass was
placed, and around, other such masses, generally about half as wide. At
this stage the edifice could be completed by a small pyramidal structure
being raised on the top, and the sides of the steps filled in, the whole
being ultimately cased, and the entrance-passage, which had of course
been continued through the masonry, securely closed ; or else the work
could be continued on the same principle. In this manner it was possible

realisation either, as such, of once-prevailing ideas among some ancient nations, of burying their monarchs *sub montibus altis*, in impressive quiet, immovable calm, and deep in the bosom of mother earth.

But was there nothing more than, or rather not by any means so much as, that inside the Great Pyramid? Did the builders there go on piling the stones of its exterior to a greater height than in any other Pyramid, when the very first requirement anywhere, of a fully excavated sepulchral chamber had never been completed, —*if they also* worked by Lepsius's Egyptologic law?

Classic Antiquity on the Interior of the Great Pyramid.

There has been some scholastic question of late years as to whether Herodotus in 445 B.C., Strabo 18 A.D., Pliny 70 A.D., and others of the more mediæval ancients, or their immediate informants, were ever actually inside the Great Pyramid; for sometimes it has been maintained that the edifice was inviolably sealed, and that what they mentioned of the interior was only on the reports of tradition; while at other times it is averred that they must have seen something more accurately than through others' eyes, in order to have described so graphically as they did; describing, however, always a vast deal more about the exterior than the interior. The very utmost, indeed, that they had to say about the latter was touching a certain removable stone on

---

for the building of a pyramid to occupy the lifetime of its founder without there being any risk of his leaving it incomplete (to any such degree or extent as would afford a valid excuse for his successor neglecting to perform his very moderate part, of merely filling up the angles, and smoothing off generally)."

Mr. James Wild is, I believe, a Swiss by birth, and is still, in his native land, greatly interested in the Pyramid subject, as I was informed in 1875 by one of his sons, engaged then professionally in rebuilding the Hôtel de Ville in Paris. Another son has been employed by this country as Secretary to the scientific staff on board the *Challenger* exploring ship.

the outside, and then a dark groping " *usque ad*," or right away to, apparently, and by one passage only, the unfinished subterranean chamber, and nothing but that — where M. Caviglia in A.D. 1820, as already mentioned, found blackened Roman letters, upon its roof;* things found in these days nowhere else inside the whole building.

To that one underground room, then, and through that then well-known entrance passage leading to it, of the Great Pyramid, occasionally (and probably only at long intervals) some individuals of the classic portion of antiquity, did penetrate, aided by the removable block of stone. The machinery of the block, and the opportunity of sometimes working it, seemed to act as a safety-valve to the Pyramid-curiosity of early times, which was thus admitted on rare and special occasions to see all the supposed interior of the greatest of all the Pyramids; and prove that there was nothing there! For, after stifling exertions, in a long, dark, narrow, steep and dangerous way, men saw and made acquaintance with—what? Nothing but a subterranean chamber, *not so good as those in many smaller Pyramids.* That subterranean chamber, which *ought* to have been the first thing finished, according to both all ancient Egyptian ideas, and the "Lepsius Law" of profane Egyptian-Pyramid building,—but was not. The very chamber which ought to have contained, for a real, unmitigated, idolatrous Pharaoh, sculptured sarcophagus, mummy, paintings, and inscriptions,—but which only really held the rough, natural rock-contents of the lower part of the room, not yet cut out of the bowels of the mountain.

In short, all the classic and idolatrous nations of old (say, from 1400 B.C. to 300 A.D.) knew nothing what-

---

* Howard-Vyse's " Pyramids," Vol. ii. p. 290.

ever about the now known real interior of the Great
Pyramid's scientific and, as we shall venture also to
call it, for far other than mere science reasons alone,
sacred, design; and which interior lies altogether above,
and in quite a different direction from, the unimportant
and unfinished, subterranean chamber which profane
eyes might regard without harm and without profit
either; but about which we, as they *did* see it, have
been obliged, at starting, to say so much.

Between the Classic and the Arabian days.

After the Classic came very dark ages; and though
a revived and considerably altered school of Greek
learning did flourish for a while at Alexandria, no
additional knowledge about the interior of the Great
Pyramid was gained there. But, in fact, neither the
æsthetics and philosophy of Greece, nor the legality
and imperial rule of Rome, as the final outcome of their
long civilizations, could excuse any longer men's continued adherence to their older idolatries; and the
Great Pyramid's unadorned and truthful sides stood
out always against, and were an aversion to, idolaters
of every kind, whether learned or unlearned.

The Christian religion too, though it had appeared
in Egypt, was soon largely perverted there by the
pagan and mythologic tendencies around. It had, also,
in those days its own peculiar struggles, persecutions,
dangers to pass through; its freethinkers, moreover, to
resist, as in the case of Proclus, in or about 450 A.D.
Though an apostate from the true faith, and exceedingly
bitter against it, witness his very rationalistic book on the
eternity of the earth and Nature, entitled most malig-
nantly, " Eighteen Arguments against the Christians,"
—this same Proclus has been recently brought up with
honour by a London magazine, as a chief authority on

the Great Pyramid, and for establishing that it was built by King Cheops for promoting astrological speculations about his own life.

But there is nothing to show that Proclus had any real acquaintance with the building itself. He may have picked up from the peasants around some of the folk-lore tales, such as always grow with time about any giant edifice of the past: and then, being an astrologer himself, he claimed King Cheops, of the mighty Pyramid, as devoted to the same vanity. But he is so little of an authority to be followed, that Gibbon wrote of Proclus,—"his life exhibits a deplorable picture of the second childhood of human reason."

Mediæval Arabians take their turn.

Meanwhile poor Christianity, though it overcame its first opponents, and flourished for a while in the Egyptian land, yet in its prosperity there became utterly adulterated; and it did not succeed either in reforming Cæsar, or governing the nations; except in so far as men had already begun to mould and hypocritically pervert it to their own political purposes, in almost mockery of its real precepts and Gospel of salvation to each individual, poor, and contrite soul. Again, too, had the theotechnic arts of the old Egyptians overlaid the spiritual purity of the worship of the one God; and so-called Christian churches were filled with figures and pictures of men deified by men themselves. So the cup of Divine wrath was found filled to the brim by the time that six centuries after Christ had come and gone; when, another bottomless pit (Rev. ix. 2—11) of infinitely greater significance than the subterranean, floorless hole under the Great Pyramid, was opened, " and there came a smoke out of that pit, as the smoke of a great furnace; and the sun and the air were darkened by reason of the smoke of the pit." (Rev. ix. 2.)

"And there came out of the smoke locusts upon the earth,—in shape like unto horses prepared for battle; their faces were as the faces of men, and their teeth like the teeth of lions, and their King was *the angel of the bottomless pit*." No king, therefore, of the ordinary sort, or military-heroic type governed them, but a religious teacher of a new order, though it might be a wrong and perverse one; and teaching more by slaughtering with the sword than convincing by loving and persuasive speech.

So too it was, that Mohammed, or his general, with the Saracen horsemen behind him, soon after 622 A.D., swept over the Egyptian country, from Alexandria to Syene, like a destroying pestilence from God; visiting with instant death by the sword; slaying whoever they found, whether of old mythologists of any nation whatever, or debased Christians, who still worshipped " devils and idols of gold and silver and brass and wood and stone, which can neither see nor hear nor walk." (Rev. ix. 20.)

Then was lost, together with their idolatrous religions, even the little of what was once known by ancient Greece, Rome, and Egypt too, of the interior, and even the mode of limited entrance into the isolated subterranean chamber of the Great Pyramid. That mighty building was therefore left to itself, in the desert, apart and alone from man ; a gigantic rock, a " terrible crystal " of a former unknown time.

But the Saracenic thunderstorm of Divine and long fore-ordained vengeance passed away at last ; its days of butchery *were* shortened by Divine mercy; the Scorpion warriors with the horse-tail standards over their scimitar-armed ranks, having put down all apparent opposition, or performed their ordained parts in an idol worshipping world, began to turn towards arts of peace and the sweet enjoyment of their war-acquired wealth ; so that presently civilized human history reopened under

their altered rule, for an advancing age, with a new
people in power, and new ideas dominant. How new
they were, in Egypt more especially, must appear from
this, that the fiercest discussions concerned now little
more than the force of the simple *name* of God, and
the virtue of praying five times a day looking towards
Mecca,—a semi-spiritualized state of society in which
a conquering Alexander the Great, or equally a learned
Aristotle would have found himself out of place indeed.

The religious successors of Mohammed, the Caliphs
of Bagdad, were now the chief potentates of the world,
the most civilised too, and were daily becoming more
so. Losing, indeed, as the years went on, more and
more of their former distinctive character and divinely
allowed purpose in the world,—for they sought now, not
so much to extend the doctrines of their own almost worshipped prophet, as to enjoy themselves. Some few of
them, too, doing so rather intelligently and intellectually.
Thus at last, in 820 A.D., came the Caliph Al Mamoun,
a caliph with an inquiring turn of mind, like his father
Haroun Al Raschid, of the "Arabian Nights," but
attending to some higher things—(indeed he was said
by Gibbon to have been a prince of rare learning,
"continually exhorting his subjects," in *excelsior* vein,
"assiduously to peruse instructive writings; and who
not only commanded the volumes of Grecian sages to
be translated into Arabic, but could assist with pleasure
and modesty at the assemblies and disputations of the
learned "). When, therefore, this British-Association-
for-the-advancement-of-Science genius of his day, coming down from Bagdad to El Fostat, an earlier Cairo,
and in sight of the Great Pyramid just across the flood
of Nile, proposed to enter that monument, A.D. 820, and
behold the wonders of its interior, there seems to have
survived only a very indistinct rumour to guide him
towards trying the *northern*, rather than any other, side
of the monument.

But Al Mamoun, the directly Mohammed-descended ruler of the world of the "faithful," and of all that physically defined portion of it which produced their two most valued fruits, water-melons and dates,—was likewise, in a new kind of profanity then growing up around him, flattered almost as a god in the rhapsodies of his court poets. They, inventing some new pleasure for him every day, could only not give him, turned inside out to the light of day, the Great Pyramid itself. Emulating, however, on a basis of Coptic tradition and post-classic, folk-lore, derived from the then innumerable, though degraded and again almost idolatrous, Egyptian monasteries, the enchanting tales of Bagdad, —they tried to do so; and drew gorgeous Eastern pictures of the contents of a wonderful interior of the Pyramid; with an astounding history for that mighty and mysterious triangular masonic fact; standing, as it did, before them on the Jeezeh hill so patent as to its exterior in the eyes of all the Memphite land; so recluse as to its interior against both the world and time.

In describing these new and strange interior matters, which might have pleased another Proclus, but merely prove to us that the reciters knew nothing about the Great Pyramid,—they seemed only intent on putting into it everything of value they could possibly think of. All the treasures of " Sheddad Ben Ad," the great antediluvian king of the earth, with all his medicines and all his sciences, they declared were there, told over and over again. Others of them were positive that the founder-king was no other than Saurid Ibn Salhouk, a far greater one than Ben Ad; and these last gave many more minute particulars: some of which are at least interesting to us in the present day, as proving that amongst the Egypto-Arabians of more than 1,000 years ago, the Jeezeh Pyramids, headed too by the grand one, enjoyed a pre-eminence of fame vastly before all the other Pyramids of Egypt put together. And that if any other is alluded to after the Great Pyramid (which has always been the notable and favourite one, and chiefly was known then as the East Pyramid), it is either the second one at Jeezeh, under the name of the West Pyramid; or the third one, distinguished as the Coloured Pyramid, in allusion to its red granite, compared with the white lime-stone, casings of the other two. Those other two, moreover, from their somewhat near, though by no means exact, equality of size, went frequently under the affectionate designation of "the pair."

But what seemed more to the purpose of Al Mamoun at the time, was the very exact report of Ibn Abd Alkokm, as to things then still to be found in each of these three Pyramids; for this was what, according to that most detailed author, the primeval King Saurid had conscientiously put into them and safely locked up; though where in the scanty hollow interior of any, or all, of the Pyramids, he could have found space for so much, is more than any one now knows.

"In the Western Pyramid, thirty treasuries, filled with store of riches and utensils, and with signatures made of precious stones, and with instruments of iron, and vessels of earth, and with arms which rust not, and with glass which might be bended and yet not broken, and with strange spells, and with several kinds of *alakakirs* (magical precious stones), single and double, and with deadly poisons, and with other things besides.

"He made also in the East Pyramid divers celestial spheres and stars, and what they severally operate in their aspects, and the perfumes which are to be used to them, and the books which treat of these matters.

"He put also into the Coloured Pyramid the commentaries of the priests in chests of black marble, and with every priest a book, in which the wonders of his profession, and of his actions, and of his nature were written; and what was done in his time, and what is and what shall be from the beginning of time to the end of it.

" He placed in every Pyramid a treasurer; the treasurer of the Westerly Pyramid was a statue of marble stone, standing upright with a lance, and upon his head a serpent wreathed. He that came near it, and stood still, the serpent bit him of one side, and wreathing round about his throat, and killing him, returned to his place. He made the treasurer of the East Pyramid an idol of black agate, his eyes open and shining, sitting on a throne with a lance; when any looked upon him, he heard on one side of him a voice which took away his sense, so that he fell prostrate upon his face, and ceased not, till he died.

" He made the treasurer of the Coloured Pyramid a statue of stone, called *Albut*, sitting; he which looked towards it was drawn by the statue, till he stuck to it, and could not be separated from it till such time as he died."

Some of these features were certainly not encouraging; but then they were qualified by other tale-reciters, who described " three marble columns in the Great Pyramid, supporting the images of three birds in flames of fire made up of precious stones beyond all value and all number. Upon the first column was the figure of a dove, formed of a beautiful and priceless green stone; upon the second that of a hawk, of yellow stone; and upon the third, the image of a cock, of red stone, whose eyes enlightened all the place. Upon moving the hawk, a gigantic door which was opposite, composed of great marble slabs, beautifully put together, and inscribed with unknown characters in letters of gold, was raised; and the same surprising connection existed between the other images and their doors."

Exciting wonders, of course, appeared beyond those strange portals; but what need *we* to disentomb these Arabian romances further? In Egypt they believe pretty seriously in enchantments and Jinn or Genii of marvellous proportions and wonderful powers still; how much more then in the days of the son of Haroun Al Raschid, and when the Great Pyramid was an absolute mystery of old, still fast sealed! To ascertain, therefore, what really existed inside it in his own time was evidently a very natural idea; and why should *not* the young Caliph Al Mamoun undertake it?

Caliph Al Mamoun attacks the Northern Flank of the Great Pyramid.

He did so, and directed his Mohammedan workmen to begin at the *middle* of the northern side; precisely, says Sir Gardner Wilkinson, as the founders of the Great Pyramid had foreseen, when they placed the entrance, not in the middle of that side, but twenty-four feet and some inches away to the east, as well as many feet above the ground level. Hard labour, therefore, was it to these masons, quarrying with the rude instruments of that barbarous time, into stone-work as solid almost before them as the side of a hill.

They soon indeed began to cry out, "Open that wonderful Pyramid! It could not possibly be done!" But the Caliph only replied, "I will have it most certainly done." So his followers perforce had to quarry on unceasingly by night and by day. Weeks after weeks, and months too, were consumed in these toilsome exertions; the progress, however, though slow, was so persevering that they had penetrated at length to no less than one hundred feet in depth from the entrance. But by that time becoming thoroughly exhausted, and beginning again to despair of the hard and hitherto fruitless labour, some of them ventured to remember certain improving tales of an old king, who had found, on making the calculation, that all the wealth of Egypt in his time would not enable him to destroy one of the Pyramids. These murmuring disciples of the Arabian prophet were thus almost becoming openly rebellious, when one day, in the midst of their various counsel, they heard a great stone evidently fall in some hollow space within no more than a few feet on one side of them !

In the fall of that particular stone, there almost seems to have been an accident that was more than an accident.

Energetically, however, they instantly pushed on in the direction of the strange noise ; hammers, and fire, and vinegar being employed again and again, until, breaking through a wall surface, they burst into the hollow way, " exceeding dark, dreadful to look at, and difficult to pass," they said at first, where the sound had occurred. It was the same hollow way, or properly the Pyramid's inclined and descending entrance-passage, where the Romans of old, and if they, also Greeks, Persians, and Egyptians, must have passed up and down in their occasional visits to the useless, barren subterranean chamber and its unfinished, unquarried-out, floor. Tame and simple used that entrance-passage to appear to those ancients who entered in that way, and before the builder intended ; but now it not only stood before another race, and another religion, but with something that the others never saw, viz. its chief leading secret, for the first time since the foundation of the building, nakedly exposed : and exhibiting the beginning of an internal arrangement in the Great Pyramid which is not only unknown in any and every other Pyramid in Egypt, but which the architect here, carefully finished, scrupulously perfected, and then most remarkably sealed up before he left the building to fulfil its prophetic destination at the end of its appointed thousands of years. A large angular-fitting stone that had made for ages, with its lower flat side, a smooth and polished portion of the ceiling of the inclined and narrow entrance-passage, quite undistinguishable from any other part of the whole of its line, had now dropped on to the floor before their eyes; and revealed that there was just behind it, or at and in that point of the ceiling which it had covered, the end of another passage, clearly ascending therefrom and towards the south, out of this also southward going but descending one! (See Plate IX.)

But that ascending passage itself was still closed a little further up, by an adamantine portcullis, or rather stopper, formed by a series of huge granite plugs of square wedge-like shape dropped, or slided down, and then jammed in immovably, from above. To break them in pieces within the confined entrance-passage space, and pull out the fragments there, was entirely out of the question; so the grim crew of Saracen Mussulmans broke away sideways or round about to the west through the smaller, ordinary masonry, and so up again (by a huge chasm still to be seen, and indeed still used by all would-be entrants into the further interior) to the newly discovered ascending passage, at a point past the terrific hardness of its lower granite obstruction. They did up there, or at an elevation above, and a position beyond the portcullis, find the passage-way still blocked, but the filling material at that part was only lime-stone; so, making themselves a very great hole in the masonry along the western side, they there wielded their tools with energy on the long fair blocks which presented themselves to their view. But as fast as they broke up and pulled out the pieces of one of the blocks in this strange ascending passage, other blocks above it, also of a bore just to fill its full dimensions, slided down from above, and still what should be the passage for human locomotion was solid stone filling. No help, however, for the workmen. The Commander of the Faithful is present, and insists that, whatever the number of stone plugs still to come down from the mysterious reservoir, his men shall hammer and hammer them, one after the other, and bit by bit to little pieces at the only opening where they can get at them, until they do at last come to the end of all. So the people tire, but the work goes on; and at last, yes! at last! the ascending passage, beginning just above the granite portcullis, and leading thence upward and to the south, is announced to be free from obstruction and ready for essay. Then, by Allah, they shouted, the treasures of the Great Pyramid, sealed up from the fabulous times of the mighty Ibn Salhouk, and undesecrated, as it was long supposed, by mortal eye during all the intervening thousands of years, lay full in their grasp before them.

On they rushed, that bearded crew, thirsting for the promised wealth. Up no less than 110 feet of the steep incline, crouched hands and knees and chin together, through a passage of royally polished white lime-stone, but only 47 inches in height and 41 in breadth, they had painfully to crawl, with their torches burning low. Then suddenly they emerge into a long tall gallery, of seven times the passage height, but all black as night and in a death-like calm (see Plate XIII.); still ascending though at the strange steep angle, and leading them away farther and still more far into the very inmost heart of darkness of this imprisoning mountain of stone. In front of them, at first entering into this part of the now termed "Grand Gallery," and on the level, see another low passage; on their right hand (see Plates IX. and XII.) a black, ominous-looking well's mouth, more than 140 feet deep, and not reaching water, but only lower darkness, even then; while onwards and above them, a continuation of the glorious gallery or upward rising hall of seven times, leading them on, as they expected, to the possession of all the treasures of the great ones of antediluvian times.   Narrow, certainly, was the way —only 6 feet broad anywhere, and contracted to 3 feet at the floor—but 28 feet high, or almost above the power of their smoky lights to illuminate; and of polished, glistering, marble-like, cyclopean stone throughout.   (See Plate XIII.)

That must surely, thought they, be the high-road to fortune and wealth.   Up and up its long-ascending floor-line, therefore, ascending at an angle of 26°, these determined marauders, with their lurid fire-lights, had to push their dangerous and slippery way for 150 feet of distance more; then an obstructing three-foot step to climb over (what *could* the architect have meant by making a *step* so tall as that?); next a low doorway to bow their heads most humbly beneath (see Plates XIV. and XVI.); then a hanging portcullis to pass, almost to creep, under, most submissively; then another low doorway, in awful blocks of frowning red granite both on either side, and above and below.   But after that, they leaped without further let or hindrance at once into the grand chamber, which was, and is still, the conclusion of everything forming the Great Pyramid's interior; the chamber to which, and for which, and towards which, according to every subsequent writer (for no older ones knew any fragment of a thing about it), in whatever other theoretical point he may differ from his modern fellows,—the whole Great Pyramid was originally built.   (See Plate XVII.)

And what find they there, those maddened Muslim in Caliph Al Mamoun's train?   A right noble apartment, now called the King's Chamber, roughly 34 feet long, 17 broad, and 19 high, of polished red granite

throughout, both walls, floor, and ceiling; in blocks
squared and true, and put together with such exquisite
skill that no autocrat Emperor of recent times could
desire anything more solidly noble and at the same time
beautifully refined.

Ay, ay, no doubt a well-built room, and a handsome
one too; but what does it contain ? Where is the
treasure ? The treasure ! yes, indeed, where are the
promised silver and gold, the jewels and the arms ?
The plundering fanatics look wildly around them, but
can see nothing, not a single *dirhem* anywhere. They
trim their torches, and carry them again and again to
every part of that red-walled, flinty hall, but without
any better success. Nought but pure, polished red
granite, in mighty slabs, looks calmly upon them from
every side. The room is clean, garnished too, as it
were; and, according to the ideas of its founders,
complete and perfectly ready for its visitors, so long
expected, and not arrived yet; for the gross minds who
occupy it now, find it all barren; and declare that there
is nothing whatever of value there, in the whole extent
of the apartment from one end to another; nothing,
except *an empty stone chest without a lid*.

The Caliph Al Mamoun was thunderstruck. He had
arrived at the very ultimate part of the interior of the
Great Pyramid he had so long desired to take possession of; and had now, on at last carrying it by storm,
found absolutely nothing that he could make any use of,
or saw the smallest value in. So being signally defeated, though a Commander of the Faithful, his people
began plotting against him.

But Al Mamoun was a Caliph of the able day of
Eastern rulers for managing mankind; so he had a
large sum of money secretly brought from his treasury,
and buried by night in a certain spot near the end of his
own quarried entrance-hole. Next day he caused the

men to dig precisely there, and behold! although they were only digging in the Pyramid masonry just as they had been doing during so many previous days, yet on this day they found a treasure of gold; "and the Caliph ordered it to be counted, and lo! it amounted to the exact sum that had been incurred in the works, neither more nor less. And the Caliph was astonished, and said he could not understand how the kings of the Pyramid of old, actually before the Deluge, could have known exactly how much money he would have expended in his undertaking; and he was lost in surprise." But as the workmen got paid for their labour, and cared not whose gold they were paid with so long as they did get their wage, they ceased their complaints, and dispersed; while as for the Caliph, he returned to the city, El Fostat, notably subdued, musing on the wonderful events that had happened; and both the Grand Gallery, the King's Chamber, and the "stone chest without a lid" were troubled by him no more.

The poets of El Fostat did indeed tune their lutes once again, and celebrate their learned patron's discoveries in that lidless box of granite. According to some of them, a dead man with a breast-plate of gold, and an emerald vase a foot in diameter, and "a carbuncle which shone with a light like the light of day, and a sword of inestimable value and 7 spans long, with a coat of mail 12 spans in length" (all of them very unlike an Egyptian mummy of the usual Egyptological type), rewarded his exertions; though, according to others, the chest was really crammed to the brim with coined gold "in very large pieces"; while on the cover, which others again maintained was not there then, and is certainly not to be seen now, was written, they positively averred, in Arabic characters, "Abou Amad built this Pyramid in 1,000 days."

But nothing further of importance was actually done,

at that time or for long after, in a cause which men began now to deem, in spite of lying poets, to be absolutely worthless, and in a region more profitless to all mere sensualists than the desert itself. The way of approach, indeed, once opened, though no more traversed, by the Caliph Al Mamoun (as he presently left Egypt for his more imperial residence in Bagdad, and ended his days there in 842 A.D., about forty years before the time of our Alfred the Great), that way into the Great Pyramid then remained free to all; and "men did occasionally enter it," says one of the honestest chroniclers of that period, "for many years, and descended by the slippery passage which is in it"; but with no other alleged result, to all those benighted followers of an iniquitously false and contemptuously anti-Christian, prophet, than this, "that some of them came out safe, and others died."

CHAPTER VII.

RESEARCH CONTINUED:

From Moslem to our Own Days.

Resumption of Egyptian History.

FROM Caliph Al Mamoun's, to our own time, is more than 1,000 years; in itself no inconsiderable portion of all intellectual human history on this globe. And if the Arabo-Egyptians had continued through all that immense interval, just as practically curious and wilfully destructive as in and about 820 A.D. in the service of their then ruler, what would have been left to these times of the primeval monument in spite of its grandeur. And especially what would have remained of its one, small, contained coffer, *i.e.* the so-described empty stone chest without a lid?

But utter, complete destruction was by no means to be. The few golden days of the son of Haroun Al Raschid soon passed away; the untoward findings of that monarch were not a little sedative in Pyramid research to his subjects; and before the year A.D. 868 had come and gone, all Egyptians had far different matters to attend to and suffer under, than to push on with more archæological explorations. And yet it was out of ancient times that their newly commencing troubles came: for the day of the Lord's controversy with the giant idols of the land of Ham, with those idols and idol customs still perverting more or less the minds of the inhabitants, and causing them,

Mohammedans though they were, to keep old Egyptian customs, was not ended. And that day was to be one, in its terrors of Divine vengeance,

"When the heart of Egypt shall melt in the midst of it;
 When the Egyptians shall fight, every one against his brother,
 And every one against his neighbour;
 City against city, and kingdom against kingdom,
 And the spirit of Egypt shall fail in the midst thereof.
 And I will destroy the covenant thereof,
 And the Egyptians will I give over into the hand of a cruel Lord,
 And a fierce king shall rule over them,
 Saith the Lord of Hosts."   (Isaiah xix.)

" And it shall be the basest of the kingdoms,
 Neither shall it exalt itself any more above the nations."
                                    (Ezekiel xxix. 15.)

These prophecies had been uttered from 1,400 to 1,500 years previously, or in 650 and 750 B.C.; and this is how they were eventually fulfilled.

Egypt has to accomplish its Destinies.

In 868 A.D. the son of a slave, named Tooloon, was appointed by the Caliph of Bagdad viceroy over Egypt; but presently rebelling against his master, he made himself ruler over the land. Continued wars and troubles ensued to the inhabitants up to his death in the midst of them. Meanwhile the solitude and silence of the desert had once more surrounded the Great Pyramid; and lent it that protection, which man would not, and then could not give, to enable it to go on preserving its message for the distant posterity it had been appointed to.

Tooloon's son, who succeeded him, had similar wars through his short reign, until he was put to death by the women of his own household. The next successor came to a similar violent end, and the next, and the next, by name Haroon; but with the addition of seeing before he died, in the year 900 A.D., according to the chroniclers, " a great tempest and earthquake " desolate the country.

Haroon reigned, say these authorities, *upwards* of eight years, but gave himself up to pleasure, and was put to death by his uncles; one of whom, Sheyban, then usurped the government. The Bagdad caliph thereupon invaded the country; Sheyban went forth to meet him, but his troops deserted; the city of El Fostat, in sight of the Great Pyramid, was taken and burnt, and the women reduced to slavery, A.D. 905.

From this time to 970 A.D., when El Kahireh, or Cairo, was founded by Gohar, close to the north of the former city El Fostat,—anarchy, bloodshed, rival and short-lived rulers, invasions, desolations, slaughters and battles, form the record of almost every year; culminating in 1010 A.D., in the also short-lived but ultra-violent time of El Hakim, who, in addition to all the mere cruelties of his predecessors, made the people pay him divine honours, and altered his name from signifying "Governing by command of God" into "Governing by his own command." But ten slaves, bribed by 500 denars each, finished the wretch's career, one midnight, when he, who had thrown off allegiance to God, was engaged on the hills to the south-east of Cairo in making strange cabalistic sacrifices; to Saturn, say some; to Satan, however, say others; and they further claim him as still the special prophet of the devil-worshippers of Mount Lebanon, the Druses; who moreover expect him to come supernaturally amongst them once again, and soon, a sort of doubly miraculous incarnation of the evil one.

Desolating wars then followed between the Negroes and the Saracens, both of them in turn overrunning Egypt, and butchering after their own fashion; also between Egypt and Bagdad: battles almost every year, and in 1070 A.D., in the time of the Cairo ruler El Mustansir, came the dreadful famine still called by his name. For seven successive years the inundations of the Nile failed; the country produced no corn, and foreign armies prevented its importation from abroad. The wretched people resorted to cannibalism; and, as related by the Arab historian El Makreezee, organized bands kidnapped unwary passengers in the almost deserted streets, catching their prey principally by means of ropes armed with hooks, and let down from the over-hanging lattice windows so common still in Cairo. A pestilence followed the famine, and an invading army the pestilence.

So continues the Arab-age history of Egypt up to the one brighter and better reign of Saladin of the Crusades, from 1117 A.D. to 1193 A.D.; and then the country is plunged into a night of internecine wars and misfortunes again.

In 1301 A.D., during the reign of En Nasir, as great a persecutor of Christians as El Hakim himself, comes the record of another earthquake, so severe, that it is said to have " nearly ruined Cairo, giving it the appearance of a city demolished by a siege," and under this visitation it most probably was, that the final and complete shaking down of the remaining fragments of the already half-plundered casing stones of the Great Pyramid took place, and formed the chief mass of those hills of rubbish which we now find on each of the four base-sides of the monument. There they cover up and preserve to future ages, perhaps on every flank of the building, important proofs of the ancient, exterior, structural architecture, such as Colonel Vyse did discover a portion of, when he cut into the covering of the northern side, the only one which has been penetrated yet.

But we are anticipating. From 1320 to 1398 A.D. things grew rather worse than better; and then began the line of Slave-Sultans, their whole families nothing but slaves, and recruited by continual importation of slaves through two hundred years. History presents,

it is said, no other example of a sovereignty so ignoble
and so lasting in its features of pessimist disgrace ; and
when it presents us also, on one side with a picture
of a sultan burned by his own guards, in "a pleasure-
tower " he had built for himself on the banks of the Nile,
he, on the roof promising all sorts of concessions to
them if only they would not burn him, and they insisting on burning him then and there; and on another
side with the picture of a sultana beaten to death by
her female slaves with their wooden clogs, and her dis-
figured body thrown out and exposed for three days on
the dustheaps outside the city—the imagination itself
can hardly realize the degradation and baseness to which
the ancient kingdom of the Pharaohs had arrived.

The Acme of the Burden of Egypt.

One woe is past, and there come two more woes hereafter, says St. John (Rev. ix.) ; for this was the time
when the four angels of the Euphrates were to be loosed
at last, with their army of horsemen two hundred thousand thousand, long since prepared for an hour, and a
day, and a month, and a year (nearly four hundred
years actual) to kill the third part of men. And the
third part of men were killed by them, " by the fire, and
by the smoke, and by the brimstone, which issued out
of their mouths."

In 1453 the Turks, first employing enormous siege
guns, were, by taking Constantinople, and destroying
the long-existent Greek or Lower Roman empire there,
loosed for new and unrestrained destruction, on all sides.
Against Europe first, but next against Egypt, which
fell under their withering rule in 1517 A.D., when the
last Slave-Sultan of Cairo was crucified over the gate
of the common malefactors by Selim I., the Emperor of
the Turks.

But was that the end of the disgraces and base sufferings of Egypt? Far from it. In place of one slave-monarch, the Turks established in Egypt what amounted to a republic of petty, but innumerable slave-monarchs, to oppress the peaceable population, and fight with each other as much as they liked, so long only as certain tribute, ground by most pitiless tyranny from the peasant cultivators of the land, was sent to Constantinople.

Each Bey, says an acknowledged historian, was a tyrant in his own district, and they were all as tyrannical as their moral character was depraved. Frequently fighting with each other, often with their masters the Turks, against whom they were continually rebelling, Egypt suffered more under the Memlook Beys than through any period of its history. And this state of things continued up to the invasion of Egypt by Napoleon Bonaparte, with 70,000 burning red-republican soldiers from Paris, in 1798; when, at the battle of the Pyramids, the Memlook forces were first notably thinned. But they rose again to a head in one part of the country or another; until finally they were almost entirely extirpated by Mohammed Ali in 1811; leaving the residual and useful population of this once powerful, industrious and most densely inhabited, land of the early world to be summed up, in 1834, as no more than this:—

Muslim Egyptians (peasants and townspeople)..	1,750,000
Copts, or Egyptian Christians	150,000
Osmanlees or Turks (still the governing body) ..	10,000
Syrians	5,000
Armenians	2,000
Jews	5,000
Various	70,000

The European Mind enters into the Great Pyramid Question.

After the terrific ordeal that Egypt had passed through in Mohammedan times, it was more surprising perhaps that the population had not been entirely destroyed, than that the ancient Pyramids escaped almost unscathed. But the population of Egypt has still, by Divine command and prophecy, to exist and see far other events than any that have yet occurred in that wondrous land of old; while the Jeezeh Pyramids, though they were close at hand during all that murdering time past, were not attractive either to sabre or scimitar, being built of stone only, and planted in an actual desert land; in a rocky, sandy wilderness of a barren yellow-ochre colour, far and near, without a blade of grass or a drop of water, but with graves all around them; an entire region where no man was particularly called on to venture in at any time; and least of all in troublous, lawless periods.

Yet it was during that barbaric Turkish rule, of the almost republican Memlook Beys, that modern Europe began to move, modern science to grow, modern travel to be undertaken; and Professor Greaves's visit to the Great Pyramid in 1637 A.D. was an example which soon had imitators, increasing in numbers as the centuries passed by.

Again, too, we find the natural instinct of nations singles out the Great Pyramid as being far more interesting than any other monument of the general Pyramid kind; while in that one building again, the same empty stone chest, which had so affronted the Caliph Al Mamoun, still offered itself there in the interior, and the very farthest and crowning part of the interior too, as the chief object for explanation. Why was it in such a place of honour? Why was the whole Pyramid arranged in subservience to it? Why was it, this mere coffer-box, so unpretending and plain? Why was it empty, lidless, and utterly without inscription, continually demanded modern Europe?

Gradually the notion grew that it might be a sarcophagus; that it was a sarcophagus; and that it had been intended for "that Pharaoh who (in 1542 B.C.) drove the Israelites out of Egypt; and who, in the end, leaving his carcass in the Red Sea, never had the opportunity of being deposited in his own tomb."

But this idea was effectually quashed, for, amongst other reasons, this cogent one,—that the Great Pyramid was not only built, but had been sealed up too in all its more special portions, long before the birth even of that Pharaoh. Nay, before the birth of Isaac and Jacob as well; which disposes likewise of the attempt to call the Great Pyramid "the tomb of Joseph," whose mortal remains being carried away by the Israelites in their exodus, left the vacancy we now see in the coffer or stone box.

Then wrote some literati of 1650 A.D., "Here was buried King Cheops, or Chemmis, the Royal, and Fourth Dynasty, builder of the Great Pyramid according to the Greeks; but his body hath been removed hence." Whereupon Professor Greaves pointed out "that Diodorus hath left, above 1,600 years since, a memorable passage concerning Chemmis (Cheops), the builder of the Great Pyramid, and Cephren (Shafre), the equally royal founder of the work adjoining. "Although," saith he, "those kings intended these for their sepulchres, yet it happened *that neither of them were buried there.* For the people being exasperated against them by reason of the toilsomeness of these works, and for their cruelty and oppression, threatened to tear in pieces their dead bodies, and with ignominy to throw them out of their sepulchres. Whereupon both of them, dying, commanded their friends *to bury them in an obscure place.*"

And again, both Professor Greaves and other scholars salutarily brought up, to check the then public mania for calling the coffer Cheops' coffin, the very clear

account of Herodotus, that King Cheops could not
possibly have been buried in the Great Pyramid building above, simply because he was buried low down, in
a totally different place; viz. " in a subterranean region,
on an island there surrounded by the waters of the
Nile." And as that both necessarily and hydraulically
means a level into which the Nile water could naturally flow, it must have been at a depth of more than
fifty feet beneath the very bottom of even the unfinished
subterranean chamber, the deepest work found yet
underneath, or connected in any way with, the Great
Pyramid. Exactly such a locality, too, both sepulchral,
and with precisely the required hydraulic conditions,
has since then been discovered about 1,000 feet south-
east of the Pyramid building.   (See Plate XIX.)

The structure there found, and still to be seen, descended into, and measured, though much defiled by
the 26th and later Dynasties of ancient Egypt in its
decline,—is a colossally large and deep burial pit, on
the square and level bottom of which rests an antique,
rude sarcophagus of very gigantic proportions. But
deep as is the pit containing it, it is surrounded by a
grand rectangular trench which goes down deeper still,
cut cleanly in solid lime-stone rock the whole of the way
down; and to such a depth does it reach at last as to
descend below the level of the adjacent waters of the
Nile at inundation time. Then, as the waters of that
river necessarily percolate the hygroscopic rock of the
hill up to their own level, the lower depths of the trench
are filled with Nile water, and the grand old sarcophagus
of the interior pit does then rest in a manner "on an
island surrounded by the waters of the Nile," exactly as
Herodotus described;—and it is the only known tomb
on the Jeezeh hill which is gifted with that peculiarity
or privilege.

The Tombic Theory.

So in later years than Greaves', all the single sarcophagus propositions for the benefit of that most re-
makable stone chest in the red-granite chamber of the
Great Pyramid having failed, their remains have been
merged into a sort of general sarcophagus theory, that
some one must have been buried in it. And this notion
finds much favour with the Egyptologists, as a school;
though facts are numerously against them, even to
their own knowledge. They allow, for instance, that in
no other Pyramid is the *sarcophagus*—as they boldly call
the empty stone chest, or granite box, of other authors
—contained high up in the body of the Pyramid, far
above the surface of the ground outside; that in no
other case* is it perfectly devoid of adornment or inscription; that in no other case, not even in the exception just alluded to in the note on the Second Pyramid,
has the lid so strangely vanished; in no other case are
the neighbouring walls and passages so devoid of hieratic and every other profane mythological emblem; in
fact, they confess that the red granite coffer, with all
that part of the Great Pyramid's chambers and ascending passages where it is found, is entirely unique, was
unknown before Caliph Al Mamoun's day, and is strictly
peculiar to the Great Pyramid.

Observe also with the alleged " sarcophagus," in the
King's Chamber (for so is that apartment now most
generally termed), that there was no ancient attempt to
build the vessel up and about in solid masonry, in the
most usual and truly effective manner for securing a
dead body inviolate. On the contrary, there were magnificently built white-stone passages of a most lasting

---

* Excepting indeed the sarcophagus of the Second Pyramid, but
which is not known to have ever been occupied by a mummy.

description, ready to lead a stranger right up to such far interior sarcophagus from the very entrance itself; while, more notably still, the shapely King's Chamber was intended to be *ventilated* in the most admirable manner by the "air channels" discovered by Colonel Howard-Vyse, in 1837 A.D.; evidently (as the actual fact almost enables us to say with security) in order that men might come there in the latter day, and look on, and deal with, that open granite chest, and live and not die.

The Exclusively Tombic Theory receives a Shake.

Meanwhile, some few good men and true in scientific researches—witness M. Jomard in the celebrated " Description de l'Égypte," and Sir Gardner Wilkinson in his own most deservedly popular works—had begun to express occasional doubts as to whether any dead body either of a king or of any other mortal man ever was deposited in the open vessel of the King's Chamber.

The actual words of that most philosophic of all the Egyptologists, Sir G. Wilkinson (several years before Colonel Howard-Vyse's unknowing discovery of the grand outside hydraulic tomb; which though he called it after a mere modern Consul, " Campbell's tomb," may now be more appropriately called by the name of him who was first connected with it, viz. King Cheops), Sir Gardner's gentle words, we repeat, are: " The authority of Arab writers " (alluding to those who had described something like the dead body of a knight with a long sword and coat of mail being found in the coffer) "is not always to be relied on ; and it may be doubted whether the body of the king was really deposited in the sarcophagus " (coffer) of the Great Pyramid.

Something of a metrological kind, again, was suggested by M. Jomard, to be signified by that hollow box; and had also been speculated on by Sir Isaac Newton more than a century earlier, but not followed up. While finally, Dr. Lepsius, as not only an Egyptologist of the perverse Pharaonic order, but one whom Gliddon states, with similar rationalistic pride, "has been justly termed, by the great Letronne, *the hope of Egyptian study*," showed the usual Egyptological want of power for appreciating any higher or purer views, by temporarily planting a young palm-tree in the hollow of the ancient coffer. It was to act, he explained in his subsequent book, as a German Christmas-tree, when decorated with some baubles which he had bought in Cairo, as presents for himself and his Prussian friends; all of them copying ordinary hieroglyphics and pictures of social life from trifling neighbouring tombs.

John Taylor's Theory.

In the midst of such scenes, illustrating, unfortunately, what is actually going on, and chiefly applauded still, among the Egyptologists of the nineteenth century, comes out the late John Taylor with the result of his long and respectful researches; and suggests more or less that, "The coffer in the King's Chamber of the Great Pyramid was intended to be a standard measure of capacity and weight; primarily in a special, exclusive, or selective manner, but ultimately for all nations; and *certain* nations, he considered, did thence originally receive their weights and measures; so that those of them who still preserve, to some degree, with their language and history, their *hereditary*, *aboriginal* weights and measures, may yet trace their prehistoric connection substantially with that one primeval, standard, metrological centre for all the future world, the Great Pyramid."

Take, for instance, our own case. When the British

farmer measures the wheat which the bounty of Providence has afforded him as the increase of his land, in what terms does he measure it ?   In *quarters*.

Quarters !   Quarters of what ?

The existing British farmer does not know ; for there is no capacity measure now on the Statute-book above the quarter ; but, from old custom, he calls his largest corn measure a quarter.

Whereupon John Taylor adds in effect : " The quarter corn measures of the British farmer are fourth parts or *quarters* of the contents of the coffer in the King's Chamber of the Great Pyramid ; and the true value, in size, of its particular corn measure, has not sensibly deteriorated during all the varied revolutions of mankind in the last 4,040 years ! "

Practical Examination of John Taylor's Coffer Theory.

The above is a statement not to be implicitly accepted without a very full examination ; and something in that way can fortunately be instituted very easily ; as thus—

The first part of the problem is merely to determine the cubical contents of the vessel known successively, from Caliph Al Mamoun's day to our own, as the " sarcophagus," " the empty box," " the lidless stone chest," or more philosophically and safely, so as not to entangle ourselves with any theory, " the coffer," in the King's Chamber of the Great Pyramid.

From Colonel Howard-Vyse's important work are drawn forth and arranged, in the following table, all the chief mensurations taken between 1550 A.D. and 1840 A.D., some of the principal authors being consulted in their original writings.   Their measures, generally given in feet, or feet and inches,* or mètres, are all

* The feet of all authors, when not otherwise particularised, have been here assumed as English feet, and in some cases may require a correction on that account, but not to any extent sufficient to explain the chief anomalies observed.

here set down in British inches, to give a clearer view of the progress of knowledge in this particular matter. And now, our only bounds to exactness will be, the capability of these educated men of Europe to apply accurate instrumentation to a regularly formed and exquisitely prepared specimen of ancient mechanical art.

MODERN MEASURES OF THE GREAT PYRAMID COFFER UP TO A.D. 1864.

AUTHORS.	DATE.	MATERIAL AS NAMED.	EXTERIOR.			INTERIOR.		
			Lngth.	Brdth.	Hght.	Lngth.	Brdth.	Depth.
	A.D.		Ins.	Ins.	Ins.	Ins.	Ins.	Ins.
Bellonius . .	1553	Black marble .	144·	72·	...	...	...	...
P. Alpinus .	1591	Black marble .	144·	60·	60·	...	...	...
Sandys . .	1610	....	84·	47·	Breast-high	...	...	...
De Villamont .	1618	Black marble .	102·	...	60·	...	...	...
Prof. Greaves .	1638	Thebaic marble	87·5	39·75	39·75	77·856	26·616	34·320
De Monconys .	1647	....	86·	37·	40·	...	...	...
M. Thevenot .	1655	Hard porphyry .	86·	40·	40·	75·?	29·?	...
M. Lebrun .	1674	....	74·	37·	40·	...	...	...
M. Maillet .	1692	Granite . .	90·	48·	48·	...	...	...
De Careri .	1693	Marble . .	86·	37·	39·	...	...	...
Lucas . .	1699	Like porphyry .	84·	36·	42·	74·?	26·?	...
Egmont .	1709	Thebaic marble	84·	...	42·	72·?	...	...
Père Sicard .	1715	Granite . .	84·	42·	36·	...	...	...
Dr. Shaw .	1721	Granite . .	84·	36·	42·	72·?	24·?	...
Dr. Perry .	1743	Granite . .	84·	30·	36·	...	...	...
M. Denon .	1799	?	84·	48·	38·	...	...	...
M. Jomard and Eg. Fr. Ac. .	1799	Granite . .	90·592	39·450	44·765	77·836	26·694	37·285
Dr. Clarke .	1801	Granite . .	87·5	39·75	39·75	...	...	...
Mr. Hamilton .	1801	Granite . .	90·	42·	42·0	78·?	30·?	...
Dr. Whitman .	1801	....	78·	38·75	41·5	66·?	26·75?	32·
Dr. Wilson .	1805	....	92·	38·	...	80·?	26·?	34·5
M. Caviglia .	1817	....	90·	39·	42·	78·?	27·?	...
Dr. Richardson .	1817	Red granite .	90·	39·	39·5	...	...	...
Sir G.Wilkinson	1831	Red granite .	88·	36·	37·	...	...	...
Howard-Vyse .	1837	....	90·5	39·0	41·0	78·0	26·5	34·5

N.B.—A note of interrogation after any of the *interior* measures indicates that they have been obtained by applying to the *exterior* measures the "thickness" as given by the observer; such thickness being supposed to apply to the sides, and not to the bottom, which may be different.

Reflections on the Numbers as given above.

Look at them, then. Surely the list is not a little appalling. An ordinary carpenter amongst us uses sixteenths of an inch quite fluently, and sometimes undertakes to make a special piece of cabinet work "fit to half a sixteenth": but our learned travellers

commit errors of many whole inches; and this when
they are voluntarily, and of their own prompting only,
measuring the one and only internal object which they
found to measure, or thought should be described by
measure, in the whole interior of the Great Pyramid.

My own part here must be very gently performed;
for I have *my* measures to produce by-and-by, none of
them perfectly exact; and yet even I feel compelled to
say, that out of the twenty-five quoted authors no less
than twenty-two must be discharged summarily as quite
incompetent, whatever their mental attainments otherwise, to talk before the world about either size or proportion in any important *practical* matter.

Professor Greaves in 1638, the French Academicians
in 1799, and Colonel Howard-Vyse in 1837, are therefore the only three names that deserve to live as coffer
measurers, in the course of 250 years of legions of educated European visitors. Of these three parties thus
provisionally accepted, the foremost position might have
been expected for the Academicians of Paris. Professor Greaves lived before the day of European science
proper. While Colonel Howard-Vyse did not lay himself out for very refined measurements ; but rather went
through what he felt himself obliged to undertake in
that direction, in the same fearless, thorough-going,
artless but most honest manner in which the Duke of
Wellington was accustomed to review a picture exhibition in London; beginning with No. 1 in the catalogue,
and going through with the whole of them conscientiously to the very last number on the list.

The Colonel's measures, therefore, are respectable
and solidly trustworthy with regard to large quantities,
but not much more.

With the French Academicians it is quite another
thing; they were the men, and the successors of the
men, who had been for generations measuring arcs of

the meridian, and exhausting all the refinements of microscopic bisections and levers of contact in determining the precise length of standard scales. Their measures, therefore, ought to be true to the thousandth, and even the ten-thousandth part of an inch : and perhaps they are so, in giving the *length* and *breadth* of the coffer; but, alas ! in their statements of the *depth* inside and the *height* outside, there seems to have been some incomprehensible mistake committed, amounting to nearly *three whole inches*.

Under such circumstances, and after having failed to obtain any satisfactory explanation from the Perpetual Secretary of the Academy in Paris, I have been compelled to discharge the French Academy, also, from the list of fully trustworthy competitors for usefulness and fame in Pyramid-coffer metrology. Only two names, therefore, are left—Howard-Vyse, who has been already characterized, and Greaves, in whom we have most fortunately a host indeed.

Of Professor Greaves, the Eastern-travelling Oxford Astronomer in 1637.

Living as he did before the full birth of European science, but on the edge of an horizon which is eventful in scientific history ; with an unusual knowledge too of Oriental languages, and a taste for travelling in the then turbulent regions of the East, Professor Greaves belongs almost to the heroic time. Immediately behind him were, if not the dark ages, the scholastic periods of profitless verbal disquisitions ; and in front, to be revealed after his death, were the germs of the mechanical and physical natural philosophy which have since then changed the face of the world. There is no better a life-point that can be taken than Greaves's, whereby to judge what Europe has gained by the exercise of civil

and religious liberty, coupled with the study of nature
direct, through two and a half centuries of unrestricted
opportunity. When as much more time has passed
over the world as now separates us from Greaves's age,
then, if not rather much sooner than then—say all the
safest interpreters of the sacred prophecies—a further
Divine, and hitherto unexampled, step in the development of the Christian dispensation will have commenced.

Now almost every other visitor to the Great Pyramid,
both before and since Greaves, paid vastly more attention to the exterior, than the interior, of the coffer;
but Professor Greaves, fortunately for our present inquiry, attended chiefly to its interior, and wrote thereon
most particularly, thus :—" It is in length on the west
side, six feet, and four hundred and eighty-eight parts of
the English foot, divided into a thousand parts " (that
is, 6 feet, and 488 of 1,000 parts of a foot) ; "in breadth
at the north end, two feet, and two hundred and
eighteen parts of the foot divided into a thousand
parts " (that is, 2 feet, and 218 of 1,000 parts of the
English foot). "The depth is 2 feet and 860 of 1,000
parts of the English foot."

And he defends his rather round-about method of
statement in this instance by adding, so characteristically for his pre-Newtonian day in science: " In the
reiteration of these numbers, if any shall be offended
either with the novelty or tediousness of expressing them
so often, I may justify myself by the example of Ulug
Beg, nephew of Timurlane the Great (for so is his name,
and not Tamerlane), and Emperor of the Moguls, or
Tatars (whom we term amiss Tartars). For I find in
his astronomical tables (the most accurate of any in the
East), made about two hundred years since, the same
course observed by him when he writes of the Grecian,
Arabian, and Persian epochas, as also those of Cataia

and Turkistan. He expresseth the numbers at large, as I have done; then in figures, such as we call Arabian, ————, which manner I judge worthy of imitation, in all such numbers as are radical, and of more than ordinary use."

Greaves's and Vyse's Coffer Capacity Determinations.

Hence we have for the cubical contents of the coffer in even English inches, deduced from Greaves's original full measures, in 1838—

$$77 \cdot 856 \times 26 \cdot 616 \times 34 \cdot 320 = 71,118.$$

And by Howard-Vyse's measures, just as taken in 1837—

$$78 \cdot 0 \times 26 \cdot 5 \times 34 \cdot 5 = 71,311.$$

Several small corrections may possibly be applicable to these mere numbers as simply read off; but for the present we may provisionally accept for a *first approximation* the simple mean of the above statements, or 71,214 cubic inches, as the apparent capacity contents of the coffer of the King's Chamber.

Wherefore now, what proportion does that number bear to the capacity of four modern English corn quarters, in terms of which British wheat is measured and sold at this very hour?

Referring to the almanac for the Act of Parliament on the subject, we find that one gallon is declared to be equal to 277·274 cubic inches; which quantity being multiplied for bushels, quarters, and four quarters, yields 70,982·144 English cubic inches. Whence the degree of agreement between a quarter modern British, and a fourth part of the ancient coffer, or granite box, and possible type of a both primeval and prophetic corn-measure in the Great Pyramid, is at this present time as 17,746 : 17,804.

Qualities of the Coffer's "Quarter" Measure.

A sufficiently fair amount of agreement is this, between the things compared (viz. the Pyramid coffer on
one side divided into four from the first decently good
measures of any modern *savants;* and on the other, the
old Anglo-Saxon corn-measure, after being too often
" adjusted " by Acts of Parliament, since those halcyon
days of rest when Edgar " the peaceable " reigned over
England at Winchester, 958—975 A.D.),—sufficiently
near, I repeat, to allow friends of worthy old John
Taylor to say that so far the Great Pyramid, with its
coffer of four British corn-quarter capacity, *if originally
intended for it,* is still capable of fulfilling the purpose of
one of the *Greek* interpretations of its now world-famous
name, in *meting* out, πυρὸς, corn.

To nations in a primitive condition, the first application of capacity measures would, with little doubt, be in
the exchange of corn; and through whatever subsequent
stage of power, luxury, or refinement they may pass,
the measuring of the staff of life will probably still keep
up a permanent importance over every other object of
measuring or weighing, even though it be of drugs, or
silver, or gold,—in perfect accordance so far with our
Lord's Prayer, where the only material supplication is,
" Give us day by day our daily *bread.*"

Yet is it to be also remarked, that if any given means
for measuring corn were devised by a very superior
intelligence, they should eventually be found applicable
also, so far as principles of, and capacity for, accuracy
go, to many of the more precise purposes to which the
after progress of mankind may introduce them.

Thus, the moon, with its frequently recurring variations
and phases, serves man in the savage, and did
serve him in the primitive and patriarchal, state, as a

coarse method of chronicling time month by month. In a more developed and civilized condition, some of the larger cycles of lunations enable him to speak exactly of many years at a time, and approximate to some eclipses. In a still further advanced condition, the moon's subsidiary features of movement enable the educated mariner in the midst of the broad surface of ocean, assisted by data from the astronomer and mathematician on shore, to measure his precise longitude. Next, amongst the ablest minds of the present day, the theory of those movements and the computation of their nature, form an arena where every chief mathematician of his country may measure off his own intellectual height at the base of an infinite cliff which he may never hope to stand on the summit of. And finally, some of the most remarkable of the inspired predictions of both Daniel and St. John, as well as the Scriptural history of men in the past, are found to have been arranged by the Creator, from the beginning of all things, to be, in some almost inscrutable manner, coincident with certain combinations of Lunar with Solar-Lunar cycles, of still more lengthened period.*

In exact proportion, therefore, as man has become able to profit by God's moon, which he, man, originally believed was merely intended to slightly moderate for him the darkness of night, so has the divinely appointed luminary been found capable of more and more applications; and whenever any difficulty has occurred, it has never been any want of perfect accuracy in the lunar machinery itself, but merely in the power of man to interpret the working of it. And when at last, as in the present day, his powers in that line have become considerable, he then begins to find symptoms in the Book of Inspiration, that there was an Intelligence

* See the Rev. Grattan Guiness's recent work on "The Approaching end of the Age."

there, which knew it long ago ; and that man cannot break out of the limits appointed him by God, either in time or space or harmony of surroundings.

Is there, then, anything approaching to the same suggestive principle connected with the coffer " corn-measure " of the Great Pyramid ?

That may probably come out as we proceed with our grand research ; but wherein we may first have to descend to some of the minutest of details, if we are to arrive at satisfactory certainty at last.

CHAPTER VIII.

THE CONTAINED VESSEL:

Its Substance, Size, and Shape.

Granite the True Material of the Coffer.

A REFERENCE to the third column of the Coffer table on page 135 of the last chapter will show that travellers have assigned the coffer to almost every mineral, from black marble to red granite, and porphyry of a colour which no one has ventured to name. Yet John Taylor concluded for porphyry, and called the vessel "the Porphyry Coffer," as I did also for a time, *i.e.* in my first book *before* going to Egypt; doubting then, if anything so well known and distinctly marked as red granite would ever have been called black marble; and having been further at that period so distinctly assured about the coffer, by a railway engineer who had been much in Egypt, that " it is undoubtedly porphyry"; an assertion which he backed up by describing some of the differences in character between the material of the coffer, as witnessed by himself, and the indubitable red granite walls of the containing chamber.

This wall granite the engineer traced to the quarries of Syene, 550 miles up the river from the Pyramid; for nearer than that, there is no granite rock on the banks of the Nile, or within many days' journey from them on either side : but there, at the cataracts of the Nile above Syene, it abounds; and Syene was in fact a storehouse of granite (of the syenitic variety, but still eminently to be called granite rather than by any other mineral name equally understood by the public at large) for the supply of every dynasty that sat on the throne of Egypt subsequently to the building of the Great Pyramid.

Porphyry may not improbably be also found at Syene, amongst the veins and extravasations of granite and basalt which there abound: but the most celebrated Egyptian quarries of porphyry, both red and green, were much nearer the Red Sea than the Nile, or at and about the Gebel Dokkan and Mount Porphorytes; therefore in much closer geographical proximity to, and, perhaps, geological connection with, the granite mountains of Sinai, than the plutonic beds of Philæ and Syene.

Nevertheless, I having at last visited Egypt in 1864-5, after the publication of the first edition of this book, spent almost whole days and weeks in this King's Chamber of the Great Pyramid, until all sense of novelty and needless mystery in small things had worn away; and then decided, without the smallest hesitation, for the material of the coffer being syenitic granite; exceedingly like, but perhaps a little harder as well as darker than, the constructive blocks of the walls of the King's Chamber containing it.

Granite in the Dark, and Semi-dark, Ages now gone by.

In either case, and in every possible or even imaginable instance, such hard granite is wonderfully distinct, naturally, from the soft lime-stone (sometimes, but with less error, called marble) of the rest of the Great Pyramid's structure; and it is not a little important, in all Pyramid research there, to be able in that monument to detect for certain whenever the primeval architect abandoned the use of the lime-stone he had at hand,

and adopted the granite procured with utmost toil and expense from a distance; whether it came from Syene, as modern Egyptologists usually determine, or from Sinai, as Professor Greaves would rather infer.

Recent travellers have indeed abundantly perceived the cartouches or ovals of both King Cheops and King Chephren, or of Shofo and Nou-Shofo, of the Jeezeh Pyramids, on certain quarried rocks in the Sinaitic peninsula, near Wadee Maghara; but the "works" with which these inscriptions were connected are generally supposed to have been iron and copper mines and emerald pits; while the following original note by Professor Greaves, evidently written long before the day of mineralogy, may be useful for a different purpose. The passage runs as follows:—"I conceive it" (the material of the coffer) "to be of that sort of porphyry which Pliny calls leucostictos, and describes thus:— ' Rubet porphyrites in eâdem Ægypto, ex eo candidis intervenientibus punctis leucostictos appellatur. Quantislibet molibus cædendis sufficiunt lapidicinæ.' Of this kind of marble there were, and still are, an infinite quantity of columns in Egypt. But Venetian, a man very curious, who accompanied me thither, imagined that this sort of marble came from Mount Sinai, where he had lived amongst the rocks, which he affirmed to be speckled with party colours of black and white and red, like this; and to confirm his assertion, he alleged that he had seen a great column left imperfect amongst the cliffs almost as big as that huge and admirable pillar standing to the south of Alexandria. Which opinion of his doth well correspond with the tradition of Aristides, who reports that in Arabia there is a quarry of excellent porphyry."

Sad confusion here between granite and porphyry in the seventeenth century: while in the "unheroic eighteenth century" Anglo-Saxon ignorance of granite

culminated. No fresh granite was then being worked
anywhere direct from nature, and the monuments of
antiquity composed of it were first suspected, and then
alleged, to be factitious; as thus stated by a Mediterranean traveller in 1702 :—" The column of Pompey at
Alexandria. Some think it of a kind of *marble*, but
others incline rather to believe that 'twas built of *melted*
(dissolved ?) *stone* cast in moulds upon the place. The
latter opinion seems most probable, for there is *not the
least piece of that stone to be found* (naturally) *in any part
of the world*, and the pillar is so prodigiously big and
high that it could hardly be erected without a miracle.
I know 'tis alleged by those who believe the story of
the Rhodian colossus, that the ancients had the advantage of admirable machines to raise such bulky pieces;
but I should reckon myself extremely obliged to those
gentlemen if they would show me any probable reason
why among so great a variety of Egyptian monuments
of antiquity, there is not one of *marble* ; and by what
unaccountable accident the stone called *granite*, which
was then so common, is now grown so scarce that the
most curious inquiries into the works of nature cannot
find the least fragment of it, that was not employed in
ancient structures.

" And even though I should suppose, with my adver-
saries, that the quarries out of which this stone was
dug were by degrees so entirely exhausted that there
is not the least footstep of 'em left, and that Nature
herself has lost so much of ancient vigour and fecundity
that she is not able to produce new ones, I may still be
allowed to ask why granite was only used in obelisks or
columns of a prodigious bigness ; for if it were really a
sort of (natural) stone or marble, I see no reason why
we might not find small pieces of *it*, as well as of
porphyry and other precious kinds of marble.

" These reflections, in my opinion, may serve to confirm the hypothesis of those who believe that all these admirable monuments were actually cast in a mould; and if they would take the pains to view this column attentively, they would soon be convinced by the testimony of their own eyes that 'tis only a kind of cement composed of sand and calcined stone, not unlike to mortar or lime, which grows hard by degrees."

Another century of modern civilization rolled on, and then we find the celebrated traveller Dr. Clarke has burst his way to light; for he is then quite convinced that granite is a natural substance, and that hand specimens of it may be found by those who will search from country to country through the world. But yet was granite then so seldom met with or recognised, that he has all this further trouble in explaining to London society, of seventy years ago, what common rock material it is that he is talking about :—" By Greaves's Thebaick marble is to be understood that most beautiful variety of granite called by Italian lapidaries *granito rosso* (see ' Forbes's Travels,' p. 226 ; London, 1776), which is composed essentially of *feldspar*, of *quartz*, and of *mica*. It is often called *Oriental granite*, and sometimes *Egyptian granite;* but it differs in no respect from *European granite*, except that *feldspar* enters more largely as a constituent into the mass than is usual with the *granite* of Europe. The author has seen *granite* of the same kind, and of equal beauty, in fragments, upon the shores of the Hebrides, particularly at Icolmkill."

Sixty more years of modern civilization passed away. Macdonald at Aberdeen had by that time taught his countrymen how to work in polished granite, both red and grey, far and wide over Scotland. From tombstones to brooches, and from banks and insurance offices to kettle-holders and earrings, cut granite (poured forth since then without any stint both by the cold, pale

Queen of the North and her blushing sister of Peter-head) is now used on every side; until all society, and the children too, talk as glibly in these our days about the once awfully mysterious tri-speckled stone, "as maids of thirteen do of puppy-dogs." And yet the thing, in Nature, is not plain to all our educated gentlemen even yet.

When, for instance, my Wife and I were living through several months in a tomb of the eastern cliff of the Great Pyramid Hill in 1865, a Cambridge man, with a most respectable name in science, and a sage-looking, experienced head of iron-grey hair, called upon us and remarked (to the lady too, who knows a great deal more about minerals than I do), "What a fine *granite* cavern you are living in!" Granite, indeed! poor man! when the petrified nummulites were staring at him all the time out of the nought but lime-stone on every side! And other travellers within the last few years have confidently talked of having seen granite in the entrance-passage of the Great Pyramid, granite in the subterranean chamber, granite forming the casing-stone heaps outside, granite, in fact, anywhere and everywhere; and basalt dykes in the Pyramid hill too, though in a country of pure nummulitic lime-stone.

They, however, being free and independent writers, cannot be easily interfered with; but will my readers at least excuse me for insisting upon it, that for any would-be pyramidist scholar it is a most awful mistake to say granite when he means lime-stone, or *vice versâ*; and to see lime-stone, where the primeval architect went to infinite pains to place granite. To talk thus interchangeably of the two is, indeed, over and above saying the thing that is not in mineralogy, over and above taking hard for soft, and soft for hard; Nep-tunian for Plutonian; repletion with traces of organic existence for nought but crystals that never had a breath of life in them,—it is also on the part of such individual a depriving himself of the only absolutely positive feature that he can, or should, speak to in all Pyramid inquiry; as thus :—

Questions of amount of angle, length of line, and measure of weight are all, even in the best modern science researches, questions of degree of approximation only ; or of limits of approach to a something which may never be actually touched, or finally defined. But if white nummulitic lime-stone cannot be distinguished absolutely from red granite, or if one of those substances is said to glide so insensibly into the other, that no man can say with confidence where one begins and the other ends—the age for interpreting the long-secret interior of the Great Pyramid has not yet arrived.

But I will not consent to any such state of mind afflicting the readers of this present edition of 1879; and would rather, with them, as one amongst friends and often, in many other learned subjects, betters than myself, request their attention (before further discussing the coffer in the King's Chamber) to a prevailing feature of the *manner* in which the Great Pyramid makes its chief mechanical use of this triple rock, of strong colours and strange traditions, granite.

There is granite in the Great Pyramid, and granite in various small Pyramids; yet so far from their being therefore alike, it is on that very account, or by that very means, that most difference may be detected both in their designs and even in the very minds of their designers.

Take the third Pyramid as an example; the Egyptological world hailed it as the "Coloured Pyramid"; coloured, forsooth, because its casing-stones more than half-way up, were of red granite. That that little third Pyramid was therefore more expensive than the Great one, all its friends admit, and even boast of: but what else did it gain thereby ?   Lasting power, is the general idea; because granite is so proverbially hard.   But, alas ! granite, besides being hard, is also so very brittle on account chiefly of its tri-crystallization, and is so largely expansible by heat,* that under the influence of a hot sun by day and cold sky by night, it loosens and crushes minutely the materials of its own surface to little pieces, film by film, and age after age—until now, after 3,000 years, those hard granitic casing-stones of the third Pyramid are rounded along their edges into pudding shapes, which can hardly indicate the angle they were originally bevelled to, within a handful of degrees.   Yet the softer, and fair, white lime-stone which was chosen of old for the casing of the Great Pyramid (a variety it is of lime-stone found in the Mokattam hill on the east side of the Nile), and which was begun to be exposed to the weather before the third Pyramid or its builders were born, has, joined to that softness, so much tenacity, smallness of heat expansion, and strong tendency to varnish itself with a brownish iron oxide exudation, that it has in some instances preserved the original angle of the casing-stones within a minute of a degree, and their original surface within the hundredth of an inch.

But *because* the Great Pyramid architect found lime-stone to answer his purpose for casing-stones, did he therefore use it everywhere ?   No, certainly not.   He knew it to be too soft to keep its size and figure in places where men do tend to congregate; and where strains and wear and tear may accumulate, and have to be strenuously resisted.   In and towards the centre,

---

* Having prepared in 1873, a number of slabs of different materials, both natural and artificial, and then examined their lengths with a microscopic beam-compass both in summer and winter, I found all the harder stones, agate, chalcedony, green-stone, flint, porphyry, and marble too, afflicted with larger heat expansions than the soft, fine-grained lime-stones, such as either the white lime-stone of the Great Pyramid, or the black lime-stone of Ireland.

therefore, of the whole mass of the Great Pyramid, where strains do increase and the treasure was supposed to be kept, and where Caliph Al Mamoun in one age, and middle-class passengers from Australian steamers in another, rush trampling in to see what they can get by force,—there, whatever other purposes we may presently discover he also had, the Great Pyramid architect began to use granite in place of lime-stone. And in the deep and solemn interior of that building, where he did so employ it, there was no sun to shine and heat up by day, no open sky to radiate cold at night; but only closed-in darkness and a uniform temperature from year to year, and century to century.

There was, therefore, no tendency in granite to separate its component crystals *there;* but very great necessity for its hardness to resist the continual treading, or hammering and mischief-working by the countless visitors of these latter days. For the granite portion of the Great Pyramid (excepting only the portcullis, or stopper, blocks at the lower end of the first ascending passage) begins in the so-called ante-chamber apartment. A narrow chamber through which all visitors must pass, in order to reach that further, grander, and final King's Chamber wherein the employment of granite culminates: and wherein is to be seen standing loose and quite movable, except for its immense weight, on the open, level, granite floor, that Pyramid coffer, or long and high granite box, which is still awaiting our further and higher examination.

Why of that Size?

If we grant, temporarily, for mere present argument's sake, that the long rectangular *granite* box, or coffer, in the King's Chamber of the Great Pyramid was intended by the precise, measured, amount of its cubic contents to typify, as Mr. Taylor has suggested, a grand and

universal standard of capacity measure—can any reason
in either nature or science be shown, why it should
have been made of that particular size and no other?

In a later age the designer of such a *metrological*
vessel would have been hampered by custom, confined
by law, or led by precedent. But in the primeval day
of the foundation of the Great Pyramid, who was there
then to control its architect; or from whom could that
truly original genius have copied anything; or lastly,
what was there to prevent *his* making the coffer therein
of any size he pleased?

Of Scientific References for Capacity Measure.

This affair of the wherefore of the coffer's precise
size is no doubt a difficult question, for there is no
ready explanation lying on the surface; and if we
attempt to consider it from a theoretical point of view,
as to what *should* regulate a system of capacity and
weight measure adapted to intellectual and religious
man both living upon this earth-ball, and in worship of,
and obedience to, God, both his, and earth's, Creator,—
we are met by an alarming degree of backwardness
among all the modern science schools in developing the
cosmical relations and peculiar refinements of which
this particular subject is evidently capable.

Previous Attempts to account for the Coffer's Capacity-size.

On this present branch of our enquiry the estimable
John Taylor had ventured some ideas, but up to the time
of his lamented decease had not reached anything very
definite, or capable either of inspiring confidence in
others, or showing direct connection with the rest of
the Great Pyramid theory.

Still less can be said for the very wild and foundation-
less ideas, *first*, of Mr. Joseph Jopling (who never saw
the Great Pyramid); *second*, of Hekekeyan Bey (an

Armenian in Cairo, but who, though living in sight of the Great Pyramid, had never been into the interior of it), and *third*, of M. Dufeu of Paris (who has done little more than introduce Hekekeyan Bey's views to European readers). Little indeed then, can be urged for any yet published hypotheses, as to why the Coffer of the Great Pyramid was made of the shape and size we find it now; and indeed one reason of all their failures could not but be, the very imperfect knowledge those earlier authors had of the size and shape to be explained.

Let *us* therefore attend more painstakingly to getting up these necessary preliminary data. And immediately we begin this task, some very unexpected matters of detail present themselves.

The Ledge Anomaly of the Coffer.

How astounded, for instance, was not I, on first visiting the Coffer in January, 1865, to find that, though sure enough that remarkable vessel was still in the King's Chamber—and that no fine-art Egyptological thieves (whether aristocratic Earls of Belmore or plebeian Belzonis) had carried it off to enrich themselves or to sell to a distant museum—yet there was actually a ledge for a lid, cut out of, or into, the substance of the top of the sides of what had been styled proverbially for ages the " lidless box, or open chest, of stone!" (See Plate XVII.)

Compared with this discovery, it was nothing that the vessel was chipped and chipped again on every possible edge; that the south-eastern corner was broken away by fresh hammer fractures to an extent of eight or ten inches *more* than it was in the days of Colonel Howard-Vyse. But that ledge neatly, skilfully cut out, when was that introduced?

It has no existence in the French Academy's drawing

of 1799, and which I had unfortunately followed in my
first book of 1864 ; but it *is* found, as I afterwards discovered, in " Perring's Views of the Pyramids " in 1840.
Was the ledge then introduced by modern workers
between 1799 and 1840 ?

Those who bow down to, and almost worship the in-
fallibility of great Scientific Societies, and especially of
the French Academy, are bound to conclude so. But I
have not that ultra respect for any merely human institute, and simply consider that in this matter, as well
as the three extra inches of both height and depth already spoken of, the Associated *savants* must have made
a mistake. Wherefore, as I unwittingly tended to spread
their ledge error in 1864, it is my duty now to set forth
exactly how I found the Coffer in 1865.

The following is, consequently, an extract from my
book, " Life and Work at the Great Pyramid," published in 1867, and now revised, in order to introduce
some still later and further observations by Dr. J. A. S.
Grant, of Cairo, and Mr. Waynman Dixon, C.E.

THE COFFER, MEASURED IN BRITISH INCHES.
MARCH 20—23, 25, 1865.

This vessel, the sole contents of the dark King's Chamber, and termed,
according to various writers, stone box, granite chest, lidless vessel, porphyry vase, black marble sarcophagus, and coffer—is composed, as to its
material, of a darkish variety of red, and possibly syenitic, granite. And
there is no difficulty in seeing this; for although the ancient polished
sides have long since acquired a deep chocolate hue, there are such
numerous chips effected on all the edges in recent years, that the component crystals, quartz, mica, and felspar, may be seen (by the light of
a good candle) even brilliantly.

The vessel is chipped around, or along, every line and edge of bottom,
sides, and top; and at its south-east corner, the extra accumulation of
chippings extends to a breaking away of nearly half its height from the
top downwards.   It is, moreover, tilted up at its south end by a black
jasper pebble, about 1·5 inch high (such pebbles are found abundantly on
the desert hills outside and west of the Great Pyramid), recently pushed
in underneath the south-west corner.   The vessel is therefore in a state
of strain, aggravated by the depth to which the vertical sides have been
broken down as above; and great care must be taken in outside measures,
not to be misled by the space between some parts of the bottom and the
floor, itself also of polished red granite.

As for the under surface of the bottom of the coffer (speculated on by some persons as containing a long inscription, I felt it, near the south end, with my hand, and tried to look under it also when a piece of magnesium wire was burning there, without being sensible of any approach to hieroglyphics or engraving. But as to the inner, or upper surface, of the bottom, and also the vertical sides of the vessel, both inside and out—all the ancient surfaces there are plainly enough polished smooth, and are without any carving, inscription, design, or any intentional line or lines ; they are also all of them simple, plain, and flat (sensibly to common observation) ; excepting only the top margin, which is cut into in a manner implying that a sarcophagus lid once fitted on, sliding into its place from the west, and fixable by three steady pins, entering from the lid into holes on that western side.

The west side of the coffer is therefore lowered all over its top surface, except at the north and south ends, by the amount of depth of such ledge cut-out, or 1·72 inch ; and the other, or east, north, and south sides are, or should be, lowered to the same depth *on their inner edges*, and to a distance from inside to out of 1·63 inch. But the fulness of this arrangement cannot be seen now, because in some places both ledge and top of sides are broken away together ; and in others, though much of the inner base-line of the ledge remains—thanks to its protected position —the upper and true surface of the coffer's side has all been chipped away. In fact, it is only over a short length near the north-east corner of the coffer that the chippers have left any portion of its original top edge. And a cast of that corner recently taken by Mr. Waynman Dixon shows, as compared with my photograph (and also with the frontispiece to Vol. I. of my " Life and Work "), that a further portion of the side's top surface, indeed an awfully large conchoidal-shaped block, *has disappeared since* 1865.

The whole question, therefore, of the full depth of the coffer rests on one very small portion of the north-east wall, so to speak, of the coffer—a portion, too, which becomes smaller and smaller every year that we live.

Only at that north-east corner, too, is there an opportunity of measuring the vertical depth between the ancient top surface of a side and the bottom surface of the *ledge ;* and it was, by repeated measure, found by me = from 1·68 to 1·70 and 1·75 ; say mean = 1·72 inch.

The sides of the ledge depression appeared to me to have been vertical, or without any dovetailing; and the horizontal base-breadth of such cutout—measuring from within, to, or towards the " without " of the coffer— and restoring the sides to their original completeness before the chipping away of the edges—is—

On and near Western portion of Northern side .			=	1·65
,,	Middle ,, ,, .		=	1·62
,,	Eastern ,, ,, .		=	1·73
,,	Northern part of Eastern side .		=	1·55
,,	Southern ,, ,,		. *all broken.*	
,,	Eastern and Western parts of Southern side		*all broken.*	

Mean　　=　　1·63 in.

But this appearance of the coffer's ledge having been *rectangular*, has been, since my visit, successfully shown by Dr. Grant and Mr. W. Dixon to be a mistake. For although everywhere else all the overhangings of an acute ledge have been broken away to beyond the vertical, yet there is a small part left near the north-east corner, which speaks unmistakably to an acute-angled shape; not by any means so sharply acute as that of the sarcophagus of the Second Pyramid, but decidedly and intentionally on the acute side of rectangular.

Along the western side are three fixing-pin holes, 1·2 deep, and 0·84 in diameter, save where they are broken larger, as is chiefly the case with the middle and southern one. The three holes have their centres at the following distances from the north end : viz. 16·0, 45·3, and 75·1 respectively.

It is inconceivable how the French Academicians could have pictured the coffer, as they did, without representing anything of this ledge cut-out, or of the fixing-pin holes; unless they looked upon these traces as a comparatively modern attempt to convert the original pure coffer into a sarcophagus, and which they were therefore bound to overlook in their description of the *original* vessel. But we are to note both states.

Outside of Coffer : Minuter Details of its Figure.

The planes forming the four external vertical sides of the coffer, which have never yet been questioned by any other measurer, appeared to me to be not very true; excepting the east one, whose errors are under 0·02, or perhaps 0·01; while the north, west, and south sides are so decidedly concave as to have central depressions of 0·3 and 0·5 inches; or more particularly—

At North side, central hollow or depression of coffer's side (measured from a *horizontal* straight-edge touching the side at either end, and in a horizontal plane), or the quantity of central *depression*, near bottom, say d . . . . =	0·45
Central *depression*, near middle of height . . =	0·20
,, top. . . . . =	0·12
Mean . . . =	0·26 in.
At West side, central *depression*, near bottom . =	0·35
,, ,, ,, middle . =	0·15
,, ,, ,, top . =	0·10
Mean . . . =	0·20 in.
At South side, central *depression*, near bottom . =	0·28
,, ,, ,, middle . =	0·18
,, ,, ,, top . =	0·10
Mean . . . =	0·19

Again, when the straight-edge is applied *vertically* to the sides, east side comes out true, but the others concave—

On North side, the maxima of such vertical depression or d' . . . . . . =	0·20 and 0·28
On West side, d', at South end . . . . =	0·00
,, d', at North end . . . . =	0·20
And on South side, d', at different distances from East to West . . . . . =	0·08, 0·12, and 0·04 in.

EXTERNAL MEASURES OF THE COFFER.

The corners and edges of the coffer are so much chipped, that the steel claws I had had prepared for the sliding-rods, to adapt them from inside to outside measures, were found not long enough to span these modern fractures and reach the original polished surfaces. A method was there-fore adopted, of making up the sides of the coffer with straight-edges pro-jecting beyond it at either end; and then measuring between such straight-edges and on either side, or end, of the coffer.

LENGTH OF COFFER OUTSIDE, MEASURED WITH BAR 100 A.

	1st Measure.	2nd Measure.	3rd Measure.
On East side, near bottom . .	90·5	90·3	90·5
,, 10 inches under top .	90·15	..	..
,, above top . .	90·20	..	..
On West side, near bottom . .	89·2	89·2	89·2
,, near top . . .	89·95	..	..
,, above top . .	90·05	..	..
Mean length .	90·01	..	..

The above mean, however, represents only the mean length of the edges of the two sides, not of the whole coffer, on account of the con-cavity of the two external ends; wherefore, if we desire to state the mean length for the mean of each end surface, we must subtract two-thirds of the mean central concavity, as previously determined; *i.e.* = 0·17 for the north end, and similarly 0·13 for the south end; so that, then, the mean *length* for mean of each end of coffer = 89·71 British inches.

$$= 89·62 \text{ Pyramid inches.}$$

N.B.—An anomaly in the West side, near the bottom.

BREADTH OF COFFER, OUTSIDE.

	1st Measure.	2nd Measure.	3rd Measure.
At North end, near bottom . .	39·05	39·1	39·2
,, near top . . .	38·7	..	..
,, over top . .	38·67	..	..
At South end, near bottom . .	38·8	38·7	..
,, near top . . .	38·6	..	..
,, over top . . .	38·5	..	..
Mean . . .	38·72	..	..
Correction for curvature of West side . . .	·07	..	..
Mean breadth of mean sides	38·65	..	..
Concluded breadth . . .	=	38·65 British inches.	
	=	38·61 Pyramid inches.	

Height of Coffer, outside.

Height of coffer outside, eliminating the stone under bottom, and the sarcophagus ledge of 1·72 ; *i.e.* measuring from coffer-bottom to *extreme* ancient top of sides, is—

At North end, eastern part of it	=	41·3
Same repeated	=	41·3
At North end, north-eastern part of it	=	41·22
At other parts, no original top left.		
Mean height	=	41·27 British inches.
		41·23 Pyramid inches.

Correction in *capacity* computations for a supposed hollow curvature of under side of bottom; agreeably with three, out of the four, upright sides; and also agreeably with the construction of the under sides of the casing-stones, which rest on their circumferences, on account of a slight hollowing away of their central areas; say . . . = ·10

Concluded capacity-computation height . . . . . . = 41·17 British inches.
= 41·13 Pyramid inches.

Sides, Thickness of.

For this purpose two vertical straight-edges higher than the sides were placed opposite each other, in contact with the inside and outside surfaces of any flank of the coffer, and the distance across was measured over the top edge of the coffer; finding at successive parts of the coffer circumference, bearing from centre—

South-south-west thickness	=	6·0
South ,, ...	=	6·0
South-south-east ,, ...	=	5·95
East-south-east ,, ...	=	5·85
East ,, ...	=	5·95
East-north-east ,, ...	=	6·10
North-north-east ,, ...	=	5·95
North ,, ...	=	5·98
North-north-west ,, ...	=	6·10
West-north-west ,, ...	=	5·95
West ,, ...	=	6·10
West-south-west ,, ...	=	5·95

Mean thickness of vertical sides = 5·99 B. in.

The above measures were repeated on March 28, and proved sensibly true for this method of measurement over the top edge of the coffer; but if calipered lower down, it is probable that a slightly increased thickness would have been found there.

BOTTOM OF THE COFFER THICKNESS OF.

By difference of heights of two straight-edges of equal length, applied, one inside and one outside—the outside one being further propped up, where required, by a third straight-edge inserted under the bottom—there was found—

Under South-west corner, thickness of bottom		=	7·0
,,	East side	,,	,,	=	6·6
,,	East-north-east	,,	,,	=	6·87
,,	East-north-east again	,,	,,	=	6·90
,,	North end	,,	,,	=	6·90
,,	North-north-west	,,	,,	=	6·85
,,	North-north-east	,,	,,	=	6·80
,,	West-north-west	,,	,,	=	7·20
,,	West	,,	,,	=	6·90
,,	South-south-west	,,	,,	=	7·15

Mean thickness of bottom around the edges (the thickness of bottom in the centre cannot at present be satisfactorily or easily measured) .   .   .   =   6·92 B. in.

INTERNAL MEASURES OF THE COFFER.

The inside surfaces of the coffer seem very true and flat over the greater part of their extent; but betray, on examination by straight-edges, a slight convergence at the bottom towards the centre.

INSIDE LENGTH OF COFFER, BY SLIDER 70.

(Correction + 0·13 added to all the readings for length of this Slider.)

Distance between East and West sides of the North and South ends.	Level at which observations were taken.			
	4 to 6 inches under top.	Middle of height.	6 to 7 above bottom.	0·6 above bottom.
Close to Eastern side . {	Broken at S.E. corner }	78·08	77·93	77·68
At ⅓d breadth from East	78·06	78·06	77·97	77·56
Half-way between E.&W.	78·06	78·08	78·06	77·53
At ⅔ds breadth from East	78·05	78·09	78·06	77·59
Close to West side . .	78·03	78·06	78·01	77·57
Mean at each level	78·05	78·07	78·01	77·59

Mean of the whole, or the inside }   = 77·93 British inches.
    length of coffer   .   .   . }   = 77·85 Pyramid inches.

INSIDE BREADTH OF COFFER.

(By Slider 25, not requiring any correction.)

Distance between North and South ends, along the East and West sides.	Level at which observations were taken.				
	Near top.	Near middle.	6 to 7 ins. above bottom.	0·6 inch above bottom.	0·6 re-measured.
Close to North end .	26·68	26·69	26·65	26·40	26·39
At ⅓d length from N. end	26·60	26·69	27·00	26·72	26·54
Near middle of length .	26·64	26·80	27·10	27·05	27·05
At ⅔ds length from N.end	26·67	26·78	26·77	26·67	26·75
Close to South end .	26·78	26·78	26·63	26·49	26·49
Mean at each level	26·67	26·75	26·83	26·67	..

Mean of the whole, or the inside } = 26·73 British inches.
    breadth of coffer . . . } = 26·70 Pyramid inches.

INSIDE DEPTH OF COFFER.

The measure of this element is taken from the inside bottom of the coffer,—which is apparently smooth and flat,—up in the shortest line to the level of the original top surface of the north, the east, and the south sides; and of the west side also, *presumably*, before it was cut down to the level of the ledge which runs round the inner edges of the north, east, and south sides, and all across the west side's top.

Now, the depth of that ledge was before ascertained = 1·72 inches below the original top; a block of wood was therefore prepared of that thickness, and placed on the west side, and also on the base-surface of the ledge wherever found on the other sides, to support one end of a straight-edge, whose other end rested on some part or parts of the original top of the coffer's sides, which are still visible at and about the north-east corner.

INSIDE DEPTH FROM ORIGINAL TOP OF NORTH, EAST, AND SOUTH SIDES.

(By Slider 25, not requiring any correction.)

Part of Length where observations were taken.	Part of Breadth where observations were taken.			
	Near East side.	Near middle.	Near West side.	Mean at each part of length.
0·6 inches South of inner N. end	34·30	34·28	34·26	34·28
3·0 ,, do. do.	34·44	34·36	34·35	34·38
5·0 ,, do. do.	34·42	34·41	34·28	34·37
10·0 ,, do. do.	34·40	34·38	34·28	34·35
24·0 ,, do. do.	34·36	34·38	34·26	34·33
Mean at each part of breadth	34·38	34·36	34·29	34·34

General mean, or the inside *depth* } = 34·34 British inches.
    of coffer . . . . . } = 34·31 Pyramid inches.

COFFER, FURTHER INSIDE MEASURES OF.
DIAGONALS.

Diagonals inside the north end; from either low corner at bottom, up to a measured height of 30·0 inches, *i.e.* the greatest height quite free from fractures; then—

From low North-east to 30· high North-west = 39·71 British inches, and from low North-west to 30· high North-east = 39·70 ,,

Diagonals inside West side; from either corner below, up to a height of 30 inches measured at the sides—

or from low South-west to 30· high North-west = 83·19 British inches, and from low North-west to 30· high South-west = 83·13 ,,

CUBICAL DIAGONALS.

From low South-west to 30· inches high North-east = 87·13 British inches.
,,   South-east   ,,   North-west = 87·05   ,,
,,   North-east   ,,   South-west = 87·06   ,,
,,   North-west   ,,   South-east } = 87·11   ,,
                              temporarily supplied

These cubical diagonals give sensibly less than the diagonals computed from the lengths and breadths; on account, apparently, of the extreme points of the corners of the bottom not being perfectly worked out to the exact intersections of the general planes of the entire sides. But they seem abundantly sufficient to prove general rectangularity of figure, in all the main part of the coffer's interior.

The Sarcophagus Theory of the Coffer.

With all this accumulation of little bits of information, then, let us now try what is the size of the coffer as a whole. And on our so doing, we must, of course, let the opposition sarcophagus theory of Egyptologists be heard over again; especially when it has something to say touching shape, as well as size.

The inside dimensions of the coffer *being* by our own measures (roughly) 6·5 feet long, 2·2 feet wide, and almost 3 feet deep, are at least long enough and broad enough for a coffin; and if rather deeper than convenient or necessary, I will not object to that, as there is now proved to be a ledge cut into the top of the thick sides of the vessel, and quite suitably for a lid.

As there *is* a ledge, an intention at some time to put on a lid may or must be inferred; but it is still to be proved whether a lid ever *was* put on by the architect of

the Great Pyramid, and especially *for* sarcophagus purposes; because, first, with a sarcophagus lid of the
ordinary style and thickness fastened into that ledge,
the coffer could not have passed through the closely
fitting doorway of the room; it would have been several whole inches too high.   Second, a sarcophagus lid
fastened into that ledge would have betokened the
accomplishment of the last rites to the dead; and
they would have included among all Eastern nations,
but more especially the contemporary, indigenous, profane Egyptians, the engraving the deceased's name,
titles, deeds, and history on the coffer, both inside and
out.   But there is nothing of that kind there; so the
Great Pyramid coffer remains still the smooth-sided,
vacant, lidless chest of Caliph Al Mamoun's Arab tale;
quite capable of having been made at any time into a
sarcophagus; but testifying in the most positive manner
that it never was completely so converted, whatever
may have been the reason why or wherefore.

Considering, however, the coffer's approximate shape,
size, and situation, I am quite ready to allow it to be
"a blind sarcophagus"; viz. a deceiving blind to the
eyes of the Pharaonic and idolatrous Egyptian workmen, as well as a symbol sarcophagus to others,
reminding *them* of death, judgment, and eternity (as
well taught by William Simpson, artist, archæologist,
and traveller); but without thereby interfering one iota
with its further more exact objects and intentions.

And what are they?

Only look at the beginning of them, as the vessel tells
them off itself in number and measure, and see features
thereby which cannot be accidental; features which
have never been heard of in any other, or mere, sarcophagus; and which no Egyptologist, not even Lepsius
himself, has ever attempted to publish as his, or any other
person's, "law of Egyptian sarcophagus construction."

Taking the coffer measures, for instance, as of the whole vessel before the ledge was cut out, from the previous pages, in Pyramid inches ; then—

Length. Breadth. De. or Ht. Volume.
Coffer interior = 77·85 X 26·70 X 34·31 = 71,317·
Coffer exterior = 89·62 X 38·61 X 41·13 = 142,316·

that is, within the limits of accuracy of the modern measures, the volume of the exterior is *double* that of the interior ; and the simplest even relation between them is that of *capacity*.

Again, the mean thickness of the sides of the coffer being assumed from the measures, in Pyramid inches 5·952, and of the bottom 6·866, we have (from a formula first prepared by the ingenious Mr. Henry Perigal)—

Coffer's bottom   = 89·62 X 38·61 X 6·866 = 23,758·
Coffer's sides = 2 (89·62 X 26·70) X 34·31 X 5·952 = 47,508·
                                                      ————
                                                      71,266·

or again, we find a *duplicity* of the one quantity against the other; and the only apparent simple relation between the two, and of the sum of both with the interior of the vessel, is that of *capacity*.

If then, now we may justifiably say, that though the coffer is probably what John Taylor did not think it, viz. a blind sarcophagus and a symbolical coffin, it is also most positively what he did consider it (though we say so by means of mensuration proof which he never lived to see)—viz. a vessel at whose birth certain leading geometrical requirements both of, and for, capacity measure presided and governed :—then in that case, what is its precise capacity ?

What shall we consider the Capacity of the Coffer proved to be ?

For the coffer's length and breadth elements we can quote plenty of measures, but the equally necessary depth is a weak point; because, as already explained, every particle of the original top of the sides is cut or broken away, except some little patches near the northeast corner. Those were in place in 1865, but who will guarantee that they are there still, when men *will* hammer that exquisite gift inherited from primeval time, merely in the ignorant notion of sending their friends at home a chip of " Cheops' coffin "? When the last of those small pieces of the ancient top, which I mapped so carefully in " Life and Work," (1867,) has disappeared (and Mr. Waynman Dixon's cast shows that some of them are already gone), then comes the deluge among future coffer measures. A veritable chaos of uncertainty as to depth; in the midst of which chaos French Academicians might put on their three additional inches again, and upset all the geometrical duplications and equalities which have just been obtained by means of our having had, in 1865, a trace of the true height. But at this point of the discussion there comes in a strange use of the ledge cut out, though that feature has hitherto been thought of only for a lid and nothing else.

No lid has ever been seen by any historical individual; but every man of the present age may test the truth of the following mechanical adaptation: viz. the ledge, though acute angled, is cut out with precisely such a base-breadth and depth that a frame made to fit it flush with the ancient top of the sides would, when let down in vertical plane, and diagonally inside the coffer, just form the diagonal of said coffer's interior; and the frame's height at that moment would exactly measure the coffer's depth. Hence the breadth of the ledge, continued across the coffer from west to east, would continue to give us an outstanding test of the coffer's original depth, long after young cadets going out to India, and large holiday parties from Cairo, shall have thoughtlessly knocked away every particle of the original top of the sides.

In coffer measuring, however,—just as it usually is in all matters of science,—no two human measures ever agree exactly even on the same parts; and all that finite man can hope for is, to come within moderate limits. So then must it be with the coffer's cubic contents.

Taking the ledge breadth (from my " Antiquity of Intellectual Man," p. 300) as 34·282 Pyramid inches, then the coffer's cubic contents in cubic Pyramid inches are :—

(1) By interior length and breadth, and by depth from ledge-
    breadth . . . . = 71,258·
(2) By interior of coffer, by all direct measures . . . = 71,317·
(3) By half the exterior volume directly measured . . . = 71,160·
(4) By sum of bottom and sides directly measured . . . = 71,266·

Here then we have a vessel whose cubic contents *are* not only something, on the whole excessively near to 71,250· cubic Pyramid inches, but it was pretty evidently *intended*,—by enabling us so nearly to bring out that number in several different ways,—to carry a check and a witness thereto down through all fair accidents, even through all historic ages, to these mensuration times. While that precise quantity, and the care for that quantity, of just so many cubic inches, rather than any other, expressed in Great Pyramid measure, are so impossible for the Egyptologists to explain on any sarcophagus theory of their own, either pure and simple, or profane and ornate,—that they do not attempt it ; and we must now strive to ascertain, on methods both absolutely new to Egyptology, and which must have been totally unknown to all the Pharaonic serfs of old Egypt, what the Great Pyramid itself may have to add to this ; viz. its own preliminary setting forth of some science reason why this vessel before us, the coffer in the King's Chamber, is not only "a symbolical sarcophagus, but one adapted likewise to something further and higher connected with *capacity* measure."

CHAPTER IX.

DENSITY AND TEMPERATURE;

Of both Earth and Great Pyramid, from the Latest Measures.

THOUGH there be no inscriptions, yet is there much instruction on the interior walls of the Great Pyramid; and as the coffer, when taken merely by it-self, has proved, thus far, too hard a riddle for our full interpretation, let us try something of the teaching of the walls which precede, as well as those which sur-round, it.

Ante-Chamber Granite Symbolisms.

In order to enter the Great Pyramid's so-called King's Chamber, we have to pass, from the Grand Gallery, through the "Ante-chamber." (Plates XIV. and XV.) It is very appropriately so called, because it is a little room which *must* be passed through *before* the King's Chamber can be entered or the coffer seen; and in passing through it, the attentive eye may note many more complicated forms there, than in any other part of the Great Pyramid. Amongst these *notanda* are certain vertical lines above the southern or further doorway.

Previous travellers have contradicted each other so abundantly about the number of these lines, that I was rather surprised to perceive them instantly to be not only confined to the number four, but these distinct, regular, parallel, extending the whole way evenly from ceiling to door-top,* and no less than 107·4 inches long, 2·8 inches deep, and 3·8 inches broad, each; with six-inch spaces between, and with similar six-inch spaces also between the outer side of each outermost line, and the bounding of the ante-room's South wall containing them.

Hence the lines were subservient to the spaces, and the whole arrangement appeared to me, not so much, though it is to a certain extent, a system of *four* lines, as an example of surface divided into *five* equal portions or spaces.

As the doorway is only 42 inches high, and the dividing lines of the wall above it are apparently drawn down to the doorway's (now broken) top, a man of ordinary height standing in the ante-room and looking southward (the direction he desires to go, in order to reach the King's Chamber), cannot fail (if he has a candle with him, for otherwise everything is in darkness here) to *see* this space divided into five.   And when he bows his head very low, as he must do to pass under the said southern doorway of only 42 inches high, he bends his head submissively under that symbol of division into five; and *should* remember, that five is the first and most characteristic of the Pyramid numbers.   (See Plate XVI.)

Travellers describe the Wall-courses of the King's Chamber.

Not without reason, therefore, was it, as the intelligent traveller may readily believe, that the architect of the Great Pyramid desired to impress that division into five upon every visitor's mind, just the last thing before

---

* That is to say, as nearly as a huge fracture of that lower corner of the granite block forming the doorway allowed me easily to judge in 1865 : for within the limits of that fracture, Dr. Grant claims to have recently found proofs that the lower ends of the lines did not quite go through to the passage below, but ended in a short, curved bevel.

such visitor should bow down, previously to passing
through the low, solid doorway, cut out of granite 100
inches thick.   But after that, rising up in the midst of
the ultimate King's Chamber beyond—what should any
and every beholder witness there?

According to that usually most correct of travellers,
Professor Greaves, *he* says of the King's Chamber that
everyone may see there " from the top of it descending
to the bottom, there are but *six* ranges of stone, all
which, being respectively sized to an equal height, very
gracefully in one and the same altitude run round the
room."

Well, though that is a very pretty arrangement, and
the grace of it is perfectly true, it is not the accomplishment of a division into five ; so let us try an older
traveller, Sandys, of a curt and epigrammatic style, and
wri‍t‍ ‍in 1610.   Says he, of the selfsame King's
Chamber, " A right royal apartment, and so large that
eight floors it, eight roofs it ; eight stones flagge the
ends and sixteen the sides."   Worse and worse.

Says Dr. Pocock in 1743, " Six tiers of stones of
equal breadth compose the sides"; which account
M. Fourmont, on the part of Bourbon France, confirms
in 1755 by laying down that "the walls are composed
of six equal ranges."   The still more famous traveller,
Dr. Clarke, makes Cambridge in 1801 support Oxford
in 1639, by particularising that "there are only six
ranges of stone from the floor to the roof"; while,
finally, that usually infallible author on Egypt, Mr.
Lane, with his clever and industrious relatives, the
Pooles, *almost* natives of Cairo, seem to set a seal for
ever on the mistake by declaring, " Number of courses
in the walls of the King's chamber, six."

What *could* have blinded all these duly warned men,
and sent them following each other down one and the
same too easy rut of simple, ridiculous error ?   Dr.

Richardson, in 1817, was more original, if error apparently there must be in these dark-room investigations by candle-light in the interior of the Great Pyramid; for he chose a new and hitherto untrodden line of erring for himself, sententiously writing of the room, " Lined all around with broad flat stones, smooth and highly polished, *each* stone ascending from the floor to the ceiling."   But having once begun this new misdescription, he soon has followers; and we find the Lord Lindsay, of 1838, announcing, " A noble apartment, cased with enormous slabs of granite 20 feet high " (or a little more than the whole height of the room) ; and Sir William R. Wilde with his companion signing himself M.R.I.A., in 1837, equally publish to the world, as observed by themselves, "An oblong apartment, the sides of which are formed of enormous blocks of granite reaching from the floor to the ceiling."

And yet, will it be credited that the walls of this chamber are divided into *five* horizontal courses, neither more nor less, almost four feet high each; and that these courses are most easy to count, as they must have been undoubtedly most expensive for the architect to construct; because every course is, as Professor Greaves so beautifully indicated, of the same height as every other, except, indeed (as I believe I was the first to point out), the lowest, which course is less than the rest by nearly 1-10th part, if measured from the floor; but is the *same* height if measured from the base of its own granite component blocks, which descend in the wall to beneath the floor's level ?*   (See Plate XVII.)

* Full particulars of the measures of this room in whole and part, and parts compared against whole, are contained in my " Life and Work at the Great Pyramid," Vol. II.; but are too long to introduce here.   I have given there also the immediately succeeding measures of a young engineer—sent, I believe, by a rich man, for the salutary purpose to me, and useful to the public, of tripping me up if he could, but finally and involuntarily confirming my measures both of number and size of courses and room.

The really Pyramid Number of the King's Chamber's Wall-courses, and of Stones in them.

But I was not by any means the *first* person to find out that the courses in the walls of the King's Chamber were five only, for the same thing had been noted by Lord Egmont in 1709, and Dr. Shaw in 1721, and perhaps by some others earlier or later; though no one previously to myself had, so far as I am aware, either fought against the world for the correctness of his observation, or connected the number with both the teaching of the architect in the ante-chamber, and the quinary character of the Pyramid's first arithmetic.

Yet, quinary though it be for some purposes, it is decimal for others, as shewn here in almost juxtaposition; first, by the tenth part nearly, taken off the height of the lower course, by the manner of introduction of the floor; and then by the 10 × 10 number of stones, exactly, of which the walls of this beautiful chamber are composed. This latter circumstance was only recently announced, though on my publication of 1867, by Mr. Flinders Petrie; and does him all the more credit because, when I came to test the statement, there was one joint line, by mistake, too many in the middle course of the south wall in my engraved plate of the chamber, though the printed numbers were correct.

Since then again, Dr. Grant, Mr. Waynman Dixon, and other gentlemen have been out to the Great Pyramid specially to test this matter; and when from the floor upwards they had counted the stones of four courses, and found them 93, did they not rejoice to think what a huge error they would presently have against my statement in the second edition of this book! They did rejoice over the prospect—they have confessed that; but when they came to count the stones of the fifth and topmost course, they beheld, to their utter astonishment, that there were only seven blocks there; that seven making up the exact hundred, as well as signifying something further in that room touching 5·7, even as we shall presently be compelled to set forth.

A marked portion of the King's Chamber, and the Coffer, are mutually commensurable in Pyramid Numbers.

But the tenth part, nearly, taken off the visible height of the lower granite course of the chamber's walls; what was that for? Its first effect was to make that course, within the fraction of an inch, the same height as the coffer; and the second was, more exactly, to make the capacity, or cubic contents of that lowest course of the room, so decreased, equal to fifty times the cubic contents of the coffer, already shown to be 71,250· cubic Pyramid inches. Two separate sets of measured numbers in Pyramid inches for the length, breadth, and height, of that lowest chamber-course giving as follows, when divided by the coffer's contents—

$$\frac{412\cdot14 \times 206\cdot09 \times 41\cdot9}{71,250} = \frac{3,558,899\cdot}{71,250} = 49\cdot95$$

And

$$\frac{412 \times 206 \times 42}{71,250\cdot} = \frac{3,564,624\cdot}{71,250\cdot} = 50\cdot03$$

Hence, close as was the connection of the several parts of the coffer with each other by the tie of capacity, equally close is the connection of the coffer with the adjusted course of the granite room in which it stands, and by *capacity* measure also. While, if the multiple before was 2, and is 50 now,—is not 50 twice 25, or double the number of its own inches in the cubit of the Great Pyramid, the significant 5 × 5 ?

*Commensurabilities between the King's Chamber and the
structural Masonry-courses of the whole Pyramid.*

Neither did the fives and the tens of this chamber,
on being examined, end here; for having been greatly
struck outside the monument on contemplating the grandeur of the horizontal courses of masonry of which the
whole Pyramid is built, I began next to study them
by measure. Not at all equal to, but often violently
different from, each other are these courses in their
successive heights; but, whatever height or thickness of
stones any one course is begun with, it is kept on at
that thickness precisely, right through the whole Pyramid at that level (*i.e.* if we may judge of the unknown
interior of the stratum by the four external edges
thereof); though too the area of the horizontal section
may amount to whole acres.

To secure this equality of thickness for a course,—in
fact, just as with the equal height of the granite courses
in the King's Chamber walls, but on a far larger scale,—
it was plain that immense arrangements must have
been instituted beforehand, with the masons of many
quarries; and such arrangements imply method, mind,
and, above all, intention. Wherefore, having measured
the. thickness of every component course of the Great
Pyramid, one day in April, 1865, when ascending to the
summit, and another day in descending, I compared
and confirmed those figures with my own photographs
of the building placed under a compound microscope;
and also with similar numbers obtained from still
more careful measures by the French Academicians in
1799 and 1800; and then began to sum up the courses'
successive thicknesses to give the whole height of any
particular number of courses. (See pp. 94, 95.)

On reaching in this manner the 50th course, lo! the
total height of that stratum, or 1,690 inches, gave the

hypsometrical level of the floor of the King's Chamber as well as it has yet been ascertained directly by all the best authorities. So that the level of the 50th course of construction of the whole Pyramid is the level also of that granite floor, whereon is resting the coffer, a vessel with commensurable capacity proportions between its inside and out, and its walls and floor, in a room with 5 courses, composed of 100 stones, and with a capacity proportion (the coffer) of 50, to the lowest of those courses; which lowest course has further been made 5 inches less in height than any of the others of its fellows.

Any person could hardly but see, then, that the so-called, in the dark ages, King's Chamber, should rather have been termed the chamber of the standard of 50. Can we also say, with reference to our present inquiry,—of 50 Pyramid inches employed in capacity-measure?

But what is a length of 50 Pyramid inches in the eye of Nature; and how ought that length to be employed for the highest order of capacity-measure purposes; *i.e.* an order which shall establish a harmonious relation between man's standards of capacity and weight, and the similar properties of the earth whereon he lives?

Fifty Pyramid inches form the one ten-millionth of the earth's *axis* of rotation; or decidedly the proper fraction to begin with for capacity measure, when we have already chosen one ten-millionth of the *semi-axis* for linear measure. The reason being, that in measuring linear distances, say amongst the spheres of heaven, men measure them from centre to centre, and therefore have only to take account of the radii of each; but in dealing with either their capacity or weight, we must take each sphere in its entirety, or from side to side, that is, by its diameter rather than radius.

More Symbolical Hints from the Ante-chamber.

Such is the answer to the first part of the question ; and a hint how to deal with the second part may be gathered from some of the hitherto incomprehensible things in the little ante-chamber to this far grander chamber.   Little indeed is the ante-chamber, when it measures only 65·2 inches in utmost breadth from east to west, 116·3 long from north to south, and 149·4 high; but it has a sort of granite wainscot on either side of it, full of detail; and was to me so complicated and troublesome a matter as to occupy three entire days in measuring.   (See Plate XV.)

On the east side, this wainscot is only 103·1 inches high, and is flat and level on the top; but on the west side it is 111·8 inches high, and has three semi-cylindrical cross hollows of nine inches radius, cut down into it, and also back through its whole thickness of 8·5 to 11·7 inches to the wall.   Each of those semi-cylindrical hollows stands over a broad, shallow, vertical, flat groove 21·6 inches wide, 3·2 inches deep, running from top to bottom of the wainscot, leaving a pilaster-like separation between them.   The greater part of the said pilasters has indeed long since been hammered away, but their fractured places are easily traced; and with this allowance to researches in the present day, the groove and pilaster part of the arrangement is precisely repeated on the east side, within *its* lower compass of height.

These three grand, flat, vertical grooves, then, on either side of the narrow ante-chamber, have been pronounced long since by Egyptologists to be part of a vertically sliding portcullis system for the defence of the door of the King's Chamber.   There are no blocks now to slide up and down in these grooves, nor have such things ever been seen there : but the gentlemen point trium-

phantly to a fourth groove, of a different order, existing
to the north of all the others, indeed near the north-
beginning of the ante-chamber; and with *its* portcullis
block, they say, still suspended, and ready for work.

The Granite Leaf of the Ante-chamber.

That alleged portcullis block, however, contains many
peculiarities which modern Egyptologists have never
explained; and as it was first carefully described by
Professor Greaves under the appellation of "the granite
leaf," (from the so-called "leaf" or "slat," or sliding
door over the water-way of a lock-gate in an English
navigation canal), we had better keep to that name.

Its groove, instead of being 21·6 inches broad, like the
others, is only 17·1 broad; and in place of being like
them cut down to, and even several inches into, the floor,
terminates 43·7 inches above that basal plane; so that
the leaf's block, or rather blocks—for it is in two pieces,
one above the other—stand on solid stone of the walls
on either side, and could not be immediately lowered to
act as a portcullis, though an Emperor should desire it.
Nor would they make a good portcullis if they were to
be forcibly pushed, or chiselled down in their vertical
plane, seeing that there are 21 inches free end space
between the leaf and the north entering wall and doorway, where a man might worm himself in, in front of
that face of it; and 57· inches above the leaf's utmost
top, where several men might clamber over; and where
I myself sat on a ladder, day after day, with lamps and
measuring-rods, but in respectful silence and generally
in absolute solitude, thinking over what it might mean.

The granite leaf is, therefore, even by the few data
already given, a something which needs a vast deal
more than a simple portcullis notion to explain it. And
so do likewise the three broader empty pairs of grooves

to the south of it, remarkable with their semi-cylindrical
·hollows on the west side of the chamber. Various ideas
as to their uses have been given out from time to time,
but none commended themselves to my mind at the
place, more than that of the three dimensions necessary
to express capacity contents—the three hollow curves,
too, reminding of the curved shell of the earth's surface;
and the granite leaf with its double block (implying
double power to its specific gravity) leading one then to
think of the earth's interior, or capacity, contents; for
they are, when taken in the whole, of almost exactly
double the mean density, or specific gravity, of *that*
granite.

Earth's Mean Density already approximately indicated, but
required more exactly.

Here, then, from every side—from the coffer, the
King's Chamber, the Pyramid courses, and the ante-
chamber trappings of stone—many of the very, and
most scientific, and suitable items necessary for preparing earth reference capacity and weight measures
were gradually cropping up in 1865 A.D., before earnest
and attentive study of the actual Pyramid facts, to a
quiet onlooker, measuring-rod in hand. But no mere
linear measuring-rod can supply the further radical idea
required for weight, if it is to have an earth-globe
reference. The something else called for in this instance,
in order to be true to the grandeur of the beginning
made in the Pyramid linear system for length, could be
no other than the mean density of the whole world;
and this quantity is not yet by any means so intimately
understood by every one, that it would be generally and
instantly recognized the moment it should haply be
seen, under some symbolical figure or numerical equivalent, in the Great Pyramid.

Although, too, the earth's mean density has been for long a subject of paramount interest throughout other most important and varied branches of natural philosophy, besides astronomy (and not only in this country, but the whole world over), yet it has been practically, diligently, successfully, studied by hardly any other nation than ourselves ; and what we have done in the cause has been confined to very late times indeed.

The first special move, always excepting Sir Isaac Newton's most sagacious guess in the absence of any experiment,* seems to have been made by Dr. Maskelyne in 1772 ; and hence came the celebrated experiment on the attraction of the plumb-line by Mount Schihallion, in Scotland ; and whose ultimate computation gave for the concluded density of the whole earth 4·8 ; but with some suspicions that it might be still more.   And finally, amongst such mountain determinations, came that of the Ordnance Survey in 1855 on the hill of Arthur's Seat, near Edinburgh ; which observations yielded, when put through the necessary computations, as they were most splendidly, by Captain Ross Clarke, R.E., the number 5·316.

Another species of experiment, not far removed in its nature from the above, was tried in 1826 by Mr. (now Sir) George B. Airy, Astronomer-Royal, Dr. Whewell, and the Rev. Richard Sheepshanks, by means of pendulum observations, at the top and bottom of a deep mine in Cornwall ; but the proceeding at that time failed.   Subsequently, in 1855, the case was taken up again by Sir G. B. Airy and his Greenwich assistants,

---

* Sir Isaac's words are:—" Unde cum terra communis suprema quasi duplo gravior sit quam aquâ, et paulo inferius in fodinis quasi triplo vel quadruplo aut etiam quintuplo gravior reperiatur; verisimile est quod copia materiæ totius in terra quasi quintuplo vel sextuplo major sit quam si tota ex aquâ constaret."   A rudely correct approach this to the density of the whole earth, but by means of such a decided over-estimate of the mean density of the average materials of " mines or quarries," that it did not carry much conviction with it.

in a mine near Newcastle. They were reinforced by the then new invention of sympathetic electric control between clocks at the top and bottom of the mine, and had much better, though still unexpectedly large, results —the mean density of the earth coming out, for them, 6·565.

Natural Philosophy and Closet Determination of the Earth's Mean Density.

The subject being thus so excessively difficult to obtain a close numerical result upon, even by the best modern astronomy, good service was done to the world in the course of the last century, when the Rev. John Mitchell proposed a different and a direct manner of trying the experiment actually between the several parts of one and the same piece of apparatus. He died, indeed, before he himself could practise his acute suggestion; but it was taken up after his death by the celebrated Cavendish, and worked very successfully in 1798, with a final result of 5·450.

Nearly forty years after Cavendish's great work, his experiment was repeated by Professor Reich, of Freyberg, in Saxony, with a result of 5·44 ; and then came the grander repetition by the late Francis Baily, representing therein the Royal Astronomical Society of London, and, in fact, the British Government and the British nation.

With exquisite care did that well-versed and methodical observer proceed to his task; and yet his observations did not prosper.

Week after week, and month after month, unceasing measures were recorded; but only to show that some disturbing element was at work, overpowering the attraction of the larger on the smaller balls.

What could it be ?

Professor Reich was applied to, and requested to state how he had contrived to get the much greater degree of accordance with each other, that his published observations showed.

"Ah!" he explained, "he had had to reject all his earlier observations until he had guarded against variations of *temperature* by putting the whole apparatus into a cellar, and only looking at it with a telescope through a small hole in the door."

Then it was remembered that a very similar plan had been adopted by Cavendish; who had furthermore left this note behind him for his successor's attention— "that even still, or after all the precautions which he did take, minute variations and small exchanges of *temperature* between the large and small balls were the chief obstacles to full accuracy."

Mr. Baily therefore adopted yet further, and very peculiar, means to prevent sudden changes of temperature in his observing-room; and then only did the anomalies vanish, and the real observations begin.

The full story of them, and all the particulars of every numerical entry, and the whole of the steps of calculation, are to be found in the Memoirs of the Royal Astronomical Society, and constitute one of the most interesting volumes* of that important series; and its final result for the earth's mean density was announced as

5·675, probable error ± 0·0038

The Ordnance Survey's Arthur's Seat experiment gave the same earth's mean density as

5·316, probable error ± 0·054

And Sir George B. Airy's mine experiment declared still the same earth's same mean density to be

,6·565, probable error ± 0·018

---

* The fourteenth volume.

From which naturally conflicting data, it will be seen that modern science, whatever it implies, by "probable error," about its extreme accuracy to $\frac{1}{300}$ or less, cannot really be certain in this transcendentally difficult, but infinitely important, physical inquiry respecting the earth's mean density to nearer than about $\frac{1}{6}$th of the whole quantity.

Earth's Density Number in the Great Pyramid.

Now the *Pyramid's* earth's mean density comes out, if at all, most simply, and to an accuracy at once of three places of figures, certain; from,—the cubic contents of the coffer in Pyramid inches, divided by the 10th part of 50 inches cubed.   Whence, trusting to my measures, it is:—71,250 divided by 12,500; the quotient being 5·70; a number which modern science may confirm, at some future day, and does meanwhile include near the very centre of its best results thus far. While the grand 5·7 of the seven stones forming the 5th and topmost course of the walls of this King's Chamber, crown the conclusion on every side.*

Of Temperature Corrections, and how effected.

Some further questions, however, modern science already asks of Pyramidists, in order to ascertain whether,

* Long after the publication of the above Pyramid theorem, and after it had run the gauntlet in London of being railed against because its numbers were so very different from any of those previously brought out by modern science, the result of a new and supposed better and safer scientific method than any of the old ones, was published by the Royal Society, London; in their *Proceedings*, Vol. XXVIII., No. 190, Meeting of November 21, 1878.   The observations were taken by Professor J. H. Poynting, B.A., Fellow of Trinity College, Cambridge, in the Laboratory of Owen's College, Manchester, and though partly apologised for as to their rudeness, and proposed to be improved on by future experiments with grand apparatus, yet did when duly reduced to one single numerical expression, amount to 5·69.

and how, certain precautions, which she thinks necessary in all her own important work, were taken, and still remain effective, in those primeval operations of the so long sealed-up interior of the Great Pyramid.

For instance, if the coffer has to be considered as to its weight contents in water (and water filling is so frequently an operation connecting capacity and weight measures), strict attention is necessary to temperature, an element, or condition usually supposed to be only amenable to the thermometers of the last 200 years; yet the smallest errors on the score of uncertainties of temperature (and we may say almost the same for variations of barometric pressure), in the ancient work, would have introduced unnumbered perplexities.

These perplexities, nevertheless, are far from being found in the Great Pyramid's Coffer. Not because the Pyramid architect either had, or left behind, any very superior mercurial thermometers; but because he employed a method overriding thermometers, and beginning now to be found preferable even by the highest science of our own day, its multitudes of most excellent thermometers, and barometers too of every kind, notwithstanding.

Thus the latest conclusion of the best geodesists, in conducting their modern standard-scale experiments, is expressed in the maxim, "Have as little to do with *variations* of temperature as possible"; for temperature is an insidious influence whose actions and reactions men will hardly ever hear the last of, if once they let it begin to move, vary, or be higher in one place than in another, or at one time than another. We have seen, too, already, how this feature went close to the annihilation of the Cavendish experiment and its repetitions; and that the only source of safety was, not any attempt by power of fine thermometers to observe the temperature differences, and compute the corrections;

but, to cut down the variations of temperature themselves.

Hence that retreating into cellars, and closing of doors, and only looking in through small holes with telescopes, already described. Quite similarly too, in every astronomical observatory, where uniformity of clock-rate is prized, it has been the last, and practically the best, thing to that end yet found out,—that after the clockmaker has done everything which his art can do, in decreasing the disturbing effects which follow changes of temperature, by applying a so-called, and in truth very considerably effective, " temperature compensation pendulum,"—there is always a further improvement that can be effected in the going of the clock, by superadding certain influences of mass, simply to lessen the amount of heat-changes for such pendulum to try its artificially supplied compensating powers upon.

Thus, at the great observatory of Pulkova, near St. Petersburg, where they value an insight into small fractions of a second perhaps more than anywhere else in the wide world, the very able Russian astronomers have placed their chief clock in the "subterraneans," or cellars, of the observatory. Something of the same sort is now practised at the Royal Observatory, Greenwich ; while the Paris Observatory has beat them all by placing its clock no less than 95 feet under the surface of the ground, in the very peculiar " caves " which exist there.

Now, at the Royal Observatory, Edinburgh, there have been observations taken for many years of several large and very long-stemmed thermometers, whose bulbs have been let into the rock at various measured depths ; and it is found that, notwithstanding the possibly disturbing effect of rain-water soaking down through fissures, there is such an astonishing power in

a mass of stony matter to decrease temperature variations, that at the surface of the ground—

The mean semi-annual variation of heat amounts to = 50° Fahr.
At three inches under the surface . . . . = 30° ,,
At three feet under the surface . . . . = 16° ,,
At six feet . . . . = 10° ,,
At twelve feet . . . . = 5° ,,
At twenty-four feet . . . . . . = 1° ,,

At 95 feet, then, from the surface, in the case of the
Paris Observatory, how very slight and innocuous to
the most refined observation must be the variation of
season-temperature ! But how much more slightly
affected still, and how admirably suited to a scientific
observing-room, must not the King's Chamber in the
Great Pyramid be, seeing that it is shielded from the
outside summer heat and winter cold, by a thickness
of nowhere less than 180 feet of solid masonry !

There is not, in truth, in any country of Europe, there
never has been erected, and it does not look much as if
there ever will be erected, by any nation under the sun, a
scientific observing-room for closet experiments that can
at all be compared in the very leading requisite for such
an institution, with the King's Chamber of the Great
Pyramid ; if indeed, as we shall presently see, it had
only been allowed fair play in modern times.

Absolute Temperature of the King's Chamber in the Great Pyramid.

All the knowledge and advance, then, of the present
day, so far from improving on, or altering with advantage, cannot too much commend, copy, and adhere to,
the *uniformity* arrangements for rendering constant the
temperature of the Great Pyramid's coffer chamber.
But what is the degree of temperature so rendered
constant ?

It is apparently a very characteristic degree, and one

which possesses otherwise some singular recommendations. In the Great Pyramid, as before observed, there
is a grand tendency for numbers, things, and principles
going by "fives"; and this seems carried out even in
its temperature, for it may be described, first of all, as
a temperature of one-fifth; that is, one-fifth the distance
between the freezing and boiling points of water, above
the former.

Observed Temperatures at, and near, the Great Pyramid.

The first grounds for this belief were certain approximate observations by M. Jomard, in the "Description
de l'Égypte"; and which indicate something like 68°
Fahr. as nearly the original temperature of the King's
Chamber of the Great Pyramid, if under both ventilation and other intended normal circumstances of its
foundation. And 68° Fahr. is precisely a temperature,
by, and according to, Nature of one-fifth.

There is more, too, in the temperature numbers
resulting for the Pyramid, than the mere accident of
the mean earth-surface temperature of its particular
parallel of latitude; for that quantity would in truth
seem to be very sensibly higher, if observed at the low
level of the generally inhabited country thereabout,
than this pyramidal quantity of one-fifth. Not only,
for instance, did M. Jomard actually find it so, seeing
that he measured 25° Cent. = 77° Fahr. for the lower
part of the "well" of the Great Pyramid, and also for
several of the tombs in the open, sun-stricken plain in
the neighbourhood; but my own much more numerous
observations in 1864-5 on the temperature of wells in
and about the city of Cairo (in winter and spring, and
at a depth sufficient to give as near an annual average
as possible) yielded on a mean of 12 of them, 69·9 Fahr.
A quantity which is also the identical result for the
mean annual atmospheric temperature of the same city,

as obtained by the Austrian Meteorological Society from five years of ordinary air observation, A. Buchan, Esq., reporting.

Hence if the Great Pyramid was devised originally to stand, both in a latitude of 30° (see p. 79 to 82) and in a temperature of one-fifth, it was *necessary* that it should be mounted upon just such a hill as that whereon it does stand (and more particularly the King's Chamber level of it), in a sensibly cooler stratum of the atmosphere than the inhabited plains below; reducing thereby 69° 9 to 68° Fahr.

Thirty-seven years too after M. Jomard had measured in the King's Chamber the extra temperature of 71·6 Fahr. (*i.e.* 3·6 *extra* according to this subsequent theory), Colonel Howard-Vyse cleared out the two ventilating channels; and reported, without having heard any idea that the temperature had been theoretically too high— that instantly upon the channels being opened, the ventilation re-established itself, and with a feeling to those in the chamber of most agreeable *coolness*.

But no sooner had he left, than the Arabs most perversely stopped up the ventilating channels again. And now steam-navigation and the overland route are pouring in, day after day and year after year, continually increasing crowds of some decorous, but more uproarious, and determined Great Pyramid visitors; trooping with their candles and torches, and excited and various, but always *heat-making* (and sometimes stone-breaking, whether of walls or coffer), amusements into the King's Chamber granite hall. For they will so particularly insist on rushing in there, rather than into any other part of the Great Pyramid. Wherefore in 1865 I found that chamber's temperature more deranged than ever of old, or risen to no less than 75·2 Fahr.

On one occasion indeed, it was so much as 75·7; and

that was immediately after a large party with extra
lights, from some vulgar steamer, had had their whirling, stamping dances over, as they derisively declared,
"old Cheops' tombstone"; and had indulged to the full
their ignorant cursing of his ancient name, amid shouting and laughter, and the painful accompaniment of
the primeval coffer being banged with a big stone swung
by Arab arms; regardless that its note is said by high
authorities in that line, to be some precious standard
of musical tone. And all that time the temperature
was only 74° in the Queen's Chamber below, and 73°
at the dry-well mouth lower down still in the Pyramid.
Simultaneous temperature numbers which evidently indicate an abnormal heat-elevating force at that instant
in the King's Chamber. And no wonder! At least
to any one who should have looked in through the
smoke and stifling dust upon any of those madding
and multitudinous scenes of lurid-lighted revelry; indulged in, within so small a space and confined an
air, by so many big pipe-smoking, tobacco-stinking,
European men, and demon-like Arabs of every degree—
black, brown, and grey—waiting on them and howling
ever and anon for their own corruption of *baksheesh*.

Lamentable scenes surely to be beheld in *such a chamber*, and in the present educated and advanced age of the
world. For they were certainly sights that would have
utterly shocked poor Caliph Al Mamoun, who had,
1,000 years ago, but quite involuntarily, prepared the
arena for them. And now, no one will attempt to put
them down; for, as one informant told us, "This
Egypt, is, in the present day, every man's land; and
every one is his own master when he comes out into
the desert here; while in nothing is each individual so
tenacious as his perfect right to enjoy himself in the
Great Pyramid. The modern Pharaoh would be pulled
rom his throne, if he attempted to interfere."

Temperature and Pressure Data for the Coffer's Weight and Capacity Measure.

At the present moment, therefore, the coffer is no more of its right, or original, temperature, than its right and original size, when so much of it has been broken bodily away by the hammering of the representative men of modern money-making society and their attendant trains. But the barometric pressure in the chamber happily defies such power of disturbance, and keeps, by the law of the atmosphere over all that region, expressively close to 30·000 Pyramid inches.

Wherefore we correct our evidently perverted temperature observations slightly by theory, take the mean pressure as observed, and then have quite enough to justify us in assuming, as the original coffer and King's Chamber temperature of 4,040 years ago (and also what their temperature would be again were the ventilating channels reopened, and a strict prohibition issued in Scottish Covenanter phrase, against " promiscuous dancing" by all travellers, whether educated or ignorant; smoking narcotics,* or not)—the number 68°0 Fahr., or a temperature of one-fifth.

* If from old America came the vice of smoking, it may be from new America only, will ever come the efficient cure for it; and the following is already the manner in which the truly *per-fervidissimum ingenium* of its newest free and independent citizens has *begun* to treat the subject, at least, in its opium variety :—

Advertisement from a San Francisco Paper, 1875.

" The people of the city and county of San Francisco do ordain as follows :—

"*Section* 1.   No person shall, in the city and county of San Francisco, keep or maintain, or become an inmate of, or visit, or shall in any way contribute to the support of any place, house, or room, where opium is smoked, or where persons assemble for the purpose of smoking opium, or inhaling the fumes of opium.

" Any person who shall violate any of the provisions of this section

Wherefore at that temperature, and the atmospheric pressure previously mentioned, the coffer's 71,250 cubic Pyramid inches of capacity, filled with pure water, (though only as a temporary practical expedient for that mean earth-density of the interior of the planet which man can never hope to touch, though he may tell it in number)—do form the grand, earth-commensurable, *weight* standard of the ancient Great Pyramid.

What precise quantity of numerical weight, in our reckoning of tons or pounds, that will amount to, and what subdivisions of its grand standard the Pyramid system permits for commerce as well as science, we propose to take up further on,—after having devoted one more chapter to examining certain of our foundational Pyramid data of modern measured lengths and angles, reduced to their original values, more rigidly than ever.

shall be deemed guilty of a misdemeanour, and, upon conviction thereof, shall be punished by a fine of not less than fifty dollars and not exceeding five hundred dollars, or by imprisonment in the County Jail for a period not less than ten days, nor more than six months, or by both such fine and imprisonment.

" And the Clerk is hereby directed to advertise this order, as required by law.

" In Board of Supervisors, San Francisco, November 15, 1875.

" Ayes.—Supervisors Menzies, Pease, Henney, Ebbets, Sims, Roberts, Strother, Scott, Roberts, Lynch, Macdonald.

" Absent.—Supervisor Deering.

" Jno. A. Russell, *Clerk*."

CHAPTER X.

CONFIRMATIONS,

of the Exterior, by the Interior, measures of Great Pyramid.

IN the several theoretical conclusions arrived at thus far in this second division of our book, the interior measures of the Great Pyramid finally made use of in the research (as those for the size and shape of the coffer) had been taken almost entirely by myself; and were so preferred, simply because they had been observed more abundantly, carefully, and had been printed at far greater length and with much more fulness of detail, than any Pyramid measures to be found elsewhere. Now when some of the remarkable commensurability results derived from those observations, and ascertained at least eight or nine years ago, were quoted rather recently in a London drawing-room as deserving serious attention,—the kindly speaker was confronted by a Cambridge mathematician, who rose with authority amongst the guests, and sententiously remarked, "So this man who discovered the wonders, made his own observations ! Then what *can* his theoretical deductions be worth ?" Wherefore the previous speaker was held to be utterly extinguished by every one present (forgetful, all of them, that the argument against John Taylor in his day was, that he never observed at all, but only worked on paper from the records of others), and the Great Pyramid was that evening, and within that drawing-room, handed back to the Egyptologists as nothing but an ordinary, profane, Egyptian tomb, intended for that and *nothing* else.

Whether so-called pure mathematicians of College upbringing have reason to be suspicious of each other, or are coming, in these days, to accept a moral insinuation, in place of a geometrical or arithmetical demonstration, I know not ; but a very different rule of conduct has been for long observed among astronomers. Indeed, the efforts of such men as Francis Baily, Sir John Herschel, Professor De Morgan, and many others of the leading spirits of their time during the last forty years, have been largely directed to encourage, and almost oblige, every astronomer in a public observatory to do something more than merely observe ; more too than compute his own observations only ; for they taught that he should further apply them to theory, or theory to them ; and discover, if he could, anything further that they were capable, in that combination, of disclosing.

No doubt the observations should first, wherever possible, be published pure and simple ; though that costs money, which is not always forthcoming even in Government establishments, out of London ; and afterwards, or separately, should appear any theoretical *discoveries that either the observer or any one else may have been able to educe* out of them.   But that was exactly what I *had* done in the case of my Pyramid observations of 1865. For, by immense proportional sacrifices out of a small income on the part of my Wife and self, I had published the original observations in 1867 in Vol. II. of my "Life and Work at the Great Pyramid," in as full detail as though it had been both a Government expedition, and its printing paid for out of the national purse. And this self-taxation was especially to satisfy all those intellectualists who might wish to do the computing and theorizing for themselves; while only in Vol. III. of " Life and Work," and subsequently in my " Antiquity of Intellectual Man," did I begin to try what I myself could make out of this new and extended supply of raw material for testing John Taylor's Pyramid theory.

And yet five years afterwards a stay-at-home mathematician, without pretending that any better, or essentially contradictory, observations had been made by any one else, either before or since, and without having looked into anything of the subject,—could openly ridicule the possibility of there being any value in my *deductions*, merely because I had previously had the toil of making, and the expense of printing, the *observations* as well!

But fortunately, since the date of publication of my volumes in 1867 and '68, several free and independent spirits, often quite unknown to me, have discussed some of the measures contained in them much more minutely than I had done myself; and have made discoveries which had never entered into my head even to conceive of. Such new men in the field are, Mr. William Petrie, late Chemical Engineer; Mr. St. John Vincent Day, C.E.; the Rev. Joseph T. Goodsir; Major U. A. Tracey, R.A.; Mr. James Simpson, Commercial Bank, Edinburgh; Mr. W. Flinders Petrie; Mr. Henry Mitchell, Hydrographer, U.S. Coast Survey; the Rev. Alex. Mackay, LL.D., Edinburgh; Charles Casey, Esq., of Carlow; the Rev. F. R. A. Glover, M.A., London ; Professor Hamilton L. Smith (Professor of Astronomy in Hobart College, Geneva, New York, U.S.); W. C. Pierrepont, of Pierre Pont Manor, New York, U.S. ; Captain B. W. Tracey, R.N., London; Mr. Cockburn Muir, Civil Engineer, London ; Mr. Sydney Hall, Civil Engineer, London; the Rev. C. W. Hickson, M.A., Bristol; the Rev. Henry Morton, South Shields; Mr.

Charles Horner, London ; the Rev. Dr. Seiss, Philadelphia, U.S. ; Mr. H. L. Powers, Chicago, U.S. ; the
Rev. Dr. Joseph Wild, of Brooklyn, New York; Charles
Latimer, Chief Engineer, Cleveland, Ohio ; the Rev.
James French, Denver, Colorado ; Mr. W. Rowbottom,
of Alfreton ; and the Rev. Alfred Beer, of Hythe ; the
several parties being mentioned here according to the
dates of their researches becoming known to me; and
I proceed now to give some* of the results of *their*
examinations.

The New School of Pyramid Theorists in the King's Chamber.

Of all parts of the Great Pyramid amenable to accurate linear measure, there are none presenting such
advantages therefor as the King's Chamber, far in its
interior ; because the said Chamber is—1. Equable in
temperature ; 2. Unvisited by wind, sand, or other such
natural disturbances of the outside of the building ;
3. Of simple rectangular figure (excepting an infinitesimal angle of convergence, and a rather larger angle
of inclination, observed as yet only by myself, and
not altogether to my own satisfaction); 4. Erected in
polished, dense, hard, red granite ; and, 5. It exhibits
the longest lines of any part of the Pyramid, both in
that hard material, and in a horizontal position ; with
vertical end-pieces too, in rectangular emplacement, or
exactly as most suitable to the modern refinements of
" end-measure."   (See Plates XVI. and XVII.)

---

* It may be proper, on account of certain recent critiques, to say, that
because I have mentioned these gentlemen's names with honour, I do
not, therefore, homologate *everything* which all of them have written ;
but I shall endeavour, to the best of my ability, to point out in the course
of this book wherever they have apparently made real discoveries of valuable Pyramid truth ; and *those* matters I shall be most happy to answer
for at all times.

M. Jomard speaks of his English predecessor, Professor Greaves, having inscribed, or cut, the length of his standard foot-measure on the walls of that chamber. But I could not find any trace of such a thing; and rather suspect that Jomard must have been misled by some figurative expression of Greaves's; who wisely considered, that a printed statement of the measured length of that chamber (so constant in its size from age to age), in *terms* of his foot-measure, would be a better record to posterity of what the length of that standard must have been, than any attempt to cut one length of it there and then bodily into the hard granite by smoky candlelight, with imperfect tools, and while Mohammedan Memlook soldiers were looking on with impatience and hatred of everything done by Christian hands.

The Mensuration Data at the Disposal of the New Theorists.

Certain it is that I could not find any corporeal record of that foot-measure in the King's Chamber; nor can the Heads of Houses in Oxford find Greaves's iron measuring-rod itself, though they have the wooden box for it, safe enough. But the libraries of Europe contain many copies of the *book record;* and that runs plainly enough to the effect, that the length of the King's Chamber in the Great Pyramid, as measured by Greaves, amounted to 34·380 of his feet, *i.e.* 412·56 of his British inches, more than 200 years ago, or in 1637.

Now this is a quantity well worthy of remembrance, viz. this 412·56 inches-length of Greaves: for—

By Col. Howard-Vyse, in 1837, that chamber's length
   was stated to be, in his honest but rough manner   .   411·00
By Mr. Lane, in or near 1838, in the same sort of
   manner   .   .   .   .   412·50
By Messrs. Aiton and Inglis in 1865, similarly from
                                   411·7 to 412·1

But by myself in 1865 it was given as follows, with

particular care to reduce my inches to standard British Government inches of the present, and also, as it is believed, a long-past, historical day:—

LENGTH.

LENGTH of South side, near floor level,
11th March, first measure . . . . = 412·6
   Do.   second measure . . . = 412·58
16th March, first measure . . . . = 412·5
   Do.   second measure . . . = 412·7

North side, March 11th, first measure . . = 412·4
   Do.   do.   second measure . = 412·5
   Do.   do.   third measure . . = 412·5

Mean of South side . . . . . . = 412·60
Mean of North side . . . . . . = 412·47

Mean LENGTH of both North and South sides . = 412·54 Brit. Inch.
                                = 412·13 Pyr. do.
Assumed true LENGTH on the whole . . = 412·132 Do. do.

BREADTH.

BREADTH of King's Chamber near East end,
      first measure . . . . . = 206·4
   Do.   second measure . . . . = 206·2
Near West end . . . . . . = 206·3

Mean BREADTH of East and West ends . . = 206·30 Brit. Inch.
                                  = 206·09 Pyr. do.
Assumed true BREADTH on the whole . . = 206·066 Do. do.

FIRST HEIGHT.

HEIGHT of King's Chamber near North-east
   angle of room . . . . . . = 230·8
North side . . . . = 229·7
North-west angle . . . . . . = 229·2
South-west . . . . = 229·9
South side . . . . = 229·5
South-east angle . . . . . . = 230·8
North-east angle repeated . . . . = 230·8
The mean HEIGHT here = 230·1, but is certainly smaller than it should be ; for so many of the floor stones, from which the heights necessarily had to be measured, were disturbed and to some extent risen up (like the drawing of a tooth), as though in consequence of earthquake disturbance. Hence the true quantity must be much nearer the greater, than the smaller, limit of the measured heights, and should probably be called . . . = 230·70 Brit. Inch.
                                  = 230·47 Pyr. do.
Assumed true "FIRST HEIGHT" on the whole = 230·389 Do. do.

SECOND HEIGHT.

The above, "the FIRST HEIGHT," or that from
floor to ceiling, is so called to distinguish it
from "the second height," or that of the
granite walls themselves.   Walls fully measurable now only in the N.W. corner of the
room, where three of the floor-blocks are
taken out, and show the wall there reaching
down 5·0 inches beneath the floor-level. This
5·0 inches completes the regularity of height
for all the five courses of granite blocks
forming the walls of the room ; seeing that
each of the four upper courses certainly
measures 47·1 British inches, nearly, in
height; and the first, or lowest of the five,
though measuring only 42·1 from the floor,
yet measures 47·1, if we add on the 5 inches
observed at the only place where we can look
at the bases of the walls underneath the
floor-level.   All this justifies us in announcing as the " SECOND HEIGHT" of the King's
Chamber, or the height of the four walls of
it, pure and simple, in themselves (see Plate
XVII.) as near to.   .   .   .   .   .   235·50 Brit. Inch.
                              = 235·25 Pyr. do.
And as certainly lying between   .   235·20 and 235·50 Do. do.

DIAGONALS of floor:
    From South-west to North-east corner . = 461·0
    North-west to South-east .   .   .   . = 461·3

Mean measured floor diagonal   .   .   . = 461·65 Brit. Inch.
                                             = 461·19 Pyr. do.
DIAGONALS of East wall :
    Low North-east to high South-east corner = 309·2
    Low South-east to high North-east corner,
        substracting 1·6 inches for hole in low
        South-east corner .   .   .   .   . = 310·0

                                             = 309·6 Brit. Inch.
                                             = 309·3 Pyr. do.
DIAGONAL of West wall :
    Low South-west to high North-west corner = 310·4
Subtract 1·0 for a sunken floor-stone South-
    west .   .   .   . = 1·0
(The other diagonal not measurable on account
    of a large and deep hole in floor in north-
    west corner of chamber, whereby men enter-
    ing have gone on excavating at some time to
    underneath that part of the floor whereon
    the coffer stands ; but are not known to
    have found anything but solid limestone
    masonry and mortar.)

                                             = 309·4 Brit. Inch.
                                             = 309·1 Pyr. do.

Mr. James Simpson's Sums of the Squares.

With these measures before him, and paying more attention to those of them taken from rectangular sides than the more difficult practical case of the corners and diagonals, Mr. James Simpson, adopting what he thought the most probable numbers for length, breadth, and height, computed the several diagonals, and prepared the following theoretical numbers for the room in Pyramid inches :—

King's Chamber Lines.	Simpson's First Numbers.	Piazzi Smyth's Original Measures.	The latter Measures corrected by Simpson's Proportions.
Linear { Breadth . =	206·10	206·09	206·066
First height =	230·42	230·47	230·389
Length . . =	412·20	412·13	412·132
Diagonals of { End =	309·14		
Floor =	460·84		
Side =	472·22		
Solid Diagonal . . =	515·24		

The differences between Mr. Simpson's adopted linear numbers and my pure measures in the first division, it will be seen, amount to not more than ·07 of an inch, or within the error of an average single measure by me, and much within those of some observers ; indicating therefore that we may take his numbers as expressing well the true constructed and measured dimensions of the apartment *inter se*, such as the breadth being exactly half of the length, and the height exactly half of the floor diagonal (as discovered also independently by Professor Hamilton L. Smith), if indeed a good and locally conclusive reason can be shown for them ; and this is what Mr. Simpson does most effectively in a series of commensurabilities of squares in very Pyramid numbers.

Take, says he, half of the breadth, or 103·05, as a special unit of division ; then test and divide therewith each of the above-recorded quantities as below ; and then, squaring the results, you will have for the—

Breadth . . . 2·000 whose square = 4
First height . . . 2·236   ,,   = 5
Length . . . 4·000   ,,   = 16

Or sum of squares for linear dimensions of K. Ch. = 25 a Pyramid number.

For the end diagonal . 3·000 whose square = 9
Floor do. . . . 4·472   ,,   = 20
Side do. . . . 4·582   ,,   = 21

Or sum of squares for part diagonals of K. Ch. = 50 a Pyramid number.

Solid diagonal . = 5·000 whose square = 25 a Pyramid number.
And the sum of the three Pyramid numbers . =100 a Pyramid number.

And this is in the chamber whose walls have now been doubly proved to be composed of just 100 blocks of well-cut, squared, polished and evenly heighted, though very differently lengthed, granite.

The manner in which the long fractions of some of the simple divisions clear themselves off, on taking the squares, is especially to be noted ; and from a further theoretical consideration of his own (for the above theorem is one touching shape only, not size), Mr. Simpson considers that a more exact ultimate expression for the original sizes of the various parts of the room should be in Pyramid inches—

Breadth of King's Chamber . . . . = 206·0659
Height (the *First* height, or floor to ceiling) . = 230·3880
Length . . . . = 412·1317

Diagonal of end of King's Chamber . . = 309·0988
  Do.   floor . . . . . = 460·7773
  Do.   side . . . . . = 472·1562

Solid, or cubic diagonal, of King's Chamber . = 515·1646

Further, the grand division test of this so-called
King's Chamber . . . . . . = 103·0329

And the *Second* Height, or the walls entire,
from *under* the floor-plane up to the ceiling,
between . . . . . . 235·20 and 235·50

Hence it must now be abundantly apparent that, however limited the size of the King's Chamber may be, as compared with the whole building, it contains a remarkable power within itself for giving out accuracy of measure, to six places of numbers, nearly ; and may in that manner form a foundation and a fulcrum in Pyramid research from which we may attain to higher things.

The King's Chamber reacts on the Exterior of the Great Pyramid.

If we now multiply the chamber's length (its chief level line and the best measured, too, of the whole Great Pyramid), by the special Pyramid numbers 5 × 5, and find it to yield 10303·29 + &c., or the same row of ciphers with the decimal point differently placed, as Mr. Simpson's touchstone line of Pyramid commensurability, we may then ask further whether that larger, absolute quantity of length so implied, has any particular value or meaning *outside* that King's Chamber wherein it is now found.

Then comes the remarkable answer, that the area of the *square* base of the Great Pyramid (determined already independently to have a side = 9131·05 Pyramid inches) is equal to the area of a *circle* whose diameter = 10303·30, within ± ·01 of the same Pyramid inches. (See Plate XX., Equality of Areas, No. 1.) Thus bringing up again, though in a slightly different shape, viz. areas instead of circumferences, that practical squaring of the circle, which was one of the chief objects of the Great Pyramid's external figure ; and establishing thus a simple, but most intellectual, relation between the apparent utter diversities of a small, long-shaped rectangular room on one side, and the square-based, originally sharp-pointed, mighty Great Pyramid on the other.

Again, considering Pyramid inches in the King's Chamber to signify Pyramid cubits outside the building, the following results came out correct to six places of figures:—Take the length of the King's Chamber 412·132 to express the diameter of a circle. Compute, by the best methods of modern science, the area of that circle; throw that area into a square shape, and find the length of a side of such square. The answer will be 365·242 Pyramid cubits; a quantity which not only represents the mean of all the measures of the length of the Great Pyramid's base-side (see Chap. III., p. 36-39), but defines the number of mean solar days in a mean solar tropical year.* (See Plate XXI.)

Next consider the same King's Chamber's measured quantity (and measured, published too, in my "Life and Work at the Great Pyramid," be it remembered, before this theory came out), viz. 412·132, as the side of a square; find its area, and throw that (by modern science as before) into a circular shape. The radius of such a circle will be found = 232·520; or in Pyramid cubits, the vertical height of the Great Pyramid according to the *mean* of all the measures; and also very close, taken as in Pyramid inches, to the *mean* of the two heights, viz. those "first and second"—heights, which

---

* The following may serve as an example of a practical mode of performing this little calculation, with the usual tables of logarithms to seven places:—

412·132 = assumed the diameter of a circle . = log.	2·6150363
Find its area, 1st, by squaring . =	× 2
	5·2300726
2nd, by adding log. $\frac{\pi}{4}$ =	9·8950899
Log. area of assumed circle and } also of the square sought . } =	5·1251625
Find side of said square by $\sqrt{}$. =	÷ 2
365·242 + &c. = Nat. number of Log. . . =	2·5625812

the architect found it necessary to introduce into the King's Chamber to enable it to typify all he required.

The above calculations may be easily performed either by arithmetic direct, or by logarithms, but including always the precisely true value of π (see our " Key the First," p. xv.) ; and the following is how the Pyramid architect further exhibits that π quantity in one and the same King's Chamber :—Take the circuit of either of the principal walls of the chamber in their entirety of *granite*, *i.e.* north or south wall, and divide by the length; the result is π, equably, so far as practical measures can go, with modern mathematics.

Taking therefore, for this purpose, as the height of the room, the " Second Height," and within the limits assigned by Mr. James Simpson, viz. 235·243 ; the circuit of either north or south wall is—

$$412\cdot132 + 235\cdot243 + 412\cdot132 + 235\cdot243 = 1294\cdot750$$
$$\text{and } 1294\cdot750 \div 412\cdot132 = 3\cdot14159 + \&c. = \pi,$$

or presents to us, we may now say in plain words without stint, " the first Key of Knowledge of the Great Pyramid."

Ante-Chamber Symbolisms.

We have by no means finished with these most accurate numbers of the King's Chamber yet,—but it may be agreeable to many readers to see from another side how gradually, though surely, those numbers there discovered were led up to by previous acts and deliberate arrangements of the architect.

To reach the King's Chamber of the Great Pyramid we have to pass through the Ante-chamber; and we have already gathered some useful hints from there, yet far from all that it was capable of giving.

One of our gatherings, p. 174, 176, was from the three curved hollows in the higher, or western, granite wainscot. There are no such hollows on the eastern side, and it is moreover cut off at top to an absolutely lower level than what the western hollows descend to.

Why was the east wainscot so cut down; evidently, from its perfection of work, by the original builders?

The architect is dead, but you may still virtually question him, in such a building of number, weight, and measure, by ascertaining *how much?* *What height,* for instance, was the eastern wainscot cut down to?

So asked Major U. A. Tracey, R.A., now several years ago; and my measures in "Life and Work" answered his studious examination of them at Gibraltar, with 103·0; since assumed, within the limits of the measures, = 103·033 Pyramid inches.·

Why, said he, that is half of the King's Chamber breadth, and must therefore be important. Then examining further, he recognized that the floor of the ante-chamber was recorded by me, though by no previous traveller, as partly in granite and partly in limestone; that the length of the former portion, given in four different places as between 102·5 and 103·6, must be intended, though roughly (as all features of this ante-chamber are rough and approximative only) for the 103·033 also; and in that case here were two similar, and of the place characteristic, lengths of granite placed in rectangular position to each other. That, he added, indicates *square* measure; but what is the circular equal, *in area*, of such a square?

The length of the whole ante-chamber was then looked for, and found in my measures, thus, in Pyramid inches:—

116·2
116·7
116·1
116·2
116·2
116·2

Mean = 116·27 or 116·26

This 116·26 being made up of 103·03 of granite, and 13·23 of limestone; and 116·260, Captain Tracey pointed out, is the diameter of a circle having precisely equal area (up to its last figure at least) to a square of 103·033 in the side. Whereupon the Abbé and Chanoine Moigno exclaimed in his scientific journal *Les Mondes*, "Who could pretend now that the diversity of the materials forming the floor, and their relations and differences of length, were a brute accident on the part of the ancient architect of 4,000 years ago?" And still less when the following additional features are produced by these numbers, 103·03 and 116·26, in their Pyramid positions, and Pyramid *inch* units of measure, there :—

(1.) 103·033 $\times$ 5 (Pyramid number) = 515·165; or is the length in Pyramid inches of the cubic diagonal of the King's Chamber.

(2.) 103·033 $\times$ 50 (the number of masonry courses of the Pyramid the chamber stands upon) = 5151·65; or is in Pyramid inches the length of the side of square of equal area to a triangle of the shape and size of the Great Pyramid's vertical meridian section.

(3.) 116·260 $\times$ 2 = 232·520; or is, in Pyramid inches, the mean, nearly, of the First and Second Heights of the King's Chamber.

(4.) 116·260 $\times$ π = 365·242 + &c.; or shows the number of mean solar days in a mean solar tropical year.

(5.) 116·260 $\times$ π $\times$ 5 $\times$ 5 = 9131·05; or is, in Pyramid inches, the length of a side of the base of the Great Pyramid from a mean of all the measures.

(6.) 116·260 $\times$ 50 = 5813·0; or is, in Pyramid inches, the ancient vertical height of the Great Pyramid, from a mean of all the measures.

Hence, as the earlier of the above cases, including the 103·033, show, the uses of the east wainscot of ante-chamber, in being lower than the west wainscot, have been most remarkable. But can any object be assigned to the west wainscot being of the greater height it has been found to be by measure, viz. 111·8 Pyramid inches?

Being so signal a feature of the chamber, and executed expensively and solidly,—though, as usual with the ante-chamber, not with microscopic refinement of work (see Dr. Grant's orders of surfaces of granite, in Great

Pyramid, Plate XVIII.)—we may be sure that the architect intended something by it; and this is what Professor H. L. Smith has drawn forth:—Divide the height by 100; and call the original quantity, now 1·118, possibly 1·11803; then,

Breadth of King's Chamber × 1·11803 = Height of the same.

Now *that* height is a very peculiar quantity, as already set forth in Mr. Simpson's sums of the squares; and all the more to be attended to now that the realities of the Great Pyramid are coming to be appreciated; for hitherto the King's Chamber has been carelessly described, by too many of our educated travellers, as merely a double cube; a simple notion of architectural science which I believe they derive from very long subsequent Greek buildings. But the designer of the Great Pyramid here sets up a notice, that if the breadth of the King's Chamber = 1, then the height thereof is *not* to be the same, but to be 1·11803. Let us try it in numbers :—

$$206·066 \times 1·11803 = 230·389$$

or the exact quantity, to within the possibilities of measure, attained for Mr. Simpson's *First* height, p. 197; shown there, and subsequently, to be intimately connected with references to the size of the whole building.

Yet there may be those who object to this one case only, of a number not being taken at once as it measures in Pyramid inches, but after division by 100! The objection is not of much force, seeing that the number chosen is so very round, and even, a Pyramid number; equivalent merely to shifting the decimal point two places; and that the ante-chamber has many purposes to serve, both theoretical and practical, all of which can only be included in some such manner. But there is also more direct justification than this, in that we find the division by 100 used *again* in this room, and touching *height* also.

The measured height of the whole ante-chamber, floor to ceiling, is 149·3 or ·4 Pyramid inches; and why?

Because that number represents the length of base-side of Great Pyramid *plus* the vertical height thereof, each of them divided by 100; as thus :—

$$\frac{9131 + 5813}{100} = 91\cdot31 + 58\cdot13 = 149\cdot44.$$

Nor is this a mere chance coincidence in whole sums, for two remarkably pertinent reasons.

First. Professor H. L. Smith has shown that the whole distance is appropriately divided by the centre of the lower, and regularly formed, component of the granite leaf, so as to represent from there, upward to the ceiling, 91·3 Pyramid inches, = Pyramid base-side ÷ 100; and from the same centre downwards to the floor, 58·1 nearly, or the Pyramid vertical height ÷ 100.

The latter measure, as recorded by me, was indeed too short by nearly half an inch; but that was presently found to be already explained by Plate XI., Vol. II. of "Life and Work" (which involuntarily shows for the date of its publication when Pyramid theory had not advanced to any of these refinements), that the stone in the floor under the leaf has been disturbed by counter pressure or dislocated by modern or mediæval earthquake shocks; so that it is at least 0·3 of an inch, at present, above its fellows.

Second. In angular confirmation of the above, the venerable and still acute-minded Mr. W. C. Pierrepont (of Pierre Pont Manor, Jefferson County, N.Y.) has pointed out, that if a model of a meridian section of the Great Pyramid be conceived to stand on the flooring of the ante-chamber and its passages, and to touch with its apex the ceiling of the ante-chamber, vertically over the centre of the granite leaf, then,

North foot of such pyramidal section rests on the great step at the head of the grand gallery, exactly there where the ramp-line continued comes through; and

South foot of such pyramidal section rests on the granite floor of the passage leading from the ante-chamber onwards to the King's Chamber; and is defined there to within a tenth of an inch by a "joint" line in the granite; the only joint line too in that passage, but duly chronicled in "Life and Work," Vol. II., in 1867.

From that joint-line in the floor, then, the vertical angle to the ceiling of ante-chamber immediately over the singular and most important, granite leaf's centre = 51° 51′, or the Great Pyramid's angle of side-rise; and from the same joint-line to the centre of the lower stone of the granite leaf (which divides the whole height, into base-side and vertical height ÷ 100) the angle is 26° 18′ nearly, or the angle of all the inclined passages of the Pyramid; and concerning which angle, there will be much more to be said by-and-by.

Inches in the Granite Leaf.

The granite leaf therefore in the ante-chamber, besides being so strange a structure in itself (standing all across the room between the floor and the ceiling), is hedged about, as it were, with important symbols connected with the scientific theory of the Great Pyramid; and now we come to a still more essential and explanatory part which it has been found to serve therein.

Some objectors to the Pyramid scientific theory have said, "We do not admit the reality of your Pyramid inches with its original builders, when you can only get such inches by yourselves subdividing immense lengths. But show us a single such inch, and we may believe."

Whereupon Captain, now Major, U. A. Tracey, R.A., has pointed out that such single inch is actually marked, and in a Pyramid manner, on, or rather by means of, the above granite leaf in the ante-chamber; and it comes about thus :—

In that small apartment its grand symbol on the south wall is the already-mentioned illustration of a division into five : and if the symbol had virtue enough to extend into and dominate some features in the next or King's Chamber (as in illustrating its now undoubted number of *five* wall-courses), why should it not typify something in its own chamber as well ? But what is there, in the ante-chamber, divided into five ? " The Great Pyramid's own scientific, earth-commensurable, cubit," answers Captain Tracey; ."for here it is so divided in the shape of this projecting *boss* on the granite leaf, just five inches broad. And further, that fifth part of that cubit of the Great Pyramid's symbolical design is divided before our eyes into five again ; for the thickness of this remarkable boss is 1-5th of its breadth. So there you have the division of the peculiar Pyramid cubit into 5 × 5 inches."

This boss on the granite leaf (see Plate XV.) is another of my mere *re*-discoverings of things at the place, which, though long denied or overlooked by most visitors, both have been, and are still to be, duly seen : for the boss is marked, but not sufficiently noted or measured, in that excellent, yet unwieldy and seldom consulted, folio of enormous plates, " Perring's," or rather perhaps to be called " Vyse and Perring's," views of the Pyramids, published in London, in 1840.

But this most unique yet modest boss was not described and pictured by me with proper correctness in " Life and Work "; I having, unfortunately, made it there much too high, too accurately rectangular at its lowest corner line, too sharply and neatly defined all round ; and the workmanship fine, instead of, as it is, rather rough. This too I am enabled now to say positively, having been kindly furnished by Mr. Waynman Dixon with a cast of the boss in Portland cement taken by him in the Great Pyramid in 1872 ; and still another cast of it in plaster was obligingly sent to me by Dr. J. A. S. Grant, of Cairo, in 1874. The *one* inch thickness, however, and *five* inches breadth, of the thickest and central part being fairly measurable along the best line of each cast-boss for measuring, viz. its steep, though not absolutely rectangular, lower edge,— *they* remain untouched and perfectly suitable for Captain Tracey's analogy, which is further supported as follows : —The boss, a flat bas-relief one inch thick or protruding *from* the stone, is on the north side of the upper of the two granite stones forming that " granite leaf " which crosses the ante-chamber near its northern end. (Compare Chapter IX., pages 175, 176.) Excepting the presently broken, or boulder-line, state of the upper surface of the top stone, the formation of the whole leaf is regular, rectangular, and symmetrical ; and the working of it masterly, though rough ; *i.e.* hammer-dressed, but very finely for that method, and sensibly smoother than the walls of the ante-chamber. (See Plate XVIII., for Dr. Grant's orders of surfaces.) Why then is the boss not even approximately in the middle of the granite leaf, or in the centre between the two sides of the very narrow apartment containing it ? (only 41·21 inches broad between the granite wainscots.)

My measures of 1865, if they can be trusted here, show that the boss is just *one inch* away on one side of the centre ; and as it will be elsewhere shown that it was a Great Pyramid method to indicate a small, but important, quantity by an *excentricity* to that amount in some far grander architectural feature,—we cannot but accept this measured excentricity of the boss as an additional Pyramid memorial of the very thing which is being called for by the sceptical just now ; viz. one single, little inch memorialised by the builders of the most colossal piece of architecture in the world through-out all human time. (See Frontispiece.) All the more decidedly too, when, as Mr. St. John Vincent Day has since then shown, that very excentric position of the boss, by the amount of just *one* inch, has enabled the distance from its centre to the eastern end of the leaf itself in its well-cut groove in the granite wainscot to be, within the limits of mensuration errors, just a whole Pyramid cubit $= 25\cdot025$ British inches, or something very near to it indeed.* So that exactly here, where

---

* My measures say, p. 100, Vol. II. of " Life and Work "—

British inches.

Centre of BOSS to East side of ante-chamber room . . . $= 21\cdot5$
Centre of BOSS to West side of ante-chamber room . . . $= 19\cdot5$
P. 98, Vol. II., depth of groove in East wall . . . . $= 4\cdot0$

Whole distance from centre of BOSS to East end of granite leaf
in its groove, roughly . . . . $= 25\cdot5$

But again, on p. 93, and also p. 95, the grooved breadth of the
room is deduced in British inches at (its ungrooved breadth, or
the breadth between the two wainscots, and in so far, all the
visible breadth of the granite leaf, being nearly $41\cdot2$ inches) $= 48\cdot067$

Half $= 24\cdot034$

Add 1 inch of excentricity of the BOSS from the East wall $= +$ $1\cdot000$
Whole distance of centre of BOSS from the inside of the granite
leaf's eastern flat groove in granite . . . . . $= 25\cdot034$

The BOSS on the granite leaf is, in general shape, much like certain bosses or lugs on the ends of old Sarcophagi ; and Dr. Grant has recently discovered some large ones, apparently for lifting purposes, on some of the granite blocks of the " Hollows of Construction " ; but their measures, which is the test point in the Great Pyramid, are entirely different ; apparently accidental, and without meaning.
Further measures of the BOSS on the granite leaf, in a letter from Dr. J. A. S. Grant, Cairo, Dec. 6, 1874, describing a long and hard-working night spent in measuring inside the Great Pyramid, in company with the Rev. F. R. A. Glover and Mr. Beecher:—
" Then we measured the BOSS, and found it to jut out from its stone *one inch ;* and also to be removed from the centre of the breadth of its stone exactly *one inch ;* measurements which corroborate former measurements."

every would-be-enterer into the King's Chamber must bow the head,—we have suspended over him the whole cubit, its fifth part and its twenty-fifth part or *inch* unit; which, though so small, yet is it as *securely* monumentalized in this vast building, as anything else of any size: clearly, too, and in a manner which has lasted up to this very day.

Thus much does the granite leaf for *linear* measure; but it indicates a beginning of capacity and cubic measure also; for Captain Tracey again shows that the lower stone of the granite leaf (in this ante-chamber, which thus proves itself to be a veritable synopsis or microcosm of the metrology of the Pyramid), that this lower stone, I say, which is fairly dressed, rectangular,*

A still further and more particular account of the CUBIT of the GRANITE LEAF is given by Dr. J. A. S. Grant thus, in a later letter of 1874:—

Breadth of granite leaf from East to West   . = 48·00 inches.
Depth of the two grooves for it in the walls East
  and West   .   .   .   .   — 6·5
                                                        ─────
                                                        2)41·5
                                                        ─────
Half of the above   .   .   .   .   . = 20·75
Excentricity of BOSS; *i.e.* Distance of centre of
  BOSS to the West of centre of granite leaf   . =   1·00
                                                        ─────
                                                        21·75
Depth of groove in East wall   .   .   . =   3·25
                                                        ─────
Distance of centre of BOSS from East end of
  granite leaf within the groove in East wall . = 25·00

* My ante-chamber measures, as condensed on p. 37 of the 13th vol. of the "Edinburgh Astronomical Obs.," give:—
GRANITE LEAF, thickness North to South, on East side . = 15·4 inches.
                                          West side . = 16·0   ,,
Height of lower stone   .   .   .   .   . 27·5 to 28·0   ,,
Height of upper stone, from its straight, level base
  under the boss, to its curved, or curvilinear, or
  broken and boulder form above it .   .   . from 18·0 to 23·5   ,,
Breadth East to West, between the open walls.   .   . = 41·21 ± *x*
          ,,   between the leaf's grooves .   . = 48·05 ± *x*
Further measures of GRANITE LEAF by Mr. Waynman Dixon, announced in December, 1875:—

and the one on which the upper stone with its divisions of the cubit rests, expresses a notable division of the capacity measure of the coffer. For it presents us, within the walls of the ante-chamber, with a fourth part of that coffer vessel; or with the veritable " corn quarter " of old, and which is still the British quarter corn-measure both by name and fact and practical size.

π in the Granite Leaf.

The above conclusion for the lower stone of the leaf has been tested by various persons, and found to come very close to the numbers recorded; but quite recently a new idea was sent to me by the Rev. C. W. Hickson, to the purport that the whole granite leaf contained, of cubic inches, a number equal to π multiplied by 10,000. I tried it upon my own measures, and was rashly about to condemn the notion utterly, when looking again at the latest and most particular letter I had had from Egypt touching the granite leaf,—there was a view expressed there which seemed, involuntarily and quite unknown to the writer of it, to meet this case completely.

With any straight-sided rectangular solid, we have merely to multiply together breadth, thickness, and height, in linear inches, to obtain the contents in cubical inches. Now the granite leaf is a straight-sided, rec-

Visible breadth of leaf between walls North of it	. = 41·0
„ „ „ South of it	. = 41·5
Real breadth of leaf, or of space between groove ends, at top	. = 48·9
Thickness of leaf, North to South . . .	. = 15·0
„ groove-hollows, North to South, at top.	= 16·25
Distance from centre of boss to East wall-face .	. = 21·5
„ East wall-face to groove end .	. = 3·25
„ centre of boss to West wall-face .	. = 19·5

The difference of thickness between the leaf's general thickness and the grooves, which was thought in " Life and Work " to be filled with cement,—is considered by Mr. Dixon to be filled by an extra edge thickness of the granite leaf itself.

tangular solid in everything except the top, which top is irregular, curvilinear, and I had always supposed, broken : wherefore the original cubic contents could only be obtained by assuming a height large enough to include at least the highest fragment remaining; and that would be, measuring upwards from the bottom of the lowest stone, to the top of the upper of the two stones composing the leaf, 51·3 inches : the breadth of the sub-aërial, or visible part of the leaf, being without any doubt 41·2 inches, and the thickness 15·7 inches.

But the multiplication of these quantities gives a number so much greater than 10,000 π, leaving it in the second place of figures, that the theorem cannot be maintained for a moment by them.

If indeed we next take the smallest height of the leaf, which is near to 45·8, the mean of that and the greater height, gives 48·55, possibly inclining to 48·57; and then between these two quantities, the announced 10,000 π comes out most plainly as 31415·9, &c.

But have we any right to use a near mean of the greatest and least heights of the curvilinear summit of the granite leaf, in our inquiry as to how many cubic inches the architect *originally* intended it to represent ?

Not the slightest, *if* that curvilinear summit is the result of modern breakages ; and I, having expressed a belief that it *was* broken mediævally, if not recently, in " Life and Work," in 1867, think myself now specially called on to publish, that a totally opposite view was communicated to me in a very positive manner by a practical engineer in December, 1875. As the matter, moreover, is one where the practised eye of an engineer is of the utmost importance, and as that eye had been employed again and again in scrutinising the granite leaf, I am quite ready now, in that particular, to bow to its conclusions.

The engineer was Mr. Waynman Dixon, and the actual words of his letter are as follows :—

" The more I see of this remarkable stone or leaf, the more I am convinced that the upper irregular part is *in its original condition*, not broken away by specimen-mongers or Arabs."

In that case, the leaving an original, natural, indefinite, curved surface on the top of a solid, whose other sides were worked by man in accurate rectangular planes, may be taken to indicate an intention of exhibiting the naturally and externally indefinite end of the fractional number (see p. xv. under the head of Key the First) : at the same time that the nearest practical amount of it in whole inches, when multiplied by 10,000, was formally shown by the *mean height* of the boulder-surface side, combined with the simple measures of the other sides.

The 35th Pyramid Masonry Course.

But I must now confine myself, in this chapter at least, to only one case more ; making a new use of the ante-chamber length, 116·26 Pyramid inches, to identify that chamber with the very vitals of construction of the whole Great Pyramid.

The manner in which the Pyramid mass is built in horizontal courses of squared stone extending, each at its own thickness, through and through the whole building, has already been mentioned at p. 172; and I may now add, that the thicknesses of these courses rapidly diminish in ascending, so that from about 50 inches at the base they dwindle down to about 27 inches at the 35th course; but there they immediately and suddenly thicken, so that the 36th course begins with a 50-inch thickness once again.   (See Plate IX.)

Now this is a tremendously important fact ; for that thick, 36th, course of masonry is conspicuous on every

side of the Great Pyramid. The French measures of
the courses in 1799, showed it accurately; travellers
with an educated eye, may see it miles off; even my
smallest photographs placed under a microscope invariably show it ; and the extra amount of weight which
the builders had to raise in the 36th course as compared
with the 35th was, on that account solely, about 40,000
tons. What then *was* the extraordinarily important thing
completed in these first 35 courses, that the builders
crowned them so majestically; honoured them, in fact,
with a diadem of stone (whose 50-inch white escarpment shines afar on every side); and marked them to
all future time by the weight and size of the 36th, 37th,
and other higher courses 'of extra thick masonry immediately above them ?   (See the tables on pp. 94, 95.)
Whether the courses of the once-existing, and then
outside, casing-stones corresponded with these inner
structural courses is not now known; but ever since
the casing-stones were removed, or for 1,000 years
past, the world has had the opportunity of seeing the
sudden leap in thickness which the courses take after
the first 35,—and no one ever guessed the reason until
Professor Hamilton L. Smith, of Hobart College,
Geneva, New York, produced, if not all the reasons, at
least a sufficient one, and probably chief one, as thus:—

35 in itself, as made up of 7 times 5, is an important
Pyramid number ; while the 35 courses attain a vertical
height above the base of the Great Pyramid of 1162·6
Pyramid inches,* or ten times the length of the already
proved micro-cosmic ante-chamber.

---

* Of three sets of measures of the heights of the masonry courses of
the Great Pyramid given in " Life and Work," Vol. II., the best is that
by M. Le Père and Colonel Coutelle; for., the one of them an architect
and the other an engineer, they made themselves a special measuring
apparatus for the occasion, and gave great attention to its use. Now Le
Père and Coutelle's result for 35 courses is almost exactly 1162·6 Pyramid
inches; the other two results are smaller, but may be safely looked on
as confirmatory in the present case.

But what then ?

Simply and completely this, that at that point of height, in the middle of any side, the horizontal distance to the vertical axis of the Pyramid is 3652·42, &c., Pyramid inches. That is, when divided by 10, it records in those particular units the number of days in the year ; a grand physical fact which the profane Egyptians did not then know, nor any other men at that time on earth by their own knowledge.   While, further, without any division at all, two straight lines are given to show the proportion of the circumference of a circle to its diameter ; for 3652·42 ÷ 1162·60 = 3·14159, &c., = π.

And finally, 11626·02, or ten times the height of the 35th course, or 100 times the length of the ante-chamber, (*plus* the infinitesimal fraction in the 7th place), or in fact twice the vertical height of the Great Pyramid, represents the mean distance of the Sun from the Earth, in terms of that grand natural quantity Divinely set before the consideration of Job (see our Chap. IV., p. 68), " the breadth of the earth " ; or its measure from pole to pole.

Nor is this the only instance of the ante-chamber's numbers *when taken in Pyramid inches*, distinguishing themselves in the proportions of the sizes and distances of those orbs of the solar system which most concern man in his physical life on earth as ordained by his Creator.   For the self-same three curved hollows of the western granite wainscot, over and above the geometrical hint obtained from them on p. 174,—do also remind of something touching the celebrated problem of "the three bodies " ; *i.e.* sun, earth, and moon in physical astronomy and certain of their numerical inter-relations.

High gravitational astronomy does not, indeed, usually take account of size, only of mass (weight) reduced ideally to a point, of any celestial orb ;—though the space throughout which such mass is distributed, and the amount of surface which it thereby affords, must be everything in the daily practical question of man's life on his Divinely appointed terrestrial abode. Hence, although Mr. George F. Chambers has collected in his "Handbook of Descriptive Astronomy"* some very curious commensurabilities between the distances and diameters of Sun and planets, by the number of " 108 nearly,"—they have not yet been much attended to in scientific society; though too they are facts in the celestial arrangements of the present period of universal time, certain to last sensibly the same for more thousands of years than human history has yet endured, and of extreme *anthropological* importance. They seem, moreover, to be alluded to in the ante-chamber by the exact length of the remarkable vertical groovings of its south wall, shown on p. 167, to be close to 107·4 Pyramid inches long. Or they may be obtained still more accurately by the mean of the heights, minutely corrected by theory on pp. 201 and 203, viz. 103·033 and 111·803, of the two granite wainscots; making 107·418.

A Representative Antagonist of the Modern Scientific Theory of the Great Pyramid.

But now, after so many confirmations, both large and small, furnished by the Great Pyramid itself, as soon as we take the hard, better preserved and better measured portions (and there are more confirmations still, and of a higher class, to appear in our fourth and fifth parts), the reader may be possibly inclined to ask, "Who are the parties who still refuse to allow the force of any of these things? Who can possibly persist in saying, that they

* 3rd Edition, Oxford, at the Clarendon Press, 1877.

see in the Great Pyramid merely a common, everyday, accidental burial " mound " of those ancient, idolatrous Egyptians, who, these parties themselves protest, *knew no accurate astronomy;* and, who also if we judge by sorry sights in the chief museums of Europe, delighted in nothing so much as grovelling worship to animal-headed gods of their own invention; and idolatrous architectural memorialisation of bulls and goats, crocodiles, beetles, and almost every bestial thing ?

One of these really unhappy, but before the world flourishing and successful, recusants has, by printing a book, lately offered himself before the public for description. He is an Oxford graduate and an Angli- can clergyman, a country vicar, and a chaplain to Royalty. His book is a large octavo of travel in Egypt, already in a second edition; written throughout cleverly, fluently, scholarly, but in an outrageously rationalistic vein of the most ultra-Broad Churchism ; or possibly of no Christian Church at all ; even to the extent of his holding the Biblical history of man, in all its miraculous features and limited statements of chronology, to be utterly false. The religions both of Christ and Moses, this author perversely maintains to have been in no way differently originated from those of Egypt, Greece, and Rome. They were each and all, with him, merely the best mental product, " the *summa philosophia,*" of the wisest *men* of their time, acting by their human wisdom alone, and composing systems of religion suitable to " the politics " of their own respec- tive ages : as, too, he would now have the ablest men among us, try to do again, for these troubled and most unhinged times in which we live—times wanting, he says, a new religion, because, as he avers, that of Jesus Christ is no longer effective.

This, then, was the author who, starting for his Egyptian tour at six hours' notice only, tells us that he took no scientific instruments with him; and says, moreover, that he did not want them, as he has methods of philosophical observation overriding all science.

Thus, as to the almost endless series of mathematical and physical problems, in exact number, weight, and measure, contained in the Great Pyramid, this Oxonian graduate merely leant against the monument, with his hands in his pockets, and looking upward along its sides, declares that he got a far better notion of it in that way, than if he had made any number of instrumental and scientific observations; for, by that simple method of merely taking a look, he perceived with the greatest certainty then, there, and at once, that in place of there being any truth in all the unique numbers and mysteriously deep scientific things published about the Great Monument by the Scottish Astronomer-Royal,— the whole edifice throughout all its building was nothing but an ordinary development of ordinary human nature in history. The Egyptians, he says, built the Great Pyramid at the time, and in the manner, they did, merely because they could not help it : it was the only way that occurred to them to build it; there was no purpose in it, and there was no thinking spent upon it.

To argue with such a man would evidently be most hopeless; and I do not specially grieve myself over his aspersions of the Great Pyramid's science, for he has the same remarks ready for all science, and par ticularly for that of Cambridge. Gifted by nature with splendid parts for the study of classical languages, but little or none for mathematics, this individual would, in and by himself alone, have probably acted a dis- tinguished part in the world of *literature*, and would have modestly avoided exposing himself in *science*. But when he went to the Oxford University, and found that his classics alone were enough to gain for him there all the luxurious enjoyments of moneyed life, then that

evil principle of egotism, or selfish pride, infused with
o'er-vaulting rationalism, which enters so copiously
into all large and wealthy human institutions, generally
in proportion to their size, numbers, and rent-rolls, induced him, as a privileged member of the great Oxford
Corporation, actually to boast of his ignorance of, and
perfect incapacity for, numbers of every kind and degree;
and led him on all sorts of occasions to be even provok-
ingly voluble in expressing his contempt for them.*

Hence, when such a one went to the Great Pyramid,
and declared immediately, on his first mere look and his
own *ipse dixit*, and without making any metrical examination whatever, that it did *not* contain anything to
admire or respect in the numerical way out of the ordinary line of unthinking, vulgar, obligatory work—no
matter what any one else had painfully and laboriously
proved by positive mensuration—the only parallel to it
that I know (unless indeed it be the carelessness of the
ante-diluvians before the Flood came upon them), is
that of the starving Red Indian, as he smoked his pipe
unconcernedly, and most contemptuously near the
mouth of a great anthracite coal mine in full and profit-
able steam-working in Pennsylvania. "Indian," said the
missionary, brimming over with sympathy and anxiety
to help the perishing one, "do you understand all this
wonderful proceeding now going on in the country you
used to hunt over?" "Yes," answers the Red-skin, "I
do; Pale-face puts fire under big kettle, and up comes
coal; Indian's plan better, he no trouble to work, he
lie on his back and smoke tobacco all day long."

Or shall I quote a Professor of Greek in another University closer at hand; who, likewise, when he recently

* That such a result need not be brought about, and is not, on *every*
mind that enters Oxford, I need point to no more decisive and instructive
proof than an admirable little book, entitled "Number: a Link between
Divine Intelligence and Human," by the Rev. Charles Girdlestone, M.A.,
late Fellow of Baliol College, Oxford. London: Longmans & Co.

visited the Great Pyramid for a few hours, declined to
make a single measure of its actual facts; and yet, on
returning home, thought himself authorised, in a public
lecture before the Philosophical Institution, Edinburgh,
to condemn most utterly and scornfully all the findings
of those who had; pronouncing them again and again
to be nothing but "nonsense; all super-subtle, transcendental nonsense. He had *not* read any of the books
containing them, and did not intend to; for he never
read any book unless it *smelt right* (whatever that
meant), to begin with."

But that public teacher, in anything else then his
mere Greek verbs, barely rises above sounding brass
and is not so innocent as a tinkling cymbal, so may be
left to finish himself.   Enough, therefore, now, to
conclude this chapter by remarking, that if opposite
extremes sometimes meet, they partly seem to do so in
several of the opinions of the Oxford clergyman first
cited, and the Scottish Astronomer-Royal; though always with a difference.   They both hold, for instance,
that the Pharaonic Egyptians spent no thought on the
design of the Great Pyramid, and built it because they
could not do otherwise at that time; but in the reasons
why,—the Astronomer puts in for the *first*, because
others than Egyptians supplied the high and noble
thought, of which the indubitable numerical traces are
found by all those who look for them in the right way;
and for the *second*, because an influence went forth
by Divine inspiration (as see further in our 4th and 5th
Parts), which compelled the idolatrous and wilfully
Cainite Egyptians, even in spite of themselves, to
perform a prescribed task, for the sacred and prophetic
purposes of the very God whom they had rebelled
against in the beginning of the world; at Babel as well
as in Egypt.

While if the clergyman, again, considers that a new

religion will soon take the place of that of Christ, as hitherto taught by the Churches, almost one and all, so does the Astronomer too.   But with the addition, on the part of the latter, that the new religion will not be any invention of a few clever men, whether of Oxford or any other University, however strong they may be in Greek, or Sanscrit, or any other variety of human school learning; but, after the overthrow which will first take place of all enemies, there will be the establishment by Christ Himself, returned as Universal King, of a larger and more glorious phase of His own blessed Christianity. An advance therefore it must prove for the world in Holiness: to be inaugurated by none less than the Divine Founder of all Christianity, and in perfect con- formity to God's intentions, times, and seasons ap- pointed from the beginning of the world; as indicated in the Scriptures of truth, both of the Old and New Testaments.

The Astronomer, however, asks no one to take his mere opinion.   If the facts which he has still to unfold, do not of themselves work increased conviction of the verity of Divine Inspiration in the Holy Scriptures, and the reality of what is prophecied therein as now shortly to come to pass, neither will, nor should, all the words of hoped for persuasion which he could possibly utter.*

---

* While actually overlooking this sheet at the press, the following most important testimony has just arrived from Switzerland; and being on a post-card, has a certain freedom of publication allowed to it:—

" Monsieur,—Ayant, en 1877, publié une explication de l'Apocalypse, un ami me fit observer que vos remarquables découvertes sur la Gde Pyramide, confirmaient de point en point mes interprétations de la Prophétie; j'en ai pris connaissance, et j'ai pu déjà, en trois con- férences, démontrer l'importance extraordinaire de votre travail scien- tifique.—Je vous prie, dès lors, de me permettre de vous faire parvenir mes deux volumes sur les prophéties,

" Votre très respectueux en J.-Ct.,
" G. Rosselet d'Ivernois.
" Pasteur à Colombier, Canton de Neuchâtel, Suisse.
" 14 Oct., 1879."

Compendium of the Principal and Leading Measures connected with the Interior of the Great Pyramid, *shortly stated. For their application, see Plates VI. to XVII. inclusive.*

ENTRANCE INTO GREAT PYRAMID.

Pyr. Inches.

This is, at present, simply a hole, or doorway, or upper end of a hollow passage-way, inclining thence downwards and inwards. It is situated on the Northern flank of the Pyramid, in a very broken part of the masonry now, at a height above the ground, rudely and imperfectly considered about ..   ..   588·

Distance of the centre of that doorway-hole Eastward of centre of the Pyramid's Northern flank, as between its E. and W. ends ..   .. = 294·

Height of said doorway, transversely to length of the passage-way, of which it is the outer, Northern, end ..   .. = 47·24

Breadth of the same ..   .. = 41·56

ENTRANCE PASSAGE AND ITS FURTHER INTERIOR, DESCENDING PROGRESS.

Angle of descent of floor of the passage, Southwards .. =   26° 28′

Length along that downward, and Southward, slope, from a supposed original Northern beginning of this passage, to its junction lower down with the first *ascending* passage inside the building ..   •..   ..   ..   ..   988·

Thence to Caliph Al Mamoun's broken hole   ..   ..   214·

Thence, chiefly by excavation through solid rock, but still in one straight, downwardly inclined line as before, to the Well's lower mouth ..   ..   2582·

Thence, to the end of the inclined and full bored part of the passage ..   ..   296·

Thence, in horizontal direction to the North wall of Subterranean Chamber ..   ..·   ..   324·

Whole length of said descending Entrance Passage .. = 4404·

Part length, or from " the 2170 mark " in the upper part of the passage, to its falling into Subterranean Chamber.. = 4053·

Bore of passage always rectangular in transverse section, and in the inclined part, as with the door-way = 47·24 × 41·56 inches.

Bore, in horizontal subterranean region ; for height   .. =   36·

                                                   „ breadth   .. =   33·

SUBTERRANEAN, UNFINISHED, CHAMBER.

	Pyr. Inches.
Flat finished ceiling, length East to West .. .. .. =	552˙
breadth North to South .. .. =	325˙

Depth of walls from said ceiling, variously 40 to 160. Floor not yet cut out of the rock, and walls not full depth.

Small blind horizontal hole or passage commencement, penetrating into the rock Southwards, from South wall of this chamber, low down; length .. .. .. =	633˙
height .. .. .. =	31˙
. breadth .. .. .. =	29˙

THE ASCENDING PASSAGE ; (Lime-stone.)

Starts, in an upward and Southward direction, from a point on the descending entrance-passage, 988 inches inside the ancient building; and the first 180 inches of its length is still filled up with fast-jammed granite plugs. The whole length, from the descending passage, up to junction with, and entrance into the Grand Gallery is   1542˙4

Measured angle of the floor's ascent, Southwards .. .. =	26° 8′
Transverse height of the passage bore, now 47 to 59 ; anciently .. .. =	47˙24
Breadths now, in broken state from 42 to 60 anciently .. =	41˙56

GRAND GALLERY ; (Lime-stone.)

ALSO, AND FURTHER ASCENDING.

Length of inclined floor line, from N. to South wall .. =	1882˙
Measured angle of ascent, Southwards .. .. .. =	26° 17′
Vertical height, at any one *average* point .. .. .. =	339˙5
Overlappings of roof, in number .. .. =	36˙
Overlappings of the walls, in number .. .: .. =	7˙
Ramps, height = 21 ; breadth = 20	
Breadth of floor between ramps .. .. =	42˙
Breadth of gallery above ramps ˙.. .. .. .. =	82˙
,, between 1st overlap .. .. .. =	76˙2
,, ,, 2nd ,, ... =	70˙4
,, ,, 3rd ,, ... =	64˙6
,, ,, 4th ,; .. .. .. =	58˙8
,, ,, 5th ,, ... =	53˙0
,, ,, 6th ,, ... =	47˙2
,, ,, 7th ,, ...˙ .. =	41˙4
Great step at Southern end of gallery, vertical height of North edge .. .. =	36˙
length along the flat top, from North to South .. .. =	61˙
Lower and further exit, or South doorway-passage, height =	43˙7
breadth =	41˙4
length horizontally from G. G. to ante-chamber =	52˙5

Upper exit, at top of Eastern wall at its Southern end, height 33 ; breadth 20, nearly and roughly.

ANTE-CHAMBER; (L. S. and Gre.)

		Pyr. Inches.
Extreme length, North to South		116·26
,, breadth at top, East to West		65·2
,, height		149·3
Eastern wainscot, granite, high		103·03
Western wainscot, granite, high		111·80

Granite (density = 0·479, earth's density = 1) begins to be
employed in the course of the length of this room, and
in the *Granite-Leaf* which crosses it, at various distances,
as 8 to 24 inches, from North wall, in floor, and side walls.

Exit passage, horizontal, from ante-chamber, Southward to		
King's Chamber, in granite all the way; length .. =		100·2
height at the North end .. =		43·7
,, South ,, .. =		42·0
breadth .. .. =		41·4
Number of vertical grooves on South wall .. .. .. =		4
Length of each of them .. .. =		107·4

KING'S CHAMBER (Granite).

Structure entirely in granite, form rectangular, length .. =		412·132
breadth .. =		206·066
1st height, floor to ceiling .. =		230·389
2nd height from base of walls to ceiling .. =		235·350

The walls, in 5 equal height courses, and composed of 100
blocks.

The hollow coffer therein; measures given at pp. 137 to 143.

North-air channel, length to exterior of Pyramid .. .. =		2796·
South-air channel .. .. =		2091·
Supposed height of their exits there .. .. =		3972·

The lower parts of these air-channels just before entering the King's
Chamber, are bent at a large angle in the vertical, and the Northern
one is further tortuous in azimuth; so that they cannot be used as
a means of looking through to the daylight sky, from the King's
Chamber,—though they may ventilate it admirably when cleared of
modern obstructions.

The "hollows," or needlessly called "Chambers" of *Construction* above
this King's Chamber, are of the same length and breadth of floor,
but not above 30 to 50 inches high, except the uppermost of the *five*,
which is angular, or gable, roofed.   (See Plate XVI.)

HORIZONTAL PASSAGE TO QUEEN'S CHAMBER.

Length from North end of Grand Gallery, Southward, to the		
beginning of low part of the passage under G.G. floor =		217·8
thence to low portion of floor =		1085·5
thence to North wall of Queen's Chamber =		216·1
Average height of longest part = 46·34, of Southern deep		
part = 67·5; breadth .. .. =		41·15

QUEEN'S CHAMBER; (Lime-stone).

	Pyr. Inches.
Length from East to West	226·7
Breadth from North to South	205·8
Height at North and South walls	182·4
„ in centre of gable ridge of ceiling	244·4
Grand Niche in the East wall; height	183·0
breadth, greatest, below .. =	61·30
„ at 1st overlap .. =	52·25
„ 2nd „ .. =	41·50
„ 3rd „ .. =	30·00
„ 4th „ .. =	19·50

Excentricity of Niche, or displacement of its vertical axis
   Southward from central vertical line of the East wall = 25·000

Air channels exist in North and South walls; but blinded
   anciently inside, by a solidly left, uncut-out thickness
   of 5 inches of stone; and their out-crop on the Pyramid
   flank now, not known.

Wall courses, number of, equally heighted all round up to
   the level of the top of North and South walls.. .. = 6

Additional wall courses in the upper gables of East and West
   walls, not yet examined.

Wall courses, by Mr. W. Dixon, approximately—

1st and lowest, in height .. .. =	36·
2nd from floor, in height .. .. =	34·
3rd „ „ .. .. =	32·
4th „ „ .. .. =	30·
5th „ „ .. .. =	26·
6th „ „ .. .. =	24.

THE WELL; (Lime-stone.)

Enters near North-west corner of Grand Gallery; shaft
   square in bore; measures in length of side of bore .. = 28·

Distance of centre of entrance from the North end of
   Grand Gallery .. .. = 34·

Vertical depth to grotto in the rock, under masonry of
   Pyramid .. .. = 702·

Further vertical depth, with some horizontal distance, to
   junction with the lower part of the entrance passage
   near the Subterranean Chamber .. .. = 1596·

PART III.

NATIONAL WEIGHTS AND MEASURES, ALSO
THOSE OF THE GREAT PYRAMID.

CORRIGENDA

(1.) The length of 1878·4 Pyramid Inches in the Grand Gallery was inadvertently stated in the 3rd Edition to be " at the height marked by a groove"; it should have been " at the height of the first side overlapping."

(2.) The breadth of the top of the niche in the Queen's Chamber was given in the 2nd Edition of this book, and in " Life and Work," by estimation only, at 25 inches, but has since been ascertained, by measure, to be only 19·5 inches, as stated here on p. 224.

(3.) In " Life and Work at Great Pyramid," 1847, the figure of the boss on the granite leaf was made too high. See its correct figure here, on Plate XV.

(4.) In Plate IX. here, the horizontal passage to the Queen's Chamber is far from correctly drawn ; the proper numbers for it are given on pp. 223 & 224.

(5.) In Plates XIV. and XV., the topmost little joint-line at the upper North corner of East wall of Ante-chamber, in a narrow limestone space there, is said by Mr. Waynman Dixon not to exist ; and in Plate XV. it is further said, by the same authority, that the next little joint-line below, in the same narrow limestone space, is drawn too high up by about one-fifth part of the small stone below. I am not aware of the pressing importance of these particular corrections, but announce them as requested.

(6.) I beg to repeat here what I have stated in former Pyramid volumes, that the small-sized drawings of these very limited plates are only intended to show generally whereabouts and to what sort of forms the elsewhere written and recorded numbers of the *measures* apply ;— these measures having been taken on the stones of the Great Pyramid themselves, and corrected afterwards, if necessary, and as described in the volumes of " Life and Work," both for value of the divisions of the scale employed, and for wear, tear, or dilapidation of the stones, so far as that could be ascertained,—before being employed for theory.

PLATE II.

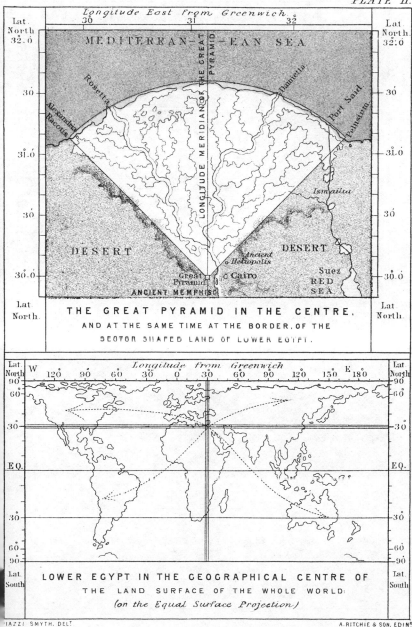

THE GREAT PYRAMID IN THE CENTRE,
AND AT THE SAME TIME AT THE BORDER, OF THE
SECTOR SHAPED LAND OF LOWER EGYPT.

LOWER EGYPT IN THE GEOGRAPHICAL CENTRE OF
THE LAND SURFACE OF THE WHOLE WORLD:
(on the Equal Surface Projection)

PIAZZI SMYTH, DEL.T   A. RITCHIE & SON, EDIN.R

PLATE III

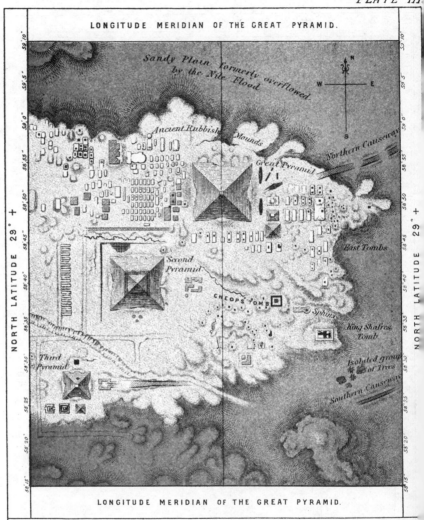

LONGITUDE MERIDIAN OF THE GREAT PYRAMID.

Sandy Plain, formerly overflowed by the Nile Flood.

Ancient Rubbish Mounds

Great Pyramid

Northern Causeway

Second Pyramid

East Tombs

CHEOPS TOMB

Sphinx

King Shafres Tomb

Third Pyramid

Isolated group of Trees

Southern Causeway

NORTH LATITUDE 29° +

LONGITUDE MERIDIAN OF THE GREAT PYRAMID.

SCALE 1/16000 NEARLY.

MAP OF THE PYRAMIDS OF JEEZEH, ON THEIR FLAT TOPPED HILL
OF ROCK, RISING JUST SOUTH OF THE LOW DELTA LAND OF LOWER EGYPT, AND
WEST OF THE NORTHERN END OF THE SINGLE LONGITUDINAL VALLEY, BY WHICH
THE NILE BRINGS ITS WATERS THROUGH 36° OF LATITUDE, FROM THE EQUATORIAL LAKES.

PIAZZI SMYTH, DEL.T   A.RITCHIE & SON, ED.

PLATE IV.

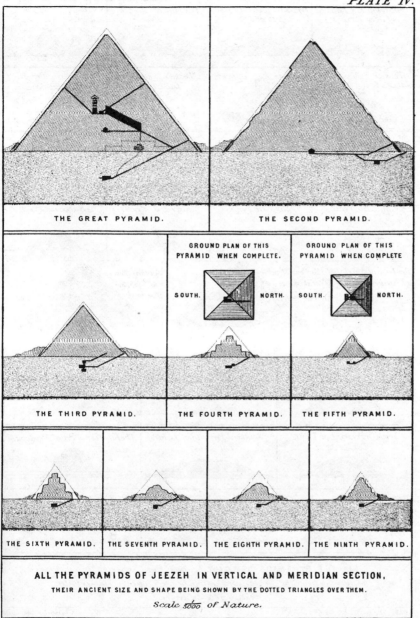

THE GREAT PYRAMID.   THE SECOND PYRAMID.

GROUND PLAN OF THIS PYRAMID WHEN COMPLETE.

SOUTH.   NORTH.

GROUND PLAN OF THIS PYRAMID WHEN COMPLETE

SOUTH.   NORTH.

THE THIRD PYRAMID.   THE FOURTH PYRAMID.   THE FIFTH PYRAMID.

THE SIXTH PYRAMID.   THE SEVENTH PYRAMID.   THE EIGHTH PYRAMID.   THE NINTH PYRAMID.

ALL THE PYRAMIDS OF JEEZEH IN VERTICAL AND MERIDIAN SECTION,

THEIR ANCIENT SIZE AND SHAPE BEING SHOWN BY THE DOTTED TRIANGLES OVER THEM.

Scale $\frac{1}{5000}$ of Nature.

PIAZZI SMYTH, DEL.   A. RITCHIE & SON, EDIN.

PLATE V.

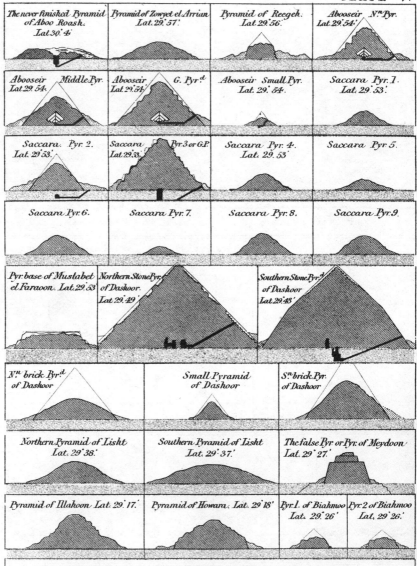

The never finished Pyramid of Aboo Roash. Lat. 30° 4′

Pyramid of Zowyet el Arrian Lat. 29° 57′

Pyramid of Reegeh. Lat. 29° 56′

Abooseir N.ᵗⁿ Pyr. Lat. 29° 54′

Abooseir Middle Pyr. Lat. 29° 54′

Abooseir G. Pyr.ᵈ Lat. 29° 54′

Abooseir Small Pyr. Lat. 29° 54′

Saccara Pyr. 1. Lat. 29° 53′

Saccara. Pyr. 2. Lat. 29° 53′

Saccara Pyr. 3 or G.P. Lat. 29° 53′

Saccara Pyr. 4. Lat. 29° 53′

Saccara Pyr. 5.

Saccara Pyr. 6.

Saccara Pyr. 7.

Saccara Pyr. 8.

Saccara Pyr. 9.

Pyr. base of Mustabet el Faraoon. Lat. 29° 53′

Northern Stone Pyr. of Dashoor. Lat. 29° 49′

Southern Stone Pyr. of Dashoor Lat. 29° 48′

N.ⁿ brick Pyr.ᵈ of Dashoor

Small Pyramid of Dashoor

S.ⁿ brick Pyr. of Dashoor

Northern Pyramid of Lisht Lat. 29° 38′

Southern Pyramid of Lisht Lat. 29° 37′

The false Pyr. or Pyr. of Meydoon Lat. 29° 27′

Pyramid of Illahoon Lat. 29° 17′

Pyramid of Howara. Lat. 29° 18′

Pyr. 1. of Biahmoo Lat. 29° 26′

Pyr. 2 of Biahmoo Lat. 29° 26′

ALL THE PYRAMIDS OF EGYPT, *(other than those of Jeezeh.)*
beginning from the North and going to the South of the country.

SCALE — ₅₀₀₀ OF NATURE.

PIAZZI SMYTH, DEL.ᵗ

A. RITCHIE & SON, EDIN.ᴿ

PLATE VI.

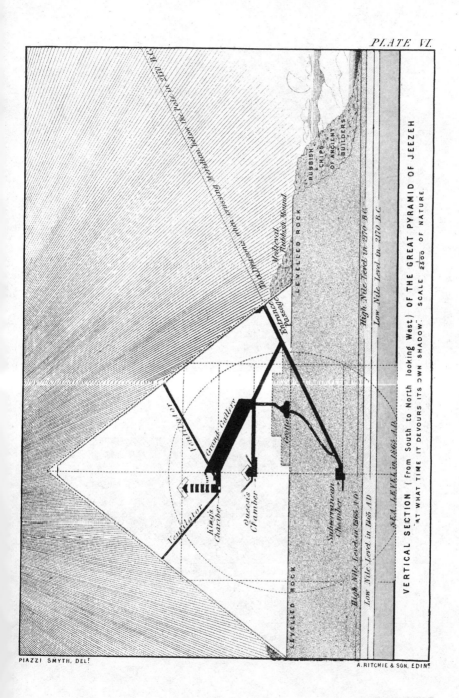

PIAZZI SMYTH, DEL.?

A. RITCHIE & SON, EDIN.

VERTICAL SECTION (From South to North looking West) OF THE GREAT PYRAMID OF JEEZEH
AT WHAT TIME IT DEVOURS ITS OWN SHADOW." SCALE $\frac{1}{2500}$ OF NATURE.

To approximate position of present meridian below N.W. face in 2170 B.C.

Entrance Passage

Vertical Rubbish Mound

LEVELLED ROCK

RUBBISH & CHIPS OF ANCIENT BUILDERS

High Nile Level in 2170 B.C.

Low Nile Level in 2170 B.C.

SEA LEVEL in 1865 A.D.

Low Nile Level in 1865 A.D.

High Nile Level in 1865 A.D.

LEVELLED ROCK

Subterranean Chamber

Grotto

Queens Chamber

Kings Chamber

Ventilator

Ventilator

Grand Gallery

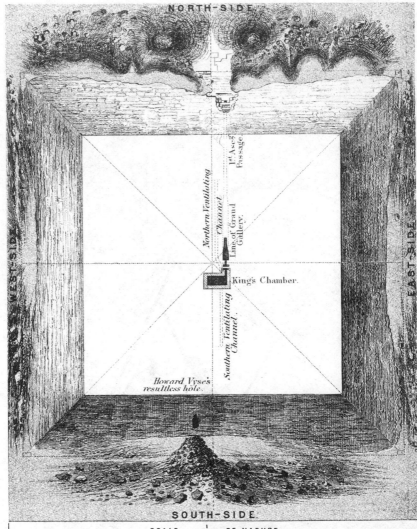

PLATE VII.

NORTH-SIDE.

1st Ascending Passage.

Northern Ventilating Channel.

Line of Grand Gallery.

King's Chamber.

Southern Ventilating Channel.

Howard Vyse's resultless hole.

WEST-SIDE.

EAST-SIDE.

SOUTH-SIDE.

SCALE $\frac{1}{2500}$ OF NATURE.

GROUND PLAN of the GREAT PYRAMID,

TOGETHER WITH ITS HORIZONTAL SECTIONAL AREA AT THE LEVEL OF
THE KING'S CHAMBER.

SCALE OF BRITISH INCHES.

1000	500	0	1000	2000	3000	1000	5000	6000	7000	8000	9000

PIAZZI SMYTH. DEL.ᵗ

A. RITCHIE & SON, EDIN.ᴬ

PLATE VIII.

EXAMPLE of the **CASING-STONES** of a **PYRAMID, SUPER-POSED.**
ON THE RECT-ANGULAR MASONRY COURSES: FROM A PHOTOGRAPH BY P.S. OF THE SUMMIT OF THE 2° PYR.

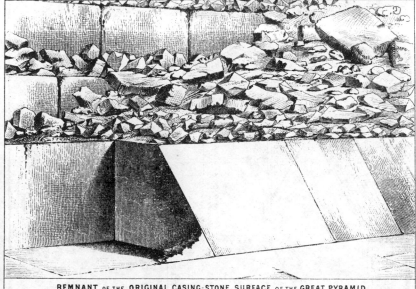

REMNANT of the **ORIGINAL CASING-STONE SURFACE** of the **GREAT PYRAMID.**
NEAR THE MIDDLE OF ITS NORTHERN FOOT. AS DISCOVERED BY THE EXCAVATIONS OF COL. HOWARD VYSE IN 1837.

PIAZZI SMYTH, DEL?   A. RITCHIE & SON, EDIN?

PLATE IX.

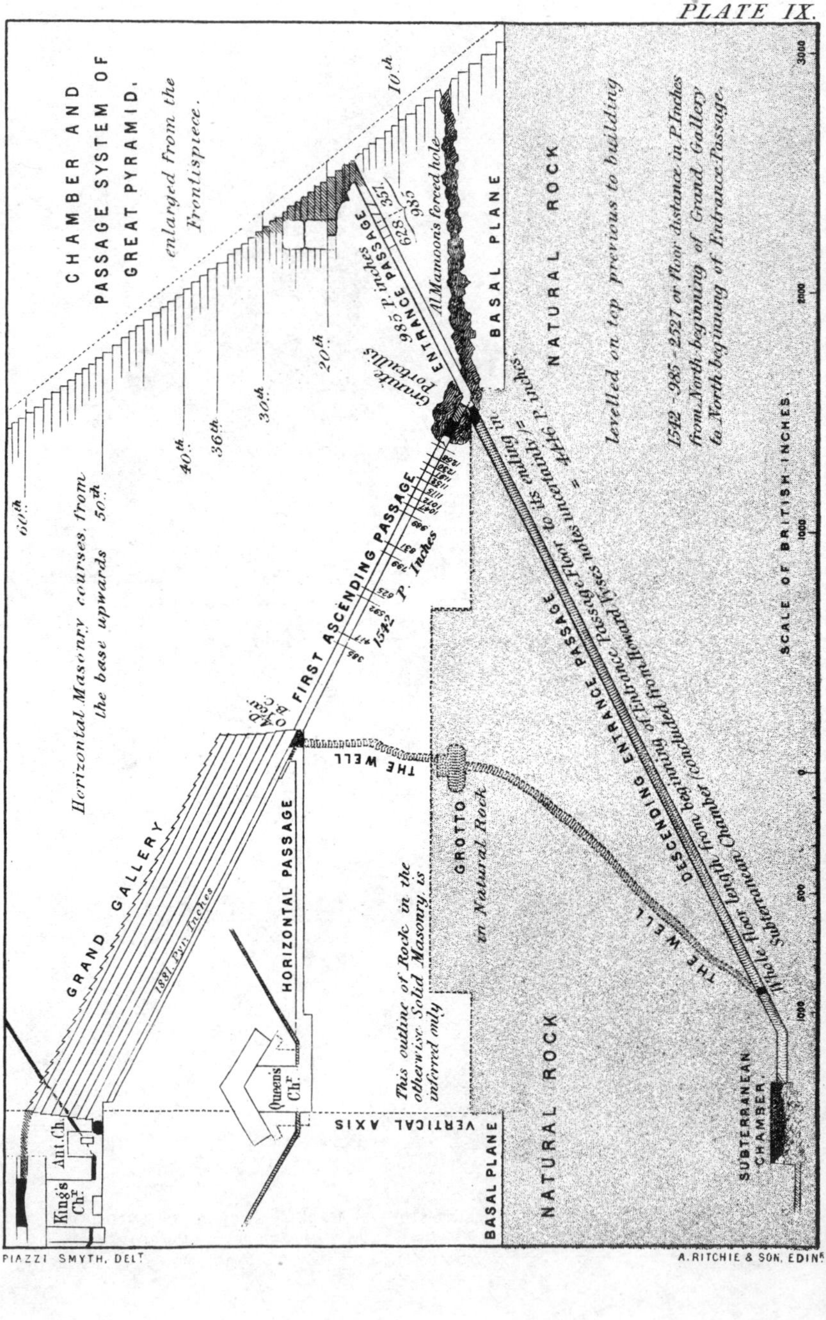

CHAMBER AND PASSAGE SYSTEM OF GREAT PYRAMID.

enlarged from the Frontispiece.

Horizontal Masonry courses, from the base upwards

10th

20th

30th

36th

40th

50th

60th

357.
628.
935.

985 P. inches ENTRANCE PASSAGE

Granite Portcullis

Al Mamoon's forced hole

BASAL PLANE

NATURAL ROCK

levelled on top previous to building

1542 - 985 = 2527 or floor distance in P.Inches from North beginning of Grand Gallery to North beginning of Entrance Passage.

SCALE OF BRITISH INCHES.

3000

2000

1000

500

0

FIRST ASCENDING PASSAGE

P. Inches

1542

OLD GATE

THE WELL

GRAND GALLERY

1881 P.m. Inches

HORIZONTAL PASSAGE

Queen's Ch.r

VERTICAL AXIS

This outline of Rock in the otherwise Solid Masonry is inferred only

GROTTO in Natural Rock

DESCENDING ENTRANCE PASSAGE

Entrance Passage Floor to its ending in uncertainty = 4116 P. inches

Subterranean Passage Floor uncertain

THE WELL

Whole floor length Chamber to Subterranean

NATURAL ROCK

SUBTERRANEAN CHAMBER

1000

BASAL PLANE

King's Ch.r

Ant.Ch.

PIAZZI SMYTH, DEL.T

A. RITCHIE & SON, EDIN.R

PLATE X.

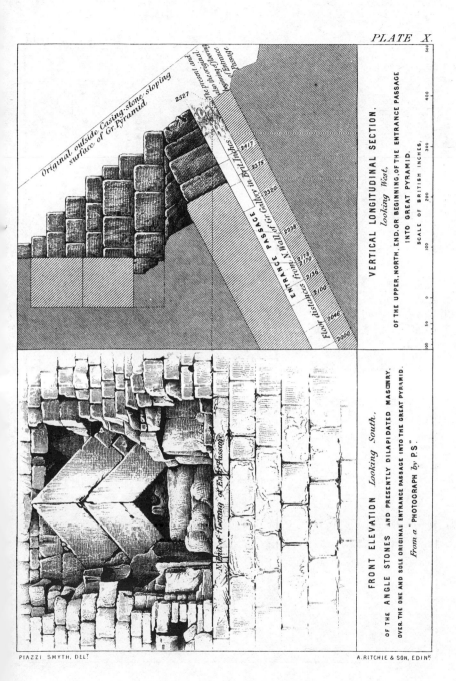

Original outside Casing-stone sloping surface of Gr. Pyramid

2527

The present and also the original floor beginning of Entrance Passage

ENTRANCE PASSAGE, from N. Wall of Gr. Gallery in Brit. Inches

Floor distances in Brit. Inches.

2417
2375
2380
2238
2175
2170
2136
2100
2046
2000

VERTICAL LONGITUDINAL SECTION.
Looking West,
OF THE UPPER, NORTH. END, OR BEGINNING, OF THE ENTRANCE PASSAGE
INTO GREAT PYRAMID.

SCALE OF BRITISH INCHES.

100   50   0   100   200   300   400   500

FRONT ELEVATION *Looking South.*
OF THE ANGLE STONES AND PRESENTLY DILAPIDATED MASONRY,
OVER THE ONE AND SOLE ORIGINAL ENTRANCE PASSAGE INTO THE GREAT PYRAMID.
From a "PHOTOGRAPH *by* P.S."

N. End or Horizon of Entr. Passage

PIAZZI SMYTH, DEL.ᵗ

A. RITCHIE & SON, EDINᴿ.

PLATE XI.

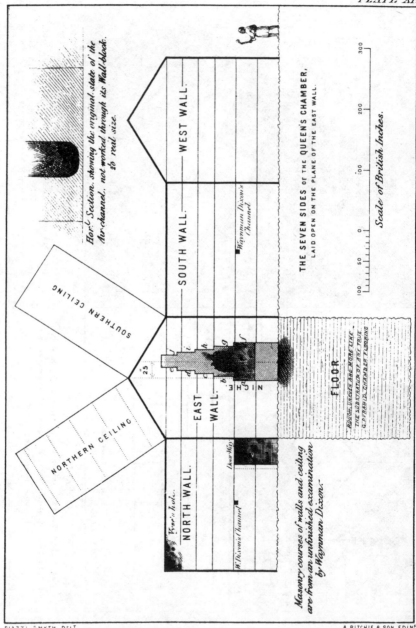

Hor.ᵗ Section, showing the original state of the Air-channel, not worked through its Wall-block. to real size.

WEST WALL.

SOUTH WALL.

SOUTHERN CEILING.

EAST WALL.

NICHE

Waynman Dixon's Channel

25

NORTHERN CEILING.

NORTH WALL.

Visor's hole.

W. Dixon's Channel

Door-Way

FLOOR

ROUGH, UNEVEN AND MORE LIKE THE SUBSTRATUM OF THE TRUE G. PYRAMID CHAMBER FLOORING

THE SEVEN SIDES OF THE QUEEN'S CHAMBER,
LAID OPEN ON THE PLANE OF THE EAST WALL.

100   50   0   100   200   300

Scale of British Inches.

Masonry courses of walls and ceiling are from an unfinished examination by Waynman Dixon.

PIAZZI SMYTH, DEL.ᵗ   A. RITCHIE & SON, EDIN.ᴿ

PLATE XII.

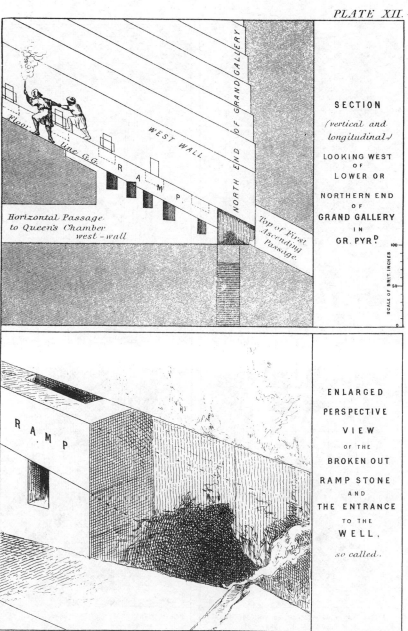

SECTION

(vertical and longitudinal)

LOOKING WEST
OF
LOWER OR
NORTHERN END
OF
GRAND GALLERY
IN
GR. PYR.ᴰ

ENLARGED
PERSPECTIVE
VIEW
OF THE
BROKEN OUT
RAMP STONE
AND
THE ENTRANCE
TO THE
WELL,
so called.

PIAZZI SMYTH, DELᵗ.

A. RITCHIE & SON, EDINᴿ.

PLATE XIII

VERTICAL TRANSVERSE SECTION. LOOKING SOUTHWARD.
FROM THE LOWER, OR NORTH END.
OR BEGINNING OF GRAND GALLERY. GR. PYRᴰ

VERTICAL TRANSVERSE SECTION. LOOKING NORTHWARD.
FROM NEAR THE UPPER, OR SOUTH END.
AND TERMINATION OF GRAND GALLERY. GR. PYRᴰ

100   50   0   100

SCALE OF BRITISH INCHES FOR THE SECTIONAL PARTS ONLY.

PIAZZI SMYTH. DELᵗ   A. RITCHIE & SON, EDINᴮ

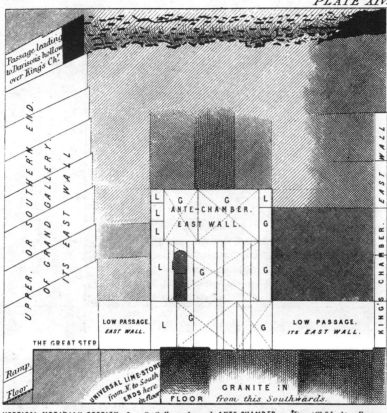

PLATE XIV.

Passage leading to Davison's hollow over Kings Chr.

UPPER, OR SOUTHERN END. OF GRAND GALLERY. ITS EAST WALL

EAST WALL

KING'S CHAMBER.

L | G | G | L
L | ANTE·CHAMBER. | G
L | EAST WALL. |
L | G | G
L | G | G

LOW PASSAGE. EAST WALL. | L | G | G | LOW PASSAGE. ITS EAST WALL.

THE GREAT STEP

Ramp

Floor

UNIVERSAL LIME·STONE from N. to South ENDS here in floor

GRANITE IN FLOOR from this Southwards.

VERTICAL MERIDIAN SECTION *from Gr. Gallery through* ANTE-CHAMBER *to Kings Chr Looking Eastward*

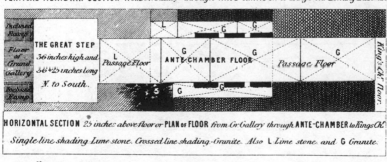

Floor of Grand gallery

THE GREAT STEP 36 inches high and 36+25 inches long N. to South. | Passage Floor | L | G | ANTE·CHAMBER FLOOR | G | G | Passage Floor | G | Kings Chr. floor.

HORIZONTAL SECTION *25 inches above floor or* PLAN OF FLOOR *from Gr. Gallery through* ANTE-CHAMBER *to Kings Chr.*

Single line shading Lime-stone. Crossed line shading Granite. Also L *Lime stone and* G *Granite.*

100   50   0   100   200   300

Scale of British Inches

PIAZZI SMYTH, DELT   A. RITCHIE & SON, EDINR

PLATE XV.

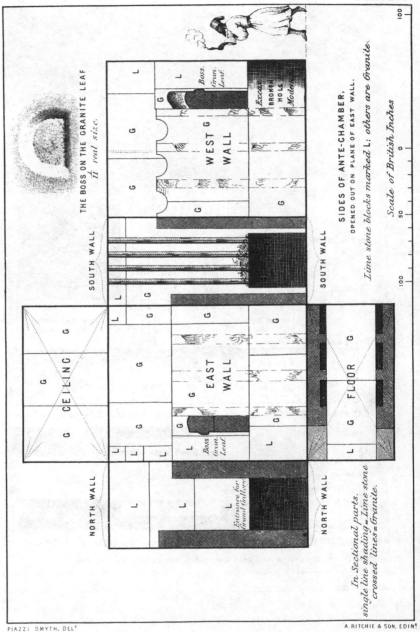

THE BOSS ON THE GRANITE LEAF
½ real size.

SOUTH WALL

WEST G WALL

SOUTH WALL

SIDES OF ANTE-CHAMBER,
OPENED OUT ON PLANE OF EAST WALL.

Lime stone blocks marked L; others are Granite.

Scale of British Inches

100

50

0

50

100

NORTH WALL

CEILING G

G

G

EAST WALL

FLOOR G

NORTH WALL

L

G

Boss.
Gran.
Leaf.

Boss
Gran.
Leaf.

Entrance for
Grand Gallery.

Excat BROKEN HOLE Modn.

In Sectional parts,
single line shading = Lime stone
crossed lines = Granite.

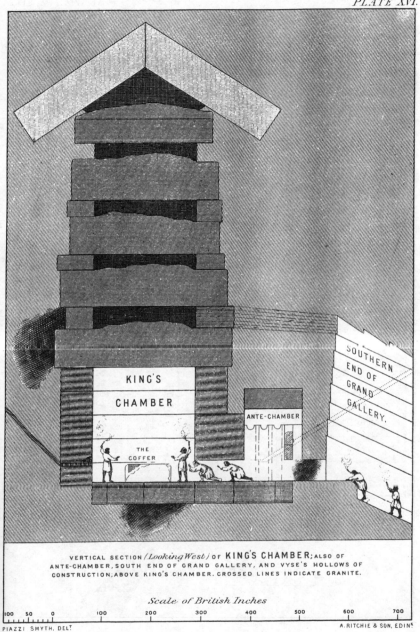

PLATE XVI.

VERTICAL SECTION *(Looking West)* OF **KING'S CHAMBER;** ALSO OF
ANTE-CHAMBER, SOUTH END OF GRAND GALLERY, AND VYSE'S HOLLOWS OF
CONSTRUCTION, ABOVE KING'S CHAMBER. CROSSED LINES INDICATE GRANITE.

Scale of British Inches

100 50 0   100   200   300   400   500   600   700

PIAZZI SMYTH, DEL.ᵗ   A. RITCHIE & SON, EDIN.ᴿ

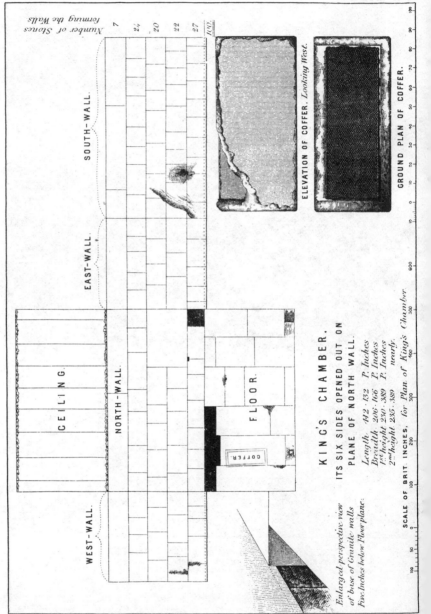

PLATE XVII

Number of Stones forming the Walls

7 24 20 22 27 100

SOUTH-WALL. EAST-WALL. WEST-WALL. NORTH-WALL.

CEILING.

FLOOR.

COFFER.

ELEVATION OF COFFER. Looking West.

GROUND PLAN OF COFFER.

KING'S CHAMBER.

ITS SIX SIDES OPENED OUT ON PLANE OF NORTH WALL.

Length 412·132 P. Inches
Breadth 206·066 P. Inches
1st height 230·389 P. Inches
2nd height 235·389 nearly.

Enlarged perspective view of base of Granite walls Five Inches below Floor plane.

SCALE OF BRIT. INCHES, for Plan of King's Chamber.

PIAZZI SMYTH. DEL.T   A RITCHIE & SON. EDIN.R

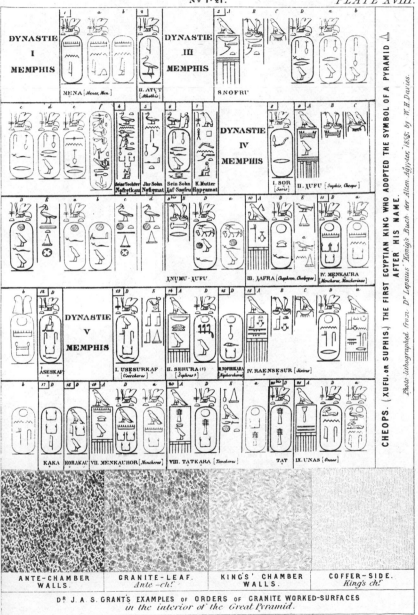

DYNASTIE I MEMPHIS

MENA [Menes, Men.]

II. ATUT [Athothis]

DYNASTIE III MEMPHIS

SNOFRU

Seine Tochter Nofretkau

Ihr Sohn Nofermat

Sein Sohn Kaf-Snofru

K. Mutter Hapramat

DYNASTIE IV MEMPHIS

I. SOR [Soris]

II. XUFU [Suphis, Cheops]

XNUMU - XUFU

III. XAFRA [Chephren, Chabryes]

IV. MENKAURA [Mencheres, Mencherinos]

DYNASTIE V MEMPHIS

ASESKAF

I. USESURKAF [Usercheres]

II. SEHU'RA (?) [Sephres ?]

N. NOFIRIKARA [Nepherchères]

IV. RAENSESUR [Sisires]

KAKA

HORAKAU

VII. MENKAUHOR [Mencheres]

VIII. TATKARA [Tancheres]

TAT

IX. UNAS [Onnos]

CHEOPS. (XUFU, OR SUPHIS.) THE FIRST EGYPTIAN KING WHO ADOPTED THE SYMBOL OF A PYRAMID △ AFTER HIS NAME.

Photo lithographed, from Dr Lepsius 'Königs Buch der Alten Ägypter' 1858; by W.H.Davies.

ANTE-CHAMBER WALLS.

GRANITE-LEAF. Ante -ch.

KING'S' CHAMBER WALLS.

COFFER-SIDE. King's ch.

DR J. A. S. GRANT'S EXAMPLES OF ORDERS OF GRANITE WORKED-SURFACES
in the interior of the Great Pyramid.

A. RITCHIE & SON, DEL & LITH

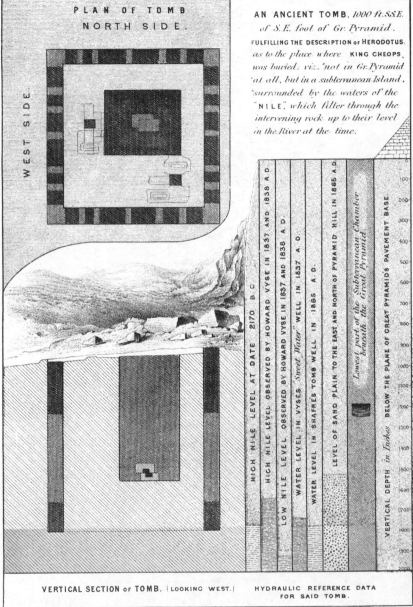

PLATE XIX.

PLAN OF TOMB
NORTH SIDE.

WEST SIDE.

AN ANCIENT TOMB. *1000 ft.S.SE.*
of S.E. foot of Gr. Pyramid.
FULFILLING THE DESCRIPTION of HERODOTUS.
as to the place where KING CHEOPS,
was buried: viz. "not in Gr. Pyramid
"at all, but in a subterranean Island,
"surrounded by the waters of the
"NILE," *which filter through the*
intervening rock up to their level
in the River at the time.

HIGH NILE LEVEL AT DATE 2170 B.C.

HIGH NILE LEVEL OBSERVED BY HOWARD VYSE IN 1837 AND 1838 A.D.

HIGH NILE LEVEL OBSERVED BY HOWARD VYSE IN 1837 AND 1838 A.D.

LOW NILE LEVEL OBSERVED BY HOWARD VYSE IN 1837 AND 1838 A.D.

WATER LEVEL IN VYSES *Sweet Water* WELL IN 1837 A.D.

WATER LEVEL IN SHAFRE'S TOMB WELL IN 1865 A.D.

LEVEL OF SAND PLAIN TO THE EAST AND NORTH OF PYRAMID HILL IN 1865 A.D.

Lowest part of the Subterranean Chamber
beneath the Great Pyramid

VERTICAL DEPTH *in Inches* BELOW THE PLANE OF GREAT PYRAMID'S PAVEMENT BASE.

VERTICAL SECTION of TOMB. (LOOKING WEST.)

HYDRAULIC REFERENCE DATA
FOR SAID TOMB.

PIAZZI SMYTH. DEL.ᵗ

A.RITCHIE & SON, EDINᴿ

PLATE XX.

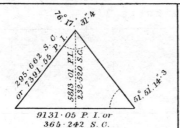

76° 17' 31".4

295·662 S.C. or 7391·65 P.I.

5813·01 P.I.
232·520 S.C.

61° 51' 14".3

9131·05 P. I. or
365·242 S. C.

**DIRECT VERTICAL SECTION OF
GREAT PYRAMID.**

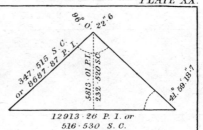

96° 0' 22".6

347·515 S.C. or 8687·87 P.I.

5813·01 P.I.
232·520 S.C.

41° 59' 18".7

12913·26 P. I. or
516·530 S. C.

**DIAGONAL VERTICAL SECTION OF
GREAT PYRAMID.**

EQUALITY OF BOUNDARIES.

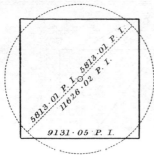

5813·01 P.I. 5813·01 P.I.
11626·02 P. I.

9131·05 P. I.

*Great Pyramid's square base,
and circle with radius =Pyr.⁸ Vert.ˡ height*

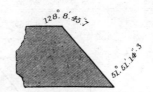

128° 8' 45".7

51° 51' 14".3

**π ANGLES OF CASING STONES OF
GREAT PYRAMID;**
*As affected by its external slope
and horizontal masonry courses.*

$\pi = 3\cdot14159\ 26535 + \&c.$
$= \log.\ 0\cdot49714\ 98726 + \&c.$

EQUALITY OF AREAS Nº I.

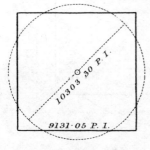

10303·30 P. I.

9131·05 P. I.

*Area of square base of Great Pyramid=
=area of a Circle whose diameter is given
÷100 in the Ante-chamber.*

P.I = PYRAMID INCHES.

EQUALITY OF AREAS Nº 2.

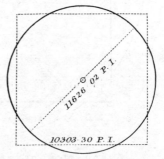

11626·02 P. I.

10303·30 P. I.

*Area of Circle with G.Pyr.ˢ height for radius=
=Area of square whose length of side is given
÷100 in the Ante-chamber.*

S. C.= SACRED CUBIT.

PIAZZI SMYTH. DELT   A.RITCHIE & SON, EDINᴿ

PLATE XXI.

EQUALITY OF AREAS N.° 3.

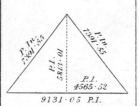

9131·05 P.I.

Direct Vertical Section of Gr. Pyr.ᵈ

Circle with Diameter
Vertᵗ. Height of G.Pyr.ᵈ

Square with side
computed by π.

11626·02 = Ante-chamber length × 100 = Sun's distance from the earth
in terms of the "breadth of the Earth" from Pole to Pole.

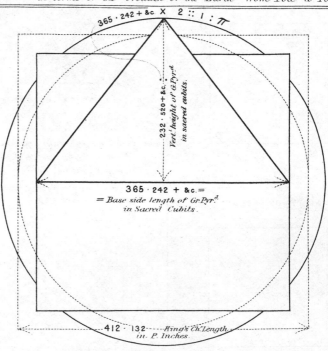

$$365 \cdot 242 + \&c. \times 2 :: 1 : \pi$$

232·520 + &c. = Vertᵗ height of G.Pyr.ᵈ in sacred cubits.

365·242 + &c. =
= Base side length of Gr.Pyr.ᵈ
in Sacred Cubits.

412·132 ····· King's Ch.ᵗLength
in P. Inches.

EQUATION OF BOUNDARIES AND AREAS.

CIRCLES AND SQUARES, INCHES INSIDE AND SACRED CUBITS

OUTSIDE GREAT PYRAMID.

PIAZZI SMYTH. DEL.ᵗ   A. RITCHIE & SON, EDIN.ᴿ

PLATE XXII

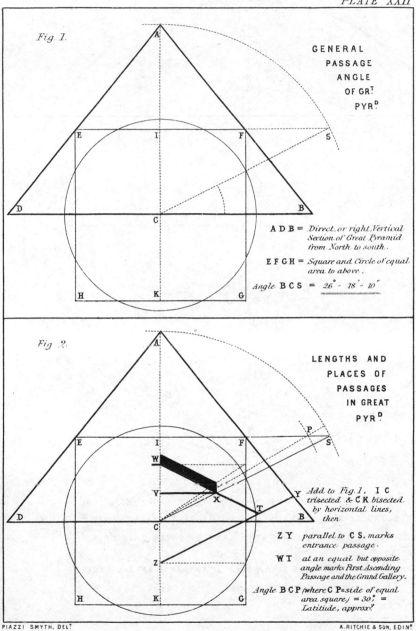

Fig. 1.

GENERAL
PASSAGE
ANGLE
OF GR^T
PYR.^D

A D B = *Direct, or right, Vertical
Section of Great Pyramid
from North to south.*

E F G H = *Square and Circle of equal
area to above.*

Angle **B C S** = 26° · 18′ · 10″

Fig. 2.

LENGTHS AND
PLACES OF
PASSAGES
IN GREAT
PYR.^D

Add to Fig. 1, **I C**
trisected & **C K** *bisected
by horizontal lines,
then*

Z Y *parallel to* **C S**, *marks
entrance passage.*

W T *at an equal but opposite
angle marks First Ascending
Passage and the Grand Gallery.*

Angle **B C P** *(where* **C P** *=side of equal
area square)* = 30°, =
Latitude, approx?

PLATE XXIII

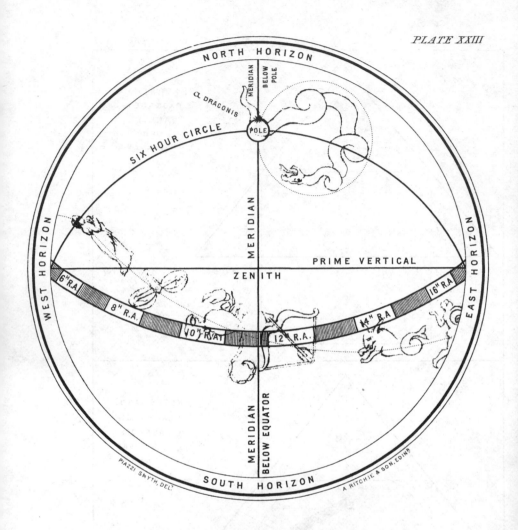

GROUND PLAN OF THE
CIRCLES OF THE HEAVENS ABOVE THE SITE OF THE THEN
UNBUILT GREAT PYRAMID; AT THE ANTEDILUVIAN DATE OF
3440 B.C.
α DRACONIS ON MERIDIAN BELOW POLE, AT ENTRANCE PASSAGE ANGLE;
PLEIADES AND VERNAL EQUINOX NOWHERE VISIBLE.

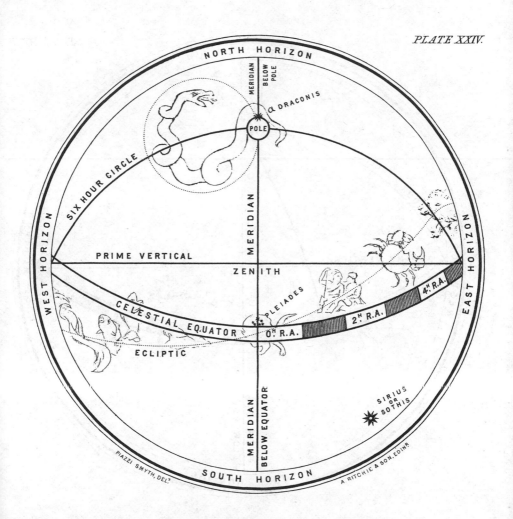

PLATE XXIV.

GROUND PLAN OF THE
CIRCLES OF THE HEAVENS ABOVE THE GREAT PYRAMID, AT ITS EPOCH
OF FOUNDATION, AT MIDNIGHT OF AUTUMNAL EQUINOX
2170 B.C.
α DRACONIS ON MERIDIAN BELOW POLE, AT ENTRANCE PASSAGE ANGLE;
AND PLEIADES ON MERIDIAN ABOVE POLE IN 0ʰ R.A.;
OR COINCIDENTLY WITH VERNAL EQUINOX.

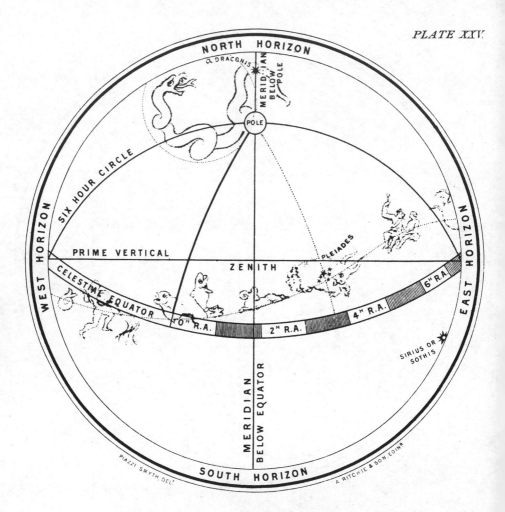

PLATE XXV.

GROUND PLAN OF THE

CIRCLES OF THE HEAVENS ABOVE THE
PRESENT GREAT PYRAMID

IN THE AUTUMN OF

1881 A.D.

α DRACONIS ON MERIDIAN, BELOW POLE, BUT AT SEVEN TIMES EN. PASS. ANGLE;

PLEIADES FAR FROM MERIDIAN, EASTWARD;

VERNAL EQUINOX FAR FROM MERIDIAN, WESTWARD;

BUT THE DISTANCE OF THEIR MERIDIANS APART, INDICATING ON THE PRECESSIONAL DIAL

THE AGE OF THE GREAT PYRAMID.

CHAPTER XI.

BRITISH METROLOGY;

Its High Descent and Pyramidal Bearings.

NOT only has it appeared, we trust, from the previous chapters taken in the whole, that some standards of measure and weight are instruments of instant research and discovery in the Great Pyramid,—but that th੭ best units and standards for the purpose have very remarkably close approaches to certain units and examples of the British system of Metrology. More especially as that system was known in earlier historic ages than our own.

The Very Reverend Bishop Cumberland, D.D., in 1686,* devoting himself for a time to the topic of weights and measures of many nations, is strong upon both its antiquity, usefulness and *learning*. "Learning," says he, "I call this knowledge, because the first constitution of weights and measures, and the reasons and proportions contained in their mutual correspondences, do impart, not only prudent observation, which is learn-

---

* See a small duodecimo entitled "An Essay towards the Recovery of the Jewish (Israelite) Measures and Weights, by help of Ancient Standards, compared with ours of England. Useful also to state many of those of the Greeks and Romans, and the Eastern Nations. By Richard Cumberland, D.D. Ex Iædibus Lambeth, October 12, 1685." I have to thank for the voluntary gift of the above book a namesake of the pyramidally celebrated Professor Greaves, viz. T. Greaves, Esq., Birkenhead.

ing's foundation, but also some elements of geometry and staticks (which are essential parts of its superstructure) and certain mathematical notions which are as old almost as mankind. But," he complains, " such hath been the ignorance and carelessness in these matters, of many intervenient ages, by whose care these things should have been transmitted to us their posterity, that many diligent enquirers, quite despairing, have been of late almost inclined to cast the whole subject into its already prepared grave of oblivion and neglect."

These views of the worthy Bishop of Peterborough, two centuries ago, contain most salutary truth for our own times also; and if we would fully understand the weights and measures of our own land, we must begin, *at least*, with Magna Charta date. For those Metrological Institutions had existed from still earlier times, even the very earliest times known to our literature, an heirloom among the Anglo-Saxon peoples; and a late first-rate American writer, as well as statesman (John Quincey Adams), equally claiming with ourselves to be descended from that ancient Anglo-Saxon stock, but without any necessary prejudice in favour of the wisdom of modern British Parliaments, has expressed a very firm conviction that the most perfect condition of those weights and measures, even including all that was done for them by modern *savants* under the reign of George IV., was, in the earliest known times of Saxon history. Also that such perfection of British metrology connects itself much more with an ancient Royal residence at Winchester, than a modern one in London or Windsor. It may have been earlier still. At all events, the old, long-employed, ancestor-descended system had already fallen into such republican, many-headed confusion in the times of King John, that his then new Charter, to the joy of all men, said that in future there was only to be one standard of measure throughout the land;* while, to render that principle a possible one to carry out in practice, wisdom counselled, and ancient Saxon practice reminded, that grand standards both of length and weight should be immediately constructed, and copies thereof dispatched to all parts of the kingdom.

But what followed?

Those standard measures, if ever made, were lost; no copies were sent to country districts; the Magna Charta lawyers trusted in words only; † and then came a certain very natural consequence.

Practical weights and measures are not only of interest, but essential importance to all classes of the realm : for, as was well said years ago, all the productions of land and labour, of nature and art, and of every concern and condition of life, are bought, sold, or estimated by them. Hence, weights and measures have been very properly defined as the foundation of justice, the safeguard of property, and the rule of right; while the laws of honour peculiarly abhor any fraud in this respect. Yet withal, says the same authority, it is to the common people, in every country, to whom the

---

* " Measures are wanted for two distinct objects, the commercial and the scientific. The wants of natural philosophy have grown up within the last two centuries; while so early as Magna Charta it was one of the concessions to the grievances of the subject that there should be one weight and one measure throughout the land," says the late Lord Brougham's chief educational authority; not knowing, however, that the epoch of Magna Charta, instead of being primeval, is very middle-aged indeed, in the real history of British weights and measures.

† A.D. 1215.   Magna Charta, sect. 35 :—

" There shall be but one uniform standard of weights, measures, and manufactures; that for corn shall be the London quarter."

" Magna Charta," says Dr. Kelly, in his " Metrology," 1816, " points out the quarter of London as the only standard for measures and weights of that time, but we are left to guess of what measure or weight it was the quarter part." What would he have thought, a most acute man of his day, if he could have been informed, before his death, that the desiderated vessel of which the British quarter is the fourth part, is the *Coffer* of the Great Pyramid in the land of Egypt; and that it is still in existence and abundantly measurable, as see back to our pages 154 to 165.

business of weighing and measuring is almost exclusively committed.   Whence, in part, by evident necessity it comes, that weights and measures are *primarily*
affairs of the practically labouring classes of the poor,
and those who with their own hands do the daily work
of the world.

Their weights and measures too, to be fully useful,
must suit the working-men, just as naturally as the
mother-tongue is felt to do in after-life; for who is
there, unless experienced in practical matters himself,
who knows how suddenly and immediately in many of
the constant affairs of the working world, an unexpected
exigency occurs; when, without books, or scales, or
balances, or compasses, the labouring man, whether
sailor or coal-miner, whether agriculturist or engineer,
has to look some natural danger in the face; and his
only hope of plucking the flower, " safety," from the
event, is in his then and there instantly conciuding,
without instrumental assistance, without time for
serious thought or metrical examination, upon a nearly
correct estimate of some measure of weight, or length
of space, or strength of material, or angle of slope,
before the catastrophe arrives ?

So what was the consequence when the restored
king and government of A.D. 1215, having got the rule
of the country once again into their power, did *not* send
the promised standards to every town and village in the
land ?   Why every town and every village began in
self-defence to make standard measures for themselves
in their often very isolated provincial communities.

History of British Weights and Measures from Magna
Charta times to the Georgian Era.

Within a certain range, that was tolerable enough ;
because all those earlier examples *pro tem.* were more

or less closely founded on, or were tolerably representative in some way or another of, the original Saxon
standards; and were named with short, pithy names
derived from the same effective language. But after
that first beginning of going a little astray, then as
civilization progressed, wealth asserted its interests too
powerfully. Whence the tendency arose to substitute
legal deeds, in place of material examples; and lawyers
were always attainable, to frame any number of acts of
parliament to secure rent and taxes being drawn from
the working poor in any and every denomination; but
to prevent their deriving profits from their work, unless
a statute standard was rigidly adhered to by them.

Unfortunately, however, the powers that were, went on
framing their acts of parliament without either defining,
actually making, or in fact identifying any such standard. The taking of practical scientific steps really to
do that, seemed to men of over-refined education in both
classic literature and high mental philosophy, a base
mechanic operation, which their ethereal line of studies
placed them far above the level of. It was a drudgery
they would not submit to; and even up to the other
day (1814), when at last it was impressed on the governing bodies, that, in the material matter of weights
and measures, there must be material standards,—they
grandiloquently appointed a yard, which was to bear a
certain proportion to a second's pendulum of a specially
named and legally described scientific order,—but what
length that pendulum was of, in very fact, they did not
know and did not inquire; for they said "any expert
watchmaker could ascertain that"; and yet up to the
present time neither watchmaker nor philosopher, nor
government official of any kind or degree, has fully
succeeded in that little, but found at last to be a transcendentally difficult, problem.

So the confusion of weights and measures only grew

worse in the kingdom, and the fault was attributed to the wrong parties, or the working men; as when a Parliamentary Committee reported in 1758, that of those uneducated beings, but who had hitherto borne all the toil and burden of the work, "only a few of them were able heretofore to make proper measures or weights; standards were carelessly made by them and destroyed as defective, and the unskilfulness of the artificers, joined to the ignorance of those who were to size and check the weights and measures, occasioned all sorts of varieties to be dispersed through the kingdom, which were all deemed legal, yet disagreed."

Other independent-minded persons, however, ventured to counter-report, and perhaps more justly, that another cause of this confusion was " the prodigious number of acts of parliament, whereby the knowledge of weights and measures became every year more and more mysterious." In 1823 it was stated by Dr. Kelly, in his examination before the House of Lords, " that there had been upwards of two hundred laws enacted without success in favour of conformity, and five hundred *various* measures in defiance of those laws." Both sets of acts of parliament, too, were in opposition to that law of the practical nature of things, which ordains that everything in connection with weights and measures shall be done in direct reference to *material* examples thereof.

The Georgian and William the Fourth Eras.

But, in 1824, a standard yard and a standard pound were at last deposited in the House of Commons; and the Legislature enjoyed the advantage of having a moderately accurate example before them, of the practical thing they were legislating about. This pleasure, however, only lasted about ten years; for in October,

1834, both yard and pound perished in the Great Fire which consumed the two Houses of Parliament.

Then was made another lamentable attempt to get on without any standards at all ; to collect revenue by the threat of a standard, and yet have no standard to refer to.   Lawyers, therefore, had it all their own way in this pleasant fiction ; and in an act of parliament (5 and 6 William IV. c. 63), which passed both assemblies in the following year, " the standards were referred to as if still in existence, and quoted as authorities to be appealed to on every occasion, although they had been actually destroyed a twelvemonth before, and no other standards submitted in their stead."

Both Houses of Parliament certainly *appeared* to have been wholly ignorant of this actual non-existence of the objects on which they were legislating; and Government itself was not aware of the state of ruin and neglect into which certain other standards, more hereditary than legal, had fallen into, in their own Exchequer Office.

In 1742, when some inquiries were set on foot by both the Royal Society of London and the Paris Academy of Sciences, those Exchequer standards (one of them an ell, and the other a yard, of the time of Queen Elizabeth), were then in a respectable condition, and seemed to be treated with attention and care, by the high officers and clerks of the establishment.   But no one had heard of them again for a long interval.   And when their habitation was at length revisited in 1835, to see the only real foundation on which the government of good King William was then legislating, Mr. Baily reports of the then single standard shown to him, the Elizabethan yard,* " that it was impossible to speak of it too much

---

* Since the above was written, an unusually good parliamentary report has appeared, drawn up by Mr. Chisholm, chief clerk in the office of the Comptroller-General of the Exchequer, on " The Exchequer Standards of Weight and Measure"; mentioning a yard rod, a gallon, and two bushels of Henry VII. ; a yard measure and an ell, together with pints, quarts,.

in derision and contempt. A common kitchen poker, filed at the end in the rudest manner by the most bungling workman, would make as good a standard. It has been broken asunder," he writes, "and the two pieces have been *dovetailed* together, but so badly that the joint is nearly as loose as a pair of tongs. The date of the fracture I could not ascertain, it having occurred beyond the memory or knowledge of any of the officers at the Exchequer. And yet, till within the last ten years, to the disgrace of this country, copies of this measure have been circulated all over Europe and America, with a parchment document accompanying them (charged with a stamp that costs £3 10s., exclusive of official fees), certifying that they are true copies of the British *standard*."

These are severe remarks; and yet partly help to answer the noted difficulty which Dr. Kelly found himself confronted with, after all his historical researches up to his own time; viz. that in England there is nothing that has a greater tendency to grow worse, or, curiously enough, more obstinately resists improvement, than weights and measures. Yet the Exchequer itself has indicated the full truth of Mr. Baily's critique, by publishing the Astronomer-Royal's very similar views; first, on the error in the general theory of British legislation on the subject of standards as shown in "the entire apathy on the part of Government towards the matter, whereby it acts only when pressed by popular demands"; and second, the error in the practice of the

gallons, bushels, and troy and avoirdupois weights of Queen Elizabeth, besides several other weights and measures of the early Norman kings, and not regarded as standards.

Of the above Exchequer standards, so called, the yard rod of Henry VII. is that which was expressly stated, in 1743, to have been for a long time disused as a standard; the ell rod of Queen Elizabeth is that which also dropped into disuse between 1743 and 1835; while the yard rod of the same queen is that which was reported on by Mr. Baily to the Royal Astronomical Society in 1835, as horrible in workmanship, and with its length shortened by a dovetail.

British Executive, which is, within its functions, not much unlike the above.

Since then, however, some members of Her Majesty's Government have advanced in metrological knowledge : a new office has been created for weights and measures, furnished with princely apartments, numerous assistants, a large revenue, and placed under a chief, with the title of " Warden of the Standards." Hence too, a gentle current of interest has so decidedly begun to flow towards the subject, that one or two of the oratorical leaders in politics have encouragingly intimated, that when that current shall have become decidedly stronger, they may then find it worth their while to utilise its motive power for their own purposes ; and perhaps at the same time consider what can be done for, or with, our British hereditary weights and measures.

The outbreak of Modern Agitators and misplaced love for the French Mètre.

Too late! too late! for while those politicals were selfishly dallying with their national duties, a mine has been sprung beneath their feet. The merchants and manufacturers of the country, with a section of the scientific men, chiefly of the electrician and chemical stamp, have burst into the arena, and declared that they cannot wait for the slow improvements of Government. The creed that they almost worship consists in " buying in the cheapest, selling in the dearest, market," and making money with the utmost speed !* and as they fancy that the further and indefinite extension of their operations receives a momentary check in some foreign countries, by the different metrological systems there and here,—so immediately, without allowing the

---

* See Mr. John Taylor's work, " Wealth the Number of the Beast."

mass of the population to have a voice in that which is *their* affair, which is as ancient and necessary to them, the people, as their very language and all their other national and hereditary institutions; and without considering whether, by breaking down the barriers between France with Frenchified countries and ourselves, they may not be raising up other obstacles between ourselves as so altered, and Russia, America, and Australia,— they, these new intruders into the metrological scene, are interestedly calling out and loudly demanding that *French* weights and *French* measures shall be instantly adopted by force of law and police from one end of Great Britain to the other. Under pains and penalties, too, of the most compulsory order; and to be enforced at all risks of national resistance by a new and special description of highly paid officials to be appointed for that sole purpose.

In the midst of such a headlong pursuit of mere wealth,—as this unprecedented throwing overboard of the pre-historic possessions of our nation, for such a purpose, would be,—the poor are unfortunately the first to go to the wall. They may have been somewhat curbed and bridled in past times by kings and barons and government servants,—but what is that to the oppression of merchants and mill-masters, of the present generation only, hasting to be rich; and freely sacrificing thereto any patriotic sentiments or historical associations which their mere " hands " may presume to indulge in?

The Committee were indeed told, from the reports of the Astronomer-Royal at Greenwich, and elsewhere, "that the said forcible introduction of foreign weights and measures into Great Britain would be to the *excessively great inconvenience* of 9,999 persons out of every 10,000 of the population, and the gain to the one person in 10,000 only small; and that any interference of Government for compelling the use of foreign measures in the ordinary retail business of the country would be *intolerable ;* that they could not enforce their penal laws in one instance in a thousand, and in that one it would be *insupportably oppressive.*" Yet all the effect that this wise, and truly charitable information produced on the merchants of peace professions but money-making practice was, in the very words of Mr. Cobden, the teacher of Free-Trade, "to look forward to a comprehensive and exact system of inspection, and the establishment of an efficient (*i.e.* a tyrannous) central department to give force and unity to local action." In fact, for a few Englishmen to act in Great Britain, like a German, or even a Russian, army in undisputed possession of a foreign country; and put down at all costs, amongst the British people, any national feelings for certain historical institutions of their own. Or for things which, however they may have been meddled with in petty ways by modern acts of parliament, are still substantially the same as those which the *origenes* of the nation received, no one now knows exactly how, or where, or precisely when ; though every one is aware that we have possessed them for as long as we have been a nation at all; and the mass of our working-people understands the outside, physical world familiarly, intuitively, only in terms of them ; *viz.* of their ancient, hereditary weights and measures.

The late near domination of Great Britain by the French Mètre.

Thus far, nearly, was written in the first edition of this book, published in 1864 ; but now, in 1877, what is the state of matters ?

Well, their condition is surely most passing strange; for, bill after bill has been brought into Parliament,

agitators have been at work throughout the land ; and
men who a few years ago gave the most splendid testimony that to force foreign measures on the British
people would aggravate them to the extent of civil war,
—have now been signing propositions on the other side;
and even assisting in putting up at the Palace of West-
minster, side by side, copies of the British and French
standards of length, as though the Government of
France ruled already over half of the British people ;
—and still the change of weights and measures has
not really taken place yet.

Other renegades, encouraged too by some of the chief
scientific societies in London, have been publishing new
text-books in science for, if possible, all the rising generation of the empire; in which books, though the
authors still condescend to use the English language,
they scorn to be loyal to British authorised weights
and measures ; but speak of everything in the wide
heavens above and broad earth below in the imported
French metrical terms; which they seem to have sworn
together they *will* make the people of this country accept,
whether they like them or not.*   While in the elementary schools which are now springing up under Government School Board management all over the country,
teachers are urged from some secret quarter to take
time, with its *expected* political changes, by anticipation,
and teach all the children within their reach at once the
French weights and measures; or when they cannot do
that, to have some printed representation of the French
system suspended in sight, as though it were soon *going*

---

* In the letters which have appeared in *Nature*, from H.M.S.
Challenger's scientific expedition, carried on at an expense of not less
than £20,000 a-year, for four years together, to the British tax-paying
people, those contemned and much-suffering individuals have the distances
steamed over by their British ship, by means of British coal, described
to them in *kilomètres;* and even a little shapeless piece of chalk,
brought up by the dredge from the ocean-bottom, is defined for size to
British readers by being recorded in minute fractional parts of a *mètre*.

to be the law of the land ;—but yet the change has not been allowed.

More threatening still were the proceedings of the late Gladstonian Government ; for if they did advise Mr. Benjamin Smith to withdraw his Parliamentary pro-French-Metric Bill in 1873, it was under the promise that they would bring in a Bill themselves in 1874-5. They had already, under the headship of the Duke of Argyll in the India Office, introduced the Anti-British metrical system into India, in the most sweeping fashion of thorough-going, red, revolutionists, by arbitrary and unprecedented enactments ;* and now, apparently they contemplated doing the same thing for the British

* I have before me, in a pamphlet printed in Calcutta in 1871, a copy of " The Indian Weights and Measures Act, xi. of 1870 " :—

Head 1, declares, " This act may be called the Indian Weights and Measures Act, 1870, and extends to the whole of British India."

Head 2, declares, as to *Standards* :—
    That the primary standard weight shall be one which "when weighed in a vacuum, shall be equal to the weight known in France as the Kilogramme des Archives."
    That the primary standard of length shall be called a mètre, and shall be a distance on a rod of metal, which, " when measured at the temperature of melting ice, is equal to the measure of length known in France as the Mètre des Archives."
    The unit of measure of capacity shall be a measure containing the equivalents of one French Archives' kilogramme " of water at its maximum density, weighed in a vacuum."

Head 3, treats of " the use of these new weight and measures."
Head 4, of " Wardens " to be appointed to attend them.
Head 5, of " Penalties "; and
Head 6, " Miscellaneous," " Commencement of Rules," " Recovery of Fines and Fees," &c.

Writing now, in 1877, I am told that this system is not yet fully in force, that it never can be enforced without, at least, a frightfully overpowering increase of our army and police; and that, in so far, it has only added another element to the difficulties existing in India before.

What the expense has been on the part of Government, and the complaints of the 300 millions of the Indian people in their own homes at the heartless experiment of a few doctrinaires in London being tried off upon them,—referring them, in the tropics, to the temperature of melting ice, and at the sea-level base of the whole atmosphere to a vacuum, for testing their new and alien standards,—it would be instructive indeed to ascertain ; but will it ever be given out ?

people themselves. But to have extra power wherewith high-handedly to force French weights and measures down the throats of a free British people, Mr. Gladstone not only appointed himself Chancellor of the Exchequer as well as Prime Minister, but must needs also go to the country for a greater Parliamentary majority than that he already had. He went; and now we all know how he fell, his opponents came into power instead ; and are there still in 1879 A.D.

Breadth of the Principles really concerned in the establishment of a nation's Weights and Measures.

This culminating case almost opens up a possible view of whence came the controlling influence which caused all the former bills before Parliament to fail. They were broken without hand ; and no one at the time saw why. Certainly they were not defeated by any visibly sufficient efforts of men. For though *two* good speeches were delivered against the last bill, what were they to the torrent of now fiery, now persuasive, now flattering declamation on the other side, —claiming, too, to be the side of liberal opinion, of modern science, of political advance, of mercantile wealth, of organized industries, of all civilization, and indeed of everything but—nationality, history, and religion.

Those three ought, of course, to be a powerful trio ; but the two latter of them were not invoked in Parliament at all. Indeed they were apparently not understood by either party as belonging to the subject, though they inevitably must be allowed their due place in its discussion before long ; so that whatever political ferment has been made hitherto by the metrological question, it is nothing to what will come.

Just now, or up to the present time, the fight has merely been between the would-be introducers of the new French metric system and the defenders of the British national system as it is.   These latter men will have no change, simply because they dislike all change ; and have been getting on after a fashion, they think, well enough hitherto.   But they cannot expect on those principles to have the victory in future fights always given into their hand : especially when they can neither pretend to prove that the existing British metrology is everything that it might be to suit the advanced wants of the present high state of civilisation ; nor demonstrate that it is still, all that it once historically was, in that primeval time when the system was first given as an heirloom to the Anglo-Saxon race, *before* they came to these islands; and where were they then?

When writers of the Georgian era are found complaining that through all our modern history, our weights and measures had always been growing worse, rather than better,—strange that none of them should have risen to the necessarily resulting idea that at some primeval age, they must have been of strange and even surpassing excellence.   And yet such appears to have been the actual fact.   Nor is it any detraction from much of the intrinsic merits of those early weights and measures to have it now suggested, that they were adapted to one nation only, and were in use by the common people there; whereas the present highly educated class desires a cosmopolitan set of weights and measures for its own ultra-refined use, no matter what their foreign nomenclature, and anti-British origin; for the whole of this idea is, in principle, a mere resuscitation of a cruel fallacy of the Middle Ages ; viz. to try to keep up Latin as a common language among all scientists, whatever language their poor fellow-countrymen might speak.   A suicidal fallacy too; because it was found in

practice infinitely more important, patriotic and charitable, as well as successful in science also, for each
scientific man to have no secrets, no mysteries from the
masses of those poor, but often most religiously minded
men around him ; his own countrymen ; and whose
friendly encompassing of him in that manner, was the
very source of the quiet and leisure and command of
means which he enjoyed for the prosecution of his
peculiar studies. Wherefore the first professor who
gave a scientific lecture in the vulgar tongue in a
German university, was rightly held to have made
almost as precious, useful, and fruitful a reform there,
as that truly Christian priest who began the system of
publicly praying, and reading the Scriptures, in the
language of the people.

There is, indeed, *something* to be said for a little final
regulation of the details of weights and measures
coming from the side of science. But, as for the mass of
the question, the people were in the field before science.
Neither is it in the power of any scientific men, with
all their science up to its very latest developments, to
invent a truly national set of weights and measures,
any more than they can make a national language and
a national people.

The beginning of the Religious Element in Weights and Measures origination.

Before the Flood, according to the Bible, there was
no division of mankind into nations ; *that* was a Divine
appointment afterwards, together with the creation of
their tongues, the appointment of their bounds, and,
there are good reasons for believing, the assignment
of their weights and measures. And if that *was* the
case, a direct and intentional effort by men to subvert
them now entirely, is not likely to succeed, however

many scientists and scientific societies too, even like the wealthy Royal Society of London, put their shoulders to the wheel.

But the French metrical system, in its acts and ambitions, is precisely such an attempt in these days to dethrone the primeval systems of weights and measures among all nations; and make all mankind speak in future in that new and artificial metrological language, invented only eighty years ago in Paris. So that if there is sound reason for believing in the Divine appointment of the ancient systems,—and also, that one of the engines and methods of the final and chief Antichrist in destroying the salvation of mankind, is to induce them to set up *human associations* in the latter day in opposition to the revelations of God's will,*—this new antagonistic metrological system *ought* to have been ushered in under some very evil influence.

How, then, was it brought to the light of day?

By the wildest, most bloodthirsty, and most atheistic revolution of a whole nation, that the world has ever seen. And, attempt to conceal it as they may, our present meek-looking but most designing promoters for introducing that very French system amongst us, cannot wipe out from the page of history, that, simultaneously with the elevation of the metrical system in Paris, the French nation (as represented there), did for themselves formally abolish Christianity, burn the Bible, declare God to be a non-existence, a mere invention of the priests, and institute a worship of humanity, or of themselves; while they also ceased to reckon time by the Christian era, trod on the Sabbath and its week of seven days, and began a new reckoning of time for human history both in years of their then new French Republic, and in *decades* of days, so as to conform

---

* "The Last Vials," Fifth Series, by a Clergyman. 1850. London: Seeley, Fleet Street.

in everything to their own devised new metrical system, but with the old Natural decimal division, rather than to revelation.

Mere human telling, in the first edition of this book, was not enough to remind our British metrical agitators of those fearful things: so they have had them, not sounded again only, but repeated too in fact, within the two years following the Franco-German war, in blood and fire and blackest of smoke throughout the same city of Paris,—when the Commune, on getting for a time the upper hand, immediately re-established the Republican era as against the Christian, and declared war against every traditional observance and respect of man.* While since then, the still more savage and merciless proceedings of the Spanish Commune, wherever it has had an opportunity of rising in their cities, shows that the heart of man, unregenerated in Christ, is no whit better in the present day than at any epoch throughout all antiquity.

Now, perhaps,—and without pursuing any further this historic part of the subject of weights and measures, which, though as old as Cain and Seth, if not Abel also, is by no means yet played out on the stage of time,—it may be given to a favoured, predestined few, to begin to understand, on a figure once used by Dr. Chalmers, what extensive armaments of what two dread opposing spiritual powers may be engaging in battle around our little isle, contending there—on this subject, too, as well as many others—for mighty issues through all eternity. So that not for the force of the sparse oratory emitted in defence of British metrology before Parliament, were

---

* " How did you get on during the German siege ? " I asked of my old friend M. S———n, in Paris, in 1875. " Very well," said he ; " I bought a horse, salted him down, and went on with my work as usual." " And how during the time of the Commune ? " " Oh ! " he replied, as if too well re-membering scenes of danger, " I then fled from Paris, with my wife, my son, and all that I could carry with me ! "

the bills of the pro-French metrical agitators so often overthrown, but for the sins rather of that high-vaulting system itself; and to prevent a chosen nation, a nation preserved through history thus far by much more than the wisdom of its own native rulers, and for more glorious purposes than have ever yet occurred to them,— to prevent that nation unheedingly robing itself in the accursed thing, in the very garment of the coming Antichrist; and Esau-like, for a little base-pottage, for a little temporarily extra mercantile profit, throwing away a birthright institution which our Abrahamic race was intended to keep, until the accomplishment of the mystery of God touching all humankind.

The outcome, and devotion of all that science alone was capable of, in its country's Metrological cause.

A very close approach to the dangerous cliff was made only a dozen years ago, when the Government's own Standards Commission, not content with the yard in place of the inch being pronounced a new British unit, must also propose to drop the original inch entirely; inventing new names for multiples of 1,000 and 2,000 of their new unit yard, to take the place of the British mile; and sub-dividing it again as a concrete quantity into a totally unheard-of set of small lengths, such as neither we nor our fathers ever knew, to supersede and obliterate what have hitherto well served all the smaller, and most of the exact, purposes of Anglo-Saxon life and existence.

But happily the Commissioners' hands were stayed; and one of their number—the highest approach to the ideal of a philosopher since the days of Newton whom this country has produced, the late Sir John Herschel— was presently gifted to see, that of all the various length-measures now on the statute-book, the inch (which was then in such imminent danger) is by far the most really important; because, not only was it the true and original unit and source of almost all the others, but he found it to be possessed also of cosmopolitan excellencies fitting it for the use of all the nations of the world.. This idea too seemed continually to grow in Sir John Herschel's mind. For, through the inch, and water, he perceived that all the hereditary British weights and measures might be easily made (once again perhaps) most scientifically earth-commensurable ; and without the popular value of any of the chief units or standards, or even their names being interfered with.

That grand principle, too, of earth-commensurability, or that there should be a complete and harmonious scale of round, and even, numerical relations connecting the small units employed by man in his petty constructions on the earth, with the grander units laid out by the Creator in the sky, Sir John Herschel stood up splendidly for: and argued and wrote for the glorious idea really belonging, and to have belonged of old, to British metrology ; but in vain ! His colleagues on the Standards Commission could see no beauty nor desirability in that which he esteemed so highly : unless it was those of them who claimed something of the same earth-commensurable principle, though in a less perfect form, for the newly invented French mètre : and *they* wished to abolish the entire and ancient British system. So after doing all that he could to convince, demonstrate, persuade, with the effect only of finding that the majority were determined to sacrifice everything British to France, he took the only final course for a great and honest man to take—he gave up what had been an honour to fifty years of his life, his place at the Standards Commission, his prospects of power or influence in government appointments,—and went out from amongst them all, alone. Lowered, perhaps, in the eyes of time-servers; but raised in his own conscience, and nobly nerved to carry on the battle single-handed, in the open world outside, against the pro-French metrical mania of the day. That mania, a strange intellectual disease which Sir John Herschel (the equal to whom, not Cambridge herself could show at the greatest of all competitive mathematical examinations) deemed not only anti-national, but, in spite of all that is so frequently said for it, not of the highest order of science either.

This was a case indeed of a scientist who would willingly suffer in place, power, and worldly social dignity, for opinion; and did so:—a man, therefore, in whom a great nation might trust when any dire emergency should arise; and who, when the last pro-French metrical bill was about to be urged before the House, came to the defence of his country's cause with the following letter to the Editor of the *Times* :—

" Sir,—

"As Mr. Ewart's Bill for the compulsory abolition of our whole system of British weights and measures, and the introduction in its place of the French metrical system, comes on for its second reading on the 13th proximo, I cannot help thinking that a brief statement of the comparative *de facto* claims of our British units and of the French on abstract scientific grounds may, by its insertion in your pages, tend to disabuse the minds of such, if any, of our legislators who may lie under the impression (I believe a very common one among all classes) that our system is devoid of a natural or rational basis, and as such can advance no *à priori* claim to maintain its ground.

" *De facto*, then, though not *de jure* (*i.e.* by no legal definition existing in the words of an act of parliament, but yet practically verified in our parliamentary standards of length, weight, and capacity as they now exist), our British units refer themselves as well and as naturally to the length of the earth's polar axis as do the French actually existing standards to that of a quadrant of the meridian passing through Paris, and even in some respects better, while the former basis is in itself a preferable one.

" To show this I shall assume as our British unit of length the imperial foot; of weight the imperial ounce; and of capacity the imperial half-pint; and shall proceed to state how they stand related to certain prototypes, which I shall call the geometrical ounce, foot, and half-pint; and shall then institute a similar comparison between the French legally authenticated mètre, gramme, and litre in common use with their (equally ideal, because nowhere really existing) prototypes supposed to be derived from the Paris meridian quadrant, distinguishing the former as the practical, the latter as the theoretical, French units.

" Conceive the length of the earth's axis as divided into *five* hundred million equal parts or geometrical inches.

" Then we will define :—1. A geometrical foot as twelve such geometrical inches ; 2, a geometrical half-pint as the exact hundredth part of a geometrical cubic foot ; and, 3, a geometrical ounce as the weight of one exact thousandth part of a geometrical cubic foot of distilled water, the weighing being performed, as our imperial system prescribes, in air of 62° Fahr., under a barometric pressure of 30 inches.

" In like manner the theoretical kilogramme and litre of the French are decimally referred to their theoretical mètre on their own peculiar conventions as to the mode of weighing.

" This premised—(1) the imperial foot is to the geometrical in the exact proportion of 999 to 1,000 (nine hundred and ninety-nine to a thousand), a relation numerically so exact that it may be fairly considered as mathematical ; and (2) and (3), the imperial half-pint and ounce are, each of them, to its geometrical prototype as 2,600 to 2,601.

" Turn we now to the practical deviations from their theoretical ideals in the case of the French units. Here, again (1), the practical mètre is shorter than its theoretical ideal. The proportion is that of 6,400 to 6,401. The approximation is, indeed, closer, but the point of real importance is the extreme numerical simplicity of the relation in our case, more easily borne in mind, and more readily calculated on in any proposed case. (2) and (3). Any error in the practical value of the mètre entails a triple amount of aliquot error on the practical kilogramme and litre, so that, in the cases of these units, the proportion between their practical and theoretical values is not that of 6,400 to 6,401, but of 2,133 to 2,134. Here, then, the greater degree of approximation is in our favour ; and it is to be observed that in our case this triplication of error does not hold good, since, by a happy accident, our standard pound has been fixed quite independently of our standard yard, and our gallon is defined as 10 lbs. of water.

" I am, Sir, your obedient Servant,
" J. F. W. HERSCHEL.

" COLLINGWOOD, *April* 30, 1869."

This is very clear so far : but its able author did not go far enough. For while his grand fountain and source of earth-commensurability for the British measures was based, even by him, upon, not the foot, which he ultimately used, but the *inch*, being an evenly earth-commensurable measure, and by the particular number of *five* hundred millions of them,—yet he afterwards drops out of view both the inch, the *five* times of so many parts, and says nothing about his new *cubit* standard, which he was at that very time proposing for the British nation, and prescribing that it should consist of 5 × 5 of those inches, in place of the nation's present yard of thirty-six inches. Nor does the exceedingly eminent astronomer attempt to show that either the earth-commensurability or the terrestrial fiveness of the British inch was anything more than accidental. At all events, he does not explain how, or when, or through what, or by whom, that unit first came about. And though he alludes to English history as far back as any printed acts of parliament may extend, he shows no faith capable of tracing the fortunes of our nation back, and still further back, even up to those dim periods of primeval story where the Bible is the only book worth consulting.

Perhaps it was well, though, that Sir John Herschel stopped where he did : for time is required to enable mankind at large effectually to receive the whole of any very new idea ; and had he, the most brilliant representative of modern exact science, gone on further still, and been the propounder of the Great Pyramid Divinely inspired source of the cosmic wisdom so long latent in our ancient measures : and announced that they had been monumentalized by Palestinian Shepherd Kings in the early Siriad land before history began, but yet in the most perfect earth and heaven commensurability, and in a manner never known to the subsequent profane Egyptians ;—the sceptical modern world would hardly have consented to believe, but that the excellencies of such a system were Sir John Herschel's own transcendent inventions ; and had arisen much more through *his* brilliant grasp of modern academical science, than by any simple readings in that primeval stone-book of Revelation which still stands on the Jeezeh hill, ever open, though hitherto illegible to all mankind.

But for John Taylor, who never pretended to be a scientific man, to propound the grand idea ;—and for the Scottish Astronomer, with scarce pay enough to exist

upon, and merely a few old, worn-out, instruments, and
one new but only half-completed one (though in a so-
called Royal Observatory, but of an ancient kingdom
treated very lightly now in London Government offices),
at his hand both for professional work, and to follow up
the Great Pyramid clue—was, and is, quite a different
matter.   Such plan was, indeed, hardly other, than to
let the stones of the Great Pyramid themselves cry out
to a heedless generation.

And now they are beginning to appeal to, and notably
moving as well, the millions of Anglo-Saxons in the
United States of North America ; and even more fervidly
than those of Great Britain.

Ancient Anglo-Saxon Metrology in America declares for its Pyramidal, as well as Biblical, derivation.

The same almost unexplainable activities of a particular class of revolutionary agitators have of late been
troubling the people of the United States, as well as
those in England ; and trying to induce them, in an
unguarded moment, to throw away their, as well as our,
birthright of ages, in their hereditary and traditional
weights and measures, and to adopt the newly invented
measures of France instead.   But now, at last, the
people there are getting their eyes open to the real nature
of the change which it was proposed they should make;
and how do they express themselves upon it ?

Following a pamphlet recently (August, 1879) published in Cleveland, Ohio, by Mr. Charles Latimer,
Chief Engineer of the railway there,—he finds that
the people of the United States are not for the change;
nor the Government thereof; nor are any reasons for
the said change adduced, that will bear the light of day.

" If we look abroad," says he, " we can see no evidence of decay in our civilization, or prosperity, or dimi-

nution of our business, because we have not adopted
these French measures. Certainly our Centennial
exhibited a most wonderful spectacle; and did we
notice that the French were in advance of us? Is
their flag seen in every port on the face of the globe,
because of the superiority of their measures? Is not
the Anglo-Saxon world (the United States and Great
Britain) in advance to-day? What superiority or advantage can the French point to on account of their
system?"

Then seizing happily the *religious* thread of the
matter, Mr. Latimer exclaims, to the Boston Society of
Engineers he was then addressing, and who had very
nearly been inveigled a few days before into petitioning
Congress to make the adoption of French measures
compulsory over the whole United States, "Gentlemen," he exclaimed, "you may rely upon it that these
pilgrim ancestors of yours are not resting easily in
their graves on account of your action. They were
sticklers for Magna Charta; they loved just weights and
measures; and the words of John Quincey Adams,
delivered in 1817, are just the words they would give you
now. I beg you not to make the mistake of taking the
advice of the young men (like those who surrounded
Rehoboam), and ignoring the counsel of your fathers.
Think for a moment. This French system came out of
the 'Bottomless Pit.' At that time and in the place
whence this system sprang, it was hell on earth. The
people defied the God who made them; they worshipped the Goddess of Reason. In their mad fanati-
cism they brought forth monsters—unclean things.
Can you, the children of the Pilgrim Fathers, consent to
worship at such a shrine, and force upon your brethren
the untimely monster of such an age and place?

"Surely not. Say rather, 'Oh! my soul, come not
thou into their secret.'

" It is true indeed that our weights and measures in the present day require some remodelling; but how shall it be done ? Not by uprooting all our traditions—cutting ourselves loose from the past. No, we must come back to the perfection of the long past of sacred history; of that religion which proves that our race is not the result of a spontaneous natural development, but that man came from his Maker a living soul.

" But where shall we find such perfection?

" I answer," continues Mr. Latimer, " in the Great Pyramid of Jeezeh. For within that grand primeval pillar of stone have been found the standards of weights and measures, earth-commensurable, and so assimilated to our own ancient and hereditary system, that it does seem as if the Almighty Himself had given them to us as an inheritance, to be kept precisely for the emergency of the present day and hour. And I beg that our American fellow-citizens will most carefully examine into this subject, deeply worthy of their attention.

" Shall we indeed find our weights and measures there? I can confidently answer," says the desecndant of Hugh Latimer, " that they are there. The inch is there ; the yard is there ; the cubit or arm of 25 inches is there ; our year is there ; our Sabbath is there ; Christ is there ; our past, our present,—yea, perhaps our future.

" But let no man judge for you in this matter. The subject is too deeply important, indeed too vital to our nationality. Let every citizen study for himself."

Now this point which the children of the Pilgrim Fathers in America have just arrived at, is exactly that which we are about to essay in the next four chapters. But it is proper, before we begin upon them, to confess and point out to Great Britain, that the United States are in a remarkable position of advantage in this matter ; for they have the figure of the Great Pyramid

of Jeezeh stamped on the reverse of their National seal ;
as thus alluded to by Mr. Latimer :—

"When a man or a nation adopts a seal, it is understood that the most significant of all emblems, for them,
is placed thereon.   We look to the seal to give us the
clue to the origin or genealogy of the wearer or owner.
And if 'there is a Divinity that shapes our ends, rough-
hew them how we may,' surely a Divinity directed the
hand and inspired the mind that wrought our seal, that
of these United States,—a Pyramid unfinished, with
the all-seeing eye (set in the now invisible, New Testa-
mental, topmost corner-stone) above it.   Reminding us
perchance, of the rock whence we were hewn, and of
that Omniscience which has guided us and brought us
to our present glory and honour as a nation ; reminding
us too, that we must *look* to that wonderful monument
of stone for our origin, our history ; indeed our weights
and measures.

"What other nation has such a seal ?   Will the
Great Pyramid speak to those whose measures are not
there ?   The Pyramid speaks in inches.   Will this be
intelligible to those who have thrown away their
ancient traditional birth-right, destroyed their old
measures,—and make it a penal offence now, for their
sons to use any other than the French metrical
system ? "

In this spirit then, we are to examine, what the
Great Pyramid weights and measures, really, truly and
practically, are.

CHAPTER XII.

Pyramid Capacity Measure ;

And the Coffer's Great Pyramid authenticity.

THE grand standard of *capacity* in the Great Pyramid, as already stated, is given by the contents or internal cubical measure, of the granite COFFER at the further, or western, end of the King's Chamber; and that, the final and crowning apartment of the whole of the interior of our Earth's most gigantic monument of stone.

But the said coffer is loose, isolated, standing on a flat floor without any guide-marks to show how it should be placed, and without the smallest hindrances (except its prodigious weight) to prevent it, in its present lidless condition, being pushed about anywhere, even through the doorway, down the long passages, and out of the Pyramid altogether, *except* for the contraction of one passage-way, at one particular point; viz. the first ascending passage at its lower commencement.

Even that fact too was recently disputed, for some one had said, in spite of my measures in "Life and Work" to the contrary, that there was a quarter of an inch to spare. But Dr. Grant of Cairo, accompanied by Mr. Waller, a medical man of the same place, specially looked into that matter in December, 1873 ; and settled it there and then by direct and immediately successive measures, with the same scale on both the passage breadth at the indicated place, and the breadth of the coffer-vessel; Dr. Grant reporting the case as follows:—

"The result of my measurement confirms yours : viz. the coffer in the King's Chamber, although turned straight into the axis of the first ascending passage, could not have passed the *whole* way along it.

" LOWER END OF ASCENDING PASSAGE, MEASURED CLOSE TO NORTH
END OF PORTCULLIS, IN BRITISH INCHES.

Breadth from East to West, across top, or North edge,
 sensibly the same as the breadth of the passage
 itself at that point   ..   ..   38·38
Breadth across middle   ..   ..   38·44
Breadth across bottom, or South edge   ..   ..   ..   38·12

" COFFER IN KING'S CHAMBER.

Breadth of North end   ..   ..   38·62
Breadth of South end   ..   ..   38·75

"These," says Dr. Grant, "are my measures, and I can vouch for their accuracy *within* one fourth of an inch."

That being the case, the coffer could not have been introduced by the regular passage-way leading to the King's Chamber, neither can it be taken out that way now, on the further account of the portcullis plug still *in situ.* But might it not be got out by passing it through Al Mamoun's forced hole in the masonry to the west of the granite plug ?

By dint of immense exertions, on account of the coffer's weight, and the confined nature of the spaces through which it must be moved, it might be done.

Then in that case, why may not the real coffer have been taken away long ago, and the present one be a spurious affair of modern introduction ?

If the present coffer *had* been so introduced, the introduction must of course have been since Al Mamoun's day ; and would have been so serious a labour, that we should have been certain to have heard something about it ; over and above that such labour would have been in the way of rebuilding, refurnishing, restoring, and benefiting the Great Pyramid ; and that is a totally unprecedented thing within the last 3,000 years.   Depredations in plenty there have been up to the present hour, but no restorations.

There are, however, fortunately, far more cogent reasons to guide us, in a series of innate features of scientific measurement, never appreciated by Egyptians themselves, nor Greeks, nor Romans, nor Arabs, nor even any Europeans until now,—yet evidently, from the exactness with which these features were executed at their original date, and their many confirmations and re-confirmations of each other, they were *intended* by the ancient architect. Intended moreover for a further very necessary purpose; for though the coffer as a capacity measure is larger than anything now on the British Statute-book, being indeed *four* times the size of the *quarter* which is at the head there,—yet one, single *coffer* measure is a very small thing to set before the whole world, and ask all nations to accept it as a standard in preference to any other box or cylinder, or other shaped measure which they might have already made, or be thinking of making, for themselves.

But all this difficulty was perfectly foreseen by the inspired architect, as well as all the possible questionings as to the authenticity and contemporaneousness of the vessel with the building of the Great Pyramid, after 4,000 years should have passed over its head, and a fifth thousand had begun. Therefore it was that he identified the coffer by certain rather abstruse, yet positively identifiable, scientific features with the King's Chamber in which it is placed; and that chamber, the most glorious hall that has ever yet been constructed in polished red granite, with the enormous mass of the Great Pyramid itself; and that building with the sector-shaped land of Lower Egypt; and Lower Egypt with the centre of the inhabited land-surface of the whole world. So that, small though the coffer may be, in itself, there cannot be another vessel of such central importance in the eye of Nature, and to the whole of mankind also, when explained.

But who is to explain it?

Evidently it requires some one who has been favoured with wisdom. Others have seen and despised it, from Caliph Al Mamoun down to the uproarious visitors at the opening of the Suez Canal; but we have been already told in Holy Scripture that there are things which, though absolutely inscrutable to the world at large, yet nevertheless the *wise* shall understand them. And if the chief explanations which I am now about to quote, have been furnished by Mr. James Simpson, known only as a young bank clerk in Edinburgh, and who never had the advantage of University education,— I care not for the world's objections,—he *has* been favoured with peculiar wisdom from on high, and has been privileged to throw upon this ancient subject a light it never enjoyed before, within the history of all civilised times.

But let us come to the point and the proofs.

The Size of the Coffer, and its Pyramid Connections thereby.

For the full measures of all the particulars of the coffer, the reader must be still referred to the several pages containing them in Chapter VIII. But we may consult his convenience by repeating the chief mean results of them here,—as thus :

OUTSIDE MEASURES OF THE COFFER IN PYRAMID INCHES.

Length, from 89·92 to 89·62, corrected for concavity of sides.
Breadth, from 38·68 to 38·61   „   „
Height, from   41·23 to 41·13   „   „

INSIDE MEASURES OF THE COFFER IN PYRAMID INCHES.

Length, 77·85, supposed to be true within half a tenth of an inch.
Breadth, 26·70,   „   „   „
Depth, 34·31,   „   „   „
Thickness of bottom   ..   ..   .. = 6·91 Pyramid inches.
Thickness of sides ..   .. = 5·98   Do.   do.

Now all these numbers are necessary to be kept in mind, for they have all a part to play in the proofs to come; and from the manner in which they are given, it will be seen that I have so far neglected the ledge cut out. I *have* done so; have in fact virtually filled it up; as indeed the mere overlooking it, is quite enough to bring about; and as evidently should be done by the wise, when they thereby obtain what must have been the original form; and which, in all its apparent geometric simplicity, is yet fraught with manifold design.

We have already shown, and Professor H. L. Smith, of New York has independently confirmed, with regard to the coffer, taken in and by itself, that—

$$\left.\begin{array}{l}\text{Exterior cubic size} \ . = 142{,}316 \\ \text{Interior cubic contents} \ . = 71{,}317\end{array}\right\} = \left\{\frac{2}{1}\text{ nearly.}\right.$$

$$\text{Also that, }\left.\begin{array}{l}\text{Sides of coffer, cubic size} \ . = 47{,}508 \\ \text{Bottom of coffer, cubic size} = 23{,}758\end{array}\right\} = \left\{\frac{2}{1}\text{ nearly.}\right.$$

And these relations, so like the duplication of the cube problem among the Greeks,* are found in a vessel of

* The Rev. Henry Morton, of St. Stephen's Rectory, South Shields, brings out extremely well in his paper in "Life from the Dead" for March, 1877, that the duplication of the cube, from including an incommensurable, was just as endless a disputation as squaring the circle, among primitive men; and it is so among modern men also, when imperfect in their mathematical education. Hence, when the people of Athens, decimated by a dreadful pestilence, applied to the Oracle of Delphi to stop it—and of course the oracle only required time enough for the pestilence to, stop itself and then claim the credit for the Delphian false god—he, the oracle, set the people upon the problem of how, exactly to duplicate the cube of the pedestal of that god's statue. Wherefore, in that day, 1,700 years after the Great Pyramid's foundation, and its double practical accomplishment of a variety of the duplication problem in the coffer—the Delphian Oracle was sage enough to know the difficulty of the case, and the people of Athens were not clever enough to solve it in any finite time.

The peculiar drift of the oracle in gaining time reminds of a case described by the Rev. Dr. Moffat in Bechuana Land, in South Africa. The country was perishing from drought, and the people applied to their atheistical witch rain-maker to stop it. He promised certainly to do so if the people brought him a full-grown baboon, without spot, blemish, or injury of any kind. Now, the said baboon being one of the most active and wary of animals, and roaming over the most inaccessible rocky summits of the hills, gave the unlearned South African savages just as time-consuming a problem as the duplication of the cube was to the intellectual Athenians.

strict geometrical figure, without carvings or any other adornment than exquisitely planed, and almost true, and *smooth* surfaces, as see the copies of Dr. Grant's and Mr. Waller's cast of them on Plate XVIII.; where they, the sides of the coffer, are the *facile princeps*, in point of smoothness, of all the various examples of worked granite surfaces. But now for the connections with the red granite chamber, which the coffer is placed in; and with the Pyramid building itself.

(1.) The chief line of the whole King's Chamber is geometrically its cubic diagonal, and that has been certainly now ascertained by modern measure, assisted by computation, to be equal to 515·165 Pyramid inches. This is Mr. Simpson's base-line from which he reaches up to the Great Pyramid on one side, and down to the coffer on the other; thus:—

(2.) 515·165 × 10 = 5151·65 = side of a square of equal area with the Great Pyramid's vertical, right section.

(3.) 515·165 = twice the greatest horizontal circumference of the coffer; nearly—

(4.) $\frac{515·165}{10}$ = 51·5165 = (A.) the mean length of all the coffer's "arris," or edge lines.

= (B.) Diameter of a circle whose area is represented in the coffer's interior horizontal area; *i.e.* its inside floor.

= (C.) Side of a square whose area = mean area of the four external vertical sides of coffer.

= (D.) The diameter of a sphere, whose contents (71,588) come very near those of the hollow part of the coffer, and do, in a sense, exist there.

= (E.) The diameter of a circle in which the natural tangent of α Draconis (the Pyramid's Polar star at the date of erection) was at its higher culmination, viz. 33° 41′ 20″ — 34·344 Pyramid inches = coffer's depth.

So exactly, though extraneously, appears thus to be given the coffer's depth, that very element, which the senseless hammerings of modern travellers breaking off specimens of the material, forsooth,—have now very nearly deprived the world of seeing again in the body.

(5.) At the same time the external correlative of inside *depth*, namely, the *height*, is given simply by the tenth part the length of the King's Chamber containing it, viz. 41·213.

(6.) While the *breadth* of the coffer's base is given thus, based on the number of days in the solar year:—In a circle with circumference = 365·242 Pyramid inches, the natural tangent of 33° 41′ 20″, or the Pyramid Polar star's upper culmination = 38·753 Pyramid inches, = breadth of coffer's base; and again = ante-chamber's length 116·260 divided by 3.

(7.) The depth and height are moreover thus related:—
Depth squared : height squared : : area of side : area of side + end.

If 103·033 Pyramid inches was found an important touchstone of commensurability in the King's Chamber, bringing out Mr. Simpson's "sums of the squares there," we may expect to find it in the coffer also; where accordingly—

(8.) $103·033^2$ = area of four external sides of the coffer, nearly.

(9.) $\dfrac{103·033}{3}$ = 34·344 = depth of coffer.

(10.) $\dfrac{103·033^2}{2\,\pi}$ = height of the coffer squared.

This last theorem brings into view the invaluable quantity π, which the Great Pyramid commemorates by the shape of its whole external figure: and Mr. St. John Vincent Day had announced long since, that, profiting by small inequalities between the sides of the coffer, as shown to exist by my measures of them, it could be proved that the height of the coffer is to the length of two *adjacent* sides (viz. a side and an end) as 1 to π. And now to that good beginning, Mr. Simpson adds,—

(11.) Coffer's internal floor has a boundary whose length = the circumference of a circle of equal area to coffer's outer floor or base; a curious result this of the *long* shape of the coffer, compared with the cube, or cylinder, which it might have been for capacity measure alone, and of which more presently.

(12.) Coffer's depth multiplied by $2\,\pi$ = area of East and West (that is, the two long) sides of the coffer.

(13.) Coffer's height squared = area of $\dfrac{\text{side} + \text{end}}{\pi}$.

(14.) A circle with diameter 38·753 Pyramid inches (the breadth of the coffer's base); or again
A square with side 34·344 Pyramid inches (the depth of the coffer), has an area = the area of the external long side divided by π.

(15.) Finally, if two vertical, right, sections be made through the middle of the coffer, then such are the proportions of lengths, breadths, and thicknesses, that
(A.) Area of the sections of the walls of coffer, is to area of whole section included, as 1 to π. And
(B.) Area of sectional walls = height of coffer squared.

Then follow some most interesting correspondences, with distinctions, between these three apparently most diverse things, the pointed Great Pyramid, the enclosed King's Chamber, and the lidless granite Coffer; thus—

(16.) In each of these three structures, *one* rule governs their shape, viz. two principal dimensions added together are π times the third.

Illustrated thus :—

> In Great Pyramid, Length + breadth = π height.
> In King's Chamber, Length + height = π breadth.
> In Coffer, Length + breadth = π height.

Wherefore Pyramid and Coffer have their radii vertical, and King's Chamber horizontal.

Professor Hamilton L. Smith, of New York, has also been privileged to discover many remarkable commensurabilities between the coffer and other signal portions both of the Great Pyramid, and some natural data, such as the number of days in the year; these latter commensurabilities evidently requiring that the measures of the coffer be expressed in Pyramid inches, and in no other units of a different length from them. These discoveries are not yet fully published—some of them will be noticed in a future chapter.

Position of the Coffer in the King's Chamber.

But now, still further, for the *position* of this remarkable vessel, the coffer, in the equally remarkable room, the King's Chamber. To a certain extent I have almost foreclosed against myself the possibility of having anything of importance to say there,—having described the coffer as loose on a flat, smooth, unmarked floor, and having also spoken of one end being tilted up, by a nodule of hard jasper from the desert outside, pushed in by Arabs in modern times. It is the south end which is so tilted, and in committing that abomination

262 THE GREAT PYRAMID. [PART III.

the ignorant children of the desert of to-day, seem to
have pushed the coffer ten inches towards the north, of
where it had been intended to stand; for on subtracting
that quantity from my measured distance (see " Life
and Work," Vol. II. p. 105) from the south wall, and
adding it to what was measured from the north wall,
each distance comes out 58·2 Pyramid inches; or,
within the limits of the errors of observation, it = the
height of the Great Pyramid divided by 100.

Encouraged by this indication, Mr. Simpson considered the distance of the west side of the coffer,
from the west side of the chamber. The slued position of the coffer (see Plate XVII.), evidently indicates
that the men who recently pushed it northward while
tilting it, moved it, chiefly at the elevated south end, a
little eastward too. My present measured distance
therefore from the west, 55·0 inches, is rather too great.
What distance then ought it to have been in such a
monument as this, where everything evidently goes by
number and measure ?

What else, replied Mr. James Simpson, than the coffer's
touchstone length, 51·516 Pyramid inches ? Allowed *pro
tem.;* but what length does that leave between the eastern
side of the coffer, and the eastern side of the chamber?

Nay, said he, take it not from the far-off eastern wall
of this long chamber, but from a meridian plane cutting
the chamber into two equal halves, and then you will
find the quantity 116· inches ; sufficiently near to the
length of the ante-chamber, or to the tenth part of the
coffer's own height above the base of the Great Pyramid,
to be accepted as intentional by the architect of the
whole ; and yet sufficiently far from the 116·26 of the
ante-chamber's rigid measure to permit of a further
reason being investigated by-and-by.

Meanwhile it may be observed that we have, theoretically, divided the King's Chamber, transversely to its

length, into two equal halves.   Is anything else gained
by that ?

This most important illustration of the very groundwork of the claim of the coffer to be a vessel of capacity
having an earth-size reference.   At p. 180 we showed
its formation upon the cube of a line of the length of 50
inches, or two of the remarkable cubits of the Great
Pyramid, each of which cubits is memorable through
all science and all history as the *ten-millionth* part of the
earth's semi-axis of rotation, for the period of intellectual
man residing on this planet world.

Now that " ten-millions " is a large number, but very
round, very exact, and very characteristic ; and if we
take the precise breadth and half length of the room as
determined before (p. 194), 206·066 Pyramid inches, and
for height, the larger 2nd height also given before, say
235·5, we obtain almost exactly 10 million cubic inches,
as the contents of each half of the room ; or indicating
that something is accomplished there connected with
capacity measure, and depending primarily on a length
of two *such* cubits, as these earth-axis commensurable
ones of the Great Pyramid are, commensurable each of
them by ten millions.

The Shape of the Coffer.

The earth-size relations then of the coffer, as deduced
for itself alone, are justified by the whole King's Chamber ; and the actual size, we showed before (p. 154), is
Pyramidally recognised by the lower course capacity of
the chamber being 50 times the contents of the coffer,
and the coffer standing on the 50th course of the
masonry of the whole of the Great Pyramid from the
pavement upwards.   But the shape ; yes, the shape of
the coffer as a capacity measure—what is to justify that ?

We have already given a variety of reasons of a somewhat mathematical order at p. 163, but have no objection now to add thereto this general verbal apology :— that the shape of the coffer is to enable it, with its elemental-founded size, to typify and be most suitable to the size, shape, forces, and purposes of man; not of man trying to scale the heavens by his own might, but of man living in obedience to, and dying in harmony with, the commands of God his Creator.

John Taylor had suggested, but not very strongly, that the shape of the coffer was derived from the hot bath, the *Calidarium*, long known in the East—a long and deep box-shape in which a man might lie down at full length, or sit up ; and such a shape, he showed, had been found more convenient for a corn-holder, or large corn-measure, than a cube of the same contents.

But in presence of the 4,000 years and more, which the Great Pyramid now represents to man,—the most solemn case of lying down is that of the tomb ; and the full length, horizontal extension is as characteristic of what was ever taught in the Hebrew or Christian religion, as it was radically opposed to the wretched, bent-up, and shortened attitude of some miserable idolaters, and of the Parsees in India in the present day, or the cremation methods of Hindoos, or the ancient Egyptian plan of bringing out the mummies of their ancestors, and setting them *up* round the dinner-table at the greater family feasts.

The very look of the coffer evidently does produce in some human minds the idea of solemnly and religiously lying down extended in length, looking upwards, peaceful and strong in faith of a future awakening by the power of God.   Wherefore only this last month (1877) an American newspaper, recounting a recent visit to the King's Chamber of the Great Pyramid, mentions how the clergyman of the party, the Rev. Dr. —— insisted on laying himself down full length inside the coffer.

He had heard the Inspiration, and Scientific, Metrological theory of the Great Pyramid duly related by Dr. Grant, and had not denied it ; but so strongly was he imbued with the mere tombic idea of the Egyptians, that he held, as he lay there, with the notion that he was lying down in a Royal coffin ; and when he, Dr. ——, rose up from that open granite chest and found himself filthy, horrible, odious, with fine grey dust begriming his hair and transfusing his clothes, — he, Egyptologically, remarked, that it was " the honour-imparting dust of *King* Cheops." And yet so very far was it from being anything of the kind, that—over and above Cheops having been buried, as Herodotus relates, in quite another place (see p. 130), and the coffer having been often filled and emptied again of rubbish in modern times, as with Dr. Lepsius and his date-palm for a German Christmas-tree,—I can testify to this,—that, previously to my measures in January, 1865, I had the coffer cleared out, and *washed both inside and outside with soap and water.* Hence the detestable powdery matter which the Reverend Doctor so willingly courted, was, if not actually plebeian, at least so very modern as to be the product *in situ* of the last twelve years only : and is contributed chiefly by the limestone dust (gathered in pushing through the earlier passages and the rubbish of Al Mamoun's hole, and then shaken out of the clothes of the swarms of travellers, as they dance their violent reels in the noble granite hall), by the pungent excrements of bats startled in numbers on account of the unearthly howls, and by the slowly subsiding smoke of innumerable flaring candles. But leaving the Doctor to cleanse his garments as best he may (and he himself says he had a great deal of trouble about it ; for not until he had got right away from Egypt, and obtained the help of the steward's assistant on board ship, to give the clothes an extra beating over the waves of the rolling sea,—was the last of the penetrating powdery stuff got rid of) let us return to our metrological inquiry.

Practical application of the Coffer in Capacity Measure.

Having already said so much in point of principle and theory for the coffer, we may now approach the final object of this chapter; *viz.* the practical uses in capacity-measure of the granite coffer of the King's Chamber; a vessel measuring, as its architect originally intended that it should, 71,250 cubic Pyramid inches, or something very close thereto.

The whole quantity subdivides itself easily, after the manner of the Pyramid arithmetic and Pyramid construction, as follows:—the two most important steps being, *first*, the division into 4, as typifying the four sides of the Pyramid's base; and *second*, the division into 2,500, or 50 × 50 parts; fifty being the special number of the room, and the number also of the masonry courses of the whole structure on which that chamber, or rather the two adjoined chambers of ten million cubic inches each, of which it is composed, rest in their places.

PYRAMID CAPACITY MEASURE.

Division, or number, of each denomination contained in the whole coffer.	Inter-mediate divisions.	Capacity of each denomination in Pyramid cubic inches.	Equivalent Weight in Pyramid pounds of Water.	Name now proposed to be given to each successive portion.
1	0	71,250·	2,500·	Coffer.
4	4	17,615·	625·	Quarter.
10	2·5	7,125·	250·	Sack.
25	2·5	2,850·	100·	Bushel.
250	10·	285·	10·	Gallon.
2,500	10·	28·5	1·	Pint.
25,000	10·	2·85	0·1	Wine glass or fluid oz.
250,000	10·	0·285	0·01	Tea-spoon or fluid dr.
25,000,000	10·	0·00285	0·0001	Drop.

We begin, therefore, with the large measured and scientific quantity of the coffer; and end with a unit which, in an *approximate* form as a drop (*i.e.* the cubical space occupied by a drop of water falling freely in air at a given Pyramid temperature and pressure), is in everyone's hands, and is definable accurately upon the coffer by the stated proportion.

In contrasting this arrangement with the British imperial system, we may see at once that that modern system is merely a measure for large and rude quantities, knowing of nothing smaller than the pint (the gill being merely a later tolerated addition to suit special wants), and rendering it therefore necessary for the apothecaries and druggists to manufacture a sort of fluid and capacity measure for themselves, which they do by starting from the pint and ending in the drop; or, as they term it, with needless addition of dog-Latin, a "minim."

This apothecaries' fluid measure was established only in 1836; and we may assume, with Lord Brougham's *Penny Cyclopædia*, that such fluid ounce, when it is an ounce, is an ounce avoirdupois; although it is stated elsewhere that medical men are never to use anything but troy weight.

This incongruity renders the break between imperial, *i.e.* the present British, capacity, and apothecaries' capacity, measures peculiarly trying; followed as it is by a break of connection between apothecaries' capacity, and apothecaries' weight, measures also.

In the Pyramid arrrangement, however, there is no halting half-way; but, when it is a question of capacity, the scheme goes right through from the biggest bulks ever dealt with in commerce, and through all the measures required by the people further in dealing with coal, corn, wool, potatoes, beer, wine, peas, meal, oil, medicines, photographicals, and chemicals, up to the

smallest quantity ever judged of by capacity measures
of specified name; for when once we have arrived by
several decimal stages at "drops," no one would ever
think of subdividing them further, if he could, in any
other manner than by the tens of pure arithmetic again
and again.

But the chief unit of the *imperial* capacity system is a
pint; and it is, moreover, the very important centre of
connection between that system for large ordinary quantities, and the apothecaries' system for scientific and
medical small quantities. The pint occupies, therefore,
the position of all others on the scale which should
be round and complete, testable also at a moment's
notice by an equally round, well-known, and frequently
employed standard of weight.

So it was too in the days of the wisdom, wherever that
was derived from, of our Anglo-Saxon forefathers, or
the times of instinctive strength of our hereditary traditions; but under the reign of George IV. the pint,
from having been measured by one pound's weight of
water, was expanded into the odd quantity of 1 and ¼
pounds. And the change was attempted to be electro-
plated with brilliant proverbial mail, by giving out this
jingling rhyme, to be learned by all good subjects,—

> " A pint of pure water
> Weighs a pound and a quarter."

But we may well venture to doubt whether every
peasant does not rather still ruminate in his family
circle and about the old hearthstone over the far
more ancient and pithier rhyme,—

> " A pint's a pound,
> All the world round."

An expression, too, in which there may be vastly more
than immediately meets the eye; seeing that the Pyramid system appears to restore the principle; and, what

with the United States of North America, true to their ancient, hereditary covenant, and all the existing British Colonies too, does form, as prophecied of old, the measuring line round the whole world.

At all events, to those who now enter the Great Pyramid, and look with understanding eyes, one of the first things set before them in that microcosm of the King's Chamber, the Ante-Chamber thereto, is the Boss on the granite leaf. Which Boss, over and above having served in lineal measure to perpetuate the inch, is now found in its cubic capacity to represent approximately the Pyramid pint; the Pyramid pint too, visibly standing vertically over the lower stone of the leaf, proved already (see p. 209) to show the size of the " Quarter " measure of the system.

Almost every one of the Pyramid's capacity measures, however, over and above its pint, with its weight-equal the pound, admits of being tested by a round number of " water-pounds "; and that number is always such a one as we shall presently see equally exists in the Pyramid system of weight measure.

We have, therefore, only to conclude this division of the subject by submitting a table of comparison of each concluded Pyramid capacity vessel, with each similarly named current capacity vessel in Great Britain (and almost, if not exactly the same in America) through means of the known medium of British cubic inches. Whence it will be seen that, excepting the " coffer," (though even that is hardly altogether unknown to our nation, " chaldron " having been under Anglo-Saxon rule an expression for, and a description of,* it,) there is no need to invent any new names; for, under the existing ones, as of pints, gallons, &c. &c., the absolute capacities have often varied much more

* See Mr. Taylor's " Great Pyramid," p. 144.

than here indicated,* and without a tithe of the reason for it.

PYRAMID, AS COMPARED WITH BRITISH, CAPACITY MEASURES,

Compared through the temporary medium of British cubic inches, *exactly* suited to neither.

Coffer, Pyramid .. = 71,463·750		Four Quarters, Brit. = 70,982·144		
Quarter ,, .. = 17,865·938		Quarter ,, = 17,745·532		
Sack ,, .. = 7,146·375		Sack ,, = 6,654·574		
Bushel ,, .. = 2,858·550		Bushel ,, = 2,218·196		
Gallon ,, .. = 285·855		Gallon ,, = 277·279		
Pint ,, .. = 28·585		Pint (Old W. Pint = 28·875)		
		= 34·659		
Ounce or Wine-glass = 2·858		Ounce, fluid, Apoth. = 1·733		
Dram or Tea-spoon = ·286		Dram, fluid, Apoth. = 0·217		
Drop, Pyramid .. = ·003		Drop, Apoth. = 0·004		

INTERNATIONAL APPENDIX TO GREAT PYRAMID CAPACITY

MEASURE.

If analogues of the Great Pyramid measures are thus found in the oldest metrology of the Anglo-Saxons presently known, some traces of them can hardly but be discoverable also in the hereditary metrologies of other countries, through which the Anglo-Saxons marched before they occupied these British Isles 1,200 years ago.

* In or about 1800 it was reported that in Westmoreland the following diverse measures were used :—1st, a *Winchester* bushel ; 2nd, a *customary* bushel, equal to three Winchester bushels ; 3rd, a *potato* bushel, equal to two Winchester bushels ; and, 4th, a *barley* bushel, equal to two and a half Winchester bushels.

Without, then, attaching any particular importance to the results, I append here some of the most striking approaches to coincidence, chiefly gathered from Dr. Kelly's "Universal Cambist," published in 1821. Dr. Kelly having been an author of the most respectable class in commercial and educational science; and one who, though the French metrical system had already appeared on the horizon in his time, yet lived in the full force of the older hereditary metrological systems— systems perverted often exceedingly into provincial variations, but not then begun to be stamped out of existence wholesale, for the benefit of the mètre of Paris.

" Quarter " Capacity Corn Measures.

Country or City.	Name of Measure.	Contents in English cubic inches.
Ancona	Rubbio	17,459˙
Malta	Salma	17,678˙
Great Pyramid ..	**Quarter of Coffer** ..	**17,866˙**
Rome	Rubbio	17,970˙

" Sack " Capacity Corn Measures.

Country or City.	Name of Measure.	Contents in English cubic inches.
Amsterdam	Mudde	6,788˙
Bolsano	Scheffel	6,657˙
Deventer	Mudde	7,049˙
Genoa	Mina.	7,367˙
Hanau	Malter..	6,868˙
Great Pyramid. ..	**Sack**	**7,146˙**
Reval	Tonne..	7,219˙
Turin .. ,. ..	Sacco	7,015˙
Zwoll	Mudde	6,851˙

" Bushel" Capacity Corn Measures.

Country or City.	Name of Measure.	Contents in English cubic inches.
Calabria	Tomolo	3,119·
Greek (ancient).. ..	Medimnus.	2,712·
Maranham	Alquiero	2,772·
Mecklenburg	Scheffel	2,591·
Nancy	Carte	2,925·
Great Pyramid. ..	**" Bushel"** ..	**2,858·**
St. Maloes	Boisseau	2,697·
Sardinia	Starello	2,988·

CHAPTER XIII.

PYRAMID WEIGHT MEASURE,

Based on Earth's Mean Density.

THE weight measure of the Great Pyramid we have also to obtain from its grand Red-Granite Coffer, situated as that remarkable vessel is in the calm air, the darkness, and most equal temperature, riotous proceedings of modern visitors alone excepted, of its internal, and well-protected King's Chamber. But, as before intimated, any question of *weight*, treated in the highest terrestrial sense and for all mankind, requires the introduction of an additional and more difficult idea than mere cubic space ; and this idea is, the *mean density* of the whole earth.

Were masses of such matter directly procurable, the best representation of the Pyramid weight standard might have been a rectangular block of that substance, 5·7 times smaller than the coffer's internal capacity, set up beside it in that chamber.

But as we are not able in spite of all the wonderful resources of modern science, to delve anything like deep enough to obtain a specimen of this grand unit material which forms the foundation of our globe (if indeed it really exists as a unity, and does not rather arise from the arithmetical average density of a vast variety of elements, some of them very much heavier, and others lighter than the 5·7),—we must take the coffer's contents in water as a stepping-stone; but only as such a mere and temporary intermediary, to reach our desired result.

Thus the coffer's contents of pure water are 71,250 cubical Pyramid inches, which at the temperature of 68° Fahr., and barometric pressure of 30·000 Pyramid inches, would weigh 18,030,100 of our avoirdupois grains; (according to the estimate of the British Government that one cubical British inch of distilled water at temperature 62° Fahr. and barometer 30·00 inches, weighs 252·458 grains; the necessary reduction being performed for the different size of the inch and the altered temperature). But if the earth's mean density material be 5·7 times heavier than water, a mass of that said heavier material, 5·7 times smaller than 71,250 cubical inches, viz. measuring 12,500 cubical inches only, will also weigh, at the same temperature and pressure, the same 18,030,100 British avoirdupois grains.

That beginning made, we have next to enquire, what are, may, or should be, the subdivisions of the whole block of 12,500 cubical Pyramid inches of the Earth's Mean Density on the Pyramid *weight* system of metrology? Here we can follow no better plan than that adopted in the capacity branch of metrology; and then we are rewarded by finding, when we come to the most characteristic division of all, viz. that of 50 × 50, which *should* give us a popular unit to compare with the pint in capacity—we find, I say, that it does give us something which is excessively close, in absolute weight to the old Saxon pound; but with this further advantage, of world-wide application in the Pyramid system, and presently to be illustrated in computing weight from measured size, viz. that each such Pyramid pound* is equal to the weight of *five* cubical Pyramid inches of the earth's mean density.

* 12,500 ÷ (50 × 50) = 5.

Hence our first Pyramid weight table runs thus :—

PYRAMID WEIGHT MEASURE.

Division, or number, of each part contained in the weight standard.	Inter-mediate divi-sions.	Weight of the part so divided in Pyramid lbs.	Capacity of the parts in Pyramid cubical inches of earth's mean density.	Capacity of the parts in Pyramid cubical inches of distilled water (T. 50° B. 30˙ of Pyramid).	Name now proposed to be given to each kind of part.
I	·.	2 500˙	12 500˙	71 250˙	Ton.
4	4˙	625˙	3 125˙	17 815˙	Quarter.
10	2˙5	250˙	1 250˙	7 125˙	Wey.
25	2˙5	100˙	500˙	2 850˙	Cwt.
250	10˙	10˙	50˙	285˙	Stone.
2,500	10˙	1.	5˙	28˙5	Pound.
25,000	10˙	0˙1	0˙5	2˙85	Ounce.
250,000	10˙	0˙01	0˙05	0˙285	Dram.
25,000,000	10˙	0˙0001	0˙0005	0˙00285	Grain.

The old British Grains nearer to those of Great Pyramid, than the newer ones.

Having already stated that the Pyramid grand weight standard weighs in British terms, viz. avoirdupois measure, 18,030,100 British grains; we are met, as soon as we begin to compare Pyramid and British weights together in point of fact, with an accusation,—that the Pyramid grains must be very small, if there are 25,000,000 of *them*, to 18,000,000 nearly of the British.

But herein comes to light one of those needless pieces of meddling legislation by our too modern, or Georgian era, political rulers, which so provoked John Quincy Adams and other American writers on Saxon metrology; for whereas the old law of the land was, that the Troy pound should be divided into 7,680 grains (and which were very nearly the weight of full and fair grains of well-grown wheat), a later law said that it should be divided into only 5,760 parts or grains so called, but of no known variety of plant employed for breadstuff. Wherefore Cocker, Wingate, and other arithmeticians of that day, used to enter in their useful conpendiums for schoolboys during the transition period, that 32 real grains, viz. the old ones, or 24 artificial grains, *i.e.* the new ones, made the pennyweight troy; and when that ingenious story was pretty well indoctrinated into their obedient scholars, the notice of the old grains was dropped out altogether, and the new ones remained masters of the situation, with the word "artificial" removed, and as though there had never been any other.

Referred then now, over the heads of these new, to the genuine old, grains of Saxon metrology (so far as we can trace them back by the usual literary and historical steps, and which is, after all, not so much as a thousand years), the number of 25,000,000 of the Pyramid grains would have been measured then by 24,040,100 of the Saxon grains of that earlier, though not Pyramid epoch, day; but a sufficiently close approach, or to the $\frac{1}{25}$ of a grain, to satisfy the ordinary purposes of life.

The conflict of three different systems of weight-measure in Great Britain.

But the British legal weight measure of modern times has, over and above this item, always been, even within itself and at home, in a dire antagonism between two rival and continually jostling systems; viz. troy and avoirdupois, not to say anything of apothecaries' weight, which is little but the troy, under a different mode of subdivision. General public favour seems at last to have settled upon avoirdupois, as most worthy to be the national weight in future for things in general, and especially things on a large scale; but as it does not go lower than drachms (of many whole grains, and some fractions, each), why then, even though troy weight should be extinguished to-morrow, apothecaries' weight will have still to be kept up for dealing with smaller quantities than *such* drachms.

The Pyramid weights, therefore, which are on one system only, and go through the whole scale from tons to grains without any break, seem to offer already, at this point, an honourable mode of escape to the British nation out of the confusion it has suffered for ages. No new names are required, many close approaches to the grander standards and units of our country will be remarked, and the proportions of matter under each denomination, as used in the Pyramid, and in British, nomenclature, are approximately as follows :—

PYRAMID, AS COMPARED WITH BRITISH, WEIGHT MEASURES.

Compared through the temporary medium of the present legal English "artificial," and over-large, grains.

1 ton Pyramid	= 18,030,100·	{ 1 ton avoird.	= 15,680,000·
		1 ton shipping	= 18,816,000·
1 wey Pyramid	= 1,803,010·	1 wey English	= 1,274.000·
1 cwt. Pyramid	= 721,200·	1 cwt. avoird.	= 784,000·
1 stone Pyramid	= 72,120·	{ 1 stone meat	= 56,000·
		1 stone wool	= 98,000·
1 pound Pyramid	= 7,212·	(1 pound avoird.	= 7,000·
		1 pound, an ancient weight preserved at the Exchequer, but of unknown origin	= 7,100·
		1 pound old English and Scotch	= 7,600·
1 ounce Pyramid	= 721·20	{ 1 oz. avoird.	= 437·5
		1 oz. troy or apoth.	= 480·0
1 drachm Pyramid	= 72·12	{ 1 drachm avoird.	= 27·34375
		1 drachm apoth.	= 60·00000
1 grain Pyramid	= 0·7212	(1 grain "real," or old Saxon	= 0·75000
		1 grain modern English	= 1·00000

Specific Gravity, and its Interference with Bulk and Weight.

In no part of metrology more than in weight, is there found so much of the wheel within wheel of *natural* difficulty, tending, unless well watched and studied, to introduce perverse variations whenever uniformity is attempted ; and there are still existing some supporters of the old arguments for keeping up both the troy and avoirdupois weight systems amongst us.   For the same reasons, too, that those gentlemen believe the complication was first introduced.

And what reasons were they ?

When society was in a very primitive, or much more probably, a mediæval degraded condition, and little but grain was sold, a test for the amount of grain in any particular vessel was, the weight of water it would hold. But water and grain are of different specific gravities ; therefore, if equal bulks were taken, the purchaser got a very different real and usable quantity of what he valued most, than if equal weights had been observed ; and as some parties were more particular about bulks than weights, and *vice versâ*, two sets of weights were prepared, with such an amount of difference between them, that a pound of grain, measured by the one sort of pound, occupied exactly the same cubical space as a pound of water measured by the other variety of pound.

But in the present day, when an infinity of kinds and species of matters besides bare grain are bought and sold, and almost every one of the thousand and more substances thus dealt in has a different *specific gravity* we cannot hope to have as many different systems of weight as there are of such substances ; though by so doing, and at the same time maintaining only one system of capacity measure, there might be kept up on many occasions a specious appearance of identity between weight and bulk.   Hence, for the modern man, the only practical resource seems to be, to have one capacity, and one weight, measure pure and simple ; but to produce the identity required of old for different substances, by *calculation*.   Assisting that calculation

necessarily by some convenient table of specific gravities, wherein the point of coincidence between the
two descriptions of measure, or the point where there is
no calculation at all from bulks to find weights, shall be
in favour of the best average example of *all* the substances which have in their turn to be either weighed
or measured by man; for such plan tends to prevent
any one substance acquiring an excessive *maximum*, or
extreme *minimum*.

In the French metric system this point of coincidence
is occupied by *water;* and it is intended that the cubic
amount of water being measured, that statement shall
in itself, with the mere alteration of names, and perhaps of the decimal point, express its weight. Hence,
at a recent metrological discussion, at the Philosophical
Society of Glasgow, a pro-French metrical speaker
lauded this quality of his favourite anti-British-national
system; and enlarged upon how convenient it must be
for a merchant receiving goods in the docks, out of
many vessels from many countries, to go about among
the packages with a mere French mètre measuring-rod
in his hand; and by that obtaining their cubical bulks,
thence to know simultaneously their weights also.

"Yes," remarked another speaker, "that would answer perfectly, if British merchants imported, and
exported, and dealt in, nothing but *water*."

Now the pro-French metrical man on this occasion
was a large dealer in iron; and had made much fame
for himself, and some money too, by improved methods
of working the weighty iron plates required for modern
armour-clad war-vessels. So he being utterly overthrown by the above answer, tried to recover himself
and his theory with the remark, "Well, but you must
allow that the French metrical system is an excellent
one for ship-builders computing their displacements by."

"Yes," again answered his most truth-speaking opponent, "if ship-builders are never required to deal with *salt* water; only pure, fresh, distilled water; and can keep that always at the uncomfortably cold temperature of water's maximum density, and can also work in a vacuum as to atmospheric air;" for all these are the truly anti-practical plans for any correct weighing to be performed in the way of business on the boasted French metrical system;—a system invented by a really most unpractical, and people-despising, knot of a few closet doctrinaires.*

Atmospheric Temperature and Pressure, also to be considered in all systems of national Weight-measure.

Other speakers then came to the defence of the pro-French-metrical Briton, in his anti-British schemes; and urged that *a table of specific gravities* might be employed, when anything else than pure distilled water at a temperature of 39° Fahr. was being measured or weighed; and also that when rough commercial results only were required, both temperature and atmospheric pressure might *probably* be neglected.

Let us look each of these sides of the argument

---

* Having had an opportunity seven years ago, of discussing with a University professor in Sicily, who was also one of King Victor Emmanuel's new Roman senators, the recent adoption by Italy of the unpractical French mètre, kilogramme, and litre,—when they had such good practical hereditary measures bequeathed to them by the old Romans, as their foot, pound, and amphora—I ventured to ask how the Sicilian people liked to give up their traditional institutions and take to these new and alien-invented French weights and measures? "The Sicilians!" shouted he, with almost comical indignation; "what business have they to think for one moment about the matter?" And then I saw that the reputed liberal king, Victor Emmanuel, was obliged to act at the head of his troops with fixed bayonets, and more tyrannically than any Russian emperor, in order to fix the French metrical system upon his no longer loving subjects of the Trinacrian isle. They did break free from his rule in 1866, when the Italian army was employed against Austria on the Po; and Palermo was then really free for a time. But as soon as the Continental war was over, Sicily was overwhelmed once more by King Victor's Italian troops, poured in without stint.

straight in the face ; for they serve well to contrast
essential and inherent qualities in the French metrical,
as against the Pyramid, system of weighing.

The former, having its specific-gravity equality-point
at water, while almost all the substances dealt with by
art and science (especially the more useful and valuable
ones in modern life, such as the metals, minerals, &c.),
are heavier, far heavier, than water,—the weights first
given out by the French mètre rod are, as a rule, largely
in error.

The latter or Pyramid system, on the contrary, having
its equality-point at the earth's mean density, or *between*
stones and metals, is much nearer the truth at once and
without any specific gravity correction, for things in
general, and for precious ones in particular.

Again, the French system which makes the temperature reference close to freezing, or where men can barely
exist (and certainly cannot work to advantage), and the
atmospheric pressure reference, a vacuum where they
cannot exist at all,—must require much larger corrections on the rough measures actually taken in the circumstances of daily life,—than the analogous Pyramid
references ; which are those of the average temperature
and average air pressure under which all men upon this
earth do live, move, and have their various occupations.

Under the French system, indeed, a shopkeeper
ought to take account in summer of the large amount of
thermal expansion of his goods, from their being then
far above the ideal temperature of water's maximum
density, the wintry 39° Fahr. ; and in winter he ought
to correct all his indoor weighings, for the artificial
temperature which he keeps up there by stoves or
otherwise. While in both summer and winter he ought
to make large allowance for the buoyant power of air of
the density, more or less, of the whole atmosphere, or
30 inches pressure of mercury, as compared with o·ooo

inches of a vacuum, on the comparative specific gravities of both the material of his weights, and the usually very different material of the things weighed ;—the duly entered French tabular specific gravities, being true, according to his system, only in an absolute vacuum ; and that, too, in close proximity to an ice-house.

But under the Pyramid system, and under the British also, the ordinary weighings in the shop under the temperatures and pressures there usually experienced, either in winter or summer, will be never more than microscopically different from weighings performed under the exact and scientific temperature and atmospheric pressure references of these systems ; viz. the mean, very nearly, of what are experienced both in the shops and the general habitations of men, all the wide world over. *But of this, and others of its far-reaching consequences, see more and further, in* Chap. XV.

Pyramid weighings with '*due reference to Specific-gravities, Temperatures, and Pressures.*

Weights, then, on the Pyramid system are equally referable, as with the French system, to one given, and scientifically definable, point on both the temperature and pressure scales, when nicety is required. But that given point in the Pyramid case is an easier, pleasanter, and a better-known one; while for the rough work of the world, the Pyramid weights are calculable at once from Pyramid linear measure, without any reference to observations of thermometer and barometer at the instant, much more accurately than the French can be from theirs, under similar circumstances. The Pyramid rules, too, being expressible in the following simple manner :—

For *small* things, ascertain their bulk in cubical inches, divide by 5, and the result is the weight in Pyramid pounds—if the said articles are of the same specific gravity as the earth's average material of construction.

For *large* masses, ascertain their bulk in cubical Pyramid cubits, add ¼, and the result is the weight in Pyramid *tons*,—under the same condition of specific gravity.*

But if the matter measured in either case were not of earth's mean density, but, say, ordinary stone, the real weight would be nearer a half, and if of the more common metals, double, the amount given by the above process : the raw number first procured by it, requiring for accuracy's sake, in the case of every different physical substance, to be multiplied by its specific gravity *in terms of that of the earth's*. Hence, such tabular multiplier is 1 when the specific gravity is the same as that of the mean of the whole earth-ball's contents; a fraction of 1 when lighter; and 1 with something added to it, when heavier; as in the following table, prepared from various authorities :—

PYRAMID SYSTEM OF SPECIFIC GRAVITIES.

Earth's mean density = 1; Temperature = 68° Fahr.;

Barometric Pressure = 30·025 British inches.

Cork	·043	Bees' wax	·169
White pine (American) ..	·072	Old oak	·170
Oats (loose as in bushel)..	·088	Distilled water	·175
Larch (Scotland)	·093	Sea-water	·180
Lithium	·100	Blood	·180
Riga fir	·105	Heart of oak	·206
Barley (loose as in bushel)	·112	Cannel coal	·223
Ether, sulphuric	·129	Aloes	·239
Wheat (loose as in bushel)	·132	Chloroform	·267
Alcohol, pure	·139	White sugar	·282
Pumice-stone	·160	Bone of an ox	·291
Ice	·163	Magnesium	·310
Butter, tallow, fat.. ..	·165	Ivory	·321

* Conversely, the Pyramid weight of a body of earth's mean density being given, to find its Pyramid cubical measure—

For *small* things, multiply the pounds weighed by 5, and it will give the number of cubical inches; and

For *large* masses, decrease the ton's weight by ⅕, to find the number of cubical cubits.

Pyramid System of Specific Gravities—(*continued*).

Earth's mean density = 1 ; Temperature = 68° Fahr. ;

Barometric Pressure = 30·025 British inches.

Brick	·351	Iron ore, prismatic .. 1·29
Casing-stone, Gt. Pyramid	·367	Lead ore, cubic .. .. 1·33
Sulphuric acid, concentrated	·373	Iron, forged into bars .. 1·36
Nummulitic limestone, G. P.	·412	Copper, native .. .. 1·37
Porcelain (china)	·420	Manganese.. .. .. 1·40
Glass, crown	·439	Steel, hardened .. .. 1·37
" Common stone ".. ..	·442	Brass, cast, common .. 1·37
Desert sand, near the Sphinx	·454	Brass, cast, special .. 1·47
Aluminium	·460	Mercury, precipitated, red 1·47
Red granite (Peterhead) ..	·464	Cobalt .. .. .. 1·48
Marble (Carrara)	·477	Cadmium .. .. .. 1·50
Red granite, Gt. Pyramid	·479	Brass wire, drawn.. .. 1·50
Emerald	·487	Nickel .. .. .. 1·54
Jasper	·494	Copper wire, drawn .. 1·56
Basalt	·500	Bismuth, native .. .. 1·58
Glass, flint	·527	Bismuth, molten .. .. 1·72
Sapphire	·550	Silver, native .. .. 1·76
Diamond	·618	Mercury, brown cinnabar .. 1·79
Topaz	·621	Silver, virgin .. .. 1·84
Ironstone	·670	Silver, hammered .. .. 1·85
Sapphire, special	·701	Mercury, precipitated, *per se* 1·91
Garnet	·720	Lead, molten .. .. 2·00
Ruby	·750	Palladium .. .. .. 2·07
Loadstone	·843	Thallium .. .. .. 2·10
Silver ore	·997	Mercury, fluent .. .. 2·38
Arsenic, molten	1·010	Mercury, congealed .. 2·75
Chromium	1·04	Gold, not hammered .. 2·76
Tungsten	1·07	Gold, hammered .. .. 2·77
Tellurium	1·10	Gold, English standard,
Litharge	1·10	22 carats.. .. .. 3·31
Uranium	1·13	Gold, English standard,
Antimony	1·17	24 carats .. .. .. 3·38
Lead ore, black	1·20	Gold, English standard,
Zinc, in its common state..	1·21	hammered .. .. 3·40
Tin ore, black	1·22	Platinum, purified.. .. 3·42
Wolfram	1·25	Platinum, hammered .. 3·57
Zinc, compressed	1·26	Platinum wire, drawn .. 3·69
Tin, pure, Cornish ..	1·28	Platinum, compressed .. 3·87
Iron, cast at Carron ..	1·28	Iridium, compressed .. 3·90

No efficient system, then, of determining weights by linear measure, in the present day, can possibly go unaccompanied by some kind of table of specific gravities ; the number of items in such table being not dependent on the system, but on the richness and variety of this globe's natural products. Wherefore a few of those items at least might worthily be extracted from time to

time, and discoursed on as natural theology texts by
every schoolmaster appointed to teach weights and
measures,—for what a boundless vista does not simple
specific gravity open up into the realm of nature ! And
what thankfulness should it not excite in the mind of
man towards the Creator, for all these endless varieties of
elementary matter, wherewith He has of old stocked the
earthly abode of man; and thereby made a higher existence possible to him, than to denizens of *water* alone !

The specific gravity standard of the Pyramid weight
measure setting forth thus the mean density of all the
solid, as well as fluid, treasures of the earth,—means
thus an almost infinity of things in the history of mankind; and there appears to be further an even commensurability of a most marvellous order, between the
weight of the whole Great Pyramid and the weight of
our planet the earth.

*The Great Pyramid itself, found to be Harmoniously Com-
mensurable with the Earth, by Weight of the whole.*

The reader may perhaps not object to see some of the
steps of this calculation, especially if we obtain the numbers to be compared, viz. the respective weights or masses
of the Great Pyramid and the earth, by means of the
system of Pyramid weight measure now being described.

If we desired the weights in Pyramid pounds, we
should begin by taking the linear dimensions of each of
the bodies in inches. But as tons are usually employed
for large weights, and the weights to be dealt with are
surely large enough in this case, we had better follow
that custom (though of course our tons will be Pyramid
tons), and begin with the dimensions of the bodies
before us, in linear *cubits*, of the Pyramid (each cubit
25 Pyramid inches long, and each Pyramid inch
$\frac{1}{250}$ millionth of the earth's semi-axis of rotation).

<small>LINEAR ELEMENTS OF SIZE OF GREAT PYRAMID.</small>

Vertical height of Great Pyramid	.. = 232·52	Pyramid cubits.
Inclined height of Pyramid face ..	.. = 295·72	,,
Side of square base of Great Pyramid ..	= 365·24	,,
Transverse thickness of the ancient casing-stone film .. .. =	4·00	,,

<small>CUBICAL ELEMENTS OF SIZE OF GREAT PYRAMID.</small>

Cubical Pyramid cubits in the whole building, computed from the above linear elements	10,339,850
Subtract for hollow internal spaces, such as the grand gallery, chambers, and passages, computed extraneously..	5,250
	10,334,600
Subtract casing-stone film's cubical contents =	861,952
Remains, for cubical contents of the general mass..	9,472,648

Now all these calculations, thus far, would have to be performed on *any* system of computing weights from linear measurements, even on the French metrical system ; and there, also, we should have still further to ascertain the specific gravity of the materials we are dealing with, *not one of them being the same as water.* But the casing-stones, of which there are 861,952 cubical cubits, have a specific gravity (ascertained by direct experiment on hand specimens) of 0·367, where unity represents the mean density of the whole earth ; while the general residual mass of the building, of which there are 9,472,648 cubical cubits, has a specific gravity, under the same circumstances, of 0·412.

<small>FOR WEIGHT OF GREAT PYRAMID.</small>

Hence the conversion of the previous data into weight, proceeds thus :—

Casing-stone cubical cubits .. .. .. =		861,952
Add ¼ (see p. 283) .. .. =		215,488
		1,077,440
Multiply by specific gravity 0·367.. .. = tons		395,420
And, Residual mass in cubical cubits .. .. .. =		9,472,648
Add ¼		2,368,162
		11,840,810
Multiply by specific gravity = 0·412 .. = tons		4,878,414

Wherefore, 395,420 + 4,878,414 = tons 5,273,834 = weight of whole Great Pyramid.

Next let us proceed to ascertain the mass or practical
weight of the whole earth.

For Weight of the Earth.

LINEAR ELEMENTS OF THE EARTH.

Polar diameter   ..   ..   .. = 20,000,000 Pyramid cubits.
Equatorial diameter   ..   .. = 20,070,000   „
Mean of all diameters, nearly .. = 20,047,000   „

CUBICAL ELEMENTS OF THE EARTH.

Cubical Pyramid cubits contained in the
earth, computed from the above linear
elements, on the usual formula, de-
pending on the value of π ..   .. = 4,218,400,000,000,000,000,000
    Now, to turn these cubical cubits into tons, we have merely to add $\frac{1}{4}$;
for as the earth itself is its own, and the Pyramid's unit of density, the
multiplier there is simply unity.   Hence—

$$4,218,400,000,000,000,000,000$$
$$+ \; 1,054,600,000,000,000,000,000$$

Weight of earth in Pyramid tons   .. = 5,273,000,000,000,000,000,000

Comparing now this weight, with that of the Great
Pyramid as given above in the same tons (5,273,834),
the first three places of numbers are found to be identical; quite as close, or rather a much closer, correspondence than could well have been expected; while the
difference in the number of places of figures, or the
number of times that the weight of the earth is absolutely greater than that of the Great Pyramid, is in the
proportion of 10^{15} to 1; or, as some prefer to express it,
$10^{5 \times 3}$ to 1.

Now this very proportion is in peculiar Pyramid
numbers, and must further be considered to have been
intended; for, had the building not been chiefly composed of a stone so much lighter than what is usually
known as "common stone," that it has the specific
gravity of 0·412 in place of 0·442, the even proportion
would not have been obtained,—without indeed altering the size, and that would have overthrown other
equally, or still more, important commensurabilities.
But now, without in the slightest degree interfering

with any of its other departments of science and cosmical reference, the Great Pyramid, still standing, from primeval ages, in the centre of all the land surface of the whole world, puts forth this additional ground of *earth commensurability in weight,* for having an unexceptional fitness to be the one and central establishment of authority and reference for *weight* measure to all men, of all nations, through the period Divinely allotted to human rule on earth, whatever that is intended to be.

INTERNATIONAL APPENDIX TO GREAT PYRAMID WEIGHT MEASURE.

Hereditary Pound Weight Measures.

Country or City.	Name of Weight.	Weight in the Modern, over large English Grains.
Aix-la-Chapelle ..	Pound	7,234
Augsburg	Light pound	7,295
Berlin	Pound	7,231
Brunswick	do.	7,206
Canary Islands ..	Libra	7,104
Cologne	Pound	7,216
Constance	do.	7,285
Dantzic	do.	7,231
Erfurt	do.	7,285
Frankfort	do.	7,210
Geneva	Light pound	7,082
Königsberg ..	Pound	7,231
Leipsic	do.	7,206
Liége	do.	7,330
Lyons	Livre, poids de soie ..	7,088
Mecca	Rottolo	7,144
Portugal	Arratel	7,083
Prussia	Pound	7,218
Great Pyramid ..	**" Pound "**	**7,212**
Rotterdam	Light pound	7,243
St. Gall	do.	7,175
Spain	Libra	7,101
Stettin..	Pound	7,219
Strasburg	Livre	7,266
Ulm	Pound	7,234
Wurtemburg	do.	7,220
Zurich	Light pound	7,233

The above twenty-seven remarkable approximations in many countries to the Pyramid pound, are extracted out of a table of 174 weights of all kinds; and the origin or centre of diffusion of the 7,212 grains, or Great Pyramid, pound, is evidently not to be sought in any of the classical profane nations; the Old Roman pound having been equal to from 4,981 to 5,246 English grains; the Ancient Greek mina, from 5,189 to 6,994 English grains; the Pharaonic Egyptian pound, or mina = 8,304 grains; and the later Alexandrian Egyptian mina = 6,886 English grains.

CHAPTER XIV.

LINEAR AND SURFACE MEASURE,

Strictly Earth-commensurable.

WE have now arrived at the commercial arrangement of the most important of all the measures
of a nation ; at that one which requires practically to
be attended to first, and which *was* first attended to, and
secured with more than sufficient accuracy, as well as
with the grandest of suitable and harmonious earth-
commensurability, in the Great Pyramid ; viz. linear,
or length, measure. And, after all that was accomplished
in laying out the exterior of the building in terms of
this standard, we have seen in Chapters X. and XII.,
that the interior arrangements of the Pyramid are
similarly laid out ; and there, both in a harder material and in a constant temperature which brings all
standards of all materials into a uniform and inter-
comparable condition, most unexceptionably.

The particular *standard* of length measure for the
Great Pyramid, viz. its 25-inch cubit, the one-ten-
millionth of the earth's semi-axis of rotation, has its
length most exactly ascertainable by modern measure
(combined with an understanding formula, so as to take
advantage of a multiple of the single standard arranged
by the Architect himself), in the King's Chamber ;
where, as Professor H. L. Smith has well shown, it is
given with surpassing accuracy by the expression: Cubic

diagonal of the room multiplied by 10, and divided by the breadth of the floor. That is, in Pyramid inches deduced from the British inches of my actual measures of the said chamber in 1865 (see Chap. X.), $\frac{5151\cdot646}{206\cdot066} = 25\cdot000$ Pyramid, or $25\cdot025$ British, inches.

This, too, is evidently the length to which, in a concrete, single, and distinctly separate shape, we were also introduced by the granite leaf in the ante-chamber, as already detailed in Chap. X.; and are still to be introduced by the Excentricity adjustment of the grand Niche in the Queen's Chamber (see Chap. XIX.). While the granite-leaf still further shows the subdivisions of a single cubit, first into five grand hand-breadths, and then each such hand-breadth into five parts (25th parts of the whole cubit), which parts we will call, in our language, "inches of the Great Pyramid."

Now any *one* of these *inches* is the unit, unit-standard if you like, of the Great Pyramid linear measure. Accurately, this inch is the 1-500,000,000th of the earth's axis of rotation; but approximately, a thumb-breadth, to any full-sized, able-bodied man who has ever lived on the earth during the last four thousand years. In that long interval of anthropological time, what mighty empires, what varied races of men, and what languages too, have arisen and have passed away again from the face of the world! Therefore, of the present words and phrases, laws and customs, which rule in modern society, whether scientific, political, or commercial, which of them can expect to continue to control the actions and thoughts of men for anything like a similar period to this rule of the *inch;* or for the next forty centuries of years?

A thumb-breadth, then, is, both chronologically and historically, no indifferent test reference of approximation, to every poor man in Great Britain, for realising, when in haste, the unit of his measure also of length;

and keeping up some identity in his works with those of his fathers from earliest history, and even before history. Wherefore it is only characteristic of human nature in the large, that the working-men of Newcastle, according to the unintended testimony of Sir William Armstrong before the British Association of 1863, have once more practically, by their deeds and in their works, pronounced indubitably for the *inch* (an inch, too, decimally subdivided), wherever extreme accuracy is concerned.

The Unit of British Long Measure, really the Inch.

It was so in our olden national times as well; viz. that the English unit was the inch, and not any of those larger measures of yards or mètres, which the wealthy have been endeavouring to get established of late.

The old Exchequer *standards*, spoken of in 1742 (strong bars of gun metal, square in cross section and slightly convex at the ends, to suit "end measure"), marked E for Queen Elizabeth, and supposed to date from 1580, were, as reported at the time, one a yard, and one an ell; but that did not make either the one, or the other, the *unit* of the country's length measure. Where the unit is small, the public standard must inevitably consist of a number of such units strung together; and the incommensurability, except through their component inches, of that pair of measures laid side by side, the yard and the ell, might have reminded men in subsequent times of the true state of the case.

But it did not; and that the efforts of the ruling classes in making so much, as they have during late years been doing, of the yard, were intended to establish it as a new *unit*, and not as a convenient number of the ancient small inch units arranged together to suit a special purpose of manufactures and commerce, the

following words of the Act (June, 1824) sufficiently
testify :—

" The straight line or distance between the centres of
the two points in the gold studs in the straight brass
rod, now in the custody of the Clerk of the House of
Commons, whereon the words and figures *standard yard
of* 1760 are engraved, shall be, and the same is hereby
declared to be, the original and genuine standard of that
measure or lineal extension called a yard ; and that the
same straight line or distance between the said two
points in the said gold studs in the said brass rod, the
brass being at the temperature of 62° of Fahrenheit's
thermometer, shall be, and is hereby denominated, the
imperial standard yard, and shall be, and is hereby
declared to be, the *unit,* or only standard measure of
extension."

Yet a yard unit would be by no means generally
acceptable, even by those desiring something large ; for
we have already seen the favour extended in Queen
Elizabeth's time to the 45-inch ell; while both the
Astronomical Society's new scale of 1835, as well as
those of Troughton, Sir George Shuckburgh, and others,
were oftener of five feet than three. At three, however, what is now by modern law, in defiance of history
and fact, the *unit* of our country's linear measure, has
been eventually settled by the last Parliamentary Commission ; * and at three feet it will legally remain until
some great constitutional exertion be made to rectify it.

* The commission of 1838 had been thorough enough to consider, at
least according to its lights at that time, all the following points :—

A, Basis, arbitrary or natural, of the system of standards.
B, Construction of primary standards.
C, Means of restoring the standards.
D, Expediency of preserving one measure, &c., unaltered.
E, Change of scale of weights and measures.
F, Alteration of the land chain and the mile.
G, Abolition of troy weight.
H, Introduction of decimal scale.
I, Assimilation to the scale of other countries, &c.

During all these twenty or thirty past years, too, that it has remained there, a most artificial quantity, and naturally incommensurable with anything grand, noble, sublime,—there never seemed to be the slightest suspicion amongst any of the Government Commissioners, until John Taylor announced it from his Great Pyramid studies, and Sir John Herschel followed with scientific confirmations, that each single one of the 36 really *unit* inches of which the modern British Government's standard, and erroneously called *unit*, yard is composed, contains within itself all that much-desiderated physical applicability and scientific perfection,—when each individual British inch is, *almost* exactly, the 1-500,000,000th of the earth's axis of rotation already referred to.

The old British Inch closer to Earth-commensurability, than the modern British Inch.

Almost, or only, and not quite though, at this present time ; for it requires 1·001 of a modern British inch to make one such true inch of the earth and the Great Pyramid. An extraordinarily close approach, even there, between two measures of length in different ages and different lands ; and yet if any one should doubt whether our British inch can really be so close to the ancient and earth-perfect measure, I can only advise him to look to the original documents, and see how narrowly it escaped being much closer ; and would have been so too in these days, but that the government officials somewhere in the "unheroic" eighteenth century allowed Queen Elizabeth's ell measure, of equal date and authority with the yard, and of a greater number of inches (45 to 36), and therefore, in so far, a more powerful standard,—to drop out of sight.

The modern inch now in vogue amongst us was derived from the Exchequer *yard* standard, through means of Bird's copy in 1760 and other copies, and was therefore intended to be one of the inches of that particular yard; but the inches of the Exchequer *ell* were rather larger inches, and there were more of them; so that if either standard was rightfully taken as the sole authority for the value of an inch, it should have been the ell. Now when these standards were very accurately compared by Graham in 1743, before a large deputation of the Royal Society and the Government,* it was found that the Exchequer ell's 45 inches exceeded the quantity of 45 *such* inches as the Exchequer yard contained 36 of, by the space of 0·0494 of an inch. A result, too, which was in the main confirmed by the simultaneous measures of another standard ell at Guildhall, with an excess of 0·0444 of an inch, and the Guildhall yard with the excess of 0·0434 of an inch; showing that at that date generally, the English inch was larger than it is now by the amount of very nearly the 0·001 of an inch which we find with the Great Pyramid inch.

Keeping, however, for minuter details only to the Exchequer standard ell; and finding that it was not, after all, the very Exchequer yard, which was subsequently made (in Bird's copy) the legal standard of the country, that said ell was compared with by Graham, but a previous copy of it, and found in 1743 to be in excess by 0·0075 of an inch, on the Royal Society's scale,—we must subtract this quantity from the observed excess of the Exchequer ell; and then we get that its 45 inches were equal in terms of the present standard inches of the country, to 45·0419.†

* "Astronomical Society's Memoirs," Vol. IX.

† This rather roundabout conclusion, but unavoidably roundabout from the nature of the only documents in existence at the time of the first edition of this book being prepared, has been directly tested since then, and almost entirely confirmed by my friend, since deceased, Colonel Strange, the eminent superintendent for Government of all scientific instruments ordered for India.

The problem set before Colonel Strange, in 1864, was, to obtain

But 45 Pyramid inches are equal to 45·0450 modern
English inches; whence it will be seen, of those earlier
English inches, that they had such a truth, a justness,
and a closely earth-axis commensurable quality, that it
required an addition of only 0·0001, or no more than the
twentieth part of a hair's breadth, or of rather less than
that still, to make one of those early English inches perfectly equal to a Pyramid inch: and will cause every well-
wisher of his country to perceive that the *inch* must be

that time, in the then legalised and Government inches of our country, a
direct measure of the Exchequer's Queen Elizabeth's standard ell rod;
i.e. the gun-metal bar decorated with the royal crown and E at each
end, and safely preserved in the Exchequer, it is believed, for close on
300 years.

Colonel Strange kindly undertook the task, and having obtained formal
leave from H.M. Exchequer and the Lords of the Treasury, proceeded
thus:—

With the aid, partly, of Messrs. Chisholm and Chaney (the Chief Clerk
and Junior Clerk of the Exchequer, since Warden and Sub-Warden of
the Standards), the exact microscopic length of the modern Government
standard yard was laid off on the old Elizabethan ell, starting from one
end of it precisely, and marking on the ell, towards the further end of it,
exactly where the other end of the yard came. That place was defined
by a very fine line, drawn with a sharp steel point; and then they had
between that line and the further end of the ell, the difference in length
of the yard and the ell, viz. 45 — 36 = 9 inches, nominally; but it might
be more or less than 9 inches, if there was any sensible difference in the
size of the inches of the ell and of the inches of the yard.—(See *Transactions of R. Society, Edinburgh*, Vol. XXIII. for 1864, pp. 702, 706.)

This plan was an excellent one, because it threw the anomalies or
accumulated small differences of all the ell's 45 inches upon the yard's
inches into the small 9-inch, nearly, space, and reduced any temperature
correction required to an infinitesimally small quantity.

The next step of Colonel Strange was, in the same skilful manner, to
transfer that residual 9-inch length, nearly, of the ell, to a slip of brass;
and then, after having again and again compared that transferred length
with the marked length on the ell, and found it certainly to agree therewith to the verge of visibility with a magnifying glass, he took it to
Messrs. Troughton and Simms's grand instrumental establishment, and
by means of well-known micrometer-microscope apparatus there, determined the exact length in modern Government inches of the apparent
9 inches, more or less, transferred from the ell.

And how much did it amount to?

To 9·039 inches. Showing that the Elizabethan ell's 45 inches were
equal to 45·039 of the present inches of the British Government; that is,
that the Elizabethan ell's inches were longer than the present English
inches, but not quite so long as the Great Pyramid inches, yet coming
almost ten times closer thereto than does the present erroneously
legalised inch of the country.

preserved. Not only and simply preserved too, but, if possible, restored to its exact ancient and Pyramid value;—when the following table of earth-commensurable lengths (in its now proposed subdivisions, chosen because apparently appropriate to the Great Pyramid's numbers, as well as suitable to human use and wont), would become possible to be the British measures in modern times also, and without dislocation to any of the more usual popular factors.

GREAT PYRAMID LENGTH MEASURES.

Division, or number of each part in the grand Length Standard.	Intermediate division.	Length in Pyramid miles.	Length in Pyramid cubits or arms.	Length in Pyramid inches.	Name now proposed to be applied.
1		4000·	10,000,000	250,000,000·	Earth's half-breadth, or semi-axis of rotation.
	1000				
1,000		4·	10,000·	250,000·	League.
	4·				
4,000		1·	2,500·	62,500·	Mile.
40,000	10·	0·4	250·	6,250·	Furlong.
100,000	2·5	..	100·	2,500·	Acre-side.
1,000,000	10·	..	10·	250·	Rod.
	10·				
10,000,000		..	1·	25·	Cubit or Arm.
(20,833,333	25·	..	..	12·	Foot.)
250,000,000	..	..	..	1·	Inch.
	10·				
2,500,000,000		..	..	0·1	Tenths.
25,000,000,000	10·	..	..	0·01	Hundredths.
250,000,000,000	10·	..	..	0·001	Thousandths.

A small standard, viz. the foot of 12 inches, is left in place; because, although not evenly earth-commensurable, and inappropriate, therefore, for scientific purposes, there is a large operative use for it; and it *is* connected at one end, though not at the other, with the Pyramid system. And if we next compare all the mutually approximating Pyramid items with the British, and in terms of present British inches (so that we may not be speaking in an unknown language), we shall have the following table :—

PYRAMID AND BRITISH LINEAR MEASURE.

Compared through the temporary medium of British linear inches.

1 earth's semi-axis of ⁄rotation, Pyr. = 250,250,000,000		
1 league Pyramid = 250,250·000	1 league British =	218,721·600
1 mile ,, = 62,562·500	1 mile ,, =	63,360·000
1 acre-side ,, = 2,502·500	1 acre-side ,, =	2,504·525
1 rod ,, = 250·250	1 rod ,, =	198·000
1 cubit or arm ,, = 25·025	2-foot rule ,, =	24·000
1 foot ,, = 12·012	1 foot ,, =	12·000
1 inch ,, = 1·001	1 inch ,, =	1·000

The first remark to be expressed on this table is the very close approach of the acre-side of the Pyramid to that of the British scale. It is a length which does not nominally figure on the usual modern linear English lists; though it exists through the square measure, and is, without doubt, the most important land measure by far which the whole community possesses ; because it is the invariable term in which all the landed property of the country is bought, sold, and "deeded."

As such an all-important quantity to this country, we cannot at all understand how an acre was ever established by Government at such a very awkward proportion in the length of its side, as it now is, to any of our linear measures ; for the fraction which it gives is rough to a degree : and yet, it will be observed, by the previous tables, that the Pyramid principle, hardly altering the real and absolute value to any sensible extent, makes the acre-side in Pyramid inches at once the easy quantity of 2,500 ; or in arm, *i.e.* cubit, lengths, 100.*

* This important principle of identifying the acre-side with the linear measures of its own country has been recently taken up, or rather arrived at independently, by Mr. Louis D'Aguilar Jackson, in his little book, " Sim-

And a second remark is, that these Pyramid linear measures lead terrestrial distances, as by leagues and earth-radii, so easily and by decimal steps, from affairs of the earth to those of the skies, that they possess another direct advantage in science. For, whether in the case of the moon, or the vastly more distant sun, astronomers express their respective distances almost always in terms of an earth-radius or earth's half-breadth—as if all men were perfectly aware of what length that was—and yet there is no indication of it in the authorised and legal long measures of the country. No! not though the sacred Book of Job indicates Divine Providence to be still waiting for the answer of self-sufficient man, as to how much he does really know, of that most proper and grand linear standard for him, in his present abode, viz. "the breadth of the earth." (See p. 68, Chap. IV.)

The really Pyramidal Scale of the present Ordnance Survey of Great Britain.

Nor does the advantage of the Pyramid principle end here, for its own mile contains 2,500 or 50 × 50, cubit lengths; and such a *proportion* has recently, though it is to be feared involuntarily, become so great a favourite

plified Weights and Measures," E. and F. N. Spon, 48, Charing Cross, London, 1876.

Accordingly, at p. 18, he speaks of its having been a custom in primitive times to have no special measures of *surface*, because the measures of length were used as corresponding with the side of a square surface, and rendering particular "superficial measures quite unnecessary."

Again, at p. 26, he speaks of the existing English expedient of Gunter's chain and other special land measures as having been introduced only "owing to the moderns having lost sight of the acre-side of ancient times, which evidently must have been once at 100 cubits, and afterwards perhaps 200 feet. And in his own proposed scheme accordingly, of not a revolutionised, but only of a wisely reformed, English table of linear measure, he recurs to what he considers original principles, and announces, 12 inches = 1 foot, 200 feet = 1 acre-side, 30 acre-sides = 1 mile.

with Government, that they have commenced a magnificent survey of Great Britain on precisely this proportion, or 1,2500th of nature.

This is by far a larger scale than either our own, or any other, country has ever been completely surveyed on yet; and infers such an infinity of drawing, copying, and engraving, that it could positively never have been thought of, even in wealthy Great Britain, but for the previous invention, *first* of photography to do all the copying, and *then* of electrotypy to multiply the soft engraved copper plates. Hence the survey on the scale of 1-2500th is a remarkable public work of the present time, and excites some curiosity to know how and why that proportion came to be adopted.

Plainly 1-2500 does not form any portion of the British imperial linear system; and when we are officially told, that the proportion was adopted to allow of the map being on a scale of 25 inches to a mile, or becoming thereby capable of representing an acre by one square inch,—we are quite assured (if the Government is still true to the legal measures of the land), that that is *not* the reason; for the map is not on that scale. It *is* truly of the proportion of 1-2500th of *nature;* but that gives, in the existing British metrology, 25·344 inches to a mile,* and 1·018 square inches to an acre.

Immense inconvenience, therefore, results to the component members of the British nation, that the grandest and most costly survey of their country which they have ever paid for, and which is now in inevitable progress, whether they like it or not,—does not fit in to their existing measures evenly, but carries these annoying fractions along with it.

---

* Agreeably with the present law of the land that 12 inches = 1 foot, 3 feet = yard, and 1,760 yards = 1 mile; then 1 mile contains 63,360· inches, which quantity being divided by 2,500 (the Ordnance map's scale of reduction), gives 25·3440, the proportion alluded to above.

Yet a single act of parliament (what high-souled, independent Member will move for it, if Government will not?) adopting the Pyramid measures for the country, — or, we might almost say, restoring the nation's ancient and hereditary measures to their proper place, and not occasioning any inconvenience to the ordinary public using the inch, the acre, and the mile,— would cause the map, without any alterations at all to its exquisitely engraved and accurately measured surface, to be at once a map on the scale of most precisely and evenly 25 of the then legal British inches to the then mile;* and of one square legal British inch to the then acre, without the smallest fraction left over or under; and would substitute truth for arithmetical falsehood, on every occasion when a Briton has hastily, and tries shortly, and without going into fractions, to mention the great national map of his country.

In my first edition I said that Britons might in *haste* stumble into that slovenly and untruthful error of speaking of 25·344 inches, as being 25·000 inches; or of the Ordnance map being on the scale of 25·000, when they should have said 25·344, inches to a mile. But I regret to have to add now, that larger experience shows that they commit themselves equally in their calmer moments, and with abundance of *leisure*, as well; for in the *Proceedings of the Royal Society of Edinburgh for the Session* 1872-3, just published, the learned President professor, Sir Robert Christison, Bart., M.D. (and positively overbearing for the anti-national, irreligious, introduction of

---

* The proportion here stated is arrived at thus:—
In the table of proposed Pyramid linear measure, p. 297, it will be seen that 25 inches = 1 cubit; 100 cubits = 1 acre-side; 25 acre-sides = 1 mile; whence, 1 mile contains 62,500 inches; and 62,500 divided by 2,500 as before, yield 25·000 exactly.

Also, 1 acre-side contains 2.500 inches; wherefore that number divided by the 2,500 of the Ordnance map's scale of reduction, necessarily yields 1·0000 inches.

the French metrical system, as well as anxious for more
accurate or convenient weights and measures for British
pharmacy and chemistry), one therefore who should
know what exactness is,—yet even he, from his presi-
dential chair and in his inaugural address for the session,
could continually speak of, and the Society subsidised by
the British Government could continually print on page
after page of their " Proceedings," " the 25-inch maps
of the Ordnance survey "; when they ought to have
fully troubled themselves to say, and *print*, on every
occasion, " the 25·344-inch maps of the same survey."

INTERNATIONAL APPENDIX TO GREAT PYRAMID LINEAR MEASURE.

Hereditary Cubit or " Cloth " Measures.

Country or City.	Name of Linear Measure.	Length in British Inches.
Algiers	Turkish pic	24·53
Ancona	Braccio	25·33
Bergen	Ell	24·71
Betalfagui	Guz	25·00
Bologna	Woollen braccio	25·00
Candia	Pic	25·11
Copenhagen	Ell	24·71
Ferrara	Silk braccio	24·75
Mantua	Braccio	25·00
Mocha	Guz	25·00
Nancy	Aune	25·18
Padua	Silk braccio	25·30
Parma	Cloth braccio	25·10
Patras	Silk pic	25·00
Persia	Guerze	25·00
Great Pyramid	**" Sacred Cubit "**	**25·025**
Trieste	Silk ell	25·22
Tunis	Silk pic	24·83
Venice	Silk braccio	24·81
Verona	Silk braccio	25·22
Zante	Silk braccio	25·37

Foot Measures.

As shown in our table on page 297, and its subsequent explication, a 12-inch foot standard introduces notable difficulties into the earth-commensurable section of the Great Pyramid arrangement of long measure. And proposals have been before the public for several years, from totally opposite quarters too, requesting Government to enact a 10-inch foot for the future use of the nation.

Such a foot would evidently harmonize at once with every branch of the Pyramid system; but how would it suit the convenience of the working men, for whose purpose mainly the foot seems to have been originally introduced, and is still kept up?

We have already seen in the note on page 31, Chap. III., that the natural or naked foot of a man is barely 10·5 inches long, though the shoed and booted foot of civilized man may be twelve inches or more; and indeed, in some parts of Switzerland and Germany, their local metrological tables state that twelve inches make, not a foot, but a "schuh," or shoe. There need be no surprise, therefore, to find, that two separate foot measures have long been known amongst mankind, one of them averaging twelve English inches long, and the other ten, though still almost invariably divided into twelve parts, or small inches of its own: In the foot of the one case, its length was twelve *thumb* breadths, and in the other twelve *finger* breadths, approximately. The ancient Roman foot (11·62 English inches long nearly) was evidently of the former class; as was likewise the Greek Olympic foot, generally known as the Greek foot *par excellence*, and = 12·11 English inches; though Greece had also another foot standard, termed the Pythic foot, which was only 9·75 English inches long.

But in mediæval and modern, or Saxon, Norman, and British times, humanity seems to have declared itself unmistakably for the larger foot. So that in Dr. Kelly's list of all the commercial peoples known to Great Britain in 1821 (see his "Universal Cambist," Vol. II. p. 244), while ten of them have feet ranging between 9·50 and 10·99 English inches, no less than seventy-four are found to have feet whose lengths are comprised somewhere between 11·0 and 13·0 of the same inches.

Hence, if any alterations should be made in future time to earth-commensurate the Pyramid foot, as now imagined = 12·012 English inches, it should rather be in the direction of making it = 12·5 than 10·0 Pyramid inches; and no harm would be done in either case, so long as the value of the inch was not interfered with.

The ancient idolatrous Egyptians of the Pharaonic period do not seem to have had any foot measure; but, for all linear purposes, to have invariably used their well-known profane cubit = 20·7 English inches long; doubling it sometimes as the royal or Karnak cubit, which was then = 41·4 English inches. In subsequent Greek Alexandrian times, those Egyptians both employed, perverted, and mixed up with their own, sundry measures of Greece, and may then have had feet, as well as small cubits = 1·5 foot: but these hybrid and short-lived standards are by no means worth our while now to inquire into, for Alexandria of the Ptolemys, never very ancient, has long since been deservedly dead and buried; while the present Alexandria is a different city, inhabited by a differently descended people, and professing a totally different religion.

Hereditary Inch Measures.

Country or City.	Name of Linear Measure.	Length in British Inches.
Amsterdam	Rhineland foot ÷ 12	1·029
Anspach	Foot ÷ 12	0·977
Austria, Vienna ..	Zoll	1·037
Basil	Foot ÷ 12	0·979
Belgium .. {	Lost its traditions and language too.	
Berlin	Foot ÷ 12	1·016
Birmah, Rangoon ..	Paulgaut	1·000
Denmark	Tomme	·1·030
France (*système usuel,* interdicted since 1840) .. }	Pouce	1·094
France (modern) ..	Destroyed its traditions.	
Königsberg	Foot ÷ 12	1·009
Leyden	Foot ÷ 12	1·028
Lindau	Long foot ÷ 12 ..	1·033
Lucerne	Schuh ÷ 12	1·030
Middleburg	Foot ÷ 12	0·984
Neufchâtel	Foot ÷ 12	0·984
Norway	Tum	0·974
Nüremburg	Foot ÷ 12	0·997
Pisa	Palmo ÷ 12	0·989
Prague	Foot ÷ 12	0·985
Prussia, up to 1872 ..	Zoll	1·030
do. since 1872 ..	Lost its traditions.	
Great Pyramid ..	**" Inch "**	**1·001**
Rhineland	Foot ÷ 12	1·029
Rome	Foot ÷ 12	0·988
Stettin..	Rhineland foot ÷ 12	1·029
Sweden	Tum	0·974
Zurich..	Zoll	0·984

The above table is prepared chiefly from Dr. Kelly's " Universal Cambist "; but inasmuch as he does not descend below foot measures, and the inches are then deduced by dividing his values for the feet by twelve : —the list is supplemented by positive inches, or their verbal equivalents, as,—zoll, pouce, tomme, tum, pollegada, pulgada, &c., as contained in Weale's Woolhouse's " Weights and Measures."

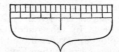

ONE INCH OF THE GREAT PYRAMID, subdivided into tenths and half-tenths, and equal in length to one 500-millionth of the Earth's Axis of Rotation.

N.B.—The above pictorial representation must be considered approximate only, on account of the expansions and contractions of the paper it is printed on, from moisture.

CHAPTER XV.

HEAT AND PRESSURE, ANGLE AND TIME,

Cosmical and Pyramidal.

A S already shown, no system of weights and measures can be complete without a reference to heat, and its power of altering the dimensions of all bodies. It would appear too, that, next to the very existence of matter, heat is the most important influence or condition in creation; and, since the rise of the modern science of thermo-dynamics, which looks on heat as a mode of motion, the measure of heat is the first step from statics to dynamics, which is the last and truest form of all science.

Thermometers and their Scales in different Countries.

A "thermometer" is therefore, in these days, one of the most widely essential of all scientific instruments, and there is probably no modern science which can advance far without its aid; unless indeed such science be assisted by some semi-natural and practical method of securing one constant reference temperature for all its observations; but which is seldom possible to be carried out completely in any modern observatories; and in fact is not. Yet the thermometer in England, though there so doubly necessary, both in, and out of doors, has been allowed to remain, as to its scale, in a most haphazard sort of guise. That is, the said scale is actually ridiculed over the chief part of continental Europe, as being both inconvenient in practice, and founded in error too : in so far as the primitive notion of Mynheer Gabriel Daniel Fahrenheit,* touching absolute cold, is seen every winter to be a mistake, whenever his thermometer descends below its own carefully marked zero ; while the all-important point of the freezing of water is left at the not very signal, but certainly rather inconvenient, number of 32° ; and the boiling-point at the not more convenient one of 212°.

Many, therefore, have been the demands that we should adopt either the German Réaumur, or the French Centigrade, *i.e.* originally the thermometer of Celsius ; in terms of any of which, water-freezing marks 0° ; and all degrees below that notable point are negative ; above, positive.

The proposed change has, except in a few chemical circles, been strenuously resisted, because—

1st. The anomalous absolute numbers chosen for freezing and boiling on Fahrenheit's scale do not interfere with the accuracy of thermometers so marked, when due allowance is made for them.

2nd. It has been against the principle of most British scientific men hitherto, in their different weights and measures, to have them showing a natural standard in themselves ; but only to have their *proportion* to the

---

* Fahrenheit was born at Hamburg as some say; at Dantzic according to others; while all allow that he afterwards lived long at Amsterdam. Exactly *when* his birth took place is not known, nor is the date of his death, but his "Dissertation on Thermometers" was published in London in 1724, not many years after the first successful introduction of quicksilver, to take the place of air, in thermometers ; and seems to have been the chief agent, over and above his own practical success in the manufacture of such thermometers, in causing his system of numbers and scale-graduation to become such an almost universal favourite in England. And yet it is now alleged that Fahrenheit was not the original inventor of the scale which bears his name; that having been really devised and first used by Olaus Roemer, the celebrated astronomer of Copenhagen, about 1709.

said natural standards numerically determined, and then recorded in writing elsewhere.

3rd. This system has been carried out in its integrity in Fahrenheit's thermometer *when* it is written, that 180 even subdivisions shall exist between freezing and boiling ; and the commencing number for freezing shall be 32°.

4th. In the fact that the distance between freezing and boiling is divided into 180 parts in Fahrenheit's thermometer, but only 100 in the French thermometer, and 80 in the German instrument, eminent advantage is claimed for every-day purposes ; even among the chemists too, as well as all other members of the community,—because a greater number of different states of temperature can be quoted in even degrees without reference to fractions of a degree ; and—

5th. It is said that the proposed change would be subversive of all ordinary ideas of steady-going individuals as to what the new numbers really meant ; because, what honest country gentleman would appreciate in his heart that a temperature of 40°, when a French system should be established amongst us, meant an over-powering, exhausting summer heat of 104° Fahrenheit ?

Some of these objections have weight, but others are of doubtful importance ; and in all that can be said about the British scientific principle (as established by recent Governments) not founding its measures on natural standards direct,—that is proved to be baseless for our nation's early, and more than historic, origin,—by reason of the real British length unit, the inch, having been found, after all, to be an even, round fraction of the earth's semi-axis of rotation ; and the Great Pyramid building bearing witness, that the matter was by no means accidental, but grandly in earnest intention.

The ultra-scientific upholders too of Fahrenheit, have,

in the instance of the best practical zero of temperature, received a notable correction from the poorer classes of our land; the very classes for whom alone all working measures should be primarily arranged; seeing that every gardener, and probably every ploughman who thinks of such things at all, is accustomed in his daily toil to speak of the more *rurally* important and biologically trying cases of temperature (as well as the physically marvellous one of the universal fluid becoming a solid, and hardening both earth and water), not in terms of alien, and over-lauded, Mr. Fahrenheit's scale by any means, but as so many " degrees of frost " or "heat."

The practical importance, therefore, of having the British thermometrical zero at the freezing-point of water, is thus incontestably proved, and from the right direction; while, if it be desirable, as no doubt it is, to have the space from freezing to boiling divided into a greater number of degrees than either the French or German systems offer,—why then, let the nation take for the space between the two natural water units, not even the 180 of the clever Amsterdam Dutchman, Fahrenheit, or rather of Olaus Roemer, the Danish Astronomer, but the 250 of the Great Pyramid scale; for by so doing, not only will they reap that one advantage above mentioned to a still greater extent, but they will suffer less shock, as it were, in their feelings, when talking of summer temperatures, than even if they retained the size of the Fahrenheit degrees, but placed the o at freezing; as simply illustrated by the following numbers, giving the same absolute temperatures in terms of five different thermometric scales :—

Fahrenheit.	Modified Fahrenheit.	Centigrade.	Réaumur.	Pyramid.
122°	90°	50°	40°	125°
104°	72°	40°	32°	100°

But now for the finishing off of this last temperature scale, in the manner in which the Pyramid system so often ends with reference to the four sides of its base, and to the first four simple sections of such a Pyramid. Multiply, therefore, the 250° of water-boiling by 4, making 1,000, and where are we landed?

At that most notable and dividing line of heat, where it causes bodies to begin to give out light; and registered with confidence by the Diffusion of Useful Knowledge Society, in Vol. II. of their "Natural Philosophy," p. 63, under title of " Iron Bright Red in the Dark," as being 752° Fahrenheit, which amounts to 1,000° of the Pyramid precisely. And multiply this 1,000° again by 5, and where are we? At 5,000° of the Pyramid, or that glowing white-hot heat, where the modern chemists of several nations would place the melting-point of the most dense and refractory of all metals, platinum. Or descend again to —400° Pyramid, and we find a point regarded by some existing chemists as the absolute zero of temperature: though natural philosophers are more inclined to prefer their theoretical base of the air thermometer at —682° Pyramid; but as none of them have yet approached nearer than about half-way thereto, no man among them knows what physical obstacles may lie in the still long and entirely untried portion of their path. And that there may be many such difficulties, we have not to look far for an example.

French Academicians of the first Revolution despise the interests of the people in their temperature standard; and are met by unexpected difficulties.

Thus the French metrical temperature reference was originally intended by its exceedingly scientific authors, admirable for their day, to have been the freezing-point

of water; on the arithmetical and mathematical, rather
than physical and experimental, conclusion—that they
would find water in its densest condition when coldest,
or immediately before passing into the state of ice.
But lo! when they began to experiment, nature refused
to be bound by human ideas, and water was discovered
to be of the greatest density at a very sensible distance
of heat above freezing, or at 39°·2 Fahr.

When this discovery was once made, able men found
in it a most beneficent influence to promote the ameni-
ties of human life upon the surface of the earth; seeing
that but for the anomalous expansion of water with
cold, when the temperature descends below 39°·2 Fahr.,
our lakes and rivers would freeze at the bottom instead
of the top; and would, in fact, accumulate beds of ice
below, until in the winter they became entirely solid
blocks; which blocks no summer sun would be able to
do more than melt a small portion of the surface of, to
be inevitably frozen hard again the next cold night, to
the destruction of all the fish.

The discovered fact, however, of what really does
take place, when water approaches the freezing-point,
had the inconvenience of utterly breaking up the uniformity of the Academy's arrangements for temperature reference in the French metrical system.   For the
Parisian philosophers still desired to refer some observations to freezing; yet could not but conscientiously
admit the superior propriety, at least for all measurements wherein the density of water entered, of employing their newly corrected temperature of 39°·2 Fahr.,
rather than their former 32° Fahr.

Accordingly, at page 21 of Roscoe's "Lessons in
Chemistry," where the best possible face is put upon
employing French measures for the British nation, we
are told that the French unit of weight is a cubic centi-
mètre of water at a temperature of 4° *Centigrade*.   But

at page 147, a table of specific gravities is given, where it is stated that water at the temperature of 0° *Centigrade* is to be taken as unity; and no temperature reference at all appears for length measure; perhaps because the author knew that that reference is just now, for the metre of the Archives, a still further deviation from the originally intended uniformity; being actually an uncertain quantity somewhere between 6° and 12° C., on account of an error in the mètre's length.

Again, at pages 361 and 362 of Prof. Roscoe's handy little book, extensive tables are formally given of comparisons between the English and French measures of all kinds (descending, where weight is concerned, to the sixth place of decimals of a grain), but no mention at all is made either of temperature or atmospheric pressure for any of them; though the former condition must vary between the two systems occasionally by 60°, and the latter by the extent of the whole atmosphere.

In fact, the too learnedly artificial character of the French temperature and pressure references is such, that they cannot, in practice, look the light of day in the face; while they are, above all things, and for other reasons as well, totally unsuitable to the working-man. You cannot, for instance, attempt or pretend to use them in practice, without breaking their most important provisions continually; as well as introducing huge errors, such as the omission or introduction of the whole atmosphere, and all for the purpose of guarding against mere microscopic errors depending on minute and almost totally insensible variations of the atmosphere as it exists about, and is breathed momentarily by, all mankind.

On that unhappy *doctrinaire* French system, strictly carried out, if there should arise a difference of opinion at a market, as to which is the longer of two measuring-rods, or which is the heavier of two weights, you must

carry both of them away from what they were being
employed for, and bring the rods down by any possible
refrigerating method to the 6° or 12° C. point, and place
the weights by some difficult and expensive contrivance
in a vacuum, and also at a temperature of 0° C., or
perhaps 4° C. All these being out-of-the-way conditions where no one, except an occasional *savant*, ever
wants to use either rods or weights; and where you
may find that their relations to each other (from
different *rates* and characters of heat expansibility)
are actually and totally different from what they were
at any of the degrees of natural temperature, wherein
they are being every day really and practically employed by the mass of the people; and which degrees
never differ much from their mean quantity all the year
through.

Nature's Standards of Temperature and Pressure, for all men.

Indeed the extreme narrowness of the range both of
temperature and atmospheric pressure, within which all
the best, and the most too, of human work is performed,
has begun at last to excite intelligent and interested
attention.   Wherefore thus, an able and scientific
American observer, field-geologist, and eloquent author,
Mr. Clarence King, leaving everyone to find out for
themselves, if they have not done so already long ago,
that they cannot write neatly with frozen fingers, holds
forth, in his recent book entitled "Mountaineering in
Sierra Nevada," California,—on the importance to man
of a certain standard degree of *pressure of the atmosphere;*
when he, Mr. King, has descended again to the inhabited and low plain country, after a long sojourn on
duty upon the high and snowy flanks of the upper parts
of Mount Shasta :—

" The heavier air of this lower level soothed us into a pleasant (laziness) (frame of mind) which lasted over Sunday, resting our strained muscles and opening the heart anew to human and sacred influence. If we are sometimes at pain when realising within what narrow range of *latitude* (temperature) mankind reaches finer development,—or how short a step it is, from tropical absence of spiritual life to dull boreal stupidity,—it is added humiliation to experience our still more marked limitation in *altitude*. At fourteen thousand feet, or with 17 only, in place of 30, inches of atmospheric pressure, little is left me but bodily appetite and impression of sense. The habit of scientific observation, which in time becomes one of the involuntary processes, goes on as do heart-beat and breathing; a certain general awe overshadows the mind; but on descending again to lowlands, one after another the whole riches of the human organization come back with delicious freshness."

By what blinded impulse then could it have been, that the philosophers of Paris did not accept their position on the earth, *under, or in, the atmosphere,* as given them by God to breathe, and to flourish in. And they *know* that they cannot do without it. Yet have they in spirit rebelled, and instead of making the delightful mean annual temperature and wholesome and necessary mean annual pressure of the atmosphere on and in their abodes, the standard references for those features in all matters of their country's metrology,—they must rush off to a horribly chilling, an actually freezing, benumbing zero; to a theoretical absence of all vital atmosphere, which would, in fact, be instant death to the bravest amongst them; and to a host of smaller physical difficulties which they have not even yet overcome or got out of the maze of.

Or by what mere flock-of-sheep idea of irrationally

following *some* leader, is it, that now, so many of our British scientific men, — after having made their own barometrical observations at temperatures between 50° and 80° indoors, and having received others from abroad also confined within the same pleasing limits of temperature, and knowing that the Russians reduce all their extensive barometric observations to 62° Fahrenheit, can think of no other mode of bringing them all to one common temperature point of comparison, than by carrying every one of them right away, as the French metrical men do, to the distant and outlandish and horrible freezing-point. Though too they have to apply for that purpose so large a correction to the numbers read off from each barometer, that the original observer fails to recognize, in his *computed* observations, those standard heights of quicksilver which he used to identify in his daily experience with particular conditions of weather, or warnings of approaching storms? Yet the London Government and the British people are daily paying, by the counsel of certain of their unpatriotic scientists, and metropolitan scientific Societies, of Gallic proclivities, for this extravagant correction being applied to innumerable British meteorological observations.

The Great Pyramid's Zone of 30° Latitude, and its bearing on the same Earth-Atmosphere Standards.

But all these anomalies are corrected at once at the Great Pyramid; for its position on the earth's surface in that parallel of latitude (30°) which, by the geometry of a sphere, has an equal amount of terrestrial *surface* between itself and the equator on one side, and itself and the Pole on the other, evidently points to something like mean terrestrial surface temperature as the proper central point of comparison in the affairs of men.

Equally too does the Pyramid point to 30 of its inches of mercurial pressure of the atmosphere, as the international reference in that department of Nature. Exhibiting the quantity also as the very clear and distinctly separating line between good, and bad, of the weather all the world over; above 30 inches of the barometer meaning dry weather, sun-shine, and bracing Polar air; below 30 inches, rain, clouds, moisture, and electric equatorial gales ; while the French metricalists can only say, that the same grand bounding line, or pathway between the serene and the stormy, of terrestrial meteorology is marked amongst them, by the indistinct number of 761·99 millimètres.

The Pyramid reference indeed for pressure would not be exact, if observed very scientifically and microscopically in its own latitude and longitude *at the sea-level.* But that needlessly low-down reduction of all meteorologists, is only another case of their going on one side, instead of to the middle, of the fact ; for the bulk of mankind does not live at that most dangerous level, when every gale might submerge whole cities and drown the inhabitants by myriads of myriads,—but much more nearly at such a mean, and perfectly safe height above it, as that of the King's Chamber of the Great Pyramid, viz. 4,297 inches. A height which both gives out, on an annual mean of barometric observations, the required 30 inches ; and at the same time makes the temperature observed there, under normal circumstances, the true Pyramidal $\frac{1}{5}$ between boiling and freezing of water ; and not the slightly higher temperature of that latitude and longitude, if reduced to what does not exist there the sea-shore and its level.

The said King's Chamber temperature of $\frac{1}{5}$, is further the mean-temperature (and therefore the proper reference point for all men) of the whole *anthropological* earth. Not of the whole earth simply, for that includes frozen

Polar lands in either hemispheres of such excessively
low temperature that they are not, and cannot, and
never will be, permanently occupied by man.   Lands
too, which with their six-months' Arctic nights ignore
the Great Pyramid's very first and foundational teaching, or of 365·242 solar days and nights as numbering
the length of the year, and defining the diurnal circumstances under which human labour is to be performed
and human rest enjoyed, until the time for setting down
in the Kingdom of God.   Lands, moreover, as those so
often sunless Polar ones, which in their perpetual cold,
and " whitening in eternal sleet," may represent that
Divinely implied impossibility to Job,—

> " Hast thou entered into the treasures of the snow?
> Or hast thou seen the treasures of the hail,
> Which I have reserved against the time of trouble,
> Against the day of battle and war ? "   (Job xxxviii. 22, 23.) *

And on making such very proper Polar exception in
our earth-surface enquiry, the mean temperature of all
man-inhabited countries does again appear to be, just
that very same beneficent and most suitable quantity of
the Great Pyramid generally, and of the King's Cham-
ber thereof more particularly,—viz. $\frac{1}{5}$, or in the special
number of that Chamber itself, 50 ; here to be called 50
degrees of temperature.

Hence we seem now to be Pyramidically justified in
giving out, as almost cosmical in their bearings, in the
following general table (reduced or translated from
various modern sources), the numbers which would be
read off for the phenomena there alluded to, upon any
well-graduated Pyramid thermometer to be.

* When the late grand Government expedition was preparing in 1874,
almost to take the North Pole of the earth by storm, through profuse
expenditure on all the promising, vaunting and most powerful means of
modern science,—I ventured, in a paper for *Good Words* to quote that
solemn warning to Job,—as an argument that nothing would come of
the attempt.   And the country is probably *now* pretty well satisfied that
such has been very nearly the result.

TEMPERATURES IN PYRAMID THERMOMETER DEGREES.
Atmospheric pressure = 30 inches, except when otherwise stated.

Phenomena.	Number on Scale.	Phenomena.	Number on Scale
	Degrees		Degrees
Platinum melts	5000	Stearine melts	138
Wrought-iron melts ..	4000	Spermaceti melts ..	122
,, ,, ..	3750	Summer temperature at } Great Pyramid.. }	100
Steel melts	3500		
,, ,, ...	3250	Ether, common, boils ..	92
Cast-iron melts ..	3875	Blood heat	91·5
,, grey, melts ..	3130	Butter and lard melt ..	82
,, white ,, ..	2625	**Mean temperature**	
Gold, pure, melts ..	3125	**at level of King's**	
,, alloyed as in coinage	2950	**Chamber in Great**	
Copper melts	2875	**Pyramid.**	
Silver, pure, melts ..	2555		
,, ,, ,, ...	2500	**Pyramid temp. = T$\frac{1}{5}$**	
Bronze melts	2250	**Mean temperature**	**50**
Sulphur boils	1100	**of all lands inha-**	
Antimony melts	1080	**bited by man, and**	
Zinc melts	1028	**temperature of the**	
,, ,, ...	900	**most suitable de-**	
Iron visible in the dark ..	1000	**gree to man.**	
Mercury boils	882		
,, ,, ...	875	Ether boils	28
Sulphuric acid, strong,		Mean temperature of } London .. .. }	25
boils	815		
,, ,,	812		
,, melts	815	Low winter temperature } at Great Pyramid }	20
Cadmium	788		
Phosphorus boils ..	725	Water freezes	0
Bismuth melts	575	Freezing mixture, snow } and salt .. .. }	—50
Water boils under 20 at-			
mospheres	535	Sulphuric acid freezes ..	—87
,, ,, 15 ,,	500	Mercury freezes	—98
,, ,, 10 ,,	450	Greatest Arctic cold ex-} perienced .. . }	—125
,, ,, 5 ,,	381		
Spirit of turpentine boils..	325	Greatest artificial cold, } nitrous oxide and car- bonic disulphide, *in* vacuo. }	330
Acetic acid boils	290		
Sulphur melts	278		
WATER BOILS	250		
Sodium melts	238	Absolute zero (Miller's } Chemistry) .. }	—400
Benzol boils	200		
Alcohol, pure, boils ..	198	Theoretical base of air	
,, ,, ,, ..	195	thermometer, or air	
Stearic acid melts ..	174	supposed to be so ex-	
White wax melts	170	cessively contracted in	
Wood spirit boils ..	166	bulk by cold, as at last }	—682
Potassium melts	158	to occupy no space at	
Yellow wax melts ..	155	all, and in that case to	
Greatest observed shade } temperature .. }	139	become of infinitely great specific gravity! }	

Angle.

No sooner has man in the course of his scientific development begun to contemplate the skies, than he feels the necessity of having angular, as well as, or even rather than, linear, measure to refer to for distances; and the same demand for angular measure is soon afterwards experienced in each of the purely terrestrial sciences as well.

Therefore it was, that the French *savants* of the Revolution attempted to introduce into their decimally arranged metrical system an *angular* graduation where the quadrant contained 100, and the whole circle 400, degrees.   But, after trying it for some years, they had to give it up; for the influence of "Great Babylon," which is, by some persons, believed to have originally invented, and then fixed on the world, our present sexagesimal system, or 360° to the circle, and 60 minutes to the degree, was too powerful for modern Paris to contend successfully against.

But there could have been no more community in ancient days of feeling or idea between most idolatrous Babylon, and the totally non-idolatrous Great Pyramid in their goniometry, than in their methods of astronomical orientation, which we have already seen were entirely diverse.   What system, then, for angle was more probably employed at the Great Pyramid?

A system apparently of 1,000° to the circle; 250° to the quadrant.

This conclusion has been ventured to be deduced from the following features at the Pyramid :—

(1.) The angle of rise of the Pyramid's flanks, and the angle of descent or ascent of its passages, are both very peculiar angles, characteristic of the Great Pyramid; and though rough and incommensurable on either the Babylonian, or French, or any known angular system, are in a practical way evenly commensurable on the Pyramid system.

PYRAMID FEATURE.	SYSTEM OF ANGLE MEASURES.			
	Babylonian.	French.	Vulgar.	Pyramid.
A whole circumference	360°	400°	32°	1000°
Angle of side with horizon .. .. }	50° 51′ 14″	57°·62	4°·61	144°·05
Angle of passages ..	26° 18′ 10″	29°·23	2°·34	73°·08

(2.) Whereas the King's Chamber has been in a manner utilised as the chamber of the standard of 50, and the Queen's as that of the standard of 25, and are both of them witnessed to by the number of the Pyramid courses on which they stand, the subterranean chamber may be considered the chamber of angular measure; and does,* at its centre, view the whole Pyramid side, at an angle of 75° 15′ 1″ Babylonian, but 209°·03 Pyramid. And though there are now only 202, there are shown to have been in the original finished Pyramid somewhere between 208 and 212 complete masonry courses; or agreeing, within the limits of error of those researches, with the angular result of 209°.

(3.) And then there follows a useful practical result to Navigation, and its peculiar itinerary measure, the "knot," or nautical, or sea mile; viz. the length of a mean minute of a degree of latitude.

At present there is much inconvenience from the large difference in length between our land and sea miles; for they measure 63,360· and 72,984· inches respectively.

* See my "Life and Work," Vol. III. p. 209.

But, granted that a Pyramid knot shall be 1-25th part of a Pyramid degree,—then the respective lengths of a Pyramid land, and a Pyramid sea, mile will be the comparatively approaching quantities, in inches, of 62,500· and 62,995·.

Money.

The French metrical system included *money;* and its francs, issued accordingly, have deluged the world to such an extent, that when a prize was recently proposed to all nations by the Queen of Great Britain for a certain artistic manufacture, viz. a fan, to be competed for at the South Kensington Museum of Science and Art, the money value of that prize was, by the advice of some most unpatriotic officers of that magnificently supported British Government Institution, publicly advertised in London in "francs."

Wherefore many inquirers have demanded, "What about money on the *Pyramid* system also?"

I can only answer them, that I have not been able to find out anything about that subject in the Great Pyramid.

And is that to be wondered at? Only look at any piece of money whatever: whose image and superscription does it bear? That of some earthly Cæsar or other. Therefore is money of vain human inventions, and of things speedily passing away. But all the Great Pyramid measures hitherto investigated, being evenly commensurable in every case, either with the deep things of this planet world, or the high things of heaven above, are to be considered as virtually impressed rather with a typical effigy of some of the attributes of the creation of God; in praise moreover and honour of God alone.

Far be it from me, however, to circumscribe by my

small knowledge, the bearings of any part of the Great Pyramid system. And, just as several other portions thereof have yielded fuller returns and more definite answers on taking into account the experiences of the Anglo-Saxon population of the United States of America, —so here, there is something further to be learned.

The coinage of that grand family of Republics is the only example of the money of a truly great people without the effigy of a Cæsar: and is also the only one known which bears certain internal numerical relations to the King's Chamber of the Great Pyramid, when the dimensions of that chamber are expressed in British inches.

This astonishing coincidence has but recently been recognized and given to the world, by the acute Dr. Watson F. Quinby, of Wilmington, Delaware, U.S., and has been expressed by him nearly in these words:—

"Our (U.S.) silver coinage corresponds in grains to the measures of the King's Chamber in the Great Pyramid, in British inches. So that the length of that chamber being 412·5 of those inches, the standard weight of the "Dollar of the Fathers" is 412·5 grains; the half-dollar, weighing 206·2 grains represents the breadth of the same chamber = 206·25 British inches; and the quarter-dollar of 103·1 grains represents in inches the half breadth of the same chamber, or the 'touch-stone' length as it has been called of so many of the Great Pyramid's measurements.

"At the same time the grander golden coin, the American Eagle, contains 232·5 grains of pure gold, or the number of Pyramid Cubits in the vertical height of the Great Pyramid; and the 'half-eagle' contains 116·25 of the same gold in grains, equal almost exactly to the length of the Antechamber of the King's Chamber in the same Pyramid expressed in Pyramid inches."

Time.

Time is an admitted subject in every good system of metrology; and yet is it an absolute imponderable; one, too, of which, says the moralist, we take no account but by its loss. And if this be true, how all-important for us to know " how much there is of it"; and more especially how much still remains, of that finite section already told off by the Eternal, to witness the present manner of dominion, perhaps trial, of men upon the earth!

Hitherto, these questions have been utterly above unaided man's intellect; and though the metaphysicians, following up their verbal disquisitions on the infinity of *space*, desire to make out also an absolutely infinite extension of *time*, and that both for time past and time to come,—the researches of the scientists are more to our purpose, for they dwell rather upon the unlimited *divisibility* of time. Divide it, for instance, into ever such minute portions, and it is time still; and not like the chemical elements of matter, which, after a certain amount of subdivision, exhibit, to the mathematician, their component atoms with totally different properties from what are possessed by larger portions of the same substances.

But whether time be long or short, and past, future, or even present, the human senses, unassisted by reference to the material world, are far more liable to error in this than in any other branch of all metrology. To some men, time slips away almost unheeded, unimproved too, until the end of life itself be reached; while with others, time is regarded as the most precious of all the usable gifts of God to men. With time and plenty of it, what splendid achievements may be realised; and into a short time, how much *can* be packed away! While the involuntary action of our thinking system, even exceeds the utmost straining of our voluntary efforts in matters of time; so that a single second between sleeping and waking has enabled a man to pass, without desiring it, through the multitudinous experiences of a long and eventful life.

On one side, again, in the study of time, the Natural History sciences give us the sober biological warning, that man, as he exists now, in materially uninterfered-with possession of the earth, is not going to last for ever; for there is a settled length of time for the whole duration of a species, as well as the single life of an individual therein. But on the other side, the too exclusive study of certain of these very sciences has led their out-and-out votaries, in late years, to talk more flippantly of time than of anything else under the sun. A few hundred thousand millions of years accordingly are at one instant created, and at another destroyed, or at another still totally disregarded by some of these gentlemen, just as their theories of the hour prompt them: and it is only the astronomer who stands up in rigid loyalty to this real creation by God alone, and tells mankind that time is one only; that it is the chief tester of human truth, or error; and, even down to its minutest subdivisions, it cannot be safely disregarded. The same eclipse, for instance, of sun by moon, as seen from the same place, cannot occur at two different times, only at one time; and that one epoch is capable of the sharpest definition, even down to a fractional part of a second.

To astronomy therefore only, of the modern sciences, can we reasonably look for some safe guidance in the practical measuring of time.

In the broadest sense, time is said to be measured by the amount of movement of some body moving at an equable rate. And the most equable motion by far, the only motion that has not sensibly varied *within the period of human history*, is, I might almost say, the favourite, or at least the fundamental, Pyramid phenomenon of the rotation of the earth upon its axis.

Not that even *that* movement is absolutely uniform through all possible time, in the eye of theory; but that, tested practically in the most rigid manner, or by the determination of the length of a *sidereal* day, no certain alteration has been perceived by practical astronomy during the last 2,300 years. The next most equable movement too, but of far longer period, is a secular consequence of that diurnal rotation, combined with the spheroidal figure, obliquity of axis, and an active disturbing element, the gravitation attraction of the sun and moon; producing thereby the " precession of the equinoxes"; whose whole cycle is performed in about nine and a half millions of these days, or turnings of the earth upon its own axis before a distant fixed star; and of which grand cycle not more than a sixth part has been performed yet, within all the period of human history.*

But though these two very distinct, and most different, phenomena,—the sidereal day, and the precessional period, of the earth, may be the grand storehouses for reference in the regulation of time for high science,—some easy, simple, yet striking modification

* This precessional phenomenon of long duration will come up again in future chapters of this book, being, in a manner, the grand historical dial of the Great Pyramid. And those who have not mastered the subject yet in principle, should read forthwith some of the numerous excellent treatises on Astronomy in our language by authors of repute, such as Sir John Herschel's " Outlines of Astronomy," or Professor Simon Newcomb's (United States) " Popular Astronomy "; and should be very careful how they listen to any private teaching of a contrary tendency by one or two individuals only. For the subject is one where single enthusiasts occasionally go as completely and absolutely wrong, as they still more frequently do on the exact numerical value of π; and there, neither the Great Pyramid nor modern science can *tolerate* any divergence from the one and only truth.

of each is required for the practical purposes of man in general. And then comes in the evident propriety of using, for the shorter period, a solar, rather than a sidereal, defined day ; and in place of the excessively long precessional period,—but without losing sight of its aptitudes for historical purposes,—the more moderate cycle of a year ; *i.e.* the time of the earth's revolution round the same solar orb. Such annual motion, moreover, we *must* adhere to, although it is a movement experiencing many minute perturbations ; and though it both is, and has been through the whole human period of development of the universe, a by no means nearly even multiple of the other, or daily, movement, whether we define the year by reference to either sidereal *cum* solar, or purely solar, phenomena.

Of different kinds of days upon this Earth.

These are practical points on which it is well worth while to spend a few more words, in order to try to make the Pyramid case clearer to those of our readers who desire further information. Let us begin then with the days.

As the sidereal day is defined, in *apparent* astronomy, to be the interval elapsing between a star leaving the meridian of any place, through the earth's diurnal revolution on its axis, and returning to it again (+ an excessively small correction for the slow, precessional movement in the interval) ; so a solar day is the time elapsing between the sun being on the meridian of any one place and seeming to return to it again. And *that* portion of time is equal to a sidereal day + the amount, measured by the rate of solar annual motion, that the sun has, in the diurnal interval, *apparently* retrograded among the stars, but by the really onward motion of the earth in its ceaseless annual orbit around the sun's

splendid light-, and heat-, dispensing sphere.   Hence a
solar day of the earth is longer than a sidereal one; and
in such proportion, that if a year contain 365¼ of the
former, it will contain roughly 366¼ of the latter.

When absolute diurnal equality is required from day
to day, the solar days have to go through a computation formula to reduce them from real solar days (as
they may appear to an observer, and therefore also
called *apparent*) to what are termed *mean* solar days; or
the successive places that the sun would occupy in our
sky if, in place of the earth revolving in an elliptical
orbit with a variable velocity, it revolved in a circular
orbit with a constant velocity, the time of a whole
revolution remaining the same.   But as this is only a
residual correction, which does not alter the beginning
or ending of the year at all, or the beginning or ending
of any day sensibly to the mere beholder of the general
features of nature,—we may consider it at once as
adopted; and then proceed to contrast the only really
opposing kinds of day, viz. the sidereal and the solar,
together, as to their relative aptitudes to promote the
greatest good of the greatest number of mankind.

Of the beginning of a *sidereal* day, then, hardly more
than a dozen persons in the kingdom are aware; and,
as it begins at a different instant of solar time each
day (in the course of a year passing through the whole
24 hours), even those few *doctrinaires* can only inform
themselves of the event by looking at their watches
under due regulation.

But, of the far more easily distinguishable beginning
of a *solar* day, it was thus that a devout, though not
sacred or inspired, poet of the Talmud wrote centuries
ago; and he will probably be equally heart-appreciated
still by 9,999 out of every 10,000 of the population:—

" Hast thou seen the beauteous dawn, the rosy har-
binger of day ?   Its brilliancy proceeds from the dwell-

ings of God : a ray of the eternal, imperishable light, a consolation to man.

"As David, pursued by his foes, passed a dreadful night of agony in a dreary cleft of Hermon's rock, he sang the most exquisitely plaintive of his Psalms :— ' My soul is among lions : I lie in the dark pit among the sons of men, whose teeth are spears and arrows, and their tongue a sharp sword.   Awake up, my glory, awake lute and harp, I myself will awake right early.'

" Behold ! the dawn then broke ; heaviness endured for a night, but joy came in the morning.   With sparkling eyes ' the hind of the morning,' the soft and rosy twilight, sprang forth, skimmed over hill and dale, bounding from hill-top to hill-top further than one can see ; and like a message of the Deity, addressed the solitary fugitive on the sterile rock : ' Why dost thou complain that help is not near ?   See how I emerge from the obscurity of the night, and the terrors of darkness yield before the genial ray of cheerful light ! '

" David's eye was turned to the brightening hue of the morn.   Light is the countenance of the Eternal. He saw the day-dawn rise, followed by the sun in all its matutinal splendour, pouring blessings and happiness over the earth.   Confidence and hope returned to his soul, and he entitled his Psalm in the Cave of Adullam, ' the roe of the morning, the song of the rosy dawn ! ' "

If any species of *day*, then, is marked in the Great Pyramid's metrological system, is it likely, after what we have already seen of that building's kindly feelings for man at large, its general objects and methods, its earth's annual orbit round the sun, and its sun-distance, —is it likely, I say (for it has been doubted by some), to be any other than the earth's *solar* day (the mean solar day, too, if it be represented evenly in the base-side of the grand immovable building, by a cubit length)?

And for the same reason, the Pyramid *year* can be no other than the mean *solar tropical* year; or that which is defined by the sun returning to the same tropic or place of turning in its apparent motion in the sky; bringing on, therefore, the winter and summer, the typical night and day of the year, in the same self-evident, powerful, beneficent manner to all mankind. And of the previously concluded mean solar days, in such a solar *tropical* year, there are contained at present, according to modern astronomy,

$$= 365 \cdot 242242 + \text{\&c.}$$
$$= 365 \text{ days, 5 hours, 48 minutes, } 49 \cdot 7 + \text{\&c., seconds;}$$

a length said to be nearly 25 seconds shorter than the similar year in the time of the Great Pyramid.

The next succeeding arrangement, however, of time, in all Biblically-religious, and some other, metrological systems, after *days*, is not this grand, natural, yet most inconveniently incommensurable, one of a *year;* but the short, and, by days, perfectly commensurable, one of, a *week;* commensurable, however, not by the Pyramidal 5 or by 10, but by the peculiar, and other than mere arithmetically impressive, number 7.

Indeed, the week of 7 days is something so important in itself, and forms, when further taken with its Sabbatic impressment, so decided a stage of time, whereon tradition conflicts with science, sacred opposes profane, and the Deistic contends with the rationalistic,—that we cannot address ourselves too earnestly or too carefully to ascertain what the primeval Great Pyramid may have to say further, if anything, touching this spiritual, as well as the other natural, subdivisions of time for the ruling of the life, and regulation of the work, of man while on his trial here.

PART IV.

MORE THAN SCIENCE AT THE GREAT PYRAMID.

AN UNKNOWN NINETEENTH-CENTURY ATRIST'S CONCEPTION OF THE
BUILDING OF THE GREAT PYRAMID.

Courtesy of New York Public Library Picture Collection.

THE PYRAMIDS OF EGYPT, FROM AN ENGRAVING, PROBABLY FROM THE
NINETEENTH-CENTURY, BY W.G. JACKMAN.
Courtesy of New York Public Library Picture Collection.

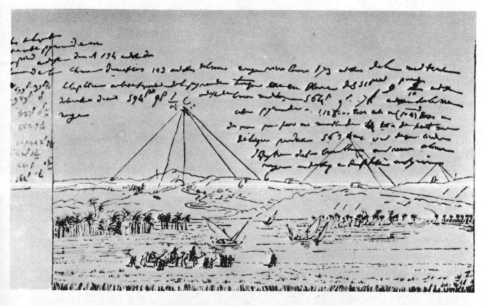

NAPOLEON'S NOTES AND SKETCHES OF THE PYRAMIDS AT GIZA.
Courtesy of New York Public Library Picture Collection.

THE MYCERINUS VALLEY TEMPLE LOOKING NORTHWEST TOWARDS THE
SECOND PYRAMID AT GIZA.

Courtesy of Museum of Fine Arts, Boston.

CHAPTER XVI.

THE SACRED CUBIT,

Of the Bible, opposes the Cainite.

IN speaking of anything in this book as simply *sacred,* I mean, to the best of my limited powers and poor ability, to distinguish such thing, as sacred to the God of Israel, or to the one and only true God who liveth for ever and ever; and I have no respect of the same kind, nor similar comprehensive word, for anything attributed to the gods of Egypt, Assyria, or Babylon, no matter what the learned Egyptologists, Assyriologists, and other scholars of the present day may say in their defence or their favour.

Hence it is no light affair for every real Christian disciple, if we should indeed find anything sacred in the above higher sense, in the Great Pyramid; and especially if we should learn that the grand standard of length, or the very governing cubit employed in the scientific design of the primeval monument was—and if it was once, it must be still—sacred to the Lord Jehovah of the Bible and all Eternity.

Of Cubits of Ancient Renown.

The mere name of "cubit" mounts up the question at once to the beginning of human affairs, for it is one of the earliest-named measures of which there is any

notice.   Not indeed that the *word* cubit is ancient in
itself; but that it is now the one English word always
used by our translators to express whatever chief measure of length, long or short, did form the working and
practical *standard* of linear measure to, or for, any and
every nation in the ancient world.   No nation could
exist then, any more than now, without having some
standard of linear measure belonging to it, and referred
to by its subjects either directly or indirectly in all
matters where lengths and breadths were concerned.
But the standard length of one nation, though called
now in our printed books by the same name, "cubit,"
was no more the necessary standard length of another
nation in a different part of the world and in a different
age, than the yard of the British Government, or two-
foot rule of the British people, is of the same exact
length, identical origination, and social force as the
mètre of the French nation, the Chinese chik, or the
Turkish pike.   National standards they are, each and
all of them, legal, discriminating, and politically omnipotent in their own respective countries; but every one
of a different length from the other, and their legal and
commercial powers depending only, and precisely, on
the absolute length of each.

Hence, under the one mere, and often misleading,
word, or name, of *cubit*, improperly used for *standard*
(which word *by itself* discriminates no linear dimensions
whatever), our translators have heaped together a number of totally different measures of length, conflicting
metrological symbolisms, and diverse national distinctions, as if they were all of one and the same length.
They have even done worse; for most persons having
Latin enough to derive cubit from *cubitus*, the elbow,
they measure off 18 inches, more or less, from their own
elbow to the end of the middle finger; and say, with a
peculiarly knowing smile, whenever a so-called "cubit"

of any time or nation whatever is mentioned,—*that* was
the length of *their* standard of linear measure.

Yet, though both the cubitus of the Romans and
πῆχυς of the Greeks were very close to the length of
18 inches, the standard measures of other and older
nations were very different in length.

What names, then, were they called by; or were
there different names for different lengths of national
standards, in *those* days?

In Egypt the linear standard was called, from 2170
B.C. through all their long historical period and down
to 100 A.D., according to different modern Egyptologists
"mah," "meh," "mahi," or "mai:" and signified,
according to the late W. Osburn, "justified" or "measured off."

Amongst the Assyrians, according to Mr. Fox Talbot
and Dr. Norris, their standard measure was generally
termed, in the age of Nebuchadnezzar, or 700 B.C.,
"ammat;" and in more ancient times, "hu."

Among the Hebrews, again, the standard measure
was called "ammah."* There is discussion still
amongst scholars whether this was the original, or
Mosaic Hebrew, word, for the thing to which it is now
applied; for some authors maintain that ammah is an
Assyrian word, and introduced only by Ezra when he
was recopying the Scriptures in Babylon during the
captivity. But they cannot prove the case absolutely;
and meanwhile, although there *are* some who will have
it that the word alludes to "the fore part of the arm"—
though too we are otherwise, and most practically,
assured that the Hebrew standard was of a totally different length from such part of the arm, being rather, if
the arm be alluded to at all, representative of its whole
length,—there are others who maintain that the word
rather implies, "the thing which was before *in point of*

* See *Edinburgh Astronomical Observations*, Vol. XIII. pp. R 79 to R 82.

time," the thing which was "the first, the earliest, the 'mother,' measure," and even "the foundation of all measure."

But these disputations of philologists are not in my line, neither are they sufficient for what we require now to know, quite apart from any particular words; viz. what actually were the lengths of the several linear standards of the chief ancient, though *idolatrous*, nations, in terms of modern British inches. And we need, moreover, to be quite certain of these, before we can presume to say that there is anything *peculiar* in such other length as we shall afterwards find to characterize the one *Sacred Cubit*, both Hebrew, Christian, and of the Great Pyramid also.

Now the cubits of Greece and Rome (mediæval, however, rather than ancient, as compared with the times of the early Pharaohs) were, in length, 18·24 British inches nearly, as every one, I believe, allows.

The cubit of Egypt, a far older land than Greece or Rome, was always longer, and close to 20·68 (sometimes for shortness spoken of as 20·7) British inches, by almost equally unanimous and universal testimony. And hence we see at once that the word cubit, as now used even by the learned, signifies merely a national standard of measure, and gives no idea of exact length, unless we prefix some other word, as Greek, Roman, Phœnician, or Egyptian, &c.

But when such word *is* prefixed, it is most important to our present inquiry to know, that the then double word becomes one of immense power in primeval history; because cubits of *intended* different lengths were so few: and each cubit was so long-lived. Through all the old and new empires of Egypt, for instance, under native princes, there was but one length (20·68 inches nearly) for the Egyptian cubit handed down most carefully from father to son, monumentally and agriculturally.

There has, indeed, been a notable attempt in modern London society, during the last few years, to assert that there was a second cubit, of the same short length as the later Grecian, viz. 18·24 British inches, in use in ancient Egypt; though reserved there, the hypothesis-markers said, for the one purpose of measuring land. They even declare that such employment of it was fully as early as the day of the Great Pyramid, and even had the honour of deciding the size of the base of that most unique monument.

This is an assertion, so directly in opposition to whatever has yet appeared in the present book, that we cannot but inquire into it with fulness, as follows.

Of the one old, profane Egyptian Cubit : and the recent attempt to say there was another, much shorter.

The whole case for there being, or ever having been, another cubit in historic profane Egypt, than the 20·68 British inch one, seems to have grown up thus.

The Director-General of the Ordnance Survey of Great Britain (1874), after having twice tried in the *Athenæum* to establish against the conclusions in my " Life and Work at the Great Pyramid," two other hypotheses for accounting for the length of the base-side of that ancient monument, he using a *different* length of base-side with each hypothesis, he at last brought out a *third* Great Pyramid base-side length, and a *third* hypothesis to account for it. This last assumed length was 9,120 British inches, and its explanatory theory, or rather hypothesis only, was the gratuitous statement that that 9,120 length was *intended* to be five hundred times the length of " the Egyptian land cubit"; and as that cubit was stated, after having been called into existence by him, to have been 18·24 British inches long,—of course 18·24 × 500 = 9,120.

By itself, perhaps I might have passed this statement by as unworthy of serious notice; but when it
was presently not only adopted and followed by "the
Warden of the Standards" of Great Britain, printed
and reprinted by the Royal Society of London, and
quoted as irrefragable by an appointed Lecturer (the
late Professor Clerk-Maxwell of Cambridge) at a meeting of the British Association for the Advancement of
Science—the matter was becoming too prominent. And,
further still, when the Rev. F. R. A. Glover, M.A., who
had been deeply studying the mensurations of the Great
Pyramid, attacked me with the remark—

"Did not you say in ' Our Inheritance in the Great
Pyramid,' Chap. II. of Second Edition, that the length
of the Great Pyramid's base-side, according to the best
means of all the socket-defined measures, was 9,140
British inches; and that the length of the sacred,
scientific, cubit of the Great Pyramid's inspired and
anti-Egyptian design was settled hereby?"

"Certainly."

"And now here is the Royal Society publishing that
the length is only 9,120 British inches, and you are a
Fellow of that Society. So you are implicated in, and
consenting to, telling the world one thing in the Society's book, and quite a different thing in your own
book. Pray which of them am I to believe?"

Such, nearly, were the words in which Mr. Glover
brought the case home to my individual, human responsibility. So, having ascertained from the Professorial
Lecturer at the British Association's meeting at Bradford, that he had drawn all his information from the
printed " Proceedings " of the Royal Society of London,
I represented in a formal paper to be read before that
learned Corporation, that if the Director-General had
got 9,120, by taking a mean of certain two base-side
measures of the Great Pyramid giving respectively

9,110 and 9,130,—he had obtained it by improperly
throwing out of view two other at least equally scientifically measured, and well-known, results giving 9,163
and 9,168 of the same inches; and which results, properly combined with the others, gave 9,140 for the base-
side length, rather than 9,120.*

How the Council of the Royal Society thereupon absolutely refused to let my paper appear before an open
meeting of the Society; how I then sent in a condi-
tional resignation of my Fellowship, to be read in public
together with the reasons *why* I so resigned; how the
Council held back those reasons, and merely announced
that I *had* resigned; how I therefore printed a pamphlet giving the *whole* case, and sent a copy to every
member of the Society; and how the next annual
general meeting of all the Fellows was held, and no
move was made by any one (so far as I have yet heard)
to question the Council's proceedings, or vindicate the
true size of the ancient Great Pyramid; and how in
fact the whole of the members have now homologated
everything done by the Council in supporting one side,
and suppressing the other side, of Great Pyramid
measures—all that, I might perhaps have written here
some forcible remarks upon, but have not, because I
would rather refer readers to Appendix II., at the
end of this book, as being an independent opinion from
America on the case.

But in the meanwhile I desire not to conceal from
any one, that the great, the wealthy, the powerful, and
numerously organized association almost worshipped in
the London world of science, the Royal Society, has
now in fact, though not in its own words, pronounced for
the Great Pyramid's base-side length being only 9,120
British inches, as well as having been anciently and

* See Chap. III., pp. 36 and 39.   See also Chap. X., p. 199, for confirmations from the King's Chamber.

even primevally *intended* to be that.   Wherefore I find
myself opposed by the whole Society, by its wealth,
power, Government influence, by each and all of its
600 or so, of Fellows, and by some unknown number
of officers or referees whose names are not disclosed.
That *is* the fact ; therefore any one who is influenced
by a crowd, by numbers, by reputed authority, mysterious agencies and worldly success, may, and many no
doubt will, join them.

But shall I *therefore* yield the ancient point ; and submissively allow, that the Royal Society was justified by
all the learning of the time and the facts of the case, in
keeping out of view everything that tended to show that
the Great Pyramid's base-side length was 9,140, rather
than 9,120 British inches ?   No !   For although I knew
well that I was, when still F.R.S., one of the least of
those so honoured scientifically; and know also that
the ranks of the Society contain numerous men almost
infinitely learned in difficult sciences which were, and
are, strange to me,—yet the present question *was*
within my moderate compass, had been the subject
of my special attention, under the open sky in Egypt,
as well as in the closet at home; and is rather one of
simple honesty than scientific difficulty,—one, therefore,
which a single human mind, with a soul to be saved
and an immortal hereafter, must form a far higher tri-
bunal for judging, than any Society, Corporation, Secret
Council, or any Association which, as such, is the work
of man and not of God, and has no soul belonging to it,
nor any future in heaven before it.

Having therefore already indicated (pp. 36—39 and
337) how little of observational and true foundation there
is for any one asserting the Great Pyramid's base-side
length to be 9,120 British inches only, let us here go
forward to the next part of the question ;—and which
asserted, with most astonishing anachronism, that there

was in ancient profane Egypt, besides its undoubted 20·68-inch cubit, another cubit only 18·24 British inches in length: so that, when multiplied by 500, such a short cubit should yield exactly 9,120 of the same inches.

This second assertion turned out to be simply a literary mistake of the late Director-General of the Ordnance Survey, when reading a passage in Herodotus; which passage, in reality, says the very opposite; as thus—

Herodotus, that charming relater of history as a pleasant family tale, we must remember, is telling his story to the Greeks; and amongst other particulars of what he saw in Egypt, informs them of an allowance of land to each of the soldiers there; a liberal and highly prized allowance too, of so many cubits square; to which account he appends the explanatory remark, evidently for the benefit of his then hearers, the Greeks, —that the *Egyptian cubit is of the same length as that of Samos.*

Of what length then was the cubit of Samos?

"Of the same length as the Greek cubit, viz. 18·24 inches," instantly asserted the surveying military chief at Southampton; and now is implicated in the same assertion the Royal Society, London.* But was it so in very fact?

As there is no other scrap of ancient authority now existing in the world, so far as I am aware, touching the *absolute* and material length of the cubit of Samos in the time of Herodotus, 445 B.C. (except that slight verbal comparative notice of his, identifying it with the

---

* I do not mean that the Royal Society has published such an opinion, in so many words, as its own conclusion; but I do mean that it printed that particular conclusion in a paper by one of its Fellows in both their "Proceedings" and "Transactions," and rejected a paper with opposite conclusions. Whether, using that amount of discrimination as to what they shall, and what they shall not, and do not, print out of all that comes before them, they are fully justified before God in holding that "they never give their opinion, as a body, upon any subject, either of nature or art," that comes before them,—let a man with a soul, rather than a society without one, attempt to define.

Egyptian, and not with the Greek), we must endeavour
to ascertain from him, himself, what *he*, Herodotus,
meant,—when *he* explained to a Greek audience in
Athens, that the length of the Egyptian cubit was the
same as the cubit of Samos.   Why, for instance, did he
not say that the Egyptian cubit was the same as the
Greek cubit, if he meant it; and was speaking to Greeks
themselves, who would of course know what the length
of their own cubit was ?

By turning to his book " Thalia," 55, we shall find
that Herodotus there makes a Lacedæmonian refer to
the Samians (in their isle so close to Asia Minor and so
far from Greece), not as Greeks, but as "foreigners."
And again, in " Thalia," 56, he himself speaks of a
siege of Samos by the Lacedæmonian Dorians as " their
(the Greeks') first expedition into Asia."   " Words,"
writes the Rev. Professor Rawlinson, in a note to his
excellent translation, " which are emphatic.   They
mark the place which the expedition occupies in the
mind of Herodotus.   It is an aggression of the Greeks
upon *Asia*, and therefore a passage in the history of the
great quarrel between Persia and Greece, for all Asia
is the king's " (i. 4).*

Samian, then, in the mind and feelings of Herodotus,
eminently meant Asiatic or Persian, the antipodes of
everything Greek ; and the phrase was a rather delicate
mode of that admirable describer telling his polite
Athenian audience, that the cubit of the strange and
far-off Egyptians he had been travelling amongst, was
of the same length as that of their hated and dreaded
foes, the Persians ; but without offending Attic ears by
the sound of the detested and threatening Eastern name.
For Samos was but a poor little island, in itself altogether innocent of plotting any aggressions on such a
combination of states as Greece ; and since its actual

* See also *Edinburgh Astronomical Observations*, Vol. XIII. p. R 70.

invasion by the Lacedæmonians, was much better known
to Greeks than the continental and somewhat mysterious country of the Persians themselves.

Now, the Persian cubit, at and about the times of
Herodotus, say from 332 B.C. to 600 B.C., according
to Dr. Brandis, of Berlin (whose investigations into
the Babylonian measures, weights, and money before
Alexander the Great, are original and most valuable),
was somewhere between 20·866 and 20·670 British
inches.

Don Vincent Queipo, in his "Metrology" (Vol. I. pp.
277—280), makes the same Persian cubit to be 20·670
inches long.   M. Oppert establishes the same length for
the Babylonian cubit in the times of Darius and Xerxes.
Dr. Hincks makes that same cubit, equally too of the
Babylonian, Persian, and Assyrian empires, chiefly from
cuneiform inscriptions = 21·0 inches.   All of them,
therefore, within their limits of error, coinciding sufficiently with a mean length of 20·68 inches nearly, for
the Persian cubit of and about 500 B.C.   And that
cubit length, we may be sure, the said Persians established in Samos for as long as they had the upper hand
there ; seeing that from the same Herodotus we learn
(Book VI. ch. 24), that no sooner were the Ionian cities
under Histiæus conquered by Artaphernes, than he
took the measurement of their whole country in *para-
sangs* (a Persian measure of length, based on the Persian
cubit), and settled thereupon the tributes which they
were in future to pay.

Hence the Samian cubit alluded to, could have been
no other than the Persian cubit of the day of Herodotus ;
and that cubit having now been proved of the length of
20·68 British inches nearly, by all modern research, we
may immediately see how close to the truth was the
Father of History, when he declared the length of the
Egyptian and Samian, *i.e.* Persian, cubits to be the

same,—for the profane Egyptian cubit has been found by all Egyptological explorers to be within a few tenths, or even hundredths, of an inch, that very quantity; viz. 20·68 British inches.

Thus Sir Gardner Wilkinson, in his "Manners and Customs of the Ancient Egyptians" (Vol. IV. pp. 24—34, third edition, 1847), expressly declares against the idea of there having been intentionally two different-lengthed cubits in Pharaonic Egypt; and gives the following as measures of accidental variations of the one and only profane Egyptian cubit belonging to any, and every, period between 2200 B.C. and 320 B.C. :—

> 20·47 British inches.
> 20·58   ,,   ,,
> 20·62   ,,   ,,
> 20·66   ,,   ,,
> 20·62   ,,   ,,
> 20·75   ,,   ,,
> 20·65   ,,   ,,

And other more recent measures by other investigators, some from cubits, and some from ancient monuments where certain parts seemed to have been laid out, so as to be even multiples of 2, 4, or more cubits,—have yielded 20·73· and 20·66 British inches.

Hence it must surely now be perfectly clear,—in spite of even the Royal Society and what that body has been pleased to issue in its two publications, and is tacitly supported in by all its six hundred members,—that while there was in *ancient* Egypt a cubit 20·68 British inches long, there was no such thing nationally there *then*, as a cubit 18·24 British inches in length; and whose multiple by 500 should, or could, amount to 9,120, as first erroneously assumed by the Director-General of the Ordnance Survey, in connection with, or in furtherance of, alas! degrading theories of the original scientific design of the primeval Great Pyramid.

But time presses, and I will now beg to call attention

to an unexpected, and all the more important, because unexpected, result of the inquiries I have been obliged to make, in pure self-defence from attempted extinguishment, in as I firmly believe, a most righteous cause.

Origination of the one Sole and Profane Cubit of the earliest East, 20·68 British Inches long.

The unlooked-for result alluded to above, is this, that not only was the cubit of Samos of the same 20·68-inch length as that of all ancient Egypt, from one end of that land to the other,—but the same identical length characterized the cubits of Babylon, Nineveh, and apparently all Mesopotamia, Persia, Assyria, and Syria, with the coasts and islands thereof.

That could hardly have been accidental in its origin, and still less so in its immense duration; for it survived those countries' wars, their empires, and even their languages ; and could only have been kept up by some most active and powerful system of surveillance, on which they were all agreed ; and were even sworn to uphold more fervently, more passionately, than any national distinction or political difference among them.

Now, what could such a system have been ?

Something more or less connected with religion ; not with its outward forms, for these had different idols, with different names and very different figures as well as attributes in every different country,—but with its original and inmost foundation, its mysteries, freemasonries, and secret abominations. And when looked at in this manner, we see immediately that all the countries holding to that 20·68-inch cubit were, through all history, arrayed in religion against Israel and against Israel's God. But on what special point of antithesis did they chiefly unite ?

Self-righteousness *versus* admitted guilt and the need
of a Divine atonement.

That very part of the Egyptian Dead-book so scrupulously inserted in the coffin of every profane mummy
throughout the Pharaonic empire, and which is intended
to enable the soul, almost first and foremost of all
things, to declare before Osiris that its owner had never
been guilty of *shortening the cubit*,* puts a long string of
other declarations into his mouth, protesting him to be
also perfectly free from any and every other possible sin,
great or small, that was ever heard of.   And whether
such unhappy being also believed and trusted, as most
of them did, in idols of animal-headed gods, of whom
there were sometimes more, and sometimes less, in the
Egyptian Pantheon, all *that*—dreadful as it is for human
beings with souls to be saved, and special instruction
from the Creator—sinks into comparative insignificance
before this unblushing assertion of whole self-righteousness.   For *this* principle lasted through all their varying
theogonies; and not only shows the innate, settled
Cainite direction of their thoughts, but their continual
antagonism also to the religion of Abel, and to the
whole Revelation doctrine of the lost condition of man,
with the consequent Christian necessity of an atonement by sacrifice and pardon through the blood of a
Divine Mediator.

Similarly also proceeded the inhabitants of Babel,
from the time when they first collected together, and
said (Gen. xi.), " Go to, let us build a city and a tower,
whose top may reach unto heaven ; and let us make us
a name, lest we be scattered abroad upon the face of the
whole earth," down to the days when (Dan. iv.) Nebuchadnezzar walked in the palace of the kingdom of

* See "Seven Homilies on Ethnic Inspiration," by the Rev. J. T.
Goodsir, published by Williams and Norgate in 1871. And specially see
the Appendix therein containing a then new translation of the Egyptian
Dead-book, by the now late William Osburn, of Leeds.

Babylon, and spake and said, "Is not this great Babylon, that I have built for the house of the kingdom by
the might of my power, and for the honour of my
majesty?"

All the above doctrine, with the history also, besides
being found under absolute condemnation in the Bible,
appears to some extent in Josephus's account of
Genesis times also; but *where* he obtained his further
particulars of Cain, and how far they are to be, or
should be, trusted, I know not. Yet he is a great
author before the Church and the world, and his
remarks on this case, or rather the traditions which
he hands on from an earlier time, are pertinent to the
present question, and run thus; viz. that after Cain's
expulsion from a more blessed society, and after the
mark was put upon him, he went on from one wickedness to another until he at last invented "weights and
measures"; using them however as instruments of
rapacity and oppression against all the peaceably inclined inhabitants round about him.

In self-defence therefore, implies Josephus, the descendants of righteous Seth, in whose line afterwards
came Noah, Shem, Abraham, and Moses, betook themselves to studying *astronomy*, with the special approval
and help of Almighty God; and when they had perfected those discoveries, he says, they set forth from
their own land (which was probably in Mesopotamia),
to the land of Siriad (that is, the Siriadic, or Dog-star
land of Egypt), and inscribed their discoveries there on
two pillars, one of stone and one of brick.

They did not therefore seek either to teach or enforce
these things on the Cainite Egyptian people whom they
found there; they merely recorded their astronomical
discoveries in their own monumental way, for their own
internal satisfaction in that land, because it was in some
way a more suitable land for that purpose than their

own ; or they had received a Divine command to make the record there, and obeyed the command in *faith*, like all the good patriarchs of old. And what such discoveries in astronomy could have been, to enable them to have a counter-effect to the bad weights and measures of Cain, unless they were connected with a principle of earth and heaven commensurability in all their standards, leading them to think lovingly, harmoniously, and Abel-like, of God, and with God, in all His wondrous works for the benefit of man,—it is difficult to conceive.

In fact, according to the *nature* of the things said to have been inscribed, the above alluded to *stone* pillar, or monument (which Whiston, wholly ignorant of hieroglyphic interpretation, proposed unhappily to identify with a Cainite obelisk of an idolatrous king of Upper Egypt in Thebes during the long-subsequent 19th Dynasty),—can be no other than the Great Pyramid as now coming to be understood and interpreted by modern science. While the similar *brick* monument, said to have been erected by the same Sethite parties, must, if ever really in existence, have gone the way of all the brick Pyramids of profane Egypt; viz. subsided into a heap of decaying mould, leaving the stone Great Pyramid of Jeezeh, the only witness in the latter day to the God of Israel, in the midst of a Cainite land.

Hence, without by any means trusting entirely to Josephus, there is, with the help of his history of primeval times, a very suggestive view opened up of a world-wide metrological contrast, entirely agreeable with Biblical characteristics in religion, though depending on scientific refinements, or minute differences of measure only understood by modern men within the last century. And it tells us, I venture to remind, of a continued and most radical opposition between Cain and Abel having been carried by their descendants through the Flood : as well as of these parties having been openly distinguished before the world (whatever were the mysteries of certain of them in their secret conclaves), by the most opposite kinds of weights and measures. And when we further find by later researches that the anti-Israel, and decidedly Cainite, nations in religion, spread abroad even from the Nile to the Euphrates, though often warring vehemently with each other, were yet banded together to employ one and the same profane cubit length of 20·68 of our inches, we must look upon that measure as the Cain-invented, Cain-descended, cubit or standard. When, too, we find that that length is apparently incongruous to the measures of both the earth and the heavens, we may at once allow that that was just what might have been expected of Cain, and any rationalistic human efforts in that age to act without God in the world.

But then, again, that very fact excites the most intense anxiety to inquire by any independent means that may be available in the case, whether the cubit of the descendants of Seth, in the line of Abraham, Moses and David, as especially representative of the cause of righteous, and God-obeying, God-acknowledging, Abel, was anything essentially different.

The Sacred Cubit of the Sethites and Hebrews.

And here, alas for the Churches ! from the time of Bishop Cumberland of Peterborough, down to the Bible Dictionaries of Kitto and Smith, down to most of the annotated Bibles of the Government printers, and even the earlier maps of Jerusalem prepared for the Palestine Exploration Association by the Ordnance Survey establishment at Southampton. For all these hitherto supposed unquestionable authorities merely indicate, lazily,

I am sorry to say, and ignorantly (both as Christians and scientists), something as follows :—" The ancient Hebrew measures are impossible to find out by the mere words of the Bible or of any book, so *we* go to the Egyptians (Cainites though they were, and desperate idolaters) : and we take from their architectural monuments, and give you, *their* self-righteous, pagan, God-defying measures, and bid you accept them as the Inspired, Sacred measures of God's chosen people from the beginning. And such numbers of inches too as these modern most blinded and misleading men give, even under that profane Egyptian guise, are not very ancient, being more often derived from mediæval, or Grecianised, or Romanised, but still idolatrous, Egypt, than the Egypt of her earliest day ; and range anywhere between 16 and 22 inches. Very recently too, or in the "Quarterly Statement of the Palestine Exploration Fund" for October, 1879, at pp. 181, 184, a lamentable paper has appeared on " The Sacred Cubit " ; endeavouring to show that it was only 17˙7 British inches long ; but by means of merely mediæval tests; latter-day things which can only bring out the then fallen condition of Jerusalem ; and prove that it had adopted the Greek cubit, as well as the Greek language when it culminated in its rebellion against every institute of God, by crucifying His Christ, the Saviour of mankind.*

In this dilemma of the flock's desertion, or misguidance, by its intended shepherds, how thankful should we be, that it pleased God to raise up the spirit of Sir Isaac Newton, and enabled him to make it one of the most important discoveries of his riper years,— that while there undoubtedly was in very ancient, pre-Grecian, pre-Roman, times a cubit of 20˙68 inches nearly, characterizing the idolatrous nations of Egypt

* See *Banner of Israel*, December 10, 1879.

Assyria, Babylonia, and Phœnicia, and which cubit
Newton was gifted to call unhesitatingly "the profane
cubit"; there was another which he equally unhesitatingly speaks of as "the *sacred* cubit of the Jews"; and
shows that it was decidedly much longer, by several
inches, than the above, and was most earnestly preserved, treasured up, and obeyed, among some very
limited branches of the house of Shem. The exact
date of its promulgation Newton does not attempt to
fix, but alludes to the certain fact of its having become
the " proper and principal cubit " of the Israelites, *long
before they went down to Egypt*.*

Now this is precisely what it is important to get at;
and the measured size of this remarkable cubit, and
which seems eventually to have remained in the sole
possession of the early Hebrews, and to have been, after
the Egyptian captivity, employed by them for sacred,
Biblically sacred, purposes only, Sir Isaac Newton
attempts to ascertain in various modes thus :—

1. By notices from Talmudists and Josephus in terms
of Greek cubits, which on calculation give, as limits,
something between 31·24 and 24·30 British inches.†
Very rough or rude limits, but indicating without
doubt something so much greater than, as to be
describable to the general public as, quite a different
size from, that of the Cainite 20·68-inch cubit.

2. From Talmudists by proportion of the human body,
giving as limits, from 27·94 to 23·28 British inches.

3. From Josephus's description of the pillars of the
Temple, between 27·16 and 23·28 British inches.

4. By Talmudists and "all Jews' " idea of a Sabbath
day's journey between 27·16 and 23·28 British inches.

5. By Talmudists' and Josephus's accounts of the

* See Sir Isaac Newton's " Dissertation on Cubits," reprinted in
Vol. II. of my " Life and Work at the Great Pyramid."

† On the mean determination by many authors that 1 Attic foot = 12·15
British inches ; and one Roman uncia = 0·97 British inches.

steps to the Inner Court, between 26·19 and 23·28 British inches.

6. By many Chaldaic and Hebrew proportions to the cubit of Memphis, giving 24·83 British inches.   And,

7. From a statement by Mersennus, as to the length of a supposed copy of the *sacred* cubit of the Hebrews, secretly preserved amongst them, and concluded = 24·91 British inches.

In all these seven methods any one may observe that the Cainite cubit length of Egypt and Babylon, viz. 20·68 inches, has no standing-place whatever; neither beside the single determinations, nor within the widest limits of the double determinations.   It is something totally and absolutely different.   Still more decidedly are both the Greek and Roman profane cubits of 18·24 inches long, or anything shorter, excluded.   What *is* indicated by the whole of the numbers appears to be,—either 24 inches with a large fraction, or 25 inches with a small fraction, added to it, or something between those two near limits; and though Sir Isaac himself concluded for 24·88 inches being the probable length, yet he expressly warned his readers that he was not certain of the *precise* quantity; and that that must be left to future measurers to settle.

There Sir Isaac Newton stopped.   Further light and correct local information were then wanting.   In fact, he was furnished with so few, and some such bad measures of the Great Pyramid (the base-side length for instance 70 feet short) that in the very same " Dissertation " where he so happily arrives close upon the really Sacred cubit of Genesis,—he concludes for the Great Pyramid to have been merely a sepulchre, and built according to the profane cubit of Egypt.   But had he enjoyed our means of information, and come to know by accurate mensurations and full descriptions that the data he went by then, were chiefly a blind of the builders in the eyes of the Pharaonic Egyptians, similarly with their subterranean sepulchral chamber never finished for sepulture (pp. 100, 105); and that the secretly monumentalized cubit of the grand structure in its entirety as well as the minutest, particular, had not only no resemblance at all to the Cainitc, Egyptian, *profane* cubit of 20·68 inches, but was identical with the latest result now deduced from his own data for the *sacred* cubit of the Israelites before they went down to Egypt, —viz. 25·025 inch more or less,—the sacred, scientific, and Israelite theory of the *one* Great Pyramid would have been opened two centuries before its appointed time.

But that could not be, in a world ruled over by God who keeps times and seasons in His own hand. Sufficient then for us to confess, in our day, that the Newton-determined length of the Sacred Cubit of the older Israelites, improved now from 24·88 to 25·025 British inches, being the same as that of the only recently disclosed interior design of the Great Pyramid, must have been, like it, earth-commensurable and nature harmonious in the best conceivable manner even of the highest science yet arrived at by man; or in term sand exactitudes which, as we have already shown in the first part of this book (pp. 39—48), could not have been intentionally arrived at by any race in that early, pre-Mosaic, age, without their having been favoured by the assistance of Divine Inspiration to that special end.

But that is precisely what the Bible tells us the Hebrew race did continually receive in early days. We need have therefore no longer any difficulty as to whence came the superhuman, wisdom and meaning of their measures, as compared with those of the idolatrous Egyptians. Indeed a still further question is answered, almost as soon as it is asked : *viz.* whether the Hebraic most significant metrological possession of a cubit the 10^7th of the Earth's Polar radius in

length, may not after all have come to the said early
Hebrews originally in the manner, more or less, indicated by Josephus ; *i.e.* through primeval Divine assistance accorded to Seth, as represented in his earlier
descendants ; and whether it was not also granted,
before the building of the Great Pyramid by a Sethite
architect, specially to strengthen them against the both
politically and religiously opposed descendants of Cain,
banded together in nations, as they were, under their
20·68-inch standard, for the oppression of those of an
opposite principle in religion.

The Egyptians were Cainites not only from what has
already been shown from their own " Dead-book," but
from Biblical history indicating that they had, like
Cain, refused the sin-offering lying at their door, and
had scornfully conspired together, to consider the
Divinely appointed means of reconciliation " an abomination unto them."*   Therefore, when Israel was in
Egypt, Abel and Cain typically met once again, and
we all know with what results of cruelty within the
power of Cain to inflict.   We also know in a parallel
manner, by monumental and metrological research,
that that Mizraite Cain held then, and continued to
hold through all his national existence, to his 20·68-
inch standard measure ; while, through Sir Isaac
Newton, the astounding information first came, that
the Hebraite Abel at the same time likewise kept true,
through all his persecutions, to his oppositely derived,
Seth-descended, better standard, of, as we have shown,
25·025 British, but 25· Pyramid, inches in length.

The two largely opposing cubits, therefore, after con
tinually warring together in the Promised Land among
the Canaanites in Abrahamic days, clashed together
still more signally in Egypt, B.C. 1542, and God gave
the final victory then to Abel's.

* John Taylor's " Great Pyramid," p. 217.

But they met together again, as Sir Isaac Newton himself points out, *after* the Exodus, and even in the very presence of the Tabernacle in the wilderness. For the Israelites *would* occasionally employ the Egyptian cubit of 20·68 inches long for many of their ordinary purposes; though Moses was always most precise, and apparently successful, in seeing that in their *sacred* work they employed only their truly and peculiarly *sacred* cubit, viz. the earth-axis commensurable cubit of 25·025 British inches long.

The Mixed and Opposing Presence of the Two Cubits, Sacred and Profane; or the 25·025 Inch, versus the 20·68 Inch.

But it may be asked, Why did the Israelites continue to employ two cubits? If, as Sir Isaac Newton states, they brought their own sacred cubit, which they had possessed of old, down with them into Egypt, preserved it when there, and took it out with them again,—why was that one not enough for all their purposes?

The first answer to this question is by Sir Isaac himself.

" They, the Hebrews, brought," says he, " their own sacred measure to Egypt with them ; but living for above two hundred years (four hundred according to some chronologists) under the dominion of the Egyptians, and undergoing a hard service under them, especially in *building, where the measures came daily under consideration,* they must necessarily learn the Egyptian (20·68 inch) cubit."

The second answer is, " Did the Israelites succeed in freeing themselves at the Exodus from every other taint and sin of the Cainite people they had been sojourning amongst? Nay, indeed, were they free from the sins of many innate, born, and predestined Cainites among themselves? Search the Scriptures, and the proof comes up too plainly."

It was not, apparently, the purpose of God to create even His chosen people absolutely immaculate; or to make it impossible for them to sin, even if they should try. Therefore was it that temptations to evil (though in a measure only) were left to prove them; and amongst other forms of seduction, the insidious Cainite 20·68-inch cubit, as well as the true cubit of Abel with the 25·025 British-inch length.

Now, exactly as these two cubits were contending with each other, and either ensnaring or saving men's souls in the very camp of the Israelites ruled by Moses, so is it still even in this Christian country wherein we, their descendants, dwell.

If the Book of the Revelation of St. John assures us so clearly that even in these present times, on the now closely approaching termination of the Turkish mission to destroy the worshippers of idols, that idolatry shall yet raise its head, and that men will not yet repent of the works of their hands, that they should not worship devils, and idols of gold and silver, and brass and stone, and of wood; which can neither see, nor hear, nor walk,—so we may be certain that the Cainite cubit will not be forgotten, or unreverenced, by them either.

Nor was it, rather ominously and unhappily, at the already-mentioned lecture before the British Association for Science at Bradford, in 1873. For the lecturer there, who might have done either thing,—*elected* to hold up to the admiration of his audience, and as the best possible example of a long-lived, well-cared-for, and in the present day to be imitated, and in the present Christian country, loved and respected, ancient standard of linear measure, not the sacred 25-inch cubit of Seth (and, as we shall show more positively in Chapter

XVIII., equally of Noah, Moses, and Solomon), with
its lasting monument, the Great Pyramid, central to
all the inhabited land-surface of the earth,—but the profane 20·68-inch cubit of both the once idolatrous and
now Divinely crushed, Egyptians ; and of Babylonians,
whose boastful city and impious nation have altogether disappeared.　Yet much did the lecturer enlarge
on the most exemplary care, far exceeding anything
known until very lately among Christian communities,
with which metrical commissioners from Egypt,
Babylon, Nineveh, and other such idolatrous empires
in primeval time, must have travelled about from
country to country, with examples of that horrible
Cainite cubit for instruction, comparison, and regulation ; keeping every one of those heathen kings, governments, and peoples,—whether worshippers of Isis,
or Astarte or the Phœnician Fishgod or any other,—
true to their ancestral, but anti-Israel's God, covenant
in metrology ; binding them moreover, for secret and
unhallowed reasons, to respect that 20·68-inch* cubit
and no other.

*Of the views of Moses and the Bible, touching " the
sacred cubit of the Jews."*

But shall our British, Christian people,—under the
plea of being taught science, in grandly adorned halls
where fashion and wealth do congregate,—be exposed

---

* The lecturer referred chiefly to the double form of this cubit 41·36
British inches long, adorned in modern times by the name of "the Royal
Cubit of Karnak," because such a double cubit rod was found recently
on pulling down part of an old idolatrous temple at Karnak in Egypt,
where it seemed to have been accidentally dropped in by a working
mason at the time of the building.　But, just as with the English workman's 2-foot, or 1-foot rule, both of them speaking equally of the English Government and the English people,—so the 41·36 inch, or double
cubit rod, of old Egypt, means politically and religiously the very same
thing as the 20·68-inch single cubit rod of the same land at the same
time.

to the temptation, the danger of unknowingly admiring, following, and patronising the profane, instead of the sacred, example in metrology ?

The attempt will be made upon them, they may be sure, again and again ; and in various ways ; one of which is showing itself in part just now, by its being circulated in various quarters, that though Sir Isaac Newton spoke of " the sacred cubit of the Jews " (as to this last name, however, meaning no doubt Hebrews or Israelites, and not the exclusive subsequent people to whom we now more properly restrict the name of Jews), he nowhere says that those Jews themselves used the term " sacred cubit" ; and that such a compound word is not to be found in all the writings of Moses.

Certainly ; for Moses did not write a treatise on metrology, and mentioned any such matters only incidentally.   Yet he did so in a *spirit* which is perfectly unmistakable.

Does he not, for instance, expressly state in Exodus, that the instructions to make the several parts of the Tabernacle in so many *cubits* of measure, were given to him by his *God*, viz. God, the only, one, and true living God, on Mount Sinai ?   And that this further instruction was impressed upon him, Moses, from the same unique Divine source,—" And look that thou make them after their pattern, which was showed thee in the Mount ? "   (Exod. xxv. 40.)

If that is not enough to prove to any unprejudiced person that *of course* those cubits so announced were sacred cubits of the Lord God of Israel, and not the profane cubits of idolatrous Egypt; let the doubter read *first* the inspired Prophet's words and terrific denunciations when the children of Israel fell away from those Mount-announced commandments he had given them, and made themselves by preference a golden calf after the fashion of the animal-worshipping Egyptians. And *then* let the same doubter compare therewith, on the other hand, the holy approval of Moses when at length the whole work of the Tabernacle, cubit by cubit of it, according to his original numerical instructions, had been faithfully completed; completed, too, by workmen specially called to it by God, and stated to be filled by Him for that very purpose " with the spirit of God, in wisdom, in understanding, and in knowledge, and in all manner of workmanship" (Exod. xxxv. 31): and then—

" Moses did look upon all the work, and, behold, they had done it as the Lord had commanded, even so had they done it : and Moses blessed them."

While finally came the still higher approval of Divine condescension, in that " the glory of the Lord filled the Tabernacle."

Hence, though the *word* " sacred cubit " be not written in the Bible, it is surabundantly implied; but always as restricted to a certain cubit of a 25·025 inch, or most opposition, length to the Cainite 20·68-inch cubit; and if the term be used here by ourselves, it is not as a quotation, but as a corollary. As such, too, it is indeed so largely deducible from whole sections of the Sacred Book, that the full spirit in which that 25·025-inch cubit we have here called sacred, was looked on by Moses, cannot be expressed, or even indicated, by us in any less positive terms than the most decided and powerful ones we have been privileged to employ.*

Moses, too, as we have already hinted, did not write on Metrology, but on Religion; and therefore had no occasion to give an account of the sacred, the 25·025 British inch, or the earth-commensurable, and God's creation harmonious with, cubit in and for itself alone.

---

* See in Chapter XVIII., correspondences between the Great Pyramid and the Ark of Noah, the Tabernacle of Moses, and the Temple of Solomon as described in the Bible, when the 25·025, and not 20·68, British inch length is employed for the cubit mentioned there.

The Great Pyramid, on the other hand, *is* largely a treatise on metrology; and therefore, being as to its design inspired from the same supernatural source, has at last taught us how to speak of appropriately, and reverently to understand, the one and only cubit used by Moses after he came down from communion with Omniscient, Omnipotent Divinity, on the Mount.

CHAPTER XVII.

TIME MEASURES,

And the Fixation of Absolute Dates.

WHAT affairs of mankind can prosper without attention to time? and what is history with an uncertain, or perhaps an utterly erroneous, chronology?

It is, I fear, very much like the history of ancient Egypt, as composed by the modern Egyptologists from the profane, hieroglyphic-bearing monuments which they study: *none of which*, according even to those gentlemen's own confession, *are capable of fixing an absolute date*. And yet on the strength of their learning in these things, the said gentlemen go on assigning dates, and have gone on continually *increasing* them too during the last 30 years; until it has recently been anounced, that " possibly more than seven thousand years have passed over the pyramids of Egypt."

As the Great Pyramid is not a hieroglyphic-adorned monument, it does not of itself lead anyone into any of *those* errors touching exact chronology. But has it any better method of pronouncing on time?

On this important question there is but one mode of inquiry, viz. attention to the measures of the whole built monument, and its parts; coupled with the quality of the work concerned, and followed by the theory, whatever that may ultimately prove to be, which explains the greatest number of facts.

Now one *time* measure has already been indicated in

the circumstance that the sacred, Hebrew, or Pyramid
cubit is of such a length that it measures the base-side
of the Great Pyramid by the number of days, and
fractions of a day, that do actually exist in a year of
the earth; while another includes a practical demonstration of our modern leap-year arrangement in the
exhibition of the four sides, or years, which make up a
cycle of years complete to the nearest even day.   (See
Chapter X. p. 180.)

But a still grander time measure of that kind is obtained by viewing the whole Pyramid's base periphery
in the light of its equivalent circle, struck with a radius
equal to the vertical height of the Pyramid ; which
height, by its sun-distance commensurability, sym-
bolises the sun in the centre of that circle ; for then the
interval of twenty-four solar hours, or the time elapsing
between the sun apparently leaving the meridian of any
place and returning to it again, by virtue of the rotation of the earth on its axis before the sun, *i.e.* a mean
solar day,—is measured off on that circle's circumference by 100 Pyramid inches evenly.

But if this first time-symbolism of the exterior of the
Pyramid is thus clear and simple enough, that of the
interior presents many difficulties.

The entrance-passage has indeed already been elsewhere shown to be connected with the meridian transit
of a circumpolar star ; but why did the builders make
both that passage and the first ascending passage so
excessively low, that a man can hardly pass through
them, even crawling on his hands and knees ; and
another, the Grand Gallery, so astonishingly high, that
the blazing torches of Arab guides seldom suffice, in its
mere darkness rendered somewhat visible, to show the
now smoke-blackened ceiling to wondering visitors ?

No approach to a sufficient answer to these questions
has yet been given anywhere ; and all that violent, and

apparently unreasonable, contrast of heights, remains the most mysterious thing in its origin, at the same time that, in its existence, it is one of the best-ascertained facts about the whole Great Pyramid.

Professor Greaves describes the Time Passages of the Great Pyramid.

Where many great men have failed, we must proceed with caution indeed ; and commencing therefore at the beginning, with what has been known to, and confessed by, most travellers for ages, I will, at present, merely call attention to the extraordinary pains that were taken by the original builders with the structure of all these passages.

Even with the first, or entrance passage, the most used and abused of the whole, both in mediæval and modern times,—yet the regularity and beauty of its fabric, composed of whiter, more compact, and homogeneous stone than is to be seen anywhere else, and in enormous blocks admirably worked, seem to have been ever the admiration of all beholders. Professor Greaves, in 1638, exclaims (with almost a Tennysonian feeling of the romantic belonging rather to 1860 A.D.), on beholding this passage some 3,800 years after its builders had been laid in the dust, and their spirits had returned to God who gave them, " The structure of it hath been the labour of an exquisite hand."

Yes, truly ; and then the Savilian professor goes on methodically to describe the mechanical elements of that excellence which he had noted ; such as, " the smoothness and evenness of the work," " the close knitting of the joints," and the accuracy with which the exact breadth of 3·463 of the English foot* is kept up through

* Equivalent to 41·51 Pyramid inches. My measures at the place in 1865 gave for extremes 41·58 and 41·46, and the mean of all, 41·49 of the same inches; or differing from my Astronomical predecessor, after two centuries, by only $\frac{1}{2000}$ of the whole.

a length of 92·5 feet.   But when he comes soon afterwards over against a portion of that rough fragment of
a side-passage forced in barbarous times of spoliation
by Caliph Al Mamoun, he correctly describes that as
" a place somewhat larger, and of a pretty height, but
lying incomposed; an obscure and broken place, the
length 89 feet, the breadth and height various, and not
worth consideration."   And again, " By whomsoever
(among the moderns) it was constructed, is not worth
the inquiry; nor does the place merit the describing;
but that I was unwilling to pretermit anything, being
only an habitation for bats, and those so ugly and of so
large a size, exceeding a foot in length, that I have not
elsewhere seen the like." *

When, on the contrary, the same Professor Greaves,
by aid of the yawning hiatus in the masonry to the
west of the portcullis, got round and above that granite
block obstruction between the entrance descending, and
first ascending, passages proper, and reached this latter
work of the ancient builders,—a passage of the same
breadth nearly as the entrance passage,—he then
resumes his more graceful imagery, and writes, " The
pavement of this rises with a gentle acclivity, consisting of smooth and impolished marble (lime-stone),
and, where not smeared with filth, appearing of a
white alabaster (cream) colour; the sides and roof, as

* Murtedi, an Arabian author, declares, " As big as black eagles; "
and that gives at once a measure of Arab veracity, to any one who will
now visit the hole by day; and, catching some of the still numerous bats
asleep, or tapping them down as they try to fly past,—ascertain their
length precisely from tip to tip.   Professor Greaves evidently did not
recognise in 1638, neither indeed did Dr. Clarke in 1800, that this " incomposed hole" was the inner part of the quarried path of forced entrance
made by the early Arabian Caliph Al Mamoun; and it required Colonel
Howard-Vyse's clearing away of the rubbish-mound outside, in 1837, to
prove the fact, by exhibiting the outer end of the long hole as well.   But
the very circumstance of Professor Greaves not being acquainted with
these latter-day demonstrations, makes his correct description of the
interior, as he saw it, and we now doubly know it to be, all the more
creditable to him.

Titus Livius Burretinus, a Venetian, an ingenious young man, who accompanied me thither, observed, were of impolished stone, not so hard and compact as that of the pavement, but more soft and tender." And I, in my turn, have now, 235 years after King Charles the First's professor of astronomy left the Pyramid, to report, as an apparent consequence of that tender softness described by him, that the upper part of the walls, and more especially the roof of much of *this* passage, have exfoliated or decayed to the extent of a foot or more in many places,—while the floor, on the other hand, has rather hardened to the feet (usually naked feet, though) of Arabs, and exhibits a peculiar change in the surface of the limestone; hardening as it does there, until it actually verges upon the consistence of flint, yet keeping nearly true still to the ancient test-marks of the floor-level on either side wall.

And then when he arrives in the far freer and much more elevated space of the *second* ascending passage, or the *Grand Gallery*, the fine old Oxford professor, who well knew what architectural beauties were, speaks of *it* as "a very stately piece of work, and not inferiour either in respect of the curiosity of art, or richness of materials, to the most sumptuous and magnificent buildings." And again, "This gallery or corridor, or whatsoever else I may call it, is built of white and polished marble (lime stone), the which is very evenly cut in spacious squares or tables. Of such materials as is the pavement, such is the roof, and such are the side walls that flank it; the coagmentation or knitting of the joints is so close, that they are scarce discernible to a curious eye; and that which adds grace to the whole structure, though it makes the passage the more slippery and difficult, is the acclivity and rising of the ascent. The height of this gallery is 26 (more nearly 28) feet; the breadth 6·870 feet, of which 3·435 feet are to be allowed for the way in the midst, which is set and bounded on both sides with two banks, like benches, of sleek and polished stone ; each of these hath 1ʹ717 of a foot in breadth, and as much in depth."*

" Upon the top of these benches (the 'ramps' of Col. Howard-Vyse), near the angle where they close and join with the wall, are little spaces cut in right-angled parallel figures set on each side opposite one another, *intended, no question, for some other end than ornament.*"

" In the casting and ranging of the marbles (lime-stone), in both the side walls, there is one piece of architecture in my judgment very graceful, and that is that all the courses or ranges, which are but seven (so great are these stones), do set and flag over one another about three inches ; the bottom of the uppermost course overflagging the top of the next, and so in order the rest as they descend."

In the edition of Greaves's works by Dr. Birch in 1737, from which I quote, there is an attempt to repre-sent these things graphically, the book being " adorned with sculptures," and "illustrated with cuts by a curious hand " ; and in the great French work some efforts in a high class of design are engraved in line, to represent perspective views looking both upward and downward in the Grand Gallery ; but they are all of them to some extent failures. The circumstances are above the scope of orthodox pictures by reason of the narrow breadth, the lofty vaulting height, and the very peculiar sloping angle of the long floor ; a floor, when one looks from its north end southward, ascending and ascending through the darkness apparently for ever ; and with such steep-

---

* By my measures in 1865, in Pyramid inches, and taking a mean of all the variations caused by the tile-setting of the stones forming the ceiling or roof, the vertical height between sloping floor and parallel sloping roof was = 339ʹ2, and the computed transverse height = 304ʹ1, the greatest breadth being 82ʹ2 ; the lower breadth between the ramps = 42ʹ0 ; and the ramps themselves 20ʹ07 broad, and 20ʹ96 high in the transverse, or shortest, direction. (See "Life and Work," Vol. II. pp. 69—91.)

ness, that no artist's view of it, painted on a vertical
plane, could ever hope to represent more than a small
part of that floor, rising upward through the whole
canvas, and going out at the top. While on looking
horizontally northward again, from the south end of the
gallery, you lose the floor instantly, and see on the level
of your eyes, in the extreme distance, part of the steeply
descending ceiling; descending, too, still further, and
going out at the bottom of the picture, if your means of
illumination extend so far. (See Plate XIII.) Otherwise, it is the solemn overlappings of the high dark
walls (very dark now, because blackened by the smoke
of travellers' torches during a thousand years), passing
you by on either side, to draw together in dim and
unknown perspective beyond, above or below, which
mysteriously case you in on every hand.

Modern Measures of the Passages.

In the first edition of this book, I was positively
puzzled to make out, let alone the architecture of the
Grand Gallery, the simple sizes of the smaller passages ;
and erred considerably in choosing among the conflicting
testimonies of former travellers. But a four months'
residence on the spot, most completely settled all that
class of difficulties; and enables me now to speak
confidently thus : Although there are some pieces of
horizontal passage in the Great Pyramid, their united
length is as nothing compared with the length of the
inclined passages. The angle of the inclination in a
vertical plane of these passages is 26° 18′ nearly, being
the same whether the passages are ascending or descending (within errors partly of construction amounting
to 1-120th of the whole) ; and the transverse size, that
is, breadth and height, excepting only the utterly diverse
Grand Gallery, being also the same ; or at least having

certainly been so, before the abrading and exfoliating
of the more " soft and tender " of the stones began.
Confining myself, however, to well-preserved portions
of the ancient surface, and just now to the entrance-
passage alone, I obtained the following measures for *its*
breadth and height : —

ENTRANCE PASSAGE.

Breadth and Transverse Height as measured in 1865.

Place where the measure was made referred to the floor-joints.	Breadth from East to West.		Transverse Height.		Notes
	Near bottom of walls.	Near top of walls.	East side of passage.	West side of passage.	
	Brit. ins.				
4th joint from north, or upper end of passage	41·61	41·63	47·27	47·24	{ The peculiar little hollows of rough decayed surface avoided.
7th do.	41·51	41·41	47·30	47·23	
8th do.	41·59	41·50	..	..	{ Supposed to be Professor Greaves's place of measure, which gave him 41·56 of his English inches.
11th do.	41·59	41·51	47·32	47·30	
15th do.	41·59	41·46	47·18	47·16	{ Broken holes in this part of the floor from 12 to 18 inches deep, along its central line.
21st do.	41·46	Chipped	47·14	47·28	{ The top of wall measured as such, was what was indicated by the plane of the roof produced.

The manner in which these numbers run, will of
itself indicate to any practical man the degree of opportunity which the Great Pyramid still presents for
respectable accuracy of measure, when the measuring-
rods are applied by those who will trouble themselves
to seek out the best-preserved parts, and endeavour to

do them justice.   But what is the meaning of the word
height in the above table being qualified as " transverse
height ? "

These Pyramid passages being all of them inclined,
have two sorts or kinds of height : ˙First, *transverse
height*, or the shortest distance between floor and ceiling, and which was the easier kind of height to measure
accurately with the sliding scales which I had had
constructed for the purpose ; and, second, *vertical height*,
or height in the direction of a plumb-line, and the more
usual, indeed almost the universal, mode of measuring
heights in any masonry structures elsewhere.

Now, putting all the observations together, I deduced
47·24 Pyramid inches to be the *transverse* height of the
entrance-passage ; and computing from thence, with
the observed angle of inclination, the *vertical* height,
—that came out 52·76 of the same inches.   But the
sum of those two heights, or the height taken up in
one way and down in the other, = 100 inches : which
length, as elsewhere shown (p. 360), is the general Pyramid linear representation of a day of 24 hours.   And the
mean of the two heights, or the height taken one way
only, and impartially to the middle point between them,
= 50 inches ; which quantity is, therefore, the general
Pyramid linear representation of only half a day.   In
which case let us ask, what the entrance-passage has
to do with half, rather than a whole, day ?

Astronomy of the Entrance Passage.

If you descend at night some long distance down the
sloping floor of the entrance-passage, and then turn
round and look upwards and northwards to its open
mouth, you will see just there any large star whose
distance is 3° 42' nearly from the Pole, if it should
chance to be crossing the meridian at that moment in

the lower part of its very small daily circle :—always supposing that there is at this present time a star at that Polar distance, bright enough to be easily seen by the naked eye ; and indeed there is such a one very nearly in the required position, viz. δ Ursæ Minoris, 3° 24' from the Polar point.

But that star was not always there; being in reality in continual slow movement, year after year, quite inde-pendently of diurnal rotation; so that it is, to all appear-ance from this earth, carried on and on, cumulatively, together with all the other stars, through an immense celestial round at the rate of several whole degrees for every thousand years, by that grand mechanism of the earth and the apparent heavens called amongst astro-nomers the precession of the equinoxes;—the most important too of all celestial phenomena, for fixing the exact and absolute chronology of the earlier periods of man upon earth.   (See Chapter XV. p. 324.)

It was Sir John Herschel who, in answer to a letter from Colonel Howard-Vyse on his return from his im-mortal Pyramid explorations in Egypt, in 1837-8, first laid down the application of this essential astronomical law with regard to the Great Pyramid.   And, indeed, he did more ; for, assuming *the prevailing idea of his then time*, that the Great Pyramid's foundation was somewhere about 4,000 years ago, he searched the starry heavens, as moving under the influence of pre-cession, and found that for two thousand years before, and as many after, that time, only one notable star had been at the required Polar distance, viz. the distance of 3° 42' ; so as to look down the descending entrance-passage of the Great Pyramid (descending at 26° 18' from the horizon, in a latitude of 30° 0', neglecting small corrections) at its—the star's—lower meridian culmi-nation ; and that star—α Draconis by modern name— was in that critical position somewhere about 2160 B.C.

That date, therefore, made up with 1840 A.D. (and excluding for the time all question about one or more possibly unrecorded years at the beginning of our era), 4,000 years ago as the epoch of the passage-angle being laid; and then evidently to suit a chronological phenomenon of excellent astronomical kind, and peculiar to the Pyramid builders' day.

This near agreement of computations by modern astronomy, with the results of Egyptological scholarship as it was in London in 1840 A.D., took the English world by a storm of admiration ; and every one allowed, for awhile, that the whole affair of the date of the Great Pyramid was quite settled. But, alas ! those were simple, innocent days under good King William and the quiet Queen Adelaide. The up-springing of German critical and philosophical theology in this country, and the demands of natural-history science overleaping itself, and calling out everywhere for long dates, began soon after that. Presently too certain Syro-Egyptian antiquarians objected in their line that the astronomy of Sir John Herschel's paper must have been only an *accidental* coincidence with the passage-angle. And why ? Because said passage, having been made, *as they knew,* merely to slide a sarcophagus down to its resting-place, and having been filled up choke-full to its mouth, after that was done, with solid blocks of stone,— it could never have been used as an observatory by any ancient astronomers.

The first answer to this earliest Egyptologic dictum was easy enough. Sir John Herschel had not said that the passage was intended to serve as a permanent observatory ; but that its cream-coloured, stone-lined, long, long tube seemed to *memorialize,* or further still, to *monumentalize,* the once occurrence, of a particular phenomenon of the day when it was being built, and of that day only ; a record, therefore, once for all, by

memorial and *monumental* astronomy (whatever other
practical use the passage may, or may not, have afterwards served), of a former special sidereal fact, but
whose memory was destined to become increasingly
important in distant ages for the purposes of exact
chronology.

That explanation holds perfectly true yet. But with
regard to the other part of the question, as to whether
Sir John Herschel's astronomical conclusion is still to
be held as confirming, and confirmed by, the date arrived
at by the very latest studies of the present Egyptologists ; alas ! what a change had passed over London
society by the time that it had come to be my privilege
to go out to the Great Pyramid in 1864, and my turn to
print upon it in 1867, 8, and 9 !

Then to talk, in ordinary scientific society, of 4,000
years ago for the Great Pyramid's date of foundation !
All Egyptologists of any pretension, and the world
following at their heels, had learned to scorn such a
petty conception ; and had begun to assert entirely new
Egyptological epochs, ranging, most of them, anywhere
between 5,200 and 6,600 years ago. Whereupon Sir
John Herschel was left, with his astronomy alone, in
violent discrepance from, instead of singular agreement
with, the Egyptologists of our present universities and
museums.

Moreover, as soon as I came to extend Sir John
Herschel's computations, it appeared that when the star
α Draconis had in a manner chanced to come to that
passage-angle distance of 3° 42' from the Pole in about
2160 B.C.,—it was from a nearer, instead of a further,
Polar distance which the star had previously occupied.
In which case, the said star must have passed through
the passage-angle on a previous occasion also, or somewhere about 3440 B.C.

Here then was a most divided duty : 3440 B.C. might

satisfy *some* of the Neologians among our most learned
Egyptologists of the last ten years; though certainly
not all.　But then, what case could be made out, independently of all Egyptology of the profane monument
order, for choosing 3440 B.C., as better than 2160 B.C.,
or *vice versâ?*　There were no astronomical reasons
then known applying to one occasion, more than the
other; Colonel Howard-Vyse was dead; John Taylor
also; Sir John Herschel remained silent; a noisy
military man would persist that Sir John had given up
his former views, and now agreed with him in maintaining, that the peculiar passage-angle was chosen for
easy sarcophagus sliding alone; and the astronomical
world, whatever the reason why, would give the subject
no attention.

The Great Pyramid's use of a Polar Star.

But there was happily more in the ancient Great
Pyramid than any one had suspected, and it began to
manifest itself thus :—

Did not the very entrance passage, chiefly concerned
in the affair, speak by its 50, in place of 100, inch
height, to a half, and not a whole, day; or a 12-hour
interval for some purpose unknown?　And did not the
axis of the passage point, neither to the one, central,
Pole of the sky (30° Alt.), nor to an upper culmination
(33° 42′ Alt.) of a close Polar star,—but to a region of
lower culmination only, at or near 26° 18′ Alt. ?

This was indeed the fact; and no one had yet
anxiously inquired, " Why did the builders memorialize,
out of the two meridian passages of their circumpolar
star, at 12-hour distances of time in occurrence from
each other, only the lower, less visible, culmination of
the two?"　Neither had any one yet suggested scientifically, " What did any able astronomer, whether of the

Pyramid or any other, day intend or mean, if *time* was his object, by observing the transit, whether above or below the Pole, of a *close circumpolar* star; and of that kind of star only?"

Why! such a star moves so slowly, by reason of the very small size of its daily circle in the sky, that the instant of its passing the meridian is difficult to observe and decide on even with modern telescopic power : and no observer in his senses, in any existing observatory, when seeking to obtain the time, would observe the transit of a circumpolar star for anything else than *to get the direction of the meridian to adjust his instrument by.* But having done that, he would next turn said instrument round in the vertical plane so ascertained towards the South, and observe there any quick-moving, nearly equatorial, star when crossing that part of the meridian. And then such astronomer would obtain the time with proper accuracy and eminent certainty.

Now to myself, who have been an astronomical transit observer for a great part of my life, it immediately occurred that the narrow entrance-passage of the Great Pyramid directed up northward, looked very like a meridian *Polar* pointer ; while the grand gallery rising up southward at an opposite, and so far wrong, angle of altitude, but in the *right meridian plane*, and with its high walls scored with broad bands, looked amazingly like a *reminder* of the wide equatorial zone. This too it did, though not pointing to the angular height of the equator ; nor indeed having any aperture in its truly southward direction for actual observing astronomy of any kind or at any altitude; but having all that quarter blocked out by 200 feet in thickness of solid masonry. Wherefore I then ventured to argue thus:—

The ancient architect's reason why the entrance-

passage points to the *lower* or less important culmination only, of its Northern Polar star, α Draconis, must
be because another and more important star was, at
the moment so defined, at its upper culmination ; or was
crossing the meridian above the Pole ; and for chronological purposes, such more important star could be
no other than a nearly equatorial one, *South* of the
Zenith.   Was there then, at either the earlier date
3440 B.C., or the later 2160 B.C. (at each of which
dates, but at no other for 25,827 years, α Draconis was,
when crossing the meridian each day below the Pole,
Northward, equally at the entrance-passage's angle of
height), was there any notable equatorial star in the
exact *southern* vertical plane of direction of the Grand
Gallery ?   (Not at the *altitude* angle of the said gallery
in that plane ; for such an altitude would imply a declination for the star 34° South of, or below, and distant
from, the Equator, and very unfit for either time observation or time symbolization.)

Now here was a question put by the Pyramid's actual
construction, and to be answered by astronomy alone;
or without any of the Egyptologists, with all their
learned lore of false gods and animal idolatry, being
consulted.

The answer too might have come out, either that
there was no signal equatorial star in such a position
at either date ; or there might have been such stars at
both dates, and then no discrimination could have been
effected.   But the answer that did come out was, that
no such star existed at the circumpolar star's lower transit of 3440 B.C., but that there was one most eminently
and exactly in position at the 2160 B.C., or rather, as
it turned out a little more exactly in my calculations,
2170 B.C., circumpolar transit ; and that well-fitting
and then very nearly *equatorial* star was Alcyone. (See
Plates XXIII. and XXIV.)

The Pleiades Year.

Now Alcyone, or η Tauri as the stricter astronomical observers choose at present to call it, is not a very large or bright star in itself, but then it is the centre of a group of stars more bound up with human history, hopes, and feelings than any other throughout the sky, viz. the Pleiades; and there have been traditions for long, whence arising I know not, that the seven over-lappings of the grand gallery, so impressively described by Professor Greaves, had (though not pointing to them in altitude) *something* to do with the Pleiades, those proverbially *seven* stars of the primeval world, though already reduced to six (*i.e.* six visible to the ordinary naked eye), so early for certain as the time of the Latin poet Virgil; and probably, according to poetic tradition, as the siege and burning of Troy.

Here then is what those overlappings in the deeply built-in Grand Gallery had to do; viz. to symbolize, or remind of, the Pleiades in that early and still sep-tennial day of their's, both on the celestial meridian and to the south (though not at their then actual and enormous altitude therein; *viz.* more than 60°, or vastly too much for any passage flooring to be ascended by visitors), and as part of the memorial, rather than observing, astronomy of the Great Pyramid; for the Pleiades evidently were *de facto*, the superior, high southern and equatorial, or time star to be taken in concert with the inferior transit of the low circumpolar α Draconis star on the opposite or northern side of the sky, and 12 Polar hours distant the Pleiades from. And how well they performed their part, as well as how capable they were of it, appeared from this further result of calculation, that when they, the Pleiades, crossed the meridian at midnight above the Pole, at the same instant that α Draconis was crossing below the Pole, and *at the particular distance from the Pole indicated by the entrance-passage*,—then in the autumn season of the Northern hemisphere of that one year (2170 B.C.), *the meridian of the equinoctial point of the heavens, coincided with the Pleiades.** That autumn night, therefore, of that particular year, was not only, in the primeval fashion, the beginning of that year,— but that year was, with the Pleiades to lead it out in that significant manner, the beginning of the first humanly noted example of a period of *the precession of the*

---

* We have spoken of only one equinoctial point, when of course every one knows that, from the opposite intersections of two great circles of the sky,—if there is one, there must be two such crossings; and these two are already popularly termed the *vernal*, and *autumnal* equinoxes. Which of these two, then, are we alluding to?

To that usually, but in a manner incorrectly as to the best time of observation for it, called the vernal. And from inattention to this practical condition of stellar *observation*, some needless difficulties have arisen elsewhere in certain pre-historic studies of mankind.

Thus M. Thomas Brunton, of Paris,—finding by his otherwise most praiseworthy researches that it is *the* equinoctial point in the constellation of *Taurus*, which was generally referred to in primeval times, and which is now denominated "the Vernal Equinox" by the moderns (basing on the Alexandrian-Greek, or Pagan, Astronomy),—he at once declares that the beginning of the ancient year of mankind, and indeed the epoch of the creation of Adam, must have occurred in the *springtime of the northern hemisphere*. Whereby he, M. T. Brunton, fights against both much of ancient tradition, as well as the Bible itself; which describes that the evening and the morning, not the morning and evening, were the first day; therein leading to the idea of the sacred Biblical year beginning for the Northern hemisphere residence of the Patriarchs, with its evening or autumn, not its morning or spring.

But the Great Pyramid method of observing settles the whole difficulty. For in place of vainly trying, like the Greeks, to see what stars the sun was amongst, and whereabouts exactly, when the sun *was* amongst them and was extinguishing their light right and left of him through the whole breadth of the sky, by his brilliancy of daylight; the Great Pyramid Architect observed the anti-sun, or the point of the heavens *opposite* to the sun at midnight. Wherefore his *time of the year* for making *his* observations of those Taurus stars which the sun is amongst in spring, is evidently in the *autumn*. He observed them in the crucial position of the meridian cutting through the crossing of the invisible, but yet definable, equatorial circle, at midnight on the 21st of September: or in the autumn of the hemisphere of the earth containing the Great Pyramid, the Holy Land, and the whole of the countries wandered over by Abraham, Isaac, and Jacob.

equinoxes ; a cycle destined not to repeat itself, in that manner, until 25,827 years shall have come and gone.

This peculiar celestial cycle, the grand chronological dial in fact of the Great Pyramid,—so much is its architecture found to base upon it, is further defined at that Pyramid, but at no other throughout all Egypt, by, amongst other intentional features, the length of the two diagonals of the base, which so eminently lay out its whole position; when their sum is reckoned up in *inches*, at the rate of a Pyramid inch to a year. For each diagonal, duly computed, gives 12,913·26 of those units ; or the two, 25,827 nearly.

Further still, this feature is memorialized again at the King's Chamber's level of the Great Pyramid ; for that chamber's floor being by measure 1,702 inches above the base of the whole building, Professor H. L. Smith has shown, that the circuit of the Pyramid at that level = 25,827 Pyramid inches. And if the whole vertical height of the Great Pyramid, 5,813 inches, typifies the sun-distance (See pp. 56, 57), the partial vertical height from the King's Chamber level upwards, 4,110, indicates the radius of the precessional circle of the equinoxes, in years.

During the very little portion of human history which is all that modern astronomy can claim to have flourished in, the following are some of the principal attempts of mankind to state the full length of this period of the precession of the equinoxes :—

By Tycho Brahe	= 25,816 years.	
,, Ricciolus	= 25,920	,,
,, Cassini	= 24,800	,,
,, Bradley	= 25,740	,,
,, La Place	= 25,816	,,
,, Bessel	= 25,868	,,

No one whatever amongst men, from his own, or school, knowledge knew anything about such a phenomenon until Hipparchus, some 1,900 years after the

Great Pyramid's foundation, had a glimpse of the fact ;
—and yet it had been ruling the heavens for ages, and
was recorded by measure, and utilized too, in Jeezeh's
ancient structure.

Virgil, 200 years later still than Hipparchus, just as
might be expected of a poet, was greater in tradition
than astronomical observation; and when he uses the
phrase,* that it is " the constellation of the white Bull
with the golden horns which opens the year," many of
our own scientific commentators have wondered what
Roman Virgil could mean, by claiming as a phenomenon
for his own day, that which the precession of the equinoxes had caused to cease to be true 2,000 years before
his time, and had, during his day, given to the next
zodiacal constellation, *Aries*, instead.

No profane philosopher or academic observer of any
country in the world is known to have lived at the epoch
when that Virgilian phrase about Taurus *was* true.   In
fact, as recently well shown by M. Thomas Brunton, of
Paris (who has proposed that the angular place of the
equinoctial point in the zodiac, for the time being, shall
form a general chronological system for all nations),
the location or presence of the equinoctial point in
Taurus was chiefly a feature of Antediluvian times.
Thus it was in the front part of the constellation, the
very tips of the horns, at the Biblical date of the Creation of Adam; and from thence it proceeded backwards
through the zodiacal figure as yet drawn on our globes ;
so that at the date of the building of the Great Pyramid,
the equinoctial point, though still in Taurus, was at that
last part of the figure, just issuing out of a cloud, where
the Pleiades stars appear.

Now hereupon, we may all well wonder how it came
about that, according to the invaluable researches of
Mr. R. G. Haliburton, of Halifax, Nova Scotia, that

* " Candidus auratis aperit cum cornibus annum Taurus."

amongst the *origines* of almost all nations, and among
many unaltered savage tribes still, such as Australians,
Fijians, Mexicans, and many others (peoples never
reached by the Greeks or Romans), a similar beginning
of the year to that described by Virgil is still perpetuated;
the Pleiades, or the star group chiefly characterizing for
those nations the constellation of Taurus, being annually appealed to for the purpose; and in Australia, most
strange to say, by precisely the Pyramid method, in so
far that the natives there do begin their year on the
night when " they see most of the Pleiades"; otherwise,
when they continue to see them all the night through,
from their rising at sunset to their setting at sunrise;
and that must be when they, the Pleiades, cross the
meridian at midnight.*

But, just as the Romans adhered to those stars in
themselves alone, and saw not that they had left the
fiducial and chronological test of coinciding with the
meridian of the equinoctial point by two hours of the
equator (equivalent to a month of error on the autumn
equinox),—so the Australians adhere to them still,
implicitly, not seeing that the same point is now more
than three and a half of those hours (or 7 weeks behind
the true autumnal day) removed from them; and also,
that on account of the residual, or transverse, effect in
declination, of 4,000 years of precession, the Pleiades
stars, though so admirably seen by us in the north because they are now 24° above the Equator, no longer
rise high and gloriously in those southern skies.   But

---

* The New Zealanders, a more inventive race, seem to have departed
further than the Australians from the primitive practice, but yet greatly
astonished the Venerable Archdeacon Stock, of Te Aro Parsonage,
Wellington, New Zealand, by remarking, on the conclusion of the last
Colonial war, that that was a most auspicious occasion for making peace,
because it was *the beginning of the year*.   " The beginning of the year,"
asked the Archdeacon, " in the month of May ? " " Yes," answered an
old chief, " because the year which we hold to amongst ourselves, and as
our fathers did before us, is regulated by an appearance of the Seven
Stars (the Pleiades)."

that, in itself, is a test, in so far, of *when* those peoples first received the Pleiades system of sidereal chronology to hold; a system grandly adapted for the longest, most difficult, national periods, and which is only found in all its completeness, as well as with testimony to the date of its beginning, and equal fitness *then* for all inhabited lands, both South and North of the Equator laid up in the Great Pyramid building. (See Plates XXIV. and XXV.)

Transcendentalisms of the Great Pyramid Astronomy.

Now the only source from whence one uniform system of sidereal chronology, and which, though endued with *some* change in respect to the seasons, yet alters so slowly year by year and generation after generation as to require 25,827 years before it passes through all the seasons,—the only source, I say, from whence it could have emanated in that early age of the world, and been impressed upon the *origines* of all races of mankind, is, was, and ever will be, Divine inspiration; and the Divine intention touching that mystery of God, the human race on earth.

But not by any means implying, that the terrestrial human race is the only object cared for by God, throughout all the sidereal universe. For had it been so, the stars might have been created for man's chronological purposes alone,—instead of man being taught, as in this case, to make the best practical use of pre-existent, pre-created means.

Here, accordingly, what we are called upon to note, may rather remind us of that which Josephus records of the descendants of Seth, viz. that no Creation miracles were wrought for them, but that they, though favoured with Divine assistance, had to study astronomy in the laws of the stars as they already existed. And on pushing our calculations to the extreme of modern science, we shall undoubtedly find that those stars were by no means in themselves absolutely perfect for this one end alone. But take them as they were 4,000 years ago, and after they had been already set in motion by the Divine power æons on æons of ages before the Pyramid day,—and you will find that they did, at that epoch, come quite near enough to form an excellent practical chronological system of the kind indicated ; and no better mode of utilizing those actual phenomena of the starry sky, nor any better choice among the stars, ever has been imagined since then, in any country of the world.

Thus, to moderate observation (and with far greater accuracy than the annals of the profane history of mankind have been kept to), all these hereinafter-following features may be said, in *ordinary* terms, to obtain,—

1. The Great Pyramid is astronomically oriented in its sides; and its passages are in the plane of the meridian.
2. The entrance-passage, with its alt. angle of 26° 18' nearly, points 3° 42' vertically below the Northern Pole of the sky.
3. In the year 2170 B.C. α Draconis was 3° 42' from the Pole of the sky, and therefore looked down the axis of the entrance-passage, when at its *lower* culmination.
4. When α Draconis was so looking down the entrance-passage in the North, then η Tauri, the chief star in the Pleiades group, was crossing the local terrestrial meridian, towards the South; in the vertical plane of direction of the Grand Gallery, but at a point high up in the sky, near the equator.
5. At the same moment of that year, 2170 B.C., the celestial meridian of the Vernal Equinox also coincided with that same η Tauri star, and gave

it for the time an extraordinary, chronological,
super-eminence over all others.

6. That whole stellar combination had not taken
place for 25,827 years previously, and will not
take place again for 25,827 years subsequently.
It has not consequently repeated, or confused,
itself yet in all the history of the human race;
though the Sothiac cycle, the Phœnix cycle, and
other chronological inventions of the profane
Egyptian priests, men long after the Pyramid
day, and supposed generally to have been the
most learned of the ancients,—have done so
again and again; to the lamentable confounding
of dates in the old Pagan, and modern Egyptological, world too.

But if the calculations on which the above Pyramid
results are founded, shall be pushed to much greater
refinement, or to portions of space invisible to the naked
eye,—it then appears that (1) the Pole-star, when it
was 3° 42′ from the Pole, (2) the equatorial star opposite
to it, and (3) the celestial meridian of the equinox, were
not all of them on the Pyramid's meridian, below and
above the Pole, *precisely* at the same instant, either in
the year 2170 B.C., or in any other year.

But this difficulty is not by any means entirely dependent on the stars, in their places, not being as exact
as if they had been created originally for no other than
the above purpose ; for there are hindrances also to
modern astronomy, in precisely realising every single
thing in number, weight, and measure, that has taken
place in Nature during the last 4,000 years. Two
astronomers, for instance, using the same data, may
compute back the place of a given star 4,000 years ago
from its present place, and they shall agree to a second
in the result ; but it does not therefore follow that the

star was as precisely there at that time, as though a contemporary astronomer had observed it then; because proper motion, and variations of proper motion, may exist, quite unknown to the short period of surveillance over the stars yet enjoyed by modern astronomy. Some of the quantities, too, of the celestial mechanics concerned, such as the precise amount of the very precession of the equinoxes itself, and its accompanying phenomena of nutation and aberration, may have been erroneously assumed, and never can, or will, be ascertained perfectly by man. The accepted numerical values of such quantities do, in fact, vary at the same time between one astronomer and another (unless both were brought up in the same school, and then both may differ from truth), and also between one generation and another of astronomers in the same place.*

After, therefore, doing my best with the Pyramid star calculations, and publishing my result, together with a repetition of Sir John Herschel's, so far as it went, I advertised, after a manner, for help or criticism from other astronomers,—in the way of each of them computing the whole of the quantities with the data he now thinks best, and also with the data most approved in the astronomical world of his youth, as well as with the quantities thought correct at the end of the last century.

But none of them have ventured to expose to modern society the weaknesses of their favourite science, multiplied by 4,000 years; and I should have been left without anything whatever to show from any other modern

* In *Nature*, No. 491, Vol. XIX., for March 27, 1879, is an admirable letter by Professor Asaph Hall, of the United States Washington Observatory, setting forth, that although " a few years ago the remark was frequently made that the labours of astronomers on the solar system were finished,—yet to-day the Lunar theory is in a very discouraging condition, and the theories of Mercury, Jupiter, Saturn, Uranus, and Neptune, are all in need of revision." And this is because the very recently prepared Tables of the Planets by the late celebrated M. Le Verrier, and the present distinguished Professor Newcomb, " are already beginning to differ from observation."

quarter, but for the kindness of Dr. Brünnow, (late) Astronomer-Royal for Ireland; who, kindly and without needing any second asking, performed the first part of my request: that is, with the quantities which he then, in 1871, thought should be adopted as correct, he most ably, and by special methods of astronomy which no one in all the world understands better than himself, computed the following numbers :—

(1) α Draconis was for the first time at the distance of 3° 41′ 50″ from the Pole in the year .. .. = 3443 B.C.

(2) It was at the least distance from the Pole, or 0° 3′ 25″, in the year .. .. = 2790 ,,

(3) It was for the second time at the distance of 3° 41′ 42″ from the Pole in the year .. .. = 2136 ,,

(4) η Tauri (Alcyone of the Pleiades) was in the same right ascension as the equinoctial point in the year = 2248 ,, when it crossed the meridian above the Pole, 3° 47′ north of the Equator, with α Draconis crossing below the Pole, nearly, but not exactly at the same instant; and α Draconis was then nearly 90° (89° 16′) from Alcyone in the meridian, measured through the Pole.

(5) α Draconis and η Tauri were exactly opposite to each other, so that one of them could be on the meridian above the Pole, and the other on the meridian below the Pole, at the same absolute instant, only at the date of .. .. = 1574 ,, but when all the other data diverged largely.

We have now to deal with the last three dates. Of these three, the first two evidently include between them my own previous mean quantity of 2170 B.C.; but the third differs extravagantly. Nevertheless, the visible effect in the sky of that one apparently very large difference in absolute *date*, is merely this, according to Dr. Brünnow's computation; viz. that when η Tauri, or the Pleiades, were crossing the meridian above the Pole, at my Pyramid date of 2170 B.C., α Draconis was not doing the same thing, *exactly* beneath the Pole, at the same instant; for the star was then at the distance of 0° 17′ *west* of the meridian. But it would have been doing the same thing perfectly, according to *an entrance-passage observation of it*, if the northern end of that passage had been made, by the builders, to trend 17′ westward, still keeping to its observed angular height in the vertical plane; viz. 26° 18′.

Whereupon comes the question whether,—granting temporarily that Dr. Brünnow's excellent calculations in modern astronomy replace everything that has happened in Nature during the last 4,000 years,—whether that 17′ of the Pole-star's *west* distance from the meridian was a thing of moment;—and if so, is this the first occasion on which the divergence has been discovered ?

Seventeen minutes of space, or less than the thousandth part of the azimuthal scale, is but a small quantity for any one to appreciate in all the round of the blue expanse, without instruments; and the first effort of Greek astronomy 1,800 years after the Pyramid was built, is reported to have been the discovery that the Pole-star of that day, then 6 degrees from the Pole, was not as *they*, the Greeks, had previously held, *exactly* on the Pole.

Greek and other profane nations, then, had been in the habit of overlooking, long, long after the epoch of the Pyramid, an error twenty times as great as this which is now charged on the Great Pyramid astronomy, by the present day science of precision, which has been at last elaborated amongst men after a further consumption of 4,000 valuable years.

And yet it was not all error either, on the part of the Great Pyramid. For here we should take account of the results of my observations in 1865, when I succeeded in comparing the directions of both the outside of the Pyramid, the internal axis of the entrance-passage, and the axis of the azimuth trenches* separately and successively with the Polar star. These observations were made with a powerful altitude-azimuth instrument, reading off its angles with micrometer-

* See " Life and Work," Vol. II. pp. 185—196.

microscopes to tenths of seconds; and the conclusions from them were, that everything at the Great Pyramid trended, *at its, north end towards the west*,—the azimuth trenches by 19 minutes, the socket-sides of the base by 5 minutes, and the axis of the entrance-passage by more nearly 4 minutes and a half.

What *could* all these features have been laid out for with this slight tendency to west of north? was a question which I frequently pondered over at the Great Pyramid, and sometimes even accused the earth's surface of having shifted with respect to its axis of rotation during 4,000 years. But now the true explanation would appear to be, that the Seth-descended architect, knowing perfectly well the want of exactly the 12 hours, or 50 inch, correspondence between his Polar and Equatorial stars (though they were the best in the sky), had so adjusted in a minute degree the position of the Great Pyramid when building it, as to reduce any error in his Pleiades system of chronology, arising out of the stellar discrepance, to a *minimum*. Whence the fact of the *western* divergence of the north pointing of the entrance-passage, as detected by the modern astronomy observations in 1865, combined with the computation in 1871, —becomes the most convincing practical proof of intention, and not accident, having guided all these time arrangements at the Great Pyramid.

Further still too I may perhaps be allowed to mention in this Edition, that on discussing recently with some of the astronomers who were sent to Egypt in December, 1874, to observe the Transit of Venus (as a stepping-stone towards attaining a knowledge of the sun-distance),—the palm of merit for the best time observations seemed to be unanimously accorded to those of them who had adopted a new method of using their transit instruments, recently elaborated by M. Otto Struve, of the Central Russian Observatory; and which consisted in observing, not exactly in the plane of the meridian (as usually done or tried to be done), but *in the vertical of the Pole-star at the instant;*—or, as nearly as possible, on the very method of ultra-refinement adopted at the ancient Great Pyramid.   Hence the object of this chapter is now fully obtained ; for not only does the ancient monument fix an absolute date for itself, viz. something very close to 2170 B.C., which all the profane monuments were confessed to be incapable of even approximately attempting, but it does so by methods unknown of old elsewhere, and only recently begun to be appreciated in the best *European astronomy.*

APPENDIX IN 1879.

In the *Contemporary Review* of September in the present year, has appeared an Article entitled, " The Problem of the Great Pyramid," by that unceasing writer in scientific periodicals, Mr. R. A. Proctor, B.A., Cambridge.   It touches on the subject of the present chapter, and, I am told, calls for remark.

Mr. Proctor cannot deny the measures, observations, star conclusions and general astronomy here just set forth ; but he is anxious to take up with the Egyptologists in their long dates, wherefore he endeavours to show that the Pyramid's entrance passage must have memorialized the earlier of the two appulses of the α Draconis Pole-star ; viz. that of 3300 B.C., and not that of 2170 B.C.

To this end he is content to lose, abolish, or be blind to, all the invaluable Pleiades traditions of the early families of mankind ; all the unique astronomical perfections of the Equinoctial coincidence with the Pleiades in 2170 B.C., as well as their nearly Equatorial place then ;—and makes everything hinge upon one other star without any traditional memorial, with a fabulous

Greek natural-history name (*a Centauri*); far from the
Equinoctial Meridian, and unsuitable for time work,
being 34° away from the Equator, and in the very low-
altitude direction of the Grand Gallery, which is further
impenetrably sealed towards the South by 200 feet in
thickness of solid masonry.

For the removal of this remarkable difficulty, Mr.
Proctor invents a scheme of a temporary observing
having been carried out, when the Great Pyramid
might have been less than half built. But as that
would not be very useful in scientific astronomy, he
borrows an astrological excuse from the mediæval Con-
stantinopolitan, Proclus (480 A.D.); he, a mystical philosopher of that day, who knew in reality nothing of
the Great Pyramid and its very ancient builders; but,
while following in the steps of the Emperor Julian the
Apostate, against Christianity, perverted, paganised,
and diabolised whatever he touched. Under this sorry
and dangerous leader then, Mr. Proctor declares in
London, with the most astounding improbability in
the history of the human mind, that King Cheops of
the Great Pyramid must have been an astrologer; and
observed stars in the once half-finished Grand Gallery
there, when it was still open to the South, in order to
compute the horoscope of his own life, in the dark,
mediæval manner that was coming into fashion in the
corrupt society of Byzantine cities in Proclus' own day,
and on his peculiar pattern.*

So hollow and far-fetched a scheme for making the

---

* In the intervals of his deep studies of morals and metaphysics,
Proclus, says Gibbon (Vol. VII. p. 149) *personally* conversed with Pan,
Æsculapius, and Minerva, in whose mysteries he was secretly initiated,
and whose prostrate statues he adored; in the devout persuasion that
the philosopher, who is a citizen of the universe, should be the priest of
its "various deities." Proclus died at the age of 73, A.D. 485; or as his
anti-christian friends preferred to mark it,—124 years απο Ιȣλιανȣ
βασιλεως; for "the pagans reckoned their calamities from the reign of
their hero."

Great Pyramid lengthen out its dates from 2170 to 3300 B.C., really needs no answer: though I am happy to point out that its author does one good thing towards the end of his essay, on his own sound knowledge of modern practical astronomy and its methods of calculation.

This good thing is, that he computes the date for the Pleiades stars being in the position described in No. 4 of Dr. Brünnow's list (p. 383); and says that he finds it, not 2248 B.C., but more nearly 2140 B.C. To which I can only say for the reasons pointed out on pp. 381, 382, very probably.

CHAPTER XVIII.

MOSAIC, AND EGYPTIAN, WISDOM,

Derived from opposite sources.

IN the circles of those very learned men in modern society who go on studying with zest the idolatrous contents of the Egyptian galleries in the British, and many other, museums (and are known as hierologists, hieroglyphiologists, Egyptologists, and though calling themselves Biblical archæologists, are much more Anti-, than Pro-, therein), are found the doughtiest of those champions who are so ready in these days to insist, that " whereas Genesis was written by Moses, and Moses was for many years of his life a priest among the Egyptians, (who were a wealthy and civilized nation when the progenitors of the Israelites were still merely wandering shepherds; while moreover, according to the New Testament itself (Acts vii. 22), Moses was learned in all the wisdom of the Egyptians,)"—that therefore Moses must have borrowed all the best things he has put into Genesis, and his other books also, from the Egyptian priests.

On this question, much defence of the Divine inspiration, *versus* the Egyptian education, of the responsible author of the Pentateuch has been written in the modern world, from the literary side ; but not always with so much decided effect as might have been done from the scientific point of view, as now established by the Great Pyramid investigations.

Mere literature, indeed, has well set forth that as to the points of community, or similar complexion, claimed by the hierologists between the Egyptian and the Mosaic laws, they exist only in certain subsidiary forms required for social order and political independence; and are such as a common humanity, with a like geographical position, chronological epoch, and traditional information from Babel, would have infallibly produced, more or less, amongst any set of people endowed with ever so little desire to amend their position in the world. And then there comes also, to every real believer in the fundamental doctrine of Christianity, this further and grander result, flowing from an inductive investigation into the two systems as wholes; viz. that the real religious essence of the Mosaic law is as totally distinct from that of the Egyptian, as any two antagonisms in this world can possibly be. For while the Egyptian system bases on Cainite assertions and reassertions of self-righteousness, and a multitude of gods, half animal and half man—some of them, too, not a little abominable—who is there, of those who have felt the saving grace of Christ's Divine sacrifice, who cannot see, as the ruling principle in Moses, the most magnificent, and particular rebellion against all the would-be power of man to theo-technicize heavenly things, and a grand assertion both of the one, true, only living God, the Creator of all things, and the sinfulness of man in *His* sight? Over and above which, how grandly distinct is the great preparation, promised to Abraham, and practically begun in the time of Moses, of setting aside a peculiar people in the midst of whom, or rather of one section of whom, Christ Himself was to appear and suffer 1,500 years afterwards as the Divine Mediator and all-essential Atonement; and in the midst of the other sections of which people and His Church, He is still to appear as Universal King on earth!

The holy zeal, too, of Moses, his earnest self-sacrificing for the cause of God, and his anxiety to show Him at once accessible by prayer, through an appointed method of *sin-offering* and *mediation* to every one, both rich and poor, are the liveliest contrasts that can well be imagined to the sordid routine of an Egyptian priesthood, placing itself immovably, for its own gain, between the people and their gods, such as they were.

Of the Number Five.

But the most decided overthrow of the modern hierologists comes involuntarily from themselves, when they attempt to handle the mechanical part of the question; for, to a great extent, what they, the hierologists, have succeeded at last in proving,—is precisely that which enables us to say most positively that a cubit measuring-rod of the Mosaic, and Newton-proved, length of 25 Pyramid inches nearly, and which has such extraordinary scientific value in its earth-axis commensurability, and was made so much of by Moses in the Tabernacle of the Wilderness,—was no part or parcel of the wisdom of the profane Egyptians during any portion of their historical career ; and could not, therefore, have been learned or borrowed from *them* by either Moses or any one else.

And though the best ethnological theory of the Egyptians be that which makes them, not Ethiopians descending the Nile from the interior of Africa, nor Indian Aryans migrating by sea from Bombay and landing on the eastern coast of Africa,—but North Asiatics and Caucasians entering by the Isthmus of Suez into Lower Egypt, and *ascending* the course of the river—there seems no reason whatever to conclude that *they* had *previously*, wherever such previous existence had been passed, either received or adopted that peculiar measure of 25 inches, which Sir Isaac Newton considers the *Israelites* possessed, long before *their* going down into Egypt.

Not only, too, may it be further said, from this cubit-measure side of the question, that recent researches have proved the astonishing vitality of standards of measure through enormous intervals of time : and that an involuntary change of a free people's standard from the undoubted Egyptian 20·68, to the Hebrew and Pyramid 25·0 inches, or *vice versâ*, was never yet seen in the history of the classic world; but it may be argued, that the ancient Egyptians, whatever faults they may have had, were both politically and socially a most conservative, methodical, and orderly people, with an immense taste for mechanics, a most commendable industry, and a marvellous appreciation of measure; so that they would be the last nation in the world, let alone their religious ideas on the topic, to lose or mistake their hereditary standards.   In fact, one of the chief accusations which a late French writer brings against those ancient Egyptians is, that they had no genius, no invention, no love of change; that they were only dull plodders at routine work; and, besides never having produced a great poet or a first-rate warrior, they were actually so low in the scale of his own Gallic ideas of advancing, civilized humanity, so debased in fact amongst mankind, as never to have had a *revolutionist* of any kind or degree amongst them.

We may therefore with perfect safety, and hierologists' support too, regard the length of 20·68 inches as the veritable and admitted hereditary measure of all Pharaonic, Cainite, idolatrous, Egyptians; and the one which, if they had been really copied from by any other nation or individual, would have been the length imitated and faithfully reproduced.

Moses, consequently, in making the distinguished and

by implication (see p. 357) *sacred*, use which he did, not of that length of 20·68, but of the very different length of 25 inches, was decidedly not taking anything there out of the known wisdom-book of the Egyptians.

And not only so, too; for if, with the absolute length of the Pyramid standard, Moses adopted its Pyramidic subdivision also into 5 × 5 parts, and wrote his whole laws and legislation in five books, or a "Pentateuch,"— he was adopting an arrangement which was particularly hateful to the Egyptians. Why it was so, does not appear; but Sir Gardner Wilkinson speaks of 5 as being the "evil number" in Modern Egypt* still; it is marked by o on their watches; and 5 × 5, or anything made up of 5, would seem to have been always repulsive there.

Particularly galling, therefore, to the old Egyptians it must have been to have seen the Israelites, when they escaped from bondage and went out of the country "with an high hand," itself a symbol of 5,—especially galling to their spirits to see their late slaves go up, marshalled by " 5 in a rank," out of the land of Egypt; for so is the literal translation of the word expressed " harnessed," in Exodus xiii. 18, of the English Bible.

But Moses had none of this unwise and anti-Pyramid hatred of 5, and times of .5; and though his first arrangement of years was the Sabbatical one of a "week of years," his next, and by far the most important one, the grand standard, in fact, of sacred time, was the jubilee of 5 × 10 years; a number which, with the similar arrangement of days for the feast of Pentecost, brings up again the number of inches frequently referred to as an important standard in the King's Chamber and the passages of the Great Pyramid.

And when we further find that in other important things, Moses was likewise going directly against the

* Murray's 1864 " Handbook for Egypt," p. 142.

standards of the Egyptians, but coincidently with those of the Kosmos of God and also the long secret, but now being manifested, design of the Great Pyramid; of those very innermost parts of it, too, which the Egyptians knew nothing about, and which he, Moses, *as a man*, could never have seen—when we meet with all these telling circumstances, and so many parallel features between the inspired writings of the Bible, and the construction by number, weight, and measure of the Great Pyramid; they two on one side, *versus* on the other all profane Egypt, together with Babylon, Assyria, and Greece also, it certainly would appear that we must be coming close to the Biblical Sethite, or Israelitic, source of the truly high and transcendent knowledge displayed by that mighty, unique, and *non*-Egyptian fabric.

While as to the oft-repeated quotation that Moses was learned in "all the wisdom of the Egyptians,"—the particular question which that most provokes in the mind of one who has closely studied the Great Pyramid, and compared it carefully by mensuration and science against every known work of those same idolatrous Egyptians when working freely and voluntarily for themselves,—is, and pray what did *all* the wisdom of the Egyptians amount to? Must it not have been something extremely moderate, if Moses knew it *all*, besides his own superlative stores of higher wisdom, which Egyptians were by no means burdened with?

Moses knew therefore, doubtless, that the profane Egyptians believed the earth to be flat, and represented it in their hieroglyphics, still to be seen, as a thin cake of bread: and had no ideas of earth and heaven commensurability for their own cubit measure. But Moses was not led, by knowing that ignorant wisdom of the Egyptians, to follow it,—rather, on the contrary, to avoid it, and fight against it; arming himself therefor out of the very treasuries of Divine wisdom imparted to him from

on high.   And, first of all, let us see how he proceeded
in that particular matter of his, or his God's, *sacred*
cubit length, as expressive of the earth we live on;
first in size, and next with its contents and all that is
therein.

Of the Sacred Ark of the Covenant.

The length of the Great Pyramid's cubit having been
25·025 British inches cannot, I presume, now, after all
that has preceded in this book,* be resisted; and, to
all minds capable of grasping the subject, Sir Isaac
Newton's testimony for the Mosaic cubit having also
been close to that length,† is probably equally conclusive; yet at the same time, those able minds may desire
to hear, if there is any further direct *Biblical* evidence
for that end, over and above what Sir Isaac Newton
adduced in his invaluable Dissertation.   Now something of this sort there does appear to be in the Pentateuch's account of the Ark of the Covenant, the most
sacred feature of the whole of the Tabernacle's arrangement under Moses.

That ark was kept in the Holiest of Holies, occupied
its chief place of honour, and was never to be looked on
by any but the High Priest alone, even during a journey.
Near it was placed an ephah measure; and immediately
outside its compartment, as Michaelis has shown, were
various other standards of measure; though no metrological purpose, that I am aware of, has been hitherto
assigned to the Ark itself.

As its original name, *arca*, implies, the Ark was a box
or chest; and its first stated purpose as such was, to
hold the Divine autograph of the law written on stone.

This Ark-box, then, made of shittim, or acacia, wood,
was further lidless, so far as anything attached to it was

---

* Chap. X. pp. 199, 208; Chap. XIV. p. 291.   † Chap. XVI. p. 351.

concerned: though a crown of gold was afterwards added round about the rim, and a separate or loose lid was made for it of pure gold, called the Mercy-seat. The actual seat, however,—said to be occasionally occupied as a throne, by an expression of the Divine presence—was not that lid, but was formed by the wings of two angels, constructed in gold, at either end of the lid; which lid, at such time, together with the Ark below, then formed the *footstool*.*

With the lower part only of this arrangement, or the Ark itself, have we now to do; and the Ark, on its loose lid of gold being removed, was merely a box—a lidless rectangular, and rectilinear box, made of a hard and tough wood common to the hills of Sinai.

Now in so far, there was nothing new or peculiar in this arrangement of Moses; for of boxes there was already an abundance in the world, even in the very temples of Egypt, when time had waxed so late in human history as 1500 B.C. In fact, those very purposes of " rapacity," in subservience to which Josephus relates that Cain invented weights and measures, would seem to require that he should have made big and strong chests, wherein to keep the fruits of his organized spoliation and oppression of mankind; as well as the stone strongholds, banks, or " oers," of which more presently, for the custody of the said chests.

The only feature, therefore, of distinctive importance which we need expect to find in the particular box constructed by Moses for a sacred purpose, should be something akin to that which distinguished his sacred cubit from the profane cubit of the Egyptians. Mere mea-

---

* The lid, or cover, of the ark was of the same length and breadth, and made of the purest gold. Over it, at the two extremities, were two cherubim, with their four faces turned towards each other, and inclined a little towards the lid (otherwise called the Mercy-seat). Their wings, which were spread out over the top of the ark, formed the throne of God, the King of Israel, while the ark itself was the footstool." Exod. xxv. 10—22; xxxvii. 1—9.)—*Kitto's Bible Cyclopædia*, p. 214.

suring-sticks were both of them to the outside, con-
temptuous world ; and yet one, not only of a different
length from the other, but implying by the amount of
that difference a commensurability with the Divinely
grand in nature, far too difficult for man to have discovered for himself, or even to have fully appreciated
when explained to him, in that age. Now the size of
that Ark-box of Moses is given in Holy Scripture as
being 2·5 cubits long, and 1·5 cubits broad, and 1·5
high ; which measures being reduced to Pyramid inches,
on Sir Isaac Newton's, or more exactly our own, evalua-
tion of the sacred cubit of Moses, = 62·5 × 37·5 × 37·5
of those inches.

But was this outside measure, or inside measure ? for
that must make a very material difference in the cubical
result.

Outside measure, without a doubt, and for the two
following reasons :—

1st. Because the vertical component is spoken of as
height, and not depth.

2nd. Because the lower lid of gold, or the Mercy-seat,
being made only of the *same* stated length and breadth
as the Ark itself, it would have stood insecure, and run
a chance of tumbling down to the bottom of the box, if
that length and breadth had signified the top of the
box's inside, and not its outside, area.

Hence, with the true length of the sacred cubit (obtained now after so many mediæval ages of error), and
the above understanding how to apply it, we may now
approach the cubical contents of the Covenant's Ark.
We are not, indeed, informed in Scripture what was
the thickness of the sides, and therefore do not know
exactly how much to subtract from the outside, to give
the inside, dimensions ; but the outside having been
given, and the material stated, the limits within which
such thickness must be found are left very narrow

indeed.   Let the thickness, for instance, be assumed 1·8 Pyramid inches; then the length, breadth, and depth will be reduced from an outside of 62·5 × 37·5 × 37·5 to an inside of 58·9 × 33·9 × 35·7; which gives 71,282 cubic inches for the capacity contents of this open box without a lid.

Or, if we consider the sides and ends .1·75 inch thick, and the bottom 2 inches,—also very fair proportions in carpentry for such a sized box in such a quality of wood,—then its inside measure would be 59·0 × 34·0 × 35·5; which yields for the cubical contents 71,213 cubic Pyramid inches.

Thus, in any mode almost of practically constructing the Ark-box, on both the name and number data given by the Bible, and the sacred Hebrew cubit value first approached in modern times by Sir Isaac Newton, we cannot avoid bringing out a cubical capacity result almost identical with that of a still older box, known for several centuries past to moderns as a lidless box, but never known at all to the ancient Egyptians; viz. the coffer in the King's Chamber of the Great Pyramid.

Wherefore, with that coffer's cubic capacity, (ascertained by the modern measures already given in Chapter VIII. p. 165, and amounting to 71,250 cubic Pyramid inches,) the Ark of the Covenant immediately acquires all the commensurabilities of that coffer's interior with the capacity and mean density of the natural earth as a whole : a something both utterly distinguishing it from any profane Egyptian box yet measured ; and most appropriate to the Scripture-stated use of the Ark under circumstances of Divine presence as a *footstool ;* agreeably with the words of the Lord in Isaiah and Acts, " the earth is My footstool."

Such, then, looked at in the light of science, 3,300 years after its day of construction, must have been the sacred Ark of the Covenant, built according to the inspiration commands received by Moses *after* he had left Egypt for ever ;—and that was the Ark which subsequently overthrew the idol gods of the Philistines, and was a source of safety to Israel, *when used by permission of God*, on many and many a national occasion. Yet what eventually became of it, or what was its latter end, Scripture does not inform us. The Eastern Churches have their traditions, but I do not know on what really secure data they found them.

The Abyssinians, too, have much to say about the Ark, and I believe claim it to be now in their country: while the Apocrypha, on the contrary, declares that, together with many other sacred vessels of the Temple, it was carried away and hidden by Jeremiah in Mount Nebo, to prevent its falling into the hands of Nebuchadnezzar at the destruction of Jerusalem by him.

Meanwhile the rising tide of national thought, inquiry, and growing belief in this country, touching the identity of the British nation with the lost ten tribes of the kingdom of Israel, is now leading, under the guidance of Mr. Edward Hine, Rev. F. R. A. Glover, Mr. E. W. Bird, and others, to the conclusion, that subsequently still to what is described in the Apocrypha, the Ark of the Covenant was brought, together with a daughter of the Royal House of Judah in the hereditary line of David, to these Isles of the West, by Jeremiah, in his latter days ; and was finally deposited by him in the hill of Tara in Ireland ; and is there still, in very secure masonic preservation for an expected day of bringing to light once again.

Papers on this subject are appearing almost every week in Mr. Hine's special Anglo-Israelite journals, *Life from the Dead*, and *The Nation's Glory Leader*, as well as in the *Banner of Israel*, under the unexceptionable editorship of Mr. E. W. Bird (Philo-Israel). Subscriptions, too, have even been sent in, though not desired yet, to pay for the expense of a search by excavation.

If this most remarkable, really miraculous, Biblical relic should ever be found, either at Tara or anywhere else, it is evident from all that has been already written here, that by its exact and scientifically-measured *size* it may prove its own case. And in the same category I may as well mention a further piece of solid information made out by the metrological researches of John Taylor and others in past years; viz. that within narrow limits of uncertainty, the brazen lavers of Solomon's Temple were also of the same cubic capacity as the coffer in the Great Pyramid; and measured on the Hebrew system, 40 baths or 4 homers; while each of those *homers* was equal to the Anglo-Saxon "quarter," used for corn-measures amongst that people, viz. our own forefathers. Those lavers, then, through the coffer, were— what no human science could have intentionally made them in that day—*i.e.* earth-commensurable incapacity, combined with weight.

Of Solomon's Molten Sea.

But there was still a far larger capacity vessel in the same Temple of Solomon: was it, also, earth-commensurable, and harmoniously proportioned with the world of God's creation?

This vessel, by name the "Molten Sea," was grandly cast in bronze, though of a shape and size which have defied all essayists hitherto to agree upon. Even in the Bible, something of what is there said about it, is stated variously in different books thereof; as in that of Kings, the cubical contents are given as 2,000 baths, while in Chronicles they are set down as 3,000. The latter account being but fragmentary, I adhere to the former; and then find, according to the simple statement in baths, that the "molten sea" would have contained the contents of a laver 50 times; or a Pyramid number at once.

Next we are told (1 Kings, vii. 23—26) that the "molten sea" "was ten cubits from the one brim to the other; it was round all about, and his height was five cubits; and a line of thirty cubits did compass it round about; and it was an hand-breadth thick."

The first point here, is to realize the shape. Some good men have imagined it cylindrical; some of a swelling caldron form; but the greater numbers, a hemispherical shape; and this, perhaps, is most agreeable (1) to the phrase "round all about," (2) to its diameter being twice its height, and (3) to the traditionary testimony of Josephus that it *was* hemispherical.

This point settled, are the measures given, of the inside, or outside, denomination? By the rule established for the Ark, the breadth and *height* are outside, of course; but in that case, what is the meaning of a circle of 10 cubits in *diameter,* having a *circumference* of 30 cubits? That is a total impossibility; and wholly against the chief part of the teaching of the Great Pyramid itself, which proves in various ways that the circumference of a circle having 10 for diameter, cannot be less than 31·4159, &c.

In this dilemma, I venture to conclude (especially as here an indication of the thickness of the vessel is given, viz. at a hand-breadth) that the *inside* circumference was alluded to, but the *outside* diameter.

Take, then, a hemisphere with an inside circumference of 30 Pyramid cubits, its diameter would be 238·73 Pyramid inches, giving, with an outside diameter of 10 cubits, nearly 5·5 inches for the thickness (or a space which the hand of a strong man spread out would easily cross). The cubic contents, then, of such internal hemisphere will be 3,562,070 Pyramid cubic inches; and divided by the Pyramid number 50, give 71,241 of the same cubic inches; *i.e.* within a seven-thousandth part the same as either the Ark of the Covenant, or the coffer of the Great Pyramid.

But why did Solomon go to such pains and expense in making the " molten sea " so very much larger than his already large brazen vessels, the lavers; and larger, too, by the exact multiple of 50?

No profane Egyptian would have chosen that number, as we have already seen; but in the Great Pyramid, planned certainly by a Seth-descended, God-inspired teacher,—the lowest course of the King's Chamber has been so adjusted in height, by the removal from sight of its lower 5 inches, that the cubic contents of that lowest course, as it now stands above the floor, amount, as already shown at p. 171, to 50 times the coffer's contents; or, as we now see, were exactly equal to the contents of Solomon's molten sea; unless we should rather say that Solomon's molten sea was made to be equal to the lower adjusted course of the King's Chamber of the Great Pyramid. The cubit used by Solomon at the building of the Temple being also of the same 25-inch, and earth-commensurable, length as that employed by Moses on the Tabernacle in the Wilderness; and that again identical with the cubit chiefly monumentalized in the design of the Great Pyramid.

Yet if we have been already obliged to conclude that Moses, though he lived long in Egypt, could never have been inside the Great Pyramid, and had, therefore, no opportunity of *humanly* copying its cubic contents of the coffer; or *humanly* supplying himself with a note of the length of its cubit; vastly more certain may we be that King Solomon was never inside the Great Pyramid either, or in a position to note the exact amount of cubic contents of the lower course of the coffer's containing chamber, or to copy the Pyramid cubit length and its subdivisions from the granite leaf in the ante-chamber.

Whence, then, came the metrological ideas common to three individuals in three different ages; and involving reference to deep cosmical attributes of the earth, understood by the best and highest of human learning at none of those times? And the answer can hardly be other, than that the God of Israel, the Creator of the Earth, who liveth for ever, equally inspired to this end the Seth-descended architect of the Great Pyramid, the prophet Moses, and King Solomon.

The Ark of Noah.

Wherever, too, throughout the Bible, Divine commands, for spiritual purposes of high degree, were given in terms of linear measure, we may now confidently expect that one and the same length of cubit is always alluded to, viz. the " sacred cubit," or the cubit 25 Pyramid inches long; and this equally in the parts of Scripture referring to the still unaccomplished future, as the primevally remote past.

Hence, when in Ezekiel (chap. xl. 5) the descriptions are given of the future temple which is still to be erected on the mountains of Israel, when her two houses, Judah and Ephraim, are once more to be joined together under one king,—the cubits of the measuring-rod employed are expressly described as "the cubit and an hand-breadth"; that is, the profane and undoubtedly 20·68-inch cubit of the Babylonish country (see p. 341) Ezekiel was then in, and a hand-breadth added to bring it up to 25· inches.

And hence, also, when in early Genesis the most important event, next to the appearance of Christ, in all the history of man upon earth is being prepared for,—viz. the Deluge for cleansing the earth of the wicked,—the commands of God to Noah respecting the size and shape of the Ark of Safety which he was to build, being given in *cubits*, they cannot be reasonably expected to be any others than the sacred 25-inch cubit of the Great Pyramid, the Tabernacle, and the Temple.

But can it be *demonstrably* shown that the cubits were the same?

I believe that it can, in a line first opened up by Mr. F. Petrie, though afterwards and independently discovered and more fully worked out by the Rev. C. W. Hickson, of Bristol.

Contrasts and comparisons between Noah's Ark and the Great Pyramid have long been indulged in by many. Both of the constructions evidently were primeval in date, but one, the greatest work ever executed in *wood* for floating temporarily on the waters; and the other, the loftiest and heaviest work ever prepared in *stone* for standing securely on the solid rock almost for ever.

Both of them have been attempted to be surpassed in their own lines within recent years by modern wealth, numbers and power, though with more of misfortune than success to those concerned. But the earlier ancient one lives only in story, the Divinely inspired story of Genesis, handed down by writings copied from writings indefinitely; while the other, little mentioned and only indirectly alluded to in the Bible, offers itself still in all the solid fact of existence for scientific modern measure throughout all its parts. One of them is everything for those who believe by faith; the other is for the Thomases of the latter day, who must still practically test and prove for themselves.

In the simplest manner, however, or by lineal measure, there is, at first sight, not the least apparent agreement between the two grand works; the three hundred cubit length of the Ark having no likeness to the 365·242 cubit length of a base-side of the Great Pyramid.

But what if we take them by *capacity* measure, for there may be identity there, though no ostensible similarity in linear dimensions. Over and above which

known law, while the whole purpose of the Ark of
Noah was eminently its large internal capacity, in
order to be an Ark of Safety to all those appointed,
—the Great Pyramid is equally remarkable for being
nearly solid; and yet the exceedingly contracted hollow
space which it does contain, centres about a small, empty
box or vessel, the coffer, whose chief value as we have
already shown, again rested in its precise amount of
capacity. On the principle, therefore, of like with like,
in species, quality, and purpose, the great Ark of Noah
may be compared in matter of interior contents of space
with the relatively very small, but most exactly sized
Ark-box or Coffer of the Great Pyramid; and when that
is done, behold the one is exactly commensurable with
the other by the sacred and precise Pyramid number
of 100,000 or 10^5; that is, however, *only* when we assume
that the cubits which were commanded to Noah by God
were the Newton-derived sacred cubits of Israel, and
had nothing to do with the much shorter profane and
Cainite cubits of Egypt, Babylon, and Nineveh. For it
thus comes about :—

The capacity contents of the Great Pyramid's coffer
are 71,250 cubic Pyramid inches.   (See Chapter VIII.)

The capacity contents of Noah's Ark are to be found,
from the Biblical statement, $300 \times 50 \times 30$ cubits; and
these being reduced to Pyramid inches, at the rate of 25
for each cubit $= 7,500 \times 1,250 \times 750 = 7,031,250,000$.

That quantity, however, is, so far, by no means exact;
and does not, as yet, include a very peculiar addition
which the Bible describes to the Ark, viz. "and a window shalt thou make to the ark, and in a cubit shalt
thou finish it above."

It was well enough for the coffer, in the well-ceiled
interior King's Chamber apartment of the Great Pyramid, to remain so long an open lidless box; but that
would not have been suitable to the Noah's Ark's far

larger box, whose very object was to float outside, and there afford shelter to those within it from the preternaturally heavy rains which were to descend from above, and, with the other miraculously supplied waters, destroy all the rest of men.

Of this window, the venerable John Taylor had already written in his book, " The Great Pyramid," p. 308 :—

" The window extended, probably, the whole length of the Ark, along the roof, and acted as a ventilator, being covered over by a ridge roof." And Mr. Hickson further imagined a double but low sloping roof, extending lengthwise, open at the ends, and raised along its middle line to the same height, "in," or within, a cubit.

If, moreover, we ask, how much within, we can hardly do otherwise than remember the Pyramidal 5-inch space taken off the height of the walls in the King's Chamber, and say therefore 5 inches. In which case 20 inches are left for the central longitudinal height; and with that, computing the additional capacity contents which such a window-roof would give, it amounts to 93,750,000 cubic Pyramid inches. Now this number, added on to the larger quantity obtained before for all the hollow box part of the Ark, gives for the final result 7,125,000,000 Pyramid cubic inches. That is, exactly 100,000 times the 71,250 measured cubic inches of the interior of the Great Pyramid's coffer-box or ark; and if of that, then also of the Ark of the Covenant in the Tabernacle of Moses, and the lavers in the Temple of Solomon as well.*

* Some further important Pyramidal connections by number and measure on one side, and by symbol and shape on the other, with both Noah's Ark and Christian Churches, on the other side,—have lately been developed by Major Tracey, R.A., out of the Scripturally-recorded measures of Solomon's Temple and other buildings; and may be found either in *The Banner of Israel* Volume for 1878; or Philo-Israel's " The Great Pyramid of Egypt," a pamphlet published in London during the present year.

Of Stone Sanctuaries, " Oers " and Pyramids.

So far for the vessels contained in the several sanctuaries, whether Pyramid, Tabernacle, or Temple. But
something now requires to be said, touching these sanctuaries themselves ; and chiefly on account of the new
light thrown on them by Mr. Henry Tompkins.*

The chief instrument with which he *voluntarily* works
is indeed linguistic only, and therefore rather outside
my methods of procedure ; but *involuntarily* he brings
to bear certain necessary business features essential to
the very existence of any, and every, community of
men, whether large or small. All such, for instance,
must have amongst them, in whatever age they live or
have lived, something approaching to a safe, or treasure-
stronghold ; even, and perhaps much more so, if they
be a community of robbers, rather than of peaceful
men.

Now the first builder of such a safe, according to this
new author, was Cain ; and Moses told us of it long
ago : though bad Hebrew translations have hidden the
fact from our eyes, by speaking rather of " the city"
which Cain built in the land of Nod. Yet Moses only
said an " oer," meaning thereby, some chambered
tumulus of earth and stones, which one man might
possibly, or even easily, have built single-handed ; and
might then with full right " call it after his son's name."
Such an " oer " was rude probably, yet exactly adapted
to serve both as a stronghold and strong room, or a
necessary practical addition to what Josephus tells us
of Cain, at that very period of his life, too, when " he
invented weights and measures, and used them for the
purposes of rapacity and oppression."

* " The Pyramids and the Pentateuch," by Henry Tompkins, of
2, Augusta Place, Lansdowne Road, Clapham Road, London, October 22,
1873.

Hence every few Cainites might well have an " oer "
amongst them, but not " a city "; and in freeing us
from this latter word, where Moses wrote " oer," Mr.
Tompkins seems to have done excellent service; though
when he proceeds further, to call every " oer " a Pyramid, he wanders from the provable stone facts.

The word Pyramid (by sound, of course, rather than
by letter) is not very distinctly read in any of the early
Pharaonic hieroglyphics, nor proved to have been known
before the visit of Herodotus to Egypt in 445 B.C. There
too, the word Pyramid,* when used at last, was applied
to a particular form of the " oer " seen nowhere else;
and the progress of mathematics since then has still
more strictly confined the word's application.   Hence,
when we read in Genesis of the rebellious and Cain-
following men, after the Flood, uniting together to build
" a city and a tower whose top may reach unto heaven,"
according to King James's translators,—and when
Mr. T. tells us rather to read, "Let us build a Pyramid,
and one of great extent, whose top," &c.,—let it be our
part to endeavour to ascertain mechanically, to some
extent, what *was* built.

Nor is this very difficult; for though Babel's old
structure may long since have been buried in the soft
alluvial earth of its foundations, yet the researches of
Layard, Botta, Loftus, and others in Mesopotamia, all
unite in showing, that the buildings which served the
purposes of " oers " next in order of time to Babel, and

* The verbal derivations from Egyptian to signify division into " ten,"
and from Greek to signify " Corn-measurer," or " Flame-measurer " are
well known, but the following conclusion of Dr. Brugsch, one of the
best hieroglyphic scholars of the day, has been recently communicated
by my friend, Dr. Grant, of Cairo; and is probably more Egyptologically important, so far as that may go :—
" The Egyptians signified a pyramid by a certain group of hieroglyphic
characters, which give the sound *abumer*, and meant a vast tomb.   The
Greeks, by a kind of metastasis, made it *aburam*, then *buram*, and next
buramis, or πυραμίς, a *pyramid*."

were evidently a locally favourite form in that part of the world, were invariably oblong, elevated, and eccentrally terraced temples; structures therefore not to be called pyramids in any degree; while their astronomical orientation was of the very opposite kind to the memorable example set by the Great Pyramid of Jeezeh.

Similarly, too, the chambered tumuli of the Lydians, Etruscans, Pelasgi, and many other early people, were all of them " oers," and many of them treasury " oers " too, but not one of them a pyramid. In Egypt only did the "oers" become truly pyramidal; and though in that land, their primitive Cainite purpose of strongholds for treasure rapaciously acquired, was gradually overshadowed by sepulchral service, yet they were not always wholly merged therein, whatever the modern Egyptologists choose oracularly to declare. For,—

Besides the many early local traditions, which can hardly but have *some* foundation, of treasure having been deposited in the Egyptian Pyramids by kings who lived close after the Flood,—Colonel Howard-Vyse and Mr. Perring (on pp. 45, 46, of the former's 3rd vol. of " Pyramids of Gizeh "), give an account of a chamber in the Great, terraced, and rather oblong, Pyramid of Saccara, closed in the ceiling by a granite stopper; of the shape of what is employed in a " stoppered " glass bottle of the present day, but of four tons weight: and that peculiar chamber was confidently declared by those authors to have been " a treasury," " a secure and secret treasury," and one that had certainly " never been put to tombic use."

To the intense Cainites, that all Egyptians were, some form of " oer " was most necessary in their early national life; and though they did perhaps begin in two or three small examples with chambered tumuli, or Babel terraced temples, or in fact the so-called Great Pyramid of Saccara, or circular Lydian mounds, or

even round towers,* the captivating, crystalline, example of the Great Pyramid, as soon as that appeared,
led them off at once into that shape alone ; and they
put *its* mark so effectually on themselves, that the
uniquely Sethite character of the Great Pyramid was
soon lost to general view in Egypt, among the numbers
of newly pyramidized Cainite " oers " there.

*Of the Epi-methean construction of profane Egyptian
Pyramids, and the Pro-methean features of the Great
Pyramid alone.*

And yet to a deeper insight there was, even in the
mere putting together of the material, the most essentially different character in the one Great Pyramid
original, and all its supposed subsequent copies.

The Egyptians, for instance, according to Dr. Lepsius's *law* of their Pyramid building (pages 103 and
105), proceeded in exactly the same *exogenous* manner as
all Cainites with their chambered tumuli ; *i.e.* beginning
with a chamber centre, and extending the structure
around and above, more or less, wider or higher, but
continuously, merely as opportunity offered ; and terminating at last at such a distance, as accident of some
kind or another determined in the end.

But the Great Pyramid, as testified by the facts of
construction and measure, detailed through the whole
of this book, and by all the accounts of Herodotus
also, collected at the place as to the actual history and
course of proceeding,—was commenced on the opposite,
or *endogenous* method ; viz. by laying out the external
boundary of a long previously settled plan, procuring all
the materials carefully beforehand, and then building up
rapidly within the given outline only.

* The round towers standing beside Christian churches in Ireland are
an architectural picture of Cain and Abel over again.

While, therefore, the Cainite Egyptian Pyramids were " Epimethean," or such as spoke to hasty act, and then, *after* that, thought, when thought was too late to be of any real service,—the Great Pyramid was essentially Promethean, or the result of *previous* wise and provident thought; and then, careful act following thereupon. And it was still more than that ; for,—

The Epimethean, even according to classic tradition, brought infinity of ills on all humanity ; but the Promethean told mysteriously, from far earlier ages than those of the Greeks, of One who should, in the fulness of time, voluntarily sacrifice Himself in order that He might (in antagonism to the false gods of heathen idolatry), bring down sacred fire, or regeneration life, from heaven to men. In fact it told of the first coming of Christ as the Messiah, to save mankind from their sins, though by suffering Himself, the Divinely innocent for the human guilty, nailed to the accursed tree.

But of this primeval and inspired phase of the long subsequent Promethean myth, long before the Greeks polluted its purity and branded its chief actor as impious, because he was opposed to all their own invented obscene rout of gods and goddesses of Olympus,* we shall have further positive evidence, on studying more advanced features of construction found only in the Great, the most ancient, the Promethean, Pyramid of Jeezeh, and utterly unknown to profane Egypt throughout all *its* historic days and amongst its innumerable Epimethean Lepsian-law buildings.

APPENDIX OF 1879.

Again, within the short interval of a year, the progress of society requires an addition to the cubit portion

---

* See " Seven Homilies on Ethnic Inspiration," by the Rev. Joseph Taylor Goodsir ; and " The Religions of the World," by William Osburn.

of the above, and previous, chapters; and the necessity
has come about thus, on the present occasion :—

The Palestine Exploration Fund's Journal, or " Quarterly
Statement " for September, 1879, contains on its pages
181—184, an essay on " The Sacred Cubit—Test Cases ";
and declares for the said cubit having been, after all,
only 17·72, and not 25·, British inches long.   But how
does the Society, or their author Mr. S. Beswick, obtain
that short value ?   Have they discovered practical examples in any kind of sound material, or ancient monument, contemporary with the primal age in which the
real Sacred Cubit first became known to the chosen
Patriarchs as God-approved ; and have they compared
their absolute examples with the earliest Scriptural
metrological statements ?

Nothing whatever of the kind !   They start merely
with Mr. Beswick's verbal statement that he thinks
17·72 inches is the length, and that he is also of an
opinion, which would make any virtue in that Sacred
measure equally common to all the Cainite and idolatrous nations.   (See *Banner of Israel*, December 10,
1879.)   He then compares the measures of some of the
mere latter-day ruins of sinful, crucifixional Jerusalem,
as recently taken in British inches, against two older
statements of them in cubits of their day.   But as one of
these cubit statements is an Arab MS. of only 1444 A.D.
date, it may be passed on one side at once ; and as for
the other, it is merely Josephus' vernacular description,
in about 70 A.D., of a bridge on which Titus stood
on a particular occasion.   But that was a time closely
following the period when, not only had the Jews been
for generations Greecised in language and customs,
and had then submitted to Roman masters, but had
culminated at last in sin, by their crucifying the Lord's
Christ, and positively desiring the guilt of His blood to
remain for ever on themselves and their children.

How horrible, if they had then possessed the really Sacred 25·025-inch Cubit of Noah, Moses, Solomon, and the Great Pyramid, amongst them, and professed to use it in all their works!   But they had it not; or at least the cubit they did then employ, and put themselves under the domination of, is now shown, involuntarily proved, by the Palestine Exploration Fund to have been still more different from the truly Sacred Cubit of Biblical Inspiration, than even the 20·68 inch Cainite Cubit of profane Egypt and idolatrous Babel (pp. 353—355), being barely 18 inches long.   A length which shows it evidently to be a comparatively modern affair; and to have been rather the representative standard of Greece in the days of Alexander the Great and his generals, as well as of both the " great red dragon " powers of the Apocalypse, Rome and Constantinople, during their lengthy Imperial military rule over all that region.

Wherefore, to behold in these days the truly Sacred Cubit of the early Patriarchs approved by the God of peace and love, and undisturbed from Abraham's day, we must betake us, as already explained in this book, to the great "oer" and primeval spiritual treasure-house of Jeezeh's Great Pyramid,—wherein none of the popular military conquerors of the earth, and their destroying legions, ever entered; and which had no hand in the crucifixion of our blessed Lord and Saviour Jesus Christ.

CHAPTER XIX.

MECHANICAL DATA,

In Channels, Passages, and Chambers.
Air Channels.

FROM time to time in the modern history of the Great Pyramid, faults have been found, or improvements suggested, or difficulties raised with regard to its construction ; and where such remarks have been the produce of able minds, it is well for instruction's sake, even in the present day, to turn back to their very words. Also, if such criticisms have, since they were uttered, been answered by further discoveries at the Pyramid, to note *how* they have been answered.

A case in point is offered by the conversation of Dr. Harvey, the learned discoverer of the circulation of the blood, with Professor Greaves, in or about 1640 A.D. The doctor, unable to leave his patients in this country, had revolved at home in his truly capacious mind, and from his own peculiar scientific point of view, one of the descriptions given to him by the great Eastern mathematical traveller of that day, and had seen a difficulty which had not struck *him*.

To one so well versed in biological phenomena (though living long before the day of a knowledge of oxygen, or the nature of gases, or, indeed, any sort of scientific chemistry), it seemed strange to Dr. Harvey, " how several persons could have continued so many hours in the Pyramid and live. For," said he, " seeing that we never breathe the same air twice, but still new air is required to a new expiration (the *succus alibilis* of it being spent in every expiration), it could not be, but by long breathing, we should have spent the aliment of that small stock of air within the Pyramid, and have been stifled; unless there were some secret tunnels conveying it to the top of the Pyramid, whereby it might pass out, and make way for fresh air to come in at the entrance below."

Now that was a remark full of wisdom in every way, and if duly received and respected, might have led to invaluable discoveries at an early period,—but Professor Greaves, an unusually good oriental linguist, and with eminent dexterity at solving algebraic equations, unfortunately could not see the vital or chemical importance of Dr. Harvey's *succus alibilis* of common air; neither had he considered very accurately the motion of aëriform fluids of different specific gravities, when he thought that both the old air might so easily go out, and new air as easily come in, by one and the same lower entrance-passage, of small bore and crooked, almost "trapped," in the course of its length; and finally, he was certain, as one who had been at the Pyramid twice, and was therefore not to be lightly contradicted, that, " as for any *tubuli*, or little tunnels to let out the fuliginous air at the top of the Pyramid, *none could be discovered within or without.*"

To this Dr. Harvey replied most discreetly, " They might be so small, as that they could not be easily discovered, and yet might be sufficient to make way for the air, being a thin and subtile body."

But Professor Greaves curtly answered, " The less they, the *tubuli*, were, the sooner they would be obstructed with those tempests of sand, to which those deserts are frequently exposed"; and considered that he thereby obliged the stay-at-home medical doctor, in a popular Oxford University phrase of that day, "To shut up all."*

Yet what would Professor Greaves have thought, if he could have known before he died, that 200 years after his remarkable conversation with the discoverer of the most important anatomical and physiological fact even yet known to science,—Colonel Howard-Vyse would actually have proved the existence of, and found, exactly two such *tubuli*, leading to the upper parts, one to the north and the other to the south, of the Great Pyramid: and formed for no other purpose than that which Dr. Harvey had indicated, *i.e.* to serve as ventilating channels: and that he, Professor Greaves, had himself actually seen their lower extremities in the walls of the King's Chamber; and proved the fact, by inditing the following almost photographic likeness of them:—

"The ingenious reader will excuse my curiosity,† if, before I conclude my description of this Pyramid, I pretermit not anything within, of how light a consequence soever. This made me take notice of two inlets or spaces, in the south and north sides of the chamber, just opposite to one another; that on the north was in breadth 0·700 of the English foot, and in height 0·400, evenly cut, and running in a straight line six feet and further, into the thickness of the wall. That on the south is larger, and somewhat round, not so long as the former, and, by blackness within, it seems to have been the receptacle for the burning of lamps."

But the blackness so adverted to would seem to have been caused mainly by the fires which were occasionally made in the hole, since Caliph Al Mamoun's time, by Arabs of an inquisitive turn of mind. While, during the two following centuries, a further fashion grew up,

* Page 161, Vol. I. of "Greaves," by Birch.
† The exact meaning of this word has altered greatly within the last two hundred years.

for each visitor and tourist to conclude his sight-seeing of the Great Pyramid, by firing his pistols into this hole,—" to give himself," says Danish Captain Norden in 1740 A.D., " the pleasure of hearing a noise that resembles thunder." And for nothing further; for, according to the Captain, immediately after that act, every then visitor being perfectly satisfied that there was nothing more to be discovered in the building, " resumed the way by which he came, and returned in the same manner, as well as with the same difficulty."

Innumerable persons, therefore, besides Professor Greaves, had had portions of the air-channel system in their hands; but, through not respecting sufficiently the *design* of the great Pyramid, they went away no wiser than they came; and the realising at last of the best-ventilated, or rather, as it has now relapsed into, ventilable, room in the world, remained to another age.*

Ceiling of King's Chamber.

Again, certain early authors of a critically mechanical turn, looked up at the ceiling of the King's Chamber, formed of horizontal beams of granite blocks, and expressed their thoughts in the manner of a judgment and condemnation, that " those beams had a vast weight to bear " (all the weight of the upper two-thirds of the Pyramid above them) ; and, with some allusion to the " arch," and no knowledge of any of the numerical and

---

* The following further detail is from Dr. J. A. S. Grant, under date March, 1877 :—" I wrote you about the zigzag course of the lower portion of the northern air-channel of the King's Chamber, through the solid masonry. In my opinion this favours much your theory about the King's Chamber being intended for a physical and scientific observing-room, for the tortuous course of the channel would thoroughly cool down the outside hot air coming along it. At the same time it is manifest that the builders must have had some important end to fulfil, by introducing such a disturbing element as a zigzag channel into the solid masonry. Ventilation alone did not require tortuosity."

physical symbolisms required in this chamber, nor the
means of relief adopted by the architect above that
ceiling, they rather hinted "that *they* could have made
a better disposition of the material."

It has been supposed that the boastful legend inscribed
by King Asychis on his pyramid of brick at Dashoor,
one thousand years after the building of the Great
Pyramid, referred to the invention or earliest known
construction of arches in brick.

Contemporary science applauded that invention, and
seemed to think it perfect; but contemporary science,
even up to the present hour, is always marvellously
well pleased with its last and latest performance, however imperfect the next generation may find it to have
been; and in the case before us, 4,000 years have reduced nearly all the brick pyramids, arches and all, to
rubbish : giving us reason for thanks, that *that* scientific improvement was not invented early enough to have
been adopted in the Great Pyramid.   By itself, of sound
material and in quiescent times, no doubt the arch
was good; but on occasions of earthquakes, the arch,
"which is said never to sleep," is in an instant antago-
nizing its buttresses and all about it, to the ruin of
many a building of antiquity in the East; wherefore
neither a brick arch, nor an arch of little stones, has
stood so long as a beam of solid granite in circumstances
similar to those of the King's Chamber.*

But these circumstances are very peculiar, or were
wisely planned; and our Plate XVI., prepared from
Colonel Howard-Vyse's explorations and discoveries,

* Although Egypt is generally considered a non-earthquaking country,
yet it is visited at intervals by such phenomena even still.   So that Mr.
Sopwith records in his " Notes on Egypt," in 1856-7, finding the house
of his friend the railway engineer between Alexandria and Cairo, partly
in ruins from the effect of a then late earthquake.   And more recently,
in December, 1874, Dr. Grant, of Cairo, informs me that on the evening
of the day of the Venus Transit, three distinct shocks of earthquake were
felt in that city, and excited much alarm.

gives an idea of the arrangement adopted, as thus :—
Besides the large, and pyramidally typical, number of
five hollow, closed spaces or *pseudo*-chambers, one over
the other, and the topmost one roofed with opposed
sloping plates,—it will be observed that the upper surface of every set of long horizontal blocks, in place of
being formed into a flat floor, is left rough, and even
rising into natural hummocks; though the under surface is true and square enough.

The latter feature was necessary for the solidity and
steadiness of the structure; but the former, while a
saving of labour and no loss for strength, was a further
proof of these closed spaces not having been intended
for chambers for any human beings to enter and walk
over.

Modern Promiscuous Quarrying.

Then again, no one seems hitherto to have had any
respect for, and that because no understanding of, why
the mass of solid masonry was so overwhelmingly large,
compared with the hollow portion of the Pyramid; the
latter being only about 1-2000th of the former.

Firmness of construction, they thought, would have
been given by a far less amount of solid substance ;
wherefore, and for that mere fancy, bred of their own
brain alone, feeling sure that there must be many
chambers still undiscovered, they immediately began
ruthlessly boring and cruelly blasting here, there, and
everywhere into the exquisitely arranged, squared, lime-
stone blocks, and to a depth often of a great many feet,
merely to see what blind chance might possibly lead
them to. Forgetful, also, of a really very sage piece of
advice, said by an Arab tradition to have been engraved on the ancient casing-stone surface of the
Great Pyramid by its unknown architect : " I have
built them, and whoever considers himself powerful

may try to destroy them. Let him, however, reflect that to destroy is easier than to build."

But the travellers went on with their mischief; and even the excellent Sir Gardner Wilkinson, when describing the Queen's Chamber in the Great Pyramid, says with the most inimitable calmness, and without a pang on his conscience for the destruction he had committed in that white-stoned chamber of precious symbolisms, "I excavated in vain below in quest of a sepulchral pit." * And an awful pit, indeed, I found in 1865 he had made it!

A Secret Doorway in the Entrance Passage.

Yet infinitely more blamable were those before Sir G. Wilkinson, who made similar, but yet more destructive excavations in the same Queen's Chamber, with the absurd idea of finding a passage leading to the Sphinx! As if there was any community in science or religion, feeling or age, between the pure and blameless Great Pyramid and the much later carved stock, stone, or idol-rock called the Great Sphinx.

As if, too, I may add, there was anything in the original design of the Great Pyramid's structure, and of importance for men to know of in this latter day, which had not had both a proper and a regular access prepared to it, requiring no smashing with sledge-hammers or splintering by cannon-balls (such as the French are said to have used on one of the smaller Pyramids), when the proper time should arrive, to open it up to view and use.

The passages lined, or rather built, with blocks of whiter stone different from the bulk of the masonry, and leading thereby right on to the ultimate point required through the whole mountainous mass of the building,

* Murray's " Handbook for Egypt," p. 167.

are a case directly in point; and are admitted by, and
known now to, every one, including the Egyptologists.
But there are more minute features also, not so generally known; yet showing equal design and intention,
in these very Pyramid passages.

Thus every one has been told how Caliph Al Mamoun,
after blasting his way from the middle of the northern
side into the solid fabric of the Great Pyramid for six
weeks, was just about to give up the research when he
heard a stone fall in a hollow space close on one side;
and breaking on further in that direction, he presently
found himself in the entrance-passage; while the stone
which had fallen at that precise instant, was a *prism*-
shaped * block that had been anciently inserted in the
ceiling.   There it had for ages formed, to all external
appearance, a merely ordinary part of the ceiling, and
yet was covering all the time the butt-end of the
granite portcullis at the bottom of the first ascending
passage, so entirely unknown to Herodotus and all his
age, but now at last exposed to view.

Would that first ascending passage, then, *never* have
been discovered, if that faithless, perhaps timeous, block
had not fallen out, whether in Al Mamoun's or any
other day?   Let the following facts indicate :—

When measuring the cross joints in the floor of the
entrance-passage in 1865, I went on chronicling their
angles, each one proving to be very nearly at right
angles to the axis, until suddenly one came which was

---

* In earlier descriptions, this stone has been miscalled a *triangular*
stone; and much did the phrase stick in the throat of an elderly gentleman who was at the Great Pyramid in 1865, but could not make out how
a triangular stone could ever have filled up "that hole" which he then
saw in the ceiling right before him; for that hole was four-sided, and
nearly square.   "Yes," I answered him, "the space to be filled up by
the *base* of the stone is square, but the two sides, parallel with the walls
of the passage, require to be triangular, on account of the angle at which
the bottom of the portcullis block of the ascending passage meets the
ceiling of this entrance, and descending, passage."   But "prismoidal"
would meet the case exactly.

diagonal; another, and that was diagonal too; but after that, the rectangular position was resumed. Further, the stone material carrying these diagonal joints was harder and better than elsewhere in the floor, so as to have saved that part from the monstrous central holes and ditches perpetrated in other parts of the same inclined floor by some moderns. Why then did the builders change the rectangular joint angle at that point, and execute such unusual angle as they chose in place of it, in a better material of stone than elsewhere; and yet with so little desire to call general attention to it, that they made the joints fine and close to such a degree that they had escaped the attention of all men until 1865 A.D. ?

The answer came from the diagonal joints themselves, on discovering that the stone between them was *opposite* to the butt-end of the portcullis of first ascending passage, or to the hole whence the *prismatic* stone of concealment, through 3,000 years, had dropped out almost before Al Mamoun's eyes. Here, therefore, in a peculiar relation of position to something concealed, was a secret sign in the pavement of the entrance-passage, appreciable only to a careful eye and a measurement by angle, but made in such hard material that it was evidently intended to last to the end of human time with the Great Pyramid, and *has* done so thus far.*

Had, then, that ceiling-stone never dropped out at all, still the day might have come when the right men at last, duly instructed, would have traversed the entrance-

---

* This matter has been looked into in 1871-2 still further by Mr. Waynman Dixon, who finds that the interstitial stone, between the two diagonal joints, is composed of a sensibly different material, and harder quality of stone, from that which is employed on either side of them; though still to be esteemed of limestone only. The introduction of granite there, for mere hardness, we shall soon find, would have been fatal to the spiritual and historical symbolizations under which that stone is elsewhere introduced into this building.

passage; understood that floor sign; and then, simply
and quietly, removing the one, prismoidal, ceiling-stone
opposite to it, would have laid bare the beginning of the
whole train of those ascending and subaërial features of
construction, which exist in no other Egyptian Pyramid,
and are the chief magazine of the Great Pyramid's
further messages to man in many times now past, and
others still to come.

A once-concealed Chamber, now open, and called the Queen's Chamber.

But if in this simple manner of a small trap-door in
the ceiling of the descending entrance-passage, it came
to pass that the *ascending* system of the Great Pyramid
was so long concealed,—there was once, a considerable
distance further on in that ascending system, viz. at or
just inside the Northern end of the grand gallery, and
in, or beneath, the rising floor thereof,—a more extensive
trap-door, which then concealed all access to the now
so-called Queen's Chamber and the horizontal passage
in these days leading so clearly to it.

At present, when the traveller enters the north end
of the grand gallery from the sloping difficulties of the
first *ascending* passage, he is delighted to meet with a
level floor; but following that southward, he finds that
it guides presently, not to the farther end of the grand
gallery, but to a hole under a steep escarpment, only a
few feet further on, formed by a cleft broken down of
that gallery's true floor; in fact, to the beginning of
the low horizontal passage leading to the, in modern
times, so-called Queen's Chamber. (See Plates IX.,
XII., and XIII.) The floor surface of the grand gallery
itself is inclined upwards at the typical angle of 26° 18';*

---

* This floor of the grand gallery being the longest and best constructed
of the inclined surfaces of the interior of the Great Pyramid, I was at
much pains to introduce larger and more powerful instruments to measure

and did once run from the lowest north end, directly
up, through 150 feet of distance, to the great step at
the south, or upper, and further, termination of the
gallery, in one continued slope.   But now we are met,
at the very beginning by a great hole, or absence of
gallery floor.   Yet there are traces still visible in the
masonry on either side of that hole, well interpreted,
first by Mr. Perring, and more recently by Mr. Waynman Dixon, engineers both ; showing, that a neatly
laid and joist-supported flooring, nine inches thick, did
once exist all along over that hole, completing thereby
the grand gallery's floor; and in that case entirely
concealing and utterly shutting out all approach to, or
knowledge touching the very existence of, the Queen's
Chamber.

Who amongst mediæval men pulled away that concealing floor, removed its supporting cross-beams, and
pushed on into the Queen's Chamber, under the Grand
Gallery, is not known now; any more than why it
was so concealed by the original builders.   Mr. Perring
imagined that the said shut-up chamber must have been
used as a store-room during the building of the Pyramid,
for the big blocks of stone which were, at the finishing,
slided down into the first ascending passage until, from
the portcullis at its lower end, that passage was full up
to its very top ; and the workmen then escaped by the
deep well mouth in the north-west corner of the Grand
Gallery, and its subterranean communication with the
lower part of the entrance-passage.

Quite willing am I to allow to the honest working engineer, that such a store-room purpose may have been

---

the angle accurately, both from one extreme to the other, and at short
intervals all the way along, than had ever been employed before.   The
instruments themselves being fully described, and all the observations
given in Vol II. of my " Life and Work," I may confine myself here to
stating that the mean resulting angle from observations was 26° 17′ 37″;
and the signification of this angle will be shown further on.

temporarily served; but was that *all* that the Queen's Chamber was intended for? And if so, to what end are all the following features; features, too, which are much more certain than that use; for the features exist still, and can be seen every day; but who ever witnessed the alleged use?

1. The central axis of the niche in the east wall (and that niche this Queen's Chamber's only architectural adornment, but a most noticeably grand one) is strangely not in the central vertical line of that wall, but is removed southward therefrom, and by just the quantity of 25·025 British inches; or one scientific Pyramid, and equally sacred Hebrew or Israelite, cubit length.* (See Plate XI.)

2. The height of the niche, multiplied by that grandly fundamental quantity in the Great Pyramid, π, and that multiplied by the Pyramid number 10 = the height of the Great Pyramid; or 185· $\times$ π $\times$ 10 = 5812, in place of 5813.†

* This result was stated as only approximately indicated by my measures in the second edition, and accompanied by the statement that the top of the niche appeared to be the same. But the last turns out to be a mistake, and, as indicated in " Life and Work," Vol. II., was a guess only at a part not then within hand reach, and therefore not actually measured; and its real breadth is only 19·65 inches, as now stated in our compendium of interior measures at p. 224. The fact was ascertained in 1874 and 1875 by Dr. J. A. S. Grant, of Cairo, Mr. Waynman Dixon, and their friends, on several visits of great enthusiasm, for the special purpose of inquiring into this error, and making a point of it; so that there can be no doubt about the result. And, by the obliging consent of the editor, who further had a woodcut specially prepared to assist the illustration, I printed the unexceptionable information so obtained in the London *Athenæum* Journal, on May 13th, 1876. Mentioning also, that decidedly as all the measures disproved a sacred cubit breadth for the top of the niche, so did they all the more establish precisely that length, for the eccentricity or displacement of the niche out of the vertical of its containing wall; the last mean actually giving the measurers, even to their own surprise (for their individual measures were rather rough), 25·025 British inches exactly.

† This very close approach must, however, be accidental, for the height of the niche is uncertain, on account of the roughness of the floor, by 2 or 3 inches; and though mensuration quantities of a remarkable order are *indicated*, they are never demonstrated in this Queen's Chamber with its soft and salt-incrusted stone to anything like the close accuracy which is found with the clean and hard granite surfaces of the King's Chamber.

3. The height of the niche, less the height of its inner species of long shelf, equals similarly the half of the base-side length of the Great Pyramid ; or $185 - 39\cdot6) \times 10\ \pi = 4568$, in place of 4566 inches.*

4. The height of the north and south walls of the Queen's Chamber measured $= 182\cdot22$ Pyramid inches ± 1 inch, and assumed $182\cdot62$, give—

(1) $\dfrac{182\cdot62 \times 100}{2} = 9131 =$ length of Great Pyramid's base-side in P. in.

(2) $182\cdot62 \times 2 = 365\cdot24 =$ solar days in solar tropical year.

5. The breadth of the Queen's Chamber measured $= 205\cdot6$, assumed $205\cdot0$, gives—

$182\cdot62 : 205 :: 205 : 230\cdot1 =$ height of King's Chamber from floor to ceiling; *i.e.* the first height there.

6. The square root of 10 times the height of the north or south wall, divided by the height of the niche $= \pi$; or,

$$\pi = \sqrt{\dfrac{182\cdot62 \times 10}{185}}$$

All the above theorems, save the first, are the discoveries of Professor Hamilton L. Smith (of Hobart College, Geneva, New York), who, without having been to Egypt, and without any other Pyramid measures than those contained in "Life and Work," has, by successfully interpreting them, constituted himself in a most unexceptionable manner the chief authority on the Queen's Chamber.

A fuller account of his researches has appeared in the November number of the American *Journal of Science and Art,* for 1873. Some of them will indeed be shaken, by my unfortunately erroneous breadth of both the top of the niche and the smaller overlappings immediately

* The shelf's height is, by the very rough measures, between 38 and 40 inches.

underneath it. But quite enough remains to justify
Prof. H. L. Smith's remark in a private letter,—that,
even half of the scientific findings really proved to be
contained in the lasting masonry of this chamber, were
enough to form a most serious dilemma of two horns;
on either one or other of which he left the opponents of
the sacred and scientific theory of the Great Pyramid
to impale themselves, as they preferred.

"Either," said he, "there is proof in that chamber of
supernatural inspiration granted to the architect; or—

"That primeval official possessed, without inspiration, in an age of absolute scientific ignorance, 4,000
years ago, scientific knowledge equal to, if not surpassing, that of the present highly developed state of science
in the modern world."

Newly discovered Air Channels in the Queen's Chamber.

Now in what is just passed, we have seen a whole
series of connections between the actually existing
measurable facts of the Queen's Chamber, and scientific
portions of the ultimate, and originally secret, design of
the Great Pyramid. Therefore, although some of the
early travellers have spoken fearfully of "the grave-like
smell and noisome odour of this room, causing them
to beat a rapid retreat," the room must have acquired
that revolting character from modern vilifying, rather
than ancient construction; for what its builders put
into it, as we see above, is not of a nature to experience
any fleshly corruption.

Indeed, in its ancient planning, the Queen's Chamber
would appear to have been *intended some day* to be remarkably well ventilated. For the chief item of latest
discovery at the Great Pyramid, is that one which was
made in 1872 by Mr. Waynman Dixon, in company
with his friend Dr. Grant, and with the assistance of

one of his English workmen from the bridge he was
then erecting over the Nile; and is to the effect, that
this Queen's Chamber has, in a peculiar state of readi-
ness, though never yet brought into action, two ventilating channels in its north and south walls, nearly
similar to those in the King's Chamber.

Perceiving a crack (first, I am told, pointed out by
Dr. Grant) in the south wall of the Queen's Chamber,
which allowed him at one place to push in a wire to a
most unconscionable length, Mr. W. Dixon set his
carpenter man-of-all-work, by name Bill Grundy, to
jump a hole with hammer and steel chisel at that place.
So to work the faithful fellow went, and with a will
which soon began to make a way into the soft stone,
when lo! after a comparatively very few strokes, flop
went the chisel right through into somewhere or other.
So all the party broke away the stone round about the
chisel hole, and then found a rectangular, horizontal,
tubular channel, about 9 by 8 inches in transverse
breadth and height, going back 7 feet into the wall,
and then rising at an angle of about 32° to an unknown
dark distance.

Next, measuring off a similar position on the north
wall, Mr. Dixon set the invaluable Bill Grundy to work
there again with his hammer and steel chisel; and
again, after a very little labour, flop went the said
chisel through, into somewhere; which somewhere
was presently found to be a horizontal pipe or channel
of transverse proportions like the other, and, at a distance within the masonry of 7 feet, rising at a similar
angle, but in an opposite direction, and trending indefinitely far.

Fires were then made inside the tubes or channels;
but although at the southern one the smoke went away,
its exit was not discoverable on the outside of the Pyramid. Something else, however, was discovered inside

the channels, viz. a little bronze grapnel hook; a portion of cedar-like wood, which might have been its handle; and a grey-granite, or green-stone ball, which, from its weight, 8,325 grains, as weighed by me in November, 1872, must evidently have been one of the profane Egyptian *mina* weight balls, long since valued by Sir Gardner Wilkinson at 8,304 grains.*

These relics approached so nearly in character to the ordinary nick-nackets of most men's modern archæology, that they excited quite a *furore* of interest, for a time, in general antiquarian, and dilettante, circles in London; but nothing more has come of them. The ball and the hook are supposed to have been dropped down the channels unintentionally by some of the mason's labourers or boys at the passages' upper ends, when the place of those ends was still open and accessible. But the things thus strangely found, belong merely to the forced labourers, the hodmen of profane Egypt; not to the architect and head administrator of the scientific and inspired design of the Great Pyramid; and which design had supplied, even in those very air-channels, a much more serious problem for solution, as set forth below.

An Unexplained feature in the Queen's Chamber's Air Channels.

This *chief* mystery of these newly discovered air-channels of the Queen's Chamber, may be described thus:—

When their inner ends, or ports, were proved to have been separated from the air of said chamber merely

---

* Thin flakes of a very white mortar, exuded from the joints of the channels, were also found; and on being recently analyzed for me by Dr. William Wallace, of Glasgow, were proved to be composed not of *carbonate*, as generally used in Europe for mason's mortar, but *sulphate*, of lime; or what is popularly known as " plaster of Paris " in this country.

by a thin* plate of soft limestone (so easily pierced
by Bill Grundy's chisel), every one leaped to the conclusion that they had originally been in use, but had
been stopped up by some mediæval interloper with a
paltry stone patch.   But this was not the case ; for
Dr. Grant and Mr. Dixon have successfully proved that
there was no jointing, and that the thin plate was a
"left," and a very skilfully and symmetrically left, part
of the grand block composing that portion of the wall
on either side.

That block, therefore, had had the air-channel tube
(9 × 8 inches) sculptured into it (from the outside direction as of the whole building), neatly and beautifully so
far as it went; but that distance was not quite through
the whole block and into the room, by the typical quantity in the Great Pyramid of *five* inches.   The whole air-
channel then, save that little unopened bit, was in place;
but could never have been used.   Not, too, that it had
been tried, found inconvenient, and was then stopped
up by the original builders; for they would in that case,
acccording to their usual style of masonry, either have
filled the port with a long plug, or would have replaced the whole block carrying the inner end of the
channel, with another block quite solid.   But, as before
remarked, the whole air-channel is in place, yet with a
left film of stone over the inner, or chamber, end of it,
absolutely preventing its being used as a practical
channel of communication, until a little something
additional be done.

How far the channel's courses are carried through
the 300 feet of masonry which separate this chamber
from the outer air, is not yet known.   But, in the meanwhile, what we do know of the channels in the walls

---

* Thin by comparison with the colossal masonry around, but really
five inches thick, by subsequent measure, and equally of the north as
well as the south air-channel tube.

and immediate neighbourhood of this chamber may, in a building like the Great Pyramid, be suggestive in a variety of ways of man's life upon earth,—and may be taken more especially as reminding of a deaf, perhaps wilfully deaf, ear. There you see before you the tubes for the conveyance of sound, but the entrance to them is *veiled*.

This idea would go for very little in a purely scientific explanation of the Great Pyramid; but we shall find before long that many of its symbolisms, and this one among them, yield to religious conclusions alone.

Scheme of the Masonry in First Ascending Passage.

Besides the above strange discovery, made in concert with his friend Dr. Grant, of Cairo, Mr. Waynman Dixon performed an arduous work *in the first ascending passage* of the Great Pyramid, or that one leading up into the North end of the Grand Gallery.

My examination of that passage in 1865, was confined to little more than its angle of slope and its floor length, joint by joint, on the floor alone. This was partly on account of the bewildering varieties of the wall jointing, as they appeared to my non-engineering eyes on a cursory examination. But Mr. Waynman Dixon, in 1872, applying himself long and steadily to this special task, and mapping down everything measurable, presently perceived a most admirable order pervading the apparent disorder, and tending also to hyper-excellent masonic construction. For the chief discovery was, that at stated intervals the smaller blocks forming elsewhere separately portions of the walls, floor, and ceiling of the passage, were replaced by great transverse plates of stone, with the whole of the passage's hollow, or square bore cut clean through them; wherefore, at those places, the said plates formed walls, floor, and ceiling, all in one piece.

As an engineer he admired the binding and solidity of this masonry.   But he had not perceived, until I was recently enabled to point it out on his own careful measures, that the intervals of passage length at which these remarkable stone *plates* were introduced, were roughly, no other than *breadths of the King's Chamber*.

The first interval, indeed, at the top of the passage was a double one, and when measured from the beginning of the passage, to the further side, not the middle, of the stone plate, equalled, though approximately only, the *length* of the King's Chamber ; but the plate there was followed by three others with that chamber's breadth, or 206 inches, nearly, between every pair of similar surfaces ; and after that, or in the lower part of the passage, near the granite portcullis plugs, the grand, enclosing plates were contiguous.*

* The above arrangement is shown approximately in the lines and numbers engraved on the entrance-passage of Plate IX.
    A more detailed description, furnished by Mr. Waynman Dixon, is as follows:—
    From the top, or southern beginning (though, according to others, the end) of this said passage, the walls are composed of nine ordinary stones, and then as the *tenth* comes one of the transverse plates, whose south face measures 385, and its north face 417, inches from south beginning of the passage.
    Then come four ordinary stones, and for the *fifth*, a transverse plate, whose sides, measured as above, are at 592 and 625 inches from the zero of these measures.
    Four more stones, and for the *fifth*, a transverse plate, at 799 and 831 inches.
    Four more stones, and for the *fifth* a transverse plate at 989 and 1,047 inches.
    Then follow four transverse plates in contact with each other, and found at 1047 to 1096, 1096 to 1133, 1133 to 1171, and 1171 to 1212.
    The next space, 1247 to 1289, is jointed regularly; but after that the contiguous plates seem to begin again, but cannot be traced far, on account of the granite portcullis plug still in place.   The upper or southern end of the granite portcullis is now fragmentary, and is near the 1291 inch of floor distance; while its lower or northern end is at 1470 inches of the same distance.
    On the east side of the wall small stones are let in, at distances from the top of the passage, of firstly 235 inches, and secondly 645 inches. While similar let-in stones appear on the west wall at 442 and 860 of distance.   Approximately, again, at differences of distance equal to the King's Chamber length; but not with much accuracy, nor with the more skilled workmanship of the more significant portions of the Great Pyramid.

This unexpected illustration of the builders working, not only by measure, but in terms of that one chamber which is now confessed to be the focus of the whole scientific design,—was followed soon after by Professor H. L. Smith pointing out, most successfully, that one of the special natural problems of the Great Pyramid the exact number of days of the solar year in the human period, is brought out by the application of *that* chamber's standard of measure to *these* passages when taken at their peculiar angle of inclination.

This angle had been determined for them long since, as will presently be explained, at

$$26° \quad „ \quad 18' \quad „ \quad 10''$$

And if you lay off, along exactly such a slope, twice the length of the King's Chamber, viz. 2 × 412·132, as already well determined by modern measure (see Chap. X. p. 195), you will find that the vertical amount by which the floor has risen, at the end of that distance = 365·242, or the true number of solar days in a solar year. While if you lay off again just one King's Chamber breadth, viz. 206·066 Pyramid inches, the perpendicular so formed with the horizontal base will be 91·310 Pyramid inches; or the hundredth part of the length of the base side of the Great Pyramid.

A striking discovery was this, which Mr. James Simpson further capped with the following π relation of the whole system of passages :—"From the top of the entrance-passage down to the beginning of the first ascending one" (988 inches), said he, there is only one line of passage, only one passage communication with the outside air; but from that point there are two lines, one ascending and the other descending. The total length of the ascending line is by measure = 1542 + 1881 = 3423 : and the length of the descending line, starting from the same point of bifurcation, is *believed* to be also 3423, but has not been so well measured.

Take, however, the 3423 known, and divide it by π (viz. 3·14159, &c.), and you have 1089·6; which is the length as close as it has yet been measured, from the bifurcation along the floor of the *single* entrance-passage upwards, and past its present termination (at 988 inches), to the ancient finished face of the Pyramid.

Here then is a proportion in *science* for the length of either passage as a *whole*. While the 365·242 result previously detailed, gives a similar reason for the twice of the King's Chamber length, marked on one of the same passages, referring to that Chamber as a whole, in harmony with all its numerous scientific relations with Coffer, Pyramid and Nature by numbers of inches, —rather than being intended for merely a length of 40 profane Egyptian cubits, and nothing more.

It has long been said in certain quarters, having been commenced even by Sir Isaac Newton, but by him on most imperfect traveller's accounts,—that the King's Chamber length would cut up into 20, and its breadth into 10, profane Egyptian cubits ; and that that was all the reason for its size.

But in that case, why was the third dimension of the room, its height, made so absolutely different, that it is quietly left out of the problem by the Egyptologists ? Why also were the length and breadth not made more exactly equal to the real profane cubit multiples, in place of being very sensibly shorter ?

The fact is, such gross subdivisions, of some only of the given lines, come near enough to act as a blind to allow of Egyptologists, who are anxious so to do, to go on deceiving themselves to the end of the chapter. Just as the subterranean chamber, is still accepted by them, as it was by the old profane Egyptians, for sepulchral use,—though unprejudiced scientific observers have no difficulty in perceiving that it was never used for such purpose, and could not have been (p. 102).

Details of the Entrance into the Great Pyramid.

We have now reached a portion of the mechanical details of the exterior of the ancient monument more discussed of late in the world than any other; viz. what sort of entrance had the Great Pyramid originally ?

The front and chief gate, or door, of almost every other species of public building, from temples to churches, and castles to palaces, is usually the most elaborated and ornamental part of the whole of the structure to which it belongs ;—but, excepting only the obscure mention of a movable stone in Strabo's time, by which a man might just creep into the descending entrance-passage,—it is believed there was nothing to mark any entering-in place at all at the Great Pyramid; but that the smooth planed-down surface of the casing-stones covered, and concealed, all that region ; and in fact did most effectually hide the essential point from any one who approached without traditional information to guide him.

In the present day, indeed, men do point to the grand anticlinal stones which are seen over the doorway (shown in Plate X.), and expect, on the experience of other buildings formed for totally different purposes, that something like that Cyclopean gable must have been on the exterior of the building too.   But these stones are far within the ancient face of the Pyramid, and so were also two or three other sets of similar stones once in front of them, on piers or abutments which are still to be seen ; and so is also the end of the white-stone flooring of the entrance-passage. Nothing, therefore, of what we see *now* connected with the internal masonry and constructive arrangements, ever projected through the casing-stone film ; and the very fact of Caliph Al Mamoun making his excavation in a different place, may be taken as a proof that nothing ever did, in any conspicuous manner, externally mark the spot.

Then why did the builders commemorate the one and only outside entrance, not on the exterior, but in the *interior* masonry; and so grandly, with at least those four inclined stones, which we see now?

Not to relieve the entrance-passage's roof from the superincumbent weight of the Pyramid; for, as Colonel Howard-Vyse well demonstrated in his day, there is no great weight to support at the place where the gable stones are, so much closer to the exterior than the centre of the fabric. Moreover, as the basement for these stones is horizontal, in place of inclined parallel with the passage, their trend would rapidly leave the line of descent of the entrance-passage, if they went much further into the building. But that, they do not; for, according to Mr. Perring, there is ordinary course-masonry at the back of the single set of stones, the last of their fellows, which we see now. Why then, again, if there was no mechanical advantage to be gained from them, and no necessary connection with the outside entry into the entrance-passage, and no visibility from the exterior, or the country round about in ancient days, why were those most Cyclopean blocks built in just there?

Chiefly to typify, in a subsequent day of partial dilapidation and then of revealing of secrets, said Professor H. L. Smith, the ruling angle of the great π Pyramid; the angle enclosed by the stones being, he considered, twice the angle of rise of the sides of this π Pyramid, viz. 51° 51′ 14·3″.

That idea was sent out to some friends in Egypt, who measured the angle *under* the stones, and pronounced it too small for the hypothesis. But the stones, though grand, are rough, and somewhat out of adjustment; and, as they were really only backing stones to at least two other sets, which were once in front of them—though within the outer surface of the Pyramid—much accuracy was not to be expected. At all events, the measurers were subsequently requested to kindly measure also the middle and the upper angle lines as well as the bottom one; and likewise the angles to which the stones themselves are cut at the parts where they bear against each other.

As these further measurements have not yet been taken, I have specially examined a large copy on glass of one of my original photographs of the front of the Great Pyramid; taken, indeed, from the ground below, but from a considerable distance off, and with a *levelled* camera, so that I do not immediately see that there is any necessary perversion of the angle of the stones one way or the other, their front face being vertical. Now there are eight corners to have their angles measured, four acute, and giving the angle as required at once; and four obtuse, or yielding the same angle only when subtracted from 180°. And this was the result of the measurings, with an ordinary transparent protractor :—

The two acute angles on the *right*-hand side ..	52° and 52°
The two acute angles on the *left*-hand side ..	51° and 52°
The lower obtuse angle on the right ..	129° — 180 = 51°
The upper obtuse angle on the right ..	128° — 180 = 52°
The lower obtuse angle on the left ' ..	128° — 180 = 52°
The upper obtuse angle on the left ..	129° — 180 = 51°

Whence, apparently, Professor Smith's idea is borne out on the whole, at least as well as could be expected from such very rough work; and we *may* regard these stones *now*, as the centre of a symbolic diadem over the forehead of the interior scientific design of the primeval monument. A riddle set up on high 4,000 years ago ; kept secret for 3,000 of those years, but exhibited to mankind during the last 1,000, and guessed by no one until three summers since.

Emplacement of the Entrance into the Great Pyramid.

Supposing the entrance-passage of the Great Pyramid continued upwards and outwards from its present known residual, inner, portions, until it should reach the ancient air surface of the building,—it would evidently find itself there both very high up above the base, and a long way on the eastern side of the middle vertical, meridian plane of that flank; wherefore the question is, in the present metrical age, how much, either way?

I regret to say that neither of these quantities is accurately known in the existing day; nor will it be, until the rubbish-heaps are cleared away on the north side of the building, and the whole is well and thoroughly surveyed. For the present, therefore, we must assist such measures as we have, by theory.

The theory which I propose to employ is that which is exhibited on Plate XXII., and to which I was led in 1864; and have had the satisfaction of seeing since then its chief feature, viz. a square of the area of the Pyramid's vertical meridian section, and 5151·65 Pyramid inches long in the side, recognised by Mr. James Simpson and other calculators as being, when divided by 10, exhibited with almost absolute precision by the cubic diagonal of the King's Chamber and various other Coffer, and internal features.

By placing that square centrally and symmetrically on the centre of the base of the Pyramid's section in that plate, trisecting its upper semi-diameter, and bisecting its lower, a remarkable approach is at once and simply gained to the general positions of all the chambers. While by taking into account, in the manner there shown, the height of the building as well, together with its π circle, we obtain the dominant angle of all the inclined passages, viz.:—

$$26° \ 18' \ 10''$$

This is the theoretical angle; and my measured angles in 1865 came out thus : *—

Entrance-passage, descending angle, 1st method = 26 27 0
                              2nd   „   = 26 28 7
                              3rd   „   = 26 25 20

First ascending passage, angle   .. 1st method = 26 5 30
                              2nd   „   = 26 6 40

Grand gallery, ascending angle   .. 1st method = 26 17 28
                              2nd   „   = 26 17 4
                              3rd   „   = 26 17 53

None of the passages are, therefore, far from the angular expectation; while the Grand Gallery, the longest, best preserved, and most suitable for measuring, comes out the closest of all; and the exact theoretical angle is *amongst* the observed ones,—as near an agreement as could be expected.

The linear vertical height, on the other hand, at which the floor of the angularly inclined entrance-passage would, if produced, cut the ancient casing-stone surface is less certain; depending as it does, without altering the angle or being altered by it, on some further points, which can only be obtained with accuracy by a close study of the building itself. Howard-Vyse's rough measure of this vertical height, duly corrected for the missing portions of the Pyramid face, would amount to about 650 inches. This is nearly 20 inches different from my theoretical conclusion, and not professing to much exactitude.

But the Colonel's measure of the eastern horizontal displacement of the whole plane of the passages, from the vertical meridian plane of the building itself, not having to deal with one end of a degraded and sloping line, but with the two well-preserved walls of the entrance-passage, running *parallel* with the plane from

* The details of these measures are given in full in Vol. II. of " Life and Work," published in 1867.

which they are to be measured, cannot be so much
in error.   He accordingly makes that eastern displacement =

296 inches.

And if a new theory should say that the quantity was,
or should be, 300, or more exactly 300·216 Pyramid
inches, then, looking to the percentage of error on the
Colonel's measure of the length of the northern base-
side, I should say that his evidently roughly measured
24 feet 6 inches, in this case, may be taken as not
overpoweringly opposing the theory.   But what is that
theory ? for whatever is described on Plate XXII. has
evidently nothing to do with *horizontal* displacement.

Mr. Cockburn Muir's Hypothesis of the Passage-plane's Side Displacement.

Many theories have been started to account for the
quantity by which the passage-plane of the Great
Pyramid is to the east of the central meridian plane
of the building, but none have fully commended themselves to my mind, or justified the measures, except
one recently brought out with signal effect in the
February number (in 1877) of Mr. Hine's *Life from
the Dead*, by Mr. C. Muir, C.E.

The view which occurred to him was, that the displacement concerned had reference to a memorialization of the obliquity of the earth's own axis to the axis
of the ecliptic,—as being the main agent in producing
the contrasts of summer and winter, while the earth
annually revolves around the sun.

The merely typifying rotation on the axis and revolution round the sun, so as to mark the length of a
24-hour day and a 365·242-day year, as already abundantly proved, was enough for mere chronology.   But

the physical life of man demands more; and if the
passage height was lately held to indicate (see page
367) a 12-hour interval only, with height up and the
same height down, or 12 hours of daylight and 12 hours
of night ; and the scheme of the Great Pyramid was
further considered to be rich in showing all the chief
agencies of God in preparing the earth as the abode
of intellectual man,—where was there anything typifying the night and day of the year, or the winter and
summer of the whole terrestrial revolution round
the sun, so necessary to the repair of the activity of
the vegetable world first, and of animal existences
next?

A glance primarily at the plane of the equator on a
terrestrial globe, passing centrally through the largest
part of the earth ; and then at the latitude plane of the
northern tropic, parallel with the equator, but at a little
distance from it, and passing through a smaller section
of the earth,—is no bad approximation in idea to the
central vertical meridian plane of the Great Pyramid
passing through its largest part, and the plane of the
passages parallel thereto, but passing through a smaller
part, *i.e.* a part of the Pyramid less high than the
central portion. And the place of the plane of one of
the tropical latitudes on a modern geographical globe,
is simply an expression of the obliquity of the ecliptic
at the present time.

But the obliquity now, is not what it was in the day
of the Great Pyramid ; and though we may compute it
accurately from modern astronomy, that will be of no
practical importance to this question, unless we can
also obtain an equally accurate measure of the Pyramid
passage displacement; and there is no such measure
made yet, or likely to be made for years.

Under these circumstances a happy idea seems to
have struck Mr. C. Muir. He had seen, in my own

unworthy hands, the marvellous help which the re-
action of the interior, on the exterior, of the Pyramid
lately gave, when the well-measured length of the
King's Chamber was shown to typify the length of the
base-side of the whole monument. Therefore he now
likewise sought the exact expression of the displacement of the passage-plane, in the same interior King's
Chamber.

In Plate VII., combined with Plate XVII., the reader
may see that the *eastern side* of the coffer in the King's
Chamber (proved by the measures on p. 156 to be of
exquisite accuracy) is apparently in the central meridian
plane of the whole Pyramid building; and as the parallel
passage-plane enters that same chamber by the low
Northern doorway, then, from the centre of that doorway to the east side of coffer produced up to the same
north wall,—there exactly is the displacement sought
for, if the coffer's existing position can be guaranteed.

In the present day it cannot be, as already indicated
at pages 261 and 263; but is yet excessively close to
some remarkable symbolic quantities: the north side,
for instance, when corrected for a push, is at the 100th
part of the Pyramid height from the north wall; the
south side the same from the south wall, and the west
side the 100th part of the side of square of equal area
(see pp. 261, 263) from the west wall. But the other
estimate of another symbolic quantity between the
east side of coffer, and the central transverse plane of
the room, did not exactly suit, though by the quantity
only of a fraction of an inch.

Then, said Mr. C. Muir, let us place the *east* side of
the coffer the 100th part of the base-side length of the
Pyramid from the *west* wall of the chamber, which only
alters the former symbolical and measured position of
the west side, from the west wall, by a little more than
an inch; and the coffer has the King's Chamber's flat

floor to be moved about upon, seeming to offer thereby
a still more powerful method of solving many problems
in a very contracted space, than even the two heights
of the walls of the said chamber, already enlarged on in
Chapter X.   But everything is to be circumscribed in
this case within the length of the King's Chamber,
known now to be 412·132 Pyramid inches.

Subtract, therefore, from that quantity half the
already well-measured breadth of the doorway, viz.
20·606 Pyramid inches, at the east end, to get the place
of the central plane of the passages themselves; and
then subtract from the other end 100th of the Pyramid's
base-side, or 91·310, and we have left 300·216 Pyramid
inches, as Mr. C. Muir's *believed* displacement of the
passage-plane, east of the meridian plane of the whole
Great Pyramid; and he believes it also to be the horizontal distance from the north-east corner of the coffer
to the central vertical axis of the Pyramid, in meridian
direction.   That is not at present to be tested accurately,
but it cannot, by our former plate, be far from the
truth; and if it places the north-east corner of the coffer
in a very remarkable position vertically over the Great
Pyramid's base, it reminds us also that the north-east
corner socket of the four corner sockets of the base, is
the largest of the whole of those sockets; and that, of
the north-eastern socket's own corners, its north-east
one is the most accurately finished; and is *the* one
which defines the ancient position of the north-east
angle of the whole basal plane.   (See Plate VII.)

What then shall we make of the 300·216 Pyramid
inches quantity obtained in this manner?

The first use is to multiply it by 10, as with the cubic
diagonal of the King's Chamber, to translate it into
whole Pyramid proportions; and then to use it as the
sine for its actually overlying radial quantity, the inclined height of the Great Pyramid, otherwise deter-

mined = 7391·55 Pyramid inches; when it yields the angle = 23° 57' 50". Which is within 49 seconds of arc, says Mr. C. Muir, of what the obliquity of the ecliptic was in 2170 B.C., the date of the Great Pyramid's foundation.

This 49" of difference follows from Mr. C. Muir's computed obliquity for that date being 23° 58' 39". But the same element computed both independently, previously, and far more carefully, by Mr. John N. Stockwell, M.A., United States, printed also in the Smithsonian Contributions to Knowledge for 1872, amounts to 23° 57' 50·2"; which is a closer agreement with the 23° 57' 50" of the Great Pyramid, than there is between the best modern authorities on the present observable obliquity of the ecliptic in the heavens of our own times.*

Of the Compression of the Earth at the Poles.

Next, seeing that the above result comes out by means simply of the *proportion* which the displacement of the passage-plane bears to the slanting height of the Great Pyramid, and has no dependence on the units of measure employed, let us see what may be further indicated by using the *very numbers* given by the Pyramid unit of linear measure, the inch.

That quantity is 300·216; and considering the symbology of the parts to which it is applied, may be taken as $\frac{1}{300·216}$, to express the compression of the earth at the Poles: or rather, when we assume, in the Pyramidal manner, the Polar diameter to be foundational, it is the protuberance at and about the equator. The proportion

---

* The obliquity of the ecliptic at present is stated by various authorities at from 23° 27' 18·98" to 23° 27' 17·88" by modern observation; and its limits of variation through its cycle of about ten thousand years, are computed by physical astronomy to be between 24° 35' 58" and 21° 58' 36". The rate of decrease at present is further stated to be 48·980" per century; and the rate at the Pyramid day of 2170 B.C. = 38·2" per century.

of such protuberance, or the increased length of the earth's equatorial, over its polar, radius,—has long, and otherwise, been known to be something excessively close to $\frac{1}{300}$, and is an essential agent in that grandly slow, but awfully regular, and unceasing angular movement of the earth's axis, producing those apparent displacements of the stars known to astronomers as the precession of the equinoxes; for, as Mr. Stockwell truly writes, " Were the earth a perfect sphere, there would be no precession or change of obliquity arising from the attraction of the sun and moon."

In the Great Pyramid therefore, where the precession of the equinoctial point among the stars, is the very dial of the Monument's grandest chronology for the history of the whole human race (see Chapter XVII, pp. 375, 379), a monumentalization of the terrestrial agency concerned in bringing it about, is to be expected; and the amount here stated of $\frac{1}{300 \cdot 216}$, though just at present rather more, has been within a few past years less, than the results of the best modern science : and that will hardly attain its final figures until the 4,000 latitudes of President Barnard, or 100 times all its results hitherto, shall have been obtained (see pp. 53, 54), in some age long future, if ever.

CHAPTER XX.

SABBATIC, AND MESSIANIC TIME;

In Queen's Chamber, Grand Gallery, &c.

The Queen's Chamber and its Seven-marked Approach.

NOW touching the well-supported piece of special flooring in the Grand Gallery, near its northern end, concealing from view the horizontal passage leading to the Queen's Chamber. Its existence was mentioned in the last chapter, p. 423 ; but there was a manner of performing the work peculiar to the Great Pyramid, which still remains for description, assisted by Plates IX., XII. and XIII.

Thus the supporting beams or joists, as shown by the holes for them on either side, within and below the level of the ramps, were 5 in number; a Pyramid, and a human hand, 5, too, inasmuch as one of them was larger and thicker than the other four. But more noteworthy is the height of the present beginning of the Grand Gallery's permanent stone floor just beyond the former site of that now vanished, once supported, piece, and looking almost like a little cliff; for, together with the dark passage mouth it overhangs, it measures no less than 86·25 inches high to any one standing on the level area in front of it.* But that rather rough though level space is 6 inches higher, nearly, than the very beginning of the Grand Gallery; † and the escarpment

* " Life and Work," Vol. II. pp. 70 and 71 ; also for height, p. 59.
† Ibid Vol. II. p. 61.

itself is under-estimated at its extreme northern end by the amount of nine inches, that depth having been removed for a short distance to allow of an overlapping of the special floor which once covered the present hole or pit. The entire height, therefore, of the remarkable frontal cliff for symbolical purposes is not much short of 101·25 inches; and this quantity, though in rough approximation only, stands before us here very much in the guise of the leading Pyramid symbol for a day: viz. 100 inches.

But is there anything else at this point concerning a day?

If of days at all, it should be of seven days, seeing that the feature of the Grand Gallery most usually attractive to travellers, next after its commanding height, is, the seven overlappings of its walls.

Now the Pyramid's entrance-passage has already been shown to have something to do with days, and the inclined passage which enters the north end of the Grand Gallery is very similar in size, being by measure 53·2 inches high vertically. The passage, however, which exits from the south end of the Grand Gallery, is only 43·6 inches high vertically; and as we cannot use either one or other exclusively in referring to the Grand Gallery between them, we have to take the mean of the two, or 48·4; and then find, that that quantity goes seven times, exactly to a hundredth, into 339·2, which is the vertical height of the Grand Gallery at a mean of 15 points in its whole length; specially measured, too, with a grand 3 to 400 inch slider measuring-rod, presented to me for this very purpose by Andrew Coventry, Esq., of Edinburgh, in 1864.*

* See "Life and Work," Vol. II. p. 84—86. Former travellers' measures of the height of the Grand Gallery vary from 270 to "about 600" inches, and are given without detail. The inclined floor length being by my measures 1881 Pyramid inches, the angle 26° 17′ 37″, and the horizontal length computed 1686·4 Pyramid inches, Mr. James Simpson has

Now this result may, or it may not, be intended in
this part of the Pyramid to assist in typifying 7 days
(more strictly 7 half-days taken twice over) ; and is of
only subsidiary importance in itself; because 7 days
merely, is a pagan mystical number which any one
might hit upon, and without its having anything to do
with the Sabbatical week of Scripture ; for that was an
institution which, though including or spanning over 7
days in its entirety, was far more notable for commemo-
rating 6 working days *and* one day of rest ; that one
day, too, being endued with a totally distinct character,
and having a special ordination by inspired command
to be held sacred to God, the Creator of all.

The Biblical Week.

We have not, therefore, yet found anything in the
Great Pyramid touching, in any clearly discriminative
manner, on the week of the Bible. But if we now
follow along that level passage which has the hundred
—inch day—symbol overhanging its entrance, viz. the
horizontal passage leading to the Queen's Chamber,—
the last part of that passage is found to be one-half
nearly greater in depth than the rest ; and the length
of that deeper part is *one-seventh* of the whole length of
the floor from the beginning of the Grand Gallery up to
the Queen's Chamber itself.* This looks like a beginning of a possible Sabbatical week symbolism ; and has
this further link of connection with the Queen's Chamber, that the seventh and deepest part of the passage,

pointed out that the typical fifth part thereof = 337·3 Pyramid inches: a
close approach to the 339·2 measured, seeing that the variations, in
places, amounted to anything between 333·9 and 346·0, by reason chiefly
of the tilt of each of the long roof-stones to the general slope of the whole
roof.

* See 'Life and Work,' Vol. II. pp. 55, 61. The whole distance
= 1517·9, and the smaller distance with the lower floor-level = 215·9
Pyramid inches, with an inch of possible error.

and which has a length of 215·9 inches, is found to be roughly a mean between the length and breadth (226·5 and 206·) of the floor of that chamber on the same deeper level.* (See Plate XI.)

In that chamber behold we a fair, white stone apartment, exquisitely built originally (except as to its present floor, which, for some reason or other, is rough, and composed of mere rudely worked building blocks); but with this special and overriding feature accompanying and distinguishing it from the other Great Pyramid Chambers; viz. that by reason of its having for ceiling a double inclined slope, the whole room may be said to have *seven* sides; of which seven, the floor, which has not had a tool lifted up against it within the building (though the others, of more finished character, had), is decidedly larger, grander, than all the rest in area.

Those other sides, however, are not quite equal and similar amongst themselves, unless reductions are made, founded on some features which do exist, marked into the wall ;† but whose full signification has yet to be accurately made out. It may be better therefore, at present, to conclude this part of the argument for the Sabbatical week of Scripture being indicated in this chamber, from Mr. James Simpson's sums of the squares, and which are given by the chief proportions of the room to a higher, though not an absolute, degree of certainty.

Taking the room, then, first with an artificial ceiling, assumed in place just beneath the angular beginnings of the roof (or at the greatest height to leave the apartment with six sides, such as ordinary rooms possess), the sums of the squares of its radius into every dimen-

---

* Salt incrustations prevent very accurate measures in this room, but the 206· width is almost a reproduction of the King's Chamber breadth ; which feature would have been lost, if the chamber had been made 216. square in plan.

† "Life and Work," Vol. III. pp. 229—232.

sion amount to 60 ; or, says Mr. Simpson, to 6 working
days of 10 each. But next take the major height, or
that central and superior height which effectively gives
the room its seventh side, and the sum of the square
there, and there alone, is 7 ; * or typical of the divinely
ordained day of rest ; and without interfering with
what has already been ascertained for this chamber's
indicating, for science alone, the π proportion of the
Pyramid, its angles, its absolute size, and the length
of one, single, sacred cubit = 25 Pyramid inches.

In connection with this last feature, not only does this
chamber stand, with its original, or apparently once intended finished floor, on the 25th course of masonry
composing the whole Great Pyramid, but its cubic contents, carefully computed by Mr. James Simpson, after
allowing for the saline incrustations of the walls, which
had made my measures the fraction of an inch too
small, amount to ten million cubic Pyramid inches.
A result to be compared with the King's Chamber,
taken as typifying a length of two sacred cubits, or
50 inches; and found to be standing on the 50th

* Mr. Simpson's sums of the squares are not quite so cogent in the
Queen's as the King's Chamber, already given in Chapter X.; and his
radius length for it, 92·17 inches, is not so well proved ; which indeed is
not much to be wondered at in this chamber of soft white stone and
saline incrustations; not so well adapted, therefore, for scientific proofs
of precision, as for some general symbology in religion of which more will
appear further on.   The proportions, however, which are more certain
than the absolute lengths, run thus :—

Height, divided by radius of chamber	..	.. = 2·	square =	4
Breadth	..	.. = 2·2361	,, =	5
Length	..	.. = 2·4495	,, =	6
Sums of the squares	..		=	15
Diagonal of end	..	.. = 3·	,, =	9
Diagonal of side	..	.. = 3·1623	,, =	10
Diagonal of floor	..	.. = 3·3166	,, =	11
Sums of the squares	..		=	30
Solid diagonal	..	.. = 3·8730	,, =	15
Sums of the squares of all the dimensions, except the major, or gable, or central height of the chamber			} =	60
Major, or gable, or central height	..	.. = 2·6458	square =	7

masonry course, and to be of the cubic capacity of two ten-millions of cubic Pyramid inches. (See pp. 172, 263.)

Grand Gallery's Cubical Commensurabilities.

Let us now return from this Queen's Chamber, so called (which to ordinary corporeal research is a *cul-de-sac*, even in spite of its newly discovered air-channels), and we shall find a certain amount of connection between it and the Grand Gallery. Only a small amount, but of a somewhat similar kind to what there is between a week and a year; inasmuch as both of them are measures of time, though the week does not march along evenly and decimally with the year in questions of history and the chronological fixation of events.

In this manner, then, while the Queen's Chamber, with its cubit-defining niche, contains cubic inches to the typical number for that cubit of ten-millionth earth-radius, reference—the Grand Gallery contains 36 millions of cubic inches; or one million to every one of the 36 inclined stones forming its long sloping roof.

The number of these Grand Gallery roof-stones had been given in 1837 at 31 by Colonel Howard-Vyse, and at 30 by the great French work, so that I was a little disconcerted in 1865 at finding them 36. But as those authors gave no particulars, and as I took much pains (duly described in " Life and Work," Vol. II. pp. 86—88), there can be very little doubt about the larger number. And in 1872, Mr. Simpson seems to confirm it as an intentional feature of the architect, by finding the round number of one million cubic inches to be repeated just 36 times in the contents of the whole Grand Gallery, carefully computed for every overlapping.

Mr. Simpson has a further speculation on the probable

50-inch length of each roof-stone. As the *successive* lengths of the stones struck me at the place as *irregular*, there is not much importance probably to be attached to that conclusion. Yet it may come out on a mean of the whole; for he has shown (in a letter, dated January 8, 1879) that if 36 such stones, be set with a tile-tilt of 10·96 inches to each other the inclined line, or hypothenuse of each triangle so formed will be 51·236 inches; and 36 times that will be 1844·5 inches, or the exact length of the roof of the Grand Gallery, as recently ascertained by Dr. Grant of Cairo, by direct mensuration between two plummets.

Wherefore the only question that remains, is to ascertain by independent measure, whether the amount of tilt of a Grand Gallery roof stone can ever be so large as 10·96 inches. It certainly does not *look* so from the floor; but then that is a deceptive sort of observation on account of the angle and the darkness; but the note on p. 448 will show, that when I was actually pushing up the point of a long measuring rod, against the roof stones, differences were found to so great an extent as 12·1 inches, which I did attribute chiefly to that very cause.

The Ramps, Ramp Holes, and the Well's Upper Mouth.

Let us next attend to the ramps, or inclined stone benches on either side of the Grand Gallery's floor, running from the very north-end right up to the great transverse step which forms the south-end thereof. They are alluded to so conflictingly in the great French work, as containing sometimes 26, and sometimes 28 holes, that I recorded, in "Life and Work," several sets of measures of various kinds, to place this very simple point beyond all dispute.

If the ramps are supposed to include the great stone

step at their upper or southern end—and which stone
step has an almost similar kind of hole at either inner
corner—then there are actually and positively 28 holes,
clear and distinct, along the eastern wall of the Gallery
(27 in the ramp itself, and 1 on the step); and there
are as many along the western wall; for though the
lowest and northernmost hole is not very clear, that is
merely from the greater part of the end ramp-stone
which once held it being now broken away. Of these
28, too, on either side, 25, viz. all except the lowest two
and upper one, are distinguished by a piece of stone
something like 13 inches broad and 18 high, but with
considerable variations, being let into the wall vertically and immediately over them; while of those 25, no
less than 24 (on either side) are crossed slantingly, says
Dr. Grant, not by another let-in stone, but by a broad,
transverse, shallow groove, measuring more or less
about 22 inches long, 12 broad, and 1 deep; with its
lower edge about three inches above the ramp's
surface. (See Plate XII.)*

Something may come of that, in the hands of future
explorers; but meanwhile we have to notice another
feature, and a most important one, already established
or brought to light by the removal of part of the ramp-
stone in the lower north-west corner of the Grand
Gallery; for the removal of that mass just there, long
ago disclosed a constructional secret of the original
builders; viz. a rather small and low West-going
outlet, leading to the upper end of a very deep and
solemn kind of shaft, usually called "the well," in
the annals of early Pyramid exploration.

At those times nothing was known of the Pyramid's

---

* This matter was particularly reported on by Dr. Grant on December 6, 1874, after an examination, and statement for every ramp-hole.
Of the 25 holes on either side which have the vertical let-in stone, the
single one of them which has not the transverse broad groove is the third
from the north end of the gallery, as shown in Plate XII.

Entrance-passage further down its course than its junction with Caliph Al Mamoun's forced hole and the entry to the first ascending passage. Therefore, when men ventured to look into the well-mouth from close to the north-western corner of the Grand Gallery, near the broken ramp-stone as above, they found themselves overhanging a dark and dismal abyss, no one knew how deep or where leading to.

What Caliph Al Mamoun and his immediate followers thought of it, is not recorded ; but soon after his time, " the well " begins to figure in Arab accounts, as an open pit of preternatural depth and fearful qualities. A party of twenty men, from the Faioum district, was once formed to investigate the mystery, but was frightened by one of their number falling down the aperture such a terrible distance, that he was said to have been three hours in the act of falling.

Again, a Sultan of Cairo, of impatient character, and determined to know all the secrets of the Great Pyramid in his own day, elected to blow it up by filling this same well with gunpowder : and only relinquished the design on being assured by his Italian architect, that the explosion of so vast a quantity of powder would endanger the safety of all the buildings in Cairo.

Again, at a later age, the celebrated Cambridge traveller, Dr. Clarke, visited the place with a large military party, and on throwing a stone down the well, and hearing it end by splashing, as they all considered, trusting to their fallacious ears, in *water*,—he called impressive attention to the admirable truth and perfect faithfulness of *classic* authors ; for had not Pliny duly written that there was a *water-well* in the Great Pyramid, 80 cubits deep ?

Again, in 1818, Signor Caviglia cleared out the entrance-passage of the Great Pyramid throughout the whole distance right down to the deep subterranean chamber; and lo, near the bottom of it, on the western side, was a low doorway leading into a dark passage: by pushing into which, and following its lead, and clambering in the darkness higher and higher, and yet higher, or 170 feet vertical altogether, he at length found himself at the same well-mouth where Dr. Clarke had dropped in the deceiving stone, and entering the lower north-west corner of the Grand Gallery. Very thirsty, too, as well as hot and tired was he, for not a particle of water existed in any portion of the so-called well; the whole of which, including the lower end of the entrance-passage and the subterranean chamber, is far above the level of the Nile inundation, the only source of water in that scorched and almost rainless land. (See Plate XIX.)

Again, in 1830 and 1837, came in the age of explorations, i.e. Egyptological and builders' explorations, with Sir Gardner Wilkinson, Colonel Howard-Vyse, and Mr. Perring. For they set forth, as already indicated, that the ancient workmen who had filled up with stone plugs the first ascending passage, above the granite portcullis, must have afterwards escaped by this long and deep well-like hole, or vertical shaft, to the lower part of the entrance-passage; and then by ascending its long northward slope, have attained to the outward air once again.

The Missing Ramp-stone.

Perhaps they did. But in that case let us ask, " In what state would they have left the ramp-stone over the well's mouth ? "

Certainly not blown from within outwards, as if by uncontrollable explosive force, breaking off part of the wall with it, and leaving the hole's mouth exposed; for that would have defeated their whole object. They would, on the contrary, have contrived a temporary support for the stone when in a position impending over the hole, partly in the floor and partly in the wall; or a support such, that when the last man had come away, the prop would be easily withdrawn, and the stone would fall neatly into a seat already cut for it, and cemented round the edges with freshly applied lime to make the work permanent and secure. For then such stone would be flush with the rest of the ramp, and would utterly conceal from any one who should ever enter the Grand Gallery by the regular method of the first ascending passage, that there was any well-mouth whatever behind the surface of the ramp. (See Plate XII.)

The original builders, then, were not those who knocked out, from within on the well side, that now lost ramp-stone, and exposed the inlet to the well-mouth as it is presently seen, near the north-west corner of the Grand Gallery. Neither was Al Mamoun the party, for no one could have done it except by entering the well from the very bottommost depths of the subterranean region; and he, the son of Caliph Haroun Al Raschid, and all his crew, did not descend further down the entrance-passage than merely to the level of his own forced hole, which is not subterranean at all. Nor is the credit claimed for any of his Arab successors, who rather allude to the well as an already existing feature in their earliest time, and one they did not understand; in large part, too, because they had only seen, and only knew of, the upper end of it in the north-west corner of the Grand Gallery floor; and there it was simply a deep hole, the beginning of darkness and the shadow of death.

Who then did burst out that now missing ramp-stone?

Who indeed! For the whole band of Egyptological writers we have mentioned, appear to be convinced that ages before Caliph Al Mamoun made his way by blundering and smashing,—long ages, too, before Mohammed was born, and rather at and about the period of Judah being carried captive to Babylon,—the Egyptians themselves had entered the Great Pyramid by cunning art and tolerable understanding of its mere methods of construction ; and had closed it again when they left.

Either some fanatics of the later dynasties of Ethiopic intruders, or the following Persian conquerors, are considered to have been those spoilers and sealers-up again ; and not only of the Great, and all the other Pyramids too, but of every royal tomb throughout Egypt, in whatever style of architecture it may have been built, whether subterranean or subaërial. The spoilers also they were, and at the same time, of those far more repulsive tombs and bigger sarcophagi, the profanely sacred ones of the deified Egyptian bull Apis ; recently brought once more to the worshipful regard of all Egyptologists by Mariette Bey's too successful excavations of ancient idolatries.

Precisely who those earlier men were, as Colonel Howard-Vyse well remarks, who committed that first spoiling, "will never be known"; but that the royal tombs *were* spoiled, and that both early Mohammedan and later Christian explorers throughout both Upper and Lower Egypt, equally found nothing but emptied sarcophagi, is positive matter of fact. By the aid, too, of features still existing, it can be mechanically demonstrated how those mysterious intruders may, in the case of the Great Pyramid, have descended to the subterranean depths of its entrance-passage, entered the bottom of the well, ascended the said well to its mouth, knocked out part of the closing ramp, ascended the then clear and open Grand Gallery, entered the King's Chamber, made what changes they could there ; and then, descending again the same way, closed all the passages (except that one and most significant ramp-stone hole) behind them so effectually that no one else

ever attempted to follow their steps, until after a lapse
of 2,000 years, or close within our own times.

Of the Sacred, touching the Great Pyramid.

That is the end, then, of the first use which the Great
Pyramid's Grand Gallery's deep well, but not a water-
well, and the entrance-passage, served. But that was
evidently not all which those features were intended for.

In the course of the summer of 1872, in a correspondence with Mr. Charles Casey, of Pollerton Castle,
Carlow (then preparing his work "Philitis" *), that
straightforward and vigorous thinker considered himself called on to tell me, that while he had followed
and adopted all that I had attempted to explain as to
the metrology of the Great Pyramid being of more than
human scientific perfection for the age in which it was
produced,—yet to call it therefore Divinely inspired or
sacred, seemed to him to be either too much, or too
little. It might have been sufficient in a previous day,
but not in these times in which we live; for with
rationalism continually extending on every side, the
only vital question left in religion, the only question
really, efficiently, sacred, is, " What think ye of Christ ?
Whose Son is He ? " The question to which we must
all of us, sooner or later, come at last.

" Now," said Mr. Casey, " unless the Great Pyramid
can be shown, besides being fraught with high science,
to be also Messianic (*i.e.* unless it can be shown to have
some acknowledgment of a testimony to the real
Divinity of Christ), its ' sacred ' claim is a thing with
no blood in it; it is nothing but mere sound. That
idea seized me the other night," said he, " when I was
thinking on my bed, and took me with such a giant's
grip that I have never been able to get quit of it since."

* "Philitis: A Disquisition." By Charles Casey, Esq. Published by
Carson Brothers, Grafton Street, Dublin, 1872. Fifth Edition in 1879.

" You are not the first student of the Great Pyramid," I was obliged to reply, " to whom the same idea has been vouchsafed; for it has long formed a matter of frequent and earnest discussion among several of them : but they have not published on it yet, thinking the necessary preliminary part of the subject, or the Pyramid's attestation to superhuman *scientific* abilities for its age, not yet brought up to the required degree of exactness to command the respect of, and induce assent from, sceptically minded men of education and ability."

At the time I wrote to Mr. Casey, the uncertainties of the base-side measure of the Great Pyramid, by modern surveyors, were simply horrible; the best of them both erring to almost any extent between 9,100 and 9,170 inches, and laying the fault thereof upon the Pyramid. At that period, therefore, the only solution of the difficulty seemed to be, to beseech some superlatively rich men, and such petitions were accordingly presented, to expend of their spare thousands, first in clearing the four base-sides of the Great Pyramid from their impracticable hills of rubbish, and then in measuring between the terminal points with proper accuracy. And there, at those rich men's luxurious doors, the matter stood; and had stood uncared for by them or treated with base contumely for seven long years, until at last the Pyramid's purpose could wait no longer.

So, partly in 1872, and still more signally in July, 1873, the ancient monument passed them all by; and in revealing the reason why the King's Chamber was made in measured length 412·132 Pyramid inches, has shown both the true base-side length and the vertical height of the structure, its π theory and the inch and cubit metrological system, to a degree of accuracy*

---

* Compare Chapters III. and IV. with Chapter X. pp. 199, 200, also Chapter XIV, p. 291.

some 700 times greater than before obtained: combined, too, now with a proved certainty of *intention*, which leaves nothing more to desire; and makes Great Pyramid studies quite independent henceforth of all those rich men and their long wasted or squandered or unused riches, confided to them by Providence for some better purpose than mere luxurious living. They had had, in this Pyramid cause, such an opportunity of doing high, pure, and noble good to all the ages, as wealth had never enjoyed before, since the foundation of the world; but the opportunity has from this time departed from them for ever.

One rich man, indeed, and with some most noble feelings in his heart, has rushed to the rescue of his peers in this matter since then; and in 1874 or 1875 ordered a superlatively accurate triangulation of the four sides of the Great Pyramid's base to be made by his then astronomical assistant. But it was too late. Such degree, only, of service was not then wanted; and no practical success has followed the effort; for no numerical result has yet been announced to the world. Wherefore the least that can be said is in terms of James v. 1—3, "Go to now, ye rich men, weep and howl for your miseries that shall come upon·you. Your riches are corrupted, and your garments are moth-eaten. Your gold and silver is cankered; and the rust of them shall be a witness against you." But mankind may well rejoice, for the flood-gates of the Great Pyramid's sacred history, or the last pages of what that primeval monument has to tell,—and has had, in "the sure word of prophecy," to relate, ever since the beginning of human life and story,—are henceforth open to all.

The Sacred pronounced to be Messianic.

It was in 1865 that a letter reached me at the Great Pyramid, transmitted, with some high recommendations of its author, by that most upright, knightly man, the late Mr. Kenmure Maitland, Sheriff Clerk of the county of Edinburgh. "He is a young ship-builder," said he, "a son of a ship-builder, an accomplished draftsman, and I hear that he lately turned out, from his own design, one of the most perfect ships that ever left Leith Docks: and from his childhood upwards he has been an intense student of whatever could be procured concerning the Great Pyramid; and though his family surname is now Menzies, he has reasons for believing it to have been originally Manasseh."

This Israelite, then, but no Jew, it was, who first, to my knowledge, broke ground in the Messianic symbolisms of the Great Pyramid, so intensified subsequently by Mr. Casey: and, after long feeling his way in a humble and prayerful spirit,* at length unhesitatingly declared that the immense superiority in height of the Grand Gallery over every other passage in the Great Pyramid, arose from its representing the Christian Dispensation, while the passages typified only human-devised religions, human histories, or little else.

From the north beginning of the Grand Gallery floor, said Robert Menzies (who was called to his rest in the end of 1877), there, in southward procession, begin the years of the Saviour's earthly life, expressed at the rate of a Pyramid inch to a year. Three-and-thirty inch-

---

* "———that most mysterious edifice, the Great Pyramid, which has been a puzzle to all ages. It is a very serious view indeed which I entertain of its purpose, and not one to be approached in a spirit of levity. I have endeavoured, largely led by a careful perusal of Mr. Taylor's book, and your own upon the subject, to follow out much further than you do, the Scriptural allusions to the Great Pyramid, with a result which appears, slightly as I have dipped into it, truly astonishing. Extreme caution is requisite in Biblical research, for, as Peter says, 'No scripture is of private interpretation.' I have humbly and prayerfully endeavoured to avoid anything which may he misconstrued, and if my humble remarks are of any assistance to you in the elucidation of this grand and holy mystery, I shall be truly glad.

"(Signed) ROBERT MENZIES.

"Sea Cot, Leith, *February 25th*, 1865."

years, therefore, or thereabout, bring us right over
against the mouth of the well, the type of His death,
and His glorious resurrection too; while the long, lofty
Grand Gallery shows the dominating rule in the world
of the blessed religion which He established thereby;
over-spanned above by the 36 stones of His months of
ministry on earth, and defined by the floor-length in
inches, as to its exact period to be. The Bible fully
studied, shows that He intended that first Dispensation
to last only for a time; a time, too, which may terminate very much sooner than most men expect, and
shown by the southern wall *impending*.

Whereupon I went straight to the south wall of the
Grand Gallery, and found that it *was* impending; by
the quantity too, if that interests any one, of about 1°;
while the Coventry clinometer I was measuring with,
was capable of showing 10″; * and *where* the writer
could have got that piece of information from, I cannot imagine; for the *north* wall is not impending: he,
too, was never at the Great Pyramid, and I have not
seen the double circumstance chronicled elsewhere.
The first ascending passage, moreover, he explained
as representing the Mosaic Dispensation. I measured
it, and found it to be, from the north beginning of
the Grand Gallery, the assumed natal year of Christ,
to its junction with the roof of the entrance-passage
northward and below, or to some period in the life of
Moses, 1,483 Pyramid inches: and when produced
across that passage, so as to touch its floor, 1,542
inches.†

* See "Life and Work," Vol. II. p. 90.

† The Rev. W. B. Galloway, M.A., Vicar of St. Mark's, Regent's Park,
in his "Egypt's Record of Time to the Exodus of Israel," after deeply
studying the question, more from Alexandrian Greek than Egyptian profane sources, makes the date of the Exodus 1540 B.C. (see his p. 371).
And at p. 429 he arrives at the conclusion that the birth of our Saviour
was actually in the course of our reckoned year B.C. 1, and needs only a
fraction of a year to make the dates A.D., as usually given, truly continuous with the patriarchal.

The Floor Roll of Human Religious History.

But the chief line of human history with Robert Menzies was the floor of the entrance-passage. Beginning at its upper and northern end, it starts at the rate of a Pyramid inch to a year, from the Dispersion of mankind, or from the period when men declined any longer to live the patriarchal life of Divine instruction, and insisted on going off upon their own inventions; when they immediately began to experience that universal " facilis descensus Averni " of all idolaters; and which is so sensibly represented to the very life or death, in the long-continued descent of the entrance-passage of the Great Pyramid, more than 4,000 inch-years long,* until it ends, at a distance from the top of the passage equal probably to 4,404 Pyramid inches, in the symbol of the bottomless pit; a chamber deep in the rock, well finished as to its ceiling and the top of its walls, but without any attempt at a floor.

One escape, indeed, there was in that long and mournful history of human decline; but for the chosen few only, when the Exodus took place in the first ascending passage, which leads on into the Grand Gallery: showing Hebraism ending in its original prophetic destination—Christianity.

And the *manner* of progress of that first ascending passage is noteworthy. " The name of the Lord is a

---

* The full length of the entrance-passage of the Great Pyramid is not so well known by modern measure as it might be. My own very careful measures in duplicate, and sometimes triplicate, of every joint-line from the northern beginning downwards, described in " Life and Work," do not extend further than Al Mamoun's hole, or a third part only of the whole length. Under these circumstances Colonel Howard-Vyse is the only authority for the further and lower portions; and I have endeavoured in the table on p. 221, to connect his numbers with mine, through the medium of the place of junction of the first ascending, with the descending entrance passage.

strong tower : the righteous runneth into it, and is safe" (Prov. xviii. 10). And so in the earlier part of the passage, representing the Theocratic period of the Hebrew people under their judges, the great stone plates which surround that lower end of it, and make walls, ceiling, and floor, all in one piece (see p. 431), are close one to the other, almost continuously. In the middle of the passage, representing the regal period, David, Solomon, and Hezekiah, and other occasional kings acknowledged by God, these surrounding safety plates appear only at successive *breadths* of the King's Chamber. But when the voice of prophecy was closed with Malachi, then follows the last part of the passage, where for 400 years and more (*i.e.* a King's Chamber length of 412 inches) there is no reminder of the same refuge from on high.

But it was not Hebrews alone, descended from those under Moses, who were to be saved by Christ ; for besides the special Hebrew passage,—another, though far less conspicuous mode of escape from the descent into the bottomless subterranean pit, was also eventually provided, to prevent *any* immortal soul being necessarily lost. For, before reaching the dismal abyss, there is a possible entrance, though it may be by a strait and narrow way, to the one and only gate of salvation through the death of Christ—viz. the peculiar, deep but dry, well representing His descent into Hades.

This Hades locality is not the bottomless pit of idolaters and the wicked, lying at the lowest point to which the entrance-passage subterraneously descends, but a natural grotto, rather than artificial chamber, in the course of the well's further progress to the other place. It is in fact the Paradise of the dead, which is stated to be within the earth; and where they wait in unconscious condition, either the rapturous awakening to meet their Lord in the air, before His visible return to all men as Millennial King ; or, the final trump of the day of Judgment and the great white throne.

Meanwhile here at the Pyramid, the stone which once covered that well's upper mouth is blown outwards into the Grand Gallery with excessive force (and was once so thrown out, and is now annihilated), carrying part of the wall with it, and indicating how totally unable was the grave to hold Him beyond the appointed time.

That sounds fair and looks promising enough, so far, said Mr. Casey ; but it is not enough yet to be the turning-point with me, when interests so immense are at stake. We must have more than that, and something not less convincing than a proof of this order. Measuring along the passages backward from the north beginning of the Grand Gallery, you find the Exodus at either 1483 or 1542 B.C., and the dispersion of mankind in 2527 B.C., up at the beginning of the entrance-passage. Now you have already published, years ago, that you have computed the date of building of the Great Pyramid by modern astronomy, based on the Pyramid's own star-pointings, and have found it, as nearly as you can ascertain, 2170 B.C. That date, according to this new theory, and the acknowledged measures of passage lengths, must be somewhere about three or four hundred inches down inside the top or mouth of the entrance-passage. Is there, then, any *mark* at that point ? for I feel sure that the builder, if really inspired from on High, would have known how many years were to elapse between his great mechanical work in the beginning of the world, and the one central act of creation in the birth of the Divine Son ; and, though not using any letters of inscription or devices of sculpture throughout the monument, he would have marked it there as the most positive and invaluable proof that he could give, of the truly Divine

inspiration under which the building had been planned
and executed.

The Crucial Test.

Now it had never occurred to me before to confront
the sacred and scientific theories in *this* manner ; the
idea was Mr. Casey's entirely. But if any trial was
ever to be considered a crucial one, surely it was this.
So away I went to my original notes to satisfy him ;
and, beginning inside the building at the north end of
the Grand Gallery, counted and summed up the length
of every stone (backward to the direction in which I
had originally measured them), all down the first ascending passage ; then across the entrance-passage to its
floor ; then up that floor-plane towards its mouth, and
soon saw that the 2170 B.C. would fall very near a
most singular portion of the passage—viz. a place where
two adjacent wall-joints, similarly, too, on either side
of the passage, were almost *vertical ;* while every other
wall-joint both above and below was *rectangular* to the
length of the passage, and therefore largely *inclined* to
the vertical.

This double joint fact, in itself most easy to see,
though not, I believe, recorded before 1865, has frequently since then been speculated on by various
persons as possibly pointing to some still undiscovered
chamber ; and it may do so, just as the diagonal joints
in the floor at a lower level are now clearly seen to
point, and long to have pointed before unheeding generations of men, to the upper ascending passage, and
all that it leads to. But while no such fourth chamber
has yet been discovered, and no Egyptologist attempts
to give any explanation of the anomalous joints, and
there are few important features in the Great Pyramid
which have not meaning within and beyond their first
meaning wonderfully incorporated into them,—these

quasi-vertical joints seemed from their upright position, —at least to one who believed from theory that they were symbolically very near, and shortly before, the Great Pyramid's date of building,—to have something representative of a *setting up*, or preparations for the erecting of a notable building. And we are told by Herodotus, that many preliminary years *were* consumed in preparing the stones and subterraneous excavations of the Great Pyramid; while, on the other hand, Dr. Lepsius assures us in modern times, with all the lights, whatever they may be, of the Egyptologists, and either his own, or Mr. Wild's, theory of profane Pyramid building, that preliminary preparation was never practised by any chance, in any case whatever, of all ordinary and idolatrous Pharaonic pyramid building. For their work was *Epimethean* only, or from hand to mouth (not *Promethean*, see p. 411), year by year, and each year in itself, and by, itself only, just as each king chanced to live on and on.

Neither of these *quasi*-vertical joints, however, in the Great Pyramid's entrance-passage, would exactly suit the 2170 B.C. date; they were both of them too early; and then besides that, there were two on each wall, instead of one only. But on the surface of the stone following the last of them, and containing the 2,170 distance somewhere or other within its length, *there* was a quite unique marking. Something it was, more retiring, more difficult to discover, and yet commending itself still more when discovered, though not having the slightest approach to either letter of language, or form of drawing, and certainly not to any species of idolatry.

This mark was a line, nothing more, ruled on the stone, from top to bottom of the passage wall, at right angles to its floor. Such a line as might be ruled with a blunt steel instrument, but by a master-hand for

power, evenness, straightness, and still more eminently
for rectangularity to the passage axis. I had made myself a large square at the Pyramid in 1865, a wooden
square well trussed and nearly the whole height of the
wall, and therewith tested the error of rectangularity of
every masonry joint therein; and in each case had
found some very sensible quantity of such error; but
on coming to the ruled line, I could find no certainly
sensible error in that. If I suspected it occasionally, a
reversal of the square then and there proved that heat
or strain had caused some very slight temporary twist
in my instrument's wooden frame; but it could not
positively and permanently accuse the ancient line on
the stone of *anything* wrong.*

There was one such line on either wall, the west and
the east, of the passage; and the two lines seemed to
be pretty accurately opposite each other; while the
two pairs of *quasi*-vertical joints were not exactly so;
and the other joints in the walls pretended to, and
generally had, no correspondence whatever; nor was
any such agreement required for mere mechanical considerations in the masonry simply as such; for that
was indeed rather in favour of the joints on one wall
" breaking joint " with those on the other. All things,
therefore, both in symmetry, beauty of truth, unique
circumstance and correctness of position, culminated
in favour of these two thin lines; viz. the one
anciently ruled line on the west wall, and the
similarly ruled line on the east wall; and I looked
at them with still more interest afterwards, when
there appeared good reason to consider them the
work of the very same hand that laid out, in forethought, *Promethean*, manner, the entire proportions of
the whole Great Pyramid. For when Messrs. Aiton and
Inglis excavated and (with my assistance from theory

* See " Life and Work," Vol. II. p. 29.

in finding its site) laid bare the south-west socket of the Great Pyramid in April, 1865,—there, upon the fair white flattened face of the said socket rock, while three sides were formed by raised edges of stone, the fourth and outer side was defined simply by a line ; but a line ruled apparently by the very same hand and selfsame tool which had also drawn these other truthful lines in the entrance-passage.

Yet though I had admired these lines so much,— witness the pages of " Life and Work," published in 1867,—I had never thought of them before in connection with possible indications of date, or, indeed, of anything else, by virtue of their precise and absolute *place ;* and hence it was, that when Mr. Casey required in 1872 to know exactly where, on the floor length in Pyramid inches, the line on either side-wall touched that long floor plane (as measured, too, not from the top of the entrance-passage comparatively close by on the north, but from the beginning of the Grand Gallery far away to the south), there was no ready prepared record to say. That is, nothing more than the readings of the masonry joints next above and below the spot, together with a mere memorandum that the ruled line was within " a few inches " of one of them. Every intervening measure by joints between the two extremes, and over scores of joints, had been procured, printed, and published to the world in 1867 ; and I had got abused too in London reviews for printing so many particulars about trifles which Metropolitan editors could see no use in and despised; but just the last item now required, merely the small distance from the nearest floor-joint to the drawn line, was wanting. (See Plate X.)

So I wrote out to my friend Mr. Waynman Dixon, C.E., then (1872) actively engaged in erecting his brother's bridge over the Nile, near Cairo, requesting him to have the goodness to make and send me careful measures of the distance, whatever he should find it to be, of the fine line on either passage wall at the Pyramid, from the nearest one of the two *quasi*-vertical joints; not giving him any idea what the measure was wanted for, but only asking him to be very precise, clear, and accurate. And so he was; taking out also as companion and duplicate measurer his friend Dr. Grant, of Cairo; and their doubly attested figures were sent to me on diagrams, where they were written into their places, in a manner which left no room for any misunderstanding.

With this piece of difference measure, thus happily obtained at so late a date, I set to work again on my older joint measures of the whole distance; and was almost appalled when, on applying the above difference, the east side gave forth 2170·5, and the west side 2170·4 Pyramid inches.

" This testimony satisfies me, and fills me with thankfulness and joy," wrote Mr. Casey; while I, never expecting to have measured so closely as that, along either side of those lengthy, dark, and sloping Pyramid passages (where the measuring-rods, if not tightly held by hand to the floor, have a knack of slipping away and shooting down to the bottom), I, not understanding how such apparently close agreement came about, and knowing that it was not my desert as a measurer,—can only conclude this chapter with a condensed, small-type representation of the figure work involved in bringing out the results. Results more laboriously, and also, perhaps, more rigidly, impartially, and unexceptionally gained, than can well be imagined by any one else, without going through some *conspectus* of the many details.

THE RULED LINES IN THE ENTRANCE PASSAGE OF THE GREAT PYRAMID.

TESTED FOR THEIR DISTANCE, BY FLOOR OF INCLINED PASSAGES, FROM THE NORTH BEGINNING OF THE GRAND GALLERY, AND FOR THE CRITICAL NUMBER
2170.

The small measures of these lines, merely from the nearest masonry joint, were kindly sent to me by Mr. Waynman Dixon, from Egypt, with attestations by his friend Dr. Grant, of Cairo, on August 19, 1872, thus:—

"East Wall—Entrance Passage.

"Distance of Ruled Line from masonry wall-joint north of it,
at the top of the wall . . = 13·25 British in.
at the bottom of the wall . . = 4·37 „

"West Wall—Entrance Passage.

"Distance of Ruled Line from masonry wall-joint north of it,
at the top of the wall . . = 17·80 British in.
at the bottom of the wall . . = 7·55 „

"The above distances were measured by Mr. Waynman Dixon, C.E., and checked by Dr. Grant," and were accompanied by drawings showing that the lines were assumed to be rectangular (which they are) to the length of the passage, while the masonry joints they were referred to were more nearly vertical, and were the southernmost members of a pair of such *quasi*-vertical joints on either wall.

Examination for Accuracy.

The above measures are generally agreeable to my own approximate indication of the position of the lines, though I was rather surprised to find by Mr. Dixon's numbers, that the line on the west wall is farther from its reference joint, than that on the east wall is from its reference joint there, by so large an amount as nearly 4 inches.

It became, therefore, prudent, before embarking in any speculation on the whole return, to make an independent inquiry into the degree of accuracy of Mr. Dixon's measures, in *one* feature at least, where they admitted of that wholesome scientific discipline.

Accordingly, if we subtract, in the case of each wall separately, Mr. Dixon's lower difference reading from the upper, we attain a difference of the differences, East = 8·88 inches, and West = 10·25 inches. And on the assumption of the *lines* being rectangular to the length of the passage, these residual quantities show how much the *joints* deviate from rectangularity towards verticality, as measured along the top of the wall, or they form the shortest side of a plane triangle, of which the longest side is the *quasi*-vertical joint, and the medium side the transverse height of the wall, equivalent to the length of the ruled line.

Now the shortest side of that triangle I did in a manner measure in 1865 ; for in pp. 29 and 30 of Vol. II. of "Life and Work," the deviation of each of the said *quasi*-vertical joints (from rectangularity towards verticality) is stated as being, or amounting to, at the top of the wall,— 1st, by an approximate method:—

The east *quasi*-vertical joint . . . = 8 ± x inches,
And the west „ . . . = 9 ± x inches.

2nd, by a more accurate method:—

The east *quasi*-vertical joint. . . . = 9·1 inches,
And the west „ . . . . = 10·4 inches;

while the line ruled on the east wall deviated from rectangularity by only
0·04 inch, and that on the west wall by less than 0·01 of an inch.

Now Mr. Dixon's numbers for the same two joints' deviations being—

For the east *quasi*-vertical joint   .   .   .   =   8·88 inches,

And for the west   „   .   .   .   =   10·25 inches,

they come between my two pairs of quantities, and closer to that pair of
them which was previously stated to be by the more accurate method.
The result of examination is therefore highly gratifying, and shows that
we may certainly depend on Mr. Dixon's measures, say to the tenth of an
inch, at least; and that is no more than the fortieth part of the *apparently*
anomalous difference of his absolute distances of each line from its nearest
joint at the bottom of its own wall.

That difference, then, of the absolute distances must be a real quantity
at the Pyramid; and the line on the west wall must be actually 4 inches
or so further from the joint there, than that one on the east wall is from
the joint there.   Wherefore much may perhaps depend at last on what
effect such large difference may have, in modifying the final result on a
certain whole quantity which has now, after a repose of several years,
been suddenly required, in order to furnish a test for a new hypothesis.

Trial of Mr. Casey's Hypothesis.

Mr. Casey had thus far simply announced, that to fulfil certain important
theoretical ends, the passage-floor distance in the Great Pyramid (measured
from the north end of the Grand Gallery, down the floor of the first ascending, and up the floor of the entrance-passage, to where that floor is
at last touched on either side by the lower ends of these two anciently
ruled wall lines) should amount to 2,170 Pyramid inches, neither more
nor less within the probable errors of measurement.

At present I need only state that the north end of the Grand Gallery
is a very well-preserved and sharply defined plane; a good starting-point,
therefore, for measures; and that, excepting some rather troublesome, but
by no means impossible, features at the junction of the two passages, the
whole distance is plain, clear, and perfectly amenable to modern measure.

Indeed, every inch of the way (excepting only the small piece now
supplied by Mr. Dixon) has been, at one time or another, measured by
me, and its chief portion even two or three times over, and on either side
of the passages, with results, too, which have been published before the
world for five years.   The numerical facts, therefore, are, so far, very
firm; and if the measures, as originally taken, have as yet only been
presented anywhere piecemeal, and with numbers increasing in two
different series from north to south, in place of, as now required, in one
long accumulation from south to north—that is an additional guarantee
that the measures taken in 1865 could not have been influenced by any
desire to bring out the result of Mr. Casey's hypothesis in 1872.

We proceed, therefore, to the first portion of the whole distance now
demanded, viz. from the north end of the Grand Gallery, down the floor
of the first ascending passage, until that floor produced cuts the opposing
floor of the entrance-passage.   This portion we may call A.

The elements for the length A are given in " Life and Work," Vol. II.,
in the shape,—

1st. Of the floor distances, in British inches, joint by joint, from a
specified joint near the lower end, up to the terminal joint at the upper
or southern end of the first ascending passage, and they have been
measured twice over by me on either side of the passage.

2nd. The portcullis length, from that lower specified joint downwards to the still lower butt-end of portcullis, measured only once, and on the east side of the passage only.

3rd. The distance from that lower butt-end (slantingly across the entrance-passage to *its* floor) in the direction of the supposed floor of the first ascending passage produced downwards; and given here in three portions, each of which has been measured on either side of the passage.

The following Table contains all these distances required for A, and they are finally reduced from British, to Pyramid, inches in the two right-hand columns.

TABLE I.

FLOOR-JOINT *distances from north beginning of Grand Gallery, towards lower end of first ascending passage ; or complements of the numbers in third columns of pages* 48 *and* 49 *of* " Life and Work," *Vol.* II.

NUMBER OF FLOOR JOINT.	INDIVIDUAL MEASURES IN BRITISH INCHES.		SUMMATIONS IN BRITISH INCHES.		SUMMATIONS IN PYRAMID INCHES.	
	East side.	West side.	East side 1291·2—distance.	West side 1291·1—distance.	East side.	West side.
Starting joint of first ascending passage of Great Pyramid; at the top or upper end of that passage, near the Grand Gallery . . 0	..	..	0·2	0·1	0·2	0·1
1	..	..	58·0	57·6	57·9	57·5
2	..	..	119·3	..	119·2	..
3	..	..	177·8	176·6	177·6	176·4
4	..	..	208·5	207·4	208·3	207·2
5	..	..	257·3	255·7	257·0	255·4
6	..	..	290·8	..	290·5	..
7	..	..	343·8	341·9	343·5	341·6
8	..	..	384·8	383·4	384·4	383·0
9	..	..	416·5	413·6	416·1	413·2
10	..	..	465·5	463·6	465·0	463·1
11	..	..	502·9	500·1	502·4	499·6
12	..	..	537·6	537·1	537·1	536·6
13	..	..	590·7	589·3	590·1	588·7
14	..	..	623·7	622·1	623·1	621·5
15	..	..	..	660·1	..	659·4
16	..	..	691·4	689·4	690·7	688·7
17	..	..	746·7	745·8	746·0	745·1
18	..	..	796·9	795·2	796·1	794·4
19	..	..	829·2	828·0	829·4	827·2
20	..	..	891·7	890·0	890·8	889·1
21	..	..	941·7	931·5	940·8	930·6
22	..	..	991·4	981·5	990·4	980·5
23	..	..	1044·7	1036·5	1043·7	1035·5
24	..	..	1094·7	1087·5	1093·6	1086·4
25	..	..	..	1124·5	..	1123·4
Lower part of first 26	..	..	1168·7	1161·3	1167·5	1160·1
ascending pas- 27	..	..	1209·6	1199·8	1208·4	1198·6
sage, near the 28	..	..	1246·0	1242·0	1244·8	1240·8
Portcullis .. 29	..	..	1291·2	1291·1	1289·9	1289·8

Table I.—(continued).

Number of Floor Joint.	Individual Measures in British Inches.		Summations in British Inches.		Summations in Pyramid Inches.	
	East side.	West side.	East side 1291·2— distance.	West side 1291·1— distance.	East side.	West side.
Special Additions.						
Portcullis length (see p. 54 of Vol. II. of " L. and W.")	178·8	(178·8)*	1470·0	1469·9	1468·5	1468·4
To roof of entrance-passage, or *c f* (see p. 41, Vol. II. of " L. and W.")	14·2	14·1	1484·2	1484·0	1482·7	1482·5
To axis of entrance-passage; or the quantity *f i*	29·8	30·0	1514·0	1514·0	1512·5	1512·5
To floor of entrance-passage; in direction of the first ascending passage produced downwards, or *i l*	29·8	30·0	1543·	1544·0	1542·3	1542·5
Whole distance from north beginning of Grand Gallery, down the floor of first ascending passage produced downwards to touch the floor of descending entrance-passage; or the quantity **A**, in Pyramid inches					1542·3	1542·5

We next take up the remaining portion of the whole quantity required for Mr. Casey's hypothesis, or the distance from the intersection plane of the floors of the two passages, up the entrance-passage's floor northward; to where that floor is touched on either side by the bottoms of the two ruled wall lines: a portion we shall call B.

But this portion B we must necessarily compute in two steps; first, in Table II., setting forth the readings of all the *floor-joints* of the entrance-passage on the floor, the supposed sheet of, or for, historic record; and second, in Table III., setting forth first for the east side, and then for the west side, the readings of every *wall-joint*, on the floor's above-described record-plane; this will be the B which we are in search of; and will have A added to it in the last two columns, so as there to present the quantity A + B, for the wall-joints in the entrance-passage.

Finally, to the wall-joint reading A + B, for the particular joint measured from by Mr. Waynman Dixon, we must apply his measured difference of the lower end of the ruled line therefrom.

* Not directly measured, only inferred, on this western side of the passage.

TABLE II.

FLOOR-JOINT *distances from contact plane in Descending Entrance Passage, upwards and northwards to its upper north end, or beginning.*

NUMBER OF FLOOR JOINT.	SUMMATIONS IN					
	BRITISH INCHES.				PYRAMID INCHES.	
	East side.		West side.		East side.	West side.
The starting-point being not a joint, but the contact plane with the floor of first ascending passage produced downwards, or line "*l*" on p. 42, Vol. II. of "L. & W."	987·2— distance (See p. 42, Vol. II. "L.&W.")	+ 1543·8	985 6— distance (See p. 42, Vol. II. " L.&W.")	+ 1544·0	Whole distance from north beginning of Grand Gallery.	Whole distance from north beginning of Grand Gallery.
Starting line "*l*" Joint from "*l*" low down in entrance-passage	0·0	1543·8	0·0	1544·0	1542·3	1542·5
1	46·8	1590·6	46·5	1590·5	1589·0	1588·9
2	82·0	1625·8	81·7	1625·7	1624·2	1624·1
3	106·6	1650·4	106·5	1650·5	1648·7	1648·8
4	146·6	1690·4	146·5	1690·5	1688·7	1688·8
5	195·2	1739·0	195·0	1739·0	1737·3	1737·3
6	231·6	1775·4	231·5	1775·5	1773·6	1773·8
7	284·4	1828·2	283·1	1827·1	1826·4	1825·3
8	335·3	1879·1	334·5	1878·5	1877·2	1876·7
9	375·7	1919·5	374·0	1918·0	1917·6	1916·1
10	414·5	1958·3	410·1	1954·1	1956·4	1952·1
11	467·5	2011·3	463·2	2007·2	2009·3	2005·2
12	526·7	2070·5	525·7	2069·7	2068·5	2067·6
13	578·5	2122·3	578·1	2122·1	2120·2	2120·0
The line on the wall is due somewhere between these two floor-joints.						
14	644·7	2188·5	644·3	2188·3	2186·3	2184·0
15	703·6	2247·4	703·5	2247·5	2245·2	2245·3
16	772·0	2315·8	769·2	2313·2	2313·5	2310·9
17	827·0	2370·8	824·6	2368·6	2368·4	2366·3
18	885·0	2428·8	883·5	2427·5	2426·4	2425·1
19	932·6	2476·4	931·5	2475·5	2474·0	2473·0
Near beginning or upper, or north end of the entrance-passage. 20	987·2	2531·0	985·6	2529·6	2528·5	2527·1

During all these *Floor* measurements, the scale bars had to be held fast to the floor, by the hand of an assistant: for though they did not *always* do so, yet more frequently than not, a measuring bar left to itself, with its length parallel with the axis of the passage, would slide downwards with a velocity increasing every moment, endangering both itself and any human being further down the passage.

N.B.—Had Mr. Waynman Dixon measured the lower end of the ruled lines from a *floor*-joint, we should now have been in a position, with this table, to have obtained for each ruled line the ultimate reading required. But his measure of a difference being from a *wall*-joint, we must now prepare a further tabular representation of the readings, on the floor-plane, of each of the *wall*-joints, and this for either wall separately; or thus:—

TABLE III.

WALL-JOINT *distances at their lower ends; or where they touch the floor in the* ENTRANCE PASSAGE; *reckoned from that* FLOOR'S *contact plane with the floor of first ascending passage (produced downwards), and proceeding upwards to the upper or north end of Entrance Passage.*

EAST WALL (BY ITSELF).
Floor's contact plane 987·2 British inches from its beginning at North end.
(See page 42, Vol. II. of " Life and Work.")

Number of Wall-joint, referring only to the bottom thereof.	Distance south from basement beginning. (See p. 24, Vol. II.)	Inverse distance, or distance from contact plane, north.	The same + 1543·8; or whole distance from the north beginning of Grand Gallery = A + B.	
			British Inches.	Pyramid Inches.
1st Wall-joint, above, or north of floor's cont.ct plane ..	957·8	29·4	1573·2	1571·6
2 ,, ,, ,,	917·0	70·2	1614·0	1612·4
3 ,, ,, ,,	854·2	133·0	1676·8	1675·1
4 ,, ,, ,,	821·3	165·9	1709·7	1708·0
5 ,, ,, ·,	761·3	225·9	1769·7	1767·9
6 ,, ,, ,,	717·1	270·1	1813·9	1812·1
7 ,, ,, ,,	658·9	328·3	1872·1	1870·2
8 ,, ,, ,,	605·1	382·1	1925·9	1924·0
9 ,, ,, ,,	537·1	450·1	1993·9	1991·9
10 ,, ,, ,,	501·0	486·2	2030·0	2028·0
11 ,, ,, ,,	442·2	545·0	2088·8	2086·7
12 ,, ,, ,,	387·3	599·9	2143 7	2141·6
The wall line due somewhere here.				
13! Approximately vertical ..	353·9	633·0	2177·1	2174·9
14! Approximately vertical ..	290 0	697·2	2241·0	2238·8
15, half-height	219·2	768·0	2311·8	2309·5
16, half-height	150·4	836·8	2380·6	2378·2
17, half-height	110·2	877·0	2420·8	2415·4
North beginning of basement sheet of entrance-passage..	0·0	987·2	2531·0	2528·5

A few of the measures near the *upper* end of this wall (which is the *lowest* part of our mere column of numbers) may be seen graphically represented in Plate X.; but all the joints of both floor, walls, and ceiling are represented similarly in Plate II. of Vol. II. of "Life and Work at the Great Pyramid," 1867.

TABLE III.—(*continued*.)

WEST WALL (by itself). Floor contact plane 985·6 British inches from basement beginning. (See page 42, Vol. II. of "Life and Work.")				
Number of Wall-joint, &c. &c.	Distance south from basement beginning. (See p. 21, Vol. II. "L. & W.")	Inverse distance, or distance from contact plane, north.	The same + 1544·0; or whole distance from the north beginning of Grand Gallery = A + B.	
			British Inches.	Pyramid Inches.
1st wall-joint, above, or north, of floor's contact plane	981·1	4·5	1548·5	1547·0
2 ,, ,, ,,	931·5	54·1	1598·1	1596·5
3 ,, ,, ,,	871·1	114·5	1658·5	1656·8
4 ,, ,, ,,	842·0	143·6	1687·6	1685·9
5 ,, ,, ,,	801·5	184·1	1728·1	1726·4
6 ,, ,, ,,	766·9	218·7	1762·7	1760·9
7 ,, ,, ,,	740·4	245·2	1789·2	1787·4
8 ,, ,, ,,	681·3	304·3	1848·3	1846·5
9 ,, ,, ,,	639·1	346·5	1890·5	1888·6
10 ,, ,, ,,	562·1	423·5	1967·5	1965·5
11 ,, ,, ,,	527·1	458·5	2002·5	2000·5
12 ,, ,, ,,	482·1	503·5	2047·5	2045·5
13 ,, ,, ,,	427·1	558·5	2102·5	2100·4
14 ,, ,, ,, The wall line due somewhere here	391·7	593·9	2137·9	2135·8
15! Approximately vertical .	349·4	636·2	2180·2	2178·0
16! Approximately vertical .	289·8	695·8	2239·8	2237·6
17, half-height	207·6	778·0	2322·0	2319·7
18, half-height	152·6	833·0	2377·0	23·4·6
19, half-height	110·0	875·6	2419·6	2417·2
North beginning of basement sheet of entrance-passage .	0·0	985·6	2529·6	2527·1

The absolute place, then, on the *floor's* scroll of history, in terms of our A + B, of the base of that wall-joint from which Mr. Dixon measured the ruled line, is on the

East side . . . . . . = 2174·9 Pyramid inches,
And on the west side . . . . = 2178·0 ,,

And Mr. Dixon's measured difference at the base amounting to—

On the east side . . . . . = 4·4 inches,
And on the west side . . . . = 7·6 ,,

and the signs of these quantities being negative, or showing that they are to be subtracted, we have for the absolute readings or dates of the two ruled lines, in terms of the strictest requirements of Mr. Casey's hypothesis,—

On the east side . . . . . = 2170·5 Pyramid inches,
And on the west side . . . . = 2170·4 ,,

Or exhibiting an agreement with the hypothesis to less than $\frac{1}{5000}$th part of the whole; and one side agreeing with the other to within $\frac{1}{20000}$th of the whole.

As remarked on p. 470, this is a much closer degree
of approach than I had expected my measures were
capable of; and I should have had some scruple in
publishing the case, had not the whole of the lengthy
data been so perfectly impossible to have been know-
ingly influenced at the time they were made, as well
as first printed and published. While, if there be any
large error in them, unknown to myself,—there is no
more powerful mode in modern society of enabling and
stimulating other more capable persons to bring out
more accurate measures, than thus to publish all the
minute particulars of these.

But assuming them now to be correct, until the contrary shall be proved,—the case may also be considered
to bear some testimony towards that frequently disputed
question as to whether an error of four years, or perhaps
less, was committed by the Christian framers of the
present mode of reckoning years from the date of the
birth of Christ. A mode commenced only, many hundred years after the event alluded to, when historic
particulars were few and uncertain; and leading, as
some persons occasionally maintain to this result,—
that the present year, called now by all the Christian
world 1879 A.D., may be perhaps really 1882, or even
1883 A.D.

So far as the final numbers of my actual Pyramid measurements are concerned, the measures now recorded
positively declare, that there was no such error in our
Christian era amounting to a whole year. But I do
not recommend any one to trust to them for so small a
quantity, as I am not certain of the *astronomical date*
concerned, by a much larger figure (see p. 381)—and
though I did, no doubt, years ago mentally conclude
and publish, 2170 B.C. to be most probably the year
intended to be memorialized as the foundation year, by
the architect of the Great Pyramid,—it was no rigid

deduction of scientific exactitude : and I would rather recommend all inquirers into the particular subject of the Christian era date, to such works as that of the Rev. Mr. Galloway, mentioned on p. 462, and to a study of the kind of documents there consulted.

There is, however, satisfaction, to my mind at least, in finding that even in this latest question of the true date of the birth of Christ, reckoned back from our own times, there is no sensible disagreement between the Great Pyramid as thus far, as well as quite independently, worked out, on one side ;—and on the other, the best divines and chronologists who have written on the point, as well as the actual practice and vital beliefs of the mass of the people in every Christian land. Wherefore we may now proceed to further developments of the Ancient Monument with assured spirits and trustful confidence in God, who rules over all.

PART V.

THE PERSONAL, AND THE FUTURE, AT THE GREAT PYRAMID.

"HOW SAY YE UNTO PHARAOH, I—THE SON OF THE WISE, THE SON
OF ANCIENT KINGS?

"WHERE ARE THEY? WHERE ARE THY WISE MEN? AND LET THEM
TELL THEE NOW, AND LET THEM KNOW WHAT THE LORD OF HOSTS
HATH PURPOSED UPON EGYPT."—ISAIAH XIX. 11, 12.

CHAPTER XXI.

HIEROLOGISTS AND CHRONOLOGISTS,

Pyramids and Temples, Sacred and Profane.

NO land has been so expansively treated of in the chronologies of schoolmen, as the valley of Egypt; for even if the early, pre-classical mysticisms of its so-called Divine kings during 36,500 years be rejected, there are equally, or still more, extraordinary modern theories. By some of the present rationalistic writers on, and inventors of, a probable primeval history, for instance, the earliest Egyptian kings have been pushed forward on paper far above all really ascertained *monumental* dates, at first by only 1 or 2 thousands of years, but finally by some persons up to 10,000, 20,000, and even 300,000 years ago; with the accompanying statement, too, that even at that remote epoch there were no signs of any gradual emergence out of a primitive savage condition, but only of an already highly organized and well-governed community; which must therefore, on the *human* and natural evolution hypothesis, have commenced to run its civilized course an almost infinite length of time previously.

Now if only a fragment of all this " Egyptology " be true, both Bible dates, and Great Pyramid dates must be utterly wrong. And although we may be ever so well convinced in our own minds that the measures and numbers of the Great Pyramid have proved its case, as described in our preceding chapters, surely to a very considerable amount of demonstration;—yet as we are but fallible mortals, we should not omit to consider what the world (for the mass of society is without doubt still against us and for Egyptology) has to say for those most oppositional conclusions.

To begin with some of the easiest and simplest matters,—certain geologists who went to Egypt, not many years ago, claim to have discovered proofs (in fragments of pottery dug up at a great depth in the alluvial deposit of the Nile) of an existence of first-rate human manufactures there during more than 13,000 consecutive years. And again there are many very worthy men who still attach much importance to the computations made, by French astronomers of the last century, from certain configurations of the ecliptic and equator in the celebrated zodiacs of the Nilotic temples of Dendera, Esneh, and E' Dayr; and giving to those buildings almost equal dates to the geological.

But, of the said geological evidence, it has lately been argued by the acute Professor Balfour Stewart, of Owens College, Manchester, that a solid mass of any substance of notable size, has an effective tendency to work its way downwards through a bed of finely divided particles of both similar, and extraneous, matter; wherefore it is no positive proof, ages after a big bone, or piece of pottery, or flint hammer of comparatively large dimensions, was deposited on a certain silty soil, that it should be of the same date as the smaller particles of the stratum it is subsequently found in ; for it may have worked its way downwards while those particles were still mobile.

This law its author illustrated in the case of celts immersed in finely divided silex powder; and if it is true at all, it must be especially applicable to the later Egyptian geology. For there, all the valley is not only composed of the so-called slime of the Nile (microscopically fine particles of granite, porphyry, lime-stone, and the other rocks washed and rolled over by the mighty river in its long course from the equator), but is visited every year by the inundation; which may be regarded as a grand tide of a secular order, producing amongst the slime's small component particles the same sort of lively quicksand effect, but in a superior degree, which is witnessed on the Goodwin Sands whenever an ordinary periodical, or only twelve-hour, tide rises there.

The geological evidence, then, for a very long chronology, under such circumstances, is specious in the extreme; while the supposed astronomical is considerably worse, having even had a decided refutation given to its very essence, years ago, by modern hieroglyphical readings, and in this way. The painted Egyptian zodiacs already alluded to, no matter how grossly they caricatured the positions of the stars, had been fondly considered, by those who sought a high antiquity for Egypt, to have been honourably constructed so as to represent something in the heavens as seen in their own day; and if they were found to have made a very badly drawn equator crossing the ecliptic, equally murdered, 90° from its present position, that was taken as a proof that the ceiling, or the walls containing those things, must have been sculptured when the equator did cross the ecliptic in that longitude; *i.e.* say 10,500 years ago, according to the now known rate of the precession of the equinoxes in good Newtonian astronomy.

But this, by itself, is plainly no scientific proof; for any stonemason can at any time, if you give him an order so to do, and a pattern to go by, carve you a zodiac with the equator crossing the ecliptic in any constellation whatever; and with vastly more scientific accuracy of detail than any of those profane Egyptian temple pictures have yet been accused of.

There was never, therefore, any real stability in the
groundwork for those pseudo-astronomically computed
chronologies; while during the last thirty years the
whole foundation for them has been entirely destroyed
by the earlier discoveries of the first of the new hierologists, Young, Champollion, and their followers; who
have proved incontestably, by interpreting the hieroglyphic inscriptions mixed up with the said pictures, that
the zodiac temples were the *latest* of all the Egyptian
monuments; that they dated only from the time of
the Ptolemys, and even some of the Roman emperors;
and were the work of house-painters rather than astronomers.

Hieroglyphic study, therefore, began exceedingly well.
But alas! for its later progressive development.

Egyptian Hieroglyphics versus *Greek Scholarship*.

Commenced by the discovery of the Rosetta stone in
1802; vivified by Young and Champollion about 1820;
and, since then, most ably developed by Rossellini,
Gardner Wilkinson, Birch, Osburn, Lepsius, Poole, De
Saulcy, De Rougé, Brugsch, Mariette, Chabas, and many
others,—hieroglyphical interpretation has rendered the
nineteenth century vastly more intimately acquainted
with the home life of early Egypt, than any century has
been since the times of actual Apis and Osiris worshipping by the Egyptians themselves.

The delightful ability thus unexpectedly acquired, to
read the writings of a people who departed all visible
life nearly two thousand years ago, infused at the time
extraordinary enthusiasm into all the new hieroglyphic
professors; who congratulated each other, and ancient
Egypt too, unceasingly, on the treasure-house of human
wisdom which they were so successfully opening up.

" Dark," said they—

> " ' Dark has been thy night,
> Oh, Egypt ! but the flame
> Of new-born *science* gilds thine ancient name.' "

And how has *that* science gilded it at last ? Not by
having set forth any grand philosophy or estimable literature ; for such things are so very far from existing in
the hieroglyphics, that the late Sir George Cornewall
Lewis, impatient of the Egyptological boastings, and
judging of what had been produced, from his favourite
stand-point of truly intellectual *Greek* authors,—both
condemned all the Mizraisms which had up to that
time been interpreted ; and concluded from their sam-
ple, that there was nothing, in grammar or language,
worthy of being known, remaining to be interpreted in
all the rest of the hieroglyphics of the reputedly *wise*
land of Egypt.

So if there *is* anything worth gilding at all, it is perhaps rather to be looked for in that low, yet necessary,
phase of history, " chronicling " ; for the Egyptians
were, of all men, the record keepers of the early world :
not only perpetually erecting monuments, but inscribing
them all over with their clearly-cut-out hieroglyphic
inscriptions ; while the dry climate of their country has
preserved even to these times almost whatever they
chose to inscribe, large or small.

Yet after years of study of these things, our great
Egyptologic and hieroglyphic scholars are not advanced
much in the way of certainty ; and seem truly agreed on
nothing chronological, except something like the order of
precedence, or comparative succession, of old Egyptian
kings, and dynasties of kings ;—for when they come to
give the absolute dates of any of the reigns, they differ
among themselves by 1,000, 2,000, 3,000 or more
years with the utmost facility ; just as each modern
Egyptologist chooses for himself to consider the " dynas-

ties" of Manetho to have been more or less successive, rather than coexistent, in different cities or provinces of ancient Egypt.

But while Manetho, though an Egyptian priest, was no ancient authority; for he lived only under the Ptolemys, wrote in Greek, and his arrangement of old Egyptian kings, in series or dynasties, was an invention out of his own head;—certain good Greek scholars. amongst ourselves (men who would have been thoroughly approved of by Sir G. C. Lewis and the grammarians), have, after studying the purely Alexandrian-Greek writers most deeply and extensively, and at those historic periods of Ptolemeian and Roman Emperor rule, when hieroglyphics must have been still intimately understood in that land, before they were lost in the dark ages,—they have, I repeat, raised the standard of opposition against the modern re-interpreters of the Mizraite monumental inscriptions; repudiate their favourite author Manetho utterly; and bring up a totally different arrangement of the names of old Egyptian kings, with perfectly different dates attachable thereto.*

Of the whole merits of this grand contest, neither is this book the place, nor myself the author, wherein and by whom it should be discussed. But there are certain of the results, from either side, which cannot be passed by, in connection with our proper Great Pyramid subject.

Differential Chronology of the Egyptologists.

When the Egyptologists, for instance, confess, as they have done most distinctly even within the last year, that they know, amongst all their profane monu-

* See "Egypt's Record of Time to the Exodus of Israel," critically investigated by the Rev. W. B. Galloway, M.A., Vicar of St. Mark's, Regent's Park, London.

ments of Old Egypt, not a single one capable of expressing, or giving, in its hieroglyphic inscription *an absolute date*,—while *we* have seen abundantly, from what is already set forth in this book (pp. 369—385), that the Great Pyramid does assign its own absolute date most distinctly, by a method of its own entirely unconnected with hieroglyphics; and all the more distinctly the higher exact astronomic science of modern times it is examined by,—evidently an invaluable type of separation has been ascertained between the one and only Israelite and Christianly sacred, ancient, monument in Egypt on one hand, and, on the other, the whole herd of that land's old profane monuments, the only research-ground which our modern Egyptologists seem to care for.

Again, while the leading principle, and very sheet-anchor, of the best Egyptological chronologists is, to seek out and confide in *monuments;* to consider nothing fixed in Egyptian history or fact, unless there is a monument for it to show, and that monument contemporary, or nearly so, with the facts to which it relates (please to note all these words),—they allow faithfully that they know of no monuments whatever at all earlier, or not earlier by more than a comparatively very few years, than the Great Pyramid.

Dr. Lepsius is very clear on this point. In his "Letters from Egypt," he wrote from his encampment amongst the tombs in the neighbourhood of the Great Pyramid in 1843 :—" Nor have I yet found a single cartouche that can be safely assigned to a period previous to the fourth dynasty. The builders of the Great Pyramid (Kings of that reputed fourth dynasty) seem to assert their right to form the commencement of monumental history, even if it be clear that they were not the first builders and monumental writers." And again, he says, " The Pyramid of Cheops (fourth dynasty), to which the first link of our whole monumental history is fastened immovably, not only for Egyptian, but for universal history." And in his " Denkmaeler " of subsequent years, the learned Doctor of Berlin opens that immense chronological series with, *the Great Pyramid*.

Hence we may dismiss entirely, even on Egyptological grounds, all the 300,000 paper years of civilized life in Egypt before the Great Pyramid, so rashly asserted by a late rationalistic writer, because he has no " monuments " to show for that long period. But for such period as the Egyptologists do bring up monuments ; viz. from the Great Pyramid downwards,*—there we can hardly but pay much attention to their schemes of the *differential* chronologic history of Egypt, as thus :—

---

* A new class of monuments has very lately been brought to light by the continued excavations of Mariette Bey ; said to be still older than the Great Pyramid, being of the third, possibly the second, or even the very first dynasty. These monuments are artistic, rather than scientific ; consisting in statues sometimes of hard stone, sometimes of wood admirably painted, and with eyes of rock-crystal and marble, which sparkle still with almost a living effect when a ray of sunlight shines upon them. These relics were obtained by breaking into tombs of those supposed early dates ; and they are now to be seen in the Boulak Museum at Cairo.

They are undoubtedly very ancient ; and as being facts, rather than theories, of their time, are of the utmost importance now. Two most just deductions from them have already been made (see *The Banner of Israel*, Vol. III. No. 150, for November 12, 1879 ; in an article entitled " The Times and others against the Great Pyramid ") ; and while remarkably disconcerting to the views of the rationalists, have lent a most unexpected light to the Biblical account of the Dispersion from Babel, as a true, Divinely insisted on, and Divinely assisted therefore, migration of the *origines* of families to their Israelitically appointed regions,—there to take up new characters, and form *nations* previously unknown ;—as already concluded by W. Osburn, from independent data, in his excellent " Monumental History of Egypt."

Judging then in this manner on the Boulak Museum relics, the chief testimony of those art monuments is,—that the Egyptians there represented, had only arrived in Egypt a short time before the Great Pyramid was built, from the plains of Mesopotamia : that they came in a stout-framed, brawny Assyrian people ; were physiologically changed, in the comparatively short duration of two or three dynasties only into the lank figure, and thin *physique*, of the Egyptians of later days ; and remained so (witness their innumerable portraits of themselves on later monuments) during the following thirty dynasties or more, of their long Pharaonic and idolatrous empire.

BEGINNING OF EACH DYNASTY OF ANCIENT EGYPT, ACCORDING TO VARIOUS EGYPTOLOGICAL SCHOLARS, GUIDED PARTLY BY MANETHO, WHOSE WORK HAS ONLY DESCENDED TO US IN FRAGMENTS OF SUBSEQUENT AUTHORS; AND PARTLY BY THE PROFANE AND IDOLATROUS MONUMENTS, WHICH, THEY CONFESS, DO NOT GIVE ABSOLUTE DATES.

Number of Dynasty, as assumed in modern times.	Date according to the average of				Assigned locality of the Régime.	Chief surviving architecture of those Dates.
	Lesueur, Mariette, Renan, &c.	Lepsius, Bunsen, Fergusson, &c.	Lane, Wilkinson, Rawlinson, &c.	William Osburn.		
	B.C.	B.C.	B.C.	B.C.	*	
1	5735	3892	2700	2429	Memphis	Memphian Tombs
2	5472	3639	2480	2420	Memphis	
3	5170	3338	2670	2329	Memphis	
4	4956	3124	2440	2228	Memphis	The Great Pyramid.
5	4472	2840	2440	..	Abydos	Memphian Tombs and smaller Pyramids, with but little ornamentation.
6	..	2744	2200	2107	Memphis	
7	..	2592	1800	..	Memphis	
8	..	2522	1800	..	Memphis	
9	..	2674	2200	2107	Heracleopolis	
10	..	2565	..	1959	Heracleopolis	Rock-tombs in the hills, inscribed and painted.
11	3435	2423	2100	2107	Thebes	
12	..	2380	2028	..	Thebes	
13	..	2136	1920	..	Thebes	
14	..	2167	2080	..	Xois	
15	..	2101	2080	1900	Foreign Hyksos	
16	..	1842	1800	1900	Foreign Hyksos	
17	..	1684	1776	..	Thebans	Theban Palace-temples and Rock-tombs in gorgeous architecture of columns, friezes, and frescoes covered with idolatrous sculptures and paintings of all sizes.
18	..	1591	1520	1674	Thebans	
19	1314	1443	1324	1394	Thebans	
20	..	1269	1232	1314	Thebans	

(OLD EMPIRE, SO CALLED. — Dynasties 1–15; NEW EMPIRE. — Dynasties 17–20)

* These names are chiefly derived from W. Osburn, and are varied from by other Egyptologists, who assign a rather problematic city, "This," in Lower or Middle Egypt, as the locality of the 1st and 2nd dynasties; and place the 5th and 6th dynasties on Elephantine, an island in the extreme of upper Egypt, near the Cataracts, and where there are no Pyramid remains. On the other hand, the Ptolemaic-Greek Librarian of Alexandria, Eratosthenes, who does not admit any arrangement of dynasties, but does admit most of the names of kings contained

Now when a scientific pyramidist, on the other hand, or from his point of view and his daily-increasing sources of mensurational, and positive information, confines himself to stating *relatively* that the Great Pyramid was erected in the times of the "fourth dynasty,"—he is evidently in accord with all the Egyptologists of every order and degree. But when he otherwise, further, and more particularly defines that the Great Pyramid was built at the *absolute* date of 2170 B.C., he is in chronological accord with one only of the whole of those Egyptologists, viz. William Osburn; for he alone makes the fourth dynasty to extend from 2228 to 2108 B.C.; inclusive, therefore, of the Great Pyramid's both astronomic and Entrance-Passage *memento* of 2170 B.C. (See p. 380.)

On finding this solitary case of agreement, in the course of 1866, I immediately obtained a copy of that author's two-volume work, "Monumental History of Egypt"; and was so well satisfied with the vigour and originality of his mind, his linguistic power,* and his

in Manetho's dynastic arrangement of them, entitles them all "of the Thebans, or of Middle Egypt."

* I have since then been informed by the Rev. John Harrison, D.D., that before taking up hieroglyphic studies, Mr. Osburn's forte had been that more difficult Greek of the Greek plays, the tragedies of Sophocles, Æschylus, and Euripides. After a long and painful illness, which Mr. Osburn bore up against for years with exemplary Christian fortitude, he died in his native city of Leeds in 1875 ; and I have had many interesting particulars of his life and labours from one and another of his former Sunday-school scholars, with whom the seed of religious regeneration which he had sown in the years of his activity had fructified and become permanent, to the advantage of others as well as themselves.

Indeed by their aid, and that of some of the younger members of his family, I had some hopes of bringing out an attempted biographical sketch of his very characteristic career, together with a new edition of his exemplary and powerful little work, "The Religions of the World." Which work, though merely Encyclopædic to some minds, did appear to me something penetrating so deeply to the spirit of Revealed Religion, even in the earliest ages,—that no one but an able Egyptologist, a good classical scholar, and at the same time an advanced Christian, could have written it. But sufficient materials have not yet been received, and there appears to be a copyright over the book in the hands of a London house, which cannot be interfered with, at least for the present.

conscientious labours, that I sought out every other work that he had written; and was eventually rewarded with a long correspondence with himself; and found him a man who, though he did not please his fellow-Egyptologists, yet seemed worthy to be regarded as the king of them all. Partly, too, by the light of *his* writings, reading both Lepsius and Howard-Vyse over again, I am now enabled to give the following comparative, but still only approximate, view of the Great Pyramid as it stands among the other Pyramids of Egypt; and in probable date, as well as shape and position.

TABLE OF THE PYRAMIDS OF EGYPT,

ALL STANDING IN THE LIBYAN DESERT, BUT BORDERING CLOSE ON THE WESTERN SIDE OF THE NILE VALLEY.

The base-side lengths of all the principal ones are given in Chapter III. p. 45, and the heights of all the principal ones in Chapter IV. p. 65.

Number.	NAME OF PYRAMID.	Latitude North.	Angle of rise of the faces to horizon, from How- ard Vyse.	Rude ap- proximation to the absolute Dates of Erection.
		° ′	° ′ ″	Years.
1	**GREAT PYRAMID OF JEEZEH**	29 59	51 51 14	2170 B.C.
2	Second Pyramid of do.	29 59	52 20 0	2130
3	Third Pyramid of do.	29 58	51 0 0	2100
4	Fourth Pyramid of do.	29 58	in steps	2130
5	Fifth Pyramid of do.	29 58	52 15 0	
6	Sixth Pyramid of do.	29 58	in steps	
7	Seventh Pyramid of do.	29 59	52 10 0	
8	Eighth Pyramid of do.	29 59	52 10 0	
9	Ninth Pyramid of do.	29 59	52 10 0	2100
10	So-called Pyramid of Aboo Roash, a ruined commencement only, and never an actual Pyramid either in shape, mathematics, or tombic use	30 4	no casing	x
11	Pyramid of Zowyat El Arrian ..	29 57	ruins only	2100
12	Pyramid of Reegah, with two succes- sive slopes	29 56	{75 20 0} {50 0 0}	
13	Northern Pyramid of Abooseir ..	29 54	51 42 35	
14	Middle Pyramid of do. ..	29 54	51 (?)	
15	Great Pyramid of do. ..	29 54	52 (?)	
16	Small Pyramid of do. ..	29 54	60 (?	2050
17	Pyramid 1 at Saccara	29 53	rubbish only	2000
18	Pyramid 2 at do.	29 53	52 (?)	
19	Great Pyramid, or Pyramid 3, at Saccara	29 53	{73 30 0} {in steps}	2050
20	Pyramid 4 at Saccara	29 53	ruined	
21	Pyramid 5 at do.	29 53	ruined	

TABLE OF THE PYRAMIDS OF EGYPT—(*continued*).

Number.	Name of Pyramid.	Latitude North.	Angle of rise of the faces to horizon, from Howard-Vyse.	Rude approximation to the absolute Dates of Erection.
		° ′	° ′ ″	Yéars.
22	Pyramid 6 at Saccara	29 53	ruined	
23	Pyramid 7 at do.	29 53	ruined	
24	Pyramid 8 at do.	29 53	ruined	
25	Pyramid 9 at do.	29 53	ruined	2000
26 {	Pyramid base, or mere pyramidal platform, of Mustabat el Pharaoon	} 29 53	in steps	1950
27	Northern Brick Pyramid of Dashoor	29 49	51 20 25	1950
28	Northern Stone Pyramid of Dashoor	29 49	43 36 11	
29 {	Southern Stone Pyramid of Dashoor, with two successive slopes	} 29 48	{ 54 14 46 } { 42 59 26 }	
30	The Small Pyramid of Dashoor ..	29 48	50 11 41	
31 {	The Southern Brick Pyramid of Dashoor	} 29 48	57 20 2	1900
32	Northern Pyramid of Lisht	29 38	ruinous	1900
33	Southern Pyramid of Lisht	29 37	ruinous	
34 {	The False Pyramid, or that of Meydoon, flat-topped and in steps ; well built as mere masonry, but not as a monumentalization of angle, the casing-stones being inclined to the horizon	29 27	74 10 0	1850
35	Pyramid of Illahoon	29 17	ruinous	
36	Pyramid of Howara	29 18	ruinous	
37 {	Pyramid 1 of Biahmoo, with two successive slopes	} 29 26	{ 63 30 0 } { 50 (?) }	
38 {	Pyramid 2 of Biahmoo, with two successive slopes	} 29 26	{ 63 30 0 } { 50 (?) }	1800
	(See Plate IV. for the Jeezeh Pyramids ; and see Plate V. for all the others.)			

Of the Earliest Pyramid.

But the above table requires to be compared with some special Egyptological authorities, so that the reader may be assured of having all the truest things that the best of those gentlemen can say on their side against it.

Let us refer, therefore, to Dr. Lepsius's folio book entitled "Königsbuch der Alten Aegypter," Berlin, 1858. Like all Dr. Lepsius's works, it is sterling in its way ; and both the drawing and engraving of the seventy-three large plates it contains are inimitable for

their excellence in reproducing the most exact fac-
similes of the very clever and minute drawing of the
ancient Egyptians, as condensed in the hieroglyphic
" Cartouches," or names of their kings in a circum-
scribing oval. Each of the seventy-three plates contains five rows of cartouches, and in each row there
may be five to ten of these peculiar signatures ; and
how carefully executed, may be judged of by our Plate
XVIII., which is a reduced copy by photo-lithography
of one of Dr. Lepsius's.

In the course of that plate will be seen several
instances of the symbol of a Pyramid, viz. a triangle
with a base to it ; and our first object should be to
ascertain by the testimony pure and simple of the
greatest Egyptologist of our age, when that symbol
first appears in, at all events *his* idea of, Egyptian
history.

The first four plates of the book contain the cartouches of the dynasties of the so-called Gods, before
men began to reign in Egypt.

The next fifteen plates contain the cartouches of the
first sixteen dynasties of human kings, beginning with
Menes of Dynasty I., and representing the chief part of
those dynasties whose chronology by various authorities
is attempted to be shown in the table on our page 491.
They are, moreover, generally known amongst Egyptologists as being the dynasties of " the Old Empire " of
Egypt, and their architectural remains are found chiefly
near Memphis and Jeezeh.

Then follow thirty-one plates, with the cartouches of
kings of dynasties seventeen to thirty-one, or of " the
New Empire " ; and extending from those who reigned
in Abydos, and then at Thebes, down to the destruction
of the native Egyptian royal line, and the accession of
Persian kings after the conquest of the country by
Cambyses.

Next appear ten plates, after the Grecian conquest of the country by Alexander the Great, of the cartouches of the line of the Ptolemys, Macedonian kings in Egypt.

After these come seven plates of Roman Emperors' names, coined by Egyptian priests into very complicated hieroglyphics as duly flattering the then non-resident lords of the country.

Finally, there are six plates of cartouches of various collateral branches of kings, not very ancient, and having their abode chiefly at Meroe and Barkal in Ethiopia.

When these cartouches have been copied from stone monuments erected by the very kings concerned, they are trustworthy; but not a few of them are derived from compilations of Scribes of long-subsequent times, especially from that ragged fragment of Egyptian writing, the notorious " Turin papyrus," as it is called now, merely from the city which at present possesses it. But where the cartouches of the dynasties of the gods were obtained from, is mysterious; for, in the true Egyptian monumental manner, some of these signatures should have been found on their tombs : but there are no tombs of the gods who lived before men known in Egypt, any more than monuments erected by them during their lives. And after carefully looking through all the four plates containing their alleged signatures and titles, I can confidently say that in so far no one, not even the greatest modern Egyptologist, ever accused one of *those* gods of erecting a Pyramid in Egypt,—for no such symbol appears there for them.

We are thus handed on to the fifteen plates of cartouches of human kings of the Old Empire, in our search for the Pyramid symbol; and the first of these plates is represented on our Plate XVIII. Wherefore the reader can assist us in testifying that no Pyramid symbol appears in the first dynasty beginning with

Menes ; nor in the second dynasty, nor in the third dynasty.

The symbol is first seen in the fourth dynasty under the name of Xufu, or Cheops, of Memphis, the almost universally allowed king, in whose time the Great Pyramid was built ; and whose cartouche *has* been found daubed in red paint by the workmen, as a " quarry mark " of the period, on some of the interior blocks of its constructive masonry.

After Cheops the Pyramid symbol was also used by

Shafra	of the	4th	Dynasty at	Memphis.
Uesurkef	,,	5th	,,	,,
Tatkara	,,	5th	,,	,,
Ati	,,	6th	,,	Elephantine.
Pepi	,,	6th	,,	,,
Auxues Mia	,,	6th	,,	,,
Mereura	,,	6th	,,	,,
Nofrekara	,,	6th	,,	,,
Teta	,,	6th	,,	,,
Asesa	,,	7th	,,	Memphis.
Amunehmat	,,	12th	,,	Thebes.

But after these very early kings, no others of the Old Empire used the Pyramid symbol. Neither is it once found in all the thirty-one plates of the New Empire, nor amongst the ten plates of the Ptolemys, nor the seven plates of the Roman Emperors, nor among the six concluding plates up to the latest of the Ethiopian kings.

This review, then, sufficiently establishes our position, so far as Dr. Lepsius is concerned, that the Great Pyramid commenced the fashion of Pyramid building in Egypt ; but that that fashion did not last very long.

But still more precise particulars about the Pyramid builders are given by another great Egyptologist of our time, Dr. Brugsch by name in Germany, Brugsch Bey by title in Egypt, where he now resides ; and whence the following particulars were kindly sent me by

Dr. Grant, of Cairo, in 1874, as copied from the then latest edition of Brugsch Bey's "History of Ancient Egypt":—

"The Pyramids were built chiefly in the district of Memphis, and the name of that city was expressed by a hieroglyphic group, including the figure of a Pyramid, sounding *Men-nofer*, and meaning the 'the good station.'

"Senofru, the Ameliorator, was the last king of the third dynasty. It is *supposed* he caused the Pyramid of Meidoun to be built. At any rate, it is said a Pyramid was built under this king, and was named 'the Pyramid of sunrise,' or 'of the fête,' or 'of the crown'; and it is now being looked for. This is all that is mentioned about Pyramids before the time of Cheops.

"Xufu, Cheops, first king of the fourth dynasty, succeeded Senofru, the last king of the third dynasty, and built a Pyramid called *Xut*, 'the splendid' (assumed by Baron Bunsen to have been the second Pyramid of Jeezeh, but by all the rest of the world to be the Pyramid now called the Great Pyramid).

"Xafra, Cephren, built a Pyramid distinguished by the name *Ur*, 'the Great' (assumed by Baron Bunsen to have been the Pyramid *now* called 'the Great Pyramid,' though all other authorities consider it to be the one now called 'the Second Pyramid of Jeezeh').

"Men-kau-ra, Mencheres, or Mycerinus: his Pyramid (the third of the Jeezeh Pyramids) is designated in the hieroglyphics, *Hir*, 'the Superior.'

"Sepseskaf, who succeeded Mencheres. His Pyramid has the monumental name *Gebeh*, 'the Refreshing.'

"Us-kaf, the Ousercheres of Manetho, king of the fifth dynasty. His Pyramid was distinguished by the name *Ab-setu*, 'the pure of places,' or 'the purest place.'

"Sahu-ra, the successor of Us-kaf. His Pyramid was discovered to the north of Abousir. It is called *Xa-ba*, 'sunrise of the soul.'

" Nofer-ar-ka-ra. His Pyramid is called *Ba*, 'the soul.'

" Ra-n-user, one of the successors of the above. His Pyramid is known by the name *Men-setu*, 'the most stable place.'

" Men kau hor. His Pyramid is called *Nuter-setu*, 'the holiest place.'

" His successor Assa built a Pyramid called *Nofer*, 'beautiful.'

" The last king of the fifth dynasty, Unas, built a Pyramid called *Nofer-setu*, 'the most beautiful place,' or 'the best place.'

" Teta, the first king of the sixth dynasty, and the first to be styled Sa-ra, ' son of the sun,' in the interior of his cartouche. His Pyramid was named *Tat-setu*, 'the most stable of places.'

" King Ati built a Pyramid called *Bai-u*, ' souls.'

" King Pepi built a Pyramid called *Men-nofer*, ' the good station.'

" King Mer-en-ra built a Pyramid called *Xa-nofer*, ' the good rising.'

" King Nofer-ka-ra built a Pyramid called *Men-aux*, ' station of life.'

" King Mentu-hotep built a Pyramid called *Xu-setu*, ' the most splendid place.'

All these were of the sixth dynasty.

" In the Hyksos dynasty, supposed to be the twelfth, King Amen-em-at built a Pyramid called *Ka-nofer*, ' the high and beautiful.' "

This is the last about Pyramids obligingly furnished to me me out of Brugsch Bey's last edition of his " History of Egypt " ; and it coincides on the whole admirably with the Pyramid cartouches of Lepsius, as to the early appearance of the Great Pyramid of Jeezeh, amongst the other Pyramids. Wherefore, when we read in a less trusty book, by n extra zealous, but very

new, Egyptologist,* the remark : " It has been asserted
that the Great Pyramid, and that one only of the many
constructed, as old as, or older than, itself, &c., &c."—
he may simply be relegated to learn his Egyptian
wisdom a little better.

Rude Stone Monuments.

But though there are thus proved, even by the opposite party, to be exceedingly few relics to be gathered
out of all *profane* Egypt, either to dispute the antiquity
of the Great Pyramid, or to show that the native
Egyptians were aware of that one building having anything so peculiar in its construction, as to place it in
quite a different category to the others as to number,
weight, and measure ;—another class of Archæologists
than those of Egyptology, has arisen up of late, whose
members roundly declare that certain rude stone monuments of *Europe* are much more ancient, and scientific
too, than the Great Pyramid of Jeezeh.

Being anxious to get up whatever has been written

* The above author is Mr. James Bonwick, and the book quoted his
" Egyptian Belief and Modern Thought," at p. 306. A previous work
of his is entitled " Pyramid Facts and Fancies." In one sense he is a
very able man, for he has written, in a surprisingly short time, nearly a
dozen other books, three of them at little more than three months' intervals. They are chiefly on Australia and Tasmania, sometimes the early
history of these colonies, sometimes tales of bush-rangers' exploits or
works of imagination, interspersed with his own experiences as an Inspec-
tor of Schools in Victoria, Australia. But in the Great Pyramid subject
he is a most dangerous hand, professing the utmost respect for its Inspiration theory, though struggling all the time to overthrow it ; and by the
method of virtually turning the building upside down, to stand unsteadily
on its apex if it can, instead of on its broad base. This being effected in
every department, by following up a statement, seldom perfect, of the
latest and best measures, by older and worse ones ; and finally by the
very oldest and most absurd fancies, of mere visionaries ; as though they
were the final outcome after all, of everything that had been ascertained
for certain, up to the present hour : or was ever likely to be ascertained.
Though so long at the Antipodes, he is evidently a born Egyptologist of
the old world, in sentiment ; and I see no prospect of his ever being
anything else.

on that side, it was with surprising delight that, after reading many other older works, I recently came across Mr. James Fergusson's lately published fourth volume of his grand " History of Architecture"; which volume is specially entitled, and devoted to, precisely such " Rude Stone Monuments "; and is abundantly descriptive of rough Cyclopean stone circles, such as Stonehenge, Avebury, Stanton-Drew, &c., and of all the occasional rows, or groups, of stones which, however rough, have evidently been brought to their places and set up by the hand of man, and are now known as dolmens, kistvaens, menhirs, cromlechs, trilithons, &c., &c., both in Europe, Asia, and Africa.

Mr. Fergusson, indeed, differs widely from many of the Archæologists I have mentioned, as to the great *age* of most of these erections ; for after brushing away the dust of supposed prehistoric, and with some persons even geologic, ages of antiquity; and after disestablishing the Druids from temples they were only theoretically promoted to, long after they had disappeared from the surface of the earth under the sword of the Romans—he successfully shows that the dates of all the chief examples of these rough and rude stone, or stone and earth, structures, are certainly confined within periods of from 300 to 900 A.D. In so far, then, the able architectural writer of those pages had no occasion in *that* book to allude to the Great Pyramid of the vastly earlier date of 2170 B.C. ; I therefore opened my eyes very widely indeed on finding in one of the notes, not only that the Great Pyramid *was* alluded to, but that the mention was made specially for the purpose of ridiculing the whole of the modern scientific and sacred theory with regard to it !

However, objections to a new theory by a really able man, usually have something worthy of attention in them ; and when they are printed and published to the

world by such a house as that of John Murray, of Albe-
marle Street, London, they *must* be attended to. As,
moreover, I have throughout the present work endeavoured to give the reader a full and fair account of both
sides of the question, I trust to be excused for going
into the present first-class attack upon it rather carefully.

Under pretended and speciously professed cover, then,
of following, and faithfully carrying out the method of
the modern Great Pyramid scientific theorists, Mr.
Fergusson demurely speaks of the size of his rude
stone circles being, as a rule, either 100 feet, or 100
mètres, in diameter, circles.

Whatever may be said for the feet, of course Mr.
Fergusson understands, and no one better, that the old
circle builders would not have had any modern French
mètre standard of linear measure among them; but he
asserts that such a standard is what legitimately comes
out when the present-day scientific Great Pyramid
methods of theorizing are applied to good measures
of the size of his mediæval stone circles; and that he
thereby not only obtains in a most dazzling manner a
short and easy method of classing his favourite relics,
but also of reducing to absurdity whatever has recently
been written for the sacred and scientific character of
the Great Pyramid, which he is not friendly to at all.
And yet he is so mortally afraid of his established
character being injured, forsooth, in London society,
by any one possibly supposing that he has admitted
the truth of the smallest part of the said sacred and
scientific theory, merely because he has touched on it,
contemptuously and derisively,—that although he has
" Piazzi Smyth his theories " in his index, — yet the
subject-matter so alluded to does not appear in the
large and readable letterpress of Mr. Fergusson's book
at all, but only in the almost invisible small print of a

note; and even then with the following bashful apology for so old and popular an author as himself:—

"I am almost afraid to allude to it, even in a note, lest any one should accuse me of founding any theory upon it, like Piazzi Smyth's British inches in the Pyramids, but it is a curious coincidence that nearly all the British circles are set out in two dimensions. The smaller class are 100 feet, the larger are 100 mètres, in diameter. They are all more than 100 yards. The latter measure (mètres) is, at all events, certainly accidental, so far as we at present know, but as a nomenclature and *memoria technica*, the employment of the term may be useful, provided it is clearly understood that no theory is based upon it:" and there then follow throughout Mr. Fergusson's book his frequent allusions to the stone circles, as being either 100 feet, or 100 *mètre*, circles.

Now, though in the above extract I could not but be shocked at the learned architectural D.C.L.'s triple blunder of "*Piazzi Smyth's* discovery of *British inches* in the *Pyramids*";—in place of "*John Taylor's* discovery of *earth-commensurable inches* having been founded upon in the unique, primeval, Israelitic and anti-Egyptian design of the *one Great Pyramid;*" still I thought myself bound to accept, until the contrary had been proved, that the successful and really mighty writer on architecture of all ages and all countries, Mr. Fergusson, had really alighted on a very curious numerical coincidence, *having* the degree of closeness alone recognized in modern Great Pyramid mensurations and theorizing, amongst his rude stone circles. In which case, all honour to Mr. Fergusson, no matter what the consequences of his discovery might ultimately prove to be.

With the best desire, therefore, to appreciate the truth, if any, of the celebrated James Fergusson's self-announced remarkable *find*, I have noted one after another, as they came up, the following quoted measures of the stone circles, *out of his own book :—*

Page 51, chambered tumulus, stated, in diameter . =	24	feet.
„　55, "sacred" stone circle, by scale, in diameter =	80	„
„　62, great stone circle, stated, in diameter . =	1200	„
„　62, smaller circle, stated, in diameter . . =	350	„
„　62, still smaller, stated, in diameter . . . =	325	„
„　63, two interior circles, each by scale, in diameter . . . . . . =	150	„
„　75, stone circle, stated, in diameter . . . =	138 to 155	„
„　76,　　do.　　　　do. . . =	45 to 51	„
„　78, Silbury tumulus, stated, base diameter . =	552	„
„　78,　　do.　　do.　　　top diameter . =	102	„
„　85, mound, stated, diameter . . . =	198	„
„　124, stone circle, stated, diameter . . . =	60	„
„　124,　　do.　　　do.　　. . . =	50	„
„　127,　　do.　　　do.　　. . . =	330	„
„　139, circular platform, stated, diameter . . =	167	„
„　139, rampart, stated, circumference ÷ π . . =	261	„
„　140, stone circle, by scale, diameter . . . =	140	„
„　141, tumulus, stated, diameter . . . . =	70 to 80	„
„　146, oval ring, stated, diameter . . . . =	156 to 243	„
„　149, stone circle, stated, diameter . . . =	345 to 378	„
„　149,　　do.　　　do.　　. . . =	129	„
„　149,　　do.　　　do.　　. . . =	96	„
„　158, cist circle, by scale, diameter . . . =	55	„
„　160, stone circle　　do.　　. . . =	160	„
„　160,　　do.　　　do.　　. . . =	102	„
„　161,　　do.　　　do.　　. . . =	80	„
„　161,　　do.　　　do.　　. . . =	63	„
„　161,　　do.　　　do.　　. . . =	57	„
„　161,　　do.　　　do.　　. . . =	50	„
„　161,　　do.　　　do.　　. . . =	40	„
„　182,　　do.　　　do.　　. . . =	120	„
„　182,　　do.　　　do.　　. . . =	80	„
„　182,　　do.　　　do.　　. . . =	60	„
„　182,　　do.　　　do.　　. . . =	40	„
„　194, oval mound　　do.　　. . . =	430 to 550	„
„　194, curved mound, by scale, diameter . . =	140	„
„　194, circular mound　　do.　　. . . =	110	„
„　194,　　do.　　　do.　　. . . =	75	„
„　202, stone circle, stated, diameter . . . =	333	„
„　214,　　do.　　　do.　　. . . =	116	„
„　228, circular, rampart　do.　　. . . =	580	„
„　241, stone circle　　do.　　. . . =	340	„
„　241,　　do.　　　do.　　. . . =	104 .	„
„　259,　　do.　　　do.　　. . . =	60 to 100	„
„　259,　　do.　　　do.　　. . . =	42	„
„　262,　　do.　　　do.　　. . . =	60	„
„　264,　　do.　　　do.　　. . . =	46	„
„　266, tumulus　　do.　　. . . =	70	„
„　266, stone circle　do.　　. . . =	100	„
„　266, tumulus　　do.　　. . . =	50	„
„　266, stone circle　do.　　. . . =	80	„

Now when we perceive here, that out of more than fifty of Mr. Fergusson's own examples, only one of them measures 100 feet, and not one of them 100 mètres (equal to 328·09 feet), and that the remainder vary from 24 to 1,200 feet in diameter,—it is pretty plain that instead of upsetting everything that has been recently made out for the Great Pyramid, he has only furnished to the world a positive proof that he, James Fergusson, Esquire, however strong he may be in other subjects, must have some very peculiar ideas touching exactness of measures and closeness of numbers.

But, that is not all.

The General Architectural Facts of the Great Pyramid.

In his p. 31, speaking of the Great Pyramid professionally (and because professionally with him, learnedly, authoritatively and admirably), Mr. Fergusson allows it to be "the most perfect and gigantic specimen of masonry that the world has yet seen"; and that, according to mere human methods of development and all rationalistic theories of progression, almost infinite myriads of years must have intervened between the first rude tumuli, or stone sepulchres erected, or which he believes were, or should have been, erected in Egypt, and the building of *such* a Pyramid.

But in that case there ought to be vastly more stone monuments in Egypt, representing the work of men *before* the day of the Great Pyramid, than *after* it; especially as in the dry Egyptian climate, we are told again and again that "nothing decays"; and then comes the stunning announcement, both from Mr. Fergusson, Dr. Lepsius, and every good Egyptologist, that however multitudinous may be the Egyptian monuments *after* the Great Pyramid, there are *no* monuments at all in and throughout Egypt older than the Great Pyramid. The Great Pyramid, therefore, according to all the known facts of the longest-known country on the face of the earth, led off the art of stone architecture in Egypt in a *sudden* uprise to excellency, or a totally different manner from all human experience of what always is, and must be, when man works by his own powers alone, unassisted by direct Divine inspiration.

Of this most astounding, and humanly unexplainable, abyss of nothing whatever of architectural remains before, but an abundant train after, the majestic Great Pyramid—Mr. Fergusson says in another foot-note, "It is so curious as almost to justify Piazzi Smyth's wonderful theories on the subject."

And what does Mr. Fergusson therefore do? Does he consent in any degree to the cogency of these, as well as all the other, facts of his own architectural science, and his own still more peculiar methods of philosophizing upon them in order to elicit from the monuments the mental history of man; and confess, that so far as they go, they do lead to nothing less than a Divine intervention in the history of men having here occurred in the primeval times of the human race; to the end that this, even still unequalled, glory of building, the Great Pyramid, appeared *suddenly* on the stage of history; as when the Lord says through Isaiah (xlviii. 3), "I did them suddenly, and they came to pass"?

Nothing of the kind. The unhappy, though in so many respects finely gifted, but rationalistically predestined, and predetermined, man merely wraps his mantle of prejudice more tightly than ever around him; and agonizingly exclaims—"But there is no reason whatever to suppose that the progress of art in Egypt differed essentially from that elsewhere. The previous examples are lost, and that seems all."

That all, indeed! Why, that is admitting every-thing; and implies the destruction and total disap-pearance, without leaving a wrack behind in the most preservative of all climates, of more old architecture than is now standing on the surface of the whole globe: and the admission may further worthily include what Mr. Fergusson nowhere allows (though the Great Pyramid scholars do), viz. the truth of the Noachic Deluge, the dispersion of mankind according to the Bible, and the original, innate wickedness and lost state of even the best human heart, if trusting to itself alone.

The Great Sphinx.

And now it may be remarked by some anxious readers, that though I have said so much about the Great Pyramid, and something, at least in the many tabular representations in Chap. III., IV., and XXI., touching almost every other Pyramid in Egypt also,— I have said nothing about the Sphinx.

That was just what the reviewers wrote against Pro-fessor Greaves after the publication of his " Pyramido-graphia," 230 years ago. Though, indeed, one of his querists presently answers himself by supposing that the Professor must have found at the place, that the said Sphinx, with its long recumbent animal body, had in reality no connection with the Great Pyramid.

Exceedingly right, too, was the critic in that supposi-tion; for not only has the oval of a king, 1,000 years and several dynasties later than the Great Pyramid, been found unexceptionably upon the Sphinx*—but that monster, an idol in itself, with symptoms typifying the lowest mental organization, reeks with idolatry throughout the built portion of its substance. For

* See Colonel Howard-Vyse's " Pyramids of Ghizeh," Vol. III. Plates, and pages 107—117 of Appendix.

when the fragments or component masses of its colossal stone beard were discovered in the sand excavations of 1817, behold, all the internally joining surfaces of the blocks had been figured full of the idol gods of the most profane and Cainite Egypt.

Strange, therefore, that Dean Stanley's ecclesiastic eye should have positively admired so soul-repulsive a creature; "with," as he himself further and more objectively describes, "its vast projecting wig, its great ears, and the red colour still visible on its cheeks;" reminding others more of the great *red* dragon of Revelation, the chosen symbol for a Pagan Empire : and yet he calls it an *appropriate* guardian to the white-stoned Sethite, and eminently anti-Cainite, Great Pyramid; whose pure and witnessing surface of blameless form eschews every thought of idolatry and sin.

The Recent Discovery about the Sphinx.

But the reign of the Great Sphinx, over the souls of some men, is not over yet.

Long since I had remarked that there is no agreement possible between the Great Sphinx and the Great Pyramid. Those who admire the one, cannot appreciate, and rather war against, the other.

So it was given lately to a pure Egyptologist, quite anti-Pyramidal in sentiment,—the eminent Mariette Bey, to set the whole of his world alight (for a time) with a supposed monumental proof that the Sphinx, instead of belonging, as hitherto so generally supposed, to the 11th or 15th dynasty, was far older than the Great Pyramid in the 4th dynasty ; and was, in fact, so ancient, that it had become an object of dilapidated, but revered, antiquity in the times of King Cheops himself; who immortalised his name, in his very primeval day, by repairing it.

The latest description of this case that I have seen, by Mariette Bey himself, is at p. 211 of the fourth edition of his " Catalogue of the Museum of Egyptian Antiquities at Boulak."

No. 581 is there spoken of as "a fragmentary stone which may be *supposed* to have formed once part of a wall of a certain building, or temple; some problematical ruins only of which have been found near one of the small Pyramids on the east side of the Great Pyramid." The stone is abundantly inscribed with little hieroglyphics; " in good preservation, but of *mediocre style*," euphuistically puts in Mariette Bey,—though " *more like scratches than anything else*," writes my plain-speaking friend, Dr. Grant, of Cairo.

This circumstance of bad, or of no, style, or of an idle modern scribble in place of a serious piece of deep and well-performed ancient sculpture which, wherever found, carries great weight with it in monumental research,—is not represented in the version of the inscription given with honour (and with well-cut, London, hieroglyphic types, drawn by the late accomplished artist, Joseph Bonomi, from other models) by Dr. Samuel Birch (of the British Museum) in the last volume of Bunsen's " Egypt's Place in History." The Doctor, moreover, looks only to one possible interpretation *of them*, and adopts that with positivism. No wonder either, in some respects; for a great day it must have been for the idolatry of old Egypt and its latter day, not worshippers, oh no! only sympathetic, philosophic admirers, when Mariette Bey first published his discovery of this astonishing inscription. There is good news in it for almost every one of the Mizraite false gods; so that all profanely devout Egyptologic readers may learn with thrilling interest, that the images of the hawk of Horus and the ibis of Thoth, in that problematical temple, of which this single stone may be *supposed* to have once formed a part, were of wood gilt; the boat of the "three times beautiful Isis" was in gilt wood with incrustations of jewels; that the principal statue of Isis was in gold and silver; the statue of Nephthys in bronze gilt, and &c. &c., as to many other ordinary idols; but surpassing words of admiration and adoration were added touching the Great Sphinx of Horem-Kou, the biggest idol of all, and declared to be situated just to the south of the "Temple of Isis, the Ruler of the Great Pyramid."

On showing this version of the inscription to Mr. Osburn, he instantly pronounced it to be an anachronism; the writing had, he said, nothing to do *contemporaneously* with Cheops, or the 4th dynasty either; it was merely a rigmarole by certain revivifiers of the ancient Egyptian idolatry, with additions, under the late 26th dynasty.

But William Osburn was a firm believer in the Divine inspiration of the Bible, and the rebellious human origin of the Egyptian gods; that they had even been invented, as very refuges of lies, in slavish fear of, but determined Cainite opposition to, the God of Heaven; whose supernatural acts in the Deluge and Dispersion were then recent and overwhelming to the human mind, rendering atheism in that day perfectly impossible to even the least reasonable being. Wherefore the most far-gone of the modern Egyptological scholars utterly refused to attend to *his*, Osburn's, condemnation of Mariette's wonderful stone; and preferred to go on trusting themselves entirely to its reputed statements for the implied profane nature of "the Great Pyramid, ruled over by Madame Isis," though no symptoms of either that lady or any other profanity had been found there; and though the ancient Great Pyramid is still an existency in the world, vocal with knowledge and wisdom, while the far later invention of the feminine Isis has long since faded away from the Egyptian mind like a summer cloud or the morning dew.*

At last, however, one of their own number has informed upon his fellow-Egyptologists ;. and he is the best and ablest man amongst them too ; viz. the German Brugsch Bey ; equally on the spot with Mariette Bey, and said to be " a more learned hieroglyphic scholar." For thus writes the trusty Dr. Grant from Cairo, date June 3rd, 1873 :—" I have been learning much from Brugsch Bey lately, and he tells me that Mariette's Sphinx-temple stone *bears a lie on the face of it*—that the style of sculpture is not very ancient, and that the whole inscription is simply a legend that has been scratched upon it at a late date, and that it cannot be quoted as an authority on any of the points mentioned in it."

Since then too, or in the present year 1879, the author of a new London book called " A Ride in Egypt," claiming to understand hieroglyphics well (though certainly knowing nothing of modern Pyramidology, which he is continually and most absurdly abusing)—confirms most thoroughly the non-authenticity of " the Stela of the Sphinx " ; and attributes the statue itself (though not some possibly earlier rough-shaping of the natural rock, of which the chief part is still composed) to so late an Egyptian Dynasty as the 18th.

So now that Sphinx, with its body pierced through and through with long iron rods by Colonel Howard-Vyse forty years ago, and found to be merely solid rock ; and its sculptured nose knocked off by a mediæval

---

* But the wave of idolatrous idea once excited from Egypt, as a centre, is travelling still over other lands ; so that in his recent work on Cyprus Mr. Hepworth Dixon describes meeting there with so-called Christian priests of the " Orthodox" Greek Church, wearing the peculiar conical cap of the ancient priests of the Syrian representative of Isis, Astarte ; and declaring it impious, drawing down a judgment from heaven, for any woman in Cyprus to milk a cow ;—apparently in remembrance of the sacred cow-form of Isis, in the ancient Egyptian pantheon.

Mohammedan dervish, to prevent its both ensnaring his countrymen by idolatrous beauty, and leading them to inquire too curiously (as Moses warned the Israelites against their attempting to do, on entering Canaan),— "now *how* did the people of this land worship their gods?" because the next idea of their minds would be, "for so will we do likewise";—and with its actual bulk a mere molecule at the very base of the hill, of whose summit the Great Pyramid is the pure and unexceptionable crown—that wretched Sphinx, I repeat,—being nothing but the grossest form of the worst, but by no means the oldest, period of Egyptian idolatry,—need not be referred to again by any Anglo-Saxon, or Israelite, Christian man, woman, or child, looking for religious instruction to the Biblical Rock of Ages alone.

CHAPTER XXII.

THE SHEPHERD KINGS,

The Architect of the Great Pyramid; and the Deluge Date.

Of certain Human Remains found at the Third Pyramid of Jeezeh.

IN the Third Pyramid of Jeezeh—admired by the sadly Egyptological Baron Bunsen, on account of its expensive red-granite casing, and because its hieroglyphic name amongst the old Egyptian idolaters was HIR, "the Superior," far above the Great Pyramid and all *its* intellectual excellencies—Colonel Howard-Vyse found, not only the genuine sepulchral, dark grey stone, sarcophagus, rich in carvings and adornments, like a miniature Egyptian temple in itself (afterwards lost at sea off the coast of Spain) together with parts of the carved, painted and inscribed coffin-board, but—a portion of a mummy as well.

In that case, of what, or of whom, was such mummified fragment, the very remain?

"Of King Mencheres," instantly insisted every Egyptologist, "for he, Men-kau-ra, Mencheres, or Mycerinus, it was, who built the Third Pyramid some 60 years after the Great one had been erected." Whereupon the remains were transmitted with honour to the British Museum; and the learned Baron, in his "Egypt's Place in History," has an eloquent eulogium on the "pious" king whose ancient remains, if removed at last out of their old mausoleum, are now vastly safer in the distant isle of the Queen-ruled empire whose free institutions continually preserve her liberty and renew her prosperity, than ever they were before, in the Egyptian central land and his own strong Pyramid therein.

But here William Osburn (whom Bunsen never liked) steps in with the wholesome reminder, that none of the mummies really of the Old Empire have come down to our age; their bodies, fragrant for awhile with spices and myrrh, sooner or later returned, dust to dust; and a little of such powdery matter, dark in colour, at the bottom of sarcophagi, is all that has yet been discovered in any of the tombs of the earliest period. It was reserved, says he, to the over-clever Egyptians of the New Empire, when Thebes rose above Memphis, to discover the too efficacious method of embalming with natron—a method which has enabled the bodies of that later period to last down to our times; and has thereby put it into the power of fanatic Mohammedans to treat visibly and palpably Pharaonic corpses with every contumely; so that male and female, old and young, rich and poor, are dragged out of all their decent cerements, to be exposed in these latter days on the dunghill, to be utterly cursed as "Kaffirs," infidels, and dogs, or finally broken up for fuel.

Wherefore the parts of a particular body, anomalously found in pretty tough preservation, without either spices or natron, but dried only, by Colonel Vyse in the Third Pyramid, could not have belonged to either King Mencheres or any of his subjects: or to any genuine Egyptian so early as the fourth dynasty. But presently this further discovery was made, that the cloth in which the remains were wrapped up, and loosely, rather than genuinely bandaged, was not composed of the proverbial linen of ancient Egypt, but of sheep's wool,—a textile material which was a religious abomination to all Pharaonic Egyptians.

Then wrote certain scholars, quickly framing up a theory to suit the occasion, " Both King Mencheres and all the other Jeezeh Pyramid builders must have been, not Egyptians, but of that ancient and most mysterious class of invaders of, or immigrants into, ancient Egypt, the Hyksos, or Shepherd Kings."

How little is positively known of *them*, may appear from one modern author, who writes,—

" When investigating the early history of the world, the Hyksos cross our path like a mighty shadow ; advancing from native seats to which it baffled the geography of antiquity to assign a position, covering for a season the shores of the Mediterranean and the banks of the Nile with the terror of their arms and the renown of their conquests, and at length vanishing with a mystery equal to that of their first appearance."

While the learned Dr. Hincks writes, " Later investigations have rather increased than removed my difficulties ; and, as a matter of argument, it would be indifferent to me to sustain, that the *Hyksos once occupied Lower Egypt ; or that they were never there at all.*"

A sad example this of primeval history as prepared for the world by purely literary men ; but Dr. Hincks was perhaps more of an Assyrian, than an Egyptian, scholar ; and the better Egyptologists, especially those who have travelled, and studied the larger Egyptian monuments *in situ*, have no doubt whatever about a period of Hyksos' rule in Egypt just before the time of the Israelites' captivity, and perhaps including a part of it. They consider, indeed, that there is still monumentally visible the most decided separation between the Old and New Empires of Ancient Egypt, caused altogether by the temporary domination just then of those whom they call the " Shepherds " ; for they drop the aggrandising word of "Kings," as needless, when talking of those who, if there at all, ruled on the banks of the Nile with a rod of iron through at least two successive dynasties, viz. the 15th and 16th; and caused an almost total blank or perversion for that period in the architectural history, as well as much modification in the religion, of all the Lower and Middle country.

Of the precise nature of that change and the origin of the party bringing it about, William Osburn has some special ideas, which, with more space at command, we might do well to inquire into; though now, as the limits of this book are drawing to a close, and as he agrees with nearly all the other Egyptologists as to what dynasties such party occupied, viz. the 15th, 16th, and perhaps part of the 17th,—we may rest assured that all men of those dynasties, whether they were native or foreign Shepherds, lived far too late in the world's history (viz. 300 to 400 years) to have had any hand in building the Jeezeh Pyramids under the much earlier fourth dynasty.

Hence the Shepherds whom Colonel Vyse alludes to (on the strength of the woollen-wrapped body from the Third Pyramid), if ever really existing, must have been, in order to have helped to build the Pyramids, of a period belonging to the said very early fourth dynasty; and were therefore earlier than, and totally different, in time and fact, from, all the later Shepherds so well known to Egyptologists.

That these *later*, or 15th, 16th, and 17th dynasty Shepherds did not build the Jeezeh, or indeed any of the Egyptian, Pyramids, does not by itself overthrow the whole theory, or possibility of there having been *a much earlier*, and quite distinct, Shepherd invasion, or temporary rule of Hyksos in Lower Egypt, and perhaps even during the 4th, or chief Pyramid-building, dynasty; for pastoral tribes existed in the East from the remotest times, and were much endued with tendencies to western emigration. But whether they really did enter Egypt in force during the 4th dynasty, must be settled on direct evidence of its own. Such evidence, indeed, the worthy Colonel *thought* he had obtained; though now we may see clearly that his reasoning was founded too much on the piece of flannel, and too little on the whole of the grand masonried facts of the Great Pyramid and their purity from *all* idolatry, no matter whether of Egyptians or any other of the then existing peoples of the world; whereupon he soon loses himself in illogical conclusions; arguing in a preconceived circle, thus :—

"It has been assumed (in my, Howard-Vyse's, opinion satisfactorily) by Bryant, that these mighty Shepherds (his supposed Pyramid builders in the 4th dynasty) were the descendants of Ham, expelled, on account of apostasy and rebellion, from Babel, from Egypt, and from Palestine; and who afterwards, under the name of Cyclopes, Pelasgi, Phœnices, &c., were pursued by Divine vengeance, and successively driven from every settled habitation—from Greece, from Tyre, and from Carthage, even to the distant regions of America, where traces of their buildings, and, it has been supposed, of their costume, as represented in Egyptian sculpture, have been discovered. These tribes seem formerly to have been living instances of Divine retribution, as the dispersed Jews are at present. They appear to have been at last entirely destroyed; but their wanderings and misfortunes have been recorded by the ever-living genius of the two greatest poets in the Greek and Latin languages; and the Pyramids remain, enduring yet silent monuments of the matchless grandeur of this extraordinary people, of the certainty of Divine justice, and of the truth of Revelation."

But while it is perfectly impossible that such sinful men could have been the genuine and original authors of all the pure and holy features we have found in the one, almost if not quite Israelitic, Great Pyramid,—or that Hamitic Cainites would have found any difficulty in amalgamating with the Mizraite, and also Hamitic Egyptians,—it is most satisfactory to know that the mere piece of woollen cloth found in the Third Pyramid can be explained in a much easier manner than by going up in the teeth of ancient masonried, and other physical facts, to the primeval antiquity of the world; or thus :—
" The remains found by Colonel Vyse were those of a mediæval Arab, who, having died at Caliph Al Mamoun's breaking into the Third Pyramid, was straightway wrapped up in his own burnouse, and thrust down the entrance-passage for his burial, when the Mohammedan workmen came away and closed the place up, as it turned out, for 1,000 years. And if the poor man's bones are so well preserved as to have allowed of their safe transport to London, it is on account of the short time they have been sepultured, compared with anything belonging to the real fourth dynasty and the building of *its* Pyramids."

Of Primeval Shemite Shepherds.

That simple explanation, therefore, completely settles the value of the mistaken Egyptological lumber on the shelves at the British Museum ; but leaves us still with an historical question on our hands, as to whether there were, after all, any Hyksos, or Shepherd Kings, from the East, descendants, too, of Shem, rather than Ham (for of Hamites there were always enough and to spare, keepers of their own sheep too, in the persons of the Egyptians themselves), in Egypt during the fourth dynasty ?

Some strangers from the eastern direction were, indeed, continually filtering into Lower Egypt through the Isthmus of Suez, the natural channel of immigration in all ages from Asia, and the path by which the Egyptians themselves had originally come.   But it is our more particular business now to ascertain, if possible, whether during the period of that particular fourth dynasty, say from 2300 to 2100 B.C. (or an age, distinctly and certainly, long previous to the calling of Abraham), there were any remarkable Eastern men in position of lordly rule or trusted power, or any notoriety in the Egyptian land. Were there, for instance, any notable Shemites ever there, before Abraham and before Joseph? and if so, let us inquire whether they either had, in the general estimation of all men, anything to do with the building of the Great Pyramid; or were likely to have been able to furnish any part of its design, as now being manifested by modern science?   And especially, had they any direct interest in preserving that Pyramid's religiously pure character, in the midst of an age and a nation given up to the worst forms of idolatry?

What, then, does history say to the point ?

History is scanty enough, every one will allow, for all times before Abraham; and though something may be occasionally made out for even those dates in such a land as Egypt, it is to be gained, even there, only by a conflict with difficulties.   There is actually a dispute, for instance, between the Egyptologists on one side, and Alexandrian-Greek classics on the other, whether there was ever a fourth dynasty at all; or whether the Kings, whose names the former party puts into that early dynasty, and supposed exclusive Memphian locality, did not live at Thebes, as Theban kings, and *after* other known members of the certainly very late 18th dynasty.   We must, therefore, when everything is disputed or disputable, interrogate either party very closely.

Egyptologic Details of Early Kings.

To begin with the Egyptologists: the literary foundations for what they assert of such far earlier days as
those of the building of the Great Pyramid, are confined to Manetho (270 B.C.), or to what has come down
to us of his own writings, in remnants of other authors
300 or 400 years later still; and whose words may be
conveniently examined in the valuable, though terse
(and terse because there was nothing else quotable for
very early times) volume of "Fragments," by Isaac
Preston Cory, of Caius College, Cambridge (1832 A.D.).

There then, most undoubtedly, a fourth dynasty is
mentioned; but it begins with a puzzling statement;
for while the third dynasty is simply said to be composed of so many Memphite kings, and the fifth dynasty
of so many Elephantine kings, this fourth dynasty is
stated to be composed of "eight Memphite kings of *a
different race.*"

This is a curious statement, and I do not know what
it precisely means; but the list proceeds as follows for
the kings concerned:—

    (1) Soris reigned 29 years.
    (2) Suphis reigned 63 years. He built the largest Pyramid; which
Herodotus says was constructed by Cheops. He was arrogant towards
the gods, and wrote the sacred book; which is regarded by the Egyptians
as a work of great importance.
    (3) Suphis II. reigned 66 years.
    (4) Mencheres 63 years.
    (5) Rhatœses 25 years.
    (6) Bicheres 22 years.
    (7) Sebercheres 7 years.
    (8) Thampthis 9 years.
Altogether 284 years.

This literary foundation the Egyptologists further
contend that they can confirm in all its main particulars from the monuments; by finding, even in the
Great Pyramid itself, evidently alluded to by Manetho,

rude original quarry-marks with two royal names, which they interpret Shofo and Noumshofo, and declare to be the two Suphises mentioned above; while they find the further royal name of Mencheres in the Third Pyramid, notoriously a later construction than both the Great and Second Pyramids; which Second Pyramid is elsewhere attributed to Suphis II., as the Great one is here to Suphis I.

But the rest of the sentence attached to the name of the first Suphis is a difficulty which the Egyptologists cannot altogether master. They can understand, for instance, easily enough, that he either built the Great Pyramid, or reigned while it was being built; but what was his "arrogance towards the gods"? and what were the contents of "his sacred book"?

Of all these things the Egyptologists know nothing from contemporary monuments; although they can adduce abundant proof therefrom, that Mencheres of the Third Pyramid was an out-and-out idolater of the most confirmed Egyptian type. This was the "piety" which Baron Bunsen praised; while Osburn, though he very seriously condemned, rather than praised, so far allowed what the other Egyptologists founded upon,—that he shows, at much length, King Mencheres to have been, —not indeed the original inventor and theotechnist of animal and other gods for his countrymen,—but the greatest codifier in all history, and the chief organizer into systems, of those idolatrous things. He, Mencheres, was the establisher, too, of a state priesthood for those things' continual service; and was an immense extender of the Egyptian mythological arrangements into new and mysterious ramifications; the very man, in fact, who put Mizraite idolatry into that ensnaring form and artistical condition with the woman Isis, the man Osiris, the child Horus, the monster Typhon, Nephthys, and all the rest of his human-mind inventions, in addition to the older Apis and Mnevis, bulls, and the Mendesian goat, that it became the grand national and lasting system of his country,—monopolizing the souls of all Egyptians for two thousand years, and even then dying hard; besides making the Pharaohs the anti-Israel's-God-contending kings they ever after proved to be.

Mencheres was, in point of fact, in and for the land of the Nile, just what the too eloquent author of that most misleadingly named book, "Juventus Mundi," with such longing admiration amounting almost to ill-concealed envy, describes Homer, in a far later age, to have been for the Greeks in similar "theotechny"; or in making up, out of his own mind, with some assistance from old traditions, such an enticing set of gods and goddesses, demigods and nymphs of all degrees, that his countrymen took to them at once with enthusiasm, and their descendants have not even yet, though claiming to be Christians, freed themselves from some of their trammels. Wherefore, worldly success in that theotechnic line, ethereal art, or elevated occupation, as it is according to *him*, but much more probably an abomination before God,—the late English Prime Minister (unhappily not seeing it in that light) declares to be a far more noble, more satisfying pinnacle for human ambition, than any amount of excellence or proficiency whatever, either in poetry or prose, civil administration, or even military glory.

But let us steadily pursue our own far more ancient path of inquiry into primeval Eastern, as well as early Egyptian, life.

Of King Mencheres, of the Third Pyramid of Jeezeh, we know, as already indicated, far too much for his credit among any real believers in the Divine origin of the Christian religion, and the preparations Divinely made for it "from the beginning of the world." But of Shofo the hieroglyphists can pick up but little, if anything, positively of that debasing kind of information. The worship, indeed, of bulls and goats had been already set up in Egypt during the previous (the third) dynasty, so that he found it in force on succeeding to the throne. Wherefore the practice perhaps went on during his reign also, until at least such time as he is reported, amongst the idolaters and the sons of idolaters, —on one hand to have become "arrogant towards the gods"; and on the other, to have shamefully closed their temples and stopped their public worship; as we shall presently see detailed on turning to the *Classic* authorities.

Classic Names for Early Egyptian Kings.

Amongst all these classic authors, indeed—*i.e.* men who either were Greeks or followed the Greeks, and did not know Egyptian—whether with Herodotus in 445 B.C., Eratosthenes 236 B.C., Diodorus Siculus 60 B.C., and Strabo 0 B.C., there is no fourth dynasty at all: nor, for that matter, any allusion to any dynasty or arrangement by dynasties whatever. While the chronological order of the kings by name, is at one point altogether dislocated from its sequence in the Manethoan dynasties. The kings' names of the very early fourth dynasty of the Egyptologists, and with Pyramid building accompanying them, being, with the classicists, placed *after* those which are found in the comparatively late nineteenth dynasty of the same Egyptologists.

Sir Gardner Wilkinson* explains this terrible anachronism for Herodotus (and if for him, for all his copying fellow-countrymen and successors at the same time), by suggesting that he (Herodotus) was furnished by the Egyptian priests with two separate lists of kings' names;

---

* See note to p. 199 of Rawlinson's "Herodotus," Vol. II.

and as they read out to him (through his interpreter, he not understanding Egyptian) the later one first, why he, putting them all down in faith as he heard them in one long row, of course, got the old Memphite sovereigns coming in *after* the more modern Thebans. The priests began with those recent Theban kings of the 19th dynasty, because they were fresh in their memory; and they remembered well the glorious times of their priestly order under those reigns; whereof, too, they told the innocent Halicarnassian a variety of pleasant, gossiping tales; and only when that stock of stories was ended did they touch, very unwillingly, on the early Memphite kings, chiefly of the fourth dynasty, and described the hard times the priests had had under *them*.

Some such explanation, too, of the dislocated chronology of the *Greek-related* history of old Egypt, must apparently be the true one; for the whole philosophy of architecture, as elaborated on ten thousand examples by James Fergusson, architect, makes it as impossible historically and mechanically for the Pyramids of Lower Egypt to have followed the palace-temples and sculpture of Upper Egypt,—as historically, politically, and socially it is utterly impossible, that after Thebes had once risen to supreme power in Egypt, the rulers there would have allowed by far the chief work of their age to be executed on the borders of their kingdom, in the " provinces," or near the then ancient, decaying, and conquered city of Memphis. As well might we expect the British Parliament to give its largest grants for the year to Edinburgh, instead of London; and men will most assuredly have to wait until the whole river of history passes by, and runs itself absolutely dry, before we see such a phenomenon as that; although, too, Scotland was never fairly conquered; and deserves far better of London, than ever Memphis did of Thebes.

Setting aside, then, agreeably with Sir Gardner Wil-

kinson and *all the Egyptologists* this one large fault, or
mistaken order of a group of the Egyptian kings in
Greek and classic authors,—from Herodotus in 445
B.C., down to the Rev. Mr. Galloway and Mr. Samuel
Sharpe, in 1869 A.D.,—as simply and altogether a book-
mistake of theirs, we shall find in the smaller details,
subsequently to the dislocation date, much agreement.
As, for instance, in the names of the three successive
kings of the three chief and successive Pyramids of
Jeezeh; which kings' names are always given in their
proper, or both monumental, hieroglyphic, and Manethoan sequence to each other; though the scholars
have certainly agreed to accept a remarkable variety
of names as meaning the same word or man; as
thus :—

NAMES OF THE BUILDERS OF THE THREE LARGEST PYRAMIDS OF
JEEZEH, ACCORDING TO VARIOUS AUTHORITIES.

Authorities.	Builder of the Great Pyramid.	Builder of the Second Pyramid.	Builder of the Third Pyramid.
Herodotus.	Cheops.	Chephren.	Mycerinus.
Manetho.	Suphis I.	Suphis II.	Mencheres.
Eratosthenes.	Saophis. Comastes, or Chematistes.	Saophis II.	Mescheres Heliodotus.
Diodorus Siculus.	Chembres.	Cephren.	Mycerinus.
Modern Egyptologists	Shofo. Shufu. Koufou.	Nou-Shofo. Noum-Shufu. Shafre.	Menkere. Menkerre. Men-kau-ra.

The Lives of the Kings.

But what, after all, is there in a name ? It is the
character of each individual king, no matter of how many
names, which we require; and especially if there be
any further indications thereby accessible, which may

betoken whether that royal personage could have both designed, and built, the Great Pyramid.

There the conversational style of Herodotus, dipping deep into the feelings of men, will serve us better than the bald rigidity of hieroglyphic inscriptions; though, as Herodotus gathered up everything without sifting it, and as between the purposed falsities of what the idolatrous Egyptian priests often related to him, in a language which he did not understand, and his cunning interpreter did not faithfully translate to him,—it is little more than the involuntary evidence, under cross-examination, that can be trusted. Here, however, as a beginning, are his own simple statements :—

(124) "Cheops," according to the Egyptian priests,* "on ascending the throne, plunged into all manner of wickedness. He closed the temples, and forbade the Egyptians to offer sacrifice, compelling them instead to labour one and all in his service; viz. in building the Great Pyramid."

(128) "Cheops reigned fifty years; and was succeeded by his brother Chephren, who imitated the conduct of his predecessor, built a pyramid —but smaller than his brother's—and reigned fifty-six years. Thus, during 106 years the temples were shut and never opened."

(129) "After Chephren, Mycerinus, son of Cheops, ascended the throne. He reopened the temples, and allowed the people to resume the practice of sacrifice. He, too, left a pyramid, but much inferior in size to his father's. It is built, for half of its height, of the stone of Ethiopia;" i.e. expensive red granite.

(136) "After Mycerinus, Asychis ascended the throne. He built the eastern gateway of the Temple of Vulcan (Phtha); and being desirous of eclipsing all his predecessors on the throne, left, as a monument of his reign, a pyramid of brick."

Now here we have four successive kings, each of whom erected a Pyramid; and the last of them entered into the work no less enthusiastically than the first. Therefore it could not have been Pyramid-building in itself, or as known to, and understood by, the natives, which had the discriminating effect of causing the last two kings to be approved, and the first two to be hated,

* Ch. CXXIV. p. 199, of Rawlinson's Translation of "Herodotus," Vol. II. See also a very salutary note, No. 9, on p. 205, by Sir G. Wilkinson.

by all Egyptians; and to that terrible and intense degree described by successive classic authors. This difference of estimation must have risen from some striking and radical *difference* of proceeding in either pair of kings. Now such an opposite manner is most religiously found in this circumstance, so clearly though succinctly alluded to by Herodotus ; viz. that the first two kings closed the temples, and stopped the worship of the bulls, cats, goats, beetles, and other detestable Egyptian gods ; while the last two kings reopened those temples, enlarged them, expensively beautified them, and re-established the soul-degrading theotechnic inventions of Egypt in greater splendour than ever. This too, those later kings did, with effrontery, for all those Egyptian animal gods : though it was *their* statues, of gold, and silver, of wood incrusted with pearls, of granite and basalt, porphyry, sandstone, and limestone, which were the very idols which the Lord declares in prophecy for the latter day " He will destroy, and cause their images to cease out of Noph."

The Right Man at last.

But there is more than this to be gathered from the classic records ; for next comes up among them a something most suggestive, to the extent of a ray of positive light, upon that very question which, even to the intelligent, though Pagan, Diodorus Siculus, was so much more important than who were the kings who ordered, viz. who were the architects who designed, or built, or superintended the building of, the Pyramids ; as he says in the plural ; the Great Pyramid, we are content alone to name. For Herodotus further states :—

(128) " The Egyptians so detest the memory of those (the first two) kings (Cheops and Chephren), that they do not much like even to mention their names. Hence, they commonly call the Pyramids (the Great and the Second) after Philition (or Philitis), a shepherd who at that time fed his flocks about the place."

Seldom has a more important piece of truth, than this touching Philitis, been issued in a few words. Sir G. Wilkinson, in his note to that passage,* allows at once the Hyksosian, or Shepherd-royal, character of a stranger who could be so distinguished in connection with the greatest of the monuments of Egypt; and is only anxious to guard his readers as to the particular personage alluded to, having really lived in the early *fourth* dynasty; and not having been one of those later, better known, but totally different individuals who figured as the Shepherd Kings in the 15th, 16th, and 17th dynasties. While Mr. Rawlinson, in another note on the same page, seems equally ready to allow,—not only that Philitis was a Shepherd-Prince from Palestine, and perhaps of Philistine descent,—but so powerful and domineering, that it may be traditions of *his* oppressions in that *earlier* age, which mixed up afterwards in the minds of Theban Egyptians with the evils inflicted on their country by the *subsequent* Shepherds of the later, better-known dynasties; and lent so much of actual fear to aliment their religious hate of "Shepherd" times and the Hyksos name.

If this theory of Mr. Rawlinson's be correct, we may learn something further of the Great Pyramid's fourth dynasty, Shepherd-Prince, Philitis—by attending to certain of the things which Manetho has written of the subsequent Shepherds; and especially by eliminating therefrom certain features which cannot by any possibility be true of those men such as they were in that later day. For thus wrote the Sebennyte priest : †—

"We had formerly a king whose name was Timeus. In his time it came to pass, I know not how, that God was displeased with us : and there came up from the

---

* P. 207, Vol. II. of Rawlinson's "Herodotus."
† Cory's "Fragments," p. 169. See also pp. 180—185 of Osburn's "Monumental History of Egypt," Vol. I.

East, in a strange manner, men of an ignoble race, who had the confidence to invade our country, and easily subdued it by their power without a battle."

This, it will be observed, is a very peculiar phrase; and lends much colour to the suggestion that Philitis was enabled to exert a certain amount of mental control over King Shofo and his Egyptian people; not by the vulgar method of military conquest, but by some supernatural influence in connection with the service of the one and only true God.

"All this invading nation," Manetho goes on to say, "was styled Hycsos, that is, Shepherd Kings; for the first syllable, Hyc, in the sacred dialect denotes a king: and Sos signifies a shepherd, but this only according to the vulgar tongue; and of these is compounded the term Hycsos: some say they were Arabians."

Yet if they were Arabians, why did they not return to Arabia, when they afterwards, "to the number of not less than 240,000, quitted Egypt by capitulation, with all their families and effects"? And went—where to? "To Judæa, and built there," says Manetho, "a city of sufficient size to contain this multitude of men, and named it Jerusalem." *

Now here is surely a most important tale, if anything written in books by ancient authors is worthy of modern attention. For, making all due allowance for some of the references, and much of the expressed hate and abuse being due to the more modern and largely native † Egyptian Shepherds of the 15th to the 17th dynasties (and who, according to W. Osburn, were in the end chiefly conquered and oppressed *within* the bounds of Lower Egypt by invasions of Thebans and fanatic Ethiopians), we have as much as testifies to the earlier and truer Shepherd-Prince Philitis, after having long

* Cory's "Fragments," p. 173.
† According to William Osburn in his "Monumental History."

mentally and physically controlled King Shofo during
the very time that the Great Pyramid was building,—
to that Prince, or King, Philitis, I say, then leaving
the country with a high hand, or by special agreement,
with all his people and flocks,—proceeding to Judæa,
and building there a city which he named Jerusalem;
and which must have at once taken a high standing
among the primeval cities of the earth, if he made it
large enough to contain not less than 240,000 persons.

Of some of the Earlier Divinely assisted Departures out of Egypt, before the Mosaic.

Now the man who executed such a work as that just
described, after assisting at the foundation of the Great
Pyramid in 2170 B.C., must have been a very remarkable contemporary nearly of, but rather older than, the
Patriarch Abraham, according to the best Biblical chronology. And the Bible does contain some slight allusions to certain persons having been brought out of, or
assisted to escape from, Egypt at that very early time
by the special favour of the God of Israel.

In Deuteronomy, chap. ii., for instance, there appears
something possibly of this kind; when Moses (in 1542
B.C., or rather later), encouraging the Israelites to be of
good heart in their march, under Divine favour, out of
Egypt into Palestine,—mentions two other and long-
preceding occasions on which God had shown similar
favour to other peoples, and they were established
successfully in consequence.

First " the children of Esau "; and afterwards, " the
Caphtorims, which came forth out of Caphtor."   Or, as
alluded to again, long after the times of the Exodus (in
Amos ix. 7), " Have not I (the Lord) brought up Israel
out of Egypt, and the Philistines from Caphtor ? "

This Caphtor alluded to on both occasions, is generally

considered to mean Egypt, the Pyramid region, too, of Lower Egypt; and although, in the one instance, the people are spoken of as Caphtorim, that may imply, not necessarily native Egyptians, but men who had been sojourning in their country for a long season; even as the testimony of Herodotus infers that Philitis (a name looked on by some as implying a Philistian descent or country), with his flocks and herdsmen (appropriately then called Philistines in Caphtor), had been doing, during all the thirty years occupied so Prometheanly, first in the preparations for, and then the building up of, the Great Pyramid as a Prophetical Monument: a lasting record in stone which was only to be understood in the latter days of the world; but was then to bear signal witness to every fact of the Christian Dispensation having been ordained, established, and prepared for in primeval times, before the beginning of history.

In short, the Biblical evidence, possibly touching on the architectship of this mighty monument of sacred and prophetic purport, is deserving of more intimate and peculiar study than we have yet bestowed upon it. As a preliminary part of it too, we may at once take up a point connected with the earliest chronological date possible for any of the remains of religious man upon this earth, wherein the Great Pyramid seems to furnish forth most useful and salutary guidance.

The World's Chronology previous to the Great Pyramid's date.

Up to the present chapter, and except for the purpose of disproving the enormous dates asserted by the Egyptologists for the Great Pyramid itself (see p. 491), we have not ascended higher in real time than the Pyramid's own simple, and true, date, 2170 B.C.—a date entirely agreeable with Biblical chronology.

But the Bible dates begin at a far earlier epoch than
that. As both learnedly interpreted and philosophically
explained by Archdeacon Pratt, in his " Religion and
Science Not at Variance," the Bible dates commence
with an allusion to an indefinitely great antiquity for
the creation of matter; then give a vastly more modern
date for the appearance of Adam; assign a not very
great interval from Adam to the Deluge of Noah;
another still less interval to the Dispersion; and
another similar one from thence up to the appearance
of Patriarchs, whose Biblical epoch is conformable to
the Great Pyramid's own statement for itself; viz. the
2170 B.C. before alluded to.

But the Great Pyramid's record of time, as shown by
our Plate X. (and at p. 477, where the 2170 B.C. date is
far down the entrance-passage), extends up to considerably earlier times than itself. Not, indeed, to the sublime
beginnings of the Bible, but *first* to the Dispersion, supposed to be marked by the top of that entrance-passage
floor as occurring in 2528 B.C.; and *second* to the Deluge.

The latter reference, which might almost have been
anticipated in a chronological building, wherein had
already been recognized a harmonious commensurability between its Ark-box, or Coffer, and the Ark of
Noah (see pp. 403 to 406) was first approached through
the astronomy of the Great Pyramid, in Vol. III. of my
" Life and Work at the Great Pyramid," published in
1867; and at p. 493 thereof it will be found approximately stated at 2800 B.C., more or less; and at 2790
B.C. at p. 383 here. But a far exacter number seems
to have been lately ascertained by the Rev. Alfred
Cachemaille, of the Parsonage, Oldham.

He had remarked acutely, that inasmuch as the Great
Pyramid building itself ends in a manner with the
entrance-passage, carrying the Dispersion date of 2528
B.C. on the very floor end, upwards and outwards, of

that passage,—some device in the way of doubling back was evidently necessary for indicating, within the building, and on the eminently white-stone lining of its entrance-passage, any still earlier date.   Now there was to his eye, most precisely such a doubling back, in the shape of the double wall courses, both east and west, of the first part of, but nowhere else along, the entrance-passage (see pp. 21 to 26 of Vol. II. of "Life and Work.")   And the mean result for the eight different measures there detailed of the four different factors to the ultimate result, is, to the nearest inch year, 215. Wherefore 2528 B.C. + 215 = 2743 B.C., as the directly measured and most easily measurable Great Pyramid date of that most notable re-commencement of the course of humanity, whose further religious history the Great Pyramid was to trace.

But now what is the Bible date for the same event ?

There, unfortunately, mankind in the present age cannot speak very decidedly as to the exact figure; for the earliest known copies of the Sacred Scriptures differ from each other, anywhere between 2327 B.C., and 3246 B.C.; and Divines still hotly dispute which of these two, or any intermediate numbers, are the most trustworthy.   In this dilemma, I ventured to write to the Archbishop of Canterbury, and received from Lambeth Palace, in May, 1866, the following positive information :—

(1.) The Church of England has assigned no date to the Noachian Deluge.

(2.) The Church has not fixed any dates between which it must have taken place.

(3.) The Church of England has not authorized the insertion into the authorized copy of the English Bible, of any system of dates.

Being thus thrown back on my own weak resources, I searched out the dates arrived at and stated to be the Scriptural ones, *i.e.* founded partly on the words and partly on the figures actually to be read piece-meal in various copies of the Scriptures, and finally summed up by various Divines of repute; and then took an average of the whole, thus (see p. 489 of Vol. III. of " Life and Work ") :—

Authorities.		Date of Deluge, in Years, B.C.
Septuagint, Alexandrine (Kitto's *Palestine*) ..	.. =	3246
Jackson	.. =	3170
Hales	.. =	3155
R. Stewart Poole (Smith's *Bible Dictionary*)	.. =	3129
Samaritan (Kitto's *Palestine*)	.. =	2998
W. Osburn (Monumental *History of Egypt*)	.. =	2500
Elliot's *Horæ Apocalypticæ*	.. =	2482
Browne's *Ordo Sæclorum*	.. =	2446
Playfair	.. =	2351
Ussher	.. =	2348
Petavius (Smith's *Bible Dictionary*)	.. =	2327
Mean of the whole	=	2741

This 2741 B.C. was therefore printed by me in 1867 as the best result of all the foremost Bible authorities known to the community, for that most important event in Biblical history, the Noachian Deluge. And in 1878, the Great Pyramid's chronology, further interpreted by the Rev. Alfred Cachemaille, gives 2743 B.C.

CHAPTER XXIII.

SCRIPTURE TESTIMONY,

And the Christian Prophetic Grand Gallery.

Biblical Views of Metrology in General.

VIEWING the Great Pyramid first of all as a monument of metrology alone, that subject has been shown from Scripture by many writers (as Michaelis, in Germany; Paucton, in France; and more recently, John Taylor, in England) to have been deemed worthy of Divine attention, or of Providence, for the good of man. Such instructions as the following having been issued through the approved medium of inspired men honoured with the commands of Revelation, viz. :—

" Ye shall do no unrighteousness in judgment, in meteyard, in weight, or in measure.

" Just balances, just weights, a just ephah, and a just hin, shall ye have: I am the Lord your God, which brought you out of the land of Egypt.

" Therefore shall ye observe all my statutes, and all my judgments, and do them : I am the Lord."—Leviticus xix. 35—37.

" But thou shalt have a perfect and just weight, a perfect and just measure shalt thou have: that thy days may be lengthened in the land which the Lord thy God giveth thee."—Deuteronomy xxv. 15.

" A false balance is abomination to the Lord: but a just weight is his delight."—Proverbs xi. 1.

" A just weight and balance are the Lord's: all the weights of the bag are his work."—Proverbs xvi. 11.

" Thus saith the Lord God ; Let it suffice you, O princes of Israel : remove violence and spoil, and execute judgment and justice, take away your exactions from my people, saith the Lord God.

" Ye shall have just balances, and a just ephah, and a just bath.

" The ephah and the bath shall be of one measure, that the bath may contain the tenth part of an homer, and the ephah the tenth part of an homer : the measure thereof shall be after the homer."—Ezek. xlv. 9—11.

This was a department of the Holy Service which
King David had appointed, in his days, a portion of the
Levites to attend to ;* and his splendid son and successor, Solomon, established the grand standards of
measure in the noblest proportions : † while Moses had
been, in his still earlier day, exceedingly particular in
all his metrological institutions, as well as impressive
in his method of carrying them out ; ‡ his chief standard
measures being, as already shown, the earth and heaven
founded standards of the Great Pyramid itself (see
pp. 347, 355, 395) ; if they were not also those which
had been originally elaborated (according to Josephus)
by Seth and his descendants in opposition to the bad
inventions of Cain, and under the direct approval of
the Almighty.   (See pp. 345 and 352.)

With the structure of the Great Pyramid building,
indeed, in its main design and ultimate purposes
(though never so distinctly or categorically alluded to
in Scripture, as thereby to give men any excuse for
turning aside to it, for any kind of spiritual worship),
the inspired writers of both the Old and New Testaments have evinced a very considerable acquaintance.
And not dry knowledge only ; for those men, " gifted
with thoughts above their thoughts," have shown an
amount of feeling, only to be explained by a holy
consciousness of the part which the monument is one
day to serve, in manifesting forth in modes adapted to
these and the approaching times, the original and inef-
fable inspiration of Scripture,—as well as the practical
reasons for expecting, both the rapture of the true
church to meet the Lord in the air, and after that

---

* I. Chronicles xxiii. 29.
† I. Kings vii. 29 ; and II. Chronicles iv. 5.
‡ See John David Michaelis, of Göttingen, " On the Plans which
Moses took for the Regulation of Weights and Measures," at pp. 454—
470 of Vol. II. of his " Hebrew Weights and Measures."   See also my
" Life and Work," pp. 498—507 of Vol. III.

His glorious return with his perfected saints following Him to an undoubted personal reign, through a long miraculous season over the entire earth.

Old Testament Witnesses to the Great Pyramid.

So well, too, were the mechanical steps for the foundation of the Great Pyramid understood (those steps being the heavy preliminary works of preparation and subterranean masonry described by Herodotus as having characterized the Great Pyramid; and declared by Lepsius (and his "law" so universally approved by all Egyptologists), to have been eschewed in every other Pyramid erected altogether by, and for, Cainite Egyptian idolaters—see pp. 103, 410);—so well, I say, were those features understood by the inspired writers, that the mysterious things of Nature visible to, but not easily apprehended by uninstructed men in the early ages, were occasionally described in Scripture in terms of those simpler features of the Great Pyramid.

Thus, when we read in Job xxxviii., marginally corrected, that the Lord answered the patriarch out of the whirlwind, demanding with power,—

" Where wast thou when I laid the foundations of the earth ? declare, if thou knowest understanding.
" Who hath laid the measures thereof, if thou knowest ; or who hath stretched the line upon it ?
" Whereupon are the sockets thereof made to sink? or who laid the corner-stone thereof ;
" When the morning stars sang together, and all the sons of God shouted for joy ? "

—it is quite plain (since at least John Taylor first pointed it out; for to him we owe almost entirely this branch of the subject) that if the creation of the earth is here alluded to, it is described under a type of something else, and not as the earth really was created ; or both as we know it by modern science to be, and as it

was described in chap. xxvi. of the same Book of Job,
in the following words :—

"He stretcheth out the north over the empty place, and hangeth the
earth upon nothing."

The earliest of the first-quoted descriptions might
apply to the building of any ordinary house ; but as
successive practical features are enumerated, the building of a stone pyramid by careful measure, and in the
Promethean, or forethought, manner of the Great
Pyramid, on a previously prepared platform of rock, is
the only known work that will fully correspond.

The stretching of the line *upon* it, is more applicable
to the inclined surface of a pyramid with an angle to
the horizon of 51° 51', than to the vertical walls of any
ordinary house ; and—after the pointed and most appo-
site question, " Canst thou bind the sweet influence
of Pleiades ? "—the further Divine interrogation,—
" Knowest thou the ordinances of the heavens ? Canst
thou set the dominion thereof in the earth ? "—has been
happily explained very lately by the Rev. F. R. A. Glover.
For he shows it to be, the Great Pyramid's chronological use of the grand celestial cycle of the precessional
movement of the Pleiades, taken at a particular epoch
in connection with a special polar distance and meridian
transit of the circumpolar star α Draconis ; the memorial of which stellar positions in the heavens, made
" dominant in the earth," is exhibited by the lower
portion of the entrance-passage of the Great Pyramid,
set backwards and downwards into, and deep, deep
into, the solid rock of the hill ; but in precisely such a
direction as to suit the critical position of those two
stars under the influence of precession, at the very epoch
of the Pyramid's foundation.   (See pp. 371—387.)

But what was meant by " the sockets thereof being
made to sink,"—might have been uncertain, had it not

been for the researches of the French *savants* at the
Great Pyramid in 1800; for they described, without
reference to this sentence, the remarkable *sockets* which
had been formed in the previously levelled area of rock
on which this Pyramid stands; and (with the assistance
of the more modern investigations in 1865) the manner
in which each of the lower four corner-stones of the
Pyramid were fitted into these prepared hollows in the
rock,—causing them to become at once the fiducial
points from which all good measurers have, ever since
then, stretched their measuring-lines on the building.
(See pp. 23, 38, 336.)

Four of the five corner-stones of the Pyramid are thus
indicated as of Scriptural notice; while the fifth, which
is, in fact, of an entirely diverse character and greater
importance, being not one of the foundations, but the
topmost portion of the whole building, is alluded to in
Job separately; more gloriously; and even as being the
finishing and crowning portion of the whole intended
work. For when that topmost corner-stone, emphatically
called "*the* corner-stone," was finally placed,—it is said
that the act was greeted by "the morning stars singing
together, and all the sons of God shouting for joy."

The Biblical interpretation of the personages here
alluded to is, with little doubt, as John Taylor pointed
out, "the faithful and the true converts"; "as many
as are led by the spirit of God, they are the sons of
God."   And all such who were present at the time,
rejoiced in seeing the completion of the Great Pyramid
with a joy far exceeding what the erection of any
ordinary building, however palatial, might have been
expected to give them; for their cry, when the *headstone* of this one " great mountain was brought out
with shoutings," took the exquisite form of " Grace,
grace unto it ! " *   And if they so cried, and it is so

* Zech. iv. 7.

reported in the Holy Bible, was it not because they recognised that that stone had been appointed by Divine wisdom, and in the mystery of God's primeval proceedings towards man, to recall some essential ideas connected with the one central point about which all Scripture revolves; viz. the Son of God; His early care for the human race, in several temporary Theophanies; His mediæval incarnation and sacrifice, as the God-man Jesus Christ, for the salvation of all sinners; and, finally, His future Kingly and Divine rule over all the nations of men? But of this elevated Scriptural Centre, we shall be instructed more clearly in the New Testament.

New Testament Allusions to the Great Pyramid.

From a practical worker like St. Paul, we have even a most methodical illustration, in the use which he makes of certain constructive differences between the four lower corner-stones, and the single corner-stone above; constructive differences which, if applicable to any other building at all, are only *fully* applicable to the awe-inspiring Great Pyramid; for his words are—

" Ye are fellow-citizens of the saints, and of the house-hold of God; and are built upon the *foundation* of the apostles and prophets, Jesus Christ himself being the *chief corner-stone, in whom the whole building fitly framed together, groweth unto an holy temple in the Lord.*" *

This fitly framing of the whole building as it grows from a broad, four cornered, four socketed, base upwards into one corner-stone above, and which is called the chief, the upper, corner-stone,—was shown by John Taylor to be an unmistakable allusion to the Great Pyramid; and this same noble figurative employment of that particular topmost stone, viz. its representation of the Messiah, and His crowning the scheme of the

---

* Eph. ii. 21. See also J. Taylor's " Great Pyramid," pp. 208—243.

redemption of individual man,—is one frequently employed in Holy Scripture ; as in Psalm cxviii. 22 ; in the Gospels, and the Epistles.* The stone is there alluded to, not only as the chief corner-stone, "elect and precious," made " the *head* of the corner" (which is only perfectly and pre-eminently true of the topmost angle of a Pyramid), but as having been for a long time "disallowed by the builders," and existing only as "a stone of stumbling and a rock of offence to them."†

The simile is easily and perfectly applicable to our Saviour's appearance on earth ; yet evidently, from the very principle of all such figurative allusions, a something bearing on the nature of the figure made use of, must, Mr. Taylor urged, have been existing on the earth before ; or it would never have been employed.

Now we know that the Great Pyramid did stand on its desert hill before any of the inspired authors wrote ; and also, that they seem to have been spiritually conversant with many principles of its construction, although they were not visitors to the land of Egypt ; and it is they who allude to some notorious objections by the builders against the head corner-stone, while their work was in progress.

What were these ?

The stones required for building the Great Pyramid were evidently, from the quarry-marks and instructions to the masons still legible upon some of them, prepared

---

* Matt. xxi. 42 ; Mark xii. 10 ; Luke xx. 17 ; Acts iv. 11 ; 1 Peter ii. 4.

† In the important theological work by the Rev. John Harrison, D.D., "Whose are the Fathers," there is, at pp. 163—172, a very able representation of the special exigences of mere ecclesiasticism in the narrow, albeit learned, view which ecclesiastics take of all these texts, and all this long line of symbology founded in all architecture and all history. For the one point to and for which everything else is there made to exist, is, the personal phrase of nominal commendation used by our Lord to Peter (Matt. xvi. 18) ; and what advantage the Roman Catholic Church has, or has not, though it is denied by Protestants that it has any, over other Christian Churches (whether State-paid and State-supported for political uses, or purely voluntary congregations of worshippers meeting for the Gospel's sake alone),—in consequence of it.

at the quarries according to the architect's orders a long time beforehand. For the vast majority, too, of stones, nothing but one unvarying figure, rather flattish and chiefly rectangular, was required. But amongst them, and different therefrom, one was ordered which did not chime in with any of the Egyptian building notions; certainly not of their temples, tombs, or palaces. For, in place of being cubic, or with nearly parallel sides and rectangular corners, this single stone was all acutely angled; all sharp points; so that turn it over on any side as it lay on the ground, one sharp corner, or edge, was always sticking up in the air; as, too, could not but be the case when the stone was a sort of model pyramid in itself, with five sides, five corners, and sixteen distinct angles.*

Such a stone was of course "a stone of stumbling and a rock of offence"† to builders whose heads did not understand, and hearts did not appreciate, the work they were engaged upon. It was to them "the terrible crystal;"‡ the pointed stone "on which whosoever shall fall, shall be broken;" and so huge a stone as a coping for the vast structure of the whole Great Pyramid, that "on whomsoever it shall fall, it will grind him to powder." §

Yet when once this unique, five-cornered, and many-angled stone was raised up to its intended place on the summit of the Great Pyramid, the propriety of its figure must have appeared evident to every impartial beholder; though the Egyptian workmen, as may be gathered from Herodotus, notwithstanding that they were forcibly prevented from breaking out into open opposition, yet went on concealing sinful hatred in their hearts; and did—after the deaths of Cheops and Chephren, and after the Shepherd-Prince Philitis had

* John Taylor's "Great Pyramid," pp. 262—275.   † 1 Peter ii. 8.
   ‡ Ezekiel i. 22.   § Matt. xxi. 44.

left the country—return with renewed vehemence to their bestial idolatry under Mencheres, "like dogs to their vomit, or the sow that was washed to her wallowing in the mire." *

For such determined resisters of grace was surely prepared, in their very midst, that type of the bottomless pit, the not sepulchral, but really unfinished and floorless subterranean chamber in the Great Pyramid (see pp. 100, 106, 222, 434), yawning to receive them :—

"For they are all delivered unto death, to the nether parts of the earth, in the midst of the children of men, with them that go down to the pit."
"This is Pharaoh and all his multitude, saith the Lord God."—Ezekiel xxxi. 14 and 18.

But again, and now for the instruction of backsliding Israel, this prophetic and historic monument—which had no similar predecessor—was without architectural parentage or descent; and yet took rank at once as the most kingly of all architecture up to the present time (see p. 505),—this more than historic monument, I say, seems to speak to us in the words of the only wise Architect :—

"I have declared the former things from the beginning; and they went forth out of my mouth, and I showed them; *I did them suddenly*, and they came to pass."
"I have even from the beginning declared it to thee; before it came to pass I showed it to thee; lest thou shouldest say, Mine idol hath done them, and my graven image and my molten image hath commanded them."—Isaiah xlviii. 3 and 5.

Never, then, was there any building so perfect as the Great Pyramid in fulfilling both the *earliest* words of the Lord given by Inspiration, and also the *latest* types of the Messiah. And if the Great Pyramid is not mentioned by actual name in the New Testament, that may arise from—as circumstances still to be related will indicate—its being connected, not so much with the First

* 2 Peter ii. 22.

and now long past, coming of Christ (which indeed the New Testament was mainly to chronicle, expound and recommend to man),—as for His Second, and still future coming for the benefit of nations. An event of little practical importance in the personal Christianity and Gospel ministrations to each individual soul for its own salvation, eighteen centuries ago;—but of the utmost consequence to all, both collectively and individually now, if the time be really close at hand.

Of the Future in the Great Pyramid.

If there is any subject wherein we should pay special attention to that truly Christian warning, "Be not high-minded, but fear," it ought to prevail in any attempt to read what it has pleased Divine Inspiration to record of the future, whether in writing or monumentalization.

But though the danger of erring be great, we are not, therefore, instructed not to make any attempt; on the contrary, "The Revelation of Jesus Christ,"* was given unto him by God, in order "to show unto His servants things which must shortly come to pass": and those particular servants were promised blessing, who should both read and hear the words of that prophecy, and struggle in spirit and wrestle in prayer to understand its mysterious sayings even in number. Indeed, as the time of the end draws near, it would even seem to be a growing duty of the present day to compare the end, thus far arrived at, with what was said of it in the beginning; and thereby realize more Scripture miracles (viz. its having prophesied future events truly) in our own day, and before our own eyes; together with such positive, and irresistible proof that there is no God like our God of Israel and the Bible.

* The Revelation of St. John the Divine, i. 1.

The Grand Gallery Prophecies of the Christian Religion.

Now we have already, in Chapter XX., concluded that the north wall of the Grand Gallery represents the date of the Birth of Christ; and that thence, upwards, along the said gallery's inclined floor, stretches Christian religious history since that time. Not that we are to expect to meet with markings to show every, or even any, event of mere human ecclesiastical arrangements; for the region begins with the birth of the Son of God, as Jesus Christ our Lord and Saviour; and thereby bids us look to the supernatural and the Divinely Inspired only.

But if it so begins, how does the said region, viz. the Grand Gallery, end?

The long-continued floor line, passing between the ramps and their ramp-holes on either side, is interrupted only by a modern dilapidation or two, including some shallow foot-holds, until we arrive at the great step, 3 feet high; and then, at 61 inches horizontal beyond that, comes the south end of the Grand Gallery. And a positive end, too, it is of the said Gallery; for though there may be on the step-level, a low passage leading on further to the Ante-chamber and King's Chamber (see Plates XIV. and XVI.), and a still smaller and ordinarily quite inaccessible passage-way leading from very high up, or close under the ceiling of the Grand Gallery to the lowest of the hollows of construction over the King's Chamber,—yet neither of these narrow ways can represent the majestic Grand Gallery, with the seven overlappings of its walls, its 36 roof-stones, and 28 ramp-holes on either side. All these things end above that great 36-inch step, and are ended inwardly and positively upon themselves with the " impending " south wall (see p. 462); and without the slightest symbolization of anything like uniform perpetuity; or of the higher, religious, history repeating itself mechanically through indefinite ages.

Hence for all those who have already accepted the beginning of the Grand Gallery, for the beginning of the Christian Dispensation which commenced 1,879 years ago, and under which we are still living,—there is nothing for it but also to accept that a period, distinct and finite, was appointed to that Dispensation by God, and that that end is close upon us. Not an end of the world, or of nations, or of men; or unhappily of armies and slaughterous wars; but of some of the arrangements and forms of religious service to God, as required by the personal Gospel published 1,850 years ago.

How close then, is such an end? The answer to that question must depend solely on the length of the Grand Gallery by measure in Pyramid inches.

As usual with the accounts of travellers at the Great Pyramid, there are many various results in print; and even Howard-Vyse, whose length of the external base-side of the monument was too great, has published a length for the Grand Gallery equal to only 1,872 Pyramid inches, or a time which is now past: while Mr. Lane, on the contrary, gave one equal to 1,894 Pyramid inches. My own measures, however, taken in 1865, at a far greater sacrifice of time and labour than theirs, amounted to, for the length up to the great step, 1813·0 Pyramid inches; and thence up to the end wall, in the line concluded for the slanting floor, 68 inches farther, = 1881·0 Pyramid inches in all; or, as computed more exactly by Mr. H. A. Powers, of Cincinnati,* 1881·4.

---

* My measures ought to have been of the floor. For practical convenience they were taken on the surface of the ramps, and would have given the same result as the floor, but for the "impending" of the south wall of the Grand Gallery, which makes the correction furnished by Mr. Powers. This, I fully agree in: but I am not equally disposed to accept certain different modes of using my own measures, adopted both by Mr. W. Rowbottom in his "The Mystery of the Bible Dates solved by the Great

Something, then, seems to be appointed to take place at that particular time, and it is much easier to say what it is not, than what it is. It is not, for instance, as just stated above, "the end of the world,"—for there is a "passage-floor," leading on from the great step, to the Ante-chamber; through that also, and onwards into the King's Chamber, the granite-lined and most glorious part of the whole interior of the building. And equally it is not Christ's second coming, neither is it the Millennium beginning, for there is rather a cessation, or at least a decrease, than an exaltation, of the Christian faith, though but for a short time only, indicated at that 1881·4 A.D. point of the progress of time and history.

In fact, it is rather like the unexampled days of future trouble which our Saviour himself announced should immediately precede His second, but which must as certainly succeed the dispensation of His first, coming.

Of the unutterable anguishes of those most exceptional days to come, we read (Mark xiii. 19) that "there shall be affliction, such as there was not from the beginning of the creation which God created unto this time, neither shall be." But its duration will not be long; "for," continues the Saviour, "except the Lord had shortened those days, no flesh should be saved; but for the elect's sake, whom he hath chosen, he hath shortened the days."

The severities of those times are Pyramidally expressed at the place by the exit passage from the south end of the Grand Gallery being lower still than any of the low passages which marked the troubles of the profane world

Pyramid "; nor again the rather different results brought out by Mr. Geo. N. Walsh, in his "Israel's Chronology." But I do not actively object to them; for some of their principles of divergence seem fair enough, in cases where it is difficult to maintain one opinion only; while the final and positive test for every one is, the future. Mr. Walsh, I should perhaps add, by measuring over the surface of the Grand Gallery's step, in place of through it in continuation of the floor-line, increases the length of the whole, from 1881·4 to 1910 Pyramid inches.

in early times.   Those passages were 47 inches in transverse, and 52 in vertical, height; painfully low, therefore, for any full-sized man to creep through; but the
passage after 1881·4 A.D. is only 44 inches in vertical
height, and is the most trying part of the whole passage
system.   But this excruciating portion is exceedingly
short; for after no more than 53 inches in length, it
enters into the freedom of the Ante-chamber, its quiet,
peace and presently *granite* protection.

Of the Upper way of Escape from the further End of the Grand Gallery.

But the final reception into the Ante-chamber is not
the only mode of mitigating the threatened horrors of
that lower, middle, passage; for before entering that at
all, there is a very peculiar mode of possible entire
escape, from the summit end of the Grand Gallery itself;
though only for a few, and not by their own power.

This escape is by the doorway of exit into the small
passage, at the upper south-east corner (or rather upper
Southern end of the East wall) of the Grand Gallery,
and is no less than 27 feet above the history-recording
floor; only therefore, accessible to something approaching
more to winged, and flying, rather than walking, beings;
and leading to a sort of retreat, more than apartment
for earthly life, immediately over the grand and final
granite hall, the so-called King's Chamber.   (See, again,
Plate XVI.)   That said retreat is one of the five hollows
of construction which Colonel Howard-Vyse found to
exist above the King's Chamber; but while the upper
four had been absolutely closed in, and about, with solid
masonry, the fifth and lowest was furnished as above
described with the passage-way leading to it from the
almost inaccessible top of the southern end of the Grand
Gallery, on the eastern side thereof.   Why it was so

furnished there is nothing either in the scientific, or Egyptologic, theories to show; though in the sacred and historic symbology it immediately reminds of what the Evangelists in the New Testament promise, viz. of the angels being sent to gather up the elect before the dread period of wars and tribulations on earth begins; and also of those elect thus saved, meeting the Lord in the air, and being retained with him in heaven for awhile before His second coming to the earth; this time to establish His visible Kingdom; the Kingdom of stone cut out without hands, ordained to rule over nations in truth, righteousness, and universal extent, by grandly supernatural means, of which the world under the present Christian Dispensation, however Divine its precepts, knows absolutely nothing practically.

The date of the rapture of the saints is necessarily therefore one thing, perhaps now impending, but not to be certainly known as to day and hour by any man; the return of Christ, the Lord, with His glorified saints to commence the Millennium, is quite another, and perhaps a more certainly fixable, time;—as indicated in the Pyramid by the greater proximity of its markings to the chronicling floor-surface.

But all these things, protest resistingly many devout readers, have been continually expected every single year since the Ascension, 1845 years ago. Not a few, too, of the most excellent Evangelistic preachers, have occasionally announced, that all the miraculous raptures of the saints,—away from this earth and into the air to meet the Lord,—might take place before the conclusion of their then discourses; but they never have. Can, therefore, any special reason be now shown from Scripture, as well as from the Great Pyramid, why, at all events, this first of the latter-day miracles should be more likely to occur in, or near to 1881·4 A.D., than to any of the long past years.

Those who have studied prophecy earnestly, must be aware that a very great number of results have been brought out, all converging on the year 1881 A.D.; but for the present I will confine myself to one, the latest, as given in his Mongrelian pamphlet, by Dr. Watson F. Quinby, of Wilmington, Delaware, U.S.; and founding, as a matter of course, upon that most chronologically rich and exact of all the prophets, Daniel.

" The rise and fall of the three great empires mentioned by name, the Babylonian, the Persian, the Grecian, and the fourth so well described as evidently to refer to the Roman, have all taken place as foretold ; and the time seems approaching for the setting up of the fifth and final kingdom. A ' great day of preparation for this event is foretold,' when ' many shall run to and fro,' and ' knowledge shall be increased,' which may well refer to our own day.

" When shall these things be ?   In the book of the prophet Daniel it is said, ' Seventy weeks are determined upon thy people, and upon thy holy city.' Seventy weeks of years would be four hundred and ninety years, at which time (from the decree to rebuild it) Jerusalem *was* destroyed by Titus. In another vision, though near the same time, he says, ' How long shall be the vision concerning the daily sacrifice and the transgression of desolation, to give both the sanctuary and the host to be trodden under foot ?   And he said unto me, Unto two thousand and three hundred days.'   These days are usually considered to mean years. Now Jerusalem was destroyed in Anno Domini 70.   In order, then, to bring the date to the commencement of our era, the seventy years must be taken from the four hundred and ninety years, which leaves four hundred and twenty years.

" Four hundred and twenty years taken from two thousand and three hundred years, leave eighteen hundred and eighty years, which brings us to the year eighteen hundred and eighty-one. ' Then shall the sanctuary be cleansed,' whatever that may mean."

And, on the other side, as an additional testimony to how the Grand Gallery measures for total duration to a most miraculous event, *may* be taken, the Rev. J. J. B. Coles, writes thus from Calcutta :—" If you let fall a plumb-line from the entrance of the way of escape at the S.E. top of the Grand Gallery, it will intersect the top of the great step. So that then, instead of continuing an imaginary line of floor distance measurement through the step, measure up the step, and along the top to the spot where the plumb-line would intersect, and I fancy the measurement would be $1813 + 36 + 31 \cdot 2 = 1881 \cdot 2$."

The Two Pathways, and the Two Religions (Christian and Christless), at the Commencement of the Grand Gallery.

But before proceeding further with the great step, at the Southern, or unaccomplished,—let us return for awhile to the Northern and historically accomplished, end of the Grand Gallery,—to endeavour to understand a certain large arrangement there ; viz. the *horizontal* passage which breaks away from that gallery's *ascending* line of floor, at the date assumed of Christ's birth, and continues thence on a dull *level* southward until it ends in the solitary, closed-in, Queen's Chamber.

" The Queen's Chamber," argues Mr. Hartwell A. Powers, U.S. (in a most eloquent private letter, and still keeping up all the metrical features for metrical purposes already found in it), " is symbolical of the House of Judah and law of Moses, *set aside* during the dispensation of the Christian religion; *i.e.* the Christian Grand Gallery's progress upwards and onwards." (See Plates IX. and XI.)

" Paul, the apostle, says that that law of Moses was

'holy, just, and good' (Rom. x.) ; but he also says,
'The law made nothing perfect, but the bringing in of
a better hope did' (Heb. vii. 19. See also Heb. ix.
9—11 ; x. 1). The unfinished floor of this chamber
and the passage leading thereto, in contrast with all
other floors in the Pyramid, illustrate, to my mind,
this 'imperfection' of the law; while the fine white
stone composing its walls and roof, so exquisitely
wrought on surface and joint, tell with emphatic voice
that the law was 'holy, just, and good.' Again, but
four overlappings in its niche, in contrast with *seven*,
the symbol of completeness in Scripture, in the Grand
Gallery. True, the room has seven sides, but only *six*
finished in Great Pyramid sense of the term.

" Then, what means that salt exuding so freely from
the walls of the Queen's Chamber and passage thereto ?
The law says, ' Every oblation of thy meat-offering
shalt thou season with salt; neither shalt thou suffer
the salt of the covenant of thy God to be lacking from
thy meat-offering : with all offerings shalt thou offer
salt ' (Lev. ii. 13).

" 'The Lord spake unto Aaron, Behold, I also have
given the charge of mine heave-offerings of all the
hallowed things of the children of Israel :—it is a
covenant of salt, for ever before the Lord unto thee and
thy seed with thee' (Num. xviii. 8, 19).

" Abijah said to Jeroboam and all Israel, ' Ought ye
not to know that the Lord God of Israel gave the
kingdom over Israel to David for ever, to him and to
his sons by a *covenant of salt ?* '

" This is a passage much quoted by several recent
authors, and much assisted to my understanding by
this pillar of witness unto the Lord of Hosts in the
land of Egypt, the Great Pyramid, containing salt in
abundance *only in that part devoted to the House of Judah;*
though there are slight traces of it in the Grand Gallery,

where, too, it ought to appear in order to symbolize the seed of David reigning over the House of Israel until the second coming of the Anointed."

Air Channels, and their Symbolic Allusions to past Judaism and future Christianity.

"Since I first read 'Life and Work at the Great Pyramid,'" continues Mr. H. A. Powers, "I have never been able to divest myself of the idea that the air-channels of the King's Chamber were symbolical of the second coming of Christ as King, and his reascension, 'when He shall have delivered up the Kingdom to God, even the Father; when He shall have put down all rule and all authority and power' (1 Cor. xv. 24).

"A recent re-perusal of your description of the discovery of the air-channels in the Queen's Chamber (so contrasting in some respects to those of the King's Chamber), by Mr. Dixon, has, to my mind, shed much light (from the other side) upon this theory.

"John the Baptist testified saying, 'Reform! because the Royal Majesty of the Heavens has appeared' (Matt. iii. 2); thus translated by Benjamin Wilson in the 'Emphatic Diaglott.' Mr. Wilson says in a foot note, 'Basileia means kingly power, authority, royal dignity, majesty, &c., as well as kingdom, realm, or reign.' He translates Matt. xii. 28, thus, 'But if it be by the Spirit of God that I cast out demons, then God's royal majesty has unexpectedly appeared among you;' and says in a note, 'It is not according to fact to make Jesus say that the Kingdom of God has come unto you, as rendered in the common version. The context shows that our Lord is speaking of himself. These miracles were proof of his Messiahship.'

"Now of Jesus it is written, 'He came to his own (tribe), and his own received him not.' Again it is written, 'Their ears are dull of hearing, and their eyes

they have closed,' &c. (Matt. xiii. 15; Acts xxviii. 27.)
That 'the Scriptures might be fulfilled,' concerning
the House of Judah, *their ears were closed*, and ' a veil is
upon their hearts even unto this day when Moses is
read—nevertheless, when it (House of Judah) shall
turn to the Lord, the veil shall be taken away.'

" Wherefore these *closed* air-channels of the *Queen's*
Chamber symbolize the Messiah's first coming and
ascension, unperceived by the House of Judah; nor
could these channels be opened until 'the time of the
end' symbolized by the great 36-inch step in the Grand
Gallery; when a 'man-of-all-work,' under the direction
of his intelligent master, breaks through that ' intentionally left thin plate (veil) of soft limestone.' (See
pp. 427—430.)

" But the previous labours of such men as Howard-
Vyse, John Taylor, and others, prepared the way for
Mr. Waynman Dixon to direct Bill Grundy where to
ply his hammer and chisel. And thus, doubtless, are
the previous labours of John Wilson, Edward Hine,
F. R. A. Glover, E. W. Bird, and others, preparing the
way for the instrumentality yet to be used, in breaking
through the veil yet covering the eyes, and through
the plate of stone yet stopping the ears, of the House
of Judah, ere their King shall come in his glory."

*The Great Step at the end of the Grand Gallery, and its
intimation of existing Religious History in Britain.*

Thus far, then, the admirable contribution in a private
letter from Mr. Hartwell A. Powers* on the now historic,
and accomplished, Queen's Chamber; and wherein he
is joined by many other independent investigators,
specially including the remarkable Edward Hine;
so that, in so far as rapidly growing testimony is

* A working-man in the " Eureka Co-operative Foundry Association,"
at Warsaw Pike, Cincinnati, United States.

concerned, that chamber and the *horizontal* passage on a dead level leading to it, may be taken as testifying to both the House of Judah, their Mosaic Law, and the Old Testament used as finality, for all the period from the first appearance of Christ and his crucifixion in Jerusalem, up to the present time.

But the *ascending* floor of the Grand Gallery testifies to Christianity; which, as a Canadian correspondent remarks, continually repeats in effect, "Come *up* hither." Not, indeed, those forms of the Christian faith which have forgotten to look forward to the second coming of Christ, and have made for themselves, out of the past alone, worldly temples wherein they repose on the earthly arm of State, forgetful how soon it may turn upon them. Such semi-political Christians may be relegated to share the Queen's Chamber's *cul de sac* with mammon-seeking Jews. But all true Christians desiring and expecting to see their Lord once again upon earth, and a few Jews too, looking forward to the same event and still thinking it the first coming of Messias,—they all ascend the Grand Gallery slope with time, and are ever nearer and nearer to the coming of their Lord.

And who are more particularly, the great national body of these rising, improving, and we may trust approved, Christians?

Some will claim the Church of one nation, and some another; some will argue for spiritual Israel, and others literal and hereditary Israel, whether spread among Teutonic people, or mainly confined to the British Isles and America. And who shall decide amongst them?

None but the Great Pyramid itself. Advance we, therefore, to the great step of 1813 A.D. (*i.e.* at 1,813 Pyramid inches from the North, or Christian nativity, beginning) of the Grand Gallery, and inquire *there* what is signified.

The step marks there, by that date, the most energetic advances made by Great Britain in its latter-day spread of the Bible, and its latter-day preaching of Christianity to all the world.   It marks indeed all the most peculiar and precious fruits of voluntary Christianity, apart from State Churches and their political ecclesiastic establishments.   Some most excellent officials in the Anglican Church no doubt followed in the line; but it was the Dissenters and laymen who *began* the carrying about of the pure Gospel to every thirsty soul.*

But why should we esteem Great Britain in particular as alluded to, by this unique piece of architecture, a step which is too high for a human step, at the further end of the Grand Gallery?   Because the height of this step is precisely the 36·0 inches of the linear national standard of Great Britain at that time.   And if the upper surface of the step, from its north edge up to its southern termination, is not also

---

* This mere idea, in attempted explanation of the 1813 prophetic memorialization in the Grand Gallery, was afterwards carefully, conscientiously, and most laboriously examined into by Mr. Charles Horner, London; who found by studying the records of the time, that 1813 was the very turning point in the efforts of Wilberforce and his friends, in breaking through the resistance offered officially to the introduction of the Gospel into India; and that it commenced an unexampled rise of activity, amongst all the Missionary Societies of Great Britain. Mr. Horner's valuable paper on this subject has been published several times both in America and this country.   See especially Mr. Edward Hine's *Life from the Dead*, Feb., 1878; and Mr. E. W. Bird's *Banner of Israel*, No. 61, Vol. II.; but the following may still be usefully extracted from it.

The first effort of Wilberforce in this cause was in 1793; but it was unsuccessful; and up to 1812, according to a case duly chronicled in the Madras Police Office, on May 22 of that year, all Missionaries who might arrive in India bent on preaching the Gospel to the Natives, were " at once expelled the country" by the British Government, or East India Company acting as such, with its due salaried portion of the State Church of Great Britain.

By the light of the Great Pyramid, we can now easily see that 1793 was not the ordained time.   Poor Wilberforce knew nothing of that. He only saw the grand efforts he had been making in so holy a cause, thrown out before Parliament on the third reading.   For a while he was quite stricken down; and wrote painfully, yet under Grace, in his private diary: " how mysterious, how humbling, are the dispensations of God's providence.   Defeat of the East Indian Clauses!   Oh! may not

36, but 61, inches; that is because 36 + 25 = 61; or indicates that the linear standards of Great Britain and Israel, the yard and the sacred cubit of Noah, Moses, Solomon, and the Great Pyramid, are now, or are to be before 1881·4 A.D., both of them respected as standards, not only in Great Britain, but also in all Anglo-Saxon inhabited regions around the whole globe; testifies Hartwell A. Powers, from America.

And his testimony is Pyramidally true; for, *first*, I believe my measures of the 36 and 61 inches made in 1865 under ignorance of any such explanation, are practically correct; and *second*, as previously explained at p. 299, the Ordnance Survey of Great Britain involuntarily uses at this time the 25-inch scale of the Great Pyramid *as well* as a British yard; already, too, the so-called geometrical 25-inch cubit has its followers in the land; already are the Israelite measures of old being sought out as a God-given heirloom to our race in the

---

this have been because one so unworthy as I undertook this hallowed cause, and carried it on with so little true humility, faith, self-abasement, and confidence in God through Christ?"

But the Lord had not abandoned his faithful servant, and on the contrary preserved him, even in his weak bodily health through twenty long years, until another opportunity came, and at the right time, or on June 22nd, 1813.

Then was Wilberforce's strength renewed as almost with eagle wings. "This East Indian subject," he then wrote, "is assuredly the greatest that ever interested the heart or engaged the efforts of man. How wonderful that a private individual should have such an influence on the temporal and eternal happiness of millions; literally millions on millions yet unborn! O God, make me more earnest for Thy glory; and may I act more from real love and gratitude to my redeeming Lord. O Lord, bless us; pardon our past lukewarmness and slothfulness, and make us more diligent for the time to come."

When the eventful evening in Parliament arrived, never had Wilberforce spoken with greater power, or produced a greater effect; and the clauses he had failed to carry 20 years before were now, in 1813, carried by a majority of 53, and became law in India in April, 1814. He gave the praise to God, "the good Providence of God really;" and still spoke of it as "the greatest of all causes, above even the Abolition; the cause, namely, of laying a ground for the communication to our Indian fellow-subjects of Christian light and moral improvement." While in his private diary he added, "I humbly hope that God has great designs in view for the East, and that they will be executed by Great Britain."

beginning of the world, and considered as a priceless treasure which must not be dropped,*—while Great Britain is day by day being identified, by the light of prophecy, with the lost tribes of Israel ; not Judah or the Jews, but of the remaining ten, or with Manasseh eleven, tribes; so long lost to the eye of the world, but of whom the Lord has long since announced that He will acknowledge them in the days approaching, and be glorified in them as no other nation ever was glorified from the beginning of the world.

What manner of people, then, ought not we of Great Britain now, of Israel in ages past, to be at this juncture of our eventful history ; saved above all nations by the Providence of God in a manner we have never deserved, and for Divine purposes of the future, respecting which nothing but the glorious Scriptures of Inspiration can give us any sufficient or saving idea; a halcyon time, when Ephraim shall be united once more with Judah, and both shall be on the Lord's side. And when, as well expressed by the author of that most Scriptural book, " The Last Week ; or, Things which must shortly come to Pass," p. 90, " the Apostle who received the Revelations, as also the Ancient Prophets, seems to indicate that there will be in those last days (not last of the world, but of this Dispensation only), *a concentration of the fulfilment of Bible truths.*"

* The following news from America is to the point. At a meeting held at the Old South Church in Boston, Mass., at noon, Nov. 8, 1879, Charles Latimer of Ohio was called to preside, and G. R. Hardy, of Mass., appointed Secretary. The President invoked the guidance of Divine Wisdom on the Great Work intended to be inaugurated ; and the meeting then proceeded formally to establish the
PARENT INTERNATIONAL INSTITUTE, FOR PRESERVING AND PERFECTING WEIGHTS AND MEASURES.
The primeval Great Pyramid origination was acknowledged ; an office opened, at 375, Tremont Street, Boston, Mass. ; and a tried friend, Lucien J. Bisbee, appointed Superintendent ; with a plan of action for collecting all, and radiating concentrated, light on the special object founded for.

CHAPTER XXIV.

PREPARATIONS FOR A SINGLE UNIVERSAL METROLOGY;

But of which of two most opposite kinds; and Why, and When.

THOUGH everything else may fail to convince some minds that our nation is born to noblest scripture heritages; that the short-date, Biblical history of intellectual and God-worshipping mankind (no matter what physiological discourses on protoplasm, on one side, and believers in German linguistic theories, on the other, may choose to aver) is a marvellously close approach to what was, and is, the reality; and that, too, not only for what has already come to pass in history touching the favoured family of the Hebrews, but also for the working out of such of the prophecies as still remain to be accomplished respecting the two distinct branches of that people; viz. the Israelites of the Assyrian captivity of the Samarian Kingdom of Israel on the one hand; and the Jews of the destruction of, and dispersion from, Jerusalem under Titus, after their return from their Babylonian captivity, on the other;—though everything else, I add, may fail to convince some minds, that our nation may reasonably consider itself to a large extent descended from the former (though they were lost to the view of mankind 2,500 years ago), and that it owes its present unexampled prosperity and power to the special favour of our God and His Christ, far above its own intrinsic deserts (and

should bow in humility and adoration accordingly) ;—
the most convincing proof, I say, of these things to
some minds may be,—to note in calmness and leisure
certain recent episodes of our national history; and to
mark what disasters might well have befallen us according to the ruling of our statesmen for the time being,
whether they were of one side of politics or the other,—
yet how the nation was preserved, and even strengthened,
notwithstanding.

Shall our public ministers, then, continue in their
erring courses in order that the nation may abundantly
prosper ?—God forbid.   Let every man try to do his
duty ; and. probably no one tries more earnestly to do
it, than the Prime Minister for the time being.   Yet
there is one always neglected department of that officer's
calling, wherein the very nature of the case allows of
clear and simple mathematical views, capable of all
men's understanding, being immediately introduced; and
this subject is, the Great Pyramid's special and original
one of metrology: a national, as well as sacred matter
too, though not yet studied from that latter side of the
question by any parliamentary leader.

A worthy science, indeed, though long ill-treated and
despised of almost all men, is metrology; and yet there
cannot be the shadow of a doubt, that we are now on
the eve of movements of the whole human race in connection with it; all educated communities *beginning*
now to acknowledge it to be a marvellous power, with
germs of political influence of the highest order; specially adapted, too, for the working out of some of the
grandest developments of the future,   Every nation,
until now, has had its own *hereditary* system of weights
and measures; curiously intertwined, no doubt, with
those of other nations in their distant primeval origins,
vulgarised perhaps, and even largely debased in times
of mediæval darkness; as well as pestiferously meddled

with and complicated by the doctrinaires of new-born
modern and o'ervaulting science schools, — but still
there was hitherto something more or less national to
every nation in its metrology, as in its language; and
serving the same purposes as the diversity of tongues
in keeping up the heaven-appointed institution of
nations;—the chief characteristic of all mankind from
the days of the Dispersion; unknown before that event,
but never for one moment ceasing since then. What,
therefore, is likely to be the result of man seeking in
these days, by means of his own devices, to undermine
that institution of *nations,* and even endeavouring to
quench it off the face of God's earth, for the sake
of introducing a modern French idea and making it
dominant everywhere?

Whatever the result, the action intended to produce
it, has already begun; and the first weapon agreed on to
be used, and the first breach to be made in the barriers
of national distinctions, is that of weights and measures. So that, without probably having distinctly contemplated the issue, yet most of the existing civilized
nations have for years passed been tending, not to go
forward in a Divinely prescribed path, but to bring all
men *back* to the old, universal-family state they were in
when they attempted to build the Tower of Babel; and
from which nothing drove them then, short of a supernatural manifestation of the power of God.

Progress of the Communistic French Mètre.

Several centuries ago, and even less, there were nearly
a hundred varieties of linear standards in use throughout
Europe; but one of them after another has latterly
dropped out of view, until it was reported at the French
Exposition of 1867, that only thirteen could then be
discovered; and since that epoch, all save three or four

of those, are said to have practically perished, and the
mètre to be gaining adherents from even *their* votaries,
every day.*

"There has, therefore," says the *pro*-French metric
President Barnard, "been large progress made toward
uniformity, and the most important steps, and the
most significant steps, are those which have been
taken within our own century!"—"No man not
totally regardless of the history of the past, and not
absolutely blind to what is taking place under his own
eye in the present, can possibly pretend to believe that
the world is to be for ever without a uniform system of
weights and measures; we cannot suppose that the
progress already indicated is going to be arrested at the
point at which it has now reached!"—"Of the two
systems, therefore, just now indicated as the systems
between which the world must choose, unless in regard
to this matter it shall henceforth stand still for ever,—
one or the other must sooner or later prevail!!" And
he considers that of these two, viz. the British yard and
the French mètre, the latter is certain to triumph in
the end.

This result has by no means come about altogether
spontaneously, or through unseen and only natural influences; the mind of man has had much to do with it,
and it has been the one polar point to which French
ambition has alone been steady and true during the last
eighty years; always working for it, whether sleeping
or waking; whether in war or peace; whether as a
kingdom, or an empire, or a republic; always endeavouring to throw the net of her metrical system
of weights and measures over other nations, as well as
her own people; and though not without some Imperial
ambition to chain many conquered nations to the chariot-

* "The Metrical System," by President Barnard, Columbia College,
U.S., 1872.

wheels of France, yet with the far deeper Communistic
feeling of converting *all* the nations of the earth into
one great people, speaking one language, and using but
one weight and one measure, and those of human, as
directly opposed to Divine, origination.

France had been consistent in her own case; she
had begun, at her first Revolution, by slaughtering off
all the accessible individuals of her reigning family;
who, as such, were the very type and symbol to the
French people of their being a *nation*, one amongst
many nations; or of their living under that post-Babel,
but Divinely ordained, institution. Having then, at
that dreadful close of the last century, killed off, as far
as she then could, all her royal family, her Roman
Catholic priests also, and openly abrogated belief in
the God of Scripture, she (France) could, at that time,
of all nations consistently, and with show of demon-
strable reason, become the champion of *her* metric,
and atheistic metrological system; a system since then
everywhere secretly adopted with still more intense fer-
vour by the Socialists, Internationalists, Communists
in all countries; but strange to say, by certain British
scientific men also, in some cases claiming, in others
scorning, to be reputed Christians.

The task of spreading this nationally suicidal scheme
over all the nations of the world, might seem at first
quite Quixotic; and would be, but for schemes and
forces in the destiny of man, which man knows little or
nothing about, until they have accomplished their ends,
and left them to rue their effects. So that it is owing
at least as much to those unseen influences as to the
direct action of any visible Frenchman, that the French
metric system has been going forward during the last
few years of history at a continually accelerated rate;
and that one country after another has been persuaded
to adopt it, until suddenly it has been found, to our

exceeding astonishment and practical isolation, that almost every nation in Europe, and many peoples in Asia, Africa, and America, have already been converted.

France herself, strange to say, has not profited by the system either in war or peace. In war, she has been lately defeated with greater overthrows than even the Persian empire of old ; and the fighting faculty has abandoned her soldiers almost as completely as it did the Babylonians towards the calamitous end of their once powerful independence, or the grandsons of the soldiers of Alexander the Great, when the Romans slaughtered them in battle with the utmost ease ; while in peace, France's commercial transactions, though continually being " reorganized " on metrical science principles, remain far below those of Great Britain. Yet still she (France) calls upon all nations, and so many of these nations answer her call with delight, and madly encourage each other, to clothe themselves with this latter-day invention of hers ; which, if successful, must, in so far as it goes, tend to decrease the nationality, if not to hasten on the final disappearance, of every nation adopting it.

Only three years ago there was published by a committee of Columbia College, United States, an excellent little book entitled the " Metric System." Drawn up chiefly by their Professor of the higher mathematics (Charles Davies), and approved by those then in power, —this work demonstrated unsparingly the artificial character of the French metrical system, the innumerable patches which it required in practice to make it hold water at all, the errors of its science, its inapplicability to the ordinary affairs of the mass of humankind ; and concluded with reprinting the celebrated report on weights and measures by John Quincey Adams : which report, after indulging in the utmost oratorical vehemence for saying whatever could be said as a partisan for *either* side of the question successively, concludes with recommending all good United States men to have as little as possible to do with the French standards; but to feel hopefully confident that the inevitable development of the world's history would, sooner or later, bring up some far better system for the future happiness and prosperity of mankind.

But three short years have so accelerated the growth of French metric influence, or the predestined metrological temptation and trial of the whole world,—that all the parties to that first, Columbia College, book upon the Mètre seem now to have vanished out of existence; and a new Columbia College work, of the same title as the old one, but with totally opposite principles, was produced last year (1873), to order of new governors, by the new President (the Rev. Dr. Barnard) of the same college. An enormous issue of this last book is now being thrown off for distribution gratuitously far and wide, and (as our extracts from it have already indicated) it is ecstatically in favour of the French metric system being adopted by all Americans with the utmost possible speed. And when that is brought about, the author declares that Britain, Russia, and the Scandinavian countries will be the only known dissentients among educated peoples.

Scandinavia, however, it is asserted, has already been exhibiting some leanings towards the metric system; Russia is in the hands of her German officials, who are all now metric men, both at home and abroad; and Britain herself, who has hitherto successfully resisted private Bills in the House of Commons in favour of French metricalism, is told at last (1874) that there shall be a Government Bill next year. If that be carried, Russia and Scandinavia are expected immediately to yield completely; and all the nations of the world will then have passed through the great French metrological mill, whose whirling stones will never cease to grind, until, excepting only those sealed by God, " it has caused all, both small and great, rich and poor, free and bond, to receive a mark in their right hand or in their foreheads; and that no man might buy or sell, save he that had the mark, or the name of the beast, or the number of his name " (or, in fact, has adopted the use of the atheistic, and contra-Deistic, French-metric system). Rev. xiii. 16, 17.)

Preparations made by the British Government.

Meanwhile, what have the ministers of Great Britain been doing either to fend off this dire calamity, or to embrace and make the most of this happy invention of the French brain, whichever of the two they may deem it to be ? In parliamentary bills (up to 1877) nothing at all: and in private study, there is reason to fear, as little. Our late Prime Minister's last work on the old, old subject of the poems of Homer, came out, he being then in office, almost simultaneously with the announcement from Paris of twenty nations being about to meet there in fraternal union and international congress on their growing metric system; both to arrange their schemes for fixing it unalterably on their own several countries; and, judging from the publications of a lawyer of Italian, Jewish extraction at several of our public societies,—to ridicule Anglo-Saxon peoples for slowness, stupidity, and ignorance.

Remarked William Blake nearly 70 years ago on classic following courses :—" The perverted writings of Homer and Ovid, of Plato and Cicero, which all men ought to contemn (in such a category) are set up by artifice against the sublime of the Bible:—Rouse up, O young men of the new age ! Set your foreheads against the hirelings ! For we have hirelings in the camp, the court, and the university, who would, if they could, for ever depress mental and prolong corporeal war." And then, adapting *his* words, which had reference to art, for our subject of metrological science, we may continue, " We do not want either profane Greek or idolatrous Roman, ancient Cainite Egyptian, or modern atheistical French models, if we are only true to the messages of Divine inspiration, to those words of eternity in which we shall live for ever in Jesus our Lord."

But William Blake wrote before the time appointed by Providence for the awakening of Israel; and the British country continued to drift on, as it has done almost ever since, under other guidance than that of metrologically indifferent Ministers. But things cannot, and will not, stop there: this view, the pro-French metric champion, President Barnard, makes very plain. We may, indeed, thus far have been providentially, rather than ministerially, saved from a pit of evil vastly more profound than appears on the surface; but politically we have not as yet reached any haven of metrological safety; no soundings are touched; no secure principles for anchoring to, reached; and no arguments of sufficient power to stand before the specious insinuations of French metrical agitators have yet been uttered in the House of Commons. We have our ancient national measures still, but with all their mediæval and modern imperfections on their head; and the attacks, open and concealed, of the metrical party upon them on that account, are unceasing. That party, moreover, has gained over the School Board Commission; the new office of the Warden of the Standards has been gorgeously supplied with expensive apparatus for French *vacuum* weighing and *refrigeration* measuring; and men who ought to have died rather than give up their opinions of a dozen years ago, have swallowed them all, and join now in recommending the total denationalisation of our ancient metrology.

How long will our plastic rulers, accustomed to take demagogic pressure from without, in place of principle, knowledge, and religious teaching, remain firm against such agitation?

The very anxiety of the Rev. President Barnard and the metricalists to bring on the final struggle as between the French mètre and the English yard, shows that they have good reason to know that there is weakness in the supporters of the latter. Some involuntary throbbing, moreover, in the pulse of humanity is now telling all nations, with deeper force than any philosophy can, or chooses to do, that these are the last times of this dispensation;* and that we are now or never to decide a long, long future. "If the work was to be done over again," writes President Barnard himself, with an admirable sense of what is true in science and right in justice because it is so, "the French metric system ought to adopt, and doubtless would adopt, not their superficial earth-measure, the mètre, but the Pyramid axial reference of the cubit, on account of its immense superiority in fact and geometric idea.† But it is not to be done over again," he says, "and never can or will be; we must choose the metrical system as it is now, or not at all; it has already been taken up by half mankind, and

* Since the above was first published in these pages, has appeared a most weighty work, " The Approaching End of the Age," by the Rev. J. Grattan Guiness, a book which, though I may differ from the author on some subsidiary points, yet on the larger, I cannot too much admire, and recommend to every thinking man. And if some such men find fault with it, may they be induced, and enabled from above, to write better and more thoroughly on all the bearings and Scriptural foundations of the same grand subject.

† This acknowledgment of the Rev. President Barnard, at pp. 93 and 94 of his book, does him immense honour, he being an out-and-out pro-mètre man; and it is of all the more weight that he gives an abler discussion of the present condition of the earth size and shape question by modern geodesic measure, in all its most scientific ramifications, than has ever yet been seen in print, in a readable form.

no able system of human invention will ever have such a
chance of universal adoption; while no system that cannot and will not become universal, is to be tolerated for
a moment. Now the British yard, or its third part, the
foot," adds the President, " being only the measure of one
nation, will always be resisted by the majority of nations,
— therefore the mètre must in the end gain the day."

The Stone Prepared without Hands.

But *is* the final contest only between the French
mètre and the British yard or foot ? The anti-metric
men in the House of Commons have hitherto succeeded
in establishing nothing against that idea; and the Rev.
President Barnard says, both that it *is* so, and that all
the wealth and numbers of mankind throughout all the
world are divided on these two sides only. He does,
indeed, allow in one place that there is a phantom of a
third side, viz. the Great Pyramid metrology; but
declares that that, having *only a religious foundation*,
will never accumulate any large party about it.*

Since the days of Sennacherib defying the God of
Israel, was there ever a speech more likely to call forth
proof, in its own good time, that the arm of the Lord is
not shortened ? We see in Scotland already what the
belief, that it is the Lord who appointed the chrono-

* The exact words are, at p. 56, "And one who, like Professor Piazzi
Smyth, bases his metrological theories on religious grounds, and prefers
the Pyramid Inch as his standard, as a matter of conscience, is not likely
to concentrate around him a very powerful party of opposition."
Here everything in the way of linear standards for the Pyramid system
is made by the Reverend President to rest on the inch; and he intensifies
that accusation at p. 73 by writing, " C. Piazzi Smyth almost fanatically
attaches himself to the inch, a measure which he believes with implicit
faith to have been divinely given to Cheops, builder of the Great Pyramid, and again to Moses in the wilderness ; and in what he, no doubt,
regards as the great work of his life, he uses no other term to express
the largest dimensions." I can only, therefore, refer my readers to all
that I have written in this book, as well as others, upon the grand linear
standard of the Pyramid, and the only one certainly common to it, Noah
and Moses, being the *cubit*. See especially Chapter XVI. on " The Sacred
Cubit ; also Chapter XVIII. pp. 395 to 413."

logical institution of the week, will do, to make that one time-measure binding on a whole nation; and will the men of that land not also adhere to any such other measures in the future, as they shall come in time to understand were likewise appointed from the same Divine source?

The Reverend President, in stating the conquests of the atheistic French metrical system at the utmost, bows involuntarily to the religious element; by the act of stating, not merely that the mètre has been adopted by 160,000,000 men, but by that number of civilized people "in Christian lands." Yet in that case, if those inhabitants are truly Christian,—if their Christianity is real, vital, heartfelt, and not confined to the land only, or to having ecclesiastically consecrated burial-grounds, exquisite cathedral buildings, supported by the State as part of a political compact, and alleged "holy places," —will not they all, as well as Britons, delight to obey, in the end, whatever shall be proved to have been appointed by Christ in the beginning of the world? Especially if in evident anticipation of present and future times; viz. of "the last days, when *scoffers* are to appear, walking after their own lusts, and saying, Where is the promise of His Coming (Christ's Second Coming as a King)? for since the fathers fell asleep, all things continue as they were from the beginning of creation."

Except for this predicted fact for these later times, so able an ecclesiastic as the Rev. Dr. Barnard might have stopped in his headlong career, in order to inquire of his own heart, "Will *Christ* be pleased to find, on descending from Heaven to occupy His future throne on Earth, that no less than 160,000,000 of His professed servants have thrown away their Divinely ordained inheritances; have, Esau-like, eschewed their metrological birth-rights; and robed themselves in atheistic-speaking livery instead?"

The Parties to the Final Metrological Contest.

It is, indeed, most curiously, but intimately, between the French mètre and the Messianic Great Pyramid cubit, that the *final* contest must come; for the present British weights and measures, as manipulated by recent parliamentary laws only, are evidently doomed to fall.

Now the metric and the Pyramid systems, though on every other point utterly opposed, are yet, in this one following feature, perfectly similar to each other; viz. that they both tend to break down the post-Babel separation of men into nations, and combine them all into one grand government: but then, how is this principle carried out, by whom, for whom, and to what ends, in either case?

The French metric system, though it is not a hundred years old, is wanted by its promoters to override everything else in the world, of whatever age, and whatever origin. All nations are to bow down, as well as presently to disappear, before it; and though it has been found, at every essential point, full of scientific blunders, and teeming with sacrifices of the comforts and conveniences of the poor and many, to the mere crotchets of a few doctrinaires of the upper classes, in their curiously appointed laboratories or expensively prepared studios,— it is never to be altered, never replaced in its rule over all mankind by anything else of similar or dissimilar invention;—no, not though the present order of man's life, national distinctions being supposed destroyed, goes on upon this earth, as the human prophets of the system say it is bound to do, for so very many hundreds of thousands of *millions* of years that the physical earth itself will have grown out of shape and size to that degree, as to become totally unfit to serve for a standard of reference to the Parisian mètre, the future symbol of human rule over all the earth in

man, for man, and by man himself alone. Wherefore
President Barnard already, in concert with other metricalists, though introducing that French mètre to the
world, *first* of all as a scientific earth-measure, yet *finally*
allows that he and they do not care whether it is, or is
not, of that character; for they intend, by and by, to
shut out all commensurable reference to God's heavens
above and His earth below; and simply adopt, within
the four walls of a closed chamber, a particular bar of
metal made by man, as the grand metrological unit, in
terms of which all men,—of many nations originally,
but soon, they think, to be swept together into one vast
commune of the whole human family, without kings,
and probably without churches, except for human glorifications,—shall live and move, and have any understanding of material things. Almost as well might
they, like suicides, refuse to live any longer on this
earth-ball; because its physical conditions and original
creation features in number, weight and measure, though
planned by God, do not please them.

The Great Pyramid system, on the other hand, is
the oldest metrological system in the history of the
world, still testified to by exact monumentalization; has
its traces extensively among European and Asiatic
peoples; and is next to perfect in all those scientific
points where the French system fails; besides acknow-
ledging thankfully every creation law of God for man,
as wisest, best, and happiest for him, both individually
and collectively. It is, moreover, full of benevolence
for the poor and needy; besides teaching that their
anguish and woes will last but a few years more;* for

* See in a past Chapter XXIII., at pp. 546, 548, and in the following
part of this Chapter at p. 585, that this is no reference to the almost
instant chronological termination of the Grand Gallery, with its Southern
"impending," threatening, punishing wall, and the following low passage of unutterable anguish,—but to Ante-chamber times and the period
of the Granite Leaf. Not to the 1260 terminating in 1882 A.D., but to
the 1335 of Daniel, closer to 1957 A.D.

then, agreeably with the Scriptures, Christ Himself shall
again descend from heaven, this time with angels and
archangels and glorified saints, accompanying; and
will give to man at last that perfect, peaceful, soldier-
less, and righteous government which man alone is
incapable of. And so shall the Saviour, even in this
present state of the earth as to size and shape, and
existing truth of the Great Pyramid earth-commensurable standards, reign over all nations brought under his
one heavenly sceptre, until that Divine termination
arrives, when time shall be no more.

Human, versus *Divine*, *Ultimate Rule*.

Even within the moderate bounds of only one nation,
and for a short space of a few years, how totally insufficient is the best human government to check the evils of
humankind! And that, too, even in periods of profoundest
peace; without any of the terrific aggravations of misfortune for the poor indissolubly connected with war,
and increasing, rather than diminishing, every day!

With all England's present wealth and science, or
notwithstanding it all, pauperism is increasing in the
land; rich men are richer; but poor men are more
numerous and more hopelessly poor, and chiefly in the
great cities; for there, in truth, the distressed, the
miserable, the sick, the vicious, the under-educated, the
persecuted and the persecutors of society, multiply beyond the rate of all government, all philanthropy, to
procure any permanent relief or hope of amendment.
A good *country* landlord may perhaps be able to super-
vise, help, and befriend to some limited extent every
person in his little provincial community of men of
humble ambition and simple life; but in the large towns
whence the great wonders of modern civilization emerge

—there, in precise proportion as the towns are large, and a few of the inhabitants rich beyond all measure— there the houses of the dregs of the population, and the progressive debasement of humanity, are beyond belief, and go on increasing every day;—recalling with awe the denunciations of Scripture against those who join house to house beyond human power of controlling results.*

But, throw all nations, without Divine guidance, into one vast community or family of humankind, as the universal adoption of the French metrical system would be the beginning of,—and then, the scales for doing mercantile business and the magnitude of the opportunities for speculating in every element of life, must enlarge enormously. With the inevitable result, on one side, of a few clever geniuses making more colossal fortunes, whether honestly or otherwise, than ever; but on the other side, of the wretchedness, the woe, and the degradation of the chief mass of the population going on increasing in all large centres of gathering together, and becoming more terrible in the long future ages than anything chronicled yet.

---

* " The truth is that our wealthy and upper classes do not fully realise the manifold dangers to society arising in the overcrowded dwellings of the poor. They see only the wonderful advances made every day in whatever can add to the comforts, conveniences, pleasures, and luxuries of their own living. They never dream that their wealth, splendour, and pride, are surrounded by a cordon of squalor, demoralisation, disease, and crime."

" The higher classes are slow to realise the fact, that in all our large centres of population there is an ever-increasing amount of poverty, immorality, and disease."

" From statistical returns in London, bearing on the condition of St. Giles's, it appears that there were in one district 600 families, and of these 570 severally occupied but one room each. In another, of 700 families, 550 occupied but one room each. In another district, out of 500 families, 450 occupied but one room each. In one of these rooms, 12 feet by 13 feet, by 7½ feet high, eight persons lived. In another room, 13 feet by 5 feet, by 6½ feet high, five children and their parents lived."

" In Manchester small houses are packed together as closely as possible, and in them are stowed away an enormous amount of the poorer

Contrast this inevitable outcome of human rule, increasing infinitely in disaster if continued for unlimited time, unchecked by anything above the laws of nature, or of man, as philosophers see, and make, them now, —with the sacred system of the Messiah's monarchy when He shall be in presence and power over all. A faint idea of only one of the characteristics of that kingdom was given in the happy condition of equality in health and relative prosperity, in the camp of the Israelites, when setting forth out of Egypt with Moses; not under human rule only, but under the guidance also of the Angel of the Covenant: and when " there was not one weak one amongst them."

What are all the triumphs of human learning to that glorious result in a great nation; and where has anything like it been seen either before or since?

But in place of approaching such a desirable consummation for our perishing, yet increasing, millions, modern science and the churches, politics, and our system of prisons and police, are swerving further and further from it every day. Yet poor science, in so far as it is for once truly called science, often maligned and never wealthy,—viz. the exact mathematical science of such excellent and most exemplary men as the late

part of the population. Six persons in one room,—only one room to live in, sleep in, and in which to transact all the avocations of life."

" In Liverpool 26,000 houses are occupied by families in single rooms, or a third of the whole population exists under these unsatisfactory conditions,—producing disease, immorality, pauperism, and crime; truth and honesty are, to human beings so debased, mere names."

" Our railway extensions, street improvements, the erection of new houses, public and other buildings, rendered necessary by our ever-increasing prosperity, act with the force of a screw, forcing decent families to quit comfortable homes, and in many cases they have no alternative but to accept shelter in already overcrowded and demoralised neighbourhoods, where there is little light, drainage, water, or ventilation, and no proper convenience for natural wants—and what happens? After a few weeks the strong man is bowed down, and the children are left an increase of pauperism to society."—Extracts from the " Social Crisis in England," by W. Martin: Birmingham, 1873.

Venerable Archdeacon Pratt, and which was "*not* at variance with Revelation,"*—has yet proved herself of precious service to all mankind, if she has enabled us in the present day of growing doubts, and hearts failing them for fear, to read off the great prehistoric, and prophetic, monument of Philitis in the land of Egypt; and to find that, besides scientific metrological knowledge, it utters things which have been kept secret from the foundation of the world; things which not even the Apostles were permitted to know of, 1,846 years ago, viz. times and seasons which are in God's power alone. Wherefore thus it is, that the Great Pyramid is now, and only now, beginning to announce that a termination to the greatest misery of the greatest numbers of human beings, or to their continuing indefinitely under solely human rule, whether of kings or of republics,—is at length drawing nigh. The improvement is indeed already begun.

The Rise of Manasseh.

No one looking beyond his own hearth-stone, can fail to have remarked the kindlier feelings that have grown up in America for Britain during the last few years; and why? Not only because the men of the United States are of the same race and language with us, but far more because they are of the same religion in heart and soul as well as name, the same intense Bible loving, Sabbath observing peoples; and yet infinitely more still, because they have studied and are deeply studying the still unfulfilled prophecies of the Sacred Book. For there they find, to use the words of one of their own most popular preachers, that " in the rapidly-hastening

* See the last (6th) edition of " Science and Religion not at Variance," by Archdeacon Pratt, formerly of Cambridge, latterly of Calcutta, where he died in 1871, to the deep grief of all who had ever had the privilege of meeting him.

future, England and America will stand together for Christ and liberty, against the great Anti-Christian host when it invades the land of Palestine; and on which host the Lord Himself will inflict the last decisive blow." " Wherefore," as well reciprocates an Anglo-Saxon clergyman here, " who amongst us can help feeling a peculiar satisfaction at discovering such strong grounds for the belief that not England only, but the English language, will be found at last united on the Lord's side?"

This was the first step towards the improved feeling; and even while it was establishing, the newly found identity of the British people with the Lost Ten Tribes of Israel, under the headship of, and inheriting the promises made to, Ephraim, was rapidly demonstrating amongst us.   Ephraim, the younger son of Joseph, but destined to become the greater, even as " a multitude of nations "; but in that case where was Manasseh, the eldest son ; also destined not only to survive, but to become " a great people " ?   While others were merely wondering, a remarkable man, Edward Hine, who had already added the key-stone to the arch of Anglo-Israelism by identifying the Normans with the tribe of Benjamin, and the prophecies connected there-with,—came forth at the right moment ; and showed that the great transatlantic nation, the United States of America, was the very representative we were in search of ; and that Britain and America were verily two brothers.

" Yes, two brothers," soon responded across the ocean an able American clergyman,[*] " both of them in their childhood brought up in sight, almost at the foot, of the Great Pyramid ; and though Manasseh was de-

_____
[*] The Rev. Joseph Wild, D.D., Brooklyn, New York. See his work, " The Lost Ten Tribes and 1882," published in, 1879. See also " A Miracle in Stone," by the Rev. Joseph A. Seiss, D.D., Philadelphia. Also the recently published " Supplement " to the same.

prived out there of his birthright, by a Providence
which he could not understand, and which long em-
bittered his feelings, yet he forgets not the place of
his youth; and on the reverse of the great seal of his
present country, he has engraved the figure of that
grandest monument of the world, the Great Pyramid;
with the long lost topmost corner-stone, raised aloft in
the air and bearing the all-seeing eye, over it.

The Great Pyramid then in the present day belongs
most peculiarly to the memories of Ephraim and Manasseh, of all the tribes of Israel: and Manasseh already
speaks of it thus fervently:—"This miracle in stone, so
wrought and placed as to be seen by the millions and
last for millenniums; this watchman on the walls of
time; this sentinel in charge of the secrets and treasures
of the sires of long ago; this prophet in the wilderness
in rugged garb—proclaiming the will of heaven as then
made known and now manifesting;—this Daniel, who
can interpret for us the future; this mile-stone of the
ages, in the central meeting-place for all mankind."

With their minds thus prepared, and their souls alight
to work the work of the Lord as soon as made clear to
them, is it surprising that when Charles Latimer, C.E.,
announced (as mentioned on p. 558) only a few months
ago, in the Pilgrim-fathers' City of Boston, that special
attempts of a few designing, but most able and wealthy
men were to be made next session to induce Congress to
render the atheistic French metrical measures compulsory over the whole United States, and to abolish their
own traditional and hereditary weights and measures,
—the people have flown to arms spiritual? Defence
associations,—for instructing the public, resisting the
mètre and both preserving, and perfecting by Pyramid
reference, every remnant of their own once Divinely
given metrology,—are springing up over the land. And
President Barnard may yet see, in his own country and

from his own countrymen, what a simple religious cause, when approved of by the God of Israel, may enable men to accomplish in a case which he, President Barnard, judging by human wisdom alone, had so emphatically pronounced to be hopeless only three short years ago.

The Two Sabbaths alluded to in the Great Pyramid.

Encouraged then thus, with a new encouragement, by knowing that Manasseh is now rising in his strength and heraldic dignity on the other side of the world in our, as well as his, deeply important cause,—let us, at this, the last place in our book where it can appropriately be attempted, note certain further and all-pervading characters of the Pyramid's inner time-symbolisms, when they indicate the sacred institutions of the Bible to man. Especially remembering, with Dr. Wild, that "The Bible is a growing book, being more read and better understood as the years pass by ; and, as men shall increase in knowledge and power, so the Bible will gain in influence and authority."

Now the whole way of approach to the interior of the building is by inclined passages ; men may choose either the descending, or the ascending; but accordingly as they *do* choose and follow either one, so they depart from the other, for every King's Chamber length they travel therein, by the amount of 365·242 Pyramid inches; or the solar tropical year in terms of mean solar days.

The perimeter of the whole building at the level of that chamber, 25,827 Pyramid inches, indicates the years of the precessional movement of the earth ; and the vertical height from that King's Chamber floor up to the angle of the inclined blocks of the topmost hollow of construction above it, marks, when multiplied by 10, the diameter of that precessional circle, 8221, nearly.

2 P 2

But this last portion of height, from King's Chamber floor upwards to the inclined blocks (and equal very nearly to the *seventh* part of the whole vertical height of the building) has been shown by Mr. James Simpson to contain some very instructive reminders not only of the sacred division of days and weeks, but the progress of sacred history itself in that particular matter.

1st. In the number of roofs within that space, five horizontal and similar of granite, and two superior of limestone, and set at a notable but opposite angle to each other. "May these two latter not indicate," asks Mr. Simpson, "the two Sabbaths, the old and the new; the one looking back to creation, the other forward to redemption, yet mutually supporting each other, and forming together the crown and strength of the week?"

2nd. Dividing that whole height by 7, we obtain, with some slight variation, as we take either the floor's level, or the base-of-the-wall's level, 5 inches below,—and the lower side or middle of thickness of stones above,—something between 116·3 and 117·3 Pyramid inches. Now this is not only the approximate length of the Ante-chamber, and the diameter of the circle of 365·242 days, but two of these heights are contained within the precious King's Chamber, and five of them above it, with Sabbatical renderings as before.

3rd. The same results obtain on treating the same space in cubic measure; five equal quantities outside the chamber, two within it, and each of them containing the appropriate number of 10 million cubic inches.

Now this quantity, continues Mr. Simpson, as the proximate contents of the Queen's Chamber, seemed there to typify a whole week, rather than a single day; or the seven days of the Queen's Chamber, form one day of the King's Chamber. While the arrangement by height of seven days there, in the King's Chamber, forms in its entirety a seventh of the height of the whole building. So that here is a scale of Sabbatisms rising by powers of seven, and giving 49 at once. Or if we take for their definition the exact Ante-chamber length 116·26, then there are not 49, but 50 of them in the whole height of the Great Pyramid, the 50th being perhaps no other than the chief and topmost corner-stone, and the year of jubilee in the larger cycle of the sacred reckoning of Israel; the chief, too, of all Sabbaths; and well realising—

" The stone which the builders refused is become the head stone of the corner.
" This is the Lord's doing; it is marvellous in our eyes.
" *This is the day which the Lord hath made ; we will rejoice and be glad in it.*"—Psalm cxviii. 22—24.

But it may be asked, continues Mr. Simpson, if the King's Chamber exhibits a week containing *two* Sabbaths, why does the Queen's Chamber show a week with only one Sabbath ? And then the reason which he gives, perfectly independently, confirms most admirably the House of Judah conclusions of Mr. H. A. Powers, E. Hine, and others given in our last chapter. For, says Mr. Simpson, it is because the first *seventh* of the Pyramid's height, including, therefore, the Queen's Chamber's low-level floor, represents the Old Testament Sabbath, *i.e.* the Creation or foundation Sabbath ; while the second *seventh* of the building, containing the Grand Gallery, which rises at last far above the Queen's Chamber's roof, represents the New Testament, or the Resurrection, Sabbath. And finally the third *seventh*, including the King's Chamber and the works above it, seems to be a sort of union of both.

Exactly so ; and herein is a most special piece of instruction from the Great Pyramid, for our own nation, at this very time, too, most particularly : the Pyramid emphasizing it thus,—

We are now chronologically on the surface of the Great Step in the Grand Gallery; and that surface memo-

rializes (see p. 557) both the primeval sacred cubit,
and the modern linear standard of Great Britain at the
present moment ; or, translated into Sabbath institutions of the respective times concerned, the primal
Creation Sabbath, and the comparatively recent Christian Sabbath are indicated as being both here in force.
Both are therefore obligatory upon us at this present
moment, or ever since the beginning of the step's time ;
though they were not so upon our ancestors who lived
before that date.

But these present days in which we are now living,
are when rationalistically inclined men are making their
onslaughts on the one and only Sabbath we have, and
are desiring to curtail and pervert its proper application
to sacred questions alone, by introducing science lectures, music of brass bands, and the opening of museums
and picture galleries.

The only answer to those men that can be consistently made by Christians believing in the proximate
gathering of the Church of Christ, and the supernatural
manifestations connected with the approaching end of
the present dispensation, is,—that not one moment of
the blessed Christian Sabbath shall be surrendered for
any such Cainite, or Jubal- and Tubal-Cainite, ideas:
but that the Nation should rather be induced to observe
(as the Pyramid teaches it ought now to uphold) two
Sabbaths in every week. The first of them, however,
being no other than the old Creation Sabbath ; to be
held, as the Jews do now hold it, on the Saturday ; and
then and thereon science lectures on Natural History or
Natural Philosophy may be appropriate enough. While,
when all our people are educated, as it is said they are
so soon to be, and minds have to be improved, as well
as limbs exercised, it will assuredly be found by the
lower, as it has long been already by the upper, classes,
—that five days in the week of hard work are as much

as any human being can go through, with due regard
to elevating his mind and chastening his soul on the
remaining two days of the week ; and thereby on the
whole, going forwards, rather than backwards, in grace
and favour with God and power of usefulness towards
his fellow-men.

The whole Number of Mankind.

When considering the many references contained in
the Great Pyramid to both the earliest past, and the
still future of mankind,—one cannot help thinking, says
Mr. Simpson, of man himself in the aggregate of the
world's human history.   In the pointed summit of the
building we see the unity of man's origin ; in the rapidly
increasing bulk below, the growth of his numbers to fill
the earth; and in the definite level plane, the coming
end of mere human, limited, terrestrial rule.

Now, from apex point to base, the contents of the
Great Pyramid in Pyramid cubic inches are near
161,000,000,000.   How many human souls, then, have
lived on the earth from Adam to the present day?   Somewhere between 153,000,000,000 and 171,900,000,000[*]
is the remarkable approach, and the best answer that
can now be made.

Granite, and its Religious Significations, in the ultra Grand Gallory Portions of the Great Pyramid.

Granite is first met with in the Portcullis plugs of
the lower part of the first ascending, or " the Hebrew
Exodus " passage, and is not seen again until we enter

---

[*] These numbers are arrived at by Mr. Simpson thus :—If the present
population of the globe is, say, 1,425,000,000, and we suppose the number
of past generations to be about 180, or 3 per century: then, taking the
average population at two-thirds of the present, we have a total of
1425 millions × $\frac{2}{3}$ × 180 = 171,000,000,000.
But at the more moderate allowance of three-fifths of the present number,
the result is 153,900,000,000.

the Ante-chamber.   But there it appears almost immediately, and looms large in front of us in the shape of
the granite leaf. There too the material appears in two
blocks, one resting on the other.   Is there any historic
or religious symbology in this ?

Yes, has been the answer of several inquirers,
—granite in the Great Pyramid typifies *both* of the
houses of Israel when united under Divine approval
and recognition.

Well, therefore, do we meet with it partially even in
the lower, and generally limestone, masonry of the building,—in the beginning of the Exodus Passage under
Moses; and up to some period near the establishment of
the Monarchy in Palestine.   Some period only, I venture to say, for the present latter or southern end of the
granite there, is a fractured surface, and no one can
say exactly how much further it once extended.   But
how happily, may we now see, has the immovability
of the lower granite plugs preserved for us this crucial
testimony of the religious signification of granite at, and
for, the most Divinely aided, the directly Theocratic,
part of the career of the chosen Israelite race.

Well, also, that we do *not* meet with granite in the
Queen's Chamber, which is set aside for the House of
Judah by itself.   And equally well that we do not meet
with it in the whole course of the Grand Gallery,
entirely occupied by the progress of Christianity in
general, and the Ephraimite, or Ten-tribed, and Manas-
sehite, House of Israel in particular.

But there is a day to come, which all Jews, as well
as both British and American, Israelites, look forward
to, of which the Lord has said by Ezekiel (xxxvii. 15—28),
that He will then distinctly take the House of Judah
and such children of Israel, chiefly two tribes, as may
be his companions, and that He will then also take the
House of Joseph or Ephraim and Manasseh, and such

children of all the House of Israel, or the ten tribes, as
may be his companions; and He will make them, these
two diverse houses and groups of tribes (representatively
only, a few for the many), into one nation in the land on
the mountains of Israel, and *one king shall reign over
them* (which has certainly not yet taken place from the
time of Ezekiel downwards); and they shall be God's
people, and He will be their God.

Now precisely such a day appears to be indicated inside
the beginning of the Ante-chamber, where granite com-
mences to be seen, not only in floor, walls, and ceiling,
but in the granite leaf, of two pieces; the lower piece,
with its cubic capacity of a quarter of corn, indicating
the sacred and prophetic "stick of Ephraim," while the
upper, with its almost heraldic badge of the boss, similarly indicates the stick of Judah with whom is the
sceptre. And the Lord God will rule over them; a
condition typified by the three granite stones of the
ceiling of the Ante-chamber; while the square of that
number forms the ceiling of the King's Chamber, representing a still higher expression of a Divine future
government for all the sons of men.

Again, in Isaiah (xi. 11), the day of the Lord is indicated when Ephraim and Judah shall cease their oppositions and be united; as in the granite leaf. While
the Ante-chamber itself, measuring round its walls close
under the ceiling 363, but round the walls near the floor,
behind the wainscot more probably, 365, &c. Pyramid
inches, is apparently an illustration of that very day of
the Lord; the same day that shall be a thousand years;
in fact, the very Millennium. But when to begin?

From the end of the Grand Gallery, supposed to mark
the date 1881·4 A.D., the floor distance through the low
passage onwards into the Ante-chamber and up to the
beginning of the granite in its *floor*, is only 61 inches.
But the place of granite commencement there, had to

expound by reference to the lime-stone portion, the earlier scientific subject of squaring the circle by area (see Chap. X. p. 202); and is very different from what it is in the walls; for there it is, on the mean of the East and West walls, almost exactly the difference of Daniel's two dates, 1260 and 1335 = 75 inch-years. While if we add thereto the half-week or 3˙5 years of some of the best commentators on Daniel, that brings us under the centre of the granite leaf (North and South) for a probably still more important sacred epoch; 1960 A.D.

The Measurement of the Great Pyramid in the Revelation of St. John the Divine.

But the world is not yet *historically* arrived in the Ante-chamber and its granite parts of the Great Pyramid,—we are still in the year 1879 A.D., on the great step, and not yet out of the Grand Gallery. That step exhibits the standards of linear measure of Great Britain and Israel conjoined (see p. 557), but there is no reference *there*, as yet, to Judah. And it is apparently to this very time, under the ominously impending South wall, long *after* the Apocalyptic sixth trumpet has sounded, and produced its earlier historical effects to the very letter, see Chapters VI. and VII.; long also after the Angel of the Reformation has appeared with the open book, his left foot on the southern Papal earth, his right foot on the sea, or the islands of Northern Protestant faith, and looking necessarily Westward towards America; and long after the rise of the Gospel churches bearing the message of salvation to kings and nations and peoples, for the love of the Gospel alone, but *before* the seventh and final trumpet begins to sound,—just to that very instant it is, that the 11th chapter of the Revelation of St. John the Divine addresses itself; and opens so uniquely and appropriately with the Pyramidal mensuration idea:—

"And there was given me a reed like unto a rod (measuring-rod) : and the angel stood, saying, Rise, and measure the temple of God, and the altar, and them that worship therein."

At the present epoch of history there need be no pretence among men, that they do not know what they are called on here to measure; for the Great Pyramid is the only remaining piece of architecture, temple, structure, or building prepared according to designs imparted by Divine inspiration, in visible existence; and therefore the only one of such most notable edifices capable of being now measured.   And it has, *teste* every page of the present book, on being recently measured with something approaching to acccuracy, proved by these very measures that superhuman wisdom in high science, more than 4,000 years in advance of all mankind at the time, and in its chief results not surpassed yet,—as well as fraught with religious associations of both the Old, and New, Testaments—must have presided at its arrangement and prophetical construction.

"And them that worship therein"; the command is likewise to measure *them*.   But who are they, and how are they to be measured?

This was a point that specially pressed upon Mr. Charles Horner, until he was enabled to remember, that at this present time, when the nature of the command is first perceived, — Christian history having reached the great step at the end of the Grand Gallery, it is there, and there alone, that the measurement has to be performed.

Now it is exactly there that the British, or Anglo-Israel people are specially indicated (see p. 557) by the linear standard of their country; their present country in these Isles of the West, to which Israel was appointed to escape, "and renew her strength." To what extent then, has that strength, under and by the favour of God (and not that "*we have made ourselves* a people of thus many millions," as so unhappily, and we trust accidentally, escaped from the lips of Lord Beaconsfield at a Guildhall Banquet last summer (1878)),—been renewed? Been renewed too after the loss of the many more once possessed; and equally children of Joseph; but who were appointed to escape and become "a great nation," as Manasseh is at this day in America.

At p. 583 we have already allowed that the Pyramid mensuration symbol of a human soul may be a cubic inch. Wherefore Mr. Horner takes the number of cubic inches in the British terminating Grand Gallery, and finds for its terminal date 1881·4, the number to be 36 millions: including probably the Anglo-Saxon populations of the Colonies still ruled over by the British Sceptre.*

"But the court," continues the beloved Disciple, "which is without the temple leave out, and measure it not; for it is given unto the Gentiles: and the holy city shall they tread under foot forty and two months."

That is to say, apparently, or by the light we are now receiving from the Pyramid, this injunction implies, "The country outside the Great Pyramid, even Egypt and Palestine and all the land of Arabia, measure them not; no metrical consequence of any spiritual significance shall be found there by so doing; and they are further given over by God to the Mohammedans to have, to possess, and to tread under foot for forty and two months of years, *i.e.* 1,260 years." Which period, dating from the Hegira, or the universally acknowledged effective beginning of Mohammedanism, in the year 621—2 A.D., will close of itself, without the efforts of man, in the year 1881·4 † A.D., or simultaneously with the closing of

---

* See Mr. Horner's original Paper in No. 44 of the *Banner of Israel*.

† May, 1882 A.D., as usually understood. Pasteur M. Rosselet prefers to date the 1,260 years from the taking of Jerusalem by the Saracens in 636 A.D., which would give 1896 A.D. for the close of Mohammedanism.

the first Christian Dispensation as marked in the Grand Gallery.

"And I will give power," continues the Spirit of God, "unto my two witnesses, and they shall prophesy a thousand two hundred and threescore days, clothed in sackcloth. These are the two olive-trees, and the two candlesticks standing before the God of the earth."

These two witnesses to God are now supposed to be the two Houses of Israel,—Judah and Joseph; and their testimony in sackcloth is the melancholy, though diverse, history of those branches of them in the Eastern lands which have been, and are, under the iron-heeled domination of the Mussulman power for the appointed 1,260 years.

But when that power shall fall, in 1881·4 A.D., its "drying up" as by the action of the sixth vial being already begun, shall they, those witnesses, then reign on the earth? Far from it; the low, extra low, passageway from the Grand Gallery to the Ante-chamber, as already set forth in former pages, forbids the idea; and, besides that, the Revelation of St. John expressly says, that it is at that moment "when they shall have finished their testimony, the beast that ascendeth out of the bottomless pit shall make war against them, and shall overcome them, and kill them." Though in a manner ineffectually, the next following verses declare; showing also, most emphatically, that God will interfere supernaturally for them.

But that final salvation is to be in Ante-chamber days, and the *troubles*, as the Pyramid's very low passage before that apartment indicates, are to commence previously, on all who are left on the earth after the Saviour shall have secretly and supernaturally removed his elect; and after, too, that the seventh vial shall have been poured out into the air; for it is *after* that

dread action, in accordance with the words of St. John
(xvi. 18), there shall be voices and thunders and light-
nings; and a great earthquake, such as was not since
men were upon the earth, so mighty an earthquake and
so great: and also the great hail out of heaven, every
stone about the weight of a talent, and to fall "upon
men."

These terms, as Pasteur G. A. Rosselet well remarks in his admirable work entitled "L'Apocalypse
et L'Histoire" are *symbols* of prophecy. Not vague,
mystical or fanciful, but most exact and truly descriptive to the very letter, when the meaning of the
symbols is understood : just as the signs of operation
of algebra in a mathematical work are anything or
nothing to an ignorant person, but the most perfect
expression for the things referred to that can be conceived, when read forth by an educated analyst.
Wherefore, by a wide inductive process, which in
the end cannot fail to arrive exceedingly close to the
truth, he proceeds to compare the words of St. John
with accomplished history from the Apostle's days to
our own ; and finds every jot and tittle to be capable
of full explanation on one uniform system.

But what does the Pasteur say of the days which are
still to come ?   His first note is, that "the Rapture of
the Church to the Lord in the air, will take place at, or
just before the sound of the seventh trumpet.   Let us
hold ourselves ready," says he; "the time is very near."

Yet what does a "trumpet" mean in the book of
Revelation ?   It always means, says the Pasteur, an
overwhelming invasion of barbarian soldiers.   The
first trumpet of the Apocalypse was that of the Goths.
And could the words of the Beloved Disciple have been
better chosen, or more expressive, when they are now
found so strikingly confirmed by our greatest, though
most sceptical historian of those times (Gibbon): seeing

that he has written in his Vol. V. p, 311, " On the
24th of August of the year 410 A.D., at midnight the
inhabitants of Rome were awakened by the tremendous
sound of the Gothic trumpet. Eleven hundred and
sixty three years after the foundation of Rome, the
imperial city, which had subdued and civilised so considerable a part of mankind, was delivered to the licen-
tious fury of the tribes of Germany and Scythia."

Then follow, the second trumpet for the Vandals,
the third for the Huns; the fourth the Heruli; the fifth
the Saracens; and the sixth the Turks. But whom does
the seventh trumpet, so soon to sound, announce?

Answers the Pasteur " The Russians; and when
they are let loose, after the destruction of the Turkish
Empire, and throw themselves on the more civilised
surrounding nations, we shall know that the seventh
trumpet has begun to sound, and the third ' woe' has
commenced. But though both the first and second
woes (the former including all the North-barbarian
trumpets, and the latter the two Southern ones), lasted
many centuries, the third one is not to do so, for the
word of God tells us that the third woe shall be terminated in brief : or, that the Russians shall merely be as
a passing, though for the time heavy, ' hail'; a term
also used by St. John to express the short infliction of
the first Gothic invasion of Rome, compared to the
larger and severer ones which followed it."

Mr. Sydney Hall, a Pyramid author, who is inclined
to look on the seven overlappings of the Grand Gallery
as the seven times of each species of warning in the
Revelation, after reading the last of them, which is
largely the Russian, in the seventh vial, feelingly asks,—

" Is this fearful description of coming events to have
no more weight with the mass of men than the warnings
given to the old world by Noah?

" Surely the indifference which is shown to the signs

of the times by mankind in general has been put on
record by our blessed Saviour himself,—

"'As it was in the days of Noah, so shall it be in the
days of the Son of Man. They did eat, they drank,
they married wives, they were given in marriage; until
the day that Noah entered into the ark, and the flood
came, and destroyed them all. Even thus shall it be
in the day when the Son of Man is revealed.'" "That
day" having been *then* a long future one; but is for us
so, no longer.*

ᴴ ⎩* The further and grander future of post-millennial days, as both
indicated in the closing chapters of the Book of Revelation, and symbolized in the final King's Chamber of the Great Pyramid, may be studied
with advantage in the third part of an admirable little book which has
only just come to my hands. It is by Mr. T. Septimus Marks, London;
is entitled "The Great Pyramid, its History and Teachings," and is the
extension of a Lecture delivered to an Association of Christian Young
Men at Hackney, December 12, 1877. Published by Partridge & Co.,
Paternoster Row, 1879.

CHAPTER XXV.

GENERAL SUMMATION; SECULAR AND SACRED, PERSONAL AND FUTURE.

LET us now cast a rapid glance over the principal results of our long and truly archæological research, including therein the commencement made so happily by John Taylor, in, or previously to, 1859.

So unexpectedly, too ; for when that fine old man entered the field of Christian thought and scientific research applied in that direction, the world had become tired of the Great Pyramid, and affronted with its seeming blankness to polite literature. A witness, of learning nevertheless it was, solemnly reflecting on all humanity from more than 4,000 years ago ; yet in itself unobtrusive, silent, hurting not any one, standing outside, though close to, the current ways of life and progress, whether in peace or war. But it had become odious to mankind simply for its calmness, its serenity, its purity ; and, like Aristides the Just, it must be ostracized because it *was* just, and true, and good.

Hence, long as had been the night of the world's general ignorance concerning the Great Pyramid, the darkest part of that night was only about forty years ago ; for then it had become quite fashionable openly to contemn the primeval monument. Even one of the most philosophic authors of that time—and approved, too, within the golden circle of the Court—could write : " The Pyramids ! What a lesson, to those who desire a name in the world, does the fate of those restless, brick-piling monarchs afford! Their names are not known; and the only hope for them is, that by the labours of some cruelly industrious antiquarians, they may at last become more definite objects of contempt."

That was human prophecy; and conforming thereto, though in a more decorous manner, as right and proper with a poet, came the abandonment of all hope of man ever accomplishing anything with such a lost, lost subject of primeval period, as the Great Pyramid; or as Petrocchi expressed it thus :—

> "I asked of TIME : 'To whom arose this high
> Majestic pile, here mouldering in decay?'
> He answered not, but swifter sped his way,
> With ceaseless pinions winnowing the sky.
>
> To FAME I turned: 'Speak thou, whose sons defy
> The waste of years, and deathless works essay!'
> She heaved a sigh, as one to grief a prey,
> And silent, downward cast her mournful eye.
>
> Onward I passed, but sad and thoughtful grown;
> When, stern in aspect, o'er the ruined shrine,
> I saw Oblivion stalk from stone to stone.
>
> 'Dread Power!' I cried, 'tell me, whose vast design——'
> He checked my further speech, in sullen tone:
> 'Whose once it was, I care not; *now* 'tis mine.' "

But how often is not the extremity of man the very opportunity of God! And so it was here, for the identical time when philosophers of the highest cultivation, and literary men the most erudite, and the best of modern science had totally given up the Great Pyramid,—that was the eve of its long-prophesied rise as a witness unto God in the land of Egypt.

Charged in the beginning of human time to keep a certain message secret and inviolable for 4,000 years, the Great Pyramid did so. And further appointed to enunciate that message before all men, with more than traditional force, more than the authenticity of copied manuscripts or reputed history,—that part of the building's usefulness began when John Taylor's examinations of it commenced.

The earliest results thence arrived at were, it is true, little beyond the metrological ; yet so clear, bright, and hopeful was the new light which then began to shine upon the monument, that Taylor's poet-friend of his latter days, Patrick Scott,* was constrained soon after to address the Great Pyramid, no longer as the property of Oblivion, but as then beginning in some measure to be understood :—

> " Dwelling like greatest things alone,
> Nearest to Heaven of earthly buildings, thou
>   Dost lift thine ancient brow
> In all the grandeur of immortal stone,
>   And, like the Centuries' beacon, stand,—
>   Up-springing as a tongue of fire—
> To light the course of Time through Egypt's mystic land.
>
>   'Tis not for poet to inquire
>   *Why* thou wast built and *when ?*
>   Whether, in monumental state,
> So great thyself to tomb the great
>   Beyond their follow men ?
> Or dost thou, in thy bodily magnitude,
>   Not uninformed nor rude,
> Declare the abstract ties which Science finds,
> Seen by the light of *geometric* minds,
> In fix'd proportions, each allied to each ?
> Or dost thou still, in inferential speech,
>   Reveal unto mankind the *girth*
>   Of the vastly rounded Earth ;
> And to the busy human race
>   Bequeath a rule, to guide the range
>   Of all the minor measurements of Space,
> Which Traffic gets, and gives, in endless interchange ?
>
> Enduring pile !   Thou art the link that binds
>   The memories of reflective minds—
> Vast mass of monumental rock sublime,
> That to the present Age dost join the Youth of Time."

But even the poet's eye, " in fine frenzy rolling," was all unprepared for the fulness and the majesty of the

* Author of " A Poet's Children," " Footpaths between Two Worlds," " A Personal Devil," the last being a prose religious work of singular importance and application to the present time.   See *Banner of Israel*, for a review thereof.

Great Pyramid's message, as step by step it came to unfold itself, rather than be unfolded by any one hand. And could it have been less, when the object of the building was, as declared by the Messianic Prophet Isaiah, "to be for a sign and for a witness unto the Lord of Hosts in the land of Egypt" in a day called by the Prophet "that day," or a day not yet fully arrived.

The quoted sentence cannot be improved upon in the same space. But if some persons will demand information of a longer, fuller and more detailed kind, then the answer, as to wherefore the Great Pyramid was built (without going further at present into why such a witness was required by the Lord "in Egypt"), must partake largely of a duplicate character; or thus:—

(A.) To convey a new proof to men in the present age by number, weight, and measure, as to the existence of the personal God of Scripture; and of His actual supernatural interferences, in patriarchal times, with the physical, and otherwise only sub-natural, experience of men upon earth. Or to prove in spite, and yet by means, of the mensurations of modern science, which in too many cases denies miracles, the actual occurrence of an ancient miracle; and if of one, the possibility of all miracles recorded in Scripture being true.

(B.) In fulfilment of the first prophecy in Genesis, which teaches, together with all the prophets, that of the seed of the woman without the man, a truly Divine Saviour of Mankind, the Branch of God, was to arise and appear amongst men; a man apparently, amongst men; in poverty, too, and humility; in further fulfilment thereof, the Great Pyramid was to prove,—in ages long after the first grand event, *i.e.* now, and in the years which are coming,—that precisely as the first Advent was, 1,879 years ago, a real historical event, and took place at a definite and long pre-ordained date,—so the Saviour's second Advent, when He shall descend as

the Lord from heaven, with the view of reigning over
all mankind, and ruling them all with one Divine sceptre,
and under one all-just, beneficent, omnipotent sway, that
that still greater event (because accomplishing for nations
what the first did for individuals only) will likewise be
historical. That it will also take place at a definite and
a primevally pre-arranged date. With a remarkable
series, moreover, of preliminary, and very special experiences for mankind, shortly to begin; and of the
utmost import for the faithful to be duly apprised of.

Now let us look a little closer into the first, and more
earthly of these two reasons, or purposes; viz.—

(A.)

In an age when writing was a rarity indeed, and
barely more locomotion was indulged in by any of mankind than merely to roam with flocks and herds from
summer to winter pasturage and *vice versâ*, and this
only in little more than one central region of the earth,
—in that primitive age it was announced that the day
would come, when of the multiplication of books there
should be no end,—when knowledge should be wonderfully increased, and men run to and fro over the whole
earth, even as they are now doing by railway and
steamer from London to the very Antipodes. In the
interests of commerce they do it every day; and in the
interests of science they do it from one end of the world
to the other, as was so extensively witnessed in 1874,
during the Venus transit, and by observers of every
civilized nation. (See Chap. IV., pp. 61 to 71.)
Nothing so costly had ever been attempted before or
would have been allowed,—yet passes with acclamation
now, because on all hands it is believed that the
present is the *scientific* age of the world, and that

everyone now knows more or less about science; and
that great associations of rich men can carry anything
and everything before them.

Therefore, it would seem to be, that an Omniscient
mind which foresaw in the beginning the whole history
of man, ordained that the message, arguments, proofs,
of the Great Pyramid, showing science knowledge from
quite a different source, should not be expressed in letters
of any written language whatever, whether then living
or to live;—but in terms of scientific facts; or features
amenable to nothing but hard science; *i.e.* a numbering medium for the communication of ideas, which
would be humanly known, and be generally and exactly
interpretable, only in the latter day.   The employment
of any written language moreover, would have been a
restricted mode of conveying the message essentially
and characteristically to one nation alone; whereas the
Pyramid's message was intended for all men, even as
Christ's kingly reign at His second coming is to be
universal, and not for the benefit of Jews only.

Trace, too, the several scientific steps by which this
purpose of the Great Pyramid is being, and has been,
accomplished; and note how each and every one of
those steps, while of the most important class for all
science, is yet of the simplest character to be looked on
as being any science at all :—so that the poor in intellect, and neglected in education, who are, and always
will be, the many, may partake of it; as well as the
more highly favoured who are only a very few.

Not in the day of the Great Pyramid at all, nor for
centuries on centuries thereafter, but rather since the
revival of learning in Europe, no *pure mathematical*
question has taken such extensive hold on the human
mind as the "squaring of the circle."   Quite right that
it should be so, for a time at least, seeing that it is the
basis alike of practical mechanics and high astronomy.

But as its correct quantity has been ascertained, now more than one or two hundred years ago; and, under the form of π, or the proportion of the diameter to the circumference of a circle, is found in almost every text-book of mathematics to more decimal places than there is any practical occasion for (see p. 17),—men might rest content, and go on to other subjects. But numbers of them do not and will not; hardly a year passes even in the present day but some new squarer of the circle appears. Generally a self-educated man, and with the traditional notion in his head, that the proportion of length between the one line already straight and the other to be made straight in a circle, has never been ascertained yet; and that either the Academy of Sciences in Paris or the Royal Society of London has offered a large reward to whoever will solve the problem : so down he sits to the task, and sometimes he brings out a very close approximation to the first few places of figures in the fraction, by practical mechanics ; and sometimes by erroneous geometry he produces a very wide divergence indeed. But occasionally the most highly educated university mathematicians also enter the field, and skilfully bring out perchance some new algebraic series, by which a more rapid convergence than any yet invented to the true numbers of π may be obtained; see, for instance, such a case, of the best order, in the last volume (XVII.) of that most important one now amongst the scientific serials of the world, the Smithsonian Contributions to Knowledge (Washington, 1873) ; besides its references to similarly intended formulæ in other recent and good mathematical works. Wherefore that numerical expression, 3·14159 + &c. is shown, on all hands and in all countries, to be one of the most wonderful, lasting, characteristic, and necessary results of the growth of science for all kinds and degrees of intellectual men ; and in an increasing proportion as they arrive at a high state of civilization, material progress, and practical development.

Is it not, then, a little strange, that the first aspect which catches the eye of a scientific man looking with science and power at the ancient Great Pyramid, and the Great Pyramid alone of all the pyramids in either Egypt, or anywhere else (see pp. 15—30), is, that its entire mass, in its every separate particle, all goes to make up one grand and particular mathematical figure expressing the true value of π, or 3·14159 + &c.

If this was accident, it was a very rare accident; for none of the other thirty-seven known pyramids of Egypt contain it.*   But it was not accident in the Great Pyramid, for the minuter details of its interior, as already shown (see pp. 200—212), signally confirm the grand outlines of the exterior; and show again and again those peculiar proportions, both for line and area (see pp. 27 and 202), which emphatically make the Great Pyramid to be, as to shape, a π shaped, and a π memorializing Pyramid; or the earliest demonstration known of the numerical value of that particular form of squaring the circle, which some men are still trying their hands and heads upon.

Physical Science of the Great Pyramid.

Again, in physics, as a further scientific advance on the foundation of pure mathematics, is there any question so replete with interest to all humankind as, what supports the earth; when, as Job truly remarks, it is hung from nothing; when it is suspended over empty

---

* The learned Dr. Lepsius enumerates sixty-seven pyramids; whereupon Sir Gardner Wilkinson remarks, with irresistible force, from one who has traversed the ground again and again, "But it is unfortunate that the sixty-seven pyramids cannot now be traced." A more recent author, Mr. W. J. Loftie, in his book, "A Ride in Egypt," at p. 151, speaks complacently of seventy pyramids; but leaves it doubtful whether he has actually visited, and entered into, more than one.

space, and yet does not fall ? In place, indeed, of falling destructively, the earth regularly revolves round a bright central orb ; and in such a manner as to obtain therefrom light and heat suitable to man ; making also, together with its axial rotation, day and night, summer and winter, and a secure chronology for the longest ages. What is the period, then, of that curvilinear path which the earth is ever describing ; and what is the distance of the physical-life luminary round which the earth so revolves in its annual orbit ; but into which glowing, central, mighty orb, the poor earth would fall helplessly as to its final bourne, and be destroyed by fire, if that onward movement were arrested ?

As in squaring the circle, so in measuring the distance of the earth's heating sun, both learned and unlearned in the schools of men have been working at the question for 2,300 years, and are still for ever employing themselves upon it. Hardly a month, nay hardly a week, passes now, but some new sun-distance result is brought out by some one or other, with either a greater or less figure than his immediate predecessor ; and nothing that all nations can do, whether by taking their astronomers away from other work, or enlisting naval and military officers, non-commissioned officers, and soldiers, as temporary astronomers and photographers ; furnishing them too profusely with instruments of precision of every serviceable science ; and sending them to every inhabitable, and some uninhabitable, parts of the earth, is thought too much to devote towards a hoped-for slightly improved knowledge of the exact number of miles to be set down ; and all for the future possible behoof of a world now grown scientific ; but they, the nations, are far from having arrived at even tolerable exactness yet. Nevertheless *there* of old, before the beginning of any human science, is the numerical expression for that cosmical, sun-distance, quantity, to

almost any refinement, nailed to the mast of the Great
Pyramid from the earliest ages; for it is its mast or
vertical height, multiplied by its own factor, the ninth
power of ten, which is the length all modern men are
seeking, and struggling after; in one attempt over-
shooting, in another falling below, and so going on
hundreds of times without ever hitting the mark
exactly. (See pp. 59—71.) And there also in the
base-side length from socket to socket of the building,
when measured by the sacred cubit appointed by God,
is the number of turns and parts of a turn made by
the earth on its axis, as it revolves in the equivalent
circle of that gigantic mean radial distance of the sun.
(See pp. 39—44.)

And if from enormous solar-system quantities we turn
to the very much smaller matters of our own planet
world in itself alone,—does not every educated inhabi-
tant thereof, in the present day, imagine that he ought
to, and does, know its size; and yet was not that impossible to all men, of all the early ages, to attain with
any exactness? In illustration whereof it is recorded,
that the Deity confounded Job at once with the words:
"Hast thou perceived the breadth of the earth? Declare
if thou knowest it all."*

But precisely that thing which all mankind from the
Creation up to the day of Job, or of Moses, had not accomplished, and had no idea or power how to set about
to perform it, and did not make even any rude attempts
in that direction during the following 2,500 years,—was
intimately known to the author of the design of the
Great Pyramid; and not only in size, but in peculiar
figure, or its polar compression. (See pp. 55, 214, and
444.)

How well therefore in this one Great Pyramid was
realised the description by God himself to Job, of the

* Job xxxviii. 18.

Divine Creation of the Earth; with whose proportions, the architectural work superintended by Philitis is so intimately connected by standard, and number, and meaning,—

"Who hath laid the measures thereof, if thou knowest? or who hath stretched the line upon it?

"Whereupon are the foundations thereof fastened? or who laid the corner stone thereof;

"When the morning stars sang together, and all the sons of God shouted for joy?"—Job xxxviii. 5, 6, 7.

Who but the Lord could have done all that metrological wonder, so far above men's power *then* to do?

Not fully known, indeed, as to its final numbers, even yet is the terrestrial breadth amongst men (see p. 53). And yet it was so familiar to the architect of the Great Pyramid that he made it then the basis of a system of linear measure, suitable for all mankind. Symbolizing moreover that God alone is ruler of the earth, and man is His tenant, merely for a season : bound too, as such, to act during that period in harmony with what the Creator hath long since ordained, for both the earth and the inhabitants thereof. For, "have ye not known? have ye not heard? hath it not been told you from the beginning? have ye not understood from the foundation of the world? It is He (God) that sitteth upon the circle of the earth." It is only He, also, "who hath measured the waters in the hollow of his hand, and meted out heaven with the span, and comprehended the dust of the earth in a measure, and weighed the mountains in scales, and the hills in a balance."* (See pp. 273—288.)

Who, indeed, but the God of Israel could have performed this last-mentioned still greater wonder than any mere linear measure, so far as its exceeding difficulty to men even in the present scientific generation is

* Isaiah xl. 12, 21, and 22.

concerned ; and could have actually introduced, both into the King's Chamber Coffer, and the said chamber itself, an expression for the next most important quality, after size, of the earth-ball we live upon—viz. its "mean density." (See pp. 176—180.)

On one side, too, see that grand quantity utilized, in settling for the Pyramid, on appropriately earth com-mensurable principles, the unit of its system of weight and capacity measure ; viz. 5 cubic Pyramid inches of earth's mean density = 1 pound weight of Great Pyra-mid. (See pp. 273 and 288.)

On the other side note the factor which that earth-density introduces into the larger chronology mensura-tion scheme of the building. For it is that quantity combined with size, shape, and rate of axial rotation which settles the amount and period of that *disturbed rotation,* typified in the base-diagonals and King's Cham-ber's level circuit of the building ; and elsewhere called " Precession of the Equinoxes." A period more than six times as long as the whole historic life of man yet accomplished, and the only known phenomenon for keeping longest records, suitable at once to all degrees and states of men. (See pp. 324, 367, 374 and 378.)

Accompanying Characteristics.

Simultaneously, too, with all these unique scientific discoveries, unheard of in Archæology before, came out proofs upon proofs that the Great Pyramid is likewise both spiritually and religiously separated in the most complete manner from everything hitherto known as Egyptian, and even from every one of the other Pyra-mids in Egypt ; as testified by our Plates IV. and V.; and by the Tables of measures at pp. 45, 65, 93, 221 and 493. Also just as distinct is it from the profane of all known nations ; for so witness the following points,—

(1.) By being centrally *in* Lower Egypt, which is central also to the inhabited land surface of the whole world, the Great Pyramid becomes similarly central to the Kosmos of man's earthly life and habitation; but yet has no profane Egyptian building to compete with it in architectural *intention* to be in that remarkable position; because it, the Great Pyramid, alone visibly stands with appropriate topographical attributes over the outspring of that country's thence-formed and thence-originating grand *delta*, or rather open-fan-shaped area of alluvial, and always magnificently food-producing, soil. (See pp. 85—92.) '

(2.) At, or immediately above, the sectorial centre, therefore, of physical and hydraulic origination of the Lower Egyptian natural land, rather than human, and idolatrous kingdom along the banks of the Nile, the Great Pyramid was placed. Yet by virtue of the peculiar mathematical shape of that land, is it standing both at the centre and also at the extremity (See Plate II.) ;—just as with the "altar" or " pillar," or, more truly translated, " Pyramid," " to the Lord, in 'the midst' of the land of Egypt," *and also* " at the border thereof," which Isaiah (xix. 18—20) expressly states *is to be* manifested in the last days. And for what purpose?—for anything Pharaonic, or glorifying to the reputed wisdom of the idol-serving priests of the Egyptians? Certainly not ; but to perform no less exalted a service than, as we have already intimated, to act as "a sign and a witness unto the Lord of Hosts " (Isaiah), and to be a parable and wonder to all intervening ages (Jeremiah xxxii. 18—20).

(3.) Next, please to remark, that at every structural point where the workmanship of it is examined with sufficient minuteness, ability, and knowledge, the Great Pyramid is found not only unlike the most characteristic buildings of the ancient idolatrous people of Egypt, but

is actually antagonistic to them.   Especially is this the
case in the Great Pyramid's opposition to *their* inveterate tendencies towards records in their own buildings
of animal worship, egotistic assertions of self-righteousness, Cainite boastings of themselves, with contempt
and hatred of all other peoples.   And while all these
latter native and indigenous structures, together with
the gigantic stone idols of Egypt, are doomed in the
Scriptures to bow down, to be destroyed, and their
country to become the basest of kingdoms (see pp. 122—
127),—the Great Pyramid, on the other hand, is alluded
to in the most honourable manner, both in the Old and
New Testaments.   Its headstone being even taken by
the Apostles themselves as a type of the Messiah ; and
the prospect of its being brought forth to view, having
been described by the older prophets, as a sight which
caused the morning stars to sing together, and all the
sons of God to shout for joy, with cries of " Grace,
grace unto it!"   (See pp. 537, 540.)

(4.) The Great Pyramid, in a land where all other
characteristically *Egyptian* buildings are profusely decorated and covered from top to bottom, and both inside
and out, with inscriptions of portentous length and
giant size both in writing, painting, and sculpture,—
the Great Pyramid has, in and upon its finished parts,*
no decoration, no painting, no inscription, no destination given to it, in any human language under the sun.
And yet, while no other Egyptian buildings, their
innumerable hieroglyphic inscriptions notwithstanding,
can speak to their own absolute dates, and have, by the
imperfections of their merely differential chroniclings
(such as the years of the life of the nearest reigning
Pharoah), sent all the scholars of the museums and

---

* Excepting, therefore, the oft-mentioned rude quarry-marks on the
rough stones in Col. Vyse's " Hollows of Construction." See Note
to p. 6.

universities grievously astray on impossible, ridiculous, mutually contradicting, and totally anti-Biblical chronologic schemes (see p. 491),—the Great Pyramid sets forth its own absolute date on unerring grounds of high astronomical science. (See p. 380.) Whereupon, being already allowed by the best Egyptologists to be *relatively* older than all other known buildings of any kind of pretence, whether in Egypt or any other part of the ancient world (see pp. 489, 491, 501, 505),—the Great Pyramid takes at once the lordly position of prescribing limits in time to all those other buildings, or we may say to all architecture whatever. And those Great Pyramid chronological limits are now found to be in an eminent manner confirmatory of Holy Scripture.

(5.) Not only are the Great Pyramid dates conformable to those of the Bible for its own foundation and subsequent ages; but its indications of some earlier events than those of its own time, such as the Dispersion and the Deluge (see pp. 531, 534) are likewise conformable thereto. And these agreements are rendered all the more cogent, when we find harmonious commensurability between the Coffer of the Great Pyramid by actual measure on one hand, and on the other the verbal statements in Scripture both of the Ark of Noah, the Ark of the Tabernacle of Moses, and the Molten Sea of Solomon. (See pp. 395 to 406.)

(6.) While every other ancient structure of Egypt, and in so far of the world, was built for its own time and its then owners, and has had in their day its utilisation, its attendants, worshippers, frequenters, or inhabiters, either living or dead,—the Great Pyramid has had no use ever made of *it*. It was erected in a lifeless, waterless desert; no living man could enter its stone-filled passages when finished; no dead body either was or could have been, regularly deposited, in the fondly supposed sepulchral chamber, there (p. 100); the coffer, or so-called sarcophagus, is too broad to pass in any way through the lower part of the first ascending passage (see p. 255);—the king of that time, according to triple historical tradition, and recently found local indication, *was* buried elsewhere (see p. 130, and Plate XIX.); neither, until the last very few years, was the building in any degree understood by any nation, though all nations have guessed at its hidden mystery, its parable in stone; a prophetic and portentous parable, long since thrown in the very way of the ungodly in order that, " seeing they might see and not perceive, and hearing they might hear and not understand." The real use of the Great Pyramid to mankind, in the Providence of God, may therefore for so many grand reasons, be expected still to come, rather than to have been long since.

(7.) A thousand years ago Al Mamoun broke violently into the building (see pp. 108—121), but discovered nothing of its design as now coming to be known, on the lines first opened to the world by one solitary but God-fearing, Christ-worshipping man, the late John Taylor (see Preface; also Appendix I.), and already found to be so invaluable. And though other visitors, in crowds since Al Mamoun's day, smashed many of the stones, chipped the edges of more, and performed whatever mischief man could perform with axes, hammers, pitch, profanations, and fire,—yet they have no more prevented certain grand ideas with which the whole building was fraught in the beginning of the world, coming to be appreciated in these last very few years,—than did the destruction of the Temple of Solomon and the carrying away of all its golden vessels to assist in the service of idols in Babylon, —prevent the accomplishment of the Hebrew prophecies touching their chief end, the appearance of the Saviour of mankind among the Jews in Jerusalem 1,879 years ago.

And when that event did take place, even at the appointed time, Satan himself is held by some writers to have joined with the Chief Priests in deriding the Saviour of mankind as He hung on the cruel cross ("the accursed tree" of the Bible). On a day, too, which seems proved to have been the 1st of April of that year of the Crucifixion,* and to have survived unhappily to this time as a day of mockery and derision, and "of putting forth of the finger," though it is to be hoped in ignorance, among all Christian communities. Yet precisely what Satan and the Jews did think they actually *saw* to be the ruin and defeat of Him who was their Messiah,—yet proved to be, with His following Resurrection from the Dead, the accomplishment of His then required Divine part, the entering into His glory, and the beginning of the full assumption of His power, His Father's knowledge of Times and Seasons, and everlasting dignity.

So, too, the Great Pyramid, exactly when it was most under the heel of this world, when false information concerning its foundational numbers was being upheld by the chief of modern Scientific Societies (see Appendix II.), has now been found just at that very epoch to have risen, not only to the accomplishment of supernaturally difficult scientific questions,—but to have opened a way into things still more deep, solemn, and important to humanity, than any science of the schools; and such as I next propose to allude to under the head—

(B.)

"Produce your causes, saith the Lord; bring forth your strong reasons, saith the God of Jacob.

"Let them bring them forth, and show us what shall happen: let them show the former things, what they be, that we may consider them, and know the latter end of them; or declare us things for to come."— Isaiah xli. 21, 22.

* "The Times of the Restitution of all Things," by the Rev. Tresham D. Gregg, D.D.   London: Mackintosh, Paternoster Row.   1868.

Now such acts as these are evidently impossible to any, or all of, men, by the light of merely human reason; and yet do they form the second and most notable part of the object wherefore the Great Pyramid was built; for that part, as already mentioned, appears to begin somewhat thus, viz. to show the reality, and the settled, as well as long pre-ordained, times and seasons for each of the two comings of Christ. Both for that one which has been, *i.e.* which was 1,879 years ago (which is marked prophetically in the Great Pyramid, first for a preliminary date by the Messianic lines, in the Entrance-Passage (pp. 465—479), and second, for the date itself by the noble North beginning of the Grand Gallery (p. 461); and under whose then commenced spiritual dispensation men are still living, but are not always to live; and also for that other coming in kingly glory, power, and universal peace, which is yet to beam upon mankind.

The First Coming was for the sake of inaugurating *amongst* men an opening whereby each of them might attain to personal, private, individual Salvation; in which respect it was a " finished and complete work."

The Second Coming, on the other hand, is for a tional, public, and governmental Salvation : a something which men, even with the personal Salvation of the First Coming to guide and assist them, have been wholly unable to bring about. And as one of the ex-Prime Ministers has openly said just now of his own country's historical proceedings towards other countries,—it is more like the licence of bandits than the rule of Christians; and yet is approved of by the nation.

Exactly when that Second Coming—which (and not the First Coming, nor anything depending upon it) will put an end for ever to all wars and human authorisations for man to slaughter his fellow-men, women, and children to promote his own so-called interests—is to take place, is a question towards which the Great Pyramid suggests in the Grand Gallery's Southern low passage, both thencefrom and towards the Ante-chamber,—that a beginning of the Divine preparations for it may be, in 1879, within only three or four years (pp. 546—548); though the full and grand event may not take place until after a further interval of time typified by the difference in years of the two sets of numbers imparted to Daniel, viz. 1,260 and 1,335.

Meanwhile a very great fact and serious difficulty which believers have to deal with, is this,—that a building we have thus alluded to as sacred, and as destined to be a miraculous witness to God in the latter day, especially in the mysteries of His appointed times and seasons,—stands in the generally Bible-condemned, and even hateful country of Egypt, instead of Palestine.

That is absolutely true. But does not Isaiah distinctly say that the monumental pillar which is to witness in the latter day to the Lord, is to be *in Egypt*. What God-fearing Christian can presume to quarrel with that? And are there not of Egypt in the latter day, many other incomprehensibly wonderful things recorded in the Scriptures of God. For it is apparently to be, notwithstanding its ages of baseness and deserved bitter punishments (see p. 123), the first of the latter-day chosen three,—Egypt, Assyria, and Israel: and the Lord of Hosts shall bless it, saying, " Blessed be Egypt my people, and Assyria the work of my hands, and Israel mine inheritance " (Isaiah xix. 24, 25).

But previously to that day there shall go up a great cry unto the Lord from the Land of Egypt: " for they shall cry unto the Lord because of the oppressors, and He shall send them a Saviour, and a great one, and He shall deliver them. And the Lord shall be known to Egypt, and the Egyptians shall know the Lord in that day, and shall do sacrifice and oblation; yea, they shall vow a vow unto the Lord, and perform it. And the Lord shall smite Egypt: He shall smite and heal it:· and they shall return even to the Lord, and He shall be entreated of them, and shall heal them."

The New Policy of the present Egypt.

Now what is this great cry to go up unto the Lord from Egypt, and because of the oppressors?

In earlier editions of this book the answer was difficult; but the affairs of "the approaching end of the age," have within the two last years been marching on so rapidly, that it is enough now (1877) merely to name the present Khedive; his extortions, luxurious expenditures, and o'ervaulting claim, after grinding down his own people to starvation, to rule also over all other peoples living on the course of the Nile, from its almost unknown sources South of the Equator,—down to its final passage through Egypt and junction with the Mediterranean Sea.

The main reason, as yet given forth, why modern Mussulman Egypt should have a claim to attack and take possession of the other Nile peoples, seems to be,—that Egypt is the only one of those states which has delighted mankind (but offended God) through forty centuries, with triumphs of ornamental idolatry in architecture, similar profane glories of sculpture, theotechnic mysteries of painting, and written human false wisdom. Wherefore every zealous paid servant of the Egyptian state has now to argue this case to the outside world; and to maintain victoriously against all comers,—that his Highness the Khedive, being the *de facto* successor of that arch-idolater Rameses the Great, is fully and Pharaonically justified in sending up armies to make war on all men and countries so far as they may be found eventually living on any portion whatever of the course of the Nile.   Either the Blue-Nile of Abyssinia, or the White-Nile of the further South-Equatorial Negro-land.

The scheme has a certain air of grandeur about it ; and the very notion of present-day Turks, who cannot draw at all, and are bound by their religion to eschew everything in the shape of human portraiture,—the idea of them, of all men, claiming the reward due to Egypt's ancient artistical skill, and her sculptured idolatry, too, is rich beyond expression.   But the underground wisdom wherewith the subtle measures for accomplishing the purpose are being taken, is a feat transcending diplomacy ; and yet,—" the Egyptians are men, and not God ; and their horses flesh, and not spirit, and the appointed time of Mohammedan existence is now rapidly drawing to a close (p. 588) ;"* wherefore out of those very ambitious steps and unscrupulous means, it may be that the close of the Turkish rule in Egypt's land will come.

"And though the Lord may have long tarried," the time will arrive, and the Great Pyramid indicates it to be near, when, in some supernatural manner, God " *shall send them a Saviour, and a great one, and He shall deliver them.*"

The Egypt of the Lord Christ.

If, then, the present possessors of Egypt be not those of whom the Lord Christ is likely to say (at least in their present and most unrepenting Slave-holding, False-prophet state), when His personal reign begins, —" Blessed be Egypt my people, and Assyria the work of my hands, and Israel mine inheritance,"—who are those favoured ones, in and near Egypt, likely to be ?

* Isaiah xxx. 1, 3.

Of the present localities of the ancient Assyrians, we do not know much very positively, though there is a growing idea that they have drifted with the human current of history westward from their original habitats, and are now to be found amongst those whom the ethnologists delight to call Indo-Germans. But of Israelites our nation is now becoming, even year by year, through means of the works of the late John Wilson and the existing and ever-working Edward Hine * and E. W. Bird,† far less blind than it has been through all the previous period of its occupation of these Isles of the Sea which contain us now; from whence, too, we have, under a gracious Providence, overflowed both to rule with order, enlightened justice, and a firm hand among many Eastern, Equatorial, and Southern nations, and to occupy and make to blossom the "desolate heritages" of distant parts of the earth. Our nation, moreover is already found to be acknowledged metrologically in the Great Pyramid (see pp. 554, 557), as being combined with Israel at the latter end of the Grand Gallery; while the striking resemblance in so many other points, of our earliest Saxon metrology to the system of the Great Pyramid, both gives us through Ephraim, as well as Manasseh, a species of "Inheritance" interest in that central and dominating building of Lower Egypt; and may include something else still more noble, and to be confirmed by "sealing," perhaps by the previous rapture of the Church (pp. 548, 590), in preparation for the subsequent Messianic universal

---

* See his monthly *Life from the Dead* and weekly *Leading the Nation to Glory* (for ever memorable by Mr. Hine's explanation, 1st, of the service performed to our Lord Christ by the one Israelite tribe of Benjamin, now the Norman-descended portion of England; and 2nd, of the United States as equally with the British descended from Joseph, but through Manasseh rather than Ephraim) (see pp. 576, 579); published by S. W. Partridge & Co., 9, Paternoster Row, London.

† See his weekly journal, *The Banner of Israel*, published by W. H. Guest, 120, Warwick Lane, Paternoster Row, London.

kingdom : when " all the ends of the world shall remember, and turn unto the Lord : and all the kindreds
of the nations shall worship before Him." That is,
when such final millennial kingdom of the Lord's shall
at last be established. But that is not to be immediately, by probably nearly a life-time (pp. 547, 572,
589), and before then, and more pressing for attention,
—what ?

> Destructive wars, first,
> False Philosophy, second.
> Divine Fulfilments, third.

Of the Final Wars.

If we are arrived so nearly at " the End of the Age,"
as Mr. Grattan Guiness terms it in his admirable and
weighty book, or " the close of the existing Christian
Dispensation," as the Pyramid's Grand Gallery, with
its impending south wall almost immediately over us,
intimates it to be (pp. 462, 545),—an unexampled opportunity is afforded of testing certain ideas of Christianity
which are very prevalent in some quarters still.

Thus in Dr. Livingstone's earlier travels on the Zam-
besi, when he found only wrecks of tribes, barely sur-
viving the many conquering and slaying marches of
stronger embattled tribes over them,—he held up the
New Testament, and told them confidently, that if they
would only believe that book, there would be no more
wars : and he describes how the poor suffering wretches
leapt, yearning to his words, " no more war."

But all those tribes he spoke to, even his aristocratic
Makololo, have all of them, according to Mr. Stanley's
latest gatherings, been decimated since then, driven
from their former habitats, and some of them altogether
annihilated by wars, on wars, more terrible and extensive than ever throughout South Africa ; not to say

anything of our own recent, or existing, wars with the Zulus, Basutos, and others in that land.   And what has been going on there, most unhappily has had its counterpart in almost every country of the world : while the most notable feature is perhaps, that it is Christian countries that have had the chief share of all the greater of these wars; and Christian peoples, states, and Governments, that are making, up to the present moment, the most stupendous preparations and arrangements for more gigantic wars still.

In place of all these countries being now occupied, —after 1,879 years of the *first* Christian Dispensation existing in the world, and with probably only three or four more years of it to run,—with beating their swords into ploughshares and their spears into pruning-hooks, —they are increasing their millions of armed men, as soldiers, and furnishing them with such destructive arms ; with such sulphurous engines and fiery inventions for rending the human body and murdering man wholesale, as, in size, deadliness, and number, most truly have " not been from the Creation unto this time."

What then is wrong ? The words of the New Testament ; or, the sense in which they have been taken by some persons ?

Most assuredly the latter. The Lord Christ never said that the preaching of His Gospel would put an end to the wars of nations, and inaugurate universal peace among all the governments of the earth from that time forth for ever : but quite the contrary.   Certain allusions to future peace on earth may, no doubt, be found in various parts of the Bible ; most blessed and extensive allusions too ; and in connection with Christ. But not at his First Coming, and merely knocking at the door of each single individual sinner's heart ; and teaching him if smitten on one cheek, meekly to offer the other to the smiter; but which no Government whatever does, or would be tolerated by its people, if it did. The grand peace allusions, on closer examination refer only to Our Lord's Second Coming, which is to be in a totally different guise, and with power over the nations, one and all, as such, to compel them to keep the peace.

In a recently published graphical work, " Modern Hieroglyphics of the Apocalypse and the Great Pyramid," where " the Watcher " represents the historic progress of Christendom, in figures ascending the long incline of the Grand Gallery's floor,—and at last brings the nations upon the final grand step (pp. 545, 556), marking the present time,—this piece of dreadful truth is well brought out, that they are then personified by no peaceful shepherds of Carmel, or rose growers of Sharon, but by soldiers upon soldiers, infantry, cavalry, and artillery all armed to the teeth for fiery war.

This constitutes apparently the first beast of Rev. xiii., and represents mainly military power; but the second beast, also present on the Grand Gallery's final step, is something still more dangerous; for, though having two small horns as of an innocent " lamb," it yet speaks as a " dragon," and causes all who would not worship the image of the first beast, or implicitly and passively obey military power, to be killed.

That second beast is held by some interpreters to be the peculiar junction of " civil " with military power, which has been denominated " Cæsarism," from the tactics of its beginner, Julius Cæsar,* since whose time it has never disappeared from the world. It is, indeed, that astute state-craft which brings on wars, but leaves them to be carried out in blood by others; and which, as in those continental countries where intense Cæsarism now prevails, makes every man of the population into a

---

* " 666, the Number and the Name of Antichrist." Published by W. H. Guest, 20, Warwick Lane, Paternoster Row, London.

soldier, no matter what his religious beliefs may be; which "raises itself above all that is called God," and obliges all men, on pain of death if necessary, to obey its human, sometimes most inhuman, decrees as though they were as infallible and far more binding than those of any Church. Which also is living unceasingly in another species of warfare even with its own people; the masses of whom are kept in order not by the words of Christian Gospel persuasion, but by armies of policemen, forcibly administered law-courts, and very castles of iron bars for prison-houses over the whole land.

In fact, it "exerciseth all the power of the first beast before him," and with that conjoins these other latter-day features, "that he doeth great wonders, so that he maketh fire come down from heaven on the earth in the sight of men, and causeth that as many as would not worship the image of the first beast, should be killed."

But of this image, which (Rev. xiii. 15) was enabled, by some diabolism, to *live*, in latter-day times, and may be regarded as a kind of resuscitation of the old Roman Empire in its persecuting character (very shortly to take place, but happily not to last for long)—it is written, that he "caused all, both small and great, rich and poor, free and bond, to receive a mark in their right hands and foreheads; and that no man might buy or sell, save he that had the mark, or the name of the beast, or the number of his name" (p. 566).

And, as this indicates, as we believe, the adoption of the French metrical atheistic system, when taken up by nations with the idea of advocating human, rather than Divine, rule on the earth (p. 563); a proceeding more intensely and actively sinful, the closer that the Second Coming of the Lord Jesus Christ, to reign practically as a King over all, approaches; we need not be surprised to read in Rev. xiv. 9, 10, 11, the special wrath of God on whomsoever shall receive of the beast, or his image, their mark in his forehead or in his hand.*

Yet not only has that France-invented atheistic metrology been taken up by Germany, Italy, and most of the Cæsarised countries on the Continent,—but news from Egypt (July 31, 1875) announces that the Mohammedan Turkish Khedive there (after having been unfortunately assisted last Spring by a Scottish nobleman and his then assistant astronomer, to monumentalize by a long line of frequent stone-piers, a mètre-measured, and mètre-testing, base line, on the plain near the Great Pyramid; for the control of all future surveying of Egyptian ground), has just ordered that in 1878 the French mètre shall be compulsory as the one and only linear standard measure for that whole country! Whereby, after a most remarkable existence among men through 4,000 years, the long-lived, historic cubit of Old Egypt (Cainite and idolatrous as it was in its origin) will be suddenly brought, or attempted to be brought, to a violent end within three short years; but in favour, unhappily, of the modern badge of materialistic atheism, or of human attempt to deify man, and thereby produce a chasm worse than idolatry.

Well, therefore, did the author of "Philitis" remark, in a then recent letter,—"Here is this Caliph of a false Prophet, true to the Nemesis decree of Providence, adopting a false measure!"

But that was perhaps necessary for putting the Mohammedan Pharaoh more completely into antagonism

---

* The Pasteur Rosselet, in his admirable work, "L'Apocalypse et l'Histoire" (published in 1878, at Neuchâtel; Librairie J. Sandoz), has a much more full and precise description of the persecuting empires symbolized by Daniel and St. John as "beasts" of one kind or another: and his standpoint being from a more exclusively religious side, differs somewhat from the above. But it is easily harmonized therewith, agrees very closely in its chronology, and should be read by everyone in the original.

with God, preliminarily to and justifying the sweeping vengeance necessary for fully purging and purifying the Egyptian government, land, and people against the coming day of Christ the King.   That day when Egypt is to have, by the words of Isaiah, and under help from the Lord,—Israel, not the Turk, "as a blessing in the midst of the land."

So far was written years ago, when everyone was saying, " Peace, peace," and the Khedive of Egypt was the favourite of the day.   But who will attempt to say now (April 14, 1879) what the Lord is about to bring upon Egypt.   Does the Khedive himself know ?

His country is bankrupt, his property is in sequestration—his deposition being discussed in London, Paris, and Constantinople; and he, with the miserable device of the wicked, is declaring,—that if a finger is laid on him, he will immediately proclaim a Jehad, or holy Mohammedan war against the Christian nations, his creditors.

And now once more, in December, 1879, where is the said Khedive ?   Broken, without hand; a fugitive from Egypt: prohibited from ever returning there, and living somehow on the shores of the Bay of Naples.   But that is only the beginning of the end.

Of Philosophy misapplied.

Yet, though in all the coming events,—even throughout the wars which must still be waged in Old World fashion, through the Pyramid's low passage period of still many years, before the Ante-chamber's day of the Second Advent begins, or the 1,260 have grown to be the 1,335 of Daniel, and the *granite* constructions of the Great Pyramid are entered into (pp. 572, 583)—the promises of God made to our nation of old, not for our righteousness, but as descendants from Abraham, and heirs of the promises Divinely made to him and recorded in the Scriptures of truth,—are abundant beyond all that the heart of man could desire or conceive, and may save us from the military woes of many of the Gentile continental nations; on the other hand, our peace responsibilities are most grave.

For though on one side we are Scripturally told (in connection with these very preparations for setting up the Messiah's coming earthly kingdom, the kingdom which is to fill the whole earth) that it shall be "when God has bent Judah for him, *filled the bow with Ephraim,* and raised up thy sons, O Zion (*i.e.* Israelites of all the twelve tribes, the two so long estranged being then united with the ten so long lost, and not forgetting Manasseh, (p. 576), *against thy sons, O Greece,* and made thee as the sword of a mighty man;"—on the other side we read, "the children of Ephraim, being armed, and carrying bows, turned back in the day of battle."

Such battle, against the sons of Greece, can hardly be anything else than intellectual battle; and the turning back of Ephraimites, though well armed (Manassehites, the sons of the Pilgrim Fathers, are happily not mentioned there),—nothing less than a latter-day loss of faith, by our countrymen, in the reality of the Divine inspiration of Scripture, and their acceptation of human science instead. Of human science, too, for guidance amongst those very subjects of futurity and eternity which are the province of God, and not of man.

Now this is a matter which concerns most intimately the purpose of the Great Pyramid, that inspired scientific Appendix to the Sacred Scriptures; wherefore I will endeavour, by its light, to give a short, but faithful account of one of the most able and popular of these most dangerous, intellectual and scientific books of our

time, " The Unseen Universe," *—and to indicate what
the Pyramid teaches to be the species of *correction*
required therein, for it is by no means all bad.

Science versus *Inspiration, in a new Book of the time.*

Basing on the mathematical natural philosophy of
the Universities in the present day, the authors of
this book take upon themselves to be prophetic. For
they not only proceed to explain the actions and reactions which are going on about us, but to announce
all that has occurred to this world on which we live,
and even to the elements which originally composed it,
before the earth was formed, or man created, through
infinite ages almost, in the past,—and *also* what *will*
happen to both the earth, and its combustion residues,
in the almost infinitely distant future, when burnt and
reformed into new worlds again and again and again ;
each time into long-enduring sun or planet globes, but
none of them absolutely eternal.   Man's soul, they
claim, is alone eternal; and they consider that they
have most correctly proved, by their mathematical
equations, that God has not been at work anywhere
throughout all the immense extent of the visible universe of earth, sun, and stars for countless millions of
millions, and millions still, of years or centuries, or
ages, or æons, or whatever longer period you like, if
only you do not say *for ever*.   And they also hold that
God is not, and will not be, at work, in the material,
visible universe, for at least as long, long periods to
come.   That man, therefore, will not necessarily see
God through all those awful intervals of future time,
though he, man, may be re-established in physical
existence on all those successive worlds and universes
still to be formed, and still to pass through their im-

* See review of it in *Life from the Dead*, No. 36, for November, 1876.

mense universe lives. Because, say they, during all such enormous periods of time, every step in all the successive existences of all those worlds, and stars, and suns, will be ruled, enacted, brought about, and upheld, by the natural principle of *scientific continuity* alone, and without any direct agency of God.

This is the general burden of the book, and deserves attention, because it is by the most able mathematical and natural-philosophy men of the day, and by those who have already introduced the atheistical French metric system into their text-books, and have the training of our University youth in those mathematical and mathematico-physical studies, which are becoming more and more every year the very backbone of all competitive examinations throughout the land : and such examinations give even Persian power to the examiners over the minds, studies, and the very language of those whom they examine.

Has God, then, been pushed out of his own creation, through millions of millions of years past, and as many to come, by the modern mathematical learning of men ? The authors of the remarkable book we are discussing would actually imply that they have accomplished it. And in that case, let us ask,—are the prophecies and histories of the Sacred Scriptures during three or four thousand years only, backwards and forwards from the present time, not merely flatly contradicted, but infinitely outdone in all they attempted to do or professed to relate, touching the direct, personal dealings of God with man through history,—by what man can now ascertain for himself through such far longer intervals ? These are the very serious questions which must arise to every thinking, religious mind, when reading that unblushing book; and though the authors would throw dust into the said reader's eyes by a sudden and unconnected passage, wherein they imply that they hold, as

equally true with their own demonstration just a moment before, against the possibility at any time of any
miracles of any kind or degree, through ages on ages
past, or future either,—the reality of "all the (very
recent) miracles of the New Testament ";—yet we
must put that contradictory account of themselves on
trial for what it is worth ; as well as examine the
grander statements of their disturbing essay as plainly
as we have been testing the enunciations of the Great
Pyramid from one end to the other of these poor pages.

Let us ask, then,—

1. Has the prophetic science so positively claimed
by the authors of "The Unseen Universe" book, enabled them by that method of their's which has led
them to deny all miracles through all human time,—
to independently discover, identify, and give further
particulars of any single one of the many and various Bible miracles, which those gentlemen notwithstanding profess they do believe to be true, and to have
really occurred in latter times they should be able most
easily to compute for.

And the answer is,—Not one; the philosophy of
"The Unseen Universe" book has no communion
whatever with, nor power of entering into, the Inspired
history of the Bible ; it practically contends against the
Bible at every step of its teaching ; and its authors
were only aware of any of the New Testament miracles past, or prophecies for the time to come,—not
through their own science, but, just as any peasant may
also know of them, viz. by reading in the Holy Scriptures
the words of Divine Inspiration.

2. What ideas of Christianity have and hold those
so very able Mathematico-Natural Philosophy authors
of their most mixed order of book ?

The following in fact, whatever may be their professions. At their page 199 (3rd Edition) they write

commendingly of the beauty of many " Christian hymns," and as a specimen they quote—what ? A free translation by Pope of an old Latin poem which, in itself, had no pretence of being, or trying to be, Christian in any one point or degree whatever. Nor has Pope introduced anything about Christ, and His Divine atonement for the sins of all mankind, into his translation ; but has allowed it, though amplified, to remain, as Cainite and Epicurean from one end to the other, as the original Latin-Pagan lines. Nor is this any single slip of " The Unseen Universe " authors ; for the very original Roman ode of Pope's translation, in all its undiluted rationalism of a worse than heathen man of Old Rome, is actually adopted by them, on the front of their book, as though it were, together with the atheistical French metrical terms they have elected to employ in all their educational works and scientific papers, a most appropriate index of *their* Christianity.

A would-be Historical Destroyer of Divine Inspiration.

And now, if I have succeeded in thus simply showing that these undoubtedly great educationists have not been able any better than some of the poorest peasants who do read and respect the words of Divine Revelation, to understand and enter into the dealings of God with man during actual human history as it has been, is still being, and has yet to be for some time, transacted upon this earth,—I do not wish to say one word more against them ; because they, not having yet run their whole careers in this world, may still repent in Christ, and become Pauline examples of light and truth in religion, as well as unapproachable masters in scholarship and science.*

* Up to the time of writing this review, and when " The Unseen Universe" book had reached a third edition, the authors had not divulged their names.

But with regard to the heathen Roman ode they placed at the head of their book, in a manner so misleading to New Testament Christian faith, we need have no compunction about exposing the thoroughly Anti-Christian authorship of that unhappy document. It is the Emperor Hadrian's address on his death-bed to his soul; wherein, besides improperly asking himself the questions which are to be answered by God alone, the several lines breathe only dull atheism, and a certain pale, cold, naked looking out into the future to come. This is surely bad enough in its mere literality. But who personally was Hadrian, that such miserable comfort was all that surrounded his death-bed? or what were his life-long characteristics that he either should or should not, in the present day, of all the later days of the Christian Dispensation, be again brought forth from the dust of ages, and be now prefixed with honour to a *soi-disant* Christian book, but of terribly contra-Deistic aim?

The Emperor Hadrian (born 76 A.D., died 138 A.D.) was distinguished above all the Roman Emperors, whether they were generally either good or bad, by the very special antipathy which he bore, not so much to other religions than his own, or to any religion at all, but to the records of really Divine Inspiration as given to both the *Hebrew* race and the *Christian* Church. The supernatural of the Old and New Testaments was, in fact, the object of his inveterate and abiding hatred; and source of disquietude too. Yet, at the same time, he was such an arch-idolater; a theotechnist, indeed, of most determined, but degrading order,—that he indulged from time to time in elevating his courtiers, after death, into the number of the gods of old Rome.*

* One of his favourites, a young man named Antinous, was further, after being accidentally drowned in the Nile, raised by Hadrian to the heavens of astronomers as the constellation "Antinous"; which spurious title still unhappily disfigures many of our celestial maps and catalogues

This Hadrian had a long war with the Jews, which he finished at last by not only an ordinary conqueror's military destruction of their captive city Jerusalem ; but by actually, viciously, and as modern rationalists would probably approve, attempting to stamp both the city itself, and its very name, out of existence ! To which perverse, wicked end he erected on the then, by him, utterly levelled site of Jerusalem a new city, which he called, and bade all the Roman world know only under the name of, ÆLIA CAPITOLINA, in part from himself; and then, after peopling this mushroom city with a Roman colony, he made it death for any Jew or Christian to set foot within the sacred precincts again.

Did that most Pagan, God-defying, Christ-opposing Emperor succeed in so extinguishing the name and very memory of God's Jerusalem amongst mankind?

We all know that he did not; that he failed utterly. Then what can mean the bringing up by a few extra-educated and very clever men just now, with honour and applause, in modern Christian Society, the impenitent ode of *such* a fighter against God and His Christ; and calling it Christian too ? The only answer that I can suggest is,—that the approaching "End of the Age," as typified by the near termination of the Grand Gallery of the Great Pyramid, will be the epoch of temptations innumerable ; in fact of the three unclean spirits like frogs coming forth,* with power to lure to their destruc-

of stars : but does far more serious despite to the naming of the original Constellations under Enoch and Job, as now believed for Divine Inspiration purposes to man. See the book called " Mazzaroth; or, the Constellations," by the late learned Miss Rolleston.

* The Apocalyptic relative time of these evil influences appearing, is near the end of the sixth vial : *after* the drying up of the Euphrates, or the Turkish Empire, has begun, and just *before* the pouring of the seventh vial; which, says Pasteur Rosselet, " is close at hand; and, corresponding, nearly, with the last of the Churches, the Seals, the Thunders, the Trumpets, and the Woes, will mark the close of the present Dispensation ; but not the beginning of the Second Advent in Millennial glory," —which he assigns to the date 1290 + 666 = 1956 A.D. (See p. 586, l. 10.)

tion all the inhabitants of the world in the battle of the
great day of God Almighty, unless personally assisted
to stand by their Heavenly Redeemer.

Divine Fulfilments of all promised in the past, to come.

If the present volume concerning the Great Pyramid
has taught anything, it should surely be the most solemn
respect for all records of truly Divine Inspiration. And
if there be any other *material* record besides the Great
Pyramid, of such Divine footsteps in the history of man,
existing still upon the whole surface of the earth,—it is
the site of the city of Jerusalem.

The existing so-called Holy Places there, are modern;
and therefore, and with all the present buildings and
recent excavations therein, are valueless. The sufferings,
too, of the Saviour there, 1,847 years ago, in and, by
themselves alone, are hardly either sufficient or most,
or even at all, appropriate to produce a loving regard
for the mere locality in the hearts of sincere spiritual
Christians; though His acts, whose memory may be
carried in the heart, and instructions, in the printed
Word, all the round world over, ever will, and must,
form the theme of their praise, thanksgiving, and song.
Neither again, with the Jews themselves, however much
they may have fought, bled and wailed for the city, as
being peculiarly their's, for the last 1,800 years, does
Jerusalem, as a city of the Jews, ascend to the highest
antiquity of their nation ; for it was only acquired by
them, or by any of the children of Israel, in David's
reign ; and since then how often and awfully sinned in.
But yet an inexhaustible stream of Divine favour appears
to be poured out towards Jerusalem through the whole
course of the Scriptures; nor is it ended yet !

A step into earlier antiquity than the age of even
Jacob, was decidedly given to Jerusalem when tradi-

tional records were Pyramidally collected, announcing
that the Shepherd-Prince, Philitis, after the completion
of the Great Pyramid, retired into Palestine, and "there
built Jerusalem." (See pp. 529, 530.)

That disposes at once of any claim of the Jews to the
origination of the Holy City ; yet still arises the strange
question, Why did that Royal Priest, or Prince, Philitis,
choose the peculiar site of Jerusalem for his sometime
post-Great-Pyramid abode, and for the safe emplacement
of the faithful followers he brought out of Egypt with
him ? Followers employed there in building a prophetic
monument of Christ, descriptive of the preparations for
His First Coming, His advent at the time foretold, and in
fact His whole Messianic history; the far-reaching consequences of His Gospel Dispensation, and the religious
future to come ? But here I must confess that my own
views were barren and unsatisfying, until, by some remarkable chance, I was led to a knowledge of a little
work by the Rev. W. Henderson (R.C.), entitled "An
Essay on the Identity of the Scene of Man's Creation,
Fall, and Redemption."*

Published so long ago as 1853, that little pamphlet
had been matured in quiet thought and tranquil occupation for its own pure sake, and without the smallest
reference to worldly excitements or hope of gain.
Without, too, any knowledge of the modern Great
Pyramid subject, which had not, indeed, then commenced. And long, full twenty years, did its modest
author allow his essay, after its first unsuccessful
attempt to obtain a hearing, to remain unread.

"What *can* the good man have got, or rather how
can he have anything, to say, on such a subject ?" was
my own rash idea, at first, in 1874, when the pamphlet
came in my way. But yet on beginning to read, most

* Published by Thomas Richardson and Son, 172, Fleet Street, and
26, Paternoster Row, London, 1853.

charmed was I to find how unexceptionably the first suspicion of the existence and nature of the final truth arose;
how cautiously it was examined by the light of the
earliest parts of Scripture ; how the subject expanded ;
and then how the better preserved or fuller-described passages of the New Testament were brought to bear upon
and assist the scantier records of the Old,—quite reminding me of the manner in which, as I had cause to be so
thankful for in recent years, the interior parts of the Great
Pyramid were found capable of explaining and by calculation reinstating the now almost vanished exterior.

And thus had W. Henderson proceeded, until not only
did there seem to be a most good and sufficient reason
why Philitis (as acting under Divine Inspiration, whatever his Scriptural personality may have been, Job,
Shem or Melchizedek) should have chosen Jerusalem's
very site, have dwelt there for a time and commenced
the architectural memorialization, or perpetuation, of
the place,—ages before the " city of David " appeared,
or claimed fealty from any one for that name; reason
also, quite independently of David, why Our Saviour
Himself should have chosen it as the scene of His Cross
and Passion; while a grand idea was still further given
of a general cyclical result including all mankind ; and
which may in one way or another be continually more and
more exhibited as the years roll on,—proving that God's
word is true, that everything mentioned therein has a
reason for its occurrence, and if future will assuredly have
its appointed time, as well as place, of performance, exact
to the minutest particular; while nothing which occurred
at the beginning, however remote, will be without confirmation and explanation, at the coming end.

Because Jerusalem's site, long before the building of
the Great Pyramid, long even before the Deluge, and
in a very different state of the earth's surface from what
it has been subsequently to that miraculous event, was

the " Paradise of Pleasure of God," the choice garden in which He placed our first parents, and where they sinned and obeyed the Serpent rather than God,— *therefore*, there, on that spot, W. Henderson argued, Our Saviour decided that the atonement should be made by himself; and the fountain of personal salvation should spring up, exactly there, where had been the tree of the forbidden fruit; and where Adam also had eventually been buried; viz. on Mount Calvary.

Not, too, because Bethlehem, a few miles to the south of Jerusalem, was David's natal village; but because originally, in the beginning of the world, or long before any of the sons of men had begun to call upon the name of the Lord, and on the primeval and yet untrodden site where Bethlehem was so long afterwards built, there, at that distance southward from the garden of Paradise of the Divine Pleasure, was Adam created by God; *therefore* argues, proves almost, if not quite, and most touchingly discourses, W. Henderson, P.P., therefore did the Saviour, when made flesh, choose to be born precisely there, in order fully to realise the life of man in the aggregate whom He came to save. And because Adam, when driven forth from the garden, went northward, therefore Our Saviour's early life was spent in Nazareth; and not till the fulness of time required for his sacrifice, did He seek Jerusalem; where, and close to whose walls (not because they were such, but because they occupied the site of the previous creation by God, and first habitation, of the parents of all the Adamic human kind), He chose to make the *personal*, individual purifying atonement, in order that it might be complete and perfect in its primeval historical reference, as well as each chorographical particular.*

* Some further useful considerations on "the World, Eden and Paradise," also their parallel in "Body, Soul and Spirit," may be found in a powerfully explanatory sermon by the Rev. Dr. Wild, of Brooklyn, printed in the *Champion* newspaper of New York, for December 6, 1879.

And now the time is near approaching when Jerusalem is to be visited by Divine favour once again. But for what special reason ?

The Jews will say, on their account : to re-establish them in their rights ; put them into possession of their own city ; make them a great people in the earth ; that the wealth and power of the Gentiles, and specially of Great Britain, are to be expended in that service ; and cannot be better spent. This is moreover a view which many Anglo-Israelites so far agree in, that they expect, in accordance with the prophecies of Ezekiel, that Judah will make advances to Ephraim, and both together (though representatively only, a few, and especially for Ephraim and Manasseh a very few only of their multitudes, for the many left at home), shall very speedily, or at the date indicated by the end of the Grand Gallery (pp. 546, 585), return to Palestine ; rebuild the holy city ; and, as they flatter themselves, enter upon a period of peace, plenty, and unheard-of prosperity, humanly for ever.

Something of that we believe is true, but it is not the whole truth nor the latter end ; nor should it be ; for Ezekiel also indicates that Judah or the Jews will return impenitent (and in so far ready to crucify the Saviour over again), and the new temple they erect on Mount Zion will be for the Mosaic worship ; as though the Christian experience of the world during the last 1,800 years had either never been, or had at last been discovered to be a mistake. Jerusalem will therefore then be ostensibly nothing but a Jewish monument ; will be altogether for a time given over to the Jews as such ; and in its apparently worldly success and golden prime will seduce many of all other nations and creeds ; the Anglo-Israelites meanwhile guarding the frontiers of the country for the Jews.

But what of Christianity during that retrograde

period, and St. Paul's most true assertion that it was
prepared for in, or before, the beginning of the world?
Why this; that that earliest of all known architectural
works, and in its interior peculiarly *Christian* Great
Pyramid,—in Egypt certainly, but that the very country
out of which, or from whose early nurture, says the
Lord, I have called My Son,—will stand as the calm,
enduring, white-stoned witness at the crossing-place of
all the continents of the earth, a testimony to the Lord
before all men ; assuring the nations by its symbolical
language that God is not the God of the Jews only ;
that they, though once chosen, were taken up, not for
their own merits, but chiefly for an intermediate purpose, the ultimate end whereof is Christ, the Son of
God, and His Kingly rule over all peoples ; but which
peoples must first, in prevailing individual instances,
acknowledge Him spiritually and seek personal Salvation
through his Death, Resurrection and Gospel alone.

Meanwhile the Jews, become the financiers of the world,
in Jerusalem's luxuriously resuscitated city, tried there
by prosperity, will be found (in the mass) as recalcitrant
as ever to their King; probably even with the very final
Anti-Christ among them.   Wherefore then, most suddenly, their trial will be varied.   Calamities quickly
following calamities such as the world has never known,
will befall them at what time the seventh vial of the
wrath of God having been poured out, the seventh
trumpet shall begin to sound and bring the overflowing
barbarian hosts of the North upon them, even in the
sacred city itself.   Ruin and destruction will then stare
them in the face ; nothing human will be able to save
either them or the Anglo-Israelite defenders of their
borders, from utter earthly perdition.   But precisely
then it will be, that the Saviour, whom Jews have rejected so long, will descend, both to their and Israel's
succour, with His armies of glorified saints and angels,

as well as to commence His Millennial Kingdom on earth; and they, the Jews, shall look on " Him whom they pierced," in a moment be convicted, convinced, and turned into the deepest grief for their traditional sins.

That instant, rather than the previous holiday-making of the return for sensual Jewish, and mistaken Anglo-Israelite, ends only, will be the occasion of the real, national, Christian recognition of Judah and the rest of Israel, viz., Ephraim, Manasseh, and the other tribes; and the Lord, whose mercies are infinite, will accept them all. Not only accept them, but crown them with honour, and keep them specially near Him in sacred service,—as the *granite* leaf of the Ante-chamber well sets forth (see pp. 584, 585). So that Christians all, but chiefly those of direct Abrahamic descent, will be first in the Holy presence, from the beginning of our Lord's visible reign amongst men and over the world's varied nations ;—during which gloriously supernatural reign, and not before

" The earth shall be filled with the knowledge of the Lord, as the waters cover the sea."

Then truly will *God's* Jerusalem, made thus the seat of that unprecedented kingdom, become

" A praise in the whole earth " ;

and the purpose of the Great Pyramid (Isaiah xix. 19) will have been justified, though not even then, ended.

APPENDICES.

—◦—

APPENDIX I.

BIOGRAPHICAL NOTICE OF JOHN TAYLOR OF "THE GREAT
PYRAMID."

By MRS. PIAZZI SMYTH.

THE subject of this brief sketch was born at East
Retford, in the county of Notts, on the 31st of July,
1781, and died on the 5th of July, 1864, at his residence
in Kensington, London.

Had he lived a few days longer he would have completed his eighty-third year, in full possession of
all his faculties, with the exception of his eyesight,
which became in the last two or three years of his life
so painfully defective that he could scarcely see the
characters he was tracing. Under these latter circumstances he could study but little ; yet so clear was his
memory still, that he could refer with ease to his favourite volumes, or to his commonplace-books, and
indicate precisely the page where might be found the
passage he wished or required to be read to him.

From his earliest years order, precision, exactness,
and fact were the ruling features of his mind and his
actions. Of him it may be truly said, he was one of
Nature's gentlemen; and in later years became ennobled
by Divine Grace! In appearance he was extremely pre-
possessing, with a countenance you felt you could not
only like, but trust. His bearing was benign and dig-
nified, yet simple, combined with a certain amount of

calm reserve, giving one the idea of his confidence and friendship being worth acquiring and keeping. He was a thoroughly religious man, without any pretence, though active in every good work.

Like all great and good men, John Taylor was throughout life a devout worshipper of truth. To the promotion of the truth, in politics, in science, and, more particularly during the latter part of his life, in religion, he devoted all he had, his time, his mind, and almost whatever portion of worldly means he possessed.

He fought through life a losing battle, and was denied that fame which was justly his due. But as his conduct proceeded from a disinterested wish to establish principles which he held to be most conducive to the welfare of the nation, he never lost heart; and want of success left him cheerful and happy in the consciousness of duty performed.

His genius and worth endeared him to all who had the privilege of knowing him, and there may be those still alive who could testify to his large-hearted goodness—his house, his hand, and his heart were always open, especially for the helpless. Many an aspiring poet submitted to him his verses, many a timid politician his projects, and many a young divine his theological speculations; and none went away disappointed. On some of his friends fortune had turned her back, but John Taylor never followed her example. He was a friend " born for adversity," and if any change was made by him, it was to show them more kindness and consideration; for his hands never slacked in works of charity, nor was he ever tempted, or if tempted he never yielded, to forsake the ways of a God-fearing, honest man.

Of no specially intense genius, yet John Taylor so used and cultivated his talents that he made himself master to some extent of most of the sciences of his day; and became a scholar, philologist, linguist, mathematician, poet, political economist, and of no mean order in all these branches of knowledge. With all his erudition, he was far too modest ever to obtrude his learning. Extensive and varied as was his information, clear and accurate as he was with his pen, those who knew him only as a writer knew but half the man. It was in conversation he shone the most. His manner was easy and playful, while the stores of his information were always at the service of those who sought it.

Such was John Taylor, the son of the Retford bookseller, to whom he was bound apprentice at the age of fourteen, having been sent in very early life to the Grammar School at Retford, where he got well grounded in Latin, Greek, and elementary mathematics, which placed him at great advantage with reference to his many varied studies in after-years; indeed he never could have then piled acquirement upon acquirement as he did, without the good foundation having been laid in youth; this joined to indomitable industry and imperturbable method, with ceaseless self-culture through a long quiet life, made John Taylor what he was, a man of deep, varied, and extensive information.

At the expiration of his apprenticeship with his father, he determined to try his fortune in London; and happily obtained a situation in the then great house of Lackington in Finsbury Square, the greatest publishing house of that day, and called the " Temple of the Muses. " Here he met, and formed a friendship with a young man of kindred tastes with his own, of the name of Hessey. From Lackington's, John Taylor went to Vernor and Hood's, another great publishing establishment. Here he made the acquaintance of the well-known Tom Hood, who afterwards became his sub-editor of the *London Magazine*.

When Mr. Hessey had finished his time at Lacking-

ton's, he and Mr. Taylor set up in business together at
93, Fleet Street; but on the establishment of the London University, Taylor being appointed their publisher,
he removed to 30, Gower Street, where he took up his
residence. At both these places of abode his hospitable
table and his "publishers' dinners" formed the centre
of a large circle of literary friends : not the wealthy and
the great alone, but talent and genius were ever wel-
come, for Taylor's heart and hand were always open to
help the needy. Here it was that John Clare, the poor
rustic Northamptonshire poet, had his mental gifts first
acknowledged, was first received and treated as an
equal, and introduced to several men of rank and
talent, including the late Lord Radstock. This introduction to Lord Radstock proved the beginning of a
friendship which lasted for years and spread its influence over Clare's whole life. Poor Clare was a
difficult person to manage or serve, nevertheless John
Taylor remained to the last a judicious friend, adviser,
and helper. These two men, each so remarkable in
his own special way, died within a few weeks of each
other : Clare on the 25th of May, 1864, and John
Taylor on the 5th of July, 1864. Their latest words
had a resemblance, Clare saying, "I want to go home;"
and Taylor, "I want to lie down;" and thus each
spirit passed from time to eternity. The mortal remains both of the *helped* and the *helper* were taken to
their native counties—Clare to Helpston, in Northamptonshire, and John Taylor to Gamston, in Notts, of
which parish his old and valued friend the Rev. John
Twells was then Rector. Another poet of higher strain
than Clare, was also indebted for his first encouragement to John Taylor. This was John Keats, the
author of "Endymion," who found in him not merely
an appreciative publisher but also a sympathizing
friend.

Mr. Taylor's life was a busy one. Not only had he the daily claims of his shop to attend to, but a large publication business was added to it; he being moreover his own reader, and superintending entirely that department. During this period, his commonplace-books show the vast range of his various inquiries. He had studied old English (Anglo-Saxon), Welsh, French, and Italian; he had also turned his attention to astronomy, not in the popular sense, but as a working practical mathematician. His varied extracts show the calibre as well as the minuteness of Mr. Taylor's studies, and how he trained himself by his extreme attention to details, which resulted in giving remarkable strength and precision to his future literary efforts. In 1813 Mr. Taylor first became an author, when he printed a pamphlet entitled "The Discovery of Junius," which was afterwards enlarged into a volume, under the name of "Junius identified with an Eminent Living Character." This was Sir Philip Francis, and the world seems to have since then held that the identification was decidedly correct. In 1821 Mr. Taylor became editor of the *London Magazine*, and held that office until 1825, during which period he wrote much fugitive poetry, essays, and other papers, which have not been collected.

Believing that the passing of the late Sir R. Peel's Currency Bill would prove a fatal era to the nation, he published the first of many pamphlets on financial subjects in 1819, under the title of "The Restoration of National Prosperity shown to be immediately practicable;" and from that time to the end of his life he ceased not in one form or other to urge his views on the subject of the currency upon the attention of the public. But his interest in these financial matters had not the usual effect of such topics in narrowing his thoughts in other fields of investigation. He was throughout life a student of Holy Scripture, and devoted much time and labour in its examination, as his works, "The Emphatic New Testament," 1854, and "Light shed on Scripture Truth," 1864, abundantly testify. He was likewise a careful student of prophecy, both fulfilled and unfulfilled, and he displayed great research and ingenuity in a work published in 1844, in which he endeavoured to find in "Wealth" the name and number of the beast of the "Apocalypse."

There was still another point on which he bestowed much labour, viz. : the tracing of the measures of length and of content that are in use in this country to the dimensions of the Great Pyramid of Jeezeh and of the Coffer therein. The investigation of this subject led him to collect a mass of information which he published under the title of "The Great Pyramid; Why was it built? Who built it?" To this he afterwards added a supplement called, "The Battle of the Standards." The first work was published in 1859, the latter in 1863. The preparation for these two works had occupied Mr. Taylor's time and mind for thirty years of his life; and in his old age he gave to the world the remarkable results of this long and laborious work of constant thought and calculation.

The Great Pyramid of Egypt, one of the seven wonders of the ancient world, and the only one of them which is still in existence, has occupied the thoughts of men in all ages; and many have been the speculations thereon. But it was given to John Taylor, to be the first to see, and then to make known to mankind, some of the deep and important truths really hidden for so many ages in that wonderful monument.

Soon after their publication as above, in his ever-remarkable work, "The Great Pyramid; Why was it built?" &c., a copy was sent by a mutual friend to

Piazzi Smyth, in Edinburgh. He, fancying it applied more to architecture than to his own professional line of occupation, astronomy, forwarded the book to the Architectural Institute of Edinburgh, with a request that they would look into it and report accordingly. This, however, they seem to have totally failed to do ; and, therefore, in 1863, when the same friend forwarded a copy of Mr. Taylor's second and smaller work, " The Battle of the Standards " (of linear measure), Piazzi Smyth immediately gave his mind conscientiously to it, and finding so much of well-digested matter, stated ably and fearlessly with regard to astronomically founded weights and measures and other kindred points, he at once procured a copy of " The Great Pyramid ; Why was it built ? &c.," studied it carefully, tested some features crucially, and finally came to the conclusion that on the whole Mr. Taylor had well-grounded reasons for his *bold* assertion, which had frightened away half his friends, viz. that " The Great Pyramid " must have been erected under *Divine* instructions to its architect.

Very much of this most weighty conclusion depended on correct measurements ; and as many of the Pyramid mensurations up to that date were lamentably conflicting, Piazzi Smyth, after fully examining again and again all Mr. Taylor's calculations, and trying in vain to clear up some of the difficulties, gave his first edition of "Our Inheritance in the Great Pyramid " to the public, under a kind of protest against the insufficiency of most of the then known literary data. And from that time he felt that, if possible, he must eventually go to Egypt and remeasure the grand old monument—whether his investigations should affirm, or whether they should refute, the wonderful theory of the Great Pyramid as propounded by John Taylor. Early in the year 1864, in this view, began a correspondence between the aged author of the "Great Pyramid; Why was it built?" &c.,

and Piazzi Smyth; a correspondence too early terminated
by the death of the good and wise old man.   A few extracts from these letters will best tell the touching tale
of his last days on earth.

EXTRACT FROM THE FIRST LETTER OF MR. TAYLOR
TO PIAZZI SMYTH.

February 16, 1864.—" You have nothing to regret in
the Architectural Institute having neglected my former
book when you sent it to them.   It was generally disregarded, but that gave me no great discomfort.   Your
handsome acknowledgment of the claim which ' The
Battle of the Standards ' has on your attention is ample
compensation, and I thank you most sincerely for it.
I hope, as you say, that we shall not get rid of our
hereditary measures in deference to any of the advocates
of the French mètre."

February 24, 1864.—" The examples you have given
me from the ' International Bulletin ' of the Paris
Observatory, touching the old-fashioned popular way in
which, even in France, such men as Marshal Vaillant
and M. Le Verrier speak of ' Leagues ' cannot fail to
be attended with the happiest effect, if they are quoted
in the House of Commons against Mr. W. Ewart's
motion.

" If you could give me a design for a better frontispiece I should be greatly obliged ; and any other assistance you can favour me with I shall be grateful for.   I
am now unable to proceed any further with my inquiry
in a direct line from myself."

February 29, 1864.—" Your diagram expresses all I
could wish, and I will add nothing to it for fear of
injuring it.   Sir John Herschel pointed out the imperfection of that in my book : but I told him it was
designed to represent the direction and extent of the

telescopic passage in the pyramid—about 340 feet—
which rendered a foreshortening of two of the sides
necessary, and I would insert a better if he would give
me one (this he has not done). Your first, second, and
third developments are fitted to remove the difficulties,
and I will get them engraved if you will favour me with
them.

"What you say about the Russians coming south is
a new view to me, and I will *keep* my eyes open to whatever light may arise in that direction. I will send you
a little book which I wrote in 1844 on the 'Number of
the Beast,' but it does not refer to Russia, because that
country was beyond the bounds of the old Roman
Empire."

March 5, 1864.—"In all my inquiries I was for long
baffled by the uncertainty of the (published) *Measures*
(of the Great Pyramid) and was obliged to trust to some
more than others. But I feel too poorly just now to put
on paper my answers to your queries, and must beg you
to excuse me till the beginning of next week, when I
hope to be well enough to proceed.

"I like what you say of the Russians."

March 7, 1864.—"I have spent many days in the
British Museum, looking up whatever particulars I
could meet with. Having satisfied my mind that the
purpose of the builders (of the Great Pyramid) was not
to erect a *Tomb*, the least suspicion of which would
have led me to care nothing more about the *Measures*, I
was therefore only solicitous to discover for what scientific uses that Great Pyramid could have been designed,
and these opened themselves out very gradually.

"We want better intelligence of the Coffer, and other
parts as well. I wish we had some one to go out to
Egypt on whom we could depend; but in the mean-
time the general truth must suffice."

March 15, 1864.—"Did I reply to your query about

present location of Coffer? It is in the King's Chamber of 'The Great Pyramid.'

"Have you any intention of going there? I could almost hope you have such a thought; but do not expose yourself to any risk—you are wanted at home.

"Ewart has carried his bill in the Commons; but it will never become law, or, if it does, the people of this country will deserve, like the Jews, to lose both their name and nation in return for their ungrateful conduct.

"I am not yet quite well, but I trust to revive a little when the flowers do.

"It is many months since I went out of the house, either for a walk or a ride in the fresh air, and I feel very low. But the pleasure of hearing from or writing to you restores me more than anything else."

March 23, 1864.—"*The cause* of truth is the great object. If in any way we are able, while on earth, 'to vindicate the ways of God to man,' we have not lived in vain. There is an immense deal of knowledge half hidden from our minds, which calm inquiry, if pursued in a right spirit, would open out.

"What you say of the Karnak cubit is perfectly true. The *measure* had its origin long before the *name;* and any attempt to account for the beginning of the measure is worthy of our best attention. When I have reflected on what you have said, I will try to write again."

March 24, 1864.—"I cannot to-day say more, but it seems to me that an excellent means of superseding the mention of the cubit of Karnak is afforded in the sacred cubit of 25 inches."

March 29, 1864.—"I had, as you suppose, mentioned in my book the inference deducible from the fact of a common origin of weights and measures among the most civilised nations of antiquity. It speaks irresistibly in favour of a common origin of all mankind from one source. I see no difference between the man who first gives utterance to such a remark and the man who approves it when he hears it uttered. I am a *thinker*, and I cannot do otherwise than act in my vocation. But it is necessary that many should *approve* before the thought can enter into the popular mind, and if that result ever takes place, I am only one among many who are entitled to any commendation ; nay there is no room for commendation to any one, for all do but impart what has been given them. Paul may plant, and Apollos water, but God gives the increase, if that ever takes place. I suppose that is the meaning of the Elders casting their crowns before the Throne in Revelation iv.

"Feeling a little better I have written a longer letter than usual."

During the month of April many interesting little notes were received, all breathing the same calm, patient, reflective spirit, written, both in style of composition and caligraphy, with remarkable precision and clearness. Mr. Taylor's handwriting was an illustration of his character—every letter, every word, every sentence, all were absolutely correct and conscientiously formed up to the very last one written on the 25th of April.

On the morning of the 6th of May, a letter arrived from the Rev. Dr. Francis Hessey, the clergyman of the parish, and the friend of Mr. Taylor and son of his respected partner. He writes thus : " I feel you ought to know that our dear friend Mr. Taylor has been dangerously ill; indeed for some hours his life was despaired of, but he has rallied, and is now somewhat revived." On the 11th of May, 1862, the same friend writes again: " Mr. Taylor is much better, but still sadly weak. He thanks you heartily for your appreciation of his work."

May 27, 1864.—A letter came from a lady, the

daughter of one of Mr. Taylor's oldest and dearest friends, and she writes as follows : " As an old friend I have come up for a short time to assist in nursing Mr. Taylor, who is in such a weak state, he is not able to leave his bed." On the 31st, this lady writes : " Mr. Taylor, was more pleased with your letter than I can well say. He is surprised at the points of contact between your mind and his."

June 2, 1864.—" I can only again report the extreme delight your letter gave Mr. Taylor. He feels it the more that being now laid aside, and his work in a manner nearly done, others are being raised up who will not let the subject drop. On looking over your corrections he said, ' Oh ! how well he has done it, I could never have done it now. The service that good man has done me is *incalculable*, for he is helping me just where I failed. Oh ! how thankful I feel for all these merciful dispensations.' "

June 28, 1864.—" In the midst of extreme physical weakness that wonderful mind tries to soar above its tabernacle, which seems now nearly dissolved. If he is spared until your book comes out, it will be a great pleasure to him to read it."

June 29, 1864.—" Mr. Taylor was so much pleased with your letter, and as I read it to him he was quite overcome. Tears of pleasure seldom hurt any one, so I read on to the end."

July 4, 1864.—" On Friday morning a change took place, and since that time he has been sinking. He looked much pleased when your *dedication* was read to him, but his great humility prevented him saying much about it. He will never live to see your book, which I *hoped* it might be my privilege to read to him.

" Thank Mrs. Smyth for her kind and most interesting letter. It was the last letter he heard from beginning to end."

And now the closing scene must be told in the words of this kind lady-friend, who was so favoured as to witness this lovely death-bed of a truly Christian man.

" On Friday, the 1st of July, 1864, I had just finished transcribing the little book I had come upon purpose to copy for him, when he said, ' Now, my dear, it is *finished,* but it is not *completed* ;' and he asked me to help him from the sofa to the chair, and reach him a large interleaved Bible, and he endeavoured to explain to me a part he had wished to expound, but illness prevented him. It was about the light Aaron was commanded to burn from six in the evening until midnight, when the length of the day was changed, when the Israelites came out of Egypt. He tried to grasp the Bible in his pale thin hands, and said with a smile, it seemed to have grown heavier. Whilst helping him to hold it, such a fearful panting for breath came on, I thought he was dying ; but shortly he rallied, and upon his faithful nurse (Sarah) coming into the room he said, ' Oh! *let* me lie down.' She asked him, ' Where, sir? On the sofa or the bed ?' He gave again his own sweet smile and said, moving his head from side to side, ' One place, one place.'

" All Saturday we thought he was dying—the dew of death seemed on his face—but at night, instead of sinking, delirium came on, and for thirty-six hours he wandered incessantly ; but even in delirium his thoughts were all for the glory of God and the good of man. His prayers were beautiful. Again and again he would say, ' Oh! let me lie down, let me lie down in the arms of Thy mercy, and when I awake may I enjoy Thy blessing continually. Grant this, O Lord, for Thy dear Son's sake. Amen.' The next night his prayer had changed : it was now, ' Oh! let me lie down in the arms of Thy *pity,* and *when I rise* up, may I dwell in Thy presence for ever.'

"These and many other expressions uttered in the bell-like voice peculiar to delirium were very touching. Six hours before I left him, he sank into unconsciousness, and the only thing that could be done for him was to moisten his lips with a feather. I would that I could have stayed with him to the last, but I left him with relations, and that was best.

"And thus sweetly and calmly closed the life upon earth of this most remarkable man. He suffered from a severe internal complaint, which was eventually the cause of his death. None, however, but those most intimate with him could have supposed that even when he appeared most cheerful, and seemed to enter with delight into the pursuits of those around him, he was enduring constant pain. No murmur escaped him even in his last struggles, and to those around him he seemed rather to fall asleep than to die."

Mr. Taylor never married; two sisters survived him, who were invalids at the time of his death; his eldest nephew was with him at the time of his death, and afterwards conveyed his uncle's mortal remains to the village churchyard of Gamston, near Retford, Mr. Taylor having departed this life on the 5th of July, 1864.

Some little time after his death the executors kindly presented his cherished copy of "Greaves's Pyramido-graphia," and a large bundle of supposed Pyramid-subject MSS. to Piazzi Smyth. He looked over the latter carefully, but finding that the pages were only the returned printer's "copy"—MSS. put away after reading "proofs" by a methodical hand, such as John Taylor's always was—he packed them up again, and turned with undivided attention to realising a grand practical duty, which had now devolved upon him, as follows:—

During Mr. Taylor's and Piazzi Smyth's correspondence, and as already hinted at, it became very manifest how desirable it was to have more accurate and reliable measures of many of the crucial parts of the great monument, so as to place the theory of "The Great Pyramid" on unquestionable basis, or, rather, either to establish or overturn it.

To this end my husband resolved that we should betake ourselves to Egypt with as little delay as possible, taking with us all the best instruments of mensuration we could command. This we did in November, 1864, and for months devoted ourselves to measuring every required part of the Great Pyramid. It was a laborious and fatiguing work, but a labour of love for the truth's sake.

The results of these admeasurements, after two years' further occupation in computing and printing, were given to the world in most unusual fulness of the original and actual measures, in " Life and Work at the Great Pyramid"; published by Edmonston and Douglas (now Douglas and Foulis), Edinburgh, in 1867.

The real bearing and importance of these volumes of apparently mere dry numbers was not seen by the public for many years; but when at last the books were well distributed, and had become a sort of known, tested, and unalterable documents before the world at large, then men began to read, and were most astonished to find thereby that not only was John Taylor's grandest discovery (in theory perhaps chiefly) now practically proved to demonstration; but that there is a vital, growing energy about this ancient Great Pyramid's awakening, whereby it is acquiring new strength from year to year; and a belief in its truth is spreading in the United States and Australia, New Zealand, Tasmania, and Canada, as well as in this country.

Wherefore if the public, in all these widely separated parts of the world, now demand this Fourth Edition of

" Our Inheritance in the Great Pyramid," we feel that
it ought not to be issued without containing something
more than the mere bald dedication towards keeping
up the memory, and relating something of the merits,
the labours, the virtues and the Christian piety of John
Taylor—the first of men to whom has been vouchsafed
in the modern world to discover traces of a primeval
monumental message of Divine Inspiration; given of
old with prophetic purport for the highest benefit of
man in these latter days, because to testify to the
Lord God of Israel and His Christ from the beginning
of human religious history onwards to the end still to
come.

J. P. S.

APPENDIX II.

THE ROYAL SOCIETY, LONDON;

And its published Base-side length of the Great Pyramid.

From the New York Daily Tribune *of Thursday, May 21st, 1874.*

To the Editor of the Tribune.

SIR,—Hitherto anything published under the auspices of the Royal Society (London) has been considered worthy of utmost credence. Such trust can no longer be reposed in all its official statements. I cannot believe that the Fellows at large have consented to the perversions of truth lately issued in the name of the Society, but they are none the less responsible or free from blame in permitting officers who can lend themselves to such perversions to continue in their exalted positions. I have before me a pamphlet, published in London, March, 1874, containing the correspondence between the Astronomer-Royal for Scotland, Professor C. Piazzi Smyth, and the President of the Royal Society; and the Royal Society, as represented by its officers, appears in a very unenviable position. Differences in opinion from those who, at least in their own estimation, are the leaders in the world's progress, "the advanced thinkers," cannot, it seems, be for a moment tolerated. The . . . has determined the Mutual

Admiration Society (which can permit no discovery or improvement which originates outside the charmed circle, to be worth anything) to nip at once all interference in the bud. As for justice or truth, that is altogether a secondary question.

At the late meeting of the British Association at Bradford, Professor Clerk Maxwell, F.R.S., was unwittingly led into an error, in a statement as to the length of the Egyptian cubit, in the course of his eloquent and excellent lecture on Molecules. It is true that he used the erroneous statement in such a manner that no particular harm was done; but still he had all the authority of the published "Transactions" and "Proceedings of the Royal Society" to back him, and he thought these might be trusted. To correct the unfortunate blunder, published under their sanction, the Astronomer-Royal for Scotland addressed a communication to the Royal Society, of which he was a Member, and, after a very long interval, he was informed that a sub-committee, to whom the paper had been referred, had reported it was "not of a nature suited for public reading before the Society!" Now the paper itself, which is published in full in the pamphlet to which I have alluded, is a very short one, and it certainly does present General Sir Henry James, R.E., F.R.S., in no very enviable light; and as the said "Chief of the Ordnance Survey" is one of the members of the Mutual Admiration Society, of course the paper could not come before the Royal Society at large, to be publicly read, and thus given to the world. The errors in question, published under the sanction of the Royal Society, all come from the very ridiculous theories of this gallant Knight in reference to the Great Pyramid in Egypt. The first theory, enunciated in the *Athenæum*, in a communication dated "Ordnance Survey Office, Southampton, Nov. 9, 1867," gave that the sole reason wherefore the Great Pyramid had been built of its actual basal size was to allow a side of the base to measure 360 cubits of 25·488 inches each, and so the base-side length was stated by Sir Henry James to be 764 feet = 9,168 inches—and as this was the actual measurement of Colonel Howard-Vyse, that most worthy pyramid explorer, the accord seemed perfect. It was afterwards pointed out to Sir Henry that 360 × 25·488 amounts to 9,175·68 inches instead of exactly 764 feet, as he had stated—an arithmetical blunder of 7·68 inches. Moreover, he could find no authority for the ancient cubit of 25·488 inches long, and so he let that cubit drop.

The next attempt was in the classical line, and never was the old saw, "A little learning is a dangerous thing," better illustrated. Finding somewhere—in a translation, I presume, and perhaps a quotation—the Egyptian cubit mentioned by the "Father of History" as equal in length to the Samian, he immediately jumped at the conclusion, "Samos? Why, that's Grecian! here we have it—the Egyptian and Grecian cubits are identical!" And so forthwith the Egyptian cubit was pronounced to be 18·24 inches in length, to the confounding of all the time-honoured Egyptologists, Sir Gardner Wilkinson, for example, and that learned Babylonian scholar, Dr. Brandis of Berlin, of Sir Isaac Newton, and almost all other authorities, who have supposed it about 20·7 inches in length. He was in utter ignorance that when Herodotus wrote, Samos was regarded as Asian and Persian, and the first attack upon it by the Lacedæmonian Dorians, he terms their expedition into Asia. (*Thalia*, 56 ; see, also, 55.) All of which, long ago, was expounded by the Rev. Canon Rawlinson. Now in giving this new length of the common Egyptian cubit, requiring a base-side length of the Great Pyramid to be 9,120 inches, in order that it might contain 500 of them, he ignores Howard-Vyse, his great authority before, ignores all the splendid work of the French *savants*, and the laborious measurements of Professor Smyth, and selects two of the smallest measurements he can find. Even here he puts on a par with the work of his own pet engineers that of a young engineer, who performed the work in measuring single-handed, and all to get this cooked number, 9,120 inches (which is ten inches less than his own engineers obtained), and to suit his new Samo-Egyptian cubit. To their credit be it said that the measurement of the Royal Engineers taken by itself does come nearest to what is the best mean of all the best measurements hitherto made, though still much too small, if we accord any weight to Vyse and the French *savants*.

These blunders were published in the "Proceedings" of the learned "Royal Society of London" for June, 1873. In his communication to the Society correcting them, Professor Smyth claims that the new length was brought in by its author, General Sir Henry James, R.E., by means of (1) an unfair selection among the standard modern measured lengths of the base-side of the Great Pyramid; and (2) a meaning attributed to certain words in Herodotus, making them tell the very opposite story to what they were intended to do. No wonder the Admiration Club was ashamed to let the world know of these misstatements of facts and classic blunders, and determined to snuff out the light of Piazzi Smyth instantly. . . . And here comes the sorriest part of the whole business. On the 7th of February, 1874, Professor Piazzi Smyth addressed a letter to the President of the Royal Society as follows:—

" SIR,—With reference to my letter of last October 27, forwarding to the Secretary of the Royal Society a short paper ' On the length of a side of the base of the Great Pyramid,' intended to correct the errors on the same subject printed by the Society in 1873, first in their Proceedings, and subsequently in their Transactions, and with reference also to the rejection and return of the said paper to me on the 22nd ult., by the Secretary, on the plea, by a sub-committee, of its not being of a nature

suited for a public reading before the Society, I beg to say that having
thus failed in all that I can do to open the eyes of the Society as to
whether they are seeking 'accurate measuring, truth-stating, and justice-
doing,' or the exact opposite thereof, in researches concerning the most
ancient and exalted monument of intellectual and religious man on the
face of the earth, there is nothing now left me but to come out of the
Royal Society, as I do hereby, resigning my Fellowship therein, and
hoping that you, Sir, at least, will not consider my reasons for withdrawing 'not suitable for a public reading before the Society.'—I have
the honour to be, your obedient Servant,   "PIAZZI SMYTH.
"To the President of the Royal Society, London."

Will it be believed that an honourable man, such as
we have always hitherto supposed Dr. Hooker to be,
under fear of the Admiration Club, probably under their
instruction, simply announced the resignation from the
chair, without reading the letter or giving the reasons?
When Piazzi Smyth, suspecting him to have concealed
from the open meeting of the Society that the truth of
its statements about the Great Pyramid had been most
seriously challenged, puts the question directly to him
in a second letter, Dr. Hooker states that—

"As your letter giving your reasons for withdrawal is of the nature of
a communication to the Society, and as it further appears to me to contain reflections on the motives as well as the actions of the Fellows
generally, I have considered it to be my duty to lay it before the Council,
with the view of taking its opinions as to the proper course to be adopted
with regard to it, and of which course you shall be duly informed."

In reply, Professor Smyth said that—

"Dr. Hooker was keeping back from the Fellows the part on which
the withdrawal depended—out of which it originated—which it was most
important for the Fellows to know of, and which I so pointedly requested
of you as President, and when I was still F.R.S., to read to the meeting,
and because you saw that that part of the letter was 'of the nature of a
communication to the Society!' As for any subsequent efforts that you
may only now be going to make, after I have ceased to be F.R.S., to
bring the part of my old letter you were previously silent on before your
Council, not for correcting your Pyramid errors, but under the odious
charge against me that I reflected therein on the motives and actions of
the Fellows generally (when you know perfectly well that it was the
Executive only, and their refusing to let the Fellows know what was
going on, that I was dealing with), the thing is so transparent that I shall
take no other mode of answering you than that of laying your own words
before all the Fellows and the world at the same time."

There the matter stands just now. I do not blame
Professor Smyth for withdrawing, and yet I am sure he

could have done more for the cause of light and truth
had he remained, unpleasant as it might have been for
awhile. Still, it will stir up a breeze, and, I hope, expose the facts so thoroughly, that these men who are
largely—some of them almost exclusively—supported
by the people, but who scorn to recognise any rights
outside themselves, may learn their true position, and
that the world is not yet their exclusive possession.
To use the glowing words of Professor Clerk Maxwell,
closing the very lecture which seems to have been the
turning-point in bringing about this sad state of affairs,
I hope that they " may learn that those aspirations after
accuracy in measurement, truth in statement, and justice in action, which we reckon among our noblest attributes as men, are ours because they are essential con-
stituents of the image of Him who in the beginning
created, not only the heaven and the earth, but the
materials of which heaven and earth consist."

H. L. S.

Hobart College, Geneva, New York.
April 10th, 1874.

APPENDIX III.

Time Indications of the Grand Gallery in the Great Pyramid.

By Mr. James Simpson.

Fourteen years ago, in February, 1865, a young Leith shipbuilder addressed a remarkable letter to Professor Piazzi Smyth (then at work at the Great Pyramid), in which, for the first time, and as it were by a sudden inspiration, the prophetic record of time embodied in the passage-system of the Pyramid was grandly opened out and explained. This of itself would have formed an era in the unveiling of the " witness," apart from the great work of measuring then going on. Yet seven whole years elapsed before this important discovery was *demonstrated* to be true, and the ground thus made firm for further advance. For it was only in 1872 that Professor Smyth, acting on the happy suggestion of Mr. Charles Casey, and with the ready assistance of Mr. Waynman Dixon, C.E., and Dr. Grant, of Cairo, was enabled to shew that the " ruled lines " in the entrance passage, which had been a seven years' wonder and baffling puzzle, were simply the builder's mark of the date of his work, in inch-years preceding the epoch of the birth of Christ, which is shewn at the commencement of the grand gallery floor. The absolute agreement of this date (2170 years B.C.) with that published by Professor Smyth years before on purely astronomical, or astronomico-mathematical grounds furnished as striking a proof as could be desired of the truth of the time-passage " theory." And now, after the same author had further shewn that 1,260 years from the era of the Mohammedans and the 1,881 years (or so) of the grand gallery dispensation run out at one and the same time in the very near future, it is not surprising that others should begin to look into a matter of such momentous interest to all. And hence most excellent suggestions have come from Mr. Hartwell A. Powers, of Cincinnati, leading to more accurate views both as to the length and signification of this passage; while, more recently, Mr. Charles Horner has brought powerfully before the readers of the *Banner* the exceeding solemnity of the events which appear to him to be clearly set forth as ready to be revealed to an (alas!) unready, unheeding world.

Be those events what they may, we are now less than three and a half years from the complete and sudden ending of the dispensation or age symbolized by the grand gallery with all its lofty proportions and curious "septiform" architectural features—speaking, no doubt, of the superior privileges and blessedness of this Christian age or dispensation of grace, over all that preceded, as well as emphatically over that time of judgment which is immediately to follow. For the greatest, or floor, length of the gallery, as we hope to shew, does not exceed 1,881·6 Pyramid inches; and when that number of tropical years is measured from the beginning of the Christian era—the *latest* date which can with probability be assigned for the nativity of our Lord—we do not get beyond the 6th August, 1882 (less than three and a half years from this time) as an *outside limit* for the termination of the gallery. And it is evident that even this limit must be reduced by whatever amount we place the nativity of our Lord *before* the 1st January, A.D. I.

The length of the gallery, indeed, which we are considering, is stated in "Life and Work" (Vol. II. p. 78), as only—

On Eastern side = 1882·6 British inches.
  ,, Western ,, = 1883·0   ,,   ,,

Mean = 1882·8   ,,   ,,
     = 1880·919 Pyramid inches.

But this is the *ramp* length, 23 inches vertically above the floor, and requires, on the shewing of Mr. H. A. Powers, the addition of ·4 inch, more fully ·444 on account of the impending of south wall, in order to give the real length at floor; which thus becomes 1881·363.

To this correction I would add another, required to reduce the inches of the measuring-rod used on this occasion by Professor Smyth to true British inches, according to his own very full explanation and table in the introduction to Vol. II. above cited. The rod in question, " 100 A," which should have measured 100 inches only, was found to have measured, when in Egypt, 100·016. Hence—

$$\frac{1881\cdot363 \times 100\cdot016}{100} = 1881\cdot664$$

This last number, then, is what the *measures* yield us for this most desirable-to-be-known floor-length (subject only to a small *minus* correction for inevitable error, and which may reduce it to 1881·6).

Now it is a remarkable fact that the precise length of this floor line is shewn by the Pyramid geometrically as—

$$\frac{365\cdot2422 \times 51\cdot51646}{10} = 1881\cdot5985 \text{ Pyramid inches.}$$

Two well-known and fundamental Great Pyramid numbers (numbers of *inches* too) are to be multiplied together; and their product, when divided by the Pyramid's arithmetical base-number 10, is the precise length of the gallery at its floor-line. How simple, and yet profound! Can a number so obtained have any conceivable relation to mundane chronology? It would seem that it has; yet it is difficult to understand what that relation can be precisely. The number 51·51646, so well known as unlocking many geometrical beauties in the coffer, besides connecting that vessel with the king's chamber and with the Pyramid as a whole, is itself derived from 365·2422 by the application of the quantity π in one of its forms; and hence the gallery's length may be stated more shortly, though not so simply, as—

$$\frac{365\cdot2422^2}{40\sqrt{\pi}} = 1881\cdot5985.$$

But a preferable form of the equation is as follows :—

$$\frac{206\cdot06585 \times 91\cdot31055}{10} = 1881\cdot5985.$$

In this case, the first number will be recognised as the breadth of the king's chamber; and the second number is $\frac{1}{100}$ of the Pyramid's base-side. And such, moreover, is the relation of these two numbers to each other and to the particular angle at which the grand gallery's floor ascends from the horizon (26° 17′ 37″ by measure, but believed to indicate 26° 18′ 10″), that when 206·06585 inches are measured along that sloping floor upwards, the perpendicular height attained is exactly 91·31055.

And here we may well pause to reflect, first, upon the extraordinary skill and accuracy with which the theoretic length of about 1881·6 Pyramid inches has been built into the heart of this witness of the desert, so as to last unimpaired through four millenniums; and, secondly, upon the scarcely less wonderful skill and accuracy of the measurer, who, at the end of those ages of stony silence, has been permitted to recover, record, and publish to the world these now amazingly vocal measures.

I have said "about 1881·6 Pyramid inches," because 1881·5985 is derived from a length of year = 365·2422 days; and while that *may* be its true present length, it is not necessarily the length embodied in the Great Pyramid. Now 1881·6 implies a length of year about twelve seconds greater, or the length which it is generally supposed to have had about the beginning of our era—a good mean length, therefore, for all Great Pyramid time.

What follows on the adoption of this minute correction? A very curious result. Our Saviour's earthly life is indicated at the beginning of the gallery by a space of 33 and a fraction inches preceding the symbolic representation of His death and resurrection. These inches denote years; and if we call them 33·6, we shall be in near accordance with many Biblical expositors, and in exact agreement with Mr. Grattan Guiness, who in his work, "On the Approaching End of the Age," gives weighty reasons historical, astronomical, and prophetic, for the acceptance of this very period.

Now 33·6 × 56 = 1881·6, the exact length of the gallery as above, and 56 (the product of the 7 of the old creation by the 8 of the new), is the very number which Mr. Charles Horner has lately found to be set up at either end of the gallery as if to tell of the two appearings or revelations of our Lord ; of His first appearing from the grave in resurrection glory; and of His second (and still future) appearing from heaven in the glory of His Father and of the holy angels.

JAMES SIMPSON.

Edinburgh, February 21, 1879.

The above is extracted from the *Banner of Israel* for March 19, 1879 (Vol. III. No. 116). It is followed in subsequent numbers by three other papers, chiefly on Biblical Chronology in itself; but concludes with a postscript containing the following addendum of more especially Pyramid matter, viz.:—

It may be noted that the length of the tropical year implied by our assumed length of the gallery floor (1881·6) is 365·2423396 mean solar days, a length just 12 seconds greater than the 365·2422 commonly assumed for its present value, and, therefore, *very near* the length which it must have possessed (according to astronomic records) at A.D. 0, that most central epoch of human time. It is very singular that then, and only then, did it possess the exact length from which the gallery's chronological index 1881·6 is derived (as at p. 120), the more especially as that particular number co-ordinates so readily with the cyclic numbers of prophecy. For 1881·6 × 10 = 7 × 7 × 12 × 32; 7,056 = 7 × 7 × 12 × 12; 5,880 = 7 × 7 × 12 × 10. Observe also that 18,816 + 7,056 = 25,872 (= 7 × 7 × 12 × 44), a nearer approach to the precessional period, or " year of the Pleiades," as usually quoted, than that given by the sum of the base diagonals of the Pyramid. The tropical year *must have passed through the particular length* which yields these results at some time within a century or two of the First Advent—why not at that exact epoch ?—J.S.

, The allusion to Mr. Charles Horner's labours, still in progress, is worthy of note, as being some recognition in this country of the possibly vast importance in the future of the American Dr. Milo Mahan's researches into the numeral composition of Holy Scripture ; set forth at length in his two weighty volumes, entitled " Palmoni." Acting on the well-known fact that every Hebrew word has in its letters a numerical equivalent, Dr. Mahan translates the Scriptures into number ; and then endeavours to ascertain what they imply in that manner: and he has, in many cases, obtained so nearly confirmatory expressions to the tendency of the literary rendering, as, in the opinion of many, to have placed the superhuman inspiration of the Hebrew Bible on a new basis of strength.

Now in the Great Pyramid we have the *numbers* in primeval Pyramid inches of the Ancient Architect, given us by modern measure (with more or less accuracy, according to the preservation of the part concerned). With these numbers then, in his hand, Mr. Horner seeks out the Hebrew words which they are the exact equivalents of ; and then compares such words with the destination of the part of the building, as already given by the sacred and scientific theory thereof; and some most striking confirmations are said to have been already deduced.

INDEX.

INDEX.

INDEX.

INDEX.

INDEX.

INDEX.

INDEX.

Measures of the boss on the granite leaf, 208, 269
   of exterior of Great Pyramid, 95
   of interior of Great Pyramid, 222
   of King's Chamber, 194
Measurement of Great Pyramid, order for in Revelations, 586
Mecca, looking towards, 110
Mechanical data, 414, 445
Melchizedek for Philitis, 629, 630
Memlook Beys, 127
Mensural data at the disposal of new theorists, 193
Menzies, Robert, first breaks ground in the religious symbolisms of Great Pyramid, 461
Messianic and Sabbatic time, 446-477
Messianic, the sacred pronounced to be, 460
"Metric System," by President Barnard, 53, 562, 565, 568, 579
Metrical system, preparations made for the introduction of the, 566
Metrology, National, 227-320
   American, 250-253
   British, 227-253
   French, metrical, 237
   preparations for universal, 559
   Religious element in, 243
Michaelis, J. D., on weights and measures, 536
Mitchell, Mr. H., on the geographical position of the Great Pyramid, 86
   Rev. J., earth's mean density experiments, 178
Missionaries summarily expelled from India by British police up to 1812, 556
Missionary and free Bible beginnings, in Great Britain, mainly in 1813, 557
Model of meridian section of Great Pyramid in ante-chamber, 204
Mohammed the False Prophet, 109
Mohammedanism dates from the Hegira, and ends in 1881, 588
Moigno, Abbé, length of ante-chamber, 202
   Venus transit, 67
Money not at the Great Pyramid, 320
Monumental history of Egypt, 492
Moon, lunations of the, 141
Morton, Rev. H., duplication of the cube, 258
Moses and Egyptian wisdom, 389, 413
Mosque of Sooltan Hassan, 20
Mount Schihallion, attraction of plumb line on, 177
Muir, Mr. C., hypothesis of the passage-plane's side displacement, 440
Murray's "Handbook for Egypt," 393
Murtedi, Arabian author, 362

Names of Pyramid authors, 191
   of the builders of the three largest Pyramids, 525
Napoleon invaded Egypt, 127
National weights and measures, 227-320
   British, 227-253
   American, 250-253
   French, metrical, 237
Nature, journal of science, 67
Nature's standards of temperature and pressure, 312-316

New school of Pyramid theorists, 192
Newton, Sir Isaac, guess as to earth's mean density, 177
   on the sacred cubit, 348, 350, 353
   speculated on the coffer, 133
   speculated on size of King's Chamber 434
New Zealander's beginning of the year 378
Noah, the ark of, 403
Norris, Dr., Assyrian name for linear standard, 333
Nouet, M., made refined astronomical observations, 73
Number a link between Divine intelligence and human, 218
   and name of Antichrist, 617
Numbers of the Great Pyramid, 42

Obliquity of the ecliptic, 444
Observations published pure and simple, 190
   of Greenwich, Paris, Pulkova, and Scotland, 182
Oers, places of security for treasure, 407
Olympus, gods and goddesses of, 411
Opium smoking, 187
Oppert, M., on the Babylonian cubit, 341
Ordnance map, on the scale of the, 301
   survey, 54, 339
   of Great Britain, 342
Orientation of the Great Pyramid, 73-77
Orientations, false, of idolatrous temples, 85
Orthography of the name Jeezeh, 4
Osburn, W., Egyptian Dead-book, 344
   Dispersion of Nations, 490
   hieroglyphic and Greek studies, 492
   late admirable Egyptian scholar of Leeds, 492
   monumental history of Egypt, 490, 529
   name of Egyptian linear standard, 333
   on the Great Sphinx, 510
   on the religions of the world, 411, 529
"Otia Ægyptiaca," by G. R. Gliddon, 76
"Our Inheritance in the Great Pyramid," second edition, 336
Oxford astronomer in 1637, 137
   graduate on the Great Pyramid, 216

Palestine Exploration Fund's cubit, 412
Palestine, land of, 577
Passage entrance, astronomy of, 367
Passages, angle of, 439
   lengths into angle, 433
   tabular particulars, 221
Passages of Great Pyramid, modern measures of, 366
Passages of Scripture quoted, 2, 68, 98, 108, 123, 126, 220, 226, 299, 316, 330, 356, 357, 393, 398, 401, 403, 406, 460, 482, 535, 536, 537, 539, 540, 541, 542, 543, 544, 552, 553, 554, 581, 585, 586, 592, 602 ,603, 609, 611, 613, 615, 621
Perigal, Mr. H., numerical proportions of the coffer suggested by, 163
Perring, Mr., assistant to Colonel H.-Vyse, 45
   measured heights of various Pyramids, 64

INDEX.

INDEX.

INDEX.

INDEX.